General Editor's Introduction

Asbury Theological Seminary Series in World Christian Revitalization Studies

This volume is published in collaboration with the Center for the Study of World Christian Revitalization Movements, a cooperative initiative of Asbury Theological Seminary faculty. Building on the work of the previous Wesleyan/Holiness Studies Center at the Seminary, the Center provides a focus for research in the Wesleyan Holiness and other related Christian renewal movements, including Pietism and Pentecostal movements, which have had a world impact. The research seeks to develop analytical models of these movements, including their biblical and theological assessment. Using an interdisciplinary approach, the Center bridges relevant discourses in several areas in order to gain insights for effective Christian mission globally. It recognizes the need for conducting research that combines insights from the history of evangelical renewal and revival movements with anthropological and religious studies literature on revitalization movements. It also networks with similar or related research and study centers around the world, in addition to sponsoring its own research projects.

John Smith's definitive study of the Jesus Movement, as told from the perspective of an "insider" who experienced this phenomenon of revitalization from its early onset in the 1970s, represents the premier interpretation of this important movement. While much in the public eye during its ascendancy, there has been insufficient attention given to its seminal impact in influencing revitalization within a host of denominations, para-church movements, and especially within the spiritual formation of several key theologians and ministers of the present generation. All of these features are explored, in light of the cultural setting and impact of the movement in the early post-Vietnam era. It also includes an important bibliographic chapter referencing the extant literature on radical Pietism. The publication of this important resource for scholars as well as persons interested in the sources of major twentieth century religious awakenings is congruent with the mission of the Center and addresses its research objectives.

J. Steven O'Malley
Director, Center for the Study of World Christian Revitalization Movements
General Editor, The Asbury Theological Seminary Series in Christian Revitalization Studies

Sub-Series Foreword

Intercultural Studies

The behavioral science approach to the study of revitalization movements has a long history that has developed several models. Anthropologists, among others, observed that people responded to colonialism and the expansion of the West in various ways: armed resistance, selective acceptance and passive resistance, among others. The problems of the colonial frontier led to a memorandum on acculturation written by Robert Redfield, Ralph Linton and Melville Herskovits in 1936. Elsewhere in the world, anthropologists observed "nativistic" or "cultural renewal" movements as well: cargo cults in Melanesia, messianic movements in South Africa, and political revolutions in Latin America. Anthony F. C. Wallace brought some order to this area of study with his 1956 article where he named the stages and subsumed the movements under the name of "revitalization movements." Harold Turner contributed the notion of New Religious Movements to focus on the indigenous responses to mission work seen in every continent. This can be seen as part of a larger development, from the 1960s on, to develop Social Movement Theory where people are seen as agents intentionally acting to renew and reform society by organizing others to resist or dethrone the powers that be. Such movements develop a culture and social organization that give meaning and impetus to action on behalf of the leader and/or the program.

In this book, John Smith has used the Revitalization Movements model to frame the history of the Jesus People Movement. This has been a monumental task, the first history of this scope. Smith traces the roots of the Jesus People Movement as well as the various branches that it takes both in America and Australia. Smith is an insider, looking back and reflecting at the dynamics of the movement over the last forty years. He finds lasting value in the movement, both for those involved, and for Christianity as a whole.

Michael A. Rynkiewich
Editor for the sub-series on Intercultural Studies.

The Origins, Nature, and Significance of the Jesus Movement as a Revitalization Movement

Kevin John Smith

Asbury Theological Seminary Series in
World Christian Revitalization Movements in Intercultural Studies, No. 5

EMETH PRESS
www.emethpress.com

*The Origins, Nature, and Significance of the
Jesus Movement as a Revitalization Movement*

Copyright © 2011 Kevin John Smith
Printed in the United States of America on acid-free paper

All rights reserved. No part of this book may be reproduced, or stored in a retrieval system or transmitted in any form or by any means, electronic, mechanical, photocopying, recording, scanning or otherwise, except as permitted by the 1976 United States Copyright Act, or with the prior written permission of Emeth Press. Requests for permission should be addressed to: Emeth Press, P. O. Box 23961, Lexington, KY 40523-3961.   http://www.emethpress.com.

Library of Congress Cataloging-in-Publication Data

Smith, Kevin John.
  The origins, nature, and significance of the Jesus movement as a revitalization movement / Kevin John Smith.
    p. cm. -- (Asbury Theological Seminary series in world Christian revitalization movements in intercultural studies ; no. 5)
  Includes bibliographical references.
  ISBN 978-1-60947-019-7 (alk. paper)
  1. Jesus People. 2. Church history--20th century. I. Title.
  BV3793.S49 2011
  289.9--dc23
                              2011021832

Contents

Figures		vii
Acknowledgments		ix
Chapter 1	Revival or Revitalization – In Search of the Jesus People	1
Chapter 2	The Jesus Movement – A Sign of the Times?	35
Chapter 3	Wandering Charismatics – An Apostolate to Popular Culture	59
Chapter 4	The Jesus Movement Goes to Church – Calvary Chapel	105
Chapter 5	The Jesus Movement Seeks the Church – Transfiguration	151
Chapter 6	The Jesus Movement in Australia – Radicalizing the Church	195
Chapter 7	Communalism for Empowerment – A Modernity Response	265
Chapter 8	Back to the Future – An Enduring Catholic Paradigm	301
Chapter 9	The Jesus People Movement – Revitalization and Mission	351
Appendix 1	Timeline for Developments	371
Appendix 2 (A)	Calvary Chapel Worship Liturgy	413
Appendix 2 (B)	Calvary Chapel Programs	415
Appendix 3	Calvary Chapel – Four Winds Doctrinal Foundations	417
Appendix 4	Elements of Style and Substance in Radical Jesus Movement Leadership	421
Appendix 5	CWLF, New Berkeley Liberation Program	423
Appendix 6	Berkeley Liberation Program	425
Appendix 7	New Covenant Apostolic Order	427
Appendix 8	Early Church Worship Routine	433
Appendix 9	The New Covenant Apostolic Order's Ideal Church Characteristics	435
Appendix 10	Preliminary Agreement of the EOCA and AO	437
Postscript		439
References Cited		443

List of Figures

Figure 2.1	"Dear John – Jesus is Greater than the Beatles"	40
Figure 2.2	Self-Immolation – Buddhist Response to the Vietnam War	42
Figure 2.3	A Popish Buzzard Guards the Truth	47
Figure 2.4	Ruined City Apocalypse	52
Figure 2.5	Gurus and World Religions Compared with Jesus	55
Figure 3.1	Itinerant Hippies – On the Road for Jesus	64
Figure 3.2	The Psychedelic, New Improved Truth	74
Figure 3.3	From John Lennon to Jesus	90
Figure 4.1	Artistic Hosannas to Jesus	111
Figure 4.2	Mystical, Biblical Imagery – Woman at the Well	135
Figure 5.1	Wanted Poster – A Hippie Jesus	160
Figure 5.2	Wanted Poster – The Jesus Outlaw Profile	161
Figure 5.3	An Apocalyptic Critique of Materialism	166
Figure 6.1	Larry Norman 1974 – Loved in Australia	206
Figure 6.2	Billboard Announcing a Teach-In	217
Figure 6.3	Happy Birthday Jesus – The Controversy Begins	233
Figure 6.4	Materialism – This Is Where It All Ends	242
Figure 6.5	The Sad World Awaiting Liberation	244
Figure 6.6	The Bikies Who Preach Love	247
Figure 7.1	Bikini Atoll Atomic Test – Reverse Creation	319
Figure 8.1	Multitudes in the Valley of Decision	362

Acknowledgments

Numerous friends and associates deserve honor as a significant part of the journey for this mature-aged student. For those who know they should have been mentioned my apologies under pressure to meet deadlines. This dissertation has required research in diverse physical contexts (Australia, the United Kingdom, and the United States) and has been an "on the road" experience, often interrupted by the peculiar responsibilities of a founder-leader of a complex, resource-stressed movement. It has therefore been consistently interrupted and has been a longer-than-expected scholastic "pregnancy."

The entire community of Care and Communication and its agencies – God's Squad Christian Motorcycle Club, Values for Life, Handbrake Turn, Inside Out, and the missions teams – have suffered labor pains and several false alarms in expectation of the project's final birth. The base leaders – Steve, David, Keith, Shirley, Tracey, Trevor, Kevin and Kath, Jill, Marc, Andrea and Martin, the Board (particularly chairman John Curtis), Marg and Alan, Bruce, and the other leaders and members of St. Martin's Community Churches – were burdened excessively over six years of uncertainty and increased responsibility during a period of resource scarcity.

Undoubtedly my wife Glena and children, Paul, Kathy and Lyndal paid the greatest price. To Glena, my wife and companion, critic, and stanch defender, I have no adequate words to express my gratitude. The disruption of her life as a matriarch obsessively concerned for her family cannot be measured. She relocated with me to the other side of the world while six grandchildren arrived and were largely deprived of her "Gran" administrations of adoration and generosity of spirit. Gall stone removal and a hysterectomy added to her stress in mid course. My cancer operation was a considerable stress, but full recovery and the conclusion of this project has sweetened life again.

Glena's assistance in typing – particularly thousands of pages of recorded interviews from discs – was a monumental contribution beyond my capacity to achieve in the time available. Her faithful love and commitment to me, her suffering, but tenacity to see me finish of this project, has been the essential support. Without her I would have almost certainly joined many able students who just don't quite finish the all-important dissertation and defense.

I wish to express profound gratitude to Dr. Darrell Whiteman, mentor, disciplinarian, staunch supporter, and friend, not out of protocol but out of deep thankfulness for one who believed in me before I could believe in myself. He has been a staunch believer in the project when the author's energy, focus, and hope of completion faltered. He has been a true friend and a tireless source of wisdom and relentless discipline. My gratitude is necessarily effusive.

My deep gratitude also to the other members of my committee – Dr. Howard Snyder, Dr. George Hunter III, and Dr. Matthias Zahniser (who retired during my long dissertation journey). This team of academic carers has been and will always be friends as well as disciplers. Their guidance, moral support, generous time, and broad base of seasoned knowledge kept me on the right road when my eclectic mind and pilgrim spirit threatened to lead me up numerous sidetracks (chasing rabbits as my mentor defined it). Special thanks to President Maxie Dunham for his gracious support and genius for inspired, spiritual and practical utterance. The late Professor Ev Hunt and Professor Bob Tuttle held me up at times of special need.

Asbury Theological Seminary and particularly the staff and faculty of the E. Stanley Jones School of World Mission, became a surrogate family of collegial support, and the source of inspiration, wisdom, and motivation par excellence. The collegial relationship with those far ahead of those they mentor was a communal experience, particularly as we shared on an even playing field for discussion, prayer, and creative rumination during Wednesday's early morning missiology seminars. During those international gatherings all faculty and graduate students join in theoretical, practical and passionate consideration of the state of the nations.

In the final days, the temptation to abort the project was overcome with the support and the gracious hospitality of Matt and Anne Zahniser for three months of accommodation and encouragement. Laurie Whiteman made the journey sweet for Glena and me. I will always recall the moral, practical support of a delightful crowd of colleagues in the E.S.J. School, whose own academic pressures were no hindrance to the offering of advice and motivational support during the final months.

David Di Sabatino, a non-participant but tireless historical chronicler of the movement provided much detail for this dissertation. He has been an encouraging younger friend and colleague in search of the meaning of the story. Numerous old Jesus Freaks gave hours and even days to the lengthy process of interviewing and I am most grateful for their openness and candor. Glen and Wendy Kaiser of JPUSA and Joe Peterson became companions of the Movement during the research.

Communality, the community church on High Street was an inspiration along the way. Co-planters of Communality and fellow travelers, the Leffels – Greg, Mary, Daniel, Kristin, and Rachel gave meaning and inspiration to the journey. Peter and Gweneth Tattem sacrificially provided car and technical items for research. Musical genius Dennie, and his parents Joe and Faye Kirtley became a significant inspiration and were friends in time of need. Jonathan and Rosina, faithful pioneers of church planting, our nearest neighbors sweetened our experience of alien status. Robert and Tracey Vaughan, Ray and Renee Groceer, Larry and Willie Gaumond shared the sweetness of the Spirit. Randolph Scott, Donna and Bob and the rest of the Harley Owner's Group of the Bluegrass chapter kept us in touch with our beloved biker fraternity. My mates at Tolly Ho and the Hideaway pub kept us in touch with reality. Mark and Angela Lewis and family – sweet missionaries "extraordinary" to St Croix gave me their flat for retreat and writing. Peter and Marcia and family, exiled Aussies for the marginalized Amerindian people kept us reminded of the nature of mission.

Many other friends made our stay in America an adventure and pleasure which compensated for the rigors of academia, especially Sandy and Duke Merron and Suzie and Rockley Miller. Among essential friends who encouraged us to never give up were: Toni Simpson, Ralph, Grace, Laurell and Annie Yoder, Professor David and Aureal Moore, Dana, Peter and Debbie Cotorceanus, Chuck and Zoe Payne, Rick, Luceen and Margaret Hisel, Bryan Sirchio, Scott and Roxy Seymour, Jeffrey Hiatt and his parents, John and Sandy Fitch, the late John Bailey (J.B), and "Little" John Martha and Nichole Harris.

Among my many mentors I must single out John U'ren, John Hirt, and the late Athol Gill who have been inspirational and theological companions during the long road in search of a city wherein dwells justice and peace. Numerous others have inspired me to reject the ubiquitous substitutes for true humanity – materialism, individualism, and soulless secularism – Jim Wallis, Anthony Campolo, Ched Myers, Bono, Professor Sam and Karen Murumba, Tom and Christine Sine and our community of faith in Australia.

My father Rev. Ken Smith, a fitter and turner who obeyed the call to Methodist ministry, must receive honor for that which is useful in this dissertation. In the tradition of the old working class, with self-educating tenacity he taught me to desire education for the beauty of truth rather than the acquisition of status or qualification. His love, pastoral patience, intellectual inspiration, and example of commitment to Jesus and to the people has been foundational to any good in this pilgrim or his work. His motivating life, example, and specific instruction to read the classics even before the onset of adolescence pointed the way for this cultural nomad's love of knowledge, search for meaning, and commitment to life both human and divine.

My deepest desire is that this academic journey may inspire the reader to engage at risk in those movements of human enterprise that leave the world a better place than we found it. I have sought to be open to the available wisdoms of the widest opinions of scholarship, but of all inspirations both moral and intellectual, Jesus, the ultimate wandering charismatic, remains my revitalizing source of hope, faith, and love.

CHAPTER 1

Revival or Revitalization – In Search of the Jesus People

I am making everything new . . . Write this down. Revelation 21:5.

The social revolution of the 1960s was the context and cause of a visionary change for many. Although Australia lagged behind America on the timeline of cultural upheaval, its youthful alienation and academic dissent paralleled that which occurred in the United States. Via the television we shared a window to the world. International travel, new technologies and affordable, street-level publishing via offset printing immediately connected like-minded dissenters. Counterculture musicians, protesters, and activists in new socio-religious movements soon bonded with each other internationally. The cultural gestalt was intense and observable in both hemispheres. Popular culture – music and performing arts – followed similar courses in America and Australia. For many of us, ideological and career changes were unscheduled, swift, and all consuming.[1]

> [At the Sunbury Pop Festival] there were in excess of 40,000 people for that sun-baked weekend. It started out, as Woodstock had two years earlier, with a great sense of optimism and destiny. There was a feeling that this generation could change the world for the better. We sang in those days, "We can change the world, rearrange the world" (Crosby, Stills, Nash, and Young 1970a). (Smith and Downey 1987:146)

A new religious movement of primitive Christian faith was taking root in the unlikely soil of the youth counterculture, amidst sex, drugs, and rock 'n' roll. It defied the religious establishment's anathematization of its youthful rebellion, anti-Vietnam war politics, outrageously sensual music, and social libertarianism.

> There was a creek running through the Sunbury site, and once again there were new [Jesus Freaks] who wanted to be baptized. They felt that this was the place where they could best serve notice to their contemporaries that a change had taken place in their lives. I was in the thick of things and spoke to the crowd. It was a remarkable scene. These people were standing up to their knees in the muddy waterhole, while naked and semi-naked people, who had earlier been skinny-dipping, lounged around on the banks and made off-the-cuff remarks at us all.
>
> One of those being baptized was a guy who had been part of an outlaw biker group. He had been a hard-drinking, hard-fighting reprobate, but had been personally transformed through his encounter with the counterculture Jesus Movement. After he had been pulled out of the water, he stood in mid-stream and told, in a simple and direct way, exactly what the gospel of Jesus meant to him. The audience was silenced by his sincerity and passion, and by the fact that he didn't use religious words, but language they understood. (Smith and Downey 1987:146, 147)

Living in the new context of the counterculture called for relocation to unfamiliar cultural space by the adoption of alternative symbols of dress, musical tastes, and alien associations. For my Plymouth Brethren wife, living in middle class suburbia, and occupied with the nurture of three young children, the changes were daunting.

> For Glena, this was her first proper introduction to what had, for the previous year or so, become my world. I had *gone native*. She sat on the side of the hill reading her Bible and came across some words in the book of the prophet Joel which seemed to sum up everything we had experienced that weekend. Tears streaming down her face, she showed me what she had been reading. It said, "Multitudes, multitudes in the valley of decision" [Joel 3:13-14]. She looked across this sea of people and said, "John, here they are. But where is the church?" (Smith and Downey 1987:147)

The Christian representation among this large crowd was minimal. One evangelical group, Theos, was there in fellowship with our ministry, Truth and Liberation Concern. Many young Jesus Freaks independently made the pilgrimage to the Mecca of seekers and revelers. It was an alien culture to us. The atmosphere was eclectic, optimistic, experimental, and inclusive. It was a strange, but inviting land for evangelical dissenters who had come to embrace a Jesus of the margins and the outcasts.

> The longings of the hippie world were basically admirable, but their naïve lack of understanding of the darker side of human nature left them vulnerable, and eventually self-destructive. Our entry into the counterculture and the adoption of elements of their ritual processes – change in clothing style, and relocation to the fringes of the youth culture – resulted in swift change of career and friendship networks. Our cultural conversion was a highly personal, marginalizing gestalt, but we soon forged lifelong links with some counterculture, alternative, and ac-

tivist Jesus Freaks in other corners of the globe, even borrowing some of their methods, especially the street-level, tabloid Jesus newspaper. Already, reports of a new youth movement of experimental, communal, and street-level churches were appearing in the mainstream media.

Occurrence and Context

The *Milwaukee Journal Insight* in 1971, September 12, featured in its weekend magazine a story about what had become known as The Jesus Movement. Around the same time, more prestigious magazines were heralding or critiquing what appeared to be a substantial religious movement in the United States and Canada. Mainstream international journals further stimulated the public interest.[2] *Time* (Figure 1.1) carried a Jesus Revolution cover story, June 21, 1971. Many sociological and psychological researchers responded with substantial analysis.[3]

In the United Kingdom, Australia, and New Zealand, similar movements to those in North America were gaining momentum. In the United Kingdom the British Council of Churches' Youth Department published two thoughtful assessments of the Movement (Corry 1973a 1973b). In Australia, *Vogue* (Gartner 1973), a fashion magazine, featured the Movement on several pages with photos of the God's Squad Christian Motorcycle Club meeting in The House of the New World, a radical Christian ministry in Sydney.

The dominant form of the Australian Jesus Movement was evangelical, socially concerned, and politically activist. The Movement was not limited to the English speaking world. It drew the attention of the media and scholars in several European countries (Buhl 1999; Di Sabatino 1999a:129-137). Denominational journals saw the Movement as worthy of published analysis.[4] Nondenominational journals added their critique.[5] Extreme elements, like the Children of God, gained the attention of scholars investigating cults.[6]

The Movement was variously called the Jesus Revolution (Corry 1973b; Croskery 1971; Ellis 1972; Gelwick 1972; McFadden 1972; Moyer 1972; Tuttle 1971; Wright 1971a); the Jesus Movement (Alvin Reid 1991, 1995; Bastien 1970:328; Chandler 1971; Ostling 1972; Plowman 1971j, 1972, 1975a; Richardson 1973, 1974; Simcox 1977; Vachon 1971), or the Jesus People Movement (Balswick 1974; Di Sabatino 1994; H. Ward 1972). Followers of the Movement were often called Jesus Freaks (Adler 1974; Fishman 1973; Plowman 1971g; Streiker 1971; Tracey 1970; Ungar 1973; Watts 1972:43), borrowing a term embraced by the wider counterculture as a term of distinction and of derision by skeptics.[7] *Jesus People* was the more common term.

It presented a fresh agenda for the church. The Jesus Movement, at least in its more radical expressions, went even further than the secular counterculture. It challenged not only the secular society, but also the *worldliness* of religious institutions and traditions. It was a direct response to the broad upheaval of the 1960s and related to the sociopolitical and psycho-historical movement described as the Counterculture. Miller (1997; Guinness 1994; Johnson 1971; Tipton 1982) affirm the enduring influence of this counterculture on the overall secular and religious cultural landscape of the United States. The Jesus Movement was sufficiently countercultural to convert many political dissenters, social revolutionaries, secular rock musicians, and westernized Zen Buddhists.

Tipton (1982) views the entire 1960s – 1970s counterculture movement, including the one fundamentalist element of the Jesus Movement he examined, as an alternative religious consciousness. He believes it responded to fragmentation and anomalous shifts in shared convictions concerning moral meanings, without which the social life has no coherence. Tipton argues that the youthful rebellion of the 1960s drew energy from the antecedent, ethical frameworks of earlier American movements.[8]

The dissenting minority culture served notice of its belief in the breakdown and inadequacy of the existing frameworks to cope with a changing social context. It sought to overthrow a defective, materialistic worldview, which was maladaptive with respect to moral meaning and ontological strength. It was a predictable outcome of the sociocultural mood of the time. The Jesus Movement found common cause with the self-expressive ethic, antiestablishment rebellion, and the utopian dreaming of the secular counterculture.[9]

But many rejected the autonomous individualism that lurked beneath the surface of the tribal, hippie, freedom movements. This is illustrated by the fact that a considerable number of the Jesus Movement leaders, particularly in the context of Californian human potential movements, rejected individual autonomy and self-expression, and eventually embraced a strong sacerdotal form of Eastern Christianity, through the Antiochian Orthodox Church. Others embraced an Anabaptist form of social responsibility and communalism as a way to subvert popular individualism and materialism. A full analysis of the Movement should include an inquiry into "the moral basis of social commitment in America" (Tipton 1982: xi). New religious movements often reflect dissatisfaction with existing value hierarchies and an openness to utopian or millenarian visions of a new order.

The Investigation of Cause and Effect

This project seeks an explanation of the nature and extent of those new religious groups during the 1960s and 1970s that are known collectively as the Jesus Movement. Some scholars of that era assert that secularism had triumphed. Religion was increasingly viewed as intellectually indefensible and socially impotent. Why did such a conservative movement as the Jesus Movement arise so swiftly during the decline in public allegiance to traditional faiths? What was the Movement about and why did it occur? What is its significance for the postmodern West? (See Definitions, Page 42).

Associated with the larger question of the nature of the Movement are many sub-problems. Why did many secularists find faith through this Movement without contact with traditional church? Why did confrontational Evangelicalism[10] appeal to a generation of youth intrigued by alternative, Eastern, occult, and nativistic faiths? Was there a common element in its diverse array of ideological and organizational variables?

Why did some elements embrace postmodern innovation, while others chose to retreat from activist, counterculture communalism, to the most ancient of Christian traditions, Antiochian Orthodoxy? Was the Movement a chance aberration of religious movementalism, or the reappearance of a normative process, predictable under certain cultural circumstances? Was this, as some supporters would claim, simply an indefinable miracle, an act of God in defiance of modern, secular hubris? Are there social scientific clues to the timing, form, and meaning of this modern outbreak of renewal? Was the Jesus Movement evidence of the incarnational, contextual nature of divinely appointed interaction between gospel and culture? Does the Movement supply us with useful clues to cultural innovation and change? If so, what may we learn in theory and practice from the successes and failures of this Movement to help equip the church and the wider society for further, postmodern upheavals in the twenty-first century?

Choosing a Model

Any organization of people, whether global or local, formed to cause or prevent social change, may be defined as a social movement. A movement may be caused by political or social conditions and may result from a planned, structured well-defined purpose and pre-arranged strategy. The Feminist Movement, Greenpeace, and the Animal Liberation Movement may be seen as movements focused on cognitive beliefs, seeking to generate data in support of social changes in attitude and behavior.

Some movements, such as the Civil Rights Movement, Black Power, the Feminist Movement, and the Labor Movement, are organized movements of resistance and protest. Such groups share a sense of social and moral outrage at prevailing conditions that marginalize and disenfranchise citizens on the basis of race, gender, or class. These groups are socio-politically driven, but as Jasper (1997) has proposed, movement theorists have often ignored the power of ethical and moral protest, with its accompanying emotional energy. Jasper views moral protest in movements as an art rather than a determinist, fixed, structural response to social conditions.

Emile Durkheim (1951) saw social movements as the result of anomie and social disorganization (Tarrow 1998:4). Some early theorists saw movements as expressions of mob psychology, mindless violence, deprivation, and extremism, as in the case of fascism, Nazism and Stalinism (1998:4). Thus some scholars have defined movements according to invariant causes, but movements are increasingly seen in terms of multiple rather than single, structural, social factors. The mechanisms of politics and ethical protest (Meyer 1990; Jasper 1997) have replaced the focus on social determinants.

Alain Touraine (1988) has highlighted the significance of the individual in analysis, decision-making and negotiation in movements as "the return of the actor" to central stage. Participants in movements are no longer primarily seen as unconscious respondents to unrecognized social determinants. Conscience and consciousness motivate movement members "to assert themselves as producers rather than consumers of social situations, as capable of questioning social situations rather than merely responding to them" (1988:11).

The data resulting from this research of 1960s movements, and the Jesus Movement in particular, highlights the conflict between determinism and free-will activism. Sociocultural forces, of which leaders and participants were clearly unaware, sometimes drove the Movement in directions that were unplanned and ill advised. Sometimes the reasons for their actions and the socially driven consequences were hidden from the actors as the drama unfolded. On the other hand, much of the Movement's growth was clearly strategized rationally and volitionally on the basis of conscience, in defiance of recognized social determinants and obvious, inevitable outcomes. Many decisions were made with awareness of both cause and consequence of the directions being taken.

A theoretical explanation for the rise of the Movement must embrace both the social determinants and the capacity of movements to defy prediction and apparently determinist factors. The social influences on perceived reality cannot be ignored or denied, but the role of the conscious actor on the stage of social protest or reformation also cannot be dismissed. Tarrow (1998) defines social movements as "collective challenges, based on common purposes and social solidarity in sustained interaction with elites, opponents, and authorities" (1998:4). Elements of social solidarity, collective identity, political opportunity, and cultural crisis combine to facilitate social movements.

Protest movements have been the focus of much research since the Civil Rights Movement of the 1950s and 1960s. They set a pattern of social mobilization which has continued to be a mark of postmodern society (Bowers, Ochs, and Jensen 1993; Burns 1990; Eyerman and Jamison 1998; Meyer and Tarrow 1998; Patterson 1995; Piven and Cloward 1979; Stewart, Smith, and Denton 1994). Both McAdam (1988) and Jasper (1997) have emphasized the impact of biographical tracks on activist movements as a cause of their occurrence, and an influence in movement outcomes. The individual stories of 1960s movement leaders such as Martin Luther King had significant bearing on the nonviolent emphasis of the Civil Rights Movement. The influence of another individual, Mahatma Gandhi, on Martin Luther King during his graduate student days further underscores the importance of biography for any movement theory.

A shift in emphasis has occurred, stressing the membership basis in movements, refocusing from ideology to identity (Laraña, Johnson, and Gusfield 1994). The cultural focus on a personal identity at the end of the twentieth century might have shifted the individual's involvement in movements from shared ideology to a personal search for identity and self-esteem. This ontological quest initiates engagement with movements that act as semi-communal fellowships (Melucci 1994) which affirm self-worth and vocation.

To explain the changing face of "collective action in the information age," Alberto Melucci (1996) combines the role of culture, the individual and collective quest for identity, or a meaningful code, with political participation, charismatic leadership, and the mobilization of resources. Much social action is in reaction to "a society without a center" (1996:207-228). The counterculture movements of the 1960s exhibited many aspects of collective action including strong elements of dissenting ideology, considerable influence from the biographical tracks of their founders, and the exploitation of political opportunity.

Modern movements often appear to comprise complex aggregates of participants whose involvement is motivated by multiple causes. These motivations range from ideological commitment to deep, personal, psychological needs. A participant may have a clear commitment to a cause, or have "rent-a-crowd" desire for emotional stimulation and notoriety. The Jesus Movement was no exception to the rule of complex reasons and multiple motivations. During my search for an explanatory paradigm that embraces the many aspects of social movements, the model of a revitalization movement appeared to provide the most appropriate template to accurately shape the observable phenomenon central to this dissertation. The theory is sufficiently broad to encompass all these elements, yet specific enough to explain the peculiar aspects of the Jesus Movement, as the following explanation seeks to demonstrate.

Revitalization as an Enduring Phenomenological Aid to Understanding

Given the extent, speed, and countercultural nature of the initial forms of the Jesus Movement, we require a critical theoretical framework that explains phenomena beyond the usually slower gradations of acculturation (Kraft 1996:366-373). It was in part this requirement which attracted me to the psycho-historical methodology of A. F. C. Wallace's revitalization theory. Using the critical framework of revitalization movements as articulated by Wallace and others (1952, 1956b, 1966, 1969), this dissertation will investigate the revitalizing, counterculture, and apostolic character of the Jesus Movement. It will draw implications for mission, community, and evangelism. Wallace's theory is congruent with many patterns of the Movement's sociohistoric development that became evident during my research.

Cultural Systems Innovation

Culture is a cognitive road map for social participation, but it is also a dynamic process in varying stages of change, renewal, and decay. Innovation and change usually occur in small, manageable increments, although the speed and extent of change has accelerated markedly in recent decades. Sometimes overwhelming change occurs at a rapid pace. Social movements are often the initiators of rapid change in cultures. Cultural revolutions or transformations have been the object of much speculation and theorizing, particularly since World War II (Burns 1990; Giugni, McAdam, and Tilly 1999; J. Jasper 1997; Larãna, Johnston, and Gusfield 1994; Marx and McAdam 1994; McAdam 1988, 1999; Reed 1992; Stewart, Smith, and Denton 1994; Tarrow 1998).

Wallace observed that major cultural innovations that bypassed slower patterns of enculturation by abrupt gestalt shifts have occurred regularly, but sporadically, resulting from "a deliberate, conscious effort to construct a more satisfying society" (Wallace 1956b:279; cf. Turner and Brunner 1986:183). Revitalization theory is a particularly enduring paradigm, frequently employed in the discussion of new religious movements.[11]

Chaotic Variety in Uniform Process

Wallace groups a number of major rapid, cultural systems-innovations under the descriptive category of revitalization movements. These embrace nativistic, messianic, revivalist, millenarian, utopian, revolutionary, and charismatic movements. Such movements, whether New Guinea's cargo cults in a technologically primitive society, Wesley's Methodism in the developing industrialization of the eighteenth century, or post-industrial counterculture movements of the 1960s, arose in stressful times of widespread social angst. They follow uniform patterns of growth and incorporation. "Major cultural-system innovations are characterized by a uniform process" (Wallace 1956b:264). Rapid change is the consequence of sociocultural and psychological factors (Wallace 1966:34-35), in response to pervasive social disorganization.

The Process of Revitalization

Wallace observes the following distinct, processual order in such movements, in response to widespread disillusionment and disorientation experienced by a significant proportion of citizens that may substantially revolutionize the existing social condition.

Steady State

Beginning with a steady state, during which the majority of the citizens find satisfactory values and social cohesion in the existing culture, the society is able to cope with the small minority of dissatisfied citizens, who often dwell on the fringes of society. The culture is in a state of equilibrium, so the level of stress and social deviance is manageable through corrective institutions and social restraint (Wallace 1966:158).

Increased Individual Stress

Secondly, cultural dysfunction develops due to the inadequacy of people's worldview and the alienation of people from society's institutions. When society's belief systems, ideology, ritual processes, and social arrangements become increasingly inappropriate, overcomplicated, or inadequate to meet changed physical and social needs, the percentage of disaffected citizens rapidly increases. The number of disenchanted, marginalized and socially deviant individuals multiplies. Intolerable stress from perceived systemic failure and disorganization creates an increase in psychological illness, substance abuse, violence, crime, and asocial individualism (Wallace 1966:159).

Serious Cultural Distortion

The third phase is a period of serious cultural distortion, forcing many people to face a choice. Should they remain lost in a maze of dissonance between the individual's expectations and the culture's contrary responses, or search for a new cultural map, or "mazeway" (Wallace 1956b:266-267). The prolonged nature of stress and disorder, accompanied by repeated failure of the culture to rectify the situation, leads some to believe that piecemeal adaptations of personal mazeways is futile. The *system* itself is vilified. Apathy or hostility results from disillusionment. Kinship or familial tradition breaks down; passivity, unemployment, and disregard for officialdom increases. Tribal or patriotic solidarity and pride disintegrates. This may lead to a critical mass of defectors that is attracted to charismatic leaders who offer a path to a more satisfying new culture. Such prophetic figures arise to facilitate an aggressive confrontation and penetration of the culture by a revitalization movement seeking to overthrow or replace the existing order.

Period of Revitalization

During the fourth phase there occurs "a conscious, deliberate, organized effort on the part of some members of a society to create a more satisfying culture" (Wallace 1956b:265). This revitalization movement responds to the crisis by the establishment of its own alternative order, in lively conflict but some synthesis with the wider culture. This period is highly visionary, countercultural, innovative, and to some extent exclusive.

Previously regarded deviancies become institutionalized as a corporate statement of rejection of the culturally distorted patterns and as a mark of new solidarity. This may be a time in which the movement is established outside the dominant culture, having created its own identity, or it may innovate within existing forms. It may seek to revolutionize, re-envision, or revitalize the wider culture, or it may provide a separate, distinct, alternative culture. Wallace observed that during this period participants in the attempted cultural revitalization regard the social distortions as so severe as to demand salvation or revolution. Some search for a *golden age*, a former period of social virtue and peace. For others a utopian, New World order not yet experienced by mortals may be the desired end. A new vision for "self, society, the culture of nature and body, and of ways of action" (Wallace 1956b:267) is revealed and applied to the group's social life.

Wallace argues that six functions must occur during the revitalization phase if the movement is to be successful (1966:159-162). These processes involve the reformulation of a worldview code; the establishment of communication networks and style; the setting up of an organization; adaptation to change resulting from creative movement and social reaction; the transformation of the participants in the new culture; and the routinization of the movement's life and work.

1. Mazeway reformulation. The vision of a new society is encoded as a blueprint for a new corporate identity. This Wallace calls "mazeway reformulation"

(1966:270). Wallace observes that revitalization is intensely visionary and usually religious. The newly conceived restructuring of society is "abrupt and dramatic, usually occurring as a moment of insight, a brief period of realization of relationships and opportunities" (Wallace 1966:270). Hallucinatory visions by one individual, often apocalyptic or communal in their projections, provide the focus for mass movemental, gestalt shifts similar to an individual's ecstatic conversion or *new birth* (1966:334-35).[12]

2. Communication. Evangelical fervor and the intensification of communication to potential converts and to the perceived enemies of a better society, is also a notable feature of this period. Prophetic, inspirational communication to outsiders and disciples is a significant element. Communication is primary, whether by intense personal engagement, mass exhortation, literature distribution, or artistic performance. Wallace's description of this aspect is most appropriate to the style of the itinerant, apocalyptic, and evangelical proclaimers of the Jesus Movement. This development requires major consideration of theories that help explain the success of the idiosyncratic proclaimers and the innovative methodologies such leaders and their groups employed. When we speak of the Salvation Army, we inevitably refer to Catherine and William Booth. In Methodism, Wesley's name is central. For Presbyterianism it is Knox; in Lutheranism it is Luther; and for the Franciscans, Saint Francis of Assisi. Wallace places two significant prophets, Handsome Lake (1952, 1956b, 1969) and Teedyuscung (1990[1949]) on central stage in his ethnohistory when developing revitalization theory in the context of Amerindian cultural renewal (1966:31-33, 211-213).

One notable aspect of Wallace's revitalization model is his descriptive typology of communication during the *mazeways reformalizing* of a movement's worldview (Wallace 1956b:270-273; 1966:160-161). He affirms Homer Barnett's contention that creative individuals, rather than groups, initiate major cultural innovations (Barnett 1953; Whiteman 1984:56, 57). Wallace regards prophet type-leaders as central to revitalization. He adapts Max Weber's (1864-1920) concept of charismatic authority, underscoring the importance of biography in understanding social movements.[13] The centrality of highly charismatic figures in revitalization is a model that is consistent with the Jesus Movement's pattern of leadership and growth. While embracing Weber's concept of charismatic leadership as typical of revitalization leadership, Wallace notes Weber's ambiguity as to whether the source of charisma lies in the visionary or in the power attributed to the leader by the followers (Wallace 1966:273). Horsley (1994) also uses Weber's concept of charismatic leadership, but calls for a more *interactionist concept* between leaders and followers, whereby "the catalytic function is to convert latent solidarities into active ritual and political action" (1994:141). I will revisit the work of Weber (1964:358-392; 1968:251-267) as to his analysis of charismatic leadership and his descriptive though controversial typology of it.[14] Charismatic leaders are normative, at least in the foundational and inspirational stages of revitalization. Modern "resource mobilization theory" embraces this concept for analysis of the 1960s protest movements (McAdam 1986, 1988, 1989 1999; Tarrow 1998; Tilly 1988, 1993). Research into this leadership model is particularly appropriate for analysis of the Jesus Movement and it will be pursued at length in Chapters 3 and 7.

The method by which the Jesus Movement leaders fulfilled a prophetic (Weber 1964:358-406) and apostolic calling, and the extent to which they adhered to, or deviated from orthodox, historic Christianity, varied. The damage done by cult leaders is a concern, perhaps influencing some modern communication theorists to sidestep the central issue of charismatic leadership. Many of the fastest growing new church movements in the Western and Third World contexts appear to reflect the revitalization model, and provide many examples of the type of charismatic leadership described by (Harold Turner 1979; Weber 1968). This enquiry will substantially examine the Jesus Movement's charismatic leadership style in the context of revitalization.

Jesus Movement leaders filled a vacuum at the time. They often picked up elements of communication in a process of discovery along the road. While inventing new forms, they also rediscovered age-old principles of indigenization in method and incarnational lifestyle. They intuitively espoused principles recognized by frontier academics, but often neglected or resisted in pulpit and pew. The relationship between leader and the followers is complex and interactive. Perhaps it is not so much the genius of discovery, but the power of popular diffusion by charismatic envisioning, which marked the Movement as remarkable during a period of increasing secularization.

3. Organization. The swift growth rate of converts brings with it an intense expectation of a changed order beyond rhetoric, creating an unavoidable pressure for organization. The intensity and diversity of the communal experience requires swift and astute administration. Initially the structure relies upon the talent of true believers, who are chosen, often autocratically, sometimes collegially, by the charismatic leader. Issues of dogma, authority structures, accountability, resources management, opposition, media management, public relations, daily and long-term scheduling, strategies and instigation of new programs arise very early in new movements. It is a balancing act between establishment resistance and popular acclaim. Wallace describes the early organizational structure as a tricornered relationship between formulators of policy, disciples from which leaders are selected, and the mass following. The structure is usually somewhat autocratic, but non-bureaucratic. Loyalty to the leader often transcends the significance of skills, or prior experience (Wallace 1966:161; 1956b:273-274).

4. Adaptation. This is a process of modification of belief, policy, and practice. External opposition becomes both an asset to draw disaffected citizens to the radical cause, and a threat to the survival of a low resourced and marginalized movement. The prophetic leader, responding to successful experimentation, criticism, and external threat to the group's survival, usually superintends the modification of belief and practice. This is often a period of synthesis and increasing pragmatism, whereby the alternative vision is nevertheless adapted to the social realities of the wider culture and the pastoral needs of the followers (1966:161-162; 1956b:274-275).

5. Cultural transformation. Notable transformation of the psychosocial state of the followers has become apparent as the new order has become established and a more satisfying culture, including a successful economic system, is established (Wallace 1966:162). "Extensive cultural changes" liberate followers to embark on organized projects, to establish the movement and achieve wider "social, political, or economic reform." During the cultural transformation some projects "fail not through any deficiency in conception or execution, but because circumstances make defeat inevitable" (Wallace 1956b:275).

6. Routinization. During this phase of activity, social realities require the innovative and revolutionary movement to refocus on the need for maintenance through ritual, myth, and appropriate administrative and legislative forms. The charismatic energy at this stage is to a certain extent redirected towards the aims of long term survival. As the necessity for maintenance increases, innovation wanes proportionately. The establishment of new ritual processes and social contracts becomes necessary to perpetuate the historical myth, to transmit the story to the children, to guarantee permanency of the new order, and to create a legal-rational basis for transfer of power from the prophet to the followers. Normalization of beliefs and practices is inevitable "with the mere passage of time" (Wallace 1956b:275). The timing and extent of routinization is in tension with charismatic, prophetic authority (Weber 1964, 1968), but failure at this point appears to spell death for even the most create revitalization attempts.

Return to Steady State

Since the purpose of revitalization movements is to reframe the culture and thereby to alleviate the damaging stress of cultural distortion, the final outcome requires a stable and fulfilling cultural form. The return to an overall steady state is not a re-establishment of the old order, but rather a cultural reconfiguration that combines old aspects of the culture with innovative adaptations to new social realities (1956b:275; 1966:163).

The Jesus Movement's Revitalization Timeline

If we are to use Wallace's revitalization paradigm to define the Jesus Movement, it will be necessary to show that this Movement followed the pattern laid out by Wallace. The early 1950s approximate the *Steady State*. During that *Happy Days* period parodied in the television comedy series,[15] disorganization and stress were kept at tolerable limits and the majority of the population seemed to be able to find a satisfying level of self-actualization. Family was nuclear, centered round a working dad; the economy boomed, and the middle class thrived. The churches were full, and her institutions were respected (Ellwood 1997:24-26).

From the mid-1950s to the beginning of the 1960s, the period of the "beat generation," emerging conflict was evident. The dynamic equilibrium of the immediate postwar period was now giving way to rapid cultural change and evidence of increased stress and disillusionment. Sociologist Robert Ellwood (1997, 2000) regards the 1950s as the harbinger of religious upheaval and social dissatisfaction, that approximates to the disorganization which proceeds cultural distortion. Egoism and antisocial behaviors were surfacing, reflected in the new genre of the arts, as expressed in films such as *Rebel Without a Cause* (1955), and the "beat" generation poetry. Deep divisions cracked the cultural crust. Anticommunist, cold war fears were intensified following the production of the H-bomb, the escalation of the Korean War, and the rise of McCarthyism.

Serious cultural distortion was apparent during the 1960s. It was a non-integrative and unstable period, which threatened to collapse the established order. The hostilities of the generation gap, wide dissent within the academy, fear and loathing of historic institutions, and widespread departures from traditional values and social norms destabilized the society. The long history of patriotism gave way to anti-American, anti- Vietnam War protest, draft card and flag burning, and widespread civil disobedience.

This cultural distortion set the stage for a period of attempted revitalization, which was expressed in the broader counterculture from the 1960s to the mid 1970s and in the substrata of the Jesus Movement from the late 1960s to the early 1980s. Dissenters sought to overthrow a dysfunctional order, challenge ineffective institutions, and call for a major shift in worldview. This gave rise to the birth of new ethical codes and behavior, an evangelical, fervent communication to the masses, new organizations shaped by charismatic leaders, and a re-adaptation of old values to the contemporary, social state of being. The dissenting behavior, far from being only a rejection of the existing order, reflected a belief in the possibility of cultural transformation, or revolution.

Finally, the *new steady state* emerged by the late 1970s, or early 1980s, during which the new society settled down to a satisfactory cultural matrix for the provision of healthy, vibrant and fulfilling patterns of life, with new, or revised cultural values. Jesus Freaks were established in astutely routinized, new paradigm churches, or had become incorporated in renewed local, denominational congregations. The stresses appeared to diminish, although current social indicators may reveal continuing cultural distortion.

Previous Scholarship

Much research and writing exists concerning the counterculture and the Jesus Movement, but most has been in the form of historical monographs, or sociological, psychological and ideological analysis of specific groups. Several theses and dissertations have been written concerning this movement either from an historical position (Di Sabatino 1994 and Peterson 1990a), or in the domain of sociology (Bozeman 1990; Heinz 1976a; Tipton 1982), and church growth (Miller 1997). Currently there appears to be a renewed interest in the Movement, and its *second wave* effect, or in the Movement's innovative relationship to postmodernity and popular culture.

Karol Borowski's work is the only contribution I know of that claims to be an anthropological analysis of a 1960s alternative group (Borowski 1984). But it is more a sociological analysis of a particular utopian community, describing it as a revitalization. He concentrates on the strengths and weaknesses of the communal structure and organization. Some excellent ethnography is supplied, but the outcome is a specific sociology of the Renaissance Movement, Massachusetts, which group was based ideologically on a New Age source.[16] He draws little on the details of revitalization theory, except for a reference to the stress drivers for new religious movements and the use of Wallace's theory as a structural and functional paradigm for describing communal renewal movements. Apart from the Wallace definition as an introductory guide (Borowski 1984:6, cf. Wallace 1956b:265), Borowski does not cite him again.

Personal Entry Point

This dissertation has arisen under unusual conditions. My undergraduate qualifications in education and theology, combined with a passionate, lifelong habit of eclectic reading, had initially seemed sufficient for the activist's task of Jesus Movement leadership. Bewildering conflicts within the Movement sometimes overshadowed exhilarating achievements. Reflection on the causes was inevitable. There were inevitable cultural and social causes beyond the genius and foibles of movement founders. The author has not only been a participant observer in the social science sense, but a long-term pioneer and activist leader of the Movement which he has recently sought to analyze from a more objective and academic standpoint.

During the research phase it became apparent that the semi-communal, new movements with which I am familiar had their roots in social and cultural realities larger than the passionate conviction of the participants. The opportunity to pursue doctoral studies occurred in mature years, providing the disciplines and vocational concentration essential to a serious analysis of social movements. Varied and extensive social impacts for good and ill occurred, out of all proportion to the resources, or cultural positioning of such movements. It is apparent that irrespective of whether one believes or disbelieves in a divine, supernaturalistic element, such movements arose as a direct consequence of external, sociocultural realities.

Ideology and leadership were paramount in attracting large followings of hopeful young revolutionaries, but they were not sufficient to explain either the phenomenon of rapid growth, or the dropout rate. Within the alternative subcultures of the 1960s, as within indigenous groups' responses to colonist invasion, people made choices that reflected their own personal or tribal search for a satisfactory set of beliefs and institutions to fulfill deeply felt needs. Some movements moved on to acquire substantial resources and the routinization of their charismatic energy and utopian dreams. Others, that initially appeared promising became fragmented, disillusioned, and ceased operation.

The reasons for success and failure seemed to lie in social processes, that occurred irrespective of the democratic or dictatorial style of the charismatic leaders. Stabilization or collapse was related to both internal and external forces. The manner in which each group related to the dominant cultural realities, and the extent of the acceptability of their innovations by the wider culture contributed to success or failure. Focused opposition from the controlling institutions of the society appeared to have bearing on the survival or demise of some groups. Some were collapsed by severe economic outcomes resulting from court action. If the vision was divine, the cultural realities were social, economic, and organic.

I was privileged to be introduced to the art-science of cultural anthropology at an intense stage of quandary concerning these issues. While being instructed by Dr. Darrell Whiteman, an anthropologist widely experienced in fieldwork and the academic stream (Whiteman 1983), I chose a course unit entitled, "The Change Agent in Mission." Investigation of cultural change, particularly rapid cultural innovation, led inevitably to the work of Wallace, and his revitalization paradigm. Of all the critical tools for examining the movements with which I was familiar, it seemed to be the most applicable. It was theoretically interpretive of the social movement to which I had given almost three decades. The "why" questions, rather than the "how" questions were my primary concern. Cultural anthropology, with its ethnohistoric, diachronic view of culture, placed emphasis on meanings behind the patterns of human response.

Research Methodology

This is an historical and theoretical dissertation requiring ethnographic, participant observation skills in the tradition of anthropology. I have employed an inductive approach in keeping with the anthropological method, thus preferring qualitative analysis for this purpose (Cresswell 1994; Pelto and Pelto 1978; Rudestam and Newton 1992). Quantitative methodology could reveal much that will not be investigated in this study. The full impact of economic, political, geographical, and demographic variables on typical membership, leadership styles, retention rates, and social form requires both quantitative and qualitative data, but statistically focussed, quantitative analysis encounters several substantial obstacles in the study of new religious movements. Henry Luce III, the publisher of the memorable *Time* magazine report in 1971 noted that their prime investigative journalist, Richard Ostling, "found the contrast with covering more conventional religion stories profound" (Luce 1971:9). He reported that "the movement is amorphous, evasive, going on everywhere and nowhere" (1971:9). While more data became available in ensuing years, research data relevant to the initial causes and processes of growth often remain elusive.

New religious movements frequently lack helpful and critical documentation and historical records (Balmer and Todd 1994; Borowski 1984). Such groups may have no membership lists, meeting attendance lists, or social demographic data available. Initially they often fail to keep minutes of meetings, or written records of significant meeting procedures and outcomes. Sociologist Max Weber (1864-1920) noted that charismatic authority often has "a character specifically foreign to everyday routine structures" (Weber 1964:363:392), thus enforcing significant policy changes and governing structures without legal-rational agreements (1964:329-341).

Quantitative studies of specific Jesus Movement units are available. Miller has provided demographics and statistics on social opinions of leadership and congregations of the Calvary Chapel, Vineyard, and Hope churches (Miller

1997:191-231). These were achieved by the employment of a financially underwritten research team, unavailable to most students. The samples are of ideologically and demographically similar groups, which represent only one of the several ideological variations within the Movement.

Quantitative analysis embracing all genres of the Jesus Movement would be a massive task, requiring comparisons of many case studies carried out by separate research teams, targeting a wide variety of groups. Hopefully in the future there will be a sufficient research base for broader analysis of the Movement. Joe Peterson, a past leader in the Movement, has an impressive research database on the Shiloh Movement and related groups from the Pacific Northwest. He launched an inquiry into standard demographics, but also into worldview orientation at a political level. Supplemented by his participant-observation of the Jesus Movement in Oregon and Washington, this work resulted in a comprehensive analysis of these groups (Peterson 1990a).

The antipathy felt by new religious movements to the release of their data is an obstacle particularly in early stages. Many initially effective movements served their time, but no longer exist. Interviews even with those who are disillusioned or disappointed with the collapse of their movements consistently reveal that the impact of revitalization participation endures long after the movement disappears. Much of the Movement's impact is invested in the diaspora of previous Jesus Freaks across the socioreligious terrain, long after the coffee shops, communes, Jesus papers, and street witnessing pioneers have disappeared. Tracing these stories, and obtaining primary documentation for just one movement is an arduous task. Archives are virtually nonexistent for the early years of most movements. Documentation is difficult to obtain for the majority of the numerous, smaller movements, which did not attain permanency, but together generated a wider consciousness that became the Jesus Movement.

No central leader or body of theology existed to coordinate a Jesus Movement denomination that could claim dominance, as did the Reformation, or the Evangelical Awakening of Methodism. Hagiographic references to Chuck Smith as the father of the Jesus Movement ignore the diversity and the indigenous nature of the foundation period. As Di Sabatino (1994) has demonstrated in his history of the Movement, the foundations of the Southern Californian expression predated Smith's Calvary Chapel venture.

There are positive reasons also for my choice of qualitative rather than quantitative methodology. The problem I wished to research was not so much that of social structure and constitution, but rather a holistic understanding of meanings, significance, and broader dynamics of development. Cultural anthropology provides a holistic tradition for the collection of data (Ember and Ember 1993:3; Hiebert 1983:20). It embraces language, family life, ideology, art, and artifacts, going beyond social description, to deeper meanings behind the images, ritual processes, and social constructs. Qualitative analyses of a large number of projects in multiple-case studies (Yin 1994:38-53) are appropriate for the broader purpose of comparing the Jesus Movement to the movemental model of revitalization. Consistent with qualitative design (Creswell 1994; Kerlinger 1973), the anthropological methods of ethnohistorical research and participant observation are well suited to my lengthy involvement in the Movement.

My adoption of the counterculture and the Jesus Movement was a gestalt conversion, rather than a gradual cognitive shift. This has been both a gift for intuitive understanding of the native feelings and meanings of the subculture, but also a scholarly disadvantage. Paul Hiebert (1983) differentiates between the emic and etic models of inquiry into cultural form and meaning. The etic model observes the receptor culture's world as a sympathetic outsider, applying the tools of the dominant culture's conceptual categories, basic assumptions, and scientific models. The emic model views the culture from the perspective of the native participants' interpretation of their own values and meanings (1983:50-54). It admits to a bias that I am happy to defend. The emic model requires empathy, skill in listening, cultural sensitivity, and a lengthy process of ethnographic interviewing.

Understanding the reasons and meanings behind phenomena attracts me more than the chronicling of their diversity. My shift at the end of the 1960s went far beyond sympathetic attempts to get into counterculture heads. A cynicism about mainstream cultural assumptions and methodologies was inevitable. Despite this, mainstream influences on me during the formative years until my mid-twenties, before my ideological and sociological conversion in my late twenties, encouraged me to also use the objective frameworks required in etic analysis.

Practitioners in the field of ethnography make reference to *going native* as a danger for fieldworkers (Hiebert 1983:53; Pelto and Pelto 1978:68-70), as it may militate against objectivity. Advantages are also noted. The internalization of the habits and concerns of the people being studied may provide the anthropologist with levels of information that are difficult to obtain, recognize, or understand as an outsider (1978:69). Hiebert suggests that rather than the two views being competitive, they may be complementary. The participant-convert has less difficulty in the translation of language, meaning, and symbols, having entered centrally into the culture, or subculture. *Going native* may not be less useful, but may be recognized as a basic shift in premise for interpreting the worldview and practices of the observed culture (1983:53).

My three decades of "undercover work" with the outlaw motorcycle subculture has parallels to the work of James Spradley amongst urban nomads (1970). In the closed subculture world of the outlaw motorcyclist, there is a popular saying that *if I have to explain to you why, you wouldn't understand anyway*. Countercultures and subcultures, perhaps even more than native cultures, assume hostility and ignorance on the part of observers from outside systems. An acute understanding of the subculture language of the counterculture was learnt in the process as a principal of ethnographic inquiry (Spradley 1979:17-24).

The ability to communicate at the subcultural level was learnt by participation. Symbols, ritual processes, and body language are all important in the ethnographic description of subcultures. An incorrect handshake in the clubhouse of the Sin Fein outlaw bikers in New Zealand almost resulted in physical violence. The New Zealand gang scene is divided between numerous street gangs and outlaw motorcycle clubs. Deep divisions between "Black Power" and "White Supremacist" groups further increase tensions between groups. A thumb-gripping handshake, common to black and counterculture groups during the 1960s in the United States is the norm in Australian outlaw clubs. For the Coffin Cheaters of Melbourne it is a symbol of bona fide membership in the subculture. In New Zealand however, "White Supremacist," racist clubs view this ritual as a "nigger handshake." Such experiences of the subtleties of various countercultures assisted me in the interviewing phase. Familiarity with subtleties of language, underground connections, mutual friends, shared anecdotes, and a broad knowledge of key players and concepts opened doors and reduced initial suspicion.

I have attempted to employ the critical skills of the ethnographer and the ethnohistorian in traditional ways, to balance the bias of lengthy immersion in the Movement. The principles of ethnographic interviewing discovered in reading the research literature (Emerson, Fretz, and Shaw 1995; Jorgensen 1989; Spradley 1970, 1979, 1980), reinforced what were survival principles for me as a participant in the sub-cultures. In reconsidering experiences in counterculture societies, the ethnographic literature was invaluable preparation for a more disciplined reappraisal of voluminous notes, diaries, Jesus papers, audio taped speeches, photographs of events and people, personal correspondence, and interviews collected over three decades. Scholarly literature gave order to experiences and helped in identifying transferable concepts.

A working knowledge of the primary literature, iconography, music, and cult figures of the subcultures facilitated the utmost cooperation, as if between tribal cousins. The highly existential nature of the Movement required a felt knowledge of seminal issues, and a familiarity with counterculture worldviews. Nothing is more evocative of cynicism in the counterculture than attempts by *straights* to play *cool* and *with it*, when they know a few *hip* phrases without a *soul* connection to both counterculture language and alternative perspectives.

In keeping with the tradition of qualitative methodology, the research for this project has been exploratory, spontaneous, and flexible. It has emphasized primarily interaction with significant individuals, within a wide range of expressions of the Movement, often in the natural environment. It has been a search for meanings more than processes, for human dynamics of relationships rather than organizational outcomes.

Rudestam and Newton (1992) categorize such research as inclusive of "phenomenological, hermeneutic, naturalistic, experiential and dialectal methods" (1992:32-36). From a holistic perspective, persons, programs, and situations are not isolated elements, but inseparable aspects of the human search for a fulfilling and sustaining culture. This is a naturalistic inquiry (1992:32, 36, 74-78), "a discovery-oriented approach in a natural environment" (1992:36) seeking to understand why the Jesus People saw the world the way they did, and why they responded in a manner sharply contrasting with the expected direction of the society at the time. The hermeneutic element seeks to interpret the meanings of counterculture terms and images, popularized through their underground newspapers, music, and rituals (Rudestam and Newton 1992:33-35).

Many participants chose to shift from the 1950s nuclear family to radical communalism; from the growing competitiveness of the capitalist market to the shared purse; from the wizardry of new technology to the simplicity of a "back to earth" experimentalism. The meaning of the text of the Jesus Peoples' lives, as written in the social context of the counterculture is inevitably "personal and biased." It is difficult to interpret by purely rationalist or empiricist methods. This is an interpretation by an "inhabitant" rather than the "formal and abstract work of the mapmaker" (Rudestam and Newton 1992:35). I affirm the scholarly relevance of a quantitative scientific approach, but the interpretation of meanings and reasons requires a different approach to that of the study of methodologies and measurable outcomes. The objective capacity of the scholar to explain processes is impressive. The data are analyzed and clarified out of the sometimes-confusing tapestry of events and statistics. But as a participant, who shares the reasons, aspirations and alternative worldview of the group, one is equally amazed how often *they* (the outsiders) *just don't get it*. The participants may concede the expert's findings are irrefutable, while at the same time remaining convinced of their alternative understanding and interpretations. This study seeks to tell and understand the story from the insider's point of view. No point of view is the whole story. It is a view from a point. An inductive approach embraces phenomenology, hermeneutics, and naturalistic inquiries as valid elements of scientific research. It moves from observation to recognition of patterns, as an essential element of comprehensive inquiry and theoretical proposals. This research seeks to be empathetic towards the subject of inquiry and seeks to be loyal to the experiences of the participants of the Movement. The Jesus Movement was centered in the domain of human, spiritual, and social experience, rather than cognitive, theoretical dogma.

The primary method of inquiry is a naturalistic/ethnographic model. Because I had moved freely in a variety of Jesus Movement groups at home and abroad, research questions to participants took for granted many of the descriptive elements of ethnographic inquiry into the social and organizational life of the communities. I had experienced the life and had extensive dialogue with participants over many years. This inquiry did not begin from the standpoint of a theoretical framework in search of data for its testing. The focus of this research inquiry has been a search for interpretive reflections upon the community life and a search for emic explanations. The enquiry began open ended, flexible, in the context of everyday struggles of a generation searching for adequate meaning and social cohesion in a rapidly changing world. The practical and theoretical conclusions emerged from real life interaction (Jorgensen 1989:34-35).

Even the process of academic research had begun and was motivated by personal life experience, by interaction and inquiry into the phenomena of the 1960s and 1970s. The employment of revitalization theory as an explanatory key to understanding the Movement emerged midstream. I gathered data throughout my life journey and initially asked research questions out of personal interest. But social science demands a more purposeful, coherent marshalling of data, and the choice of a paradigm to focus the inquiry and substantiate preliminary conclusions, or explanations (Rudestam and Newton 1992:74-75). The project finally evolved out of the rigors of academic discipline.

This inquiry shall draw on the "convergence of multiple sources of evidence" approach (Yin 1994:93) to show that the Jesus Movement was part of a general revitalization attempt. It is a single study, but it employs convergent data from several ethnographic studies, marshaled for the purpose of a single major conclusion. Despite the variables, the research leads to a sustainable proposition that the Jesus Movement was a revitalization movement. The evidence is consistent with the catholic or broadly applicable model Wallace has provided, with some variables expanding elements of the theory and making it more tenable, rather than diminishing its validity.

Searching for Evidence

The suspicions of informants, and the researcher's unfamiliarity with the symbols, "street" language, and subtleties of alternative value systems complicate the gathering of reliable ethnographic data for sub-culture or counterculture movements. The values of Christianized New Guinea indigenes may be more congruent with mainstream Western Christianity than the values of a Zen devotee from the University of California, Berkeley campus. In early days of revitalization documentation is often neglected through lack of process, or disdain for documentation. The apocalyptic or eschatological bent of some groups creates a disregard for time-consuming documentation of the group's history if "the end is nigh." To understand counterculture societies requires much more than standardized surveys. Effective ethnographic interviewing requires participant observation. Before lengthy, open-ended interviews can begin, orientation to the informants' world must be established in an atmosphere of mutual trust.

Interviews

I have been fortunate to be in consistent contact with many of the Movement's early and continuing leadership and followers. There has been no need for concealed agendas as a researcher, or lengthy processes of providing assurance of my goodwill to informants (Borowski 1984:9-11). I provided guarantees to interviewees that they may, upon reading the text, make factual corrections, alter that which is inaccurate, delete confidential matter, or rectify misunderstood meanings, or interpretations of the events, or social processes. Copies of the interviews were sent to respondents from whom I received no nervous or negative responses. Some corrections of dates, or biographical and typographic details were inevitable. Interviews were, with permission, recorded on mini-disc for recording clarity, archival durability, referencing access to detail, and availability to the researching community.

Formal interviews were conducted with a balance of charismatic founders of movements or ministries, long-term lieutenants exercising major influence within the Movement, and participants, or long term observers whose relatives or friends were in the Movement. I have reviewed many anecdotes, discussions, letters, emails, and phone conversations, embracing hundreds of participants over three decades of involvement. These provide a mnemonic and written tapestry of data on which to draw. The documentation of the Movement embraced the following elements.

Primary Documentation of the Movement

Despite the diversity and fragmented nature of the Movement, I was able to compile a substantial database of original materials. This included published or recorded lectures of movement leaders, correspondence between myself and activists or participants in specific groups, and written accounts of conversions. Insight into the participants' beliefs and practices was obtained in part from archival material describing doctrines, policy and social instructions, and from propaganda training manuals, communal regulations, internal news reports, and prayer bulletins. Leaflets advertising Jesus Movement-sponsored conferences, and descriptive leaflets and histories for public relations and recruitment hint at the way participants saw the world and their mission to it. Posters and advertisements indicated not only details of events but also the ambiance of the groups. These are visual impact statements that are often more definitive than written statements. Slogans, inscriptions, movement and commune names point to the groups' worldview, ideology and behavior.

Jesus papers. No documentation more clearly reveals the interactive relationships, social forms, missional initiatives, central beliefs, geographical incidence, and affective nature of the Movement than the street level Jesus papers. At the height of the Movement I was collecting samples from over 60 groups. These are invaluable now for research. I obtained all editions of Milwaukee, Wisconsin's Street Level, all of Melbourne, Australia's Truth and Liberation, many samples of Berkeley, California's Right On, and Hollywood's Hollywood Free Paper. These are complement by a host of other samples ranging from Pentecostal and fundamentalist to highly politicized, socially activist papers like The House of the New World's Free Slave, from Sydney, Australia.

Audiovisual records. Video recordings, films, and other audiovisual materials provide the most impressionistic record of the utopian hopes, the rejection of the dominant culture, and the communitas[17] experienced by the groups. The combination of audio and visual elements more accurately conveys the social and spiritual mood and affective nature of the Movement than text alone can do.

Photographs, visual arts and icons. Photographs provide highly significant records of the early stages of protest, activism, and euphoria. I seriously doubt the Jesus Movement, or the wider counterculture would have so impacted the society without the power of the media image. Photographs in the secular press, and in the Jesus papers revealed the countercultural and innovative nature of the Movement. Time magazine's image of balding, middle-aged Chuck Smith is unforgettable (Boeth, Mohs, and Ostling 1971:34). He was immortalized, beaming with affection, surrounded by thousands of counterculture converts, as he carried a paraplegic he had just baptized from the ocean at Corona del Mar State Beach (Balmer 1989:22-24; Enroth, Ericson, and Peters 1972:91-93). It was a more powerful statement and invitation to join the revolution than any sympathetic text. As I reflect upon the most significant influences on my own life, I recognize a profound shift from the text to the image. The gestalt shift in the cultural pilgrimage was certainly accelerated by a dozen or so visual images provided either by journalism – particularly Time and Life magazine releases – or television.[18]

The open-air baptisms, protest sit-ins, Jesus rock concerts, and other typical scenes were familiar to me as a Jesus Movement participant before I engaged in formal research. Photographic images stimulate memories of experiences over decades. To convey to others an emic understanding of the counterculture by text and interview alone, without its art and images is an impossible task (Hiebert 1983:50-54). The collation of media and photographs was of critical significance in developing the ethnography of the Movement. I have included a few representative images in the text of the dissertation.

Discography. For many Jesus Movement participants I know, now mostly scattered throughout traditional denominations, popular records by Barry McGuire, Larry Norman, *Wilson McKinley*, *Love Song*, Randy Stonehill, and the groups popularized through Calvary Chapel's Maranatha Music are still felt to be the most influential aspect of Jesus Movement communication. It would be easy for a researcher to overlook the seriousness of the arts, but given the power of popular culture in transforming social consciousness, and the current size of the contemporary Christian music industry, this would be a serious omission. Di Sabatino's listing of 357 records released by Jesus Movement groups (1999a:158-213), indicates the significance of music in the Movement.

Press articles. The press' fascination, which followed the occurrence of the Jesus Movement, both stimulated and reflected the public interest. It was short lived, not necessarily indicating waning significance, but rather the short media life span of any new social issue or movement. I have personally gathered a significant representation of Jesus Movement press clippings. I gave much time to examination of considerable local and regional[19] print and electronic media coverage of the Movement, at home and abroad.

For interested scholars, a Canadian, David Di Sabatino, arguably the primary Jesus Movement historian has provided a formidable and comprehensive record of media materials for the North American and European context of the Movement (Di Sabatino 1999a). He was too young to be a Movement participant, but he has tirelessly researched the almost forgotten founders, whether deceased, or retired from active involvement in Christian activity. His MA thesis provides thoroughly researched historical data, from a sympathetic, non-participant's view of the Movement. During the research phase and since, I was in close contact with Di Sabatino, interviewing him at length as a researcher who has maintained personal contact with second generation Jesus Movement leaders, particularly Chuck Fromm and Chuck Smith Jr. from Calvary Chapel.

A Southern perspective. Despite the considerable influence of the Jesus Movement in Australia/New Zealand, Di Sabatino's annotated reference volume contained no scholarly papers, press reports, or discography from that region. The movement with which I was associated was reported in approximately 900 print media articles, sometimes at considerable depth and length. I had the advantage of access to these materials, collecting not only the media releases about our own movement, but a great many other Australian press releases, positive and negative, pertaining to the Jesus Movement. Several Australian academics in church history and psychology of religion have written assessments of the Jesus Movement's impact on the Australian church and society (Breward 1988; Kaldor and Kaldor 1988).

Bibliography

The number of literary items related to the Jesus Movement as recorded in Di Sabatino's annotated bibliography (1999a) is some indication of its significance. Di Sabatino records 279 historical documents, ranging from denominational critiques, media analysis, journal interviews, historical monographs, and Jesus Movement publications (1999a:23-80). He lists a further 45 books and articles of a sociological nature, many being from scholarly journals, particularly in the fields of sociology, sociology of religion, and psychology of religion (1999a:90-91). The Movement's impact at the fringes of Judaism gave rise to 26 items listed by Di Sabatino (1999a:92-95). The media interest, in both secular and religious periodicals and newspapers, via reviews, reports, and analysis, accounts for 693 citations in his bibliography (1999a:96-129). Foreign sources, mostly French and German, provide a further 134 entries (Di Sabatino 1999a:129-137).

It was necessary to become familiar with many general works on the overall religious ferment of the 1950s to the 1990s,[20] some of which feature specific Jesus Movement groups. Of primary importance was a comprehensive study of the historical and biographical accounts of the Jesus Movement, some of which are hagiographies, while others are skilled social science.[21] Many scholarly papers and books were available providing various, objective assessments. As a participant, I had collected most of the manuals, teaching volumes, and other works of the best known Jesus Movement leaders.

While the anthropological works of Wallace are central to the dissertation, I have sought to familiarize myself with sociology of religion publications, particularly literature that focuses on the phenomenon of New Religious Movements, some of which employ revitalization theory in their analysis.[22]

Delimitations

While this study embraces a measure of historical research to fulfill the diachronic needs of ethnography, the variety and geographical spread of the Movement's incidence requires prodigious research to supply a comprehensive account of the individual expressions of the Movement in any one country. I have not provided a thorough, in- depth history of the total Movement. Di Sabatino has achieved much of this for the American stage (1994, 1999a). In Chapters 1-3, I have included representative, or archetypal leaders, and communities, to create an ideological and ethnographic sense of the total Movement. The ethnohistories of two American variations in Chapters 4 and 5 are contrasted with samples of the Australian Jesus Movement in Chapter 6.

I have provided scant description of the more extreme elements, or cults, associated with the Movement. The dividing line between indigenous, sect or cult movements is unstable. The subjective nature of social and ideological categories complicates the issue. One person's cult may be another's security, depending on the definition of orthodoxy. Orthodoxy within the typologies of social science is as porous as within theology (Melton 1998; Stark and Bainbridge 1979, 1981, 1985, 1996; Stark, Bainbridge, and Doyle 1979; Bryan Wilson 1990). It may be argued that cults are the inevitable promoters of generally unacceptable ideas, which may become mainstream orthodoxy later (Fink and Stark 1997:54-108; Stark and Bainbridge 1985:126-262).

Some elements of the Movement began as theologically orthodox, but moved toward the cult end of the movement continuum. Linda Meisner, initially a staff worker with the respected drug rehabilitation work, Teen Challenge, became an associate of David Brant Berg, in the much-maligned cult, the Children of God. During her transition between mainstream Jesus Movement leadership in the Pacific Northwest, and her shift to the Children of God (Sine 1999), she was a prime strategist and trainer of several Jesus Movement leaders (Palosaari 1999; Sine 1999). Some of these were later involved with respected movements such as the Calvary Chapel Movement, and Chicago's Jesus People USA (JPUSA) which is now a religious order within the Evangelical Covenant Church.

At the opposite end of the spectrum, historic denominations, both Protestant and Catholic were in a measure renewed through the interaction of local communities of faith within Jesus Movement ministries or communes. I have largely ignored the considerable impact of the Jesus Movement within historic denominations. The Movement's impact upon the general church community has been investigated in the United Kingdom (Corey 1973a, 1973b; Pete Ward 1996), and Australia (Kaldor 1987; Kaldor and Kaldor 1988). Alvin Reid has researched the broad effects of Jesus Movement revitalization on Southern Baptist communications, worship forms, and evangelical zeal (Reid 1991, 1995). In Australia growth and creativity occurred in Anglican, Uniting Church, Baptist, and Churches of Christ, directly and indirectly through the influence of the Jesus Movement and the infusion of converts into local congregations. A focused study on the impact of the Movement on a particular congregation could yield much data concerning the interface between new religious movements and mainstream religious institutions.

Regrettably, a chapter on the Church of the Redeemer Episcopal (Pulkingham 1972, 1980, 1973) had to be abandoned following extensive research (Smith 2000). Conclusive proof of the connection between the Charismatic Movement and the Jesus Movement requires considerably more time and space than was available for this dissertation. The Redeemer case study is unnecessary to establish the Jesus Movement as a revitalization. I found a rich source of ethnographic material there for the study of the rise and fall of one of many communitarian movements established in the 1960s (Farra 1999; McGregor 1999, 2000; Munro 1999, 2000; Newman 1999; Pulkingham 1999; Woodruff 1999). I have chosen to bypass this significant case study of a countercultural, revitalizing innovation. Communalism was a central theme of the 1960s movements, and several specific examples of these experimental communities have been documented (Borowski 1984; Bozeman 1990; Peterson 1996a, 1996b, 1990a, 1990b; Peterson and Mouss 1973; Richardson, Stewart, and Simmonds 1979).

There is some evidence that the "new paradigm" churches and "megachurches," as defined by sociologist Donald Miller (1997) and church growth analyst Peter Wagner (Wagner 1973, 1989) were in some cases also an outcome of the revitalization. Some are loosely affiliated with historic denominations, which benefited from the revitalization. This phenomenon of renewed and creative radicals, returning "home" to their origins, could supply a wealth of material to expand the theoretical constructs of the sociology of religion. Others trained by the Jesus Movement have been recruited by traditional churches as creative leaders. A dozen past primary leaders from Truth and Liberation Concern and Care and Communication Concern, the movements with which I was associated, are now pastors, chaplains, and academics serving in Baptist, Churches of Christ, Uniting Church, and Catholic contexts. I have again chosen to bypass this significant element.

I have not supplied a comprehensive description of any particular group, having been satisfied to provide a reasonable description of typical variations, for the purpose of a broader analysis of the Jesus Movement revitalization. The Vineyard and Calvary Chapel movements have published non-academic accounts of their story, with biographic and historic detail (Jackson 1999; Smith and Brooke 1992; Smith and Steven 1972).

Theoretical and Practical Worth

Some of the new wave of movemental theorists[23] regards social movements as the primary cultural force for initiating rapid cultural innovation. The importance of social movements in the transformation of culture makes research into recent movements a significant pursuit of knowledge. The impact of the counterculture movements of the 1960s, as discussed in Chapter 2, justifies further research into their causes and their meanings (Ellwood 1994; Giugni, McAdam, and Tilly 1999; Jasper 1997).

The Between Age

It has become common to view the movements of the 1960s onward as evidence of the impact of postmodernism on popular culture (Ellwood 1994:91). Postmodernism is viewed as an historic shift from the age of reason, logic, and analysis, to a new age quite distinct from that which we have ever known before. The postmodern shift is far from a "fait accompli," being perhaps an adolescent philosophical response to the dysfunction and inadequacy of scientific modernity to meet the perceived needs of current social and spiritual realities. Postmodernity is not so much a cohesive alternative worldview, as a critique of rationalism, positivism, and functionalism. Most of us live our lives daily on the basis of both modern pragmatics and postmodern perceptions. This is a temporary age of synthesis, with no clear end in sight as to the evolutionary outcomes (H. Ward 1972:27-39). Ellwood (1994:91) sees the 1960s counterculture and the Jesus

Movement as an early expression of postmodern popular culture. If as he proposes and this dissertation claims, that those movements were a first wave of popular culture postmodernity, such inquiries as this supply important foundational data for examining the changing status of social movements during the postmodern flux.

Movement theorist, James Jasper (1999) views social movements, particularly revitalization movements, as prime sources of wide-ranging, social reconstruction. Globalization tensions will most likely continue to foster further revitalization movements. I hope that reassessments of past success and failure of revitalization attempts will provide insights for future leaders and their disciples.

Unresolved Tensions

In the West, traditional institutionalized faith has given way to new, personalized forms of religious community, which may find few parallels apart from the Gnostic movements at the time of Christianity's birth (Ellwood 1994:130-131). Tension between modernity models of control in political and religious institutions and the postmodern culture of individualistic rootlessness is far from resolved. Current anti-globalization movements serve notice of ongoing cultural distortion. If movements are to successfully communicate their messages and marshal transformational forces in response to the inevitable dangers of postmodern, global realities, the lessons learned from revitalization success, or failure, may be invaluable.

Definitions

Many terms that are familiar to the author as a participant may be obscure or even misleading to the reader, particularly the counterculture terms sometimes employed.

"Beat:" Short for beatnik, this is technically the term for a group of dissenting United States writers in the 1950s who were the precursor to the hippie counterculture. They were marked by their rejection of conventional social mores, unconventional dress and behavior, and the propagation of exotic philosophies, particularly from the East (Ginsberg 1963; Kerouac 1958; Watts 1950, 1959). Their writings had considerable influence on the next generation of hippies. A recognized formula of "Beats plus LSD = Counterculture" was a popular perception in the 1960s (Unger & Unger 1998:158-160). Steve Turner (1996) provides a visual and written tapestry of Kerouac's life and his evolution into the 1960s.

Counterculture: A minority culture with values and mores that run counter to those of the dominant or established culture. The 1960s cultural rebellion in Western countries became known generally as "the counterculture," a definition particularly promoted by Californian dissident academic Theodore Roszak, in his publication of *The Making of a Counterculture* (1968), though the term is often used more generally.

Communitas: Victor Turner (1969) has popularized the term *communitas*. Following the experience of acute liminality individuals experience an intense sense of existential and timeless connection to each other, as they are re-aggregated in a new social arrangement, usually following stressful rituals. *Communitas* is not necessarily inherent in the concept of community. Turner chooses the Latin term *communitas* rather than community, to distinguish this intense special social relationship from the "area of common living" (1969:96-97). Turner notes "the values of *communitas* are strikingly present in the literature and behavior of what came to be known as the 'beat generation,' who were succeeded by the 'hippies' . . . who 'opt out' of the status-bound social order and acquire the stigmata of the lowly, dressing like 'bums,' itinerant in their habits, 'folk' in their music tastes, and menial in the casual employment they undertake. Turner speaks of the "hippie emphasis on spontaneity, immediacy, and 'existence' [that] throws into relief one of the senses in which *communitas* contrasts with structure" (1969:113).

Culture: As defined by Louis J. Luzbetak, culture is "a plan, map, or blueprint for living . . . that is always in the process of formation and adjustment" (1988:156-159). The sets of beliefs, values, and meanings enable citizens to adapt to the "physical, social, and ideational environment" (1988:157). Culture expresses itself in symbols, rituals, artifacts, language, and institutions, which shape social interrelationships. Culture is an all-encompassing design for living. Whiteman (1983) defines culture as "the complex array of ideas that man carries in his [her] head, which are expressed in the forms of material artifacts and observable behavior" (1983:27). Counterculture movements express discontent with the existing plan and blueprint. They may attempt to overthrow and replace the existing shared meanings, values, standards, notions, beliefs, rituals and the institutions that guide and consolidate the society.

Freak: Of uncertain origin, this became the affectionate slang term applied to hippies in general, but also to persons who were committed to a belief or alternative lifestyle to the point of cultural marginalization. It may be parallel to the term "Christian" in the first century AD as it is a defining term used in derision by detractors, but embraced as a term of mutual association by members of the subculture.

Jesus Freak: Jesus Freak, rather than being a generic term for Christians was the name given to hippie Christians, whose almost fanatical commitment to Jesus and hippie appearance marked them out as Jesus Movement enthusiasts, especially during the early years of revitalization.

Liminality: The term liminality is frequently used to indicate a state of "in-between-ness" uncertainty, or suspension from supporting structures (Turner 1969:166-172). Derived from the Latin root *limen* for doorway, gateway, or threshold, it has come to also mean suspension in an existential chasm, or separation at the margin of a society. Liminality or marginality (Lee 1995) is thus a state of suspension between options producing heightened awareness, tension, or even expectation. Liminality is deliberately instigated in tribal groups by extreme social and physical processes.

Hippie: [Slang] referring to a (mostly) young person of the 1960s who due to alienation from conventional society turned variously to psychedelic drugs, mysticism, tribalism, communal living and alternative lifestyles in music, hair styles, clothing and social associations.

People group: Strictly speaking it is "a people in one country with a specific language as mother tongue with unique combined identity" (Barrett and Johnson 2001:615). In missiological terms it has come to indicate a culture or sub-culture in which members share a sufficiently distinctive basis for corporate identity to be observable to non-members as well as being a self-defining aspect. "A significantly large grouping of individuals who perceive themselves to have a common affinity for one-another because of shared language, religion, ethnicity, residence, occupation, class or caste, situation etc, or combination of these" (Winter and Koch 1999:514). By this definition it is arguable that hippies during the 1960s were a distinct people group.

Postmodern: Coming after and in reaction to the modern understanding of reality and epistemology, often in reaction to scientific rationalism, literalism and objectivism. It is a rejection primarily of the Cartesian worldview that emerged from the Enlightenment. Reaction to 20th century modernism is particularly noticeable in the arts, literature, psychology, and sociopolitical analysis. In religion a rejection of dogma and denominationalism has given rise to more affective, personalized religious practices (Grenz 1996).

Postmodernism/
Postmodernity:
Interchangeable terms for the current interim philosophical worldview, which seeks to deconstruct and challenge the Cartesian/Enlightenment worldview that has dominated Western cultures since the triumph of the scientific revolution.

Primitive Church:
The term "primitive church" usually alludes to the early stages of the development of the Christian church as described in the biblical account of the Book of Acts and thus is often employed as a synonym for "early church." Revivals and renewal movements frequently draw on images of the "primitive church" for inspiration. The communalism, *communitas*, fervent proclamation, and mass conversions of that period provide a sense of divine approval and social cohesion, which attracts those who are committed to revitalization movements.

Revival:
A period of intense, popular interest in religion, usually associated with mass gatherings, highly emotional evangelistic meetings and mass conversions to the faith. Emphasis is on personal salvation rather than cultural transformation as in revitalization or major "renewals" such as the 18th and 19th century Awakenings in America.

Revitalization:
Generally used as a term for the renewal of a culture, a worldview, or even a city, but in this dissertation it is more distinctly defined according to anthropologist Anthony F. C. Wallace. As the scholar who popularized it as an anthropological term for a distinct form of social movement, Wallace defines revitalization as "a conscious, deliberate, organized effort on the part of some members of a society to create a more satisfying culture" (1956b:265). This occurs during a period perceived to be one of severe cultural decay, dysfunction, or disintegration.

"Straight":
During the counterculture period "straight" was the antonym of "hip." If you were not counterculture, you were a "straight." A regular mainline church would be a "straight" church. It did

	not always denote derision or lack of respect. There were good and bad "straights."
Third World:	The so-called "underdeveloped" or emerging countries of the world community, most of which are in the eastern and southern hemispheres in Africa, Latin America, and Asia, in contrast to the "first world" of (largely western) economically advanced nations and the "second world" of the (former) Communist Block nations.
Soft-Pentecostal:	
	Neo-Pentecostalism is a parallel term. Particularly since the rise of the denominational charismatic movement and the Jesus Movement, the theological and social separatism of the traditional Pentecostal churches has "softened." The "old" hard-line Pentecostal view of other churches, which they sometimes described as the "whore of Babylon" because of tolerance of liberalism in theology and libertarianism in behavior has been modified in "soft" or neo-Pentecostal groups. "Hard line" Pentecostals teach that "speaking in tongues" is an essential proof of salvation and others view it as an essential evidence of the "Baptism" or fullness of the Spirit. Most New Paradigm churches accept the gifts of the Spirit, including tongues, prophecy, revelations, and divine healing, but in a less strident or dogmatic manner than the traditional Pentecostals.

In Search of the Jesus People

This introduction seeks to highlight the significance of the Jesus Movement, and to propose a theoretical and practical way to gather the diverse threads of this short-lived, complex and socially transformational movement. Since it may hold valuable keys to understanding the nature of creative human response to severe cultural crisis, its history and cultural expressions are worthy of research and analysis.

While this chapter provides an outline of the intentions and methodology of this project, there remains another preparatory task prior to the examination of case studies. If, as I suppose, the Movement was a revitalization attempt, certain sociocultural preconditions must be established as historical fact. The Jesus Movement was neither separate from, nor fully congruent with the secular counterculture from which it emerged. The next chapter will explain its relationship to the historic events in the larger cultural context, and its enigmatic relationship to the counterculture rebellion from which it clearly emerged.

Notes

1. The following vignettes, adapted from the author's autobiography, On the Side of the Angels (Smith and Doney 1987), provide the context for a life journey of participant observation, resulting in this dissertation. Being written nearer to the time of the early revitalization from numerous interview tapes, it provides a counter to memory lapses on the part of the author, and its popular literary form revives the existential feel of the subculture at the time.

2. *Time* (Boeth, Mohs, and Ostling 1971:32-43); *America* (Donohue 1973); *Psychology Today* (Harder, Richardson, and Simmonds 1975:45-113); *Commonweal* 97 (1972:44-46); *The Wall Street Journal* (Gottschalk 1971:1); *U.S. News & World Report* (1972:59-65); *Look* (Cheetham 1971:15-21); *Rolling Stone* (Cahill 1973a:42-50, 1973b:50-60) and *Christianity Today* (Bastien 1970:328; Chandler 1971:332-3; Plowman 1972a:379-80). Many city newspapers of smaller circulation, such as the *Toronto Star* (Harpur 1971a:61, 1972:85); *The Milwaukee* Journal; Milwaukee *Sentinel* ran frequent items on local Jesus People.

3. *Annual Review of the Social Sciences of Religion* (Richardson and Reidy 1980:183-20); *Social Compass* (Jacobsen and Pilarzyk 1974:225-58); *Society for the Scientific Study of Religion* (Jacobsen and Pilarzyk 1971); *American Behavioral Scientist* (Richardson, Simmonds, and Harder 1977:819-838); *Journal of Social Issues* (Balswick 1974:32-42); *Society* (Adams, Lynn, and Fox 1972:50-56); *Social Compass* (Harder 1974:345-348); *Journal of Voluntary Action Research* (Richardson, Simmonds, and Harder 1979:93-111); *Youth and Society* (Richardson, Simmonds, and Harder 1972:184-202)

4. Denominational journals included Baptist, *Home Missions* (Burns 1971:47-52; Druin 1971:43-46; Marty 1971:35; Price and Hullum 1971:13-23); Reformed, *Reformed Journal* (Van Eldren 1971); Catholic, *Fides et. Historia* (Tiffin 1972, Fall: 79-85); Brethren, *Brethren Life and Thought* (Eller 1971:101-108; Moyer 1972:167-174); and Lutheran, (Lochaas 1976).

5. *Christian Century* (Berkey 1972:336-338; Lovelace 1971:1164-1171); *Eternity* (Enroth 1973:14-17, 28; Plowman 1971b:8-11, 31); *Theology Today* (Marty 1972:470-76); *United Evangelical Action* (McKenna 1971:9-14) joined such unlikely participants in the inquiry as *The Critique* (Quinn 1971). In the general field of religion, interest was also aroused, in *Judaism* (Adler 1974:287-97); *Christianity and Crisis* (McGraw 1973:87-89); *Review of Religious Research* (Perrin and Mauss 1991:97-111).

6. The inquiry into cults predates the "cultish" period of the counterculture. Stark and Bainbridge directly incorporated the 1960s and 1970s into their continuing research. In court, Stark defended the Moonies against evidence opposing cults. The following are useful texts in the difficult field of cult and sect definition: Bainbridge 1950a, 1950b, 1981, 1989, 1997:208-40; Bainbridge and Stark 1963, 1979; Prittchet 1985; Stark 1996a; Stark and Bainbridge 1979, 1980, 1981; Stark, Bainbridge, and Doyle 1979.

7. In the early days of the Movement some participants discovered the reason for the derisive use of the term "enthusiast," against the early Methodists. The English term is derived from *en theos*, "possessed of the gods," as the Greeks would describe those whose commitment to religion, or even sport, went beyond the normal patterns of social behavior, to the point of total absorption and fanaticism. Although intentionally more affectionate and positive than the epithet "enthusiast" of Wesley's day, "Jesus Freak"

shared the sense of abandonment, bordering on fanaticism for a cause, or a lifestyle. As with many subculture words, the texture of its meaning was deeply existential. For insiders to say "She's a Jesus Freak" was to say much more than "She's a Christian." Something alternative, new, and outrageously independent of the traditional, institutionalized forms of religion was implied. This was a "lifestyle" – another term born of that era – thus being a "freak" was more than the acceptance of a cognitive code of intellectual beliefs, with accompanying ritual processes. For those who gladly saw themselves as "Jesus Freaks," the name told the world that Jesus was not a sporadic experience, or a commitment centering in the few hours of attendance at religious gatherings. Jesus was the overwhelming focus of their waking hours. What I experienced in working with the Jesus People indicates that there was an existential and social fixation on Jesus, which is uncommon amongst most traditional, evangelical, liberal, or even Pentecostal adherents.

8. Tipton assumes only two flows of historic consciousness. The first was a traditional American moral culture based on biblical, authoritative religion, holding to a deontological theory of ethics (Tipton 1982:3-6), and second, a coexisting utilitarian individualism (1982:6-14). His understanding of historic, Puritan, biblical religion assumes an entrenched dualism and textual fundamentalism. In my opinion he ignores the contribution of Methodism and a range of more communitarian, indigenous American religions, such as several Mennonite groups, for whom the radical, individual voluntarism and utilitarian individualism which marked Puritan and utilitarian models, is seen as unbiblical. There is a certain reductionism about his description of biblical Christianity, as if there was only one clear philosophical expression of it. The significance of the Catholic creational view rather than a redemptive emphasis of biblical understanding is not seen as a primary force in the development of American moral consciousness, despite the obviously significant presence of such contributors as Irish, Italian, and Spanish Catholic immigrants. He sees Puritan morality and secular, utilitarian morality as both holding individual freedom to be a central value, even though they meant quite different things by it – one proclaimed the freedom to obey God faithfully, the other to pursue self interest efficiently (1982:13). Bellah (Glock and Bellah 1974) speaks of the corruption of the biblical tradition by utilitarian individualism, so that religion itself finally became, for many, "a means for the maximization of self interest, with no effective link to virtue, charity or community" (Glock and Bellah 1974:336; also See Tipton 1982:4, 309 cf. 1982:182). Tipton describes American society as continuing to invoke the rhetoric and symbols of biblical religion, even while it acts according to utilitarian values. While his description of the breakdown of traditional moral cohesion in American society as the source of counterculture revolt is well argued, he assumes there were only two counterculture responses. This was a short-lived attempt by hippies to embrace Eastern monism as a basis for holistic living. Some returned to extreme deontological, fundamentalist, biblical literalism, to resolve the ethical complexity of postmodern morality. A central element of the failure of Tipton's analysis is the academically ignored, "third way" of the Jesus Movement radical discipleship groups. Many of these were influenced by Methodist, Catholic or Anabaptist theology. They equally claimed to be a biblically based, but radically obedient to an inherent sociopolitical application.

9. The Jesus Movement cannot be understood apart from contemporary sociopolitical, religious, and psychological issues. The Movement reflected a radical contextualization of the Christian message to the times. Though based on a holistic, biblical assumption, rather than the monistic fusion of Western and Eastern thought of the counterculture, the Jesus people initially found common cause with their secular counterparts.

10. By Evangelical we refer to the acceptance of the Christian Scriptures as the basis for faith and conduct, with special emphasis on the New Testament and the person and

work of Christ. Evangelical faith emphasizes personal salvation by the grace of God, accepted by faith, and requiring personal conversion. The term Evangelical is in a state of evolution. Where once it implied a Protestant belief, Evangelicals are found in all major traditions. The acceptance of more ritual process and iconography by many Evangelicals, and the acceptance of evangelization and personal salvation by faith on the part of Catholics and other ritualistic groups has been a recent mark of considerable deregulation of denominational and theological hegemonies. The Jesus Movement was thus found to exist often in close relationship to Catholic ministries or communities, or on the other hand, Pentecostal communities of faith. Initially, in the author's experience Charismatic Catholics were more open to the Christian element of the hippie movement.

11. Edgerton 1992:29, 224n; Ember and Ember 1993:285-286, 1999:280; Hiebert 1983:394, 425, 426, 388-394; 1985:44; Hiebert and Meneses 1995:313-314; Horsley 1994:115, 120, 170; Horsley and Hanson 1999:187; Kraft 1996a:57, 107, 368, 371, 385, 438-439; Stark 1996:78-79, 211-215; Stark and Bainbridge 1985:177, 360, 430, 504, 1996:188; Whiteman 1983:173-280, 291, 301, 318#95, 319#112, 362, 387; P. Williams 1989:11, 28, 49, 57n, 61, 110, 112-113, 241.

12. Lewis R. Rambo (1993) in *Understanding Religious Conversion* explores an understanding of personal conversion as a "micro" individual revitalization.

13. Miller 1997:26; Rogers 1995:399-400; Weber 1947:363-373, 1968:48-65, 80, 138, 144, 180-181; P. Williams 1989:17, 18, 69, 105, 108-109, 112, 114, 144, 232, 241.

14. Rodney Stark is somewhat dismissive of Weber, claiming "discussions of charisma did not move beyond definitional and descriptive statements and said nothing about the causes of charisma" (Stark 1996a:24). Stark says little of the charismatic role of Paul the apostle in the Gentile, Jesus Movement revitalization of the first century, except to quote him as a commentator on certain ideas and processes of Christianity's meteoric rise (1996a:108-109). It would be advisable to further explore the processes and meanings behind charisma, rather than seeing it as epiphenomenal to the movemental issue.

15. While the production of "Happy Days" is historically a later event, the show parodies the beatnik rebellion of the 1950s when leather jackets, motorcycles, and cafés were dominant symbols. The movie "Rebel Without a Cause," (James Dean, Performer 1955) served notice that despite the "Happy Days" facade of the stable, nuclear, increasingly suburban family, all was not well by the mid-1950s.

16. Its scripture was The Aquarian Gospel of Jesus Christ: The Philosophical and Practical Basis of the Religion of the Aquarian Age of the World. Transcribed from the Akashic Records by Levi, by Levi H. Dowling 1972(1935), rather than the orthodox, biblical sources chosen by the Jesus Movement.

17. Victor Turner (1969) has popularized the term *communitas*. This phenomenon is common in new marginalized groups and cults which experience an intense existential and timeless connection to each other. It is a new social arrangement, usually following a period of intense alienation and separation from their traditional support mechanisms of belief or association. The intensity, intimacy, mystery, and existential bonding experienced are not necessarily inherent in the concept of community (1969:96-97).

18. My first experience of television coincided with its introduction to Australia for the 1956 Olympic games. It supplied indelible images of the Olympic pool, stained with human blood, as the result of the conflict between Russian and Hungarian teams, following the brutal crushing of the Hungarian attempted revolution against Soviet control. These were possibly as impacting upon my generation as the destruction of the Berlin Wall, or the Tiananmen Square image of the lone protester confronting the Chinese army tank was to my children's generation. The images that endure for me, as if seen only yesterday, include baton wielding police and dogs attacking Afro-Americans in southern

cities, the atomic test at Bikini Atoll, the aftermath of Hiroshima's destruction, the student resistance crushed by Soviet tanks in Czechoslovakia, a naked Vietnamese child aflame with napalm, a Buddhist monk self-immolating in Vietnam, and a distraught girlfriend kneeling by a slain student protester on Kent State University. They changed forever my view of politics, global economics, and personal responsibility.

19. While national or international journals would appear to provide more sophisticated analysis, local media is often of more ethnographic use in studying, for several reasons:

a. More social, personalized, lifestyle detail is included because of local content interest.

b. Frequently the local interest factor invites a serial approach, in which on-going developments are reported at regular intervals, providing a more diachronic analysis.

c. Articles are often accompanied by public reflection on the impact and acceptability of the Movement, according to both participant observers, and general public, pro and con.

d. Detail of the sociological impact on the community, and its institutions, is more likely to be provided in local media.

e. The folksy style of provincial media allows for a more contextualized analysis, rather than the reductionist analysis of a national journal seeking to subsume complex, regional variations, under a more functionalist abstract.

20. Balmer 1989; Elwood 1979, 1987, 1994, 2000; Finke and Stark 1997; Glock and Bellah 1976; Handy 1984; Heelas 1997; J. Hunter 1983; Jorstad 1990; Lotz 1989; Lovelace 1979; Martin 1996; McLoughlan 1978; Needleman 1970; Oved 1988; Roof 1993, 1999; Tipton 1982; Wuthnow 1976, 1978, 1987, 1998.

21. Balmer 1989; Balmer and Todd 1994; Blessitt and Wagner 1971; Ellwood 1976; Enroth, Ericson, and Peters 1972; Ford 1972; B. Graham 1971; Jackson 1999; Johnson 1971; Jorstad 1972b; Miller 1997; Owen and Pederson 1973; Palms 1972; Plowman 1971a; Richardson, Stewart, and Simmonds 1979; H. Ward 1972; Wind and Lewis 1994b.

22. Bainbridge 1997; Fink and Stark 1997; Giugni, McAdam, and Tilly 1999; Heelas 1997; Jasper 1997; Marx and McAdam 1994; Saliba 1995a; Stark 1996a, 1996b; Stark and Bainbridge 1985; 1996, 1997; Stewart and Denton 1994; Tarrow 1998; Touraine 1988; Whiteman 1983; Bryan Wilson 1990.

23. Giugni, McAdam, and Tilly 1999; Jasper 1997; Laraña, Johnston, and Gusfield 1994; McAdam, McCarthy, and Zald 1996; Melucci 1996a, 1996b; Meyer and Tarrow 1998; Stewart, Smith, and Denton 1994; Touraine 1988.

CHAPTER 2

The Jesus Movement – A Sign of the Times?

Swing the sickle for the harvest is ripe. Joel 3:13.

This chapter is provided to place the Jesus Movement in the broader context of the peculiar times in which it was birthed. It is a journey down memory lane to provide the reader with a sociohistorical picture from which to gain an empathetic view of the Movement. Because this is an inquiry which employs "event-analysis" (Wallace 1956b:268) exploring causes and precipitating factors, interpreted by the phenomenology of revitalization movements, it is essential to establish its relative position in the broader historical context. Its historic timing, relationship to the general culture and diversity of forms must be investigated. The Jesus Movement would not have been birthed without the turmoil of the 1950s and 1960s. It also would not have emerged but for the prior revitalization attempts of the counterculture rebellion of that era. It is significant that the hippie Christian movement thrived as the counterculture was disintegrating. Initially this began as a mission by hippies, to hippies, for hippies.

The Timing of a Revolution's Soul

The crucial events, socio-cultural responses, social indicators and the timing of counterculture movements during the 1950s to mid 1970s present compelling data for assuming the processual structure of a revitalization movement (1956b:268). I have therefore developed a timeline of events I believe to be significant from religious, political, and popular cultural perspectives, as an appendix to this volume (See Appendix 1). The turmoil of the period is evident in the extent and sequence of cultural conflicts, and in the responses of new socio-religious movements. The timeline indicates the late arrival of the Jesus Movement as a response to the failure of the counterculture. It was a revitalization challenge to many of the same inadequacies of mainstream culture that provoked the initial non-Christian rebellion, but it also challenged the alternative culture. The timing of the soul of the Jesus Freaks was intimately bound up in the timing of the nation's soul search in both the United States and Australia. The Jesus Movement was not only a religious alternative, but also a religious variation of a general theme of disaffection, utopian dreaming, and the reshaping of social consciousness.

Whether it can be proven or even confidently claimed that that period was as culturally distressed I claim here is not the issue. On the one hand I will supply numerous scholarly sources which strongly express the conviction that it was so, but the issue is not the accuracy of the perception but rather it is the extent and intensity of protest, disillusionment, and counterculture reaction that matters most. For revitalization to occur there must be a critical mass of citizens whose mutual disaffection has intensified sufficiently to create a social movement with the intent to overthrow the existing order, or provide an alternative culture. It would seem to be an anthropological norm that under such conditions passionate visionaries with a prophetic style are created by the circumstances of history.

It was a difficult birth in a dysfunctional family. Few decades in any nation's history have been marked by such contrasting hope and frustrating despair as the 1960s in the United States. The post-war period from the mid-1950s to the mid-1970s has been variously described as "the age of climax and the hinge of history" (Guinness 1994:20) and the "watershed of religious pluralism" (Di Sabatino 1999a:3). It was "a time when events went into overdrive and life blue prints were rejected, [when] people struck out on new causes" (Unger and Unger 1998:1).

> Dickens said of an earlier, similar era: "It was the best of times; it was the worst of times; it was the age of wisdom; it was the age of foolishness; it was the epoch of belief; it was the epoch of incredulity; it was the season of Light; it was the season of Darkness; it was the spring of hope; it was the winter of despair; we had everything before us; we had nothing before us; we were all going direct to Heaven; we were all going direct the other way." (1998:2)

Robert Bellah says it was "a particularly poignant moment in its [America's] historical transformation" (Tipton 1982:ix). Tipton believes "the disruptions of the 1960s occurred along old fault lines in the American terrain, particularly those separating the biblical from the utilitarian tradition" (1982:9).

A Culture of Disaffection

In every culture there are dissidents and malcontents whose self-marginalization is largely the result of personal, psychological, or physical trauma, resulting from perceived maladaptions or malfunctions of the dominant group. Sometimes a significant proportion of a society's citizens experience marginalization and disaffection as the consequence of a widespread failure of the culture to provide adequate worldviews, or institutional and social support mechanisms for reasonable security and personal fulfillment. Marginalization and disaffection are the consequence of a widespread failure of the culture to provide adequate worldviews or institutional and social support mechanisms for reasonable security and personal fulfillment.

If the culture no longer provides a satisfactory lifestyle for a growing proportion of individuals, widespread disaffection and negativity occurs. When this reaches a critical mass of citizens who share and articulate their strong disaffection with their culture, a counterculture movement, a precursor to a revitalization alternative, may arise.

This counterculture may express itself in both theoretical and practical resistance to the existing order. In defiance, it makes coordinated attempts to bring down the existing order, or establish an alternative, revolutionary subculture. Social mores, value systems, institutions, and familial arrangements may radically change during these upheavals. Scholars have recognized that such a historical event occurred in the 1960s to mid 1970s in the United States, and similarly in other Western nations.[1]

This cultural disruption arose in response to widespread disapproval of the traditions and institutions of both church and state. The materialistic worldview and the hierarchical, authoritarian culture of the older generation were targeted. Some scholars refer to that era as a Cultural Revolution, or Reformation (Amin, Arrighi, and Frank 1990; Wuthnow 1976). The counterculture movement existed in many forms, but in almost all cases it was religious, or quasi-religious in focus. The social psychology of students' lives made them a primary force in the rebellion that emerged, since they had relative freedom from economic, career, and family responsibility (Jasper 1997).

Giving clear definition to either the counterculture, or its Christian expression, the Jesus Movement, is no easy task. Whilst "counterculture" is a generic term for dissident subcultures in conflict with the dominant culture, from the 1960s it became a common designation for a general activist disaffection of diverse factions in the United States, and other Western nations. The ferment of the Civil Rights quest in the 1950s set alight more general fires of discontent in the following decades. The counterculture period was marked by anti-establishment, anti-structural protest, born of academic and youthful disillusionment with the "cold-war" society.

Generational or Ideological?

The alternative movements of the 1960s were fostered by an older generation of dissident academics, beat artists, and cult musicians in the emerging folk-rock, popular music scene. Theodore Roszak (1968, 1972a, 1972c, 1995) popularized the term "counterculture" in his seminal work on the 1960s youthful resistance to the dominant, materialistic paradigm of their parents' generation:

> [T]he young stand forth so prominently because they act against a background of nearly pathological passivity on the part of the adult generation . . . . The adults of the World War II period, trapped as they have been in the frozen posture of befuddled docility . . . have in effect divested themselves of their adulthood . . . . Which is to say: they have surrendered their responsibility for making morally demanding decisions, for generating ideals, for controlling public authority, for safeguarding the society against the despoilers. (Roszak 1968:22)

Roszak expressed the extent to which this was a serious, counterculture challenge to the alien values and structures of the mainstream culture, with passionate analysis, in a work that became a sacred text to many students.

> If the resistance of the counterculture fails, I think there will be nothing in store for us but what anti-utopians like Huxley and Orwell have forecast – though I have no doubt that these dismal despotisms will be far more stable and effective than their prophets have foreseen. For they will be equipped with techniques of inner-manipulation as unobtrusively fine as gossamer. Above all, the capacity of our emerging technocratic paradise to denature the imagination by appropriating to itself the whole meaning of Reason, Reality, Progress, and Knowledge will render it impossible for men to give any name to their bothersomely unfulfilled potentialities but that of madness. And for such madness, humanitarian therapies will be generously provided. (Roszak 1995:xli)

In his revised analysis of the counterculture, Roszak, with the hindsight of 30 years, reflects that the youthful resistance was "a footloose generation" (1995:xxvi). Their creative rebellion generated "a bright idea in Berkeley one week, [which] might be in Santa Fe the next, and Katmandu the week after that" (Roszak 1995:xxvii). Others have also referred to the counterculture as a youthful revolution (Mead 1978; Steigerwald 1995).

Margaret Mead saw an historic, unprecedented rift between youth and the older generations, which she described as the "Generation Gap" (1978:xvi-xx). Her description is compelling. The movement supporters were mostly college age and younger, but the intellectual framework underpinning the counterculture, and the charismatic leadership, was provided by an older generation of scholars, artists, and popular proclaimers. Margaret Mead was 71 years of age when she first delivered her study on the "Generation Gap." Roszak was 35 at the time of writing *The Making of a Counterculture* (1968), and 40 when he published *Where the Wasteland Ends* (1972c). The leadership icons of the Jesus Movement were not baby boomers. Jack Sparks, Arthur Blessitt, Joe Peterson, Duane Pederson, Carl Parks, Barry McGuire, and Jim Palosaari, whose ministries I shall describe in following chapters, were born during, or before World War II.

Generational language, which speaks of postwar baby boomers as if they were socioculturally the homogeneous unit responsible for the ferment, is quite misleading. David Steigerwald (1995) asserts that "the youthful generation had seized control of it" and, "the new group culture grew from the affluent society and counted as virtues, open sexuality, passivism, and egalitarianism" (1995:154). This ignores the fact that George W. Bush, William Bennett, and Pat Boone were as much a part of that generation, as were Jerry Rubin, Abbie Hoffman, Jimmie Hendrix, Janis Joplin, Theodore Roszak, and Bob Dylan. The dissidents crossed generations on all sides of the ideological and lifestyle conflict. While many dissenters were young, so was the silent majority, which abhorred the activities of "draft dodgers" and dope smokers. When a minority of older dissidents promote change during auspicious times, youth are more easily recruited than their parents, having fewer encumbrances or career risks to face.

Boomers sometimes participated in the revolution, but more often they ignored or opposed it. The majority rejected some elements of the 1960s counterculture and synthesized other aspects to their own reconfigured, cultural advantage. The percentage of that generation which motivated the cultural shifts was relatively small, even if the general population of boomers were to subsequently evidence substantial shifts in attitude towards institutions, racial and religious freedoms, multicultural homogenization, and women's rights, as an outcome of the social flux of that era.

McAdam (1999) believes "no more than two to four percent took an active part in any of the social movements of the mid to late 1960s." It seems that the "yuppies are not drawn from the activist segment of the generation, but from the other 96-98 percent of their baby boomer cohorts" (1999:119). Numerous baby boomers and older dissidents shared some elements of the gestalt shift, but the percentage of that generation that orchestrated the cultural shifts was relatively small.

The followers were primarily boomers, but the impact on the older generation leaders may have been more catastrophic than on their younger disciples. Some participants were adults birthed in the Old World but they defected and became traitors to the values that had shaped their family histories. The impact of 1960s' activists on the society and on the actors themselves, "transcends the lives of the activists" (1999:144). The radical changes in life courses, including unmarried cohabitation, long term singleness, and liberalism, initially embraced a minority of both generations, despite the media's focus on the dissenting fringe as if it were the popular norm (McAdam 1999:124-135). During the social upheaval, many boomers embraced remarkable shifts in attitude towards institutions, racial equality, religious choice, and multiculturalism, but clearly rejected the communalism and anti-consumerism of the counterculture.

The death of *Beatle* George Harrison (2002) gave rise to much media discussion concerning the "post-war baby boomers" as if Harrison was representative of that generation. Like many of the cultural icons of the era, including Dylan and Jagger, Harrison was born during World War II. It may be that the war years were a formative influence in the childhood of many counterculture icons, more than is currently recognized. But the younger generation was so overwhelmed by *The Beatles'* performances, that "Beatle mania" entered the new vocabulary of the 1960s. Several Jesus Freaks I interviewed spoke emotionally of the impact of *The Beatles* on their radicalization. Disillusionment after the groups' disbanding led some to their conversion to Jesus (Carothers 1999:1-6, 18; cf. Witherington 2000:1, 8).

Some Jesus Papers, including Spokane's *Truth* and Melbourne's *Truth and Liberation* (1972b:1, 5-6) featured an open letter to John Lennon, following his assertion that the Beatles were more popular than Jesus (Figure. 2.1). The tone was chiding but affectionate, reflecting respect for *The Beatles'* ubiquitous influence. Francis Schaeffer, conservative Christian philosopher to many itinerant seekers attending his L'Abri, Swiss study center, reportedly wept on hearing their hit song, *Hey Jude* in 1970. He concluded that it was a departure from their

Figure 2.1 "Dear John – Jesus is Greater Than the Beatles."
(*Truth and Liberation* **1972**)

previous soul-searching emphasis, and a return to the mindless love songs of their parents' generation.

The vital point remains, that the mood and tone of the cultural revolution, as well as its ideology, was not set by boomers, but by a minority of intellectuals, activists and artists, who were members of a bridging generation. Leary and Roszak were pre-war generation children. It was the passion and vision of a leadership from the twilight zone, between the Old World values and the technological society that blazed the trail (Ellul 1954, 1964; Mead 1978[1971]). There were generational issues, but the revolution was ideological and ontological, drawing devotees from Old World and New World citizenry.

From Perception to Deception

The popular perception of the counterculture is that wild-eyed, obscene radicals such as anarchist Abbie Hoffman (1968) or the strayed psychotherapist Timothy Leary (1964, 1968) fueled the fires of discontent. This is seen as indicative of an intellectual derangement of that era. Despite this, by the late 1970s a wide range of respected scholars embracing social philosophy (Ellul 1973; Guinness 1973; Rookmaaker 1970), history (McLoughlin 1978; H. Ward 1972), theology (Altizer 1964; Johnson 1971; Lovelace 1979; Pinnock 1971), and the social sciences (Ellwood 1976, 1979; Glock and Bellah 1976; Jorstad 1972b; Mead 1978; Roszak 1968; Slater 1971), recognized the shift in consciousness as a serious departure or a crucial nexus in history. Many saw the seriousness of a developing rift in Western philosophy and perception.[2] By the mid-1970s, the dissenting energy had been fragmented and overwhelmed by the politics of Vietnam (Figure. 2.2) and Watergate such that the innovative, fragile new insights into community and spirituality seemed to be brutally overshadowed by political events. Perhaps the Jesus Movement expression of the counterculture was later swallowed up in the politics of conservative fundamentalism and Pentecostalism also.

By the summer of 1968 a sad transformation had occurred, and "instead of acid and marijuana on the street, they now pushed speed and heroin" (Di Sabatino 1994:28). The openness of the counterculture movement had made it vulnerable to predators possessed of self-seeking malice (1994:27-28).

It was a sad betrayal of the innocents, as idealistic young women in particular fell prey to sexual exploitation and drugs, in the name of "making love, not war." Di Sabatino recalls San Francisco seminary student Kent Philpott's account of dramatic change by early 1967, by which time he says, "organized crime infiltrated the drug trafficking network, where local dealers strong armed their suppliers to channel their customer interest towards harder drugs" (1994:28). By 1971, several of the greatest musicians were dead, substantially because of the abuse of substances that the counterculture had initially imbibed in search of cognitive and spiritual liberation. By 1970, political assassinations had taken four of the greatest political icons (the Kennedy brothers, Martin Luther King, and Malcolm X).

42 *The Origins, Nature, and Significance of the Jesus Movement*

Figure 2.2   Self-Immolation – Buddhist Response to the Vietnam War
                  (Printed in *Right On*. Photograph source uncertain)

An Aborted Trip to the East

Equally disorienting and disillusioning was the religious confusion. A decade of "secular hope" had ended in the abandonment of social and political focus (Ellwood 1994:104-175). Artists and students turned east, to the religions of Asia and India, to mother earth, to paganism, to the occult and to new cults in search of a transcendent escape from their failed attempts to overcome the system.

> Throughout the second half of the 1960s, "fringe" religion became a boom industry with everything from pagan magic to Zen Buddhism on the market, all of it generated by the young who now complained loudly about the dead materialism of their parents. (Steve Turner 1995[1988]:50-51)

> Rock songs derided the soulless-ness of living without a higher purpose, of being well respected but lacking vision. In 1965 John Lennon chided the "Nowhere Man" who "Doesn't have a point of view, (who) knows not where he's going to" and Mick Jagger, in "Mother's Little Helper" (1966), lamented that "The pursuit of happiness is just a bore."

> The trigger for the lurch into Gnosticism, paganism and pantheism was the hallucinogen LSD, more commonly referred to as acid, which entered the British recreational drug market around 1964 with a reputation as cannabis double plus. Within three years almost all of the most influential rock 'n' roll musicians would take it – John Lennon, Paul McCartney, George Harrison, Mick Jagger, Keith Richards, Brian Jones, Pete Townsend, Steve Winwood, Eric Burdon, Brian Wilson, Roger McGuinn, Donovan, Cat Stevens, Jim Morrison, Eric Clapton, and Jimi Hendrix among them. (Steve Turner 1995[1988]:50-51)

In this context of a desperately disillusioned generation whose hopes had swiftly risen to heaven and as quickly sunk to hell, a street level Movement of *native* evangelists emerged, offering a last ditch hope for an abandoned tribe.

Jesus Freaks to the Rescue

The Jesus Movement, a product of the counterculture rebellion of the 1960s and 1970s, was not a unified theory or movement. Rather, it appears to have been many coincidental, smaller movements, which together appeared larger when they coordinated with a sense of common cause, in public demonstration, or media propaganda exercises. The Jesus Movement was a late Christian outcome of the 1960s counterculture reaction to postwar Western culture. It shared some of the contentions of a wider social discontent. No scholar or participant in the movement seems confident to locate the date or source of the names given to it. I can find no evidence of the movement's existence prior to 1966. Jesus came on stage as the curtain was falling on a bad performance.

The limits of this study do not permit a detailed explanation of the reasons for the timing of the Jesus Revolution, but the reader may find some clues by pondering upon the details of the timeline between 1964 and 1967 (Appendix 1). A mixture of despair and hope, success and failure, change and decay mark that period. On the positive side, Civil Rights was gaining in the courts and on the streets between 1964 and 1965, but Malcolm X, Viola Liuzzo, and several black students on the University of South Carolina campus were murdered. The Free Speech Movement inspired hope in 1964, but the Democratic Convention violence in 1968 wrote protest in blood on the pavement. The first combat troops were sent to Vietnam in 1961 in hope of speedy victory, but the defeat during the Tet Offensive in January 30, 1968 bred despair and loathing across America (Obst 1977; Steigerwald 1995). In 1965 Barry McGuire's song, "Eve of Destruction," which was rewarded with great chart success, boldly declared the imminent self-destruction of the nation. Drugs, violence, and philosophical confusion were compromising the counterculture by the mid-1960s. A clear shift to a variety of exotic spiritualities made Jesus an option and emboldened a small underground tribe of fresh young followers. In 1966 Harrison spent six weeks in India with Ravi Shankar – just one of many events which flagged a growing interest in a new spirituality that was conducive to Jesus Movement success. "Give peace a chance," became for many "Give Jesus a chance."

The names given to the movements which proliferated in the 1960s give us an indication of the nature of *The New Religious Consciousness* (Glock and Bellah 1976); also described as *The Consciousness Reformation* (Wuthnow 1976). From the East had come the Healthy – Happy – Holy Organization, The Divine Light Mission and the dancing, meditating, health food distributing, Krishna Consciousness Movement. Running parallel to these quasi-religious movements the Berkeley New Left and The Human Potential Movement also sought "the New Consciousness." In the Christian tradition, the Californian West Coast produced reconfigured evangelicalism through the Christian World Liberation Front (CWLF) and the Catholic Charismatic Renewal. The Church of Satan hailed the rediscovery of ancient paganism. Even some Jewish hippies were turning on to Jesus. Jews for Jesus activists were prominent on Berkeley campus.

Timothy Leary had persuaded thousands of students to *drop out* of the system, *tune in* to transcendentalism and *turn on* to hallucinogenic and LSD-inspired, communal ecstasy. The counterpart for Jesus Freaks was also to *drop out*, but for Jesus. They too *tuned in*, but to the Holy Spirit, the biblical text and the supernatural love of Jesus. They claimed to be *turned on* also, but to ecstatic, visionary, existential love, exploding within by the presence of God, and through the ecstasy of discovering New Testament communal life together. An indescribable sense of *communitas* (Turner 1969:96, 97, 109, 153-154), and an overwhelming compassion for all people was a common experience in the early days of the Jesus communes. Being "turned on to Jesus," they testified, had none of the destructive accompaniments of drug-induced ecstasy or the promiscuous pleasure experienced by their counterparts in the secular counterculture?

A Counterculture within a Counterculture

This indigenous, largely youth-oriented Movement was a Christian initiative that greatly simplified the existing theological codes of the established church, and centered its message and its lifestyle on its understanding of the revolutionary, peasant figure of Jesus of Nazareth. In appearance the Jesus Freaks were indistinguishable from their hippie counterparts, with their long hair, alternative lifestyle clothes, contemporary folk rock music, and psychedelic pamphleteering. Both the wider counterculture and the Jesus Movement shared a belief that the "system" was demonic, and beyond mere reforms, or repairs. As Roszak observed, "everything was called into question, [including] marriage, family life, work, school, and conventional politics" (1995:xxvi). The old crumbling order needed to be replaced by a more organic, holistic, humane, celebratory and creative alternative (Ellwood 1994; Peterson 1999).

The Jesus Movement arose from the ashes of a failed, wider counterculture attempt to overthrow the existing order. More specifically than the counterculture generally, it appears to have been mainly confined to the English-speaking western world. Seeking to extract itself from the unpopular traditionalism of "churchianity" and the unpalatable political and social evils of Christendom, it embraced Jesus in Eastern guru terms. Its initiators were dispirited radicals for whom the messianic figure of Jesus, the marginalized savior of disaffected outcasts, became a last ditch hope for some of the counterculture, which was disillusioned and fragmented. The timeline (Appendix 1) provides evidence of the devastating period of increasing violence and disillusionment surrounding the counterculture as the Jesus Movement emerged.

The original Jesus People were a counterculture (Di Sabatino 1994; Donovan 1972; Enroth 1983; Peterson 1990a; Plowman1971a; Sparks 1972). Like their non-Christian counterparts, they decried social arrogance (*ego-tripping*), and obsession with power, privilege, and possessions (*power trips*), which they believed were characteristic of mainstream culture. Some non-Christian analysts drew strong comparisons between first-century Christianity and the twentieth-century hippie movement.[3] They chose to live simply, more often than not in some form of communal arrangement as had their first century predecessors (H. Ward 1972; Peterson 1990b, 1996a, 1996b).

Many foundational Jesus Movement leaders had experienced no prior relationship with the Christian church, beyond the broad element of acculturation in a Christianized society. Rather than pursuing renewal within the existing order, many of the Movement's groups and their leaders innovated from well outside of the traditional church. Although Evangelical and Pentecostal scholars have generally assumed the modern American Jesus Movement to be a typical revivalist movement (Di Sabatino 1994; Fromm 1996a; Lovelace 1979), it may have more in common with its radical antecedent in the first century. The New Testament movement, based on the teaching and life of Jesus, was not a revival of a previous religious tradition, but a radical new fusion of Judaism and the "new covenant" innovations of Jesus (Jeremiah 31:31; Luke 22:20; 1Corinthians 11:25).

With a few exceptions the first Jesus Freaks were unrelated to the Asuza Street continuum of Pentecostalism (Hollenweger 1997:18-24) traditional fundamentalism, or evangelicalism (Edwards 1997:492-493; Jorstad 1972). I saw counterculture converts speak in tongues at conversion, with no knowledge of what the phenomenon was, or of its theological significance. Jesus Movement indigene, Joe Peterson, maintains the Pentecostals were the "barracudas of straight Christianity," who invaded Jesus Movement groups, introducing the first theological controversy over the essential nature of tongues to "Spirit filled" faith (Peterson 1990a:2). Some Florida-based, Pentecostal, itinerant preachers exercised a global influence on open-minded Jesus People communities. From Florida to Washington, from London to New South Wales I found evidence of their impact moving the Jesus People towards politically conservative Pentecostalism.[4]

The Jesus Movement I and II

Remarkable parallels exist between the first century Jesus Movement and that of the end of the second millennium. Both fostered creative, counterculture dissent from the prevailing social norms, and a desire for the renewal of culture along Kingdom of God values. Both Movements were simultaneously radical and conservative.

> The Jesus Movement [of the first century] rather both envisioned and, to a degree, realized an independent and revitalized local social order. It emphasized freedom and justice over hierarchical social order and domination. Its members lived in social spontaneity, instead of according to heteronomously propagated norms, and manifested a creativity that disrupted the established social order. The Jesus Movement proclaimed God's overcoming of the old unjust and unfree order, and insisted on the possibility of free, just, even creative personal and social life. It was not the Jesus Movement, but Herod and the priestly aristocracy who abandoned traditional Jewish-biblical values and norms. Their oppressive and sometimes even predatory behavior was inducing suffering and disorder. The Jesus Movement involved not abandonment or lack, but intense commitment to the renewal of traditional values: "Thy kingdom come, Thy will be done." (Horsley 1994:152)

Just so it was with the recent Jesus Movement. It extended the Christian influence to previously un-evangelized groups, creating an inclusive social milieu, while it intensified the moral norms of traditional Christianity. While Jesus People relaxed the ritual and institutional norms – pious language, male removal of facial hair, and the dress and work codes of respectable religion – they intensified the moral expectations of those who would follow Jesus (Theissen and Mertz 1991:361-372). As the Torah had been robbed of its social genius by the Pharisees of Jesus' time, the Jesus Freaks believed the Establishment's legalism and intellectualization had deactivated the Christian Bible. *Truth and Liberation* street paper carried a full page picture of an ugly buzzard, wearing a large, sparkling, papal ring on one of its claws as it sat ominously grasping the Bible, guarding it from the people (Figure 2.3).

There was a feeling abroad that the discoveries of love and peace in the teachings of Jesus had been kept from the masses, in an ecclesiastic, political conspiracy promoted by the institutional church.

Tolerance of external religious law-breaking – dancing, drinking and the use of "street language" – was often in contrast with rigorous expectations that disciples adhere totally to the Jesus ethic of love, extended even to the enemy in Vietnam. Neighbor was no longer "someone like me," but rather, as in the ethical Jesus parable of the Good Samaritan (Luke 10:25-32), the ethnically hated outsider, or whoever was in need.

Figure 2.3 A Popish Buzzard Guards the Truth from People
(*Truth and Liberation* 1973)

Inclusiveness and strict commitment to revitalized moral norms based on love became the focus of the Movement (Theissen and Mertz 1991:381-389). As the first-century movement was centered in an ethic of love, which embraced aliens, enemies and outcasts (1991:389-394), so the 1960s revitalization returned to the intense ethical norms of Christianity's founder. While prostitutes were warmly welcomed into the fold, the sexual ethics of the Jesus houses were quite puritan.

The theme song in many Jesus Houses was, not surprisingly, *They'll know we are Christians by our love*. This Movement was a grass-roots rediscovery of a simpler, first century, primitive Christianity. It was a communal, anti-materialist, socially inclusive revitalization of identity and human values. Much of Western Christianity was abandoning historic, moral absolutes, seeking thereby to attract the young. The Jesus People cried out for frameworks of renewed meaning and feeling, rather than dogmatic faith, but they reaffirmed traditional values being abandoned by liberal churches.

Revisiting a Proven Paradigm – Mission from the Margins

Joe Peterson was a first generation, indigenous convert from the Rainbow People, an itinerant hippie tribe. In his sociological dissertation on the Christian, communal movements of the Pacific Northwest he asserts: "The most unexpected eventuality for the 1960's was just beginning *within* the hippie culture itself. [It was] an event unexpected not only by the hippies and the church, but by the media and academicians as well" (Peterson 1990a:10). The twentieth-century Jesus Movement arose and briefly developed outside the hierarchies of church and state. Harold Lindsell, then editor of *Christianity Today*, Evangelicalism's prime magazine had concluded at the end of the 1960s that the Church had been "outdone" by "hippiedom." He claimed that an alarming defection of youth had resulted from the counterculture's initiatives "in drama, in music, in art, and on the printed page" (Lindsell 1969:21-22). "As the church at large wrenched its hands in disbelief, hundreds of hippies, street people, and other youth were beginning to flock to Jesus of Nazareth" (Peterson 1990a:10). Their entry point to Christian faith and experience was within the counterculture.

> [They came] not via the established churches, but rather via their counterculture contemporaries who had themselves come to the conclusion that Jesus was the Way, the Truth and the Life . . . but not necessarily as their forefathers and elders might have considered appropriate and certainly not via the established church. (Peterson 1990a:11, cf. Richardson et al., 1979:xv)

The hippie tendency to proselytize its lifestyle facilitated evangelization at the margins as the media was prophesying the demise of the church. "The focus of the youth rebellion for these young followers of Jesus of Nazareth shifted from rebellion against the Judaic-Christian heritage from the outside, to rebellion within the Judaic-Christian tradition itself – from within its own origin, the Bible" (Peterson 1990a:11). The Jesus Movement sprang from the hippie, minority tribe of seekers for a new moral and social order (Roof 1993). "Teachings, with an emphasis on the moral virtues of social justice, the ideals of the *tribe* and community, the power of love and trust . . . the miracles and charisma, and the quest for peace and joy" were attractive to the growing ranks of disaffected pilgrims (Peterson 1990a:11).

> It was an interesting time to be alive. You'd find Jesus people all over the place. There were dozens of Jesus People houses all over Seattle. The pastor would have to literally climb over the bodies of Jesus People sitting down the front going right up over the altar, because it was such a remarkable time. (Sine 1999:3)

It was as if a generation had abandoned the nuclear family home to rediscover the meaning of family itself. Having dismissed the church as an establishment, new converts, calling themselves members of "God's forever family" (Sparks 1974b) discovered to their amazement that they had spiritual relatives in the church home after all. It was the welcoming back process, by astute cross-cultural pioneers, that gave rise to explosive growth in some small churches such as Smith's Calvary Chapel. It is not surprising that the concluding music to usher in an evangelistic appeal to thousands attending Love Song Jesus concerts in Anaheim, during the early 1970s was:

> *Welcome back to the love you once believed in*
>
> *Welcome back to what you knew was right from the start*

The Jesus Movement, despite a spate of media attention afforded it in the early 1970s, was a marginal group; but groups survived more often when they were willing to compromise their radical beginnings to forge relationship with existing traditions and religious institutions.

Challenging the Status Quo – Reasserting Moral Norms

The following description of the emergence of young sects is remarkably congruent with the counterculture nature of the moral stance espoused by the Jesus Movement, both first century AD and late twentieth century.

> The young sect seeks to challenge comfortable and conventional moral assumptions and demands of the general public [in a way in which main-line churches do not] that they consider radically the meaning and purpose of living. It constitutes a moral minority in the body of a society in which there is moral flux, in which social organization is less and less underwritten by moral prescriptions, and in which there is increasing tolerance of dispositions once labeled "immoral." The sect emerges as a type of reassertion of community values in which moral consensus – albeit sometimes in totalistic mold – is reestablished. In any but a fully laissez-faire society tension between such a moral minority and the amoral majority is likely to recur. (Bruce Wilson 1990:68)

For the Jesus Freaks, Christ was countercultural in his trenchant challenge to the materialism, injustice, violence, institutionalism, and secularism of the "world's system." Yet in remarkable contrast they also viewed him as intensely personal, culturally relevant, accessible, and affirming of every race and culture. Jesus adapted his message and the mode of communication to the marginalized as his statement of unconditional love. Conservatives embraced the Jesus Freaks, tentatively at first but substantially by the mid-1970s. The Movement's agenda turned towards piety rather than political activism. Despite the initial counterculture flavor of the original Jesus Freaks, the Movement's commitment to traditional moral values and spirituality may have been a major factor in the baby boomer shift to conservatism since the Carter presidency.

Sects, New Religious Movements, and Renewal of the Old

Bryan Wilson (1990) says that public perceptions are frequently wary of New Religious Movements. He notes the "pejorative language of the media in reference to sects" and a "bias . . . revealed by scholars to be normally used by the media" (1990:6).

> The votaries of many sects do maintain standards of behavior which excel those of both other religionists and secularists; they are generally punctilious in obeying the law in the payment of taxes, in conscientiousness and integrity at school and work, but they are rarely given credit by the media, the courts, or the public for their orderly comportment.
>
> Such matters are not news worthy, and their various good works – the hostels of the Salvation Army, the (much less extensive) Home Church work of the Moonies, and the reclamation of drug addicts and wastrels by many movements – go unsung. Sects are news only when they are objects of opprobrium. It is, of course, news reporting, with all its negativity, which forges public opinion – and at times even the opinion of judges . . . .
>
> Sects and new Religious movements make news only when there is supposed scandal or sensation to report; in the "humans stories" of apostates, or the anguish of parents about children exposed to sectarian influence (whether as converts or as offspring). (Wilson 1990:6)

Even some groups that held to a traditionally orthodox, Trinitarian worldview, were initially marginalized, and viewed as sects or cults. New religious movements are often parodied so. We forget that Methodism, the Salvation Army, the Anabaptists, and the Plymouth Brethren, were once under a cloud of suspicion, and were defined as cults. Now they are mainstream, institutionalized faiths.

Today historic denominations are challenged by increasingly postmodern, popular choices between Westernized Asian and Indian religions, defensive, authoritarian, fundamentalist denominations, neo-Pentecostal, New Paradigm churches, and New Age forms of individualized spirituality.

Not all radicals who begin movements are remembered or respected by contemporaries, but some await future recognition after lengthy struggle with the dominant worldview. The Anabaptists struggled thus against the Protestant Reformers, but left behind an enduring influence memorialized in the largest Protestant denomination in America. Their influence in radical Christian theology continues through Anabaptists John Howard Yoder (1972), and Berkeley's

Graduate Theological Union's mentor, Robert McAfee Brown (1984) whose influence for change conflicts with the conservative Baptist institutions.

At a time when conventional religion lacked vision, adventure, and simplified codes to challenge the disintegration of institutions and faith-based morals, some radical movements of the 1960s and 1970s drew support from surprisingly respectable quarters. A younger Ronald Reagan initially showed support for youthful communitarian movements. Several Senators and Congressmen were supportive of Jim Jones before his tragic move to Guyana. Such events can turn the tide against innovation through fears that all dissent may lead to dangerous cult activity. Some groups left behind a legacy of disillusioned followers, but my research indicated a surprising lack of overall damage.

Apocalypse Now

The early Jesus Freaks were motivated by love, but often driven by an apocalyptic sense of imminent social, geopolitical, and ecological disaster (Figure 2.4). Literature by futurologists (Taylor 1969) socio-political analysts (Koestler 1967; Marcuse 1964; Mumford 1968; Roszak 1968, 1972a, 1972c), and popular folk singers (Baez 1971; Crosby, Stills, Nash, and Young 1970b; Dylan 1979), fueled the general counterculture's apocalypticism (Turner 1995). Liberal theologians married Eastern thought (Wuthnow 1976, 1978) and apocalypticism to the social gospel (Altizer 1961, 1964; Batstone 1992; Johnson 1971), appealing to less fundamentalist students. Evangelical, eschatological writings, particularly Hal Lindsay's *Late Great Planet Earth* (Lindsay 1970) touched an apocalyptic nerve in the youth culture (Graham 1989:249; Wallis 1982).

They went out seeking their converts, rather than calling the unconverted to come into their church or commune. There was remarkable diversity in both the application of the message and the forms of communication. They ranged from very right wing, fundamentalist Jesus Freaks to social activists ardently committed to anti-war, environmental, and social justice causes. This diversity was created variously by ideological, biographical (leadership vision), geographical, and sociocultural influences.

The beginnings of the Movement were not the consequence of traditional, institutional mission activity in the counterculture, by "straight" missionaries. Rather, as indicated earlier, the initial appearance of this counterculture expression of Christian faith was an indigenous movement, sparked by a handful of hippie and radical converts whose conversions began as an existential rather than cognitive encounter with the person of Christ. Some of these I shall describe in Chapter 3. Quite early in the developmental stage of the Movement however, some dissenting evangelists and pastors defected from mainstream Christian organizations to lead or augment the Jesus People communities.

Fallen, fallen is Babylon the great!
And she has become a dwelling place of demons and a prison of every unclean and hateful bird.
For all the nations have drunk of the wine of the passion of her immorality and the kings of the earth have committed acts of immorality with her, and the merchants of the earth have become rich by the wealth of her sensuality.
And I heard another voice from heaven, saying, "Come out of her my people, that you may not participate in her sins and that you may not participate in her sins and that you may not receive of her plagues;
for her sins have piled up as high as heaven, and God has remembered her iniquities.
Pay her back even as she has paid, and give back to her double according to her deeds; in the cup which she has mixed, mix twice as much for her.
To the degree that she glorified herself and lived sensuously, to the same degree give her torment and mourning; for she says in her heart, 'I sit as a queen and am not a widow, and will never see mourning.'
For this reason in one day her plagues will come, pestilence and mourning and famine, and she will be burned up with fire; for the Lord God who judges her is strong.
And the kings of the earth, who committed acts of immorality and lived sensuously with her, will weep and lament over her when they see the smoke of her burning,
standing at a distance because of the fear of her torment saying, Woe, woe, the great city, Babylon, the strong city! For in one hour your judgment has come.
And the merchants of the earth weep and mourn over her, because no one buys their cargoes any more.

The Apocalypse Ch. 18

Figure 2.4 Ruined City Apocalypse (*Truth and Liberation* 1973)

Defecting from the Mainstream

The author defected from mainstream society and joined the Jesus Moment counterculture at an initiating leadership level in Australia in 1971. Now some 40 years later, reflecting on an extraordinary experience of cross culture communication, I am seeking with hindsight to step back and make a holistic assessment of the Movement. The research leads me to the conclusion that out of all proportion to its resource and social positioning in society, this movement was a significant player in the 1960s and 1970s Cultural Revolution. This was particularly so in America, but to a significant extent in the United Kingdom and Australia also. As a grass-roots movement it was remarkably diverse in substance and style, but united in its disdain for the existing order and convinced the culture could be transformed. Revitalization was its aim, not revival.

It was inevitable that a Christian movement bedded in an alien culture would be forced to reassess the mainstream tradition and its dismissal of exotic lifestyles and belief systems. The growing impact of globalization on Third World nations and multiculturalism in the west has placed "the gospel and culture" debate at the forefront of theological discourse and church-media interaction (Hunsberger 1998; Hunsberger and Van Gelder 1996; Newbigin 1989; Sanneh 1989; Scherer and Bevans 1999; Zahniser 1997). Now a mainstream concern, interfaith dialogue in the popular culture was then a relational necessity for an unauthorized rabble of the street disciples of a marginal Jesus.

An emphasis on the Incarnation of Jesus as a paradigm for mission gave rise to the missional concept of "fleshing out the gospel" in more culturally human, acceptable terms for the unconverted. Vigorous debate ensued over the nature of Christ's message to the world in both word and lifestyle. To what extent was Christ anti-culture, pro-culture, transforming culture, or transcending culture? What had been a theological dilemma brilliantly expounded almost two decades before by Niebuhr (1951), was now a profoundly practical issue for alienated hippie converts. They passionately cared about a rebel culture that was initially rejected by the official keepers of the contemporary Christian tradition.

They Seek Him Here; They Seek Him There

Some Jesus Movement apostles were natural communicators to the Eastern oriented disciples, many being converts from Divine Light mission, Hari Krishna, Zen, and other popular Eastern faith movements. Perhaps they pioneered in practice the now common dialogue between evangelicals and adherents to other faiths (Fig. 2.5). While theologically untutored, these pioneers were often familiar with Eastern-oriented texts, which were of major significance to their non-Christian college counterparts.

The more reflective Jesus Freaks of the author's acquaintance read *Siddhartha* (Hesse 1951); *Steppenwolf* (Hesse 1963); *The Journey to the East* (Hesse 1968); *Zen and the Art of Motorcycle Maintenance* (Pirsig 1974). Alternative sacred texts such as *The Aquarian Gospel of Jesus the Christ* (Dowling 1972) and other Gnostic gospels, were read to keep pace with the eclectic spirit of the religious seekers to whom the Jesus Freaks witnessed daily. Converts from Hindu Guru-led communes, Zen centers, Divine Light Mission, and Krishna communities joined the Jesus Movement, further stimulating the cross-fertilization of ideas. It was significant as an early, postmodern model of religious interaction with culture. Many recollections of this inter-faith dialogue were re-inforced during research into numerous 1970s Jesus people publications. Testimonies of conversion from Zen to Jesus were typical fare in many Jesus papers. The CWLF developed a "Spiritual Counterfeits" project for the serious examination of other faiths. The group still exists in Berkeley.

Young evangelicals, sensing the collapse of their metanarrative, were delving into the treasures of previously proscribed texts in search of truth wherever it could be found (Quebedeaux 1974). In Australia, the Radical Discipleship element of the Jesus Movement delighted in the cultural explanations of the biblical text by Scottish "soft" liberal, William Barclay, who had interpreted the glossolalic miracle of Pentecost as an outburst of public enthusiasm. More radical favorites at that time were peace activist William Stringfellow, and liberation theologians, Robert McAfee Brown, and William Sloane Coffin. Latin American liberation theologians (Camera 1971; Gutiérrez 1973; Segundo 1973) were also eagerly read. Almost anything from Orbis Books was eagerly sought in the Australian Movement. It was a time of synthesis, experimentation, ideological flirtation, and cross-fertilization of ideas.

Experimental Faith

If the Movement was an early postmodern, populist movement as believed by Ellwood (1976, 1994) and H. Ward (1972), it should be more significant for culture analysts than it was for the media journalists. If it was a postmodern, valid version of Wallace's revitalization paradigm, its forms and meanings may be of great significance at this time of anti-globalization protest. Beyond their own salvation, the Jesus people applied their faith to the individual's spirituality, a kinder gentler social intercourse, and a renewed sense of the Galilean's mission to all peoples across racial and social boundaries. The Jesus Movement began as a largely independent, indigenous rediscovery of a radical, historical Jesus. It was birthed as a counterculture mission to the counterculture tribes. As secular and religious media gave positive spin to the unexpected street-level revitalization movement it became a prophetic voice to an over-complicated, institutionalized, compromised, religious establishment.

In the cross-cultural exchange between the old and the new, something was lost by both, but something was also gained. The acceptance of the Jesus Freaks by the traditional church compromised and mollified their counterculture ambiance and the message of the original Movement. Conversely, the radical enthusiasm of the movement renewed existing churches (Reid 1991, 1995) and gave rise to highly successful, seeker sensitive movements and congregations (Balmer and Todd 1994; Jackson 1999; Miller 1997). Some of their leaders were adaptive to the surprising speed of social change from the radical 1960s to the late 1980s, when a great calm-down and the renewed patriotism and radical individualism of the Reagan years reversed the effects of national discontent and

The Jesus Movement – A Sign of the Times 55

**Figure 2.5 Gurus and World religions compared with Jesus
(*Truth and Liberation* 1974)**

dissent. One result of the 1960s may have been an accelerated religious deregulation – a popular move away from historical denominational power over private faith – which the neo-Pentecostal and Jesus Movements stimulated. It may spell a deathblow to the hegemony of traditional religious institutions over the religious choices and commitments of the popular culture. Popular religion may also have silenced the more socially prophetic voice that first attracted the dissidents of the counterculture.

Some movements that will be described in Chapters 3-6 are now respected new denominations. Others, having served their catalytic purpose, disbanded having inspired thousands of re-envisioned, creative adults to become active, civic-minded citizens. These now swell the ranks of Catholic, Orthodox, and Protestant denominations. As I have sought to establish in this chapter, the situation in the 1960s had reached a point of social upheaval and cultural distortion not seen since the Great Depression. At a time of cultural frustration, and innovative abandonment of traditional restraints, the stage was set for revitalization prophets to condemn the existing dysfunctional order, and propose utopian or nativistic alternatives. A decade of unpredicted, religious and social experimentalism would occur in response to the widespread search for a more satisfying culture. In an atmosphere some believed was bordering on social chaos, visionaries were necessary to lead the seekers of a New World through a jungle of self-contradictory concepts and behaviors to revolutionize and transform the culture. Both elements espoused a common disdain for a culture which showed severe signs of dysfunction and inadequacy to meet the felt needs of many of its citizens. The next chapter will describe the creative, inchoate beginnings of the resultant revitalization, through the genius of popular, itinerant, charismatic prophets, and communal architects of social transformation who initially defected from the hippie, activist, leftist ranks to abandon the failed experiments of their peers.

The timing of the Jesus Movement's birth and creative revitalization period place it distinctly at the late stage of the Counterculture's evolution – in the late 1960s in the United States, and following the delayed socio-political response in Australia and the United Kingdom, during the early 1970s in those countries.

The Movement's communalism, rejection of social norms, radical apocalypticism, prophetic leadership styles, and anti-establishment tendencies placed it squarely in the counterculture rather than mainstream Protestantism. That much of the Movement's energy and vision was assimilated by the mainstream does not invalidate the assertion that it began as a counterculture revitalization arising from a failed secular attempt.

Rather than denying the validity of the counterculture's critique of society, and its utopian quest for a new society, the early Jesus Freaks affirmed it. The desire for peace, community, and joyous celebration was right. The direction was wrong. There was only one way – the Jesus way. Early Jesus Freaks indicated this by displaying the one way sign. They too sought a Cultural Revolution – the Jesus revolution. They too hated "ego tripping," and "power trips," but they had seen these social dysfunctions developing within their own hippie context. Thus they sought an alternative to both the establishment and the rapidly disintegration counterculture.

NOTES

1. Bellah 1982; Clecak 1983; Ellwood 1994; Fukuyama 1999; Gitlin 1987; Glock and Bellah 1976; Guinness 1994; Irwin and Unger 1998; Johnson 1971; McLoughlin 1978; Mead 1978; Miller 1997; Roof 1993; Roszak 1972b; Seligman 1990; Steigerwald 1995; Tipton 1982; Wuthnow 1978.

2. Burger and Burger 1971:23; Ellwood 1976; Friedenberg 1959; Glock and Bellah 1976; Goodman 1962; Jorstad 1972b; Keniston 1967; Laing 1967, 1976; Mead 1978; Marcuse 1964; Mumford 1968, 1969; Needleman 1970; Pinnock 1971; Reich 1970:347; Rookmaaker 1970; Seligman 1975; Tillich 1963:97, 1966:90.

3. The following extract from Theodore Roszak is surprising, given the antipathy felt by the counterculture towards establishment Christianity. It does however link the counterculture Christians to the wider youth rebellion in social and philosophical terms. I have included this lengthy quote, remembering the sympathy felt towards Roszak's radical rejection of the Enlightenment, shared by many members of the Radical Discipleship Movement, which was part of the Jesus movement:

"Toynbee has identified such cultural disjunctures as the work of a disinherited 'proletariat,' using as his paradigm the role of the early Christians within the Roman Empire – a classic case of Apollo being subverted by the unruly centaurs. The Christian example is one that many of the hip young are quick to invoke, perhaps with more appropriateness than many of their critics may recognize. Hopelessly estranged by ethos and social class from the official culture, the primitive Christian community awkwardly fashioned of Judaism and the mystery cults, [was] a minority culture that could not but seem an absurdity to Greco-Roman orthodoxy. But the absurdity, far from being felt as a disgrace, became a banner of the community. . . . It is a familiar passage from what is now an oppressively respectable source [1Corinthians 1:18-31]. So familiar and so respectable that we easily lose sight of how aggressively perverse a declaration it is . . . how loaded with unabashed contempt for a long-established culture rich with achievement. And whose contempt was this? That of absolute nobodies, the very scum of the earth, whose own counterculture was, at this early stage, little more than a scattering of suggestive ideas, a few crude symbols, and a desperate longing.

It was the longing that counted most, for not all the grandeur of Greco-Roman civilization could fill the desolation of spirit Christianity bred upon. Since we know now with an abundance of hindsight what the Christian scandalum eventually led to, the comparison with the still fledgling counterculture of our youth is bound to seem outlandish. But then, all revolutionary changes are unthinkable until they happen. . . and then they are understood to be inevitable. Who, in Paul's time, could have anticipated what would come of the brazen hostility of a handful of scruffy malcontents? And what would the nascent Christian movement have looked like under the merciless floodlights of any then-existing mass media? Would it even have survived the saturation coverage?" (Roszak 1995:43-44).

4. In Western countries, traditional, white Pentecostalism appears to be almost uniformly fundamentalist, and politically conservative. During the high tensions over apartheid in South Africa, in the late 1970s and early 1980s I was surprised to discover an aggressive protest document, signed by scores of pastors who were predominantly Pentecostal. The document, theologically competent and articulate, condemned Evangelicals

for their betrayal of the gospel by their conservative, racist, passivity in the face of South Africa's tyranny against blacks. Assemblies of God pastors were prominently involved in this "Antioch Manifesto." Further inquiries revealed the fact that most of the protesting leaders were black Pentecostals.

CHAPTER 3

Wandering Charismatics –
An Apostolate to Popular Culture

*Your sons and daughters will prophesy . . . old men will dream dreams . . .
young men will see visions.* Joel 2:28.

A.F.C. Wallace clearly outlined the process through which revitalization moves from cultural turmoil to a steady state, having substantially resolved cultural stress through the formation of a reformulated culture. Any movement has a beginning and it is in the initiation of revitalization that we find the most peculiar aspects of this particular form of social movement. Revitalization begins with self-referenced or prophetic characters whose authority to attract a following is not based primarily on reason or prior experience, although passionately declared reasons for the revolution are part of the leader's methodology. The charismatic often sets the vision of the movement as a Moses-led journey to a Promised Land. This chapter must provide evidence of this kind of driven-ness, visionary passion and ability in stressful times to captivate a following that will sacrifice and innovate "at risk" to achieve the leader's dream.

For many, the sociocultural conditions, which gave rise to the youthful rebellion of the 1960s, are living memories that remain influential. We recall the incendiary prophets, dissenting academics, counterculture preachers, political iconoclasts, folk singing social critics, and Jesus Freak troubadours who crisscrossed the land. Singing, miming, and preaching bands placed Jesus on the media's center stage for a brief period.

The naive openness and revolutionary attitudes of the counterculture prepared many for acceptance of the Jesus People prophets and apostles. The counterculture had exercised a destabilizing influence disproportionate to its relatively marginal cultural positioning and size, but its demise was approaching by the end of the 1960s. In this context of a deteriorating dream, manifested by thousands of itinerant, disconnected, and disillusioned youth a street level movement of "native" evangelists, miracle workers (Richardson et al. 1979) prophets and apostles emerged. They bore an ancient message. In counterculture terms, they offered not only personal salvation but also a restored order of universal love, psychic restoration, and communal solidarity. The Movement, a subplot in the final act on the 1960s dramatic stage, was remarkable for its impact on the flow of a "new religious consciousness" (Glock and Bellah 1976; Wuthnow 1976).

The initial sparks that fired the renewal flames are difficult to identify. Several hippie converts appear to have independently started the movement. A few sympathetic "straights," with counterculture sympathies and personal connections to alternative cultures, emerged alongside of the indigenous Jesus Freaks. Di Sabatino (1994:27) records that Kent Philpott, a seminary student at San Francisco's Golden Gate Baptist Seminary initiated one of the first missionary ventures into Haight-Ashbury. Scott McKenzie's hit song, *San Francisco*, provoked a sense of Divine call in him. As a prior fan of the Beatnik culture he felt a cultural connection to the hippies.

Jesus is on the Road Again

The concept of Jesus as a travelling revolutionary with socially marginalized followers seeking to overthrow the existing, oppressive order has been taken up as a first century model by modern scholarship (Cullmann 1970; Hengel 1971; Horsley and Hanson 1999; Stegemann and Stegemann 1999; Theissen 1978). In keeping with the 1960s, the modern movement depicted Jesus as a bearded hippie teaching a revolutionary new way of life. Posters described him as itinerant, dangerous to the materialistic culture, and in search of those who would be the vanguard to the transformation of a sick society.

The crucial role of wandering charismatics in the first century movement (Horsley 1994:15-20, 43-50; Horsley and Hanson 1999:8-27) justifies a fresh enquiry into the significance of charismatic initiators in recent social movements. Some have highlighted the significance of itinerant, apostolic preachers rather than the creation of Christian communities in the first century AD. Theissen claims, "Jesus did not primarily found local communities, but called into being a movement of wandering charismatics" (1978:8). In contrast Horsley highlights the Movement's communal aspect, asserting that "The most striking thing sociologically about the [first century] Jesus Movement was that it seems to have taken the form of local communities" (1994:106). Whatever the form of the early Christian communities, they began with the itinerancy of Jesus and his disciples. The Jesus Movement of the 1960s and 1970s appears to be an old phenomenon. The tension between itinerant prophets and intentional community was as real to the modern Jesus Freaks as it is to the Theissen/Horsley debate about the first century AD. The itinerant healing, preaching, and communalism of the early church revitalization (Acts 2: 42-47; 4:32-35)[1] were dominant aspects of the recent Jesus Movement as well.

Those who concentrated on the establishment of localized Jesus Movement communities, such as Smith at Calvary Chapel, routinized their creativity early, forming impressive local ministries and even establishing new denominations. The initial impact of the more itinerant prophets of the early Movement may have done more to influence the mainstream culture because of the ubiquitous nature of their ideas, which were spread creatively in a popular culture context by crisscrossing the land.

Wandering Charismatics – Preliminary Definitions

The prominence of charismatic leaders in revitalization is underscored by Wallace and was clearly a key aspect at the beginning of the Jesus Movement. Most of the leaders were charismatic in the sense of Max Weber's definition and prophetic in both Weber's and Wallace's descriptive terms. The counterculture was significantly itinerant. The hippie, Christian prophets, like their first century predecessors, followed that pattern in congruence with the culture they sought to evangelize, and in keeping with the centrifugal urgency of their sense of call and apocalyptic message.

Recent sociological analysis of first century Christianity has embraced the term "Jesus Movement," to describe the new movement. Their chosen typology of leadership and formation of the original movement closely parallels key elements of the 1960s-1970s movement. Some descriptive terms of reference used by biblical scholars, such as "wandering charismatics," approximate closely to an historical description of the Jesus Freaks of the recent Jesus Movement. Terms however can be misleading if not clearly defined. Clarification of some of these terms is now supplied before the description and analysis of some of the typical leaders that initiated the Movement.

Charismatic Apostles and Prophets

The nature of the Movements' leaders and their methodologies in the first and twentieth centuries are similar. Both cases are illustrations of a revitalization pattern. The manner in which counterculture movements arrive, thrive, and survive exhibits a processual structure in which a distinct style of leadership is normative (Wallace 1956b:269-275). From a social science perspective *charismatic* is a contentious but recurring term in the typology of leadership. Theologically, *apostolic* is equally contentious. While *itinerant* is a more normative term, I have chosen *wandering* for reasons that I hope will become apparent later. Although the biographies and styles of the Jesus Movement leaders bear little similarity, they hold in common a charismatic, innovating restlessness which is consistent with the typologies of Wallace and Weber, thus reinforcing the revitalization theme.

Max Weber has provided the most useful typology of the wandering charismatic apostles of the Jesus Movement. His concept of "charismatic authority" (1964:358-392, 1968:252-267)[2] has been heavily critiqued, but remains useful for discussion of leadership typology.[3] Weber saw human beings as significant participants in social movements. The emotional life and aspirations of individuals, not just abstract framing of ideas, contributes substantially to social movements. The extent to which a leader can identify with, or create meaning for seekers of change is a significant element in the creation of a following. The fountainhead of many social movements and innovative groups is in the charisma of individuals that manifest creativity and innovation (Conger 1989; Conger and Kanungo 1998; McAdam 1988, 1999; Nanus 1995).

Max Weber (1968) gave much attention to the concept of the "prophet" (1968:253-267). He defined such a charismatic/prophetic leader as "a purely individual bearer of charisma who by virtue of his mission, proclaims a religious doctrine, or divine commandment" (1968:253). Powerful proofs, often in the form of ecstatic abilities, the "gifts of the Spirit," stunning oratory, or performance of miracles validate the charismatic in the eyes of followers. Weber also noted that charismatic-prophetic leaders possessed a strong sense or consciousness of power, and the divine call of authentication (1968:254-255). He viewed the apostolic period of Christianity as one in which the social movement of Christianity was promoted by wandering, or itinerant prophets. They were "a constant phenomenon" (1968:255). While mobilization of resources for a movement is critical, it is evident that the inspirational drawing power of visionaries to frame both ideology and strategy plays a vital role across time and cultures.

The Jesus Movement in general appears to have manifested the classic style of charismatic authority as defined by Weber and Wallace. The more evangelistic and itinerant forms of the Movement, as far as I can assess, were usually created and driven by wandering or localized charismatic figures. I employ the term "charismatics" in Weber's sense, defined as prophetic individuals whose power to establish authority and attract a following is not based on either traditional or legal/rational grounds, but upon their unique sense of divine call, and personal drawing power as bearers of a message. Their extraordinary giftedness is established by the performance of perceived miracles and prophetic revelations, or their capacity to proclaim a reconfigured worldview with riveting authority to make sense of life for people in a severe state of stress.

Wanderers, Itinerants, and Performers

In speaking of the Jesus Movement charismatics as "wandering," we may again draw on New Testament and church history parallels, borrowing the paradigm of itinerancy from recent New Testament scholarship (Horsley 1994:15-18, 43-49). Theissen and Merz also employ the term "wandering radicals" (1998:353-354). This typifies the more activist leaders of the Movement in Australia and the United Kingdom (1998:223-224). I do not imply that such leaders were devoid of strategies, or itineraries developed prior to their activities, but that they improvised "on the road." (See Figure 3.1). Their restless relocation and strategic changes were itinerancies in cognitive, emotional and cultural space, not only in geographic relocation.

They were wanderers with a plan, a purpose and a mission, but many were nevertheless of "no fixed abode" during the initiating days of the Movement. The Jesus Movement's wandering charismatics were not indiscriminate in their mobility. They were driven by an apostolic sense of call, an inner compulsion of ideas, a pursuit of resources to expand their influence, and the search for a ready audience. While they certainly maintained distinct strategies rather than purely random wanderings, they did not generally fix their itinerary well ahead of publicized appearances. Rather they followed "the Spirit's leading" and the people's responses, sometimes at very short notice, as was apparent in the worldwide wanderings of Arthur Blessitt and Jim Palosaari, described later in this chapter.

They were itinerant, but unlike the mainstream itinerant evangelists like Billy Graham or Benny Hinn, they did not itinerate to fixed schedules, planned media, pre-arranged locations, pre-announced meeting times, with the engagement of well-known musical performers, or professional celebrities arranged by committees.

A precedent for the itinerant charismatic model of movement formation is seen in the itinerancy patterns of Jesus' disciples, the apostolic team-mission journeys in the Acts of the Apostles, and in the ministries of St. Martin in the Fields, St. Patrick, St. Francis, John Wesley, and Francis Asbury. St. Paul stayed in Thessolonica for a few weeks, but in Ephesus for three years. Some counter-culture apostles of the Jesus Movement resided in new locations for very short periods, but stayed for years where strategy, public response, or divine call was perceived to demand longer residence.

Synthesis of an Old Paradigm – Apostles and Prophets on a Mission from God

Many groups were led by charismatic figures whose proclamation and innovations came to be described as apostolic, and prophetic. For the Jesus People, "apostle," and "prophet" were mission concepts expressing vigorous outgoing ministry with little of life's assurances and securities. These leaders were incendiary preachers, whether indigenous or seconded from previously traditional ministries that identified with the counterculture. With a guitar or a Bible in hand, they hit the streets, schools, campuses, and festivals to an extent still not recognized by the church.

The pattern of charismatics mobilizing communally-centered groups of disciples in the early days of the Jesus Movement is remarkably similar to the New Testament. *The Acts of the Apostles* reports that the church spread its word through wandering charismatic, proclaiming, and miracle working apostles Peter, Philip, Paul and Stephen.

These charismatics mobilized, inspired, and prepared believers for ministry. Scattered by persecution, they "Preached the word [itinerantly] wherever they went" (Acts 8:1 NIV). Similarly, prophetic, apostolic proclaimers inspired thousands of Jesus Freaks to invade rock concerts, to hand out Jesus papers on street corners, university campuses, night clubs, and drug pads, thus spreading the word about Jesus in contexts alien to conventional religion in the 1950s and 1960s.

Figure 3.1   Itinerant Hippies – On the Road for Jesus
(*Truth and Liberation* 1974)

Jesus Movement evangelization combined elements of people movement mobilization with the inspirational and strategic aid of popular oratory, creating an oral mission statement and mythology. Organizational structures were often lacking but the popular following affirmed a charismatic, "legitimate authority" (Weber 1993:71-79; 1964:124-132), fostered by the power of oral tradition and tactical creativity.[4]

During revitalization the prophetic leader is often a symbol of counterculture resistance to the perceived disorder of the system. The leader sometimes uses opposition as a validation of the group's strategic power to lead the people to a new culture. On the other hand failure to control the level of persecution and make peace with destructive opponents may be terminal for a movement. Some opposition is stimulating as verification of divine approval and a motivational stimulant for the movement, but too much opposition may cause those seeking salvation from stress to abandon the vision.

As with the first century Jesus Movement, the Jesus Freaks received a mixed reception. Tom Sine laments that sometimes the existing church, as much as the secular culture did not embrace the mobile tribes of Jesus Freaks.

> My remembrance [is] of [how] the Jesus People started in Hawaii. . . . I got involved with the Jesus People Movement when it happened spontaneously in Hawaii on the Island of Maui in about 1968, 1969. There were many hippies who went west across the United States as far as San Francisco, but a lot of them made it all the way to Hawaii Islands, as that was as far west as you could get without leaving America. There seemed to be a westward migration. There were huge numbers in Hawaii. The local people hated them. There were a lot of rapes of hippies. Maui warriors, Polynesian types of people were beating them up and pushing their bands [musical instruments] over the cliffs. (Sine 1999:1)

There were exceptions, for some local churches and leaders embraced the Movement, stabilizing the itinerant Jesus Freaks and thus enlivening the local church. Significant leadership of some churches adapted to their counterculture style.

> There was a woman who had been a faithful minister of the gospel on the Island of Maui (beyond Paia down towards Haiku) named Momma Hattie Hapuna. She'd been a faithful teacher to about twenty people in a small Pentecostal Church. The hippies started visiting the church. It was one of the few places in Hawaii where the locals would welcome them, as the other locals hated the hippies.
>
> So the hippies started hanging out at the church. They liked the warmth of the fervor of the Pentecostal music. There were small groups of about twenty people, mainly older folks and mainly Hawaiian and Filipinos. They found out that at Thanksgiving there was going to be free food, so they said, "Can we come?" They got the whole tribe to come – about 30 people. It was shortly after that that all of them essentially went forward together and there was a kind of mass conversion of about thirty hippies. Some were on acid and they went down drugged and came up straight. They wound up in a little Assemblies of God church at Makawao. The church was revived. Twenty were living with this one family. Bill Phelps was in a house with one bathroom with about seventeen to twenty young people with his wife and his own two kids. My oldest son used to beg to go to

church Sunday nights. It was an amazing time to be there. It was a real time of joy and spontaneity. It was a real move of God. (Sine 1999:2)

During the 1960s the church was not recognized for its presence or success in the secular or alternative market place. The Jesus Movement's apostolic "sentness" was independent of the institutional church's program. Extraordinary events often caught the church by surprise, as they had little knowledge of the "street level" realities so familiar to the Jesus Movement leaders and converts.

In Shepparton, Victoria, Australia, a regional country town, over 1,000 young people marched the streets in 1974, chanting Jesus Movement slogans, singing, and dancing in tribal style solidarity. The spontaneity, creativity, and unabashed enthusiasm bewildered rather than antagonized the local churches. The local clergy were amazed by the youth response to the unorthodox visit in that city. They hired a hall for the Jesus People to run a separate Sunday youth service, which was packed out with youths that had no previous connection with church. The churches followed their own traditions that morning, as they confessed to complete ignorance of what to do with the spiritual ferment aroused by Jesus papers, school meetings, Christian rock coffee shops, street witnessing, and media reports. Some young converts commenced *The Salt and Light Company*, a street level outreach with a coffee shop headquarters. Despite little practical, institutional support, the group continued as an outpost, contact ministry for almost 20 years.

Revisiting an Enduring Paradigm – Itinerancy for Cultural Penetration

The apostolic model employed by the Jesus Movement was not like that of the privileged, economically driven, television-evangelist. It was a counterculture model of downward mobility, and centrifugal activity. This model was not new. It was used in the Celtic spread of the gospel through the efforts of evangelists and commune planters. One period of such mission itinerancy produced 60 monastic communities of faith in Scotland, in the Shetlands, on the Faeroe Islands, and beyond to Iceland (Sparks 1995:6-9). Itinerant prophets are not essential to revitalization. But as in some other revitalizations (the First and Second Evangelical Awakening in the United States and the early Pentecostal Movement), itinerants and their teams were a common aspect of the initiating period of revitalization. Itinerancy is a typical pattern of primitive Christianity, of innovative periods of Christian renewal, and of the Jesus Movement. Itinerancy was a significant element of the mission of St. Francis of Assisi (Edwards 1997:228-234; Latourette 1975a:429-434; McManners 1993:185, 213). The Moravians combined communalism, spirituality, and missionary itinerancy. This model inspired John Wesley (Latourette 1975b:1024-1025; 1993:292-293), who combined local cell fellowship and training with an aggressive use of itinerant preachers. They spread the gospel supremely by open air preaching (1975b:1024-1029).

The social ferment of the 1960s, the itinerant lifestyles and eclectic, searching mind of counterculture youth created an ideal context for the revival of the old model, through the itinerant mission of the Jesus Freaks. The extreme mobility of the wider counterculture marked the Jesus People lifestyle patterns also. The wandering patterns of apocalyptic preaching, and the creative dissent and innovative energy of the Jesus Freaks followed in similar fashion. The hippies "dropped out" of school and society, "tuned in" to new cosmic vibrations, and "turned on" to communal love. Ecstatic visions, drug and art-induced inner liberation were experienced by many who credulously followed Dr.Timothy Leary's acid trail. Eventually they would try anything – even Jesus.

The early Movement inspired bold communication with the non-Christian world. It was this open engagement of converted hippies evangelizing on the Southern Californian beaches, which gained Smith's attention, leading to his acceptance of a Jesus People invasion of his small Pentecostal Church. In the Jesus Movement days, the pubs, bars, schools, university campuses, and even the highways, were the foci of their missionary penetration. The youth subculture soon knew Jesus was in town. Having no access to large auditoriums or chapels, the Jesus Freaks took to the highways and byways. Hitch-hiking itinerants often evangelized their drivers as captive audiences.

During the best days of the Jesus Movement an impressive array of celebrities had direct contact with the Movement outside traditional religious locations. Musicians Bob Dylan, Santana, and Kris Kristofferson flirted with the faith (Steve Turner 1995). Enduring conversions resulted from the free flow of dialogue through communes, coffee shops, and festivals as Di Sabatino notes:

> They'd say, "We just walked out onto the street and said to anybody we talked to that they could crash at our pad and they would get saved. Charles Manson and Robin Williams came in. We had all these weird characters and everyday someone would come in and give their heart to the Lord." I would have loved to be involved in something like that. I went to JPUSA, Chicago and thought, could I do this? It's tough. That's a tough call. I come from the upper middle class. I got off the plane and within an hour I was serving food to homeless people. How can you go back to our little churches where you get into little groups and put up your hands and sing praise songs? . . . .Where are those places? There is now a new generation of non-churched outsiders who are unreached by us. (Di Sabatino 1999b:18-19)

The concept of receptor oriented communication was normative in the Jesus Movement, but it was positioned well beyond the comfort zones of the believer. This was later refined as the "seeker sensitive" church gathering.[5]

Some Significant Actors in the Jesus Movement

If we had asked the counterculture who Harry Emerson Fosdick, Billy Sunday, Amee Semple McPherson, Katherine Kuhlman, Oral Roberts, or E. Stanley Jones were, the response would have been enigmatic. But the names of Linda Meisner, Larry Norman, Carl Parks, Jim Palosaari, Lonnie Frisbee, Larry Norman, Barry McGuire, and Ted Wise would have drawn a ready response, whether positive or negative.

Many unsung, but significant leaders arose, some with only localized influence, and some of international significance. Tom Pope, admissions officer at

Asbury Theological Seminary (1999), tells of an unnamed founder of Charisma Chapel, Naples, Florida, who caught the vision to embrace the counterculture (1999:6-7). Ron Crews, middle-aged graduate student, recalls the powerful influence of Gene Sprigg at the Jesus Movement's Yellow Deli, in Chattanooga, and of sister communes in Cleveland and Dayton, Tennessee, and across the border in Trenton, Georgia (1999:9-11). The late Jim Durkin, a real estate broker and young believer, was impacted by counterculture converts and opened his life to the youth culture. He guided thousands of young people to faith and to gainful employment through the Lighthouse Ranch in an old Coast Guard station, in northern California. He extended this gospel outreach to Alaska, New York State, and beyond, to Europe, Japan, and Brazil (Sczepanski 1975:34-37; Di Sabatino 1996).

Upstate New York had disc jockey Scott Ross at the Love Inn Community (Di Sabatino 1994:40-43); the Pacific Northwest had John Higgins, David Hoyt, Carl Parks, Linda Meisner; California had Lyle Steenis at Redonda Beach, and Breck Stevens created Bethel Tabernacle; Arthur Blessitt, Duan Pederson, and Don Williams invaded Hollywood; Jack Sparks was at Berkeley; Southern California had Lonnie Frisbee and Chuck Smith; Glenn and Wendy Kaiser of Jesus People USA (JPUSA) set up in Chicago; Milwaukee had Street Level with Jim and Sue Palosaari; The Toronto Catacombs had Jim McAlister; and Brantford Ontario had Mark Woodley of Cornerstone Church (Di Sabatino 1999:b, 1999d; Plowman 1971; H. Ward 1972). The names of the charismatic figures that arose during the Movement of the 1960s and 1970s are many, and I regret the omission of numerous, impressive charismatics not recognized in this dissertation. Many of them made enduring contributions to the reconfiguration of faith and practice during the brief period of Jesus Movement revitalization, despite the lack of institutionalized monuments to their genius.

Extensive research across the United States confirmed Di Sabatino's belief that every city of significant size owned its particular expression of the Movement, with charismatic leaders to inspire and envision locally (1994:18). A comprehensive history of the thousands of ministries and cells which emerged during the revitalization is a long way from completion. The following choice of a few of the pioneers is only representative, but reflects the wandering charismatic typology.

Ted Wise – From Sail-making Priest of LSD to Fisher of Men and Women for Jesus

According to Di Sabatino (1994:4) Ted Wise, once a prominent figure in the hippie, transcendental drug subculture, was one of the earliest indigenous Jesus Movement leaders. Like many native evangelists of the Movement, this converted sail maker was still smoking marijuana when he began effective ministry. He was joined by an old hippie friend Danny Sands, who typical of many Jesus Freaks, took literally the story of Jesus' encounter with the rich young ruler. He forsook all to itinerate for Jesus.

In 1967 they set up the first Christian coffeehouse, The Living Room, on Page Street, one block from the corner of Haight and Ashbury, contacting between 30,000 and 50,000 youth (Enroth, Ericson, and Peters 1972:13). Lonnie and Connie Frisbee were converted at the Wise commune, and later met John Higgins, who established Shiloh ministries in Eugene, Oregon in 1969. The Living Room, seen by some as the birthplace of the Jesus Movement (Di Sabatino 1994:33) attracted a breadth of visitors, including Robin Williams and Charles Manson, who was repeatedly ejected for violence.

> Ted Wise and his band of Merry Pranksters hit the "Haight." These guys were very countercultural. Ted was involved in the very first experiments of communal living out in the O'Donnell project, living with Timothy Leary when he was experimenting with LSD as far back as the early 1960s. By 1967 when they got saved, [late 1966 according to Enroth, Ericson, and Peters 1972:13] this was supposedly the first indigenous group. Did anybody come and tell them? He says no. (Di Sabatino 1999b:4)

For "straights" that became cross-cultural missionaries to the counterculture, the use of "soft" drugs by new enthusiastic converts was less troublesome than the addiction to prescription drugs common amongst middle class parents. There was no normal pattern. Some converts forsook all substance use immediately. Others, obviously transformed in other ways quit dope gradually. The ability to cope with an alien hierarchy of values was essential for missionaries to the counterculture.

> Ted especially was very suspicious of any kind of "churchified" understanding of the gospel. . . . When David Wilkerson came to them and tried to anathematize them, he caught them on film with short skirts. He was trying to be the great evangelist to the youth culture and get all this money for Teen Challenge . . . . David had worked with the drug addicts. This hippie culture was a very laid back, different culture. He didn't have any effect on them [with] his straight suit and tie . . . . These guys were on Haight-Ashbury, doing their thing, being left alone by some Baptists who were giving them a little bit of money and David came in and said "This is wrong." He caught them smoking pot still. He put them on camera doing this and then went around churches and showed them that "This is not a work of God because they are doing this." So you had this real tension of "straight" verses "street." You have that pocket which was indigenously countercultural. (Di Sabatino 1999b:4)

Ted Wise remains one of the enduring pioneers of the Christian counterculture revitalization and continues in effective ministry, but with the residual suspicion of mainstream, institutionalized religion.

Lonnie Frisbee – The Pied Piper of Southern California

An almost forgotten evangelist, Frisbee was once known as the "Pied Piper of the hippie generation" and the "John the Baptist of Southern California" (Di Sabatino 1997:5). Frisbee was persuaded to join Chuck Smith at Calvary Chapel when the attendance was 150. Attendances skyrocketed to thousands within two years through Frisbee's magnetism (Plowman 1971a:44-45). Frisbee was the primary evangelist in the local Movement who it is claimed led 20,000 Californians to embrace the Christian faith, resulting in over 8,000 baptisms in two years (Di Sabatino 1997:25). He provided John Wimber with the model of a "signs and wonders" emphasis in Vineyard Ministries, which now has hundreds of congregations (Di Sabatino 1999c). There were many gifted communicators to the youth culture in the late 1960s and early 1970s who are similarly obscured by later developments of new denominations, led by more conventional leaders.

Carl Parks and the *Wilson McKinley* – Rock 'n' Roll in the Spirit of Elijah

My first direct connection to the American Jesus Movement was through correspondence with one of the many incendiary, wandering charismatics who, though unknown to mainline historical discourse, was a primary leader and communicator in the Pacific Northwest region. Carl Parks was a mercurial authoritarian yet a creative motivator of hundreds of Jesus Freaks. He put them to work on the streets, confronting people with an apocalyptic message through personal witnessing and the dissemination of thousands of copies of *Truth*. This magazine abounded in hype and photographs of hippies preaching, handing out Jesus papers on the street, getting baptized, worshiping together, and discussing faith in their high school classes. For a short period our Australian group became involved in a joint Jesus paper venture which shall receive attention in Chapter 6. We kept contact with the group for some years but for theological and sociological reasons we went in a different direction.

Carl Parks, the "dropout" son of a fire-brand father and mother evangelistic team, directed an aggressive street witnessing program, a Jesus Free Store, the I Am Coffee House, and the Jesus paper *Truth* – all under the name of Spirit of Elijah Ministries. From our first contact with the Spokane, Washington Jesus people, we built tenuous relationships with many American groups and collected samples of over 60 different street papers produced by such ministries.

Contemporary music and "hip" preaching formed a popular culture model, which the Jesus Movement used to great effect. In Chapter 7 the significance of this shall be considered briefly, in terms of historic precedent and revitalization process. The Jesus papers and personal contact with scores of groups lead me to believe that virtually every group had its musicians and/or street theater group. Carl Parks had observed the success of another leader, Jim Palosaari, in the use of contemporary music in the market place. He discovered what he needed in the *Wilson McKinley* (Parks 1971b) local cult rock 'n' roll band. It was impossible thereafter to think of the Spirit of Elijah ministry without combining Parks and *McKinley*, who exhibited a visceral style reminiscent of the early music of the Dublin-based group *U2*. The *McKinley* band was converted during an evangelistic blitz spearheaded by Linda Meisner in a park in Spokane. Though they had just returned from a successful recording session in Los Angeles, and were anticipating a national break as "one of the fastest rising groups of the northwest . . . they were miserable" (Parks 1971b:12). They were impacted by the dancing, singing, and joyous presence of a crowd of Jesus Freaks, who appeared to be "free from the burdens and hassles that had plagued [them] for so long" (1971b:12). They briefly abandoned their music to search the scriptures before coming under Parks' direction for mission.

They all knew from Jim Palosaari that you needed a rock group to gather a crowd, Carl immediately said "You are all with me. You're going to come and live in Spokane." So they became The *Wilson McKinley* of the *Voice of Elijah*. They were the cutting edge really, singing about Jesus. Nobody's going to give them acclaim because they didn't sell many albums. They weren't about getting money for their albums . . . .They were very sincere. The last album was an instrumental album of hymns. It was terrible, but that's what Carl wanted to sing – "Just a Closer Walk with Thee." It was one of the sad stories. (Di Sabatino 1999b: 7,8)

I kept in touch with them for several years. Parks and his followers mounted "The Man With a Plan" crusade in Spokane. There was much criticism from the churches because of their bearded hippie appearance and the aggressive publicity campaign depicting Jesus as a hippie on billboards and pamphlets. They altered the Jesus posters to depict him with a trimmed beard, wearing a suit. They were then accused of mockery.

Eventually they wiped their feet of Spokane because people had not responded adequately to their message. It was claimed that some people, disturbed at their unexplained, overnight disappearance, feared Jesus had returned and "raptured" them. They were there one day and gone the next. They claimed God sent them to Europe through a prophecy. Shortly thereafter I received a final communication via a card showing a Jesus sticker placed on a painting in the Louvre, Paris. Tragic division and complete disintegration of the group occurred. Parks was divorced and Di Sabatino, who has kept personal contact with several major, past leaders, including Parks, reports that he has an alcohol problem (Di Sabatino 1999d).

Linda Meisner – From Conservative Teen Challenge to the Radical Children of God

Linda Meisner had been a staff worker with Teen Challenge ministry to addicts and gangs. Tutored under the conservative leadership of David Wilkerson, she became challenged by the hippie subculture. Her influence upon youth in Seattle was powerful.

Linda is one of the most enterprising women I have ever known. She arrived in Seattle just ahead of the big drug thing in 1968 and promptly set up a Teen Center. She had been on an extensive drug-abuse speaking tour, and before that she worked for David Wilkerson with young addicts, prostitutes, and street gangs in New York City but fell out with Wilkerson, possibly because of a conflict of mission focus in her desire to shift to the hippie scene. (Plowman 1971a:51)

With no financial backing Meisner opened The Ark, a rapping post for Seattle young people who wanted to talk and pray with someone about their problems. She leased a skid row bar and turned it into a coffeehouse called The Eleventh Hour. Later she relocated to a large building across from the Space Needle and renamed it The Catacombs, reputedly the largest coffeehouse in the Movement at the time, with a nightly attendance of 400. Jim Palosaari described her to me, as a "straight" that cared passionately about the counterculture but initially had no idea how to communicate with it. He claims to have tutored her and passed the leadership of the Jesus Army to her (Palosaari 1999:1).

> Linda went into the publishing business with an underground-type give-away newspaper, *Agape*. During one of the Northwest's first big pop festivals, a three-day affair at Gold Creek Park, she rented a small airplane and dropped 10,000 copies of the initial issue on the revelers. *Agape's* front page featured the bearded face of Bud Moegling, a drug dealer active in radical politics before his conversion; inside was his testimony. Meanwhile, street Christians infiltrated the crowd and had a field day of witnessing. Desperate high school principals who were discovering that the majority of their students were on marijuana or harder narcotics welcomed Linda to assembly programs. She forthrightly singled out Jesus as the One Who could help them kick drugs and find real life . . . . Her kids were definitely counterculture because she grabbed them, as nobody else wanted to do it, or give her any support. (Plowman 1971a:51-52)

Tom Sine, an evangelical futurist and mentor to a growing population of postmodern defectors from traditional church models, recalls that at the height of Meisner's leadership of the Seattle Jesus People, nearly 1,000 youth gathered every Friday and Saturday night at a large location down by the Seattle Center. Young people were out on the streets selling Jesus papers.

> [It was a] very serendipitous place where a lot of young people who were not hippies would come, as it was a happening place. They were having dramatic conversion experiences. It was very spontaneous. Groups would blow in and they'd just play their music, making up new Christian music because they were all recent converts. It was a very energizing time. (Sine 1999:2)

The conversion of Meisner to the Children of God was a devastating blow to an effective youth ministry in the Pacific Northwest. She called together the Seattle Jesus People and announced her move to the Children of God, saying it was the only way.

> She saw the Children of God, as very regimented and very strict. Their kids snapped to attention when you asked them to. She said, "That's exactly what I need" and she got co-opted. She thought they would get them over the hump so if she went in with them she could really jump-start the Jesus Movement, and this could go Nation wide and . . . the end would come. (Di Sabatino 1999d:3)

Linda Meisner called upon all Jesus people willing to obey God to immediately join her. She abruptly departed, leaving her confused group of supporters shattered. Tom Sine was present when Meisner told her staff and followers. "It was absolutely devastating. She just said, 'This is where God's will is. I am going. If you want to be where God is, you better come now.' She just walked out and left what was a vital Jesus Movement in ruins overnight" (Sine 1999:3). She set up a competing street paper to Spokane's *Truth*, which she named the *New Improved Truth*, far more radical and psychedelic in content and style than Carl Park's contribution (Figure. 3.2). Although Brant Berg (founder of Children of God) and Meisner had come from the conservative, Christian and Missionary Alliance, they encouraged morally alien practices, including "flirty fishing," (Moses 1976:572-534),[6] whereby young girls were encouraged to employ promiscuous sexual wiles as "hookers for Jesus" to attract young men to the faith. Meisner deserted her husband and five children. Years later Di Sabatino met her in Denmark, seeking to discover why she left the mainstream Jesus Movement for the cult.

> How hard is it to figure out that you shouldn't walk out on five kids? Linda felt she was the Apostle Paul of the Movement. Pentecostalism suggests that if you can spark something you can spark the end to come and be the great thing before the end. The gospel will go out throughout the entire world and then the end will come. They based their theology on that. It's pretty ridiculous. Here she is making all these claims to be one of the two witnesses and all this weird stuff. God had given her a vision for an army of children marching down the streets of Seattle, which was fulfilled by 2,000-3,000 kids, but that's never enough. (Di Sabatino 1999b:5)

Linda Meisner left the Children of God; they soon embittered her. She had made a huge mistake when joining them in 1973 and she left them shortly after. She resides in Denmark where she claims to be leading an army of street converts in a revival (1999b:5).

John Higgins Jr. – Counterculture Communitarian on the Oregon Trail

John Higgins, an Irish, New York Catholic, moved to California and became involved in the counterculture and the drug scene during the mid 1960s. "While reading the Bible to disprove it, he was converted to his own interpreted brand of Christianity. At the time, he was convinced he was the only one in the world who truly believed the things in the Bible" (Peterson 1999a:77). Eighteen months after conversion in 1966 he met Lonnie Frisbee and in 1968 they made contact with Smith. A bond was established which was to lead him years later, after a crisis in his own ministry, to become a pastor of a Calvary Chapel. He served as elder in the first Calvary Chapel commune, The House of Miracles, opening May 17, 1968. It was an outstanding success. John Higgins also established a connection with The House of Acts in San Francisco, from which Frisbee came to join him in the Costa Mesa project (Richardson et al. 1979:6-7).

John Higgins received what he believed to be an apostolic call, which came in the form of a vision like "watching television, but without the tube. It was a whole picture, yet the surrounds of the room remained in tact." He heard a voice saying, "I have opened an effectual door to you" (Richardson et al. 1979:14). Higgins followed his vision to Oregon along the historic Oregon trail, g

Figure 3.2. The Psychedelic *New Improved Truth*

gathering fifteen disciples who settled on land provided by a wealthy Christian land developer, Ken Smith (Di Sabatino 1994:37; Peterson 1990a:46). Higgins, through a "revelation," named the new organization Shiloh in 1969, from a biblical passage Genesis 49:10, "The scepter shall not depart from Judah, nor a law giver from beneath his feet until Shiloh come; and unto Him shall the gathering of the people be" (1990a:47). This was to become Shiloh's Revival Youth Centers Inc.

"By December 1974, they had established 163 centers across America, including Alaska, Hawaii, and the Virgin Islands . . . though it is unlikely any more than 50 to 75 were functioning at any one time" (1990a:48). The life of this movement, which Peterson claims was the largest and best documented of America's Jesus people groups (1990a:3, 1999a:1), centered its life around work, worship and witnessing. Their highly successful industries, which underwrote the ministry, were to eventually draw the attention of the Internal Revenue Service (IRS) which, despite the communitarian, nonprofit nature of the movement, was to foreclose on Shiloh for unpaid corporate taxes on profits (Peterson 1990a:49). John Higgins had found himself at the top of a rapidly expanding movement, and like many of the Jesus Movement charismatics, he was highly visionary, but organizationally flawed. The power of his charisma appears to have convinced the majority of Shiloh's membership, but Shiloh's eight man Board "could not handle the capriciousness of the founder" (1990a:57). In a midnight meeting, in his absence, they removed him as President and Chairman of the Board.

Joe Peterson reports: "There had never been a previous threat to his leadership and the flock were left in a state of pandemonium, dismay, and disorganization" (1990a:59). Quoting Stark (1987), Peterson (1990a59) states: "Ineffective mobilization is chronic among new religious movements" (1990a:59, cf. Stark 1987:6). "Shiloh had effectively immobilized their mobilizer" (1990a:59). Higgins left Oregon on April 24, 1978 for New Mexico and reconnection with Smith's movement as a pastor, never to return again. He has remained in pastoral leadership since. For some years, under the leadership of Joe Peterson, his movement battled against Government litigation. Several pamphlets in my possession bear witness to outstanding educational conferences hosted at the Shiloh Study Center until the early 1980s. They reflected a radical commitment to the arts, environmentalism, "earthkeeping," and social justice. Senator Mark Hatfield, Wesley Granberg Michaelson, now a primary leader in the Reformed Church in America, and John Alexander, editor of *On the Other Side*, were speakers at Shiloh's conferences.

Joe Peterson – From Jesus Freak to Sociologist

Joe Peterson, who had been an effective leader in the Oregon and Washington Movements described above, was eventually prevailed upon to steer Shiloh through the IRS crisis and ultimately to its final dissolution. His MA thesis (1990a), his impressive collection of historical data, including media, correspondence, and sociological surveys of a sizable sample of Shiloh's membership, and the scholarly investigation of Shiloh by Richardson, Stewart, and Simmonds

(1979) provide the most extensive database of any Jesus Movement operation known to this author. While Peterson was not one of the more celebrated public proclaimers of the Movement, his leadership combines a unique mixture to Jesus Movement participation and scholarly research. He was a mature, typical, tribal, hippie agnostic when converted through a series of bizarre events.

> The next day I was a Religious fanatic. . . . I rushed right out to the Jesus Freaks who thought I was crazy. They're all 16, 18 year olds and I'm 26 with real long blonde hair, scraggly beard, 6 foot 6 inches [tall]; [I was] a terrifying creature. Then I started going up to the House of Elijah, which opened shortly before. It was just full of young kids. . . . My tribe had gone on and I decided to stay to try to figure out what's going on; [I was] looking for truth. (Peterson 1999:11)

Following conversion in 1968, Peterson experienced rejection by the established church, but a strong affirmation of his conversion by the hippie Christian community. While now pursuing a career in sociology and lecturing in the military, he maintains the clearest expression of the counterculture, anti-institutional faith I have heard in my investigations. His thesis (Peterson 1990a) combines social scientific skills with a thorough biographical knowledge of the good, the bad, the ugly, and the magnificent elements of the counterculture. His anecdotes of the impact of the Jesus Movement on the counterculture provide impressive evidence of a much more extensive movement than history has hitherto recorded. In 1971 Peterson became the leader of the House of Elijah, Spokane. This community was "a haven for drug freaks, escaped prisoners, under-aged children, and the ubiquitous Jesus people" (Gosney 1979:2).

Initially involved in Youth Speaks, an aggressive outreach program headed by Meisner, Peterson and the House of Elijah gravitated towards fellowship with Park's Spirit of Elijah ministry, as Meisner turned to more cult-style activities. They never officially linked with either group. Joe Peterson's movement began at High Bridge Park, Spokane, WA in 1969. In mid-1970, 40 Jesus Freaks began to sing and witness statewide to local dopers and establish communes (Millay 1970). In 1971, the *Yakima Valley Sun* (Patricia Brown 1971) reported that hundreds of youth "had given their lives to Christ and about 150 got baptized" (1971:16). In connection with Parks and the *Wilson McKinley* rock band, four houses embracing 70 people, provided a context for the development of Bible study, work projects, and street witnessing. A journalist for the *Yakima Herald-Republic* (Gosney 1979:2) described Peterson's counterculture group as providing a "haven for free thinking Christians and a place which eventually 'weathered the resentment' of fearful locals, through the establishment of a cooperative garden to provide foodstuffs to the elderly and the transient." It continued for 11 years, closing on September 15, 1979.

Several sociological studies of Shiloh, the House of Elijah, and a closely related, itinerant ministry, the Highway Missionary Society, have been carried out by Peterson and his colleagues, with enthusiastic co-operation of many past members of all three groups (Peterson 1990a). Under the directorship of Donald Pitzer, (the Center For Communal Studies, University of Southern Indiana, at Evansville, Indiana), and Gordon Melton (the Institute for the Study of American Religion, Santa Barbara, California), Peterson created a comprehensive survey investigating Christian youth communals. This comprehensive survey is "an in depth, scholarly, longitudinal study of a large, disbanded, communal group, utilizing those former members as the primary source" (Peterson 1990a:70). Joe Peterson reports, "a reasonably good return rate" for the 20-page survey, sent to over 500 former Shiloh members. For the respondents, the average length of time spent in Shiloh was five years. The questionnaire embraces complex questions of belief, personal goals, political orientation, education, post-Jesus Movement lifestyle, and worldview positioning. Sensitive questions regarding the communal experience and its effect on sexual and family experience are included.

The groups associated with Peterson and Higgins were typical of the early movement as they were led by indigenous converts, manifested a high level of charismatic leadership and combined the localized communal model with geographically extensive, itinerant proclamation. The widely scattered members have commenced a remarkable process of reconnection for reconciliation after bitter division following Shiloh's demise.

Duane Pederson – Psychedelic Entertainer for Jesus

Duane Pederson became a counterculture evangelist whose *Hollywood Free Paper* is claimed to have peaked at 500,000 copies per edition (Di Sabatino 1994:103). Any Christian publication achieving that today would be seen as an outstanding success. It was the most glitzy and the most popular. Pederson, a ventriloquist-entertainer-evangelist launched his paper in October 1969 in an attempt to evangelize teenagers, particularly "dopers." Like Blessitt, he did not come from the ranks of the street people, or the hippies, but was an evangelist willing to adapt to the culture. He claimed to have flirted with "drugs, booze, and about everything else" (Enroth, Ericson, and Peters 1972:74) but after conversion, put his considerable platform skills to use with a passion for counterculture youth. Today his passion for the marginalized is expressed in the form of Antiochian Orthodoxy, and through its priesthood he ministers to Hollywood street people and to the Californian prison population through Orthodox Bible study courses. The charismatics we have thus far considered were proclaimers or popular preachers, but the role of the travelling musician also became a major aspect of the spread of the revitalization message of a New World through Jesus.

The Singing Troubadours of the Jesus Revolution

Several scholars (Baker 1985; Di Sabatino 1999b; Romanowski 1990a, 1990b) assert that the huge, Contemporary Christian Music (CCM) industry was triggered by Jesus Movement performers (Di Sabatino 1999b:18-19; Rabey 1998). These included individual artists Larry Norman, Barry McGuire, Andre Crouch, Randy Matthews, Phil Keaggy, Nancy Honeytree, Paul Clarke, Glenn Kaiser, and Keith Green, and a host of popular bands including *Wilson McKinley, The Resurrection Band, Sheep, Liberation Suite, Love Song, Gentle Faith,* and *2nd Chapter of Acts.* The impact of the wandering charismatic singer-preacher is regarded by these writers as fundamental to the development of CCM, now a major industry in terms of economic turnover (Di Sabatino 1999a, 199f; Robey 1998).

The Movement engendered a new form of evangelical itinerancy by a genre of intensely counterculture singer-preachers. Of the scores of examples of this model of Jesus Freak musician-preachers, Larry Norman, blues preacher-artist Glenn Kaiser, and Barry McGuire have been enduring performers. These contrasting characters reflect continuing genres of the contemporary music scene, enduring 35 years later.

Larry Norman – Slightly off this Planet[7] (1947 –)

Larry Norman is an aggressive innovator. On a Jesus Movement website, the following report sets his contribution in its cultural context:

> It was 1969 in America. Apollo 11 astronaut Neil Armstrong walked on the moon. Nearly half a million young people tuned in and turned on at Woodstock. Mounting American casualties in Vietnam led to a growing chorus of protests against the war and the administration of Richard Nixon. At the same time, a revival was sweeping the country. The deep spiritual hunger that led millions of young people into Eastern religions, psychedelic drugs, communal living and political activism, led many straight to the loving arms of Jesus. While these 'Jesus people' loved the Lord, they had problems fitting into churches where the dress code was straight, the atmosphere structured, and the music stodgy.

> The stage was set for Larry Norman a longhaired, guitar-carrying, denim-wearing, Jesus-loving iconoclast who gave birth to contemporary Christian music with his debut recording *Upon This Rock* released in 1969. Norman bravely proclaimed that God could use rock 'n' roll, a form of music which many mainstream citizens – then and now – associated with sex, drugs and rebellion against traditional values. Or as he put it in his now-classic song, "Why Should the Devil have all the Good Music?" (Rabey 1995)[8]

It is difficult to get beyond the voluminous hagiographic mythology that surrounds this unpredictable, sensitive personality. No Jesus Movement musician is more consistently recognized in the aging memories of the revitalization participants, possibly because of the frequency and global spread of his concerts and the number of his records. Certainly he thrived on confrontation, hyperbole, and controversy.

> Larry Norman's music was bold. At a time when "Do your own thing" was king, his songs loudly proclaimed that there was only one way to God: Jesus Christ. Norman helped popularize the "One Way" hand sign, which with its index finger pointing heavenward, was the Jesus Movement's alternative to the secular youth movement's two-fingered peace sign.

> Even more radical was Norman's attempt to provide a Christian analysis of the social issues that were tearing us apart. Unlike church hymns, which largely dealt with safe "spiritual" topics, Norman's songs explored racism, militarism, secularism, the war in Vietnam, NASA's $25 billion space program, social and economic justice, free sex and sexually-transmitted diseases, and the boom in Eastern, occult and New Age religions. (Rabey 1995)

Larry Norman's relationships have been stressful. He is divorced and remarried. His theology is no doubt sincere but piecemeal, and highly individualistic, laced with extravagant conspiracy theories based on proof-texting from Revelation. Some music lovers are ambivalent about Norman's status in the Movement. His performances are electrifying, but can be frustrating because of unpredictable moods. The extent of his originality in lyrics and concepts has been questioned.[9] His mercurial, moody, unpredictable persona however, cannot obscure the enormous impact he has exercised on a generation in search of an earthy, contextualized faith. He is a memorable pioneer who maintains a global influence.

Glenn Kaiser – True Blues Disciple of Jesus

In behavior, theology, consistency, and family stability, Kaiser, blues rock musician and leader of the *Rez* (Resurrection) *Band* is in stark contrast to Norman. Though still embracing a demanding level of itinerant preaching and singing, and a fiercely anti-materialistic lifestyle, he has maintained a long-lasting, stable marriage to Wendy and they retain the respect of their children. They were led to faith and discipled by Jim Palosaari. Glenn Kaiser co-founded JPUSA on the September 30, 1971. The Kaisers learnt enduring lessons through Palosaari's failures and established an accountability model of collegial leadership, which has undergirded the lasting success of Chicago's JPUSA and is worthy of serious research. Their message is uncompromising, but their multi-story commune, meeting place, school, shop, offices, and crisis center still attracts hordes of young and old to radical faith and community. To visit JPUSA headquarters is to be bewildered by the loving intensity, speed, and volume of human interaction pouring in and out of their multi-faceted mission center. Kaiser has a disciplined, focused witness, a character of consistency and reliability, and a well-developed, mildly Calvinist, covenantal theology. Wendy Kaiser often accompanies him, singing with an energy and style reminiscent of Janis Joplin. While not making grandiose claims, JPUSA's Chicago, inner-city ministry, *Cornerstone* Jesus paper, and their large annual festival of the same name, continue to impact youth to the far ends of the earth. The Kaisers continue global, itinerant preaching, and gutsy blues-rock performances.

Barry McGuire – (1935– From Eve of Destruction, to the Day of the Lord

Barry McGuire was well known for his lead singing role in *The New Christy Minstrals*, whose song "Green, Green" topped the charts. Like many of his era, McGuire joined the counterculture in both lifestyle and message. He recounted to me during a mission together in Tasmania, Australia, that during Woodstock he had been "jamming" in a hotel with Joplin and Hendrix between their performances. They were airlifted to comfort while the crowd wallowed in the mud and drugs. His rendition of the iconoclastic song, "Eve of Destruction," bought him permanent acclaim amongst the dissenting youth, and angry reprisals from patriotic conservatives, resulting in a widespread ban across many radio stations in America. He performed a leading role in the New York nude production of "Hair," and was an anarchistic biker in a B-grade occult movie.

Barry McGuire was converted through the influence of an enthusiastic younger group of Jesus Movement kids. On stage, he often recalls his previous anti-establishment hostility with a unique turn of phrase, rich with subculture poignancy. With sadness he hints at a string of sexual relationships before conversion, and waxes eloquent on his enduring transformation through Christ. A British DJ in Birmingham was criticizing McGuire during the early 1970s for jumping on the "Jesus bandwagon." He recalls:

> At first I denied it, thinking it was a cheap shot. I was . . . off, but the Lord checked my heart. I waited for him [Jesus] to tell me what to say and I heard myself saying: "Let me tell you – it was the only wagon going anywhere. I've been on all the other wagons and they didn't go anywhere. The wheels fell of them and the horses died. We ate the horses and went lookin' for another wagon. A guy would be a fool not to get on the only wagon leavin' town when the exterminators are comin' the next day. What would you do? Just say I think I'll stick around and dig [enjoy] the exterminators." (McGuire 2000)

I was involved on several occasions with McGuire and on every occasion observed a spontaneous flow of creative, powerfully appropriate, folk responses, which never failed to place the audience in the palms of his hands. Every performance resulted in many professed conversions. The aging hippie has suffered at the hands of the Christian music industry, having no control of his award winning "Bullfrogs and Butterflies," or popular numbers, "Take This Bread," and "If My People Who Are Called By My Name." Wearied by America's materialism, McGuire relocated his family to New Zealand for some years, but returned to California, where he continues to write and produce albums on an independent label, singing on tour with Terry Talbot, brother to another pioneer in the Jesus music field, John Michael Talbot. John Talbot, formerly a Protestant-style evangelical, now a Franciscan monk, produces folk style, contemplative, worship songs.

These instigators of the Jesus Movement were variously spiritual adventurers, stump-orators, passionate preachers, folk-singing prophets, apostolic church planters and social critics whose initial countercultural impact attracted a following that was to initiate a wide variety of social experiments. Without their enormous energy, swift innovations, public personas, pop-culture savvy, and ubiquitous presence in the market place, the Movement would not have grown so rapidly or significantly impacted the culture. Two wandering charismatic archetypes will now be considered, chosen partly because of the extent and creativity with which they spread the word of a popularly acceptable Jesus. They also represent the polar extremes of the Movement.

Two Itinerant Archetypes: A Lone Ranger and A Communal Road Show Performer

More detailed accounts of the two following, highly visible, charismatic innovators will illustrate two typical models of itinerant charismatic leadership. They display elements of a spiritual Lone Ranger or an evangelistic road show. The influence of the final two wandering charismatics has been enduring and international, but they have established no abiding institutions to bear their names. Arthur Blessitt was a cross cultural missioner who "went native." Palosaari was embedded in the alternative culture before conversion. Blessitt began with a pastoral ministry, but shortly thereafter became entirely itinerant. Palosaari was itinerant, but traveled with a communal, mobile church. The first remains almost entirely individualistic in his view of "salvation." The second remains communitarian in worldview. Blessitt concentrated on contextualized proclamation. Palosaari made effective use of communal life, performing arts, street witnessing, Jesus papers, and street preaching. Both decry materialism, consumerism, and secularism.

Arthur Blessitt (1941 –)

Some Jesus Movement leaders attracted a following without seeking to establish themselves as leader of a specific community. Such charismatics sought rather to pursue an unorthodox lifestyle of proclamation and demonstration on the road. All observers were invited to participate, but this form of itinerancy built no distinct organization, or community. Such was and is Blessitt.

Arthur Blessitt claims to have been "saved" at seven (Blessitt 1999:1). Whie in many ways he became the "arch freak" of the hippie Jesus Movement, his roots were in fundamentalist ministry in Baptist churches. From a "straight" background he embraced:

> Paul's assertion to become all things to all men quite literally; Blessitt grew out his hair, shrouded himself in hippie regalia, handed out psychedelic New Testaments and reworked traditional Christian metaphors into a more hip phraseology. Though his circus-barker, evangelistic style made many uncomfortable, Blessitt is an important cog in the story of the Jesus people. (Di Sabatino 1994:79)

Arthur Blessitt informed me, "It was late in 1966 that the call of God clearly came to me, ordering me to Los Angeles. The newspapers had given much attention to large gatherings of hippies at the Griffith Park Love Inns. It was a real hippie thing" (1999:1). He arrived at the park for a rock concert and shared the relevance of Jesus with a stranger, who said, "That's heavy. Why don't you tell them on stage?" He replied that he would like to do that, but saw no way open. The stranger replied, "I'm running it." He was given time between "gigs" and asked for anyone interested in Jesus to talk with him under a tree. Over 100 came. These were not young people with religious experience of church. Arthur Blessitt, a youth evangelist at the time thought, "I'm not getting 100 fresh people in a week of revivals I'm doing. This is where I need to be" (Blessitt 1999:1).

Early in 1967, he started a ministry to the people of the streets, making California's Sunset Strip, the glamorous location which attracted many wandering American youth, the location for a 24-Hour Club, to reach exploited, counterculture kids.

Meanwhile he leased a building on the Strip and opened a combination coffeehouse and counseling center in time for the Easter vacation influx. He named it His Place, and served free coffee, doughnuts, punch, and peanut butter sandwiches. On summer nights as many as 500 young people – hippies, bikers, plastics [counterfeit hippies], junkies, teenyboppers, runaways – wandered in for the handouts and to listen to the music, testimonies, and Arthur's midnight sermons, or just to rap with one of the workers about some hang-up. Every night some prayed to receive Christ. In two years 10,000 decisions (an average of a dozen per night) had been recorded. (Plowman 1971a:47)

His Place site is now Dan Aykroyd's House of Blues (Blessitt 1999:1).

Arthur Blessitt had "pastored in Mississippi, Montana, and Nevada but his flamboyant methodology was better suited to the California Strip" (Di Sabatino 1994:79). Little known musicians at the time, Andre Crouch and Jimmie Owens joined Blessitt for a series of two-hour shows at the Sunset Strip's Godfather rock 'n' roll haunt in 1968. In 1969, facing eviction, Blessitt chained himself to his cross in protest. Joined by a supportive crowd he was eventually reinstated. He was a well-known figure in bars and pubs. Initially, many local churches vigorously opposed him.

Arthur Blessitt believes the nomination of Calvary Chapel as the birthplace of the Jesus Movement is historical nonsense. The Jesus Movement began as a street movement at least two years before Calvary Chapel was to encounter it. In his own words, "That was just the one that got commercialized [publicized]" (Blessitt 1999:1). Prior to media exposure, the freaks knew what Jesus was doing on the streets without the established church. Blessitt recounts the radical time when they mixed it with the war protesters, when they responded to the Kent State student shootings, when Jesus marches and Jesus cheers were part of a real hippie movement. Blessitt worked with a band, *The Eternal Rush*, and in the midst of all the political heat of the time, their focus remained on Jesus.

On Christmas day 1969 Blessitt reshaped his ministry, leaving his more localized Californian ministry for a journey around the nation. Early in 1970 he spent three months in Times Square, New York which initiative he claims was fought hard by the church, that disapproved of his unorthodox ways. He then left and "hit the road," somewhat in protest at the increasing domestication of the Movement. Leaving others to look after His Place, he traveled to New York and Washington. He claims he went "to every major city of America, even Louisville, Kentucky, where 20,000 gathered at Freedom Hall" (Blessitt 1999:2). This was "all before *Time, Life,* and *Newsweek* discovered the Movement existed" (1999:2). As concerts and marches became respectable, and further removed from the street into the organizational hands of parachurch agencies, he felt that he wanted to leave America.

The media, once the Jesus Movement became popular, were beginning to report it regularly. Within a few years, Christian singers began charging for their concerts and preachers began leaving the street. The free concerts, the Jesus marches, and the unscheduled proclamations that had marked the true Jesus Movement gave way to church and parachurch sponsored activities, becoming a subculture for attracting Christians.

At one stage Arthur Blessitt felt called of God to an act of silent protest against the conflict between two warring Middle Eastern groups. He sat between them in the "no-mans land," kneeling at the foot of his 100-pound, mobile, wooden cross in prayer for peace. He has dragged his cross, with a small wheel at its base, around the world for over 30 years; 33,463 miles, to 278 nations. He has used it as an open-air pulpit, and a symbol for spontaneous proclamation. His story reads like Pauline missionary journeys[10] but without the planting of churches. The largest crowd he addressed was 500,000 at the Atlanta rock festival in 1970 and a similar number at Washington, DC for a Jesus Rally in 1980. He has carried his cross across 49 war zones and remained apolitical from the beginning of his ministry, through the Vietnam protest era until now.

The transient nature of the culture, the lack of resources, networks, and personnel to follow up the alleged conversions, make assessment of his ministry's long-term outcomes difficult to verify. I was somewhat of a skeptic because of the flamboyant, public persona of Blessitt. In Amsterdam in 1984, on hearing through Youth with A Mission that Blessitt was coming to the Red Light District, I decided to investigate. I observed a typical, unscheduled Blessitt. He arrived with his cross, his unconventional appearance, and an international reputation. He swiftly gathered a crowd.

Amsterdam is a cosmopolitan city so the audience was multicultural and multiracial. Businessmen in dapper three-piece suits stood next to thinly clad prostitutes, who stepped out of their publicly viewable, shop front "slots," joined by tourists and citizens. Given Blessitt's fundamentalist persona I expected he would castigate the crowd for the sexual irregularities of the infamous Red Light District. His theology was simplistic but his method of contextualization was remarkable. He knelt at the foot of his cross, looked into the faces of the inquisitive crowd and said, "Amsterdam is known all over the world as the City of Love. Thousands of people who are lonely and lost come here looking for love. They come here for the touch of human flesh; mistakenly they believe they will find the answer to their heart's cry."

The crowd was transfixed. With an excellent employment of the "pregnant pause" he allowed the surprised crowd, perhaps like St. Paul's audience on Mars Hill (Acts 17:16-34), to grasp the fact that he was not a moral critic, but a friend and mutual pilgrim. He opened a small, well-worn Bible, and read 1 John 4:8: "He that loveth not, knoweth not God; for God is love." He proceeded, "We are all seeking love, but some of us are seeking love in the wrong place. You will never find the love you seek in anything else but God, because the Bible says, God is love." Following a classic evangelical call to Christian conversion, prostitutes and businessmen, knelt with tourists and wandering young people, at the foot of Blessitt's cross, to "find" Jesus with evident emotion.

Youth with A Mission, and other agencies picked up relationships with some of Blessitt's converts, and were able to build on the initial, emotional response. While traveling around the world, I have consistently met individuals who date the total turn-around of their lives to a bizarre encounter with Blessitt. His gospel still lacks any sophisticated application to sociopolitical issues, or to popular psychology. It is anti-intellectual, ecclesiologically messy, and organizationally chaotic, but a trail of faith has been blazed for many marginal people to find their way into the community of faith.

One might justifiably question whether such responses would be likely to endure, without immediate incorporation into a moral community (Stark 1997: 2-7, 21-30, 183-187). Pastoral experience and surveys indicate a high attrition rate for converts who are not followed up, and connected to a nurturing community of faith (Stark 1996c). Many stories are told however, of people whose initial paradigm shift through a religious experience in the Jesus Movement has matured to permanency, despite lack of nurture, even after social opposition. No research the author is aware of has tracked conversion patterns in the Jesus Movement. Anecdotal evidence reveals extraordinary religious intensity during revitalization, and an immediate sense of communal re-aggregation, and *communitas* at the point of conversion. We observed in the early days a "larger-than-life" impression on converts, and a sense of hippie tribal connection, such that even when separated from the group many were sustained during periods of disconnection from an adequate nurturing context.

Blessitt's United Kingdom Tour – Catalyst for Change

Arthur Blessitt's visit to the United Kingdom in 1971 was a headline story in the London papers, after he was televised carrying his large wooden cross. His London demonstrations coincided with The Festival of Light, which he addressed at Trafalgar Square. Many believed this was the highlight of the Festival with an impressive response of many people to his evangelistic appeal (Corry 1973a:3, 11, 14). It is remarkable that one marginal, wandering charismatic could sufficiently impact the culture of a foreign land, that he could be a major feature in two official British Council of Churches Youth Department reports. One was a published document (Corry 1973b), the other was an interim report to the Sixty-Second Meeting of the British Council of Churches by the field officer for the British Council of Churches youth department (Corry 1973a). The reports evaluate the visits to Britain by three itinerants, Blessitt, Jim Palosaari, and Larry Norman (1973a:13-17, 28-30, 34-36, 38).

Twenty-three years later, Pete Ward (1996) has provided a well-documented history of recent British church developments. He believes that Blessitt's publicity stunts combined with the music of Norman and Palosaari visit to England with his Lonesome Stone Rock Opera as the initiating Jesus Movement force, permanently reshaped the evangelical youth culture, for good and ill. Rather than founding any separate or new movement, Blessitt, Palosaari, and other Jesus Movement wandering charismatics changed the basic culture of evangelicalism in the United Kingdom. Their influence, along with the charismatic movement, introducing both laudable and questionable innovations, challenged the existing Christian order, creating an enduring evangelical youth subculture, still the dominant expression of evangelical and charismatic faith in the United Kingdom.

The British Council of Churches' typically conservative analysis described the Jesus Movement as an expression of Christianized American pop culture (1973a), saying that it would be unlikely that a Jesus Movement Revolution could appear in the United Kingdom (Corry 1973b:31-34). The official keepers of the traditional British churches assured their constituencies that Britain is not like America. The idiosyncratic sensationalism of these American prophets would have a short-lived impact upon the United Kingdom. They claimed that in Britain "there is no national identity crisis or deep social division." Typically the establishment seemed unaware that the generation gap was a global reality for Anglo-European cultures. Despite this, churches were packed to capacity for Blessitt's flying visits through London, Newcastle, Edinburgh, Glasgow, Belfast, Dublin, Cardiff, Birmingham, and Cambridge (Corry 1973a:5). A few Jesus Movement groups were started and remained but the primary impact lay in the revitalization of traditional churches and reorganization of youth movements. New, postmodern, parachurch movements resulted, Greenbelt Youth Festivals being the best known. Their annual attendance peaked at 40,000 people in the late 1980s.

The second British Council of Churches report was self-contradictory. On the positive side, it reported extraordinary public responses. A thousand people packed a Baptist church in Scotland. Enthusiasm was aroused among the church-going youth. A committee in Scotland, and the Crusader Union claimed:

> Blessitt gave a direction to these groups by emphasizing the importance of outreach evangelism. Christianity had to be brought out of the churches and into places where people congregate. Blessitt provided a focal point, and he stimulated the formation of outreach groups. His visit gave rise to a planning committee, which put young people in contact with each other in local areas and forged links between the youth and the older congregations. Counselors, follow through groups, Bible study notes and follow up rallies were part of the legacy, but the church report, perhaps a little cynically, maintained that these enabled many young people to search beyond the very simplistic view of Jesus that many had accused Blessitt of presenting. (Corry 1973a:5)

The cautiously positive sections of the report are peppered with pejorative phrases such as "Blessitt's one night stands," "his band wagon," "publicity seeking marches," and "good entertainment while it lasted," in summarizing the significance of this highly charismatic style of apostolic, Jesus Movement leader.

> Blessitt's publicity-seeking marches and rallies made the Jesus Movement a talking point in every major town in Britain and brought it within reach of most young people through an all-round handing out of stickers. Blessitt brought Jesus to them and they have not had to search for him. For many Blessitt's work has been "instant evangelism" and will have no lasting effect as the rain-washes away and the sun fades the Jesus stickers. It was good entertainment while it lasted. Yet for a few, he was the person who "turned them on to Jesus" and gave them a vision which no local church or regular evangelist had been able to give. For older Christians, he revived their commitment; offering renewed hope and confirming that the Holy Spirit is at work renewing the Church. They learnt two things in particular from him. First, what it is really like to live personally in Christ and in the Spirit – to have a natural love for every person. Secondly, to have a "loving boldness" in outreach evangelism, in which you don't have to be apologetic about what you believe. (Corry 1973a:5)

To make Jesus primary news anywhere, especially in post-Christian England, may be a notable feat. But like George Whitefield of old, he may finish a hyperactive life of street preaching with only a "rope of sand" (Hunter 1987:126) to show for it in terms of any distinct movement, or stable institution. His erratic history has left a remarkable secondary impact (Pete Ward 1996:87). As Corry sees it,

> The importance of Blessitt in relation to any Jesus Movement in Britain will probably lie in his contribution towards creating a climate of opinion in which Jesus is news. People can talk openly about Jesus and not be afraid of reading the Bible in cafes and waiting rooms. The Jesus sticker has become a point of identification and contact and an opener for conversation in a bus queue or train. (Corry 1973c:6)

The overall results add weight to Pete Ward's contention that an entirely new configuration of the evangelical youth culture resulted, even if few Jesus Movement institutions took root in the organizational sense (Ward 1996: 87).[11] Ward affirms that despite Blessitt's erratic performance and the lack of primary institutional monuments to his name, he impacted existing forms. He also has influenced multitudes of converts, existing institutions, and methodologies. Some recent socioreligious traditions in worship, youth festivals, contemporary Christian music, and youth Christian pop culture media such as *CrossRhythms* magazine owe their existence substantially to such wandering charismatics (Pete Ward 1996:87-90).

A movement leader's legacy may not lie in the establishment of new institutions, but in the cultural reconfiguration of already existing institutions, organizations, or cultural mazeways. The issue may not be the maintenance of a visible movement, but the propagation of a new matrix or worldview drawing on both old tradition and new cultural innovations. During Blessitt's United Kingdom visits, he not only obtained individual responses to the message, but also stimulated existing moral communities to organize more contemporary organizational structures for the preservation of the results. He even provided a handbook for training in ministry to every conceivable context, from laundromats to taxis and nursing homes (Blessitt 1972).

There is an important message in this for the church. While some elements of the Jesus Movement's early innovations have been taken up by a range of church traditions, the Movement itself was opposed, ignored or trivialized by many, resulting in the collapse of creative groups because of immaturity, lack of relationships, and lack of resources and stabilizing historic structures. Incendiary orators such as Blessitt did not intend to leave a legacy of organized movements, but they saw their role as apostolic and catalytic within the culture, hoping to set an example that would be voluntarily taken up by the culture and by existing institutions. While in defiance of the existing order, such creative innovators hoped for the revitalization of the dominant culture.

David Di Sabatino, currently researching the place of the "holy fool" in pre-industrial cultures (1999d), is inclined to see Blessitt as a classic "holy fool" who captivates the common people and challenges the powerful.

> Arthur Blessitt was the king of media attention . . . .He obtained a lot of media, but his understanding was not holistic. He ran for President in 1976 based on a platform of prayer and getting people baptized in the Holy Spirit. You have to admire a guy that has committed himself to a very literal rendering of the 'foolishness of the cross.' Arthur is a holy fool in the best sense of that term. (Di Sabatino 1999d:2)

Blessitt is typical of those who defected from the mainstream culture to seriously engage the counterculture rather than colonize it. His marriage of radical days dissolved. Perhaps radical itinerancy and the stress of bearing a culturally conflictual commitment are barely compatible with stable marriage. The Palosaari, Norman, Frisbee, Parks, and Higgins marriages all failed. Meisner, Blessitt, and Jim Wallace were "straight" converts to the counterculture as itinerant missioners. They fared no better.

Despite disappointments, Blessitt has remained committed to his initial call to the streets. In 1999, at 59, he still provided his home phone number on the Internet, personally answered his phone, and waxed enthusiastically about "incredible responses" to his cross carrying crusades "from Wyoming to San Antonio" experiencing the "triumph of speaking to a crowd one block away from going straight to hell" (Di Sabatino 1999d:2). He is disdainful of "easy believism" or "fast, instant McDonald's faith."

> They don't want to be obedient; to be holy. They ask me to lay hands on them and impart my charisma. I won't do it. Do they know how many years of committed tears, how many hours of prayer, how many sleepless nights spent on the ground it takes to be a holy person?

> A revival in the church for six months has no relation to the street. I preach where I'm walking. The road is my home. I'm more excited. I'm still an optimist and a dreamer. People are still responding where they are. I have recently seen whole Moslem villages come to Christ. (Blessitt 1999:2-3)

Traditional preachers institutionalized Jesus marches and left the streets and the Jesus musicians started a moneymaking industry. God's tool continued to build an incalculable legacy of revitalized lives and renewed local structures.

Jim Palosaari – Taking the Church on Tour

Jim Palosaari was more representative of the dominant countercultural model, whereby the counterculture penchant for communal clustering was combined with an equally counterculture, apocalyptic proselytism, expressed in arts, festivals, and tribal-like itinerancy.

Another product of the Pacific Northwest Jesus People is Palosaari. Despite elements of dysfunction, he has connections to the most enduring and stable community, JPUSA. An actor by trade, Palosaari was converted through a Pentecostal tent preacher. He represents an indigenous, counterculture leadership, and is still antiestablishment and counterculture though working in Tennessee as a fundraiser for Christian charities (Palosaari 1999). He was the most "direct link" between the Midwest and Northwest (Enroth, Ericson, and Peters 1972:128). He was involved in a cluster of Seattle-Vancouver communal houses while he was trained in Meisner's God's Army, which he claims he helped retool for a more indigenous and radical application.

Early in 1971, after a meeting of Jesus Movement leadership in the Pacific Northwest Palosaari and his wife Sue returned to his home territory of Milwaukee. He set up the Jesus Christ Power House as a center for Bible study and outreach meetings. He was highly charismatic, a professional actor with a strong emphasis on charismatic experience, and an apocalyptic view of a doomed society. The initial group of seven members had grown to 150 full-time members in less than a year. The *Milwaukee Journal* and the *Milwaukee Sentinel* published many enthusiastic reports on his Jesus People in 1971 and early 1972. In Australia, we connected through his Jesus paper, *Street Level*. Eschewing the shallowness of some of the revolution, he founded a rigorous Believers' Discipleship Training School. He engaged new converts in alternating weeks of class work and practical witnessing, or disciple recruitment throughout the Midwest. Seventy disciples volunteered for the first intake.

The Milwaukee Jesus People acquired an abandoned 315-roomed nursing home in Milwaukee, Wisconsin. His group was among the most anti-materialistic and rigidly controlled, patterning after Acts 2, "having all things in common." Disciples withdrew from the world, placing themselves under a "buddy" system, by which they were closely monitored and even discouraged from going home at Christmas. Lisa Carothers, age 18 when converted through Palosaari, joined Street Level at the beginning of September 1971, remaining with the movement until its disintegration around January 1975.

> When I was 18 and *The Beatles* broke up; I felt totally direction-less [Figure 3.3]. I didn't know what I wanted to do with my life or where I wanted to go. I was completely lost. I was a follower so I thought I should try it. Looking back, it was a security thing because it made me feel good when I gave my life to these people. Members gave up all their possessions. People surrendering cars and money and sharing their clothes and deodorant. I remember Jenny Howsen. We went into the bathroom and cried because she wanted to go home. I felt like I had joined the Army. This was my life. This was my calling. I submitted to it. I didn't have to make any decisions. I liked it . . . . I didn't have my own opinion. I did what they said. A part of that was fun. All you had was your knapsack. It was a very free existence. You weren't dragging stuff around and you didn't have responsibilities. You didn't have anything anyone could steal from you. It was a substitute family. (Carothers 1999:6,12)

Street Level formed a talented rock group, and recruited blues guitarist Kaiser. John Herron, Kaiser's father-in-law, with a history of infidelity like Palosaari, led an evangelistic group on tour through the Midwest. Jim Palosaari and *Sheep* formed one group; Herron, Kaiser and his band *Charity* formed another; and Bill Lowry, an old-time Pentecostal tent evangelist, with a unique relationship to the Jesus Movement, led a third group, traveling with the band *Servant*. Lowry formed The Highway Missionary Society in British Columbia and later Oregon. Remarkable stories abound from that period, including claims in *Christianity Today* of a mission involving young Kaiser in Duluth, where despite "terrible wintry weather," people attended for over 50 consecutive days and "thousands are documented as having accepted an invitation for salvation" (Di Sabatino 1994:44).

Lisa Carothers' recollections are intensely positive and negative. Typical of many participants, she believes it was the most exciting time of her life. There was a romanticism about living in a liminal state, with all of one's worldly possessions in a knapsack, with no long-range responsibilities, little of value for a thief to steal, and a creative uncertainty as to what another day would hold. For many like Carothers, the radical Christian group became a substitute family. Submission to the prophetic authority of the charismatic leader, and to the structures he put in place was virtually unquestioned.

Leo Mueller of the Finnish Christian Businessmen's Committee invited Palosaari to Finland after hearing *Sheep* and seeing their street work. In April 1972 with a team of 30 Palosaari left for Europe. According to Carothers, Palosaari faced major debts. By May 1972, the core group in Milwaukee had dissolved. They had survived for less than 18 months. The Herron-Kaiser team, having blitzed campuses and towns south to Florida, faced moral problems in the leadership and began to long for enduring community and serious ministry in the inner city of Chicago. Where Palosaari failed they were to succeed remarkably till this day as Jesus People USA.

Mueller set up the Palosaari tour team in a resort replete with a sauna for a month. In Finland, Carothers claims they saw a tremendous revival. In conjunction with the Lutheran Church, a concert in Helsinki drew a capacity audience and "the whole church came forward in response to the message" (Spransy and Spransy 1999:7). Sweden and Germany were bemused rather than impressed by the American hippie persona of the "traveling church" of "gospel gypsies" (*Street Level* 1973:1:4). In Germany, they turned a brothel into a Jesus House and, struggling for financial survival, they lost half the team. En route they picked up Swedish, German, and Danish recruits. Some drove their two equipment vans; others hitchhiked through East Germany. *Street Level* (1973) reported bizarre divine interventions, despite passport irregularities. In Holland, they were basically ignored, but they connected with local Jesus people.

Arriving in Birmingham, United Kingdom in September 1973, they announced themselves as a Jesus Movement Commune and were invited to set up a discipleship-training center. A millionaire, Kenneth Frampton underwrote their lengthy stay and later financed the Greenbelt Festival Movement. Frampton had lost two sons to the Children of God but, impressed by the Wisconsin's group music, he saw them as a healthy alternative. He endowed them with a three-story house in East London which eventually accommodated 60 people. He provided food, clothing, and two double-decker buses.

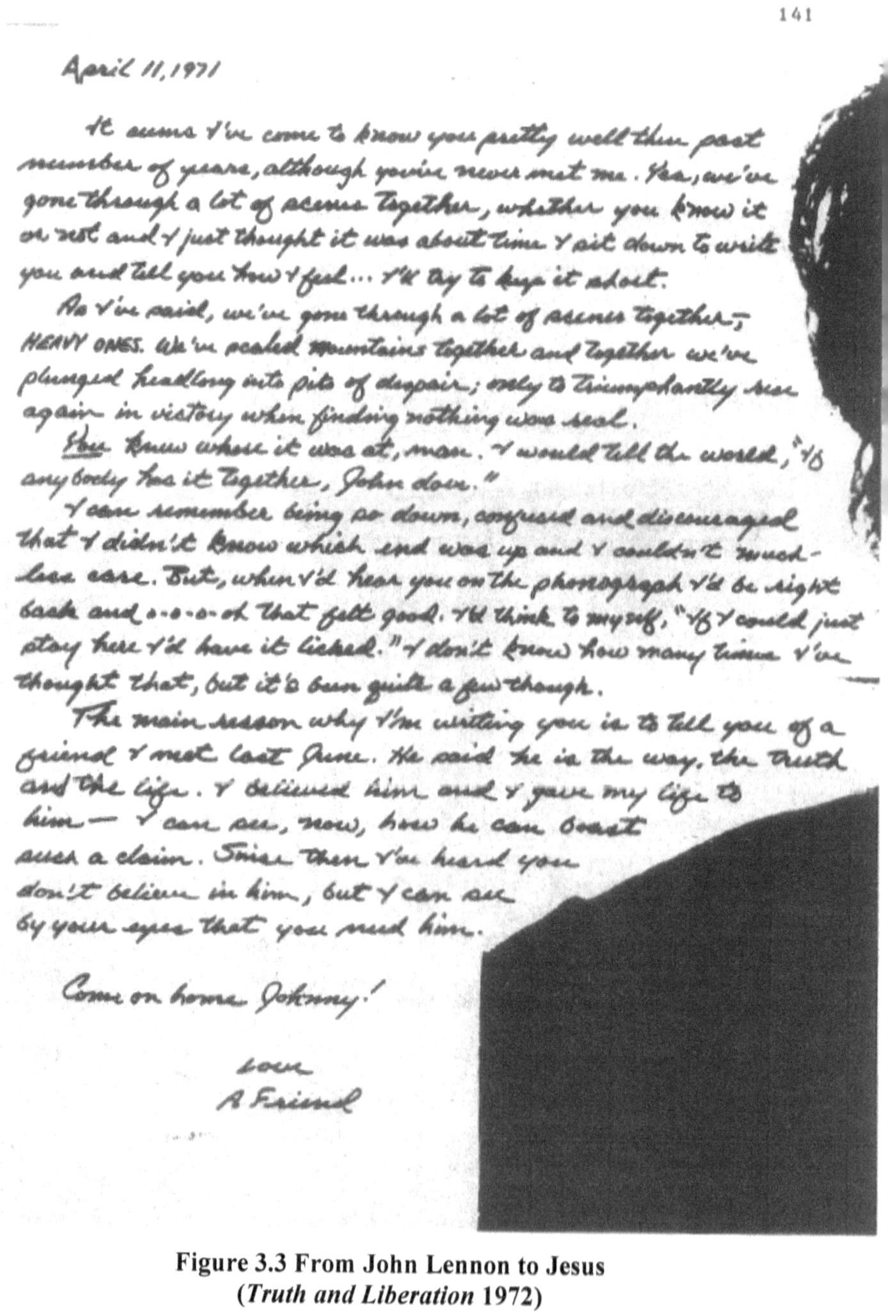

Figure 3.3 From John Lennon to Jesus
(*Truth and Liberation* 1972)

Good publicity encouraged Palosaari to produce a musical show, "Lonesome Stone" in response to "Jesus Christ Superstar" and "Godspell." The show incorporated secular favorites like "Blowin' in the Wind" and traced the history of a typical Jesus Freak, using the group's testimonies. Initial presentations in the famous Rainbow Theater, rented by Frampton, brought poor attendance and bad reviews. Actress Caroline Green, well known lead female actress in the London production of "Hair," became a Krishna Consciousness devotee through George Harrison, but was converted to Jesus through the group. With the assistance of two directors from "Hair," she re-assembled the cast of "Lonesome Stone," which then toured through the United Kingdom to some enthusiastic reviews. "The cast with an amazing past" was made up of six ex-drug addicts, two convicts, including a drug smuggler, and a convert who had made three suicide attempts. Typical of 30 regional media reviews, which applauded the performance for its creativity and power to inspire, *The Star Sheffield* said:

> "Lonesome Stone" with perhaps the oddest lineup ever, rocked into Sheffield singing a song of love and peace. Former drug addicts, drug smugglers, con men and dropouts spent two hours belting out beat numbers that had the audience stamping and clapping. It was one of those shows that made you want to join in. The theme was San Francisco's flower children's disillusionment with the world of pot and LSD. The message was peace and love but it wasn't compulsory. This was certainly no religious sermon. (*The Star Sheffield* 1974)[12]

The American Commander in Chief in Europe reported: "We are still hearing words of praise about the excellent showing of the 'Lonesome Stone' made here in Ramstein. Their Wiesbaden fans were equally enthusiastic" (Jones 1974). Protestant Air-force Chaplain, Charles Caudill reported, "[There were] 40 young people attending Bible studies as a result of the visit, requests for Bibles, continued baptisms, and a marked increase in requests for chaplain, counselor contacts, and a scheduled youth revival planned for the near future" (Caudill 1974). Conversation between university student James Holloway, and Palosaari birthed Greenbelt, a large Christian arts festival.[13]

Although Holloway's vision was ignited by the supportive conversation that he had with Palosaari, it was clearly a British initiative. The official story of Greenbelt abandons customary British, emotional restraint:

> The London summer of 1973 was memorably muggy. Long clammy weeks punctuated by the occasional spectacular thunderstorm. It was the season theater director, Jim Palosaari, who brought his hippie troupe of actors, musicians and dancers from the United States to perform their Jesus Rock Musical, "Lonesome Stone" at the capital's premier rock and roll venue, The Rainbow Theater in Finsbury Park. Sponsored by Christian businessman Kenneth Frampton's *Deo Gloria Trust*, Palosaari's dramatic band of ex-drug addicts and flower children put across a spectacular message of personal salvation through the teachings of Christ. They used slide shows, wailing guitars, dance, thudding drums and lights that flashed till your eyes streamed. It was the culture of San Francisco's Haight-Ashbury but doused in Holy Water. The good old gospel communicated with the rawness and energy of contemporary fashion; too modern for some spiritual elders, who lead their popping eyed young flocks away from this Sodomized hippodrome lest their innocent souls catch something nasty.

"Lonesome Stone" rambled into the flat wilds of Suffolk where a young musician, James Holloway, studying at Essex University, caught up with it at Mildenhall Air base. Holloway, a blues singer who stomped and boogied various venues into submission with the East Anglican band, All Things New, had a dream. It was of an Arts Festival where Christians came to present their talents before a sympathetic audience and to give God the praise for inventing self-expression in the first place. He got talking to Jim Palosaari and shared his vision with the rugged, rotund Canadian [Ward 1996:98]. Palosaari suggested he find a field. A field was found. "Then you've got yourself a festival" replied Big Jim. (Henderson 1984:1-2)

Thus, Greenbelt Festival was born at Prospect Farm, Charsfield, August 1974. Frampton's *Deo Gloria Trust* also financed this venture. Jesus People performed "Lonesome Stone" and turned up in force at the first festival (Pete Ward 1996:98-99). The indigenous element of Greenbelt produced a tradition unlike parallel festivals in America such as Ichthus, Wilmore, Kentucky, the first Christian music festival commenced in May 1970 (Burgess 2000:1), and Creation Festival. The engagement of the gospel and culture debate occurred from the earliest days with a far more eclectic representation of the arts, and of radical theological discourse and dialogue on social and cultural issues. *U2*, Bruce Cockburn, *The Alarm*, Sir Bob Geldorf and *The Boomtown Rats*, and the *Violent Femmes* are some of the secular performers to play on Greenbelt's main stage. Speakers have ranged from Anglican John Stott to *Sojourners*' Jim Wallace, and Sandinista supporting Nicaraguan, Gustavo Paragon.

On returning to America in 1974 the team was exhausted. Palosaari's personal life was under extreme stress and an attempt to kick start the movement again in America failed. Visions of a Lonesome Stone Company to travel the world dissipated quickly. Perhaps it was a case of too little routinization too late. According to Carothers, things swiftly soured and they only performed in six American cities, Duluth, Minnesota; Sioux Falls, South Dakota; Kansas City, Missouri; Davenport, Iowa; Oconomowoc, Wisconsin; and Lancaster, Pennsylvania. The show did well, but some conservative hosts, upon viewing the hip performance, ejected team members because they "were of the devil." A mass exit of supporters occurred although Carothers "stuck with it till the bitter end," as she "didn't know what else to do." The road show stressed the families who she observed "were burning out. We had been on the road with kids. It was really hard on families and marriages" (Carothers 1999:23-24).

Jim Palosaari moved 11 times in one year. Itinerancy took a toll on family life, he admits: "Every time they would go to a new house, my wife would start 'nesting.' She would paint rooms and settle down as if we were going to stay. Then we would shift again. This was very emotionally difficult and costly for her" (Palosaari 1999:1).

Memory is colored by personal elements of suffering or adventure. Carothers remembers her traveling membership as stimulating and unparalleled in terms of meaning and mission. Having been under recovery therapy for more than 25 years, she now concludes that the co-dependency produced between her, the charismatic leader, and the group was symptomatic of the social psychology of many attracted to such movements. On the other hand, the crisis that led her to the group may have concluded in suicide or substance abuse if she had not made the social connection. This was a legacy of the Jesus People, who were the only ones there for thousands of lost, at-risk itinerants.

Mary Steinke, Lisa Carothers' older sister, and mother of five children who are today all married and involved in some form of radical or frontier mission, was an early patron of the group. With her husband, Mary opened their large home to years of invasion by counterculture seekers. In her kitchen Palosaari led Carothers to faith. Mary Steinke, who was never "on the road" as Carothers had been, gave a lengthy account of positive involvement with Palosaari.

> I graduated in 1955. Jim Palosaari graduated in 1957 from the same high school just outside Milwaukee, Wisconsin. Jim went off to New York, married somebody, and lived a rough theater life. He has the gift of making people do things. He is a promoter. It is redeemed. It is useful. That is the side that I have always known. I just knew that he had weaknesses and failures. That was God's business. I am only now learning these other things. I am not one [to whom] people tell rough stuff. I'm not in denial, but I've learned what my gift is and that is to say, "You are who you are in Christ" and not listen to the same stories seven thousand times. Counselors are meant to hear that stuff over and over. (Mary Steinke 1999:23)

While not denying moral and psychological flaws in the wandering charismatic, she believes their involvement was the most productive and exhilarating period of their lives. She remains convinced the Jesus Movement was a quantum leap forward from a stagnant church in the 1950s.

> Well, the reason that was so great is because it was street level, which I like. There is a thing in all of us, especially globally with our awareness that really has to deal with that. My granddaughter cries when she sees what's going on in India. She cries when she sees the war and when she was watching Kosovo. That computes in her Bible's position and worship. Everything we are about, the Jesus people revolutionized. . . . It was consciousness raising on "what is your worldview?" Now it is all dissipated and gone. But, now it's on the news and like you said, Bible verses are used. On Highway 26, did you see that big Christian message? "Jesus. Don't leave Earth without him." In the 50s it was this hidden, quiet, private thing. It wasn't the road from Jerusalem to wherever else Jesus went, when it was confrontational. That's not how it was in America. Now you could almost anticipate that you are going to see something on a street corner. (Steinke 1999:23-24)

Siv Spransy (1999) joined the Palosaari troupe in Sweden when she was a high school student, intrigued by the hippie visitors' performance. Her experience paralleled that of Carothers as she recalls the distressing times of Palosaari's alleged, relational dysfunction and authoritarianism, of selling Jesus papers and witnessing on streets and busking for bare survival. She left, troubled by Palosaari's alleged relational irregularities, convinced they were a cult. A mother of five very talented young adult children, she wistfully recalls the rich experience of abandonment to a great cause and of deep bonding in a liminal state of itinerancy.

Siv Spransy's husband Matt Spransy (1999) who met her in Palosaari's group, performed as a musician in *Sheep*, and a later group *Servant*. He does not recall the stresses felt by the two younger women at the time. His memories are of rewarding commitment, creative, caring service of humanity, and of great success in leading people to faith. He meets regularly with a new generation, mentoring a creative rock group *Jacob's Stone*, restless for another experience of radical commitment.

Jim Palosaari has drifted through several marriages and appears to have stabilized in a fund raising occupation for charities. Perhaps the most moving and surprising postscript to the story is the feelings expressed by Palosaari's first wife Sue, long since divorced by her husband. My conversations with many similar casualties revealed how typical she is of those who have known such existential bonding, through the extreme liminality, of revitalization. Victims of the dysfunctional elements often recall a sense of high ecstasy in movement days, and unparalleled alienation and pain at the loss of the "larger than life" utopianism, communalism, and activism.

> Such a long, long time ago. Our lives are all so much the richer and complicated for it – marriages and children and jobs and directions we didn't expect to take. By now, full-bloomed adulthood has matured and flowered and sometimes been nipped. We were just little ripe beginnings then. But sometimes, when you take the time to remember, the pain of parting is just as real as if it had just happened. On that odd moment, when you allow the flood of memories and reasons why, to have some play in the front of your head, or hear an old tape or record, the agony of not being together still brings an ache. (Sue Palosaari 1998:1)

A longing for the communalism and mission focus experienced in the revitalization days has not been destroyed by divorce, or by the reconfiguration of the culture into a therapeutic materialism in defiance of all they had sacrificed to establish.

> Don't go home; stay for the night. You can still sleep on the floor, even though your bones argue the next morning. (Remember the story of Greg and Lyn sleeping on the floor in their new sleeping bags on their honeymoon – "practicing" for Europe . . . isn't that a precious memory?) You could still buy and prepare a meal for 60 cents. Old skills never die. But can you still go through a day without looking at the clock? Can you do without indoor plumbing? Can you even *find* someone like Malmberg to take care of your kids? Do you still take sharing for granted?
>
> Someday, don't go home. Tell your kids that you've decided to forsake it all for Jesus, because that's where your heart really belongs, and everywhere else you put it only makes you ache to go back; to take up his cross and walk down the road with a light step; to cram into crowded vans and juggle babies and discuss all aspects of life; to pray *long* prayers while the meals get cold; to sing about everything wherever you are. (Sue Palosaari 1998:2)

This nostalgia is not uniquely a mark of aging Jesus people. McAdam's enquiry into the state of mind for the civil rights activists of *Freedom's Summer* uncovered similar sentiments (1986, 1988, 1989, 1999). They had "to a remarkable extent . . . maintained the political vision that drew them to Mississippi."

They had "paid for this lifelong commitment with a degree of alienation and social isolation [liminality] that has only increased with time. This is marked also by a high rate of marriage collapse." The sense that "they have kept the faith while America has lost it" (McAdam 1996:659) is paralleled in many aging Jesus Movement activists. They feel that they have kept the prophetic "word" while the increasingly market-driven church has lost it. A nostalgic sense of longing for the best of the former years mingles with a salutary sense of the external and self-instigated causes of movement collapse.

> In the end, we got so full of ourselves. Authority is a difficult commodity to deal with. You can't get organized without it. Its very nature is rife with little bits of communication gaps that leave gaping chasms of retaliation between [the] beloved. None *meant* to wound or disenfranchise, and none *meant* to dismember the body we loved so well in. It just happened and we scattered. (Sue Palosaari 1998:2)

Jim Palosaari, still countercultural in his convictions, recognizes the faults and failures of leadership, but believes the sociocultural realities of America militated against the success of an alternative Christian Movement.

> The Jesus Movement was doomed from the start. It could never survive in America. Nothing could save it in this country. The moment you get a group of people together in this society, they become fanatics and dangerous. Communitarianism was at the heart of the Jesus Movement, but as they say, "The ad-man is the prophet of this generation." If you have 80 people using one ladder, or 100 people using one washing machine, then it must bring down the system. We were countercultural, perhaps mildly anarchist. If our alternative lifestyle were adopted, if we were successful, it would bring about the downfall of the Government. I still believe there is no lifestyle to compare with it.
>
> I was on my way to see Keith Green on the day of the Jonestown massacre on November 18, 1978. The next day Keith said, 'This is a dark day for the communitarian movement.' Before that, *Christianity Today* and other journals were prophesying that communitarism might become the next great movement of the church in America, but after Jonestown[14] our numbers froze. From the early 1980s we spent half our energy defending community and being diverted. Parents were sending us letters. We were doomed from the beginning because of the pressure of the culture. (Palosaari 1999:2)[15]

Whatever the fatal flaws in some leaders of the Movement, the brief decade of frenetic Jesus Movement activity has left its mark on the church and the society in terms of repositioned worldviews and innovative practices.

A Postscript: Fleeting Success

Donald Miller (1997) attributes a "reinvention of American Protestantism" concerning worship, organization, and mission focus, substantially to the paradigm shifts generated by the Jesus Movement. Robert Wuthnow observes a less institutional and more catalytic contribution of deregulation whereby "spiritual freedom and moral imagination was engendered (Wuthnow 1998:53). "In retrospect the 1960s had a dramatic impact on American spirituality. Research indicates that many people were influenced by the turmoil of these years to adopt a more freewheeling and eclectic style of spirituality" (1998:53). The relaxation of social norms and religious experimentation in the midst of clearly defined, simplified, moral paths characterized the movement for the outsider.

The Jesus Movement pioneers prepared the way and seeded the ground for a period of harvest by those of the second wave, who were prepared to reposition, refurbish, and deregulate the institutional forms for a new receptor-oriented (Wagner 1989:77-86), seeker sensitive, church growth movement (George Hunter 1992:165-167). Wuthnow further believes that much of the attraction for a previously secularizing populace was the "experiments" of the 1960s radicals, "such as communes, underground churches, and student groups" (Wuthnow 1998:58).

The "second wave" denominations and the aftermath of seeker sensitive mega-churches may be traced to the gestation period of the early Jesus Movement (Miller 1997). Perhaps most significant was the relaxation of social norms, the employment of popular culture, and an emphasis on youth which clearly arose out of the youthful rebellion of the 1960s movements. The new synthesis of evangelical, mystical, Pentecostal, counterculture, and apocalyptic elements of Christianity, with a touch of Eastern philosophy – previously incompatible elements – emerged particularly amongst educated, middle-class youth. This indefinable new spirituality is now perceived by the popular culture as a permanent worldview realignment, or new religious consciousness, as an outcome of the upheavals of the 1960s and 1970s (Ellwood 1973:132-141; Glock and Bellah 1976; Guinness 1994; Johnson 1971:132-162; Jorstad 1972b; H. Ward 1972; P. Ward 1996). Eventually, at the practical and communications level the "institutional church paid close attention to the Jesus Movement, and mainly welcomed it and even mimicked it" (Richardson Stewart and Simmonds 1979:xxvi).

Fallen and Forgotten Pioneers

The Jesus Movement's wandering charismatics are easily lost in the dominance of more traditional histories of new paradigm churches.[16] The surviving charismatics[17] could provide scholars with research data for investigating the role of pioneers in the process of social change. They catalyzed cultural reconfigurations, which are only fully recognized after routinization. They may also provide substantial support for McAdam's (1999) thesis that social movements drastically reconfigure the lifestyles of those who initiate them.[18] As with the original wandering charismatics of the first Christian social movement, those of the twentieth century Jesus Movement changed the world around them. But in so doing, they rewrote their own biographies.

There is an historic, New Testament precedent for the easily forgotten pioneers. How many of the original 72 wandering charismatics Jesus commissioned (Luke 10:1ff) exist in church history? Little may be found of organizational evidence for the long-term significance of the recent Jesus Movement pioneers' contribution to the current revolution in ecclesiology and missiology. It is every bit as significant as a child's initial moment of birth. The child may find the infancy details lost in the onward march toward maturity, but for the rarely viewed photograph album, and unprofessional family videotape.

While this social movement was a grass-roots development, it was driven by a small, but energetic genre of hyperactive leaders, which parallel the description of (Horsley 1994 and Theissen 1978) of wandering charismatics. They attracted and sometimes divided their constituencies by their tendency toward authoritarianism, or lack of organizational wisdom. Like the first-century movement, the recent Jesus Movement itinerancy often resulted in the unplanned development of local communes or churches.

The tension between the role of the charismatic founder and the engagement of the disciples in social networking and cellular growth was a significant factor in the division, reshaping, or dissolution of numerous Jesus Movement groups. Some survived leadership struggles, after massive membership hemorrhage as in the case of Ohio's Xenos (McCallum 1999a:24-25); others divided and regrouped under new organizational names and structures, as in the history of TLC and CCC (Smith and Doney 1987:239-240). Some, like the House of the New World, the House of the Gentle Bunyip, and Shiloh ministries, struggled and collapsed after the dismissal or death of their founders (Peterson 1990a:60-66).

Summary

The prophetic, charismatic experience and style of virtually all the Jesus Movement founders is congruent with the Anthony Wallace paradigm of revitalization, in which a movement is "led by a prophet who has undergone an ecstatic revelation" (Wallace 1966:158). We saw in this chapter, the collapse of many high impact, innovative groups where there was a failure to respond to relational, family, and organizational stressors by early routinization by such creative founders. In future chapters we will face the complex and crucial nature of routinization of such independent energy and visionary focus. The next three chapters will provide illustrations of the perils, paradoxes and perplexities of leadership, journeying from a vision of revolution to a durable settlement in the "promised land" of a transformed, "steady [alternative] state."

The next chapter will consider one of the most unorthodox beginnings to an enduring new paradigm denomination, born out of the street level ministry of a hippie, but routinized and stabilized by the genius of a middle-class, middle-aged, Pentecostal defector from a traditional Pentecostal denomination. The crusade to make converts is replaced by the pressing demand to provide a fold for a vulnerable new flock of counterculture refugees; it is an example of routinization and organization in revitalization.

Notes

1. The combination of itinerant proclamation and the establishment of communal living, as the strategy for extending the influence of the Movement is described in Luke's history of the early church. The following references are examples of this. Acts 8:4-8; 26-32; 11:19-25; 27-30; 13:3-5; 13-14; 42-49; 14:1-7 (note the random wandering mixed with unscheduled stays where the reception is good); 14:21-28; 15:30-35; 16:6-12; 17:1-34. The latter chapters of Acts describe the geographically extensive itinerary of Paul the Apostle and his teams. Distinct similarities exist between the Pauline Jesus movement itinerary and that of the recent Jesus Movement wandering charismatics. Paul lost and gained team members between locations, so that new names of assisting disciples and the loss of others appears in the text.

Leadership conflict and division, a common feature in the modern Movement, occurred in the Pauline itinerary also. Despite charismatic, supernatural affirmation of the team appointment of Paul and Barnabas, and miracles accompanying their public ministry (Acts 13:1-12), severe conflict divided and separated Barnabas and Paul over the apostle's authoritarianism and lack of tolerance towards a weaker team member (15:36-40). Thus Silas, also a charismatic prophet (15:32) replaced Barnabas as Paul's lieutenant, and Barnabas took the disputed John Mark with his own team. It is to Paul's credit that later in his career he publicly gives credit to John Mark's effective discipleship (II Timothy 4:11) despite his earlier dismissal of him, presumably because of earlier timidity and withdrawal from risk in ministry. Another similarity lies in the duration of residency in various locations. As with Palosaari, Higgins, and Parks, the first century, charismatic teams stayed very briefly in some locations, because of opposition (Acts 9:29-30; 14:2-7, 19-20; 16:39-40; 17:5-10; 19:8-10; 19:23-20:3) and longer in others because of enthusiastic support public acceptance of the message (14:27-28; 15:30-35), or perceived divine instruction (16:9-10; 18:9-11; 21:9-14).

2. Despite the datedness of Weber's work his description of charismatic leadership remains the most parallel to the dominant forms of leadership I have observed in the Jesus Movement. Nuances of definition may be found in Weber's typology of charisma and its routinization; I offer this particular one as indicative of my purpose in designating some Jesus Movement leaders as "wandering charismatics." Weber's definition is as follows:

> The term "charisma" will be applied to a certain quality of an individual personality by virtue of which he is set apart from ordinary men and treated as endowed with supernatural, superhuman, or at least specifically exceptional powers or qualities. These are such as are not accessible to the ordinary person, but are regarded as of divine origin, or as exemplary, and on the basis of them the individual concerned is treated as a leader. In primitive circumstances this peculiar kind of deference is paid to prophets, to people with a reputation for therapeutic or legal wisdom, to leaders in the hunt, and heroes in war. It is very often thought of as resting on magical powers. How the quality in question would be ultimately judged from any ethical, aesthetic, or other such point of view is naturally entirely indifferent for purposes of definition. What is alone important is how the individual is actually regarded by those subject to charismatic authority by his "followers" or "disciples" (Weber 1964:359).

3. It is objected that the concept is circular in its reason; "Particular religious leaders are so potent because they [have] charisma" (Stark 1996b:24), but they are so empowered because their disciples believe they possess such charisma. Weber rightly saw the social

significance of such charisma, not in its cause, but in its effect upon the followers or disciples (Weber 1964:359).

4. In the Jesus Movement the power of charismatic prophets and apostles was enhanced by the counterculture worldview of many converts, who were already prepared to abandon the economic security and the social networks of their parents. The itinerancy of the mind in search of a utopian dream facilitated their readiness to "hit the road" in radical mission. Current missioners are often heard to complain that the present generation of youth is less sympathetic to a gospel of self-abandonment.

5. While the popular, "seeker sensitive" concept is dated back to the Calvary Chapel Jesus Movement church by some researchers (Miller 1997:186-188), virtually no recognition is given to the Jesus Movement's distinctly "street level" employment of this initiative. Calvary Chapel's Smith was initially drawn to his radicalized model by observing Jesus Freaks evangelizing the popular beaches of Southern California.

6. The author collected a wide range of the numerous and frequent tract releases from Children of God during this period, including the "Flirty Little Fishy" tract. In graphic visuals a very sensuous naked young woman hangs on a large fish hook, dangling in the face of an enraptured pagan about to be "hooked" for Jesus (Moses 1976:526-568).

7. I use this phrase, as a play on the words of the title of Norman's most popular album, "Only Visiting this Planet."

8. I obtained this report from a difficult to relocate website for Norman, under the title "Old Time Religion in the Age of Aquarius." It confirmed my own experience of Norman's better aspects as I had observed them while attending performances and sharing as a preacher performer with Norman at Greenbelt (British) and DeBron (Dutch) youth festivals. Much useful material on the Jesus people musicians and their history is obtainable on the Internet: (Jesuspeople.com) but this however is a Calvary Chapel initiative or at least overly influenced by their ministry, including the mythology that Smith was the "Father of the Jesus Movement." Pagination is almost impossible to affirm because of constant change of text and repositioning of articles in the text.

9. In personal correspondence with rock 'n' roll analyst, Steve Turner, Di Sabatino (1995:3-4) affirms the primary role of Norman in the Jesus Movement, but calls to question the originality of several song titles, poetic forms, and concepts in some of Norman's creations. He also questions some of Norman's public accounts of his involvement in the founding of Vineyard ministries. The following is a sample of this critique.

"True, he was interesting, but he was far from novel. I'm not sure, but putting Christian lyrics to other people's hit songs doesn't strike me as being creative. When I listen to Larry, I hear the Stones, Van [Morrison], and [Bob] Dylan overdubbed with his vocals. After following his career rather intently for over 10 years, I'm not sure he is deserving of the accolades that he gets. Case in point: Martin Luther's epithet 'The devil should not be allowed to keep all the best tunes for himself;' Norman's song: 'Why Should the Devil have all the good Music;' or even more obvious, 'Crew cuts are bad with all that hair cluttering around your brain.' ('I let my hair grow long so's I can be wise and free to think' – also from album 'Why Should the Devil')."

"I will hand it to Larry; for the last 20 years he has basically sold and resold the same song. I'm not sure if you are in touch with him now or know what is going on with [him], but he has become a caricature of reality." In the final analysis though, "He has invented nothing, but he has infused all with fire."

"One more thing – and I trust you aren't getting too tired of reading this – but the story about Norman having anything remotely to do with the Vineyard is bogus. Kenn Gulliksen, the original founder of that string of Bible studies that turned into the Vineyard, started the first study at the home of Girard. A couple of months later, Gulliksen asked

Larry if they could use his house in Beverly Hills to start a second one. He agreed that they [could have] a meeting there [and] collected offerings totaling $36. Larry attended two of those meetings, leaving one of them early, although I think Larry believes the stories he prints on his liner notes. They are half, quarter or eighth truths. Gulliksen seems as confused about Larry's statements as anyone."

10. He claims the following, much of which can be authenticated. He was beaten and stoned in Morocco; attacked by the Civil Guardian in Spain; almost choked to death in Hollywood; pistol-whipped in Orlando. He has experienced suffering 135-degree temperatures in Chad, Yemen, and Djibouti, and frigid temperatures in Nova Scotia, the Baltic Republics, and the scientific base at Antarctica. Blessitt has suffered storms at sea near the Philippines, Papua New Guinea, and the great passage through Antarctica. His worst animal scares were a green mumbo snake in Ghana, a baboon attack in Kenya, an elephant chase in Tanzania, and a crocodile attack in Zimbabwe. He has symbolically placed his cross in Washington DC, at the Olympic Stadium in Berlin, the Coliseum in Rome, the Pantheon in Athens, Greece, and the Pyramids of Egypt. He has raised it in Cebu City in the Philippines, at Magellan's cross, on top of the World's biggest pyramid, in Cholula in Mexico, in Red Square, Moscow, and on the Great Wall of China. The friendliest military encounters were with the Israeli and Palestinian Liberation Armies.

The greatest hostility towards the cross was experienced in Amsterdam and Morocco. The coldest receptions to the cross were in New York, Montreal, and Sydney, Australia. The greatest welcome he received for his cross bearing expeditions were in South Pacific islands like Vanuatu, the Solomon's, Papua New Guinea, in communist countries Poland, and Lithuania. Spain, with its strong Catholic tradition of the cross, and religious pilgrimage festivals, welcomed him gladly, perhaps sending a message to Protestants, that engagement of popular symbolism in evangelism in Catholic countries may be an excellent communication strategy. A warm reception in India may be more surprising at first glance, but not so since festivals and high symbolism are central in Indian culture.

Seventy-two miles is the longest walk in a day. The longest continuous period of walking in a particular Continent was almost two years spent walking across African countries. He is still walking (Blessitt:1999a). He has been arrested or incarcerated 24 times and maintains his own country America, is the country he found most apt for arrest, and Hollywood the worst city. The worst jail was Concord, NH. He has walked through almost impenetrable jungles (the Darien Jungle, Panama to Colombia). He estimates he has flown 1,700,000 miles across the seas; traveled 20,000 miles on the oceans, and 233,000 miles in motor vehicles . (From Blessitt's internet website and a lengthy collaboration with him by phone in 1999).

11. In Britain God's Army still appears to be active and continues to present itself as an aggressive Jesus Movement presence, with a confident Internet web page. In the 1970s several Jesus Movement groups were well established but mostly have diffused their innovative leaders throughout mainstream ministries. The Children Of God made their presence felt in the United Kingdom, as did Outreach for Jesus, The Living Room, Every man Jesus Paper, Jesus World Liberation Teen Mission, London Festival for Jesus 1972, and One Way In Front (Ward 1996:33-35). The most enduring influence was achieved by wandering charismatics rather than institution founders. The impact of Greenbelt festivals on youth ministry in Great Britain as one example has been profound. Sparked off by conversation between Palosaari and James Holloway, it has provided huge public exposure for poets, musicians, bards, prophetic analysts, Christian comics, artists, creative worship teams and fringe preachers. The traditional spokespersons for the faith have mingled with radical theological innovators for over 25 years in a process of incalculable creativity. Greenbelt certainly was part of the ferment which Palosaari,

Norman, and Blessitt engendered in their much-publicized forays into the British youth sub-culture. A smaller but robust British group of frontier youth workers, similarly to some Australian Jesus Movement leadership established a strong, mutually creative relationship with Jack Sparks and the CWLF.

12. While I have a hard copy of the *The Star Sheffield* article speaking of the unusual makeup of the cast, obtained from Carothers, a participant in the "Lonesome Stone" production, it is a clipping that has no date or page. To pursue this regional British newspaper for this detail would require inordinate time. That it was published in 1974 is established from the itinerary of the performances given to me by Carothers.

13. As recounted by Ward (1996), Holloway had a previous vision for a Christian arts festival and shared this with Palosaari. Holloway, who played in a blues band, *All Things New*, went to see "Lonesome Stone" at an air base.

14. Several respondents believed with Palosaari that the Jonestown massacre became a powerful symbol in the evolution of the culture from interest in Communitarianism to the triumph of radical individualism, and from the pursuit of gurus and charismatics to the rejection of authoritarianism and pyramidal leadership. It was not surprising therefore to discover sociologist Robert Wuthnow sees Jonestown as significant:

> By the end of the 1970s, many of the new religions that had been formed during the preceding decade were being described as 'cults.' The mass suicide that took place in Guyana in November 1978 among the followers of religious leader Jim Jones fueled the tendency to view Religious experiments as bizarre, antisocial movements led by misguided, charismatic figures. In this interpretation, people forsook the faith of their parents, escaped the uncertainties of their own lives and allowed themselves to be brainwashed by authoritarian cult leaders. The result was submersion in a totalitarian community that resembled a theocratic family, only with higher walls against the outside world.
>
> There were plenty of examples, especially from former cult members and from so-called deprogrammers, to support this interpretation. More common however was a form of Religious experimentation that involved short-term exposure to a variety of leaders, ideas, and spiritual disciples. Typical accounts of spiritual journeys took the form; 'I tried everything from a to z . . . .'Yet the idea that spirituality needed to be pursued on one's own and perhaps in tension with social institutions did not die easily. A decade later most still thought it was important to arrive at their religious values on their own and to be skeptical of accepting the words of religious authorities.
>
> The lingering question from the standpoint of organized religion of course, is why the churches and synagogues did not oppose long – or oppose more vehemently – a cultural development that was to contribute so greatly to the weakening of religion's traditional monopoly over spirituality . . . .Individuals who left their spiritual homes also found it difficult to return to them or find alternatives . . . .Other people had returned to a sacred space more narrowly defined where they could feel safe and secure. To an outsider, they sometimes appear to have rejected the pronounced freedom offered by the 1960s, but it is clear that even their search for a spiritual home was influenced by the idea of choice.
>
> If my argument is correct, then the 1960s did not simply introduce new religions that encouraged being more eclectic in their spirituality; rather, during the 1960s the nature of freedom itself was contested and redefined. The freedom that living in a secure community of like-minded individuals offered was gradually replaced

by a freedom to exercise choice in a marketplace of ideas and life-styles. Freedom of choice was attractive to those who in fact were confronted with an immense array of alternatives. Yet most people recognized that some choices are less healthy than others, and that exercising choice for its own sake is not always the most desirable alternative. As a way of reigning in freedom of choice, a new emphasis was also placed on the dangers of external constraints, such as those imposed explicitly by government, or implicitly, by technology. In the process, freedom came to be more subjective. In spirituality, freedom of conscience thus came to mean paying attention to the inner voices of feelings, and freedom of choice meant exposing oneself to alternative experiences that would help develop these voices. (Wuthnow 1998:83)

15. It is significant that following the Jonestown massacre (November 1978) our own group, which had previously earned glowing reports from every level of the media, came under attack. A controversial but popular, liberal churchman, Ted Noffs (Uniting Church), ran a 24 hour a day drop-in center in the heart of King's Cross, Sydney's sexual Soho. He was frequently a guest of the press, and was called upon to write a feature article on the new religious movement impact on Australia for the *Sydney Morning Herald*. In this article he named God's Squad Motorcycle Club as a likely cult, and John Smith as a dangerous charismatic who could conceivably follow the example of Jim Jones. Around this time an internal tension developed over the question of the role of the charismatic leader. The designation of my role changed from leader to "one amongst equals." This euphemistic title confused the rank and file and created an ambiguous "stand-off," rather than clarification concerning the authority structure. The intense fear of cult leadership prevented more healthy, open debate. It was feared that the implied doubts about leadership were so serious in the context of revitalization/charismatic authority, they would threaten destabilization of the Movement if openly declared. Di Sabatino that there is evidence of a rapid change in public attitudes to all fringe religious groups from then on (1999d). He notes a swift and severe shift by Ronald Reagan as Governor in California and as President (1980), against experimental, communitarian groups, following the Jonestown tragedy (November 1978).

David Janzen (1996:48-50) maintains that around this time, "More overt persecution was not absent, however. Government surveillance and dirty tricks dogged the more activist Christian communities. The Reagan administration used the Internal Revenue Service to investigate and hound many non-profit organizations, *including many Christian communities*" (My emphasis). The IRS harassment of Shiloh Youth Revival Centers was a prime example of this process. Shiloh was claimed by Richardson, Stewart, and Simmonds (1979) to be one of the two largest expressions of the Movement spanning over 70 nations and representing between 300,000 and 3 million adherents (1979:xxvii). More than six years of research (1979:xviii) investigating Shiloh as an archetypal Jesus Movement expression, led them to believe that they had arrived "at a very defensible prediction that CCO [Shiloh] will indeed last for the foreseeable future" (1979:xix). A combination of paranoia about charismatic leadership after the Jones affair, IRS targeting of Shiloh's financial affairs, and the subsequent focussed attack on Higgins, the founder, led to his dismissal by the external board. Overwhelming confusion and disarray amongst the rank and file at the sudden dismissal and departure of their leader proved fatal to the group despite the valiant attempt of Peterson to sustain the Movement. His success in defeating the IRS attack left the Movement financially ruined through litigation costs.

(For more detailed accounts of the foundational and stabilized years of Shiloh read Richardson, Stewart, and Simmonds, 1979, *Organized* Miracles: A *Study of a Contempo-*

rary, Youth, Communal, Fundamentalist Organization. For the story from rise to demise from a participant leader's viewpoint read Joe V. Peterson, 1990a, "Jesus People: Christ, Communes, and the Counter-Culture of the Late Twentieth Century in the Pacific Northwest." In *Communities: Journal of Cooperative Living* 1996:92(Fall), there are brief accounts of the Shiloh Youth Revival Centers – "Christian Communities, Then and Now" (Peterson 1996a:24-27), "A Shiloh Sister's Story" (Murphy 1996:29-32) and "The Rise and Fall of Shiloh" (Peterson 1996b:60-65). For further information concerning intentional communities contact the Fellowship for Intentional Community at Route 1, Box 155, Rutledge, MO. For subscription to the journal write to *Communities*, 138 Twin Oaks Rd., Louisa, VA 23093.

16. The best example of this deconstruction of history is that of Lonnie Frisbee's relationship to the Calvary Chapel phenomenon. While historian Di Sabatino (1994, 1999a) gives Frisbee the primary credit for the phenomenal growth initially of Calvary Chapel (1994:56-63), sociologist Miller (1997) in his effusive part on the history and development of Calvary Chapel commits only one short paragraph to Lonnie Frisbee. This is despite the fact that he therein refers to Lonnie as "an important figure in the early history of the Jesus Movement" (1997:94). The "signs and wonders" theology of the Vineyard movement (Jackson 1999) was, according to Fromm (1999) and Di Sabatino (1994, 1999a), initiated more by the controversial "signs and wonders," demonstrations of Frisbee than anything else. Jackson similarly dismisses Frisbee with a few brief anecdotal pages (Jackson 1999:72-75). Di Sabatino, as the best known historian of the Movement, was asked to peruse the history prior to publication. Subsequent to his expression of strong concern about the neglected, rightful place of Frisbee in the history, an appendix concerning Frisbee, written by Di Sabatino, was included at the conclusion of the history (Jackson 1999:381-394). A prior appendix, providing three pages of a time line, embracing over 60 key events, includes only two Frisbee references – his commencement of the House of Miracles and the now legendary event when Frisbee provoked "signs and wonders," after calling, "Come Holy Spirit" (1999:377-378). By default, this history attributes the founding of both Calvary Chapel and Vineyard to the work of the two "straight" neo-Pentecostal leader – Smith and Wimber. Since the release of Di Sabatino's appendix in the Vineyard history, he has produced an unpublished, more thorough, historic monograph, detailing the rise and fall of Frisbee (1997). This includes details of Frisbee's wife's feelings about the failure of Calvary Chapel to respond adequately to her cry for pastoral help. When she sought counsel in dealing with the dysfunctional behavior of her husband, she claims she was reminded of Lonnie's God ordained ministry, and put in her place as a woman, having been made to feel she wasn't important" (1997:30).

17. One of the most charismatic Jesus Movement prophets, Lonnie Frisbee, died of AIDS on March 12, 1993. Jim Punton, a significant mentor to the European and Australasia Movements also died of AIDS in the late 1980s. Dr. Athol Gill, a major theological mentor to the radical expressions of the Movement in Australia, died of a heart attack in 1995.

18. Doug McAdam, reflecting on the biographical impact of activism, laments the "unevenness in the coverage of various kinds of impacts" in social movement research. (See "The Biographical Impact of Activism" in, *How Social Movements Matter*, Giugni, McAdam, and Tilly 1999:117-146). He believes the biographical issues to be both formative and consequential to the shape of movements. "While there are biographical consequences that appear to follow from sustained individual activism" (1999:117), movements act "as sources of aggregate levels of change in life-course patterns" (1999:117). McAdam's enquiry into the impact of the 1960s' activists in the Civil Rights Movement,

(Doug McAdam 1988) attests "to the biographical impact of movement participation." This impact is enacted upon society by charismatic leaders, and reciprocally upon the social actors themselves, radically reshaping their worldviews and life choices.

CHAPTER 4

The Jesus Movement Goes to Church – Calvary Chapel

God's salvation has been sent to the Gentiles [outsiders] ... and they will listen.
St. Paul (Acts 28:28).

My initial journey to North America, in early 1973 at the height of the Jesus Movement was to connect with the rest of the "tribe," and to assess creative models for church and Christian community rather than to survey evangelistic methods. The Jesus Movement had no problem making converts, but it did face the problem of establishing adequate, ecclesiological models and workable structures for nurture, instruction, and mutual accountability. Rob Hopkins, an airline pilot, paid my fare and said, "Go to America and see for yourself what is happening in the Jesus Movement."

In Search of Stability and Endurance

Traditional Pentecostalism, though similar in its social marginality, with its emphasis on emotional, immediate, transcendent experience, and its distrust of institutions, was surprisingly suspicious and hostile towards the "hippie" Jesus Movement (Balmer and Todd 1994:695; Peterson 1999a:11-12, 1999b:2). Many surviving Jesus Movement groups were stabilized by cross-cultural missionaries, such as Chuck Smith, Jack Sparks, John Smith, and John Hirt. They were not the initiators of the revitalization, but were bicultural change agents, and older mentors. Some experienced visionary, prophetic callings similar to the hippie initiators. Most cross-cultural missionaries to the counterculture were marginalized by traditional churches or agencies as they crossed cultures and adopted much of the culture of their pastoral charges.

As a postmodern, grass-roots Christian response to the unfolding deconstruction of Western traditions, the Movement produced contrasting ecclesial models. Several evolved into small denominations with only a few congregations. Others became mega-churches with a single congregation operating as a mini social movement. Di Sabatino (1999b) and Miller (1997) claim that the mega-church phenomenon, in which one very large congregation exhibits the marks of a localized social movement,[1] is a "second wave" consequence of the Jesus Movement. Several leaders of megachurches, including Greg Lawry, Chuck Smith Jr., and Ray Bentley were nurtured and trained by the earlier Movement (Fromm 1996a:13, 17; 1999:11, 32-36).

Successful "new paradigm churches"[2] have resulted as a direct result of the Movement (Miller 1997:1-3). These new churches are independent, de-institutionalized, postdenominational (see Endnote 2.), democratic, innovative and appropriating contemporary cultural forms (1997:1-3,20). New paradigm churches accommodate to market forces through seeker-sensitive services, relaxed, contemporary, charismatic worship, and relevant proclamation. Some Jesus Movement groups have formed sizeable new denominations such as Calvary Chapel,[3] Hope Chapel,[4] Vineyard Christian Fellowship,[5] Gospel Outreach, Verbo Churches,[6] Great Commission Churches,[7] and Alliance for Renewal Churches.[8]

In this Chapter and in Chapter 5, I will describe Calvary Chapel, Costa Mesa, CA, and Christian World Liberation Front (CWLF), Berkeley, CA, as contrasting Jesus Movement responses to the fundamental question, "How do we be church?" A third case study in Chapter 6 will examine models of radical urban and suburban church (Truth and Liberation Concern (TLC) and Care and Communication Concern (CCC) Melbourne, Victoria, Australia. A third Movement, Theos, will be added to TLC and CCC in examination of a more radical missiology in the Southern Hemisphere. In Calvary Chapel, CWLF, TLC, and CCC, the primary aim of the leadership, with varying relationship to mission, was the conservation of the revitalization outcomes in some congregational or institutional form.

The move from frontier outreach to steady state, ecclesial formation was often theologically and socially shaped by leaders who were missionaries to the culture rather than by indigenous hippies. Some of the adherents and members were from evangelical, Pentecostal, or traditional church backgrounds. Most were previously un-churched dissenters from mainstream values. Radical countercultural influences through the indigenous converts impacted and altered the values and behavior of the "straight" members of the group. Rapid growth patterns place stress on each Movement as they shift from the sole authority of charismatic leader to stable government and the routinization of beliefs, and policy, and structures. In the first two studies, an enduring institution remains, although each is considerably changed in social form and constituency from the foundational period. In the Australian examples, the radical position of the foundational period has been maintained, but the journey to routinization and organizational stability has been plagued with difficulties.

The models investigated provide insight into the peculiar nature of the 1960s' and 1970s' search for credible authority, human community, spiritual identity, and divine intervention. They also illustrate the Wallace description of revitalization process, and the order in which the various stages move from free-flowing innovation to the necessary shift in emphasis to maintenance and perpetuation of the new order.

The urgent search for a better way of being human and being community, occurring as it did during a period of severe cultural distortion, was historically associated with social conditions typical of those associated with the initiation of revitalization movements. Thirty years later the search continues, with the cultural context and the Christian church still somewhat in a state of flux, creating a new diversity of options resembling "a spiritual market place" (Roof 1993, 1999). The ferment that emerged during the 1960s produced some new and strong communities of faith, embracing many previous non-believers, reviving many traditional churches, and re-engaging traditional believers who had drifted from their religious roots. Following a dizzying pace of innovation and apostolic proclamation, the Jesus Movement had to settle down and ask, how do we be church and how do we preserve our new-found, stress-reduced lifestyle, but simultaneously maintain our mission to the world? Mission was the easy part.

Calvary Chapel, Costa Mesa, California

The first model of response is that of a soft-Pentecostal, radicalized pastor (Wind and Lewis 1994a:665, 683-684), gathering counterculture converts, re-forming them, and creating a new model of accessible, movemental, independent church from their energy, and postmodern, affective faith. Several new church movements could have been chosen, but the most publicized and documented of these is Calvary Chapel.

A Conversation with Family and Friends

To supplement earlier visits to Calvary Chapel, and familiarity with its teaching during the early 1970s, I located two long-term participants and one academic researcher with very close association with Calvary Chapel. Chuck Fromm has been involved with the development of the worship and music ministries from the earliest days and is Chuck Smith's nephew. Chuck Smith's son, Chuck Smith Jr. is a second-generation leader who offers a postmodern critique not typical of his father.

My third informant, David Di Sabatino is an outsider, but he is a respected scholar who is generally regarded as the primary historian of the overall Jesus Movement (Bill Jackson 1999:381). He has interviewed a significant representation of Jesus Movement leaders at length and in particular, he has spent many years concentrating research on Calvary Chapel. Di Sabatino currently works with Fromm on a worship music project and research into the Jesus Movement's relationship to popular culture. He has extensively investigated the life of the late Lonnie Frisbee (1999c, 1997).

I have drawn on a wealth of descriptive literature concerning Calvary Chapel, mostly written from 1971 to 1987, and the sociological analysis of (Balmer 1989:12-30; Balmer and Todd 1994:663-698; and Miller 1997). I have an extensive collection of Smith's teaching tapes, audio-tapes of interviews, and notes of personal reflections recorded during my visits to Calvary Chapel.

Scholarly investigation of Jesus Movement groups is no easy task. Even Calvary Chapel after 30 years of development and organization remains somewhat ill-defined.

> Calvary Chapel informality poses obvious problems for anyone trying to write a history of the congregation; the traditional tools of the historian are simply not useful. Because of its unique social location in the early 1970s, a number of sociologists have written about Calvary Chapel, but few have paid careful attention to its history. (Balmer and Todd 1994:663)

Calvary Chapel has no membership lists, no formally affiliated members, no archives or records. One researcher was told that such items "seemed to be just in Pastor Chuck's memory" (Balmer and Todd 1994:663). Balmer and Todd maintain there is "little discernible historical consciousness at Calvary Chapel" and "[T]he sense of belonging to the congregation is entirely self-referential . . . and, despite local and elaborate public libraries built on the ever expanding tax base of Orange County, no library in the vicinity contains a clipping file on Calvary Chapel" (1994:663-664). There is no official theological statement, policy statement, and manual for ordination or governmental appointments. The Sunday Bulletin has a brief statement of faith.9 An unofficial statement of belief has been circulated on the Internet, stating a fundamentalist, socially conservative worldview (Appendix 3). Despite the technical difficulties, personal experience of the Movement, and friendships with long-term participant-leaders, has given me a substantial basis for analysis.

An Australian Encounters Californian Revitalization

In Southern California, Calvary Chapel became an attractive alternative to traditional church during the 1970s, providing multiple entry points through its communes, its market place proclamation, and its highly contextualized, Bible teaching "raps." Psychedelic, joyous, alternative style cartoons accompanied the text of tract and hymn book. Even the envelopes provided for donations sported a cartoon hippie leaping with joy to the paraphrased text "God loveth a hilarious giver" (2 Corinthians 9:7). The Maranatha Recording Company churned out new style, hip Christian music. Several Maranatha records became personal favorites in my record collection.

A week after I arrived at Calvary Chapel in the summer of 1973, I was introduced to the business manager of Maranatha Music, Dick Hardy. Minutes after recounting my story and the purpose of my visit to America, Hardy made an unexpected resource offer. I left with a new Plymouth Fury III car on hire, a credit card to meet expenses on my host's account, with limitless time of use until the end of the investigative journey. This was typical of the situational and inspirational basis of decision making during early stages of revitalization as I observed it in this and other Movements.

My initial guide and friend was a dismissed Calvary Chapel pastor, who had been temporarily involved in the Deliverance Movement and the Shepherding Movement.[10] He was a casualty of Smith's assiduous policy of swift dismissal from leadership of anyone tainted by "Pentecostal extravagances" of doctrine, or practice. His intimate knowledge of the founding years served me well, as he showed me many aspects of Calvary Chapel's early ministry. Smith was unavailable for interviews. He was concentrating on teaching, leaving all public relations [except major media] and counseling to Pastor Romaine. This routinization policy significantly stabilized the Movement, leaving Smith to concentrate on his extraordinary teaching ability.

A Mega Sheepfold for Strays

Calvary Chapel's size, growth patterns, and influence in Los Angeles were impressive in 1973. Even in 1972 Sunday morning services were held in triplicate, with Smith speaking at all three, the first two services drawing 400 or 500, and the third service overflowing the relatively new building. One year later, a huge circus tent was the meeting venue, enabling a reduction of the number of meetings and a massive increase in attendance. The Bible studies and the evangelistic rock concerts were drawing crowds of several thousand. Calvary Chapel still possessed many of the accouterments of the counterculture. It was driven by an eschatalogical sense of the immanent return of Christ, rather than secular utopianism. To the apocalyptic, Californian sub-culture in search of a guru, Jesus was attractive, and so was Pastor Smith.

The Saturday night concerts established an enduring model of entertainment evangelism. The gentle, but obviously alternative style of West Coast, "soft" rock was presented at weekly concerts, by Love Song, Mustard Seed Faith, Seeds of Love, Honey Tree, Gentle Faith, Maranatha, and Second Chapter of Acts. Their names, in contrast to most of secular counterparts, were explicit in their expression of faith, hope, and love.

The mood I experienced was electric, inclusive, expectant, gently alternative, but carefully orchestrated in the best sense of that term. I remember eating potato chips during a "Jesus rock" concert and being gently, but firmly asked to put them away by one of the many strategically positioned ushers. A liberating sense of freedom and inclusion prevailed, counter-balanced by an uncompromising discipline and detailed control of every element of the ministry. Everywhere there were long-haired youths in psychedelic tie-dyed shirts, and literature displaying counterculture, psychedelic art forms. A new age of peace and love was about to engulf California, through the visions of young women and men (Joel 3:1; Acts 2:17-18). The ambiance created in the tent was of a gala event with popular acclaim. It was more disarming than attending a Billy Graham rally in the hey-day of the crusades. The expectant hordes of youth in alternative clothing reflected a counterculture lifestyle. "Bare footed hippies" abounded. Long hair predominated for both women and men, much to the disgust of many fundamentalist and Pentecostal churches that did not initially enter into positive relationship with the Movement. "It was a shame for men to wear long hair," they remonstrated. It was a major issue. Denims, t-shirts, caftans, and ponchos were then a soft counterculture statement. Eyes and the ears were under constant assault. Posters, stickers, and flyers sported minimal text, and maximum imagery. Everywhere one looked, it seemed somebody was literally carrying the message on his or her person.

The creative art was visually impacting, as the calligraphy was distinctly hip in its form. Psychedelic shapes and colors blended with fundamentalist text. The hymn-book was liberally sprinkled with joyous psychedelic cartoon characters praising Jesus. Today the tradition of art enhanced praise of Jesus (Figure 4.1) and love of gospel text continues. Some Chapels focus on the arts as a mission tool (Fromm 1999 28-29).

Communes of Faith and Restoration

I initially attended with the members of the House of Psalms where I stayed. It was one of many rehabilitation and discipleship communes developed by Calvary Chapel Jesus Houses. House of Psalms members related enthusiastically to other commune members on arrival at concerts. It was expected that I participate in the structured disciplines of the community as much as the new convert despite being a prominent Jesus Movement leader in my own country. One other "straight" Christian leader, who arrived at the same time, left hostile after one day, offended that his status as an ordained and experienced Christian leader had afforded him no special conditions or exemptions. "Servanthood as the basis of authority," was virtually an article of faith throughout the Jesus Movement. It had been exemplified by Smith's own serving attitudes at very practical levels. Smith had taught them that if you were not prepared to clean the bathroom or pick up cigarette butts, you were not ready to teach God's Word. Humility and servanthood were the Jesus Movement maxims in most communes.

The commune was a family, with all the tensions of working with members who wanted their own way. The constant teaching on love and servanthood combined with clearly defined lines of accountability, acted as social glue. It seemed much better than the families from which many of these social refugees had initially fled. From early in the morning until late at night, life was shaped by a social rhythm of activity. This left little time for those who came with substance abuse or relationship problems to dwell on the past. Members were discouraged from reliving the past apart from positive testimonies to the transforming power of Jesus, the Bible, and the fellowship provided by Calvary Chapel and the commune. Almost every member had a story of experience in Eastern religion, experimental sex, radical politics, psychedelic drugs, or just rootless itinerancy.

Each commune had daily Bible study, special meetings, and work schedules. Constant deprogramming occurred, as people would share their trials and joys for the day, and hopes and expectations for the immediate future. Unlike a traditional family, frequent dealing with personal problems in community made it difficult for members to live isolated from their brothers and sisters. The highly regimented life was primarily centered around establishment in biblical truth Several hours a day were spent in Bible study. "Many [had] memorized more

Figure 4.1 Artistic Hosannas to Jesus (Calvary Chapel Bible Project)

Scripture in a few months than some churchmen have learned in their lifetimes" (Palms 1972:43). On average they stayed for six months.

Each household had an elder, assisted practically by deacons. Groups of up to ten, "led by the Lord," (Enroth, Ericson, and Peterson 1972:90) were sent after training and prayer, to establish new communes. While hippie communes reputedly embraced sexual license, here the strictest regime of moral behavior was maintained. The bustling vitality, enthusiasm, and informality of the group impressed me. In the communes, Smith's grace, authority, and communication skills had already become legendary in and out of the pulpit. He had taken center stage in a Movement that was initially inspired by the work of hippies among hippies on the streets and beaches of California.

A Public Show of Faith and Communitas

One of the most visually inescapable elements of the Calvary Chapel crowd was the confident display of very large Bibles. The counterculture movement had fostered a return to creative arts and crafts, so most converts had denim or leather Bible covers, on which messages were often carved, painted or embroidered. Arm bands, crosses (particularly those made from horse-shoe nails), head bands, anklets, and leather sandals were the accessories accompanying long flowing granny dresses. Some men wore Asian sarongs. The customary attitude at Calvary Chapel was a non-judgmental acceptance that contributed to its meteoric rise in counterculture popularity. The cross became a central icon to new believers. Many of their parents had abandoned it to the Catholics. The symbol that was most prominent and expressive of the Calvary Chapel people was the minimalist, impressionistic image of a flying dove. Rock group *Gentle Faith* used the biblical image of a dove descending on Jesus, as the symbol of the Spirit of love, at the heart of Calvary Chapel faith. Coming out of the violence of the late 1960s, many found release from political strain and disillusionment through a gentle, loving, communal feeling of pietistic faith. This was revitalization's stress reduction at work.

While Smith brought with him the strong emphasis of the Holy Spirit from his Pentecostal tradition, it was expounded in pastoral, inclusive love. He had abandoned the legalism that festered in classical Pentecostalism, believing that the mark of the Spirit's activity was love. Everybody talked about love; and sought to express love; the preacher was always proclaiming love, and the musical "megaphone of the Movement" (Fromm 1996:42) was soft-rock group, *Love Song*.

High energy and creativity was expressed in innovative forms of communication. There was an abundance of "underground" print media, hippie iconography, Jesus "one way" signs, the "fish" symbols of the catacombs of the early century of the church, and psychedelic, contemporary art forms of the Westcoast. All of this created a sense of cultural innovation generated by the youthful counterculture. "Soft" Jesus rock music, reminiscent of the style of the *Eagles, Chicago, Credence Clearwater Revival,* and *Jackson Brown*, was enormously attractive to both counterculture and straight young rebels struggling with their parents' world. Many "straight" people, intrigued by the sense that "times they are a changing," flocked to the alternative worship and music driven evangelism. Intense feelings of joy, exuberant expressions of faith, and highly physical manifestations of love abounded between young and old, although the vast majority was young. While there appeared to be a constant flurry of activity, every form of gathering was casual, seemingly spontaneous, and orderly.

Calvary Chapel's much publicized mass baptisms were being held at a public beach nearby at Corona del Mar Beach. I spent an afternoon observing this extraordinary spectacle. In excess of 700 people, the majority at least appearing to be counterculture by clothing and attitudinal style, were baptized over the length of a lazy afternoon. Sometimes whole families held onto each other to be baptized simultaneously. Hundreds of hippies gathered to watch, while many other counterculture Christians mingled with them and somewhat aggressively but winsomely, evangelized the curious onlookers.

As previously noted in Chapter 1, one of the telling images in the media reports was that of balding, beaming "Pastor Chuck" carrying a paralytic into the ocean for baptism as hundreds viewed from the beach and the cliffs. This was astutely seen by Balmer and Todd as a highly visible symbol of the "the safe arrival of these prodigal sons and daughters, after a harrowing ride on the magic carpet of radical politics, Eastern esoterica, and psychedelic drugs. Wounded by their experiences but still searching, they were now safe – and forgiven – in the arms of the [alternative] church" (Balmer and Todd 1994:667).

I observed emotional conversions during the baptisms. New converts were given brief instruction and added to the number being baptized. There was something strangely reminiscent of the "Day of Pentecost." Uncontrollable spontaneity and all pervasive communality were apparent in the midst of this ritual process. The ancient and the contemporary combined, as a secular beach became the location of sacred space and sacred time. Divine presence and divine activity, combined with lingering human imperfection, was expressed poignantly in an emotional request of one candidate for baptism, who declared through tears, "Hold me under the water for a long time pastor. I've got a lot of sin to bury."

The return to a primitive Christianity was appealing. Ritual had been rationalized, formalized, and secured in the sanctuary of the traditional church. Here was first century liminality. Culturally re-located and reinterpreted rituals were a vulnerable demonstration of cultural defiance for all to see. The exercise of Calvary Chapel baptisms was natural in location and had all the appearance of a public demonstration. This was an advantage in the eyes of a marginalized clientele. The substantial numbers created high public visibility, especially at a popular, public beach. The contrasting images of a balding, fatherly Pentecostal preacher, and a longhaired, John the Baptist-type, incendiary, hippie prophet provided the media with graphics and a story line (Boeth, Mohs, and Ostling 1971). Calvary Chapel baptisms are still beach events. In the Australian Movement, baptisms in rivers and the ocean were the preferred mode. After all, public baptism for the first church was a defiant statement of civil disobedience. Caesar and Jesus could not share the patriotic allegiance of citizens of the Kingdom of God. Baptism proclaimed "Jesus is Lord!"

Transition from Tent to Temple

Before returning to Australia, after travelling to several other movements across the country, I revisited Calvary Chapel for the first public meeting in its new building, a couple of months later. The wall behind the stage sported a huge stylized dove, the most prominent icon for a movement centered not in theology but simple, down to earth, Protestant interpretation of Scripture, through the illumination of the Holy Spirit.

On a return visit a couple of years later, the counterculture was in retreat. Hippie Frisbee was long gone. In October 1971, Frisbee left Smith and Calvary Chapel (Enroth et al 1972:93) to briefly join Florida based Bob Mumford, whose authoritarian "shepherding movement" wreaked havoc in many vulnerable indigenous Jesus Movement groups. Di Sabatino quotes participants in 1971 who "thought Lonnie was the whole thing" (1997:26) having never "heard of Chuck Smith" after a year of attendance. Now Smith's middle class, highly charismatic persona had eclipsed Frisbee, who was rarely referred to by my informants in 1973. Smith had "mandated a more passive, Pentecostal theology, whereby preaching and teaching the Bible became the primary focus" (1997:31). By 1973 Smith was on the lips of all participants.

From the outset of relocation to the new building in 1973 there was a sense of stability and developing routinization. The tent was gone. So was the sense of uncharted pilgrimage. The tent, with its alternative, liminal, alternative style was replaced by the permanent architecture of a sanctuary that was the epitome of Santa Ana, middle class culture (Balmer and Todd 1994:667). Now there was a practical, homely temple to replace the portable tabernacle. The relocation from Costa Mesa to Santa Ana took it from the alternative, beach, communal culture of its birth to the heartland of materialism and self help movements. There was little sign of the prosperity apparent 25 years later, when Randall Balmer (1998) noted the vehicles in the car park ranged from "a Rolls Royce, several Mercedes Benzes, Lincoln Continentals, and Cadillac Eldorados" alongside "Scooters, and Volkswagen Vans stuffed with junk, so dilapidated as to appear unroadworthy" (1998:13). Then as now, a professed love for all predominated, irrespective of status.

Sociocultural Issues of Organizational Formation

Culture is a road map to guide the individual in acceptable behavior, appropriate to their social context. Local expressions of culture profoundly inform values and shape resultant lifestyles. For example, California has earned a reputation for media conscious and experimental religion, so it may not be coincidental that the Jesus Movement appears to have been birthed in that region. Some elements of particularity and change at Calvary Chapel have resulted from the local cultural context.

The Costa Mesa – Santa Ana Context

Calvary Chapel is located south east of Los Angeles in Orange County, one of the most affluent regions in America. In 1994 it was "the fifteenth largest metropolitan area in America, and its economy would rank thirteenth in the world if it were a separate nation. It [was] tenth in gross national product" (Balmer and Todd 1994:665). It is situated in a region well known for its thriving suburban conservatism and large conservative churches. Calvary Chapel shares the region with Robert Schuller's Crystal Cathedral, Chuck Swindoll's First Evangelical Free Church of Fullerton, Melodyland School of Theology (just by Disneyland), and John Wimber's Vineyard Christian Fellowship. Evangelicalism, married to creative individualism and the entrepreneurial spirit, has created a fertile field for popular culture churches. There is an excitement, speed, and eclecticism which outsiders sense immediately in Southern California. There is a cultural deconstruction that promotes innovation, romanticism, and casual abandon to whatever appeals to the individual. If anything, Calvary Chapel is "laid back," like its senior pastor who appears unassuming but is also all pervasive in his influence.

Even the architecture reflects the southern Californian Spanish mission style and is a "patchwork complex . . . as unassuming as the Crystal Cathedral, its neighbor to the north, is ostentatious" (1994:667). It is a very different church now compared to its Genesis days when its primary clientele decried the materialism of the older generation. Located in the vortex of suburban prosperity, while still welcoming to all and sundry, it is the happy home of the self - indulgent Californians who would rather mix conspicuous consumption with generosity and affective spirituality than to resist materialism.

The Counterculture Connection

There is a marked, alternative historical context to the Calvary Chapel phenomenon. An identity that was attached to slick appearance, conspicuous consumption, status by association, and comfortable, conformist religion provided a target for young iconoclasts. Southern California was a battle-ground for the counterculture resistance. It reflected the best and worst of the opposing forces. It is in this context that Calvary Chapel eventually bought together hippies and "straights."

It is not possible to explain the emergence of the Jesus Freaks and the meteoric rise of Smith from Pentecostal obscurity to Los Angeles media headlines without recalling again the social conditions of the era. Balmer and Todd (1994) note that rapid expansion of congregations at the end of the 1960s was not limited to Calvary Chapel, but it did excel there. Thousands of youthful visionaries had belonged to a movement intent upon revolutionizing the world, but their dreams ended "in squalor, bitterness and economic failure, augmented by violent opposition from without" (Balmer and Todd 994:668).

The intensity and extent of disillusionment was directly related to the extent of prior illusion. In California during the early 1960s, a novel perception was widespread amongst the dissenters. They believed that a confluence of human evolution, new religious transcendence, the lineup of the planets in "The Age of Aquarius," and the uprising of previously oppressed Afro-Americans seeking equality had created an irresistible force for Cultural Revolution. Those who surrounded the Pentagon in a celebrated attempt to levitate it through the power of the communal spirit truly believed they could do it. Crosby, Stills, Nash, and Young expressed the level of existential commitment with a haunting song that simply said: *"Find the cost of freedom, buried in the ground; Mother earth will swallow you; lay your body down."* The level of devotion to a new order was bordering on bizarre. For middle class kids to shave their heads, embrace rigorous spiritual exercises on Hindu paths to transcendence, and forsake the eating of the ubiquitous American steak and chicken, was evidence of the contrary belief that engulfed many of that generation.

Despite the quirks, perversions and even unjustifiable violence, "the counterculture challenged utilitarian culture at the most fundamental level. It asked what in life possessed intrinsic value, and to what ends ought we to act. Do ever more money and power add up to life's meaning, or do they obscure it?" (Tipton 1982:19). Do money and power enrich self-awareness, or is material obsession the rape of the soul? Graham Nash had sung in *Wild Tales*, "Is the money you make worth the price that you pay?"

The 1960s were not only years of political upheaval, they "also emerge as a period of intense religious experience, not only for alienated hippies, but also for many others" (Peterson 1990a:10), including mainstream but drifting middle class youth. Peterson sees the Charismatic Movement as a parallel expression of this social ferment (1990a:10). Donald Richardson writes that "apparently no social scientist predicted the onset of the Jesus Movement and related phenomena. At the time when the Jesus Movement began, most social scientists were still reeling from the shock of the also unpredicted 'student revolution'" (1973:396).

Glock and Bellah, in their examination of the era, chose the religious paradigm "as the strategic point of entry into the question of contemporary cultural transformation because we thought it potentially the most profound level of change" (Glock and Bellah 1976:19, cf. Ellwood 1992:7-8; Donald 1976b:xiii). By the end of the spiritual 1960s the experimentation in politics and religion had led to sensory overload and fragmentation. Between 1968 and 1970, disillusionment set in. Peaceful protest and nonviolent resistance were eclipsed by social dissent, violence, assassination, race riots, and substance abuse. Sit-ins and demonstrations were followed by increased numbers of bombings and arson attacks on campus (Glock and Bellah 1976:81-83). Rioting at the Democratic National Convention in Chicago in the summer of 1968, the Tet offensive in Vietnam, and the revelation of previously denied secret bombings of Cambodia, helped fuel demonstrations, strikes, administration building's take-over, and cancellations of classes in 300 colleges and universities (Gitlin 1987:377).

In 1968 Black Power fell into disarray through internal division. Congressman Adam Clayton Powell Jr. urged Californian college campuses to begin a black revolution. Three black students were shot and killed at a protest at South Carolina State College with no prosecution of the officers. Martin Luther King was assassinated. Tommie Smith and John Carlos were censored for giving black power salutes after winning first and second places in the Olympic Games in Mexico City, and Eldridge Cleaver released his angry *Soul on Ice*. The 1960s ended and a new decade began, but 1970 was little better. Whites attacked South Carolina school buses carrying black students to integrated schools; school buses were bombed in Denver, Colorado; two black women were killed and 12 wounded in a student dorm when police opened fire indiscriminately (Christian 1995:438-443). Four students were shot dead by the National Guard at Kent State University, Ohio (Christian 1995:449-451; Gitlin 1987:410). It was literally believed by many that "the State will kill its children" before it will accept social revolution (Richardson, Stewart and Simmonds 1979:xxii).

Increasingly the Civil Rights Movement, which welcomed white participation in the beginning, excluded them as the Movement began to stall, and protest became more violent and ineffectual. "Thus political action undertaken by many to alleviate strains in the structure of American society actually contributed more strain to an already stressed society" (Richardson, Stewart and Simmonds 1979:xxii). Nixon's election (1972) and the murders associated with the Charles Manson Family the previous year created despair in the hearts of many who had believed in a new society. The 1967 Summer of Love, promoted by the San Francisco City Council, had invited "the youth of the world to join a Holy pilgrimage to our city to affirm and celebrate a new spiritual dawn" (Wind and Lewis 1994a); but the sun was already setting on the hopes and dreams of the counterculture as early as the Spring of 1967 (Didion 1968:20), and it was all over by the end of 1968 (Peterson (1999a:8).

The explosive response of counterculture refugees to the conservative, apolitical, communal euphoria of the Jesus people forming the core of Calvary Chapel is only understandable if one takes seriously the level of existential angst the decade had produced. As one sun set on the hopes of radical politics, Eastern mysticism, communes, and mind-altering drugs, another sun arose on the horizon of the youthful, spiritual quest.

> As the curtain fell on the 1960s, there had been a palpable sense of defeat and loss, especially among the young. Spurred by their alienation from the larger culture, many had felt compelled to transform it. No doubt to some degree they succeeded. However, their radical program, ill-defined as it often was, proved unworkable in a society largely hostile to it. The perceived failure of the counterculture demanded redress. For some of the 1960s refugees, evangelical Christianity provided just that. A formidable tradition in the very society the young had defied, evangelicalism proved to be for many rebels both a balm for their souls and a means of continuing their protest, however muted. Its strong current of apocalypticism, in many ways a doctrine both of despair and protest coupled with its equally powerful message of hope and salvation, made evangelicalism an attractive alternative to the anomie of the late 1960s. (Balmer and Todd 1994:694)

The growing ranks of disaffected, pilgrims were an unevangelized people group, a social network overlooked or disdained by conventional religion. There was a remarkable turn to Jesus by hippie converts fleeing from rational argument to transcendent experience and from dogma to experimentalism in the Spirit. Old World values fused together with social non-conformity. Many sought moral recovery from the previous damaging free fall into promiscuity and drugs.

Calvary Chapel entered the brief period of revitalization creativity, reaping a harvest of humanity and conserving those results of mass conversions in a remarkable shift from chaotic fragmentation to vibrant Christian fellowship. The counterculture's apocalyptic, Aquarian and neo-pagan tendencies opened it to reception of a Pentecostal phenomenology. Sociologist Peterson recalls that "speaking in tongues" (glossolalia), an ecstatic phenomenon common to the Jesus Movement (McGuire 1974; Richardson and Reidy 1980, 1976; Richardson et al. 1979:7, 186, 198), had been spontaneously experienced in hippie circles prior to Christian contact, or conversion (Peterson 1999a:10). Experientially the revitalization seekers were thus strangely prepared for adoption by an unlikely ally – a disaffected, Pentecostal holiness "straight," and his small, middle-class congregation, Calvary Chapel.

The Contrasting Charismatic Characters

Before the Jesus Movement invasion, Calvary Chapel was a small Pentecostal church in Costa Mesa, a suburb of greater Los Angeles, which called Chuck Smith, a pastor in Aimee Semple McPherson's Foursquare Gospel denomination. The Calvary Chapel movement embraced the local church's name as it evolved rapidly from an alliance between the fatherly pastor-teacher Smith, and a hippie, Lonnie Frisbee of the Jesus Movement. The successful fusion of the old and the new was the consequence of the meeting of two vastly different minds, histories, and cultural formations.

In 1965 when Smith arrived at Calvary Chapel, it was a congregation of 25. The church quickly grew to Smith's optimum congregational size of 200 adults under his ministry. Smith grew up in a stable, loving family that became Christian as a result of the miraculous healing of Smith's older sister. Upon entering Life Bible College, Los Angeles in 1946, Smith fulfilled a youth camp decision to enter the ministry (Fromm 1996a:25). Taking a number of pastorates over the years, Smith speaks of enduring "17 years of denominational discomfort," when he believes that "God prepared him for what was about to happen" (Smith and Brooke 1992:12). In 1965, Smith was given a prophecy that he would "become a shepherd over many flocks . . ." to the point where his "gathering place would not be adequate to contain all of the people" (1992:15). In 1969, the church had outgrown its facilities, undertaking a building project. They erected a chapel on the border between Santa Ana and Costa Mesa. Shortly before the building project began Smith was introduced to Frisbee (Di Sabatino 1994:56).

When his oldest daughter dated a hippie convert from the Haight-Ashbury drug scene during college, Smith's dislike of hippies receded (Balmer and Todd 1994:674-675). Conversion stories of Jesus Freaks on Huntington Beach initially aroused typical establishment disdain. "Why don't they get a haircut and a job" (Di Sabatino 1994:35). He admits to "initial revulsion at the hippie movement" (1994:57; Balmer and Todd 1994:674). Despite his repulsion he "felt drawn to them" (1994:674).

Chuck Smith's wife Kay, in contrast, nursed a compassion for antiestablishment youth (1994:674). She sometimes pressured her husband to drive her to the counterculture scene. There she spent many hours in weeping and prayer for wisdom as to how this generation of dissidents could be reached with the Christian message. Fromm affirms a sequence of events that drove Smith into a new ministry.

> My uncle did not start the local Jesus Movement. It was an ongoing thing when he came to it. It [Calvary Chapel] had about 60 people, who were not involved in the Jesus Movement. Initially it was Kay his wife [who] had a real burden for hippies. They would drive down to the ocean and see these strange people. Chuck's attitude was let them cut their hair and get straightened out. Kay would intercede for these people. That's the way it started. Then their daughter Jan brings one home. (Fromm 1999:10)

Many Americans had sought meaning and reorientation in the First and Second Great Awakenings (1730-1760; 1800-1830) during the build up and aftermath of the Revolutionary War (McLoughlin 1978). Similarly, many hippies embraced the Jesus Movement revival in their bewilderment and religious disorientation and their search for a new identity. Once Smith was won to the vision of converting and pastoring hippies, he soon recognized the need for culturally adaptive changes to the church. It became a reciprocal process as the small church responded now by embracing the cultural aliens.

> They decided to have two services – one for straights and one for hippies. . . people want either a traditional service (straights) or a contemporary one (hippies), but then the love was so strong that the straights and the hippies started mixing it up. There was a real sense of community happening (love) and the straights were helping the hippies set up houses. [There were] a lot of runaways. (Fromm 1999:10)

At Calvary Chapel in 1969, only "a dozen people met . . . for the mid-week Bible study." Within two years, "during the summer of 1971, more than 1,000 people, most of them under 21 joined the original dozen for a typical Wednesday night young people's Bible study" (Enroth, Ericson, and Peters 1972:85). Investigators were told that 150 were being converted each week and monthly baptisms were normally upward of 500 people at one time (Enroth, Ericson, and Peters 1972:86-87). Monday, Tuesday, and Friday nights saw similar numbers in attendance for teaching of the faithful, rather than the drawing in of converts (1972:86). By early 1996 Calvary Chapel could boast almost 600 churches, several of which have over 10,000 members (Miller 1997:34-35), and an aggregate, denominational, weekly attendance of approximately 500,000 (Fromm 1996a:6-7; 1999:8-9).

The capacity of middle-aged Smith to forsake conservative, cultural taboos is to his credit. His values were challenged in a leadership conflict over the effect of bare, hippie feet on new church carpet. He chose the hippies over carpet. "If our plush carpet leads to closed church doors to even one bare-footed young Christian, then I believe the carpet should be removed . . . . No, let's never, ever close our church doors because of someone's appearance – never!" (Smith and Brooke 1992:27-28). "This dramatic stand contributed to a massive insurgence of young people as the older, more conservative members either left, or learned to appreciate the Jesus People" (Di Sabatino 1994:61).

Chuck Smith could have compromised, but he would have lost the hippies. It was a defining moment through which he gained credibility with many counter-culture people. The power of this simple act of advocacy was accentuated by the alienation from mainline institutions felt by the counterculture. Charles Fromm says Smith's capacity to adapt culturally remains, and it may in part explain the growth of this new denomination.

Has the inclusive ideology and practice been maintained since the gentrification of the counterculture and the cultural triumph of conspicuous consumption?[11] If I wanted to walk in now with bare feet, a solid ring in my nose and bare chested with pierced nipples, would I get the same respect? Smith's nephew says "yes."

> He'd probably think you're one of his grand kids. [On] the front page of the *Los Angeles Times* there was a picture of Chuck Jr.'s daughter, who has married a biker, a great guy and a great heart. He's a tattoo artist so Chuck Jr. and that picture was in the *Los Angeles Times*. Chuck was asked what he thought of it and he replied, 'Are you asking me as a Grandfather or [as] a pastor? As a pastor it's okay.' As a Grandfather he has other thoughts [concerning] the permanence of it [the tattoo] . . . . Nothing would surprise him. He's pretty well experienced it all with his grand kids. (Fromm 1999:19-20)

When the Jesus Movement first invaded his church confrontation was inevitable. The resolution lay in swift and unequivocal inclusiveness of the outsider, rather than the maintenance of the traditional congregation. Chuck Smith recognized a strategic moment of opportunity to break the nexus between the Old World and the new generation of searching youth. The results were explosive and immensely demanding on existing resources, particularly the human resources of trained leadership. The desire to hear teaching was not only the consequence of Smith's obviously charismatic and skilled presentation. Rather, he was available to serve an inquiring, grassroots sub-culture outside the traditional sources of religious discipling. Smith was not only a benefactor to the indigenous Jesus Movement, but a beneficiary. He was an outstanding innovator, building a middle class, upwardly mobile, alternative denomination from youth alienation.

As Di Sabatino records, "Eventually, as more and more hippies drifted into the services, Calvary Chapel was transformed into a bustling center of activities" (Di Sabatino 1994:6). Smith's initial advantage over many parallel movements was the resource of church buildings and the commitment of a considerable number of resourceful middle class congregational members. This osmotic process of the counterculture entering through the receptive membrane of a living church cell facilitated a ready and interactive absorption of new ideas, attitudes, strategies, and liberating celebration. This was a familiar pattern in those elements of Jesus Movement groups that went on to form stable churches. It appears that Pentecostal or Evangelical leaders converted to advocacy and pastoral care of the counterculture provided more permanent models than the indigenous attempts at stabilization by hippie founders. Di Sabatino confirms this pattern after much historical research into the movement.

You have this "straight" preacher and liaison [person]. Lyall Steenos at Bethel Tabernacle and Breck Stevens who was a drug addict formed an alliance. Breck would bring his heroin [addicted] friends to Lyall to teach them. Lonnie Frisbee [and Chuck Smith are another example]. [At] the Toronto Catacombs an Anglican [Episcopal] minister in downtown Toronto enjoyed the vibrancy of these Jesus kids and let them use his church to worship. Thursday nights 2,000 kids [were] praising the Lord. (1999a:9)

The enduring success of the few traditional churches and leaders with significant denominational training, who took up leadership of new Jesus Movement groups, indicates the significance of bridging between the old and new paradigms in times of revitalization. The affirmation of a charismatic hippie, Frisbee, and the incorporation of the indigenous "Freak" into the existing church, was a stroke of genius. "Lonnie was the Pied Piper of Southern California. He's John the Baptist who went out onto all the beaches and brought all the kids there" (Di Sabatino 1999a:22).

The significance of the "indigenous" element, particularly during foundational days, cannot be over-stated. The Calvary Chapel phenomenon would never have occurred if it had not been for Frisbee and the fringe people. Smith could never have initiated the movement and projected the mythological proportions of charisma essential to the movement's early development without the key involvement of the indigenous Freaks at the marginalized edge. Scarcely could one conceive of two more incompatible personalities to forge a working relationship. Cultural and theological differences complicated the arrangement.

Lonnie Frisbee's insistent prophetic orientation put him at odds with some of his friends and pastors at Calvary Chapel. Some of his critics state that he was concerned solely with obtaining conversions, insisting that converts "seek out" the baptism of the Holy Spirit, which Frisbee believed was necessarily accompanied by the evidence of speaking in tongues. His physical appearance was also a direct contrast to Smith's large-frame. Frail and soft-spoken (unless talking about Jesus), he was a caricature of the Sunday-school images of Jesus. His charismatic appeal to those in the counterculture complemented the Bible-teaching foundation of Smith. Some who were closely associated with the origins of Calvary Chapel, state that "Frisbee brought them in, and Smith taught them. Together they forged an uneasy but dynamic twosome that propelled Calvary Chapel into a worldwide ministry. Smith couldn't have started it but he certainly sustained it" (Di Sabatino 1994:56, 57).

It is difficult to find the enduring success of Jesus Movement units where a cultural liaison was not developed between hippies and straights (Richardson *et al* 1979:38). The critical mass that launched Calvary Chapel to media fame could never have been reached without the synthesis of the two worlds of Frisbee and Smith. Smith obviously reshaped Frisbee's world. The reoriented Frisbee embraced a politically conservative worldview alien to his counterculture days. If Frisbee had come into a group dominated by somebody who loved and taught the Bible well, while providing him a structure accompanied by a radical, counterculture gospel, he may have maintained his countercultural roots as Joe Peterson, Glenn Kaiser, and Jim Palosaari have done.

Perhaps the pastoral need to help Frisbee recover from drugs and counterculture hostility should have outweighed the pragmatic, missional issue of his usefulness as a wandering, radical charismatic. Di Sabatino believes he was in need of retreat.

> Internally Frisbee was so abused and broken up that I think the counterculture was really a mask for what was really ailing him. He was raped, and rejected by his father. His real father took off with another woman. Her jilted husband married Frisbee's mother. . . . The stepfather never loved Frisbee. Frisbee had clubbed feet, and was very effeminate. He was a kid trying to get away from home. He was really hurt, abused, beat up, and escaped into the counterculture. (Di Sabatino 1999a:20)

Frequently the drugs, shattered relationships, and cultural alienation of the 1960s took a terrible toll on the creative dissenters, leaving some terminally damaged even after conversion. The "heady" experience of charismatic leadership accentuated rather than alleviated the psychic and social fractures of personality resulting from the street experience. Rehabilitating highly charismatic casualties is a difficult task.

> They tried to do the best of their ability. Smith is not a counselor. He didn't know what to do with Frisbee. Lonnie was looking for somebody but at the same time he ostracized everybody in his life. One would have had to be a very strong character to handle somebody like Lonnie. He was wild. If he knew he had this unction on his life, sometimes he would lapse into "I don't need you. I can do this stuff. If you're going to ditch me, I'll go do something else." He was constantly breaking relationships, and alienating himself from the people who loved him. There were people who talked into his life and yelled at him. He would bring down curses on them. [He was] a very strange guy. (Di Sabatino 1999a:21)

Chuck Smith probably thought Frisbee had been around long enough to take responsibility for himself. The phenomenal growth of the movement and the hunger for teaching isolated Smith from "hands on" counseling. It was extremely difficult to obtain audience with Smith at the height of the growth phase; interview applicants were told he was only available for important media. His entire work was the fatherly watch over the shape of the movement and the preparation of the many public teaching sessions.

> At the end of his life Lonnie sought out counseling help, realizing how much of his life had been guided by its abuse and hurt. He was saddened that Smith and Wimber, these father figures he had latched onto, never really tried to help him. So he tried to tell them that, but they didn't want to hear. Lonnie was tough. Lonnie embarrassed them and caused them a lot of pain and heartache. They had a huge undertaking. Smith doesn't have a heck of a lot of time to counsel one guy, neither did Wimber. They were busy building an empire and [he's] only one sheep. It would be gospel to try and help him, but you've got to try to save the flock. Lonnie became too aberrant so they distanced themselves from him. (Di Sabatino 1999a:21)

It is to Smith's credit that after many years of conflict, when a penitent Frisbee returned to Calvary Chapel, in fatherly style Smith embraced him again. When Frisbee died of AIDS in 1993, at 43, Smith officiated at his elaborate funeral in Robert Schuller's Crystal Cathedral and described him in Old Testament terms as a Samson, whose life was a struggle between anointed genius and human frailty. Di Sabatino has sought earnestly to assess the significance of Frisbee, and dedicated his Masters thesis to the memory of Lonnie Frisbee, *extenuates amabitur idiom*. When asked to assess the mythological proportion attributed to Frisbee and his prophetic style of ministry, he recalled remarkable stories corroborated by less than sympathetic observers.[12] One particular story of Frisbee's legendary style is corroborated by several sources (Jackson 1999:72-74, 378; Di Sabatino 1999c, 1997).

> He (Frisbee] was asked to preach at his [John Wimber's] incipient Vineyard [church] which was at Calvary Chapel at the time. Frisbee said, "Holy Spirit come" and apparently everyone hit the floor. Someone fell down and as he was falling the microphone came to his lips and he was speaking in tongues. It just freaked out the congregation. Wimber had never seen anything like this. It was so dramatic that Wimber from that point on developed the "Signs and Wonders" theology and Lonnie came as his "go to" guy to do this stuff, to demonstrate it. John Wimber would give these talks and would ask Lonnie to come up and show them. Lonnie would demonstrate somehow. You get people who are pretty sober, even theologians [who say], I was there. (Di Sabatino 1999a:22)

Some who were influenced heavily by Frisbee are prominent leaders of the next generation of church planters and evangelists. One such leader is Greg Laurie, a pastor of a 10,000 member Harvest Christian Fellowship and an outstanding communicator. An estimated 3,000 teenagers come to faith per annum in response to Laurie's youth addresses (Miller 1997:171-172). The tradition of this genre of youth rallies began when Frisbee impacted Laurie's life.

> It was at Newport High School. Frisbee had gone there for the early morning and preaching on the lawn and Greg started mocking Lonnie and saying, "I can't believe you are a Jesus Freak." Lonnie said, "In the Name of Jesus be quiet." Apparently immediately Greg hit the ground and started speaking in tongues. (Di Sabatino 1999a:24)

Laurie is typical of some converts resulting from the Jesus Movement who were to bridge from the counterculture movement to the more centrist culture of "new paradigm" churches. These, though embracing elements of the original movement such as "seeker sensitive" meetings and casual clothing, have become domesticated, reflecting a more conservative, middle class culture.

Where traditional leaders departed from the structures of denominational tradition to create a friendly culture for the flocks of converts, two consequences were common. The new paradigm church created appropriate leadership, worship, and evangelistic models and grew rapidly in consequence. Secondly, where conservative leaders opened their church doors to hippies, there was usually a domestication of the worldview of previous radicals rather than political radicalization of the existing congregation.

Redemptive and Rehabilitating Structures

As with any cultural transformation, worldview shifts are accompanied by new forms expressive of those shifts in perception and emphasis. The rock concert and the youth festival movement were sanitized and refocused, providing a youth contact method that still thrives more than 30 years on. Some methods were short-lived despite their initial effectiveness. The coffee shop and communal movements, outstandingly effective when the counterculture was searching for revitalization, faded away as individualism, materialism and a return to the work ethic prevailed again.

Communal Living

New or readapted forms and structures undergirded the radical movement. Charismatic leaders were not the sole explanation for the popular appeal and rapid growth of the Jesus Movement. Minimal though the structures were in traditional terms, astute choices of communication methodology, leadership development, and culturally appropriate facilities played a significant role. The rock concert, the commune, and the coffee shop became standard institutions for mission, discipleship, and socialization. Communes served as the primary tool for resocialization, so we now examine the structure and effect of the Christian commune as a mission and discipleship tool.

A cross-cultural experiment. The creative genius came from the indigenous counterculture converts while the pastoral oversight, administration and regulation were provided by the church. The House of Miracles, Costa Mesa was the first Calvary Chapel experiment. Smith requested young hippies Lonnie and Connie Frisbee to relocate from San Francisco to Los Angeles in May 1968 because the Frisbees could "speak their language . . . and know better than any of us how, what and why they think and feel the way they do" (Di Sabatino 1994:58). Frisbee and another significant Jesus Movement figure, John Higgins, later the founder of Shiloh communal ministries, joined together "to form communal houses under the support of Calvary Chapel" (Di Sabatino 1994:59; Richardson et al. 1979:xv, 7-11).

John Higgins and Frisbee witnessed on the local beaches. Within one week, 35 people had made the House of Miracles their home. Other communes quickly followed with typical Jesus Movement names: The House of Psalms, Philadelphia House (the House of Brotherly Love), and Mansion Messiah. These spawned ever more communes.

A new family. The Jesus house was the entry point for socialization, a commencement for those who were attracted by the excitement, the sense of loving family, the creativity, and vision of the movement. They were also the centers of discipleship and worldview reconstruction. Converts from the counterculture who had proven themselves to be committed, enthusiastic, and deeply enamored by the overall ministry usually controlled them. Leaders were often inexperienced and definitely not professionally trained for the organizational or pastoral tasks.

Smith's Bible studies were the basic theology, the mentoring, the training manual, and the marching orders for followers and leaders. Strict attendance at all Bible teaching events was required of the household. Smith was the father who many of that footloose generation never had. His style of strict, but loving discipline, constant application of the text to the most mundane of human affairs, and his rigorous commitment to a life structured around disciplines of the faith, was reflected in the style of the young house leaders. The discipline in the communes was rigorous and the lifestyle transforming.

Therapy, discipleship, and restoration – not revolution. For Calvary Chapel, the communes were not a utopian alternative or even a permanent lifestyle model. They facilitated restoration to socio-spiritual health and reintegration to mainstream society. The term "halfway house" became common coinage to describe the network operation of such Jesus houses. These facilities provided healing, reaggregation, and reorientation for weary and blitzed refugees from the war zones of the defeated counterculture. The Calvary Chapel model was a rescue shop and a retraining tool, with none of the more socially radical overtones of communistic societies (Nordhoff 1960), the brotherhood of love utopianism (Kanter 1972:43-57), or the "counter system" of the Franciscans, the Anabaptists, or the modern "radical discipleship" Kingdom of God models (Snyder 1991:77-85).

"Rescue shops within a yard of hell." Many of the Jesus Freaks, convinced the system and even the environment was doomed, accepted Smith's expositional emphasis on the imminent return of Jesus. Building a permanent utopian house made little sense if judgment was about to fall, and the curtain of history was about to descend. To be saved, cleaned, and to save others was the purpose. These were rescue shops within a yard of hell.

> They took care of their drug addicts. They set up half way houses. There was a social element to it. Ted Wise went with Ray Stedman and started two clinics of drug rehabilitation. They [Jesus people] had drug hot lines. If kids came they took care of them and then it stopped [at Calvary Chapel] because the ultimate goal was not to get them to do anything intellectual, artistic or creative, or live their lives in a holistic way. (Di Sabatino 1999a:19)

This may understate their openness to the arts. The emphasis on joyous relationships, music, and the rich varieties of fellowship activities appears to belie this judgment. In spite of this positive lean towards creativity and relationships, the theology and sociology of the movement is clearly a "life-boat," fundamentalist form with strong emphasis upon the certain, soon return of Christ. Smith appears to hold to the irrelevance of politics beyond sexual ethics, the defense of Israel, and capitalism. Social action, apart from anti-abortion activity is not seen as advocacy for the poor, but as genuine compassion for the needy to add to the credibility of a gospel of love.

There was an atmosphere of excitement and expectation as we traveled together to Smith's teaching sessions. A mark of many of the Jesus Movement groups was the interactive fellowship that occurred en route to meetings, often in beaten up vans. Discussing the Word, sharing personal anecdotes, and singing the latest creative Jesus music bonded the community members.

Pilgrims seeking a haven, a home, and a return to normality. Many were relieved to find the structure and the security of stable, committed relationships. They readily submitted to elders who truly understood by experience. The destructive toll paid for by drug abuse, promiscuity, and worldview fragmentation led many to seek strong leadership and reforming programs. Regimentation in the Jesus houses was a point of stabilization.

There were some radicals in other Jesus Movement groups saw "normal" patterns of the materialistic society as beyond redemption. For them, communes were an alternative where the nuclear family would give way to an extended family of believers. The commune was a true expression of church, as well as the generator for power for ministry to a broken world. No commune in this sense was entirely a homogeneous unit.

Chicago's JPUSA is one of the few remaining, radical Jesus communities which has maintained the resistance against the dominant, materialistic, and individualistic paradigm of mainstream society. The primary factors mentioned as typical of the Calvary Chapel communities were common to all of the communities I have visited over the last 30 years. Reorientation, reeducation, resocialization, discipleship, and training were an integral part. These communities were often the context of conversion and the place where many received "the baptism" or "anointing" of the Holy Spirit.

It is estimated that at "its peak" the Jesus People Movement operated over 800 communal houses throughout America and Canada (Di Sabatino 1994:16; Richardson, Stewart, and Simmonds 1979:xvi). An intense sense of mission was almost atmospheric in these communities. As the Celtic communities of old, some combined the missional and the contemplative with the ancient grace of hospitality to strangers. In the best of the monastic tradition in the history of the church, these centers were often the first experience of communally-centered welfare and love to marginalized people. They were "cities of refuge," centers of hospitality for the wayfarer. With the collapse of these networks, the homeless, and the marginalized find less sociological entry point into most local churches. The Jesus Freaks knew the network of communes and drop-in centers by word of mouth and by widely distributed lists published in more than 60 Jesus papers. The Soup Kitchen is a far cry from the redemptive hospitality of the Jesus Houses.

Calvary Chapel Leadership

Miller (1997) maintains the movement is "clearly built on relationships, not centralized authority, or formal reporting structures" (1997:36). In conflict with Miller's view, the centrality of benevolent, but firm authoritarian leadership is inherent and apparent in the all aspects of Calvary Chapel.[13] At a time when charismatic leadership was declining in denominational circles, in the interest of democratization, and lay ministry, the Jesus Movement created many highly charismatic movers and shakers. A new class of leaders emerged.

> Smith is not complicated. He's a leader. He has inspired other people to be leaders. You don't have to be perfect to be a leader. Look at Abraham the first mis-

sionary. Intuitive leadership versus long range planning is the way for Smith. He started 800 churches with no church growth plan; no church growth department; only a secretary that handles communications. All he does now is go out and personify what a Calvary Chapel pastor is, just by going out and telling the stories. He hasn't had the need to market. [It is] not a seeker-sensitive model church; it is not a marketing methodology model they have adopted. (Fromm 1999:8)

The Cultivation of Charisma

One man's late maturing charisma could scarcely explain the proliferation of a next generation of leaders under Smith's influence. Some Calvary Chapels have outgrown mother church. Rarely does a figure of such legendary proportions as Smith reproduce his or her gift in significant numbers. The "uniqueness of Smith is that he was able to cultivate charisma. He has facilitated many other charismatic leaders like Mike McIntosh, and Ray Bentley of Maranatha Chapel, with 5,000 in San Diego" (Fromm 1999:36).

The mild mannered pastor, whose nephew Fromm and son Smith Jr. say makes a hobby of restoring old cars, has a strong focus on restoring broken people. His single-minded focus on individual restoration simplified the mission and the message. A focused commitment by the charismatic leader to maintain the base operation was primary. Many early Jesus Movement centers saw similar responses to contextualized teaching but failed to conserve the results.

> I would say Smith struggled with that because once they see the church numbers, you get all the invitations. Chuck would go through seasons where he'd take a bunch of speaking engagements and really kick himself for doing it. He rarely gave up Sunday morning and Thursday nights. [He did] weddings (five or six a week), baptisms, dedicating babies, hospital calls, and all the little rituals that go into pastoring. He didn't become a superstar. He stayed faithful in those things. (Fromm 1999:5)

Non-Professional, Deregulated, and Entrepreneurial Leadership

One of Smith's notable decisions was to limit any further development of congregational size, determining to facilitate new Calvary Chapel churches rather than to expand the older facility. Almost 30 years later the line has been held concerning methodology of expansion. Obesity is a form of growth. So is cancer. He decided reproduction is the healthy way to permanency.

New openness to innovation and experimentation is not the only factor, but a free association was birthed for this new paradigm church leader. Within clearly defined limits, openness to new moves of the Spirit, and to the possibility of unexpected sources of divine activity was embraced. Less emphasis was placed upon dogmatics and more on experience and relationships.

> It is characteristic of the baby boomers' generation [that they do not embrace] the polarizations of liberal and conservative. They would lean more towards the middle than their parents. They, [the parents] are pretty much more bound up by prejudice; would not enter into dialogue but would only monologue at different poles. I just think the dialogue expanded and allowed more freedom of form within worship. (Fromm 1999:67)

There is an entrepreneurial freedom in the Calvary Chapel movement which is in the context of Smith's dominant presence. New units are a franchise (Miller 1997:35-36, 141-142, 167-168). Permission is not required for experimentation. There is no established hierarchy to act as the regulator or repository of wisdom. Most Calvary Chapels started with basically no capital investment in money. Older denominational churches invest heavily in new church plants with property grants or loans and stipends for pioneering clergy. Calvary Chapel's pioneers start with little else than a sense of call. The Albuquerque, New Mexico church plant, which now has 15,000 attenders, is typical. Skip and Lenya Heitzig moved out, found secular work, and commenced a Bible study at home (Miller 1997:157-159; Fromm 1999:40).

De-institutionalization and the employment of unordained, intuitively gifted, indigenous leaders trained by mentoring is the key to their growth. There is no "how to" instruction manual for pioneers in uncharted waters. Calvary Chapel however has a second generation of highly successful leaders, but has resisted the normative pattern of producing numerous books and instruction programs as many of the mega churches are doing, preferring to maintain a mentoring, "bootcamp" training for their church planters and ministry conceptualizes.

Developing a Tribal Pedagogy – The Power of Oral Culture

The initially rapid growth resulted from conversions substantially attributable to Lonnie Frisbee's charisma and counterculture networking. The maintenance and form of the Chapel's growth results from Smith's determination and charismatic use of an oral tradition, centered around systematic, public expositions in a popular culture format. Possibly his genius lies in a postmodern return to oral culture during a receptive period in Western culture. Walter Hollenweger believes that there is a revolution occurring at Calvary Chapel and similar movements, which still evades the traditionalists.

> Academic theologians to this very day have been largely ignorant of the ever-growing Pentecostal revival. The greatest revival movement of our time is largely ignored by professional theologians, probably because its strongest side is its *oral* theology. Oral theology operates, as we have seen not through the book, but through the parable, not through the thesis, but through the testimony, not through dissertations, but through dances, not through concepts, but through banquets, not through a system of thinking, but through stories and songs, not through definitions, but through descriptions, not through arguments, but through transformed lives. (Hollenweger 1997:196)

While Bible teaching is central for Smith, its form is heavily laced with testimony, stories, and parable. It is woven into a seamless garment of word, worship, music, and the reestablishment of testimony as descriptive gospel. The radical repositioning of faith, outside the former tradition of cognitive theology has invaded the citadel of popular fundamentalism. The resultant folk culture shows no sign of diminishing in influence. Analysts of the Calvary Chapel phenomena have done so through relationship and observation, rather than literary sources. Little documentation exists but participants are eager to share their story (Balmer and Todd 1994:19-22). There is a shifting emphasis in both social science and theology, from literary to oral sources, facilitating more empathetic, and immediate investigation of new social, and religious movements. Calvary Chapel, despite its fundamentalist theology has attracted research for its highly successful revolution of traditional Pentecostal ministry.

> Until very recently, academic theology did not seem interested in what the Spirit is doing today, because the work of the Spirit has been relayed mainly in oral forms. In order to get to the roots of this Movement one has to do field research, and that not only in Europe and America. No wonder that anthropologists, ethnologists, and sometimes sociologists have been the first to discover Pentecostalism (however, mostly without seeing its theological and academic relevance). For these scholars, Pentecostals have been interesting objects of research – not teachers in a global art of communication. (Hollenweger 1997:196-197)

The centrality of Smith's exposition as an oral tradition has marked the movement from early in its development. His concentration on the divine text as the master of ceremonies has enabled Smith to establish his own imprimatur, positioning himself in the exposition of the text with his own moral authority extending from it. There is however a fixed pattern to Smith's oral tradition.

> The trademark of the doctrine of all Calvary Chapels is their verse-by-verse exposition of the Bible. In his years with the Foursquare denomination, Smith reports, he was a "topical" preacher, jumping from one passage to another as he sought to cover the major concepts and doctrines of Christianity. Every sermon was an effort to prepare, and after about two years of preaching he had to change churches to avoid repeating himself. Since abandoning this "hodge-podging" around the Bible, he has, in his words, been "cruising." Sometimes he takes a few verses and other times a few chapters. Smith's approach and that of most Calvary pastors is to read consecutively through the Bible, book by book. Smith's goal is to have "the best fed sheep" in the church. In his view, healthy sheep will want to share their faith with others, helping the flock reproduce. (Miller 1997:36, 37)

Chuck Smith's conservative and orthodox theology is "somewhere between traditional Baptist and mainline Pentecostal" according to Miller (1997:36). He promotes a relaxed, inclusive, open atmosphere of passionate enquiry into truth. Smith has educated successive waves of converts, in a communal dialogue with sacred text for guidance on every issue of life.

The people have become a "people of the Book" through oral tradition by listening to the extensive cassette library of little else but exposition. They have been pastoraly bonded to their shepherd, perceiving themselves to be well fed. They are eager to evangelize, confirming that "healthy sheep reproduce," as Smith says (Fromm 1996a:28). Loyalty to the leader is founded on a relationship of reciprocal love for the one who provides the basis for shared meanings and beliefs from Scripture. His competence and winsomeness in public presentation established an authority status on all matters of faith and conduct. Biblical exposition applied astutely to the nuances of the local, youth and young family culture was as powerful in converting outsiders as any traditional evangelism. A significant aspect of Calvary Chapel was its engagement of idealistic youth, thus effecting the next generation, shifting a portion of that generation back to the Bible.

A Vernacular Conversation between Cultures

Using the old poetic King James Version, the exposition is presented in popular, vernacular language and is dialogical in its style. Relaxed humor and folksy insertions of audience experiences help produce a sense of relational dialogue, even though the presentation is monologue. Transcendence and ancient tribal authority is inherent in the use of the traditional, "holy" language of the Authorized Version.

> The best use of Scripture in public worship was the King James Version. [For] a Bible study, obviously the King James Version is not the best, but for listening and memorizing it is captivating. For an oral society, it's poetry. The black church has never left it. (Fromm 1999:8)

The Jesus Movement excelled at evangelism through use of the vernacular, and by evoking popular images. Vernacular speech and music were the key. The process is congruent with the biblical doctrine of the Incarnation.

> The Scottish Poet said, "And the Word was made flesh. Are we to make Him word again." The Jesus Movement embraced a vernacularization of the faith and the rejection of literacy. In order to be a minister [in traditional church] you had to go to Bible College. The fact that you could take a bar [pub] band like "Love Song" meant nothing. Now all of a sudden they become communicators of faith without the certifications; [which were] the baptisms, if you will, into the literacy aspect of Christianity. (Fromm 1999:31)

Some "straights" buried themselves in the counterculture, and became students at the feet of the indigenes, learning how to communicate Jesus in the youth culture. A close relationship with hippies and their prophetic style attracted and taught Smith.

Diffusion of Innovations and Ideas

The Jesus Movement was marked by its youthful inexperience. Its counterculture leanings suggested potential for a short life. The new religious movement was highly innovative in communication methodology and social experimentation. In the realm of ideas the movement embraced apocalyptic speculation and millenarian theories, which have a long history in America. The hippie penchant for conspiratorial theories, exotic spiritualities, and the expectation of immanent disasters made the revised eschatology of the 1960s extraordinarily attractive to the young dissenters. In typical Southern Californian style, Calvary Chapel was and remains fixated by eschatology.

Surfing the Apocalypse

Traveling Californian highways, during the early 1970s, I picked up numerous hitchhikers who were drifting around the country – a mark of the Californian counterculture. I was amazed as a citizen of a far more secular country, at the intense interest in the Second Coming of Christ amongst non-Christian youth. A mixture of apocalyptic belief in the imminent collapse of corrupt Western culture, and the likelihood of a San Andreas Fault earthquake, combined with a hope of utopian alternatives, and a penchant for collecting gurus. Many were intrigued with premillennialist eschatology. The sense that the system was doomed and under judgment of nature and God led many earnest seekers to surf the waves of possible conspiracies, apocalyptic prophecies and futuristic projections. The Six Day War (1967) in the Middle East and particularly the Jewish reclaiming of Jerusalem in entirety, produced widespread expectation for believers, or fear for unbelievers, promoting a rush of speculations based on the biblical prophecy (Lippy 1989:249).

> Jerusalem shall be trodden down of the Gentiles, until the times of the Gentiles be fulfilled. And there shall be signs in the sun, and in the moon, and in the stars; and upon the earth distress of nations, with perplexity; the sea and the waves roaring, men's hearts failing them for fear, and for looking after those things which are coming on the earth: for the powers of heaven shall be shaken. (Luke 21:25-26)

Chuck Smith's focus on eschatology was central to his popularity. Balmer and Todd (1994) note "Smith frequently refers to the coming end times and counsels his auditors to prepare for Christ's coming," and "this eschatology is arguably the most strongly held and consistently taught doctrine at Calvary Chapel" (1994:685), probably a vestige of his Pentecostal tradition. It is for this reason that I have made an issue of Calvary Chapel eschatology and its link to Hal Lindsey. It is also a feature consistent with revitalization, which is related to later conclusions in this dissertation. I had many conversations with Calvary Chapel congregates and commune members and listened to hundreds of Smith's teaching tapes with my own staff. Calvary Chapel's bookstore, looking on the busy intersection of Fairview and Sunflower, depicts a rainbow arching over the clouds, a dove, and the inscription; 'God keeps His promises, Jesus is coming soon'. An entire section of the bookstore, End Times, features the works of Hal Lindsey . . . and several apocalyptic books by Smith, including *Dateline Earth: Count Down to Eternity*" (Balmer and Todd 1994:685).

Dallas Baptist Seminary eschatology is a folk tradition throughout America repopularized in the early 1970s by Lindsey's (1970) best seller, *The Late Great Planet Earth* and Smith's Bible teaching. Lindsey's primary audience has been from mid teens to 25 year olds (Lippy 1989:252), possibly accounting for the enduring impact of his "pop" theology. He is "one of the few authors to see three of his books on the [New York] *Times* best seller list at the same time" (1989:250). I was constantly confronted at Calvary Chapel by converts and seekers for whom Lindsey's book, and Smith's eschatalogical preaching content, had provided the overwhelming "proofs," they desired to verify the Scriptures and prove God's presence in history. In Paul Boyer's study of the cultural history of modern, American, eschatology (Boyer 1992), both Smith and Lindsey receive considerable attention as cultural influences.[14]

The appeal of Lindsay's book and Smith's teaching on the Second Coming of Christ to the counterculture had little to do with the previous generation's eschatalogical bent. The hippies had an apocalyptic feel born not of tradition but of intuitive responses to sociocultural perceptions of immanent disaster. The cold war paranoia and the fear of nuclear disaster were fanned by novels and movies from the 1950s. Jesus papers included cartoons and artists' impressions of global meltdown, degradation, and war. It was believed that scientific reductionism had put mother Earth and her inhabitants at risk. There seemed little debate about humanity's madness. The positioning of Lindsey's pop eschatology was historically poignant for the baby boomers (Di Sabatino 1999a:48-49; Heinz 1976a:34; Lippy 1989:247-255; Wuthnow 1998:219).

The stage was set in the 1960s for any actor who was prepared to move from the choir to the market place with a prophetic message concerning world affairs and the return of Christ. There was a massive distribution of Lindsey's book. At evangelical conference book sales in the United Kingdom and Australia, there are usually few books on eschatology. In America however, eschatology and more recently pre-millennial fiction, occupies a prominent place.

> Millennial dreams and apocalyptic nightmares are never far below the surface of the American psyche – especially now, as the third millennium approaches.... The deeper and more interesting phenomenon is the enormous role prophecy has played in Western religious and popular culture. A Newsweek Poll found that 40 percent of American adults do believe that the world will one day end, as Revelation describes, in the Battle of Armageddon.... In the 1970s, the best-selling book of the decade was Hal Lindsey's apocalyptic *The Late Great Planet Earth*, with 28,000,000 copies sold by 1990. Recently, a series of *Left Behind* novels by Tim LaHaye and Jerry Jenkins based on Christian prophecies including two published this year, have sold more than 9,000,000 copies.... "Over the past 30 years," says Bernard McGinn, a medieval specialist at the University of Chicago Divinity School, "more scholarship has been devoted to apocalypticism than in the last 300." (Woodward 1999:66-74)

Craig Miller (1992) lists Millennialism as one of the "ten essential values of a generation" (1992:105-118) in his research of "baby boomer spirituality." The Jesus Movement futurology influenced the generation towards a Smith-Lindsey paradigm. Tipton (1982) notes the disenchantment of the Living Word Fellowship led many to adopt millenarianism after political activism had failed to usher in the hoped for new order (1982:84-94).

> Both the LWF's millennial vision and its communal practices give clear evidence that disenchantment with full-scale political struggle has led sixties youth not simply to abandon it but to elaborate it symbolically and, in fact, to create alternative political institutions on a more modest scale. For all its generational specificity, the Living Word Fellowship expresses a political morality that resonates through much of America's lower middle class and through much of its Pentecostal, Fundamentalist, and Evangelical religious traditions. In this sense, the LWF represents one of three major strands of a new anti liberal consensus presently growing in American culture, this one rooted in conservative Christianity and its authoritative ethic. (Tipton 1982:94)

Lindsay was a prominent figure in the Californian Jesus Movement and primary teacher at the Jesus Light and Power House before adultery set him apart. The role of Jesus Movement groups, in spreading this influence of Lindsey's book extended to unexpected quarters in the pop culture.[15] The pre-millennial mood of Calvary Chapel, boosted by Lindsey's sensationalist books entered conservative politics also.

> The impact that [Lindsey's book] had up until Reagan's Presidency was significant. These guys were all steeped in eschatalogical thinking because of that kind of ethos they grew up in and were formed in. Hal had a huge impact at that time. In the 1970s you had Menachem Begin, Anwar Sadat, Ronald Reagan and having this concordat – I was six and being so scared Jesus was going to come back – that's what my parents thought. I don't think it was just the Christians. In the counterculture you had all these "doomsday" apocalyptic preachers talking about the end of the world and having all these predictions about what was going to happen. This [was a] whole culture of doomsday and Hal just capitalized on it. He came along and put these things in a codified belief, took all his notes from Dallas and the world stood up and took notice. (Di Sabatino 1999b:3)

Chuck Smith made great capital of the general counterculture mood, refusing to set the date of Jesus' immanent return, but some of his expositions in those early days came perilously close to predicting the decade.[16]

The Worship and Communications Revolution

The Jesus Movement was an evangelistic movement and a church growth movement. Many groups formed local churches or small denominations. Being indigenous, counterculture movements, they required the reinvention of worship forms being well outside denominational experience. Some, led by defecting denominational leaders, felt released from traditional constraints and thus able to fuse old traditions with some elements of counterculture art and imagery.

Calvary Chapel is developing sophistication of art forms, but the alternative, creative flair is still apparent in a new series of artists' impressions of biblical events for incorporation in a Bible release (Figure 4.2). Calvary Chapel was an outstanding example of the synchronization of soft-Pentecostal tradition and the alternative culture. Popular iconography was established at the grassroots, but it was swiftly incorporated at the high altars of the revitalization.

The Charismatic Movement and the Jesus Movement deregulated worship, revitalizing song writing for pop culture, opening the doors of the church to visual and performing arts in worship, and evangelism. The art and street theater of the counterculture was seconded to the sanctuary. Much has been written concerning the revolution in worship since the 1960s (Ammerman 1997:54-56, 115-116, 186-187, 251-252, 276-277, 286-287; Handy 1998:129-174; Miller 1997:80-88, 90-92; Roof 1999; Wagner 1998:125-126; Wuthnow 1994:127-150).

The influence of music, dance, drama and visual arts was to spread across all theological and ecclesiological territories in the following decades. The new wave of worship forms, incorporating contemporary music and dance, is a primary innovation of the Jesus Movement and the Charismatic Movement, Calvary Chapel being a prominent player. Traditional Pentecostals and evangelicals initially railed against the music and art forms as sensual and even demonic.

The use of rock music with Christian lyrics by innovative youth was condemned as "spiritual fornication" (Romanowski 1996:213). Many critics accused Christian rock groups of using "pagan polybeat" as a doorway to sensual abandon and demonic invasion. I recall hearing Bill Gothard and other popular convention speakers attributing youth rebellion partly to the influence of the guitar as a phallic symbol. Vernon McGee of *Back to the Bible* wrote to Fromm attacking the Jesus rock groups on the preaching platform stating "When Satan fell out of heaven, he must have fallen into the choir loft" (Fromm 1996a:41).[17] The victory of the guitar in church was a crucial innovation.

> The Jesus Movement has given validation to free worship and inventiveness. There was a period of time where the church limited which cultural elements from the mainstream culture would be allowed into the church, as expressions of belief and worship. I think if the gatekeeper's had won, the rock 'n' roll would never have made it through the doors. In [rock music] coming through, I think it's blown out the boundaries in worship and as a result not only is there a new apologetic of free worship but there's also a new apologetic for including liturgy in free worship; a blending of new elements. (Fromm 1999:38-41)

Lyle Schaller (1995), in an interview with Fromm for *Worship Leader* magazine, claimed that the contemporary versus traditional worship battle is the most divisive issue facing the church for the coming decade (1995:18). A preboomer generation of leaders marginalized themselves to bring rock singing Jesus Freaks into the sanctuary. Coincidentally, a new relationship between the arts and the preacher was born. Preachers thereby became more intuitive in their use of performing artists. At the existential moment they injected a contextualized proclamation, unrehearsed, into the flow of music.

> I remember we'd just finished a song and all of a sudden Chuck jumped up and started preaching on the subject we'd been singing about. It was incredible. These songs were just personal to us and I never thought of somebody taking the lyrics and turning them into a sermon. Afterwards he gave an altar call and a lot of people were saved. (Fromm 1996b:42)

This is typical of the Movement's paradigm shift. For a new breed of preachers, a dynamic interaction occurred between proclaimer and player. The arts became the nerve ends of the soul, incorporated in worship and mission as integral, rather than as entertainment or a "warm up" peripheral. The church has embraced a new contemporary iconography of visual arts, performing arts, and music. Rock concert evangelism is effective 30 years later.

> For the last several years, Anaheim Stadium has been filled to near capacity as upwards of 50,000 young people and families have gathered to listen to concerts of Christian rock music followed by a message from evangelist Greg Laurie, a Calvary Chapel pastor and a potential successor to the aging Billy Graham. (Miller 1997:12)

The Movement embraced a "low-culture" rather than "high culture" (Levine 1988; Romanowski 1996) expression of the arts.

**Figure 4.2 Mystical, Biblical Imagery – The Woman at the Well
(Calvary Chapel Bible project)**

People knew they did not want the religion that went with stained glass and pipe organs, but a long-haired hippie strumming a guitar and singing about Jesus' love sent a different message. According to Fromm, who was involved with Maranatha Music from its early days, the most powerful and enduring songs were written by non-professionals from the depths of their own experience. They were truckers, former strippers, and housewives who wanted to share their love of God and wrote songs such as *Father I Adore You, Seek Ye First*, and *Glorify Thy Name*. (Miller 1997:12)

While the church has still not taken the 1960s consciousness shift as seriously as it should, some commentators have concluded that "nothing was more singular about [that] generation than their addiction to music. This is the age of music and the states of soul that accompany it" (Allan 1987:68). Bloom, savagely critical of rock music in a way that I am not, still rightly states that, "Today a very large proportion of young people between the ages of ten and 20 live for music. It is their passion; nothing else excites them as it does; they cannot take seriously anything alien to music" (Bloom 1987:68).

Fromm describes Maranatha Music as the megaphone for the Calvary Chapel movement. Their tapes and records were shipped across the country and around the world. Radio stations started to play this new music and found that it had an audience. In Fromm's opinion, every social movement has its own "sound," and the Jesus Movement was marked by the guitar and a culturally current rhythm. Young people could imagine Jesus playing a guitar in a way that they could not picture him at a pipe organ or leading a choir. Fromm believes that you can tell how vibrant a social movement is by the vitality of its music. If a movement (or for that matter a local church) lacks a signature sound, he suggests, then it undoubtedly lacks cohesion at a foundational level. (Miller 1997:83)

Allan Bloom claims that Nietzsche attempted "to tap again the irrational sources of vitality, to replenish our dried-up stream from barbaric sources, and thus encourage the Dionysian and the music derivative from it" (Bloom 1987:73). Rising out of "the ashes of classical music," he believes that "this [barbaric, Dionysian quest] is the significance of rock music" (1987:73). The secular enquiry has ignored the *moral* impact of good concepts diffused throughout youth culture via rock 'n' roll. If music has the power to influence youth culture for ill, its use for good may be just as dynamic to facilitate mission and stimulate virtue. The church has concentrated on the dysfunctional behavior of rock's practitioners and often ignored the *missional impact* of pop music. Popular music was a major aspect of the Jesus Movement, but few groups developed it to the extent of Calvary Chapel. The early adoption of the popular culture is seen by Fromm as fundamental to their success. His brother's church in Yuba City California was started with concerts (Fromm 1999:36).

Most of the [Calvary Chapel] leaders are more aesthetically tuned than what you find in [the] everyday run of the mill clergy. [They are] attuned to the popular culture; to the music; they listen to music. The pastor of Warehouse Ministry in Sacramento was an Assemblies of God missionary. He started in 1972. By having concerts every Saturday night it's become a church of about 8,000. They've started ten other churches. (1999:36)

The Jesus people had rediscovered an enduring missiological principle. The Movement did not invent the missional use of popular arts and vernacular culture but they did successfully recover its popularization, in keeping with a long tradition dating back to St. Paul's use of pagan poetry (Don Richardson 1984:22-25) to address the Areopagus (Acts 17:27-29). This incarnational principle has a long and noble history in the field of mission. The Celtic church employed the arts as a major integrative factor in both mission and ritual process, even ordaining the artist. The cognitive and the affective elements were married in a cultural form that spoke to the heart of the receptor culture. The postwar generation had made a substantial shift from the enlightenment worldview. The initial effectiveness of the Movement lay in indigenous responses, often mentored by older prophets who saw beyond their own conditioning. Smith was a stabilizing mentor.

A CD and video package, *First Love* (Collins and Griesen 1998), was recently released under the title "An Historic Gathering of Artists from the Jesus Movement." Listening to *Welcome Back* (1998), I felt a powerful attraction, and a renewed memory of the affective power of the early Calvary Chapel concerts I attended, and also an alienation from my own secularized Australian culture.[18]

> *Welcome back*
> *Welcome back to the things that you once believed in*
> *Welcome back to what you knew what was right from the start*
> *All you had to do was to be what you always wanted to be*
> *Welcome back to the love that is in your heart.*
> *I know that you thought you could turn your back*
> *And no one could see in your mind*
> *But I can see that you know better now*
> *You never were the untruthful kind*
> *And I'm so happy now*
> *To welcome you back.*
> *Sometimes you just don't know what you're missing*
> *'Til you leave it for awhile.*
> *Welcome back*
> *Welcome back to Jesus*
> *Welcome back.* (Girard 1971)

The lyrics speak for themselves as they connect with American revivalist roots (McLoughlin 1978),[19] but the complex interaction between music form and cognitive content, bridges the Old and New World. There is an essentially conservative, evangelical concept implied in the song *Welcome Back*. The assumption that everybody deep within really does know that they are rebelling against God, is a culturally driven concept defended from the biblical text, and the received tradition of American revivalism. But there is a less traditionally evangelical note of inclusivism that does not assume that the acid-dropping hippie who is sleeping with his girlfriend is any different from the middle class, monogamous businessman. The outsider is not so much the rebel against truth as the deceived. In the midst of the Movement's atmosphere, they can feel welcomed and free to do what they knew "was right from the start." The Methodist doctrine of prevenient grace most approximates to this typical Jesus Movement emphasis.

Fromm, a facilitator of the innovation of evangelical witness and worship in contemporary art forms, believes the Jesus people had rediscovered a primary missiological principle familiar to the Celtic Church.[20] The radical departure from the centrality of dogma to a faith based primarily on relationship and experience, predated the 1960s and had already been well established in the oral culture of Pentecostalism, but was popularized by the 1960s cultural revolution.

A Christian Sub-culture Rather than a Counterculture

The Movement was initially marked by aggressive invasion of traditionally non-Christian territory, initiating a crossover whereby previous religious taboos collapsed. They embraced popular social forms that were previously outlawed by evangelicals. Long hair, rock music, political demonstrations, motorcycles, billiards and pool, playing cards, and wearing the "in" styles of clothing became acceptable for believers. Blue jeans invaded the pulpit. Distinctive language, behaviors, and ritual forms, once embraced as marks of separation by the counterculture, no longer evoked liminality or subcultural social intimacy for rebels. Calvary Chapel promoted the "dumbing" down of the radical culture rather than revolutionizing the system. It provided a secure and well furnished lifeboat by its theology and a socio-political mazeway, enabling members to accommodate to the secular city, rather than challenging its materialistic assumptions. The alternative, marginalized feeling so evident during my first visit has long been replaced by an affluent, aggressive, upward mobility. This is appealing to the postmodern, post-yuppie, Silicon Valley culture, now seeking a comfort zone rather than a prophetic zone.

Calvary Chapel has developed its own subculture, congruent with Southern Californian affluence, emotive self-actualization, and fundamentalist epistemology. The social variant of Smith's commitment to strict textual exposition has however preserved Calvary Chapel from the extreme Gnosticism of much Californian Pentecostalism, and New Age theory. Perhaps the sociological context of Orange County was formative in the development of a religious steady state from the confusion of the 1960s California.

> I lived in Orange County for a while. The Christianity is very shallow. The kind of counterculture thing that is holistic happens, but it's marginal. You should have seen the house I grew up in . . . .You come from a different world. It's dialectic for you. It should be for everybody. You've gone in a little bit deeper. You've said there are some ramifications that I can't get away from . . . . Certainly they [Calvary Chapel] are not having any impact on the secular culture. (Di Sabatino 1999a:17-18)

Ironically, that which began as an aggressive outreach to an alienated generation, gave rise to institutions in which successive generations of young evangelicals could be enculturated into mainstream society in terms of worldview, institutionalized into their own comfort zone (Pete Ward 1996:103-4; 161-85).

The emergence of specifically targeted Christian records, festivals, and magazines, has meant that Christian young people have been given the chance to buy into this new hip culture. As these young people have grown up, events and products have moved with them. The net result has been that changes brought about by and for young people have now passed into the mainstream life of the majority of evangelical churches in this country. (Pete Ward 1996:103)

The isolation of the evangelical subculture has resulted in the creation of separate market places, festivals, and publishers. The instant, all pervasive nature of electronic communications easily creates the false impression that numbers indicate penetration of the secular community.[21] Because of a massive contemporary Christian music industry, today's kids can enjoy all the best of the secular art forms, without engagement with the non-Christian culture. Scholars attribute this evangelical pop culture to the Jesus Movement, Calvary Chapel Maranatha Music being a primary player (Baker 1979, 1985; Di Sabatino 1999:155-213; Fromm 1996a:42, 43, 61; Miller 1997:80-85; A. Reid 1995:41-52; Romanowski 1990a, 1990b:143-70; Pete Ward 1996:80-104).

Young believers may have been led back into the world but off the streets, providing credence for the criticism that the church which was meant to be "in the world, but not of it," has now become "of the world, but not in it." "Outreach" becomes "in-drag," as the mega rally, within sanctified space, on sacred territory. It tends to attract the outsider by seeker-sensitive "in-house" productions, rather than mobilizing the believers to blitz the market place, as did the young Jesus Freaks of the 1960s and 1970s. While Calvary Chapel shows many signs of creating such a subculture it has also maintained an aggressive though winsome tradition of innovative evangelism.

One element to emerge from the 1960s was the recognition of "adolescence" by the church. The need to treat this somewhat homogeneous unit seriously, as a distinctly needy unit, was highlighted by the Jesus Movement though Pete Ward warns of isolationist consequences (1996:199-202, 161-198). Di Sabatino recalls:

> I think the most significant thing about the Jesus Movement is the development of youth evangelical culture where for the first time, you have the evangelicals taking kids seriously. You have youth pastors, worship bands, programs, and training. [We] didn't have these things before. [We] didn't have a culture that adapted to what was going on with the youth. The introduction of the guitar, the drums, and mass meetings [concerts] were innovative. You had all these baby boomers coming through like a pig in a python . . . at one time. It was just natural for the church to say "Hey, let's talk with these people". . . .The impact on the Seminaries and para-church organizations, Campus Crusade and Youth for Christ was considerable. (Di Sabatino 1999:2)

Tentative Conclusion –
Did the Jesus Freaks Come Home Too Soon?

Despite Calvary Chapel's evangelical success, Fromm says that there is disquiet amongst the emerging, postmodern substrata. Donald Miller believes that a "new reformation" or a "re-invention of American Protestantism" was initiated predominantly by Calvary Chapel (1997:11-12), but his definition lacks parallels to the Protestant Reformation, which was a major engagement of the mind with emerging modernity. The Reformation produced changes in Western culture that have taken centuries to erode. In a period of paradigm shift to postmodernity, something far more than the pragmatics of user friendly communication is required to warrant evoking the image of reformation. Revitalization may be a different issue, as I will investigate in Chapter 7. Calvary Chapel is innovative, reproductive and culturally astute, but it is not a reformation voice. A modification of manners and methods is scarcely a reformation of theology. Chuck Smith Jr. (1999:56) is firm and unequivocal when asked of the reformational status of the movement, affirming that the "life boat theology" of Calvary Chapel is neither reformational nor adversarial on behalf of the poor, despite some urban mission plants.

> I don't think it is a Second Reformation and the people are not taught to think that way. I'm thinking about . . . . Ray Bentley's rejuvenation of a city block. If I went to Ray's church, and said, 'I live in this community. I see what you've done to that city block and I'm very impressed. Cut through all the crap and tell me what is the bottom line?' He would say 'Believe on the Lord Jesus Christ and you will be saved.' It would have an evangelistic motive behind it. To be fair to Bentley, he was supporting the vision of this black guy who was very socially active. (Chuck Smith Jr. 1999:56)

Indisputably thousands have found satisfying faith and have been rescued from self-destruction through this new paradigm church. Some essential elements of the original Jesus Movement have been preserved in Calvary Chapel, including acceptance of diverse sociocultural appearance, and the belief that love, not charisma is the essential evidence of grace (1999:59-72).

Not all are currently convinced that the new paradigm is adequate to weather the storm of postmodernity. Chuck Smith Jr. is his own man, and currently is in dialogue with a disturbed new genre of Generation X leaders, such as rock band *AC.DC's* one time "sound man," Barry Taylor (Ph.D. Fuller Theological Seminary). Taylor is investigating the significant cultural role of the arts, particularly fringe expressions in music and cinema.[22] Not all are finding the Costa Mesa, conservative, small "c," charismatic subculture adequate. The church as either a lifeboat, or alternately, a prophetic voice in the outside marketplace, looms as an increasingly disturbing dichotomy. Smith Junior seriously questions the effectiveness of Calvary Chapel's penetration, even considering "disbanding the church" to "move into the culture" if by that he could have more impact on the wider culture (Smith Jr. 1999:67). With a benign but monolithic control exercised by the aging Smith Sr. and emergence of creative dissidents, Calvary Chapel's direction after Smith Sr., may be problematic.

The public perception, and the church growth movements' assessment, of Smith's Calvary Chapel (Fromm 1996a; Miller 1997; Wagner 1998) as the prototype of the best of the movement is rather uncritical. Joe Peterson, academic and early participant in the Pacific Northwest's movement, casts strong doubt on the accuracy of Smith's account of the Movement. My judgment would be tentatively similar. Peterson had been directly involved with some early Movement activists whose initiatives were lost in the more conservative church growth shaped by Smith (Peterson 1999).[23]

Although Smith may be more a beneficiary of the Jesus Movement than an initiator, at the very least, he must be recognized as one of the earliest denominational defectors to the Movement, having recognized its unique potential. He astutely perceived the danger of the established church missing both the social momentum and the divine moment of this widespread, youthful search for faith, meaning, and community. He employed the indigenous forces, while maintaining a conservative foundation for what was to become one of the most remarkable church growth patterns in post-war evangelical history.[24] He domesticated it theologically, while exploiting its cultural forms. He may be criticized, or extolled according to one's worldview. Richardson, Stewart and Simmonds observe that "routinization of charisma is likely to conservatise the dominant core of the movement while simultaneously producing increasingly radical splinter groups" (1979:335). Calvary Chapel's rapid routinization under Smith settled the movement down to a conservative socio-political and theological norm, but alienated indigenous radical, Lonnie Frisbee and birthed the "miracle"-oriented Vineyard movement. Thus, despite controversy, the movement successfully proliferated.

The ability of a leader to "reinvent" himself or herself at regular intervals becomes necessary to the extent the surrounding culture is rapidly reconfiguring, and focal points of the value system are in transition. Smith's capacity to adapt to the liminal state of the counterculture initially and to the baby boomer's radical individualism, and then to conspicuous consumptiveness a decade later enhanced his persona as Calvary Chapel's leader.

The capacity to create new social networks of individuals who have common cause, rather than skillfully exploiting traditional networks contributed significantly to the phenomenal growth pattern of such Jesus Movement groups. Growth of a movement, though exceptional in speed or volume, does not of itself assure cultural penetration and impact on existing dominant worldviews or institutions. The extent to which the Calvary Chapel movement is able to effect change in the wider culture, as well as increase its own growth remains to be seen. It appears to be self-perpetuating, rather than culture transforming, but its open system of church planting has attracted many creative, postmodern, young leaders. They may yet direct Calvary Chapel in a direction, more reflective of its early days of counterculture dissent, but suited to new postmodern demands. As with all human movements, Calvary Chapel is moving towards those institutional frameworks that are essential if a movement is to outlive the originators of it. Late last year (2001) the Xenos leadership, following an investigative visit, reported to me that systematic and sophisticated though theologically conservative education is now well established by Calvary Chapel in the study of biblical hermeneutics.

Summary

This chapter has provided a case study, which appears to be a copybook example of revitalization. A movement born in the most culturally convulsed region of the United States counterculture, captivates a stressed, searching, generation by multiple forms of outstanding communication, in prophetic judgement on the surrounding society and inclusive love for the respondents. Scarcely could a more thoroughly fine-tuned and attractive new code be formulated than that which Smith has provided to his loyal and inspired following. A military trained, disciplined assistant supplements the inspirational gifts of Frisbee and Smith, devising a process for establishing a predictable, accountable culture but open culture. Within two years of the chaotic Jesus Movement beginnings, the footloose, counterculture drifters are recovering from stress, enabled to reorder their universe in a social context that has established equilibrium. Jaded, Californian, middle class Christians find a meaning and purpose beyond the rat race of consumption, as they enter into ministry in the stimulating context of a partly alien culture of youth. While a feeling of *communitas* and apocalyptic excitement and innovation continue, the sense of a new steady state of faith, prosperity, mission focus, and competent organization has dispelled the stress and confusion of former years.

Not far away, a very different response to the drifting hordes of disaffected youths was occurring at the same time as the Calvary Chapel phenomenon. The first occurrence of a postmodern, popular culture produced its own form of alienation and fragmentation in the wake of a splintering mainframe culture. In response to the legitimate counterculture resistance and the escalating stress and liminality of the hippie dissenters, a Christian, counterculture call to solidarity, community and radical resistance was developed in Berkeley, the hotbed of disaffection and rebellion. This will be the subject of the next chapter, as we investigate the CWLF. The journey began in extreme liminality and counterculture rejection of tradition and ritual. In a classic revitalization reconstruction of their world, CWLF discovered a new set of stress-relieving rituals, not in the freedom of postmodern rebellion, but in the ancient, Eastern mystery and tradition of Antiochian Orthodoxy. The resolution of stress appears to be as great as any observed in this enquiry, but the outcomes were totally unexpected at the time of revitalization.

NOTES

1. Several new terms have been introduced to popular ecclesiology, chiefly through the church growth movement. The rapid growth and demographic spread of a new style of very large, independent church movement has also captured the attention of a number of academics. Wuthnow (1997:234-238) defines the mega church as a church with a membership ranging from 2,000 to 10,000 or more. One of the major advantages for such churches is the capacity to gather a critical mass of diversely gifted people, and sufficient financial base, to create a network of assistant pastors, program directors, and specific subcultural ministries to youth, students, the addicted, and the incarcerated. Such churches are able to mount specialist entry point ministries to the lonely, those in need of recovery movement assistance, those wishing for support concerning child rearing, and those seeking personal advice in psychology, health, and marital relations. The "group within a group" is part of the social genius of such arrangements, which provide a larger sense of social power, through seeker sensitive public gatherings of thousands of attendees, and the proliferation of specialized small groups. These provide a sense of intimacy and connectedness to others that could easily be lost in the mega-meetings.

2. Donald Miller, in Reinventing America's Protestantism, describes many of these new style churches as new Paradigm Churches (1997:37-44, 51-52, 173-174). Miller lists the Calvary Chapel movement, the Hope Chapel movement, and Vineyard Christian Fellowship, each of which have planted a number of mega church congregations as an eventual outcome of the Jesus Movement revitalization. Both Miller and Wagner (1998:8-9) have employed the term Post-Denominational Churches. Wagner includes Willow Creek Associates, Calvary Chapel, and Vineyard Fellowships as part of this movement. However, the use of the term Post-denominational was later rejected when Wagner (1998) who uses the term "New Apostolic Churches" as "some thought it (Post-denominational) linked them to past failures, or even worse, implied that some effective evangelical denominations were not in fact effective" (1998:9). Wagner changed the title to the New Apostolic Reformation. For description and analysis of Hope Chapel movement, as a "second wave" of the Calvary Chapel Jesus Movement phenomena, read Wagner's New Apostolic Churches (1998) where a personal account by founding pastor Ralph Moore is provided. Miller provides a sociologist's independent assessment of the same movement (1997:37-42).

3. Thirty years have passed since the founding of Calvary Chapel. It is difficult to obtain an on the spot description of the atmosphere and style, these being important elements for the new affective generation, unless we return to the commentaries being written at the time. Most of these initial reports are short and racy because they are incorporated in general descriptions of the Jesus Movement, embracing many different groups and styles. Enroth, Ericson, and Peters (1972:84-94) provide an overview and a good general description, which concurs with my own experience there a little later. A number of internal documents are available, describing the movement from the standpoint of the leadership. For this see Harvest (1987) Chuck Smith. The History of Calvary Chapel (1992), Chuck Smith and Tal Brooke. The Reproducers: New Life for Thousands (1972), Chuck Smith and Hugh Steven. For an internal view of Calvary Chapel philosophy of ministry, ecclesiology, and eschatology see The Soon To Be Revealed Antichrist (1976a); Chuck Smith. Snatched Away (1976b); Chuck Smith. Charisma vs. Charismania (1983). For a more in depth analysis see Mine Eyes Have Seen the Glory: A Journey into the Evangelical Subculture of America (1989); Randall Balmer. "Calvary Chapel, Costa

Mesa, CA;" Randall Balmer and Jesse T. Todd, Jr. In American Congregations, Vol.1. James P. Wind and James W. Lewis eds., (1994:663-698). See "Jesus and Jesus People." Christian Century 89(1972):336-338).

4. For a description and analysis of Hope Chapel see Donald E. Miller. Reinventing American Protestantism: Christianity in the New Millennium (1997:37-44); C. Peter Wagner, ed., The New Apostolic Churches (1998:185-198).

5. The Quest for the Radical Middle Bill Jackson (1999) is the official history of the Vineyard Movement.

6. Gospel Outreach and Verbo are related movements, claiming more than seventy churches in the Americas. They have placed their histories, vision, theology and church data online: http://www.verbo.org/site/vcm.htm

7. The title "Great Commission Churches" has been claimed by at least three small denominations that the author has contacted, including a new group in Wilmore, Kentucky. One group appears to clearly have roots in the Jesus Movement through Jesus Freak activity in Iowa. Several dozen churches have sprung from this group including the Lindworth Road Community Church, Columbus, OH. According to Greg Leffel, who had experience of this group in earlier days through his ministry in Xenos, (also in Columbus), the original group became extremely authoritarian and cultist in early days, shortly after its founding. The leadership later apologized to the people for the damage done, and appears to have achieved a remarkable recovery. They have entered into the mainstream community and have been hosting Perspectives on the World Christian Movement seminars, in fellowship with mainstream churches, including Southern Baptist, United Methodists, and Presbyterians.

8. The Alliance for Renewal Churches (ARC) is a small, but very active missional church movement, with a Covenantal, charismatic, Calvinist leaning. With a strong emphasis on grace, some of their churches have referred to this in their titles (e.g. Grace Fellowship Church, Mansfield, OH). There is an emphasis on the intellectual, theological foundation, but also an affective, experiential emphasis on the guidance of the Spirit, particularly through the leadership communally seeking God's will. Under the title of International Association of Missions mission activity has been established in Latin American countries (Brazil and Peru). ARC churches are being reproduced in Japan and in Islamic nations in South Asia. Discipleship training, systematic theology and biblical studies' courses are balanced by ministry and mission training.

Links have been made with the "Missional Church" movement represented by such authors as George R. Hunsberger, Darrell L. Guder, Alan J. Roxburgh, and Craig Van Gelder (See Darrell L. Guder ed. 1998 *Missional Church: A Vision for the Sending of the Church in North America*). The author presented a keynote address at their National Leadership Conference in 1999, at the ARC base and community of faith in Mansfield, OH. Their concentration is in the North and Northeast (Baltimore, MD; Amhurst, MA; Haslett and Port Huron, MI; St. Paul, MN; Mont Claire, NJ). Several churches have been planted in Ohio from its beginnings in Mansfield, originally through the Jesus Movement ministry of Grace Haven Farm, at which Ray Nethery, ex-Campus Crusade director served as co-leader with CWLF/Evangelical Orthodox pioneer Gordon Walker.

When Nethery defected from the house church movement of Sparks (CWLF), Gilquist, and Walker, he continued to develop a strong Calvinist, charismatic work at Grace Haven that became ARC. He provides a patriarchal presence in the movement, the leadership of which follows a central collegial form. Typical pastors were converts from the counterculture. They brought with them interest in the arts and creative outreach. This small but vigorous denomination is worthy of further scholarly investigation. A web page is available for information: http//www.arcchurch.org.

9. We believe worship of God should be intelligent. Therefore: our services are designed with great emphasis upon teaching the Word of God that He might instruct us how He would be worshipped.

We believe worship of God should be inspirational. Therefore: we give a great place to music in our worship.

We believe worship of God should be spiritual. Therefore: we remain flexible to the leading of the Holy Spirit to direct our worship.

We believe worship of God is fruitful. Therefore: we look for His love in our lives as the supreme manifestation that we have been truly worshiping Him (Wind and Lewis 1994a:681-685).

10. The Deliverance Movement was an external influence, which infiltrated the Jesus Movement all over the world. Particularly through Derek Prince, Bob Mumford, Don Basham, a strong Pentecostal influence was exerted, whereby every ailment, psychological or relational problem was attributed to specific demons and exorcism became the central ministry form. Believers were said to be subject to such forces, often related to family, or personal contact with the occult, even at a casual level. This was one of the issues that caused several pastors associated with Smith to eventually either leave, or be dismissed by Smith, who strongly held the line that no person in whom the Holy Spirit dwelt could simultaneously be dwelt by a demon. Any preachers who embraced the deliverance ministry model were dismissed. Closely associated with this was the Shepherding Movement. The innocence and vulnerability of hippie converts, longing for order out of their previous chaotic itinerancy, made them easy prey for authoritarian gurus, and also for extreme doctrines of accountability.

Tom Pope, former Asbury Theological Seminary Admissions Director was involved in the Jesus Movement in Florida, where he saw considerable confusion over these influences:

> It peaked mid 1970s in the discipleship movement. They went with every wind that came. They started as a charismatic group. Some of the charismatic leaders were real interested in that church and were steady visitors, like Derek Prince, Bob Mumford, Don Basham, Charles Price, and Simpson – the big five. So when the whole discipleship Shepherding Movement came about in the early 1970s, they went with that movement. It did damage, in that it became legalistic and it became a control issue. For instance, in that church called Charisma Chapel, each member of the church had a particular elder to whom they were responsible. That elder was responsible for them. They couldn't go to another elder. (Pope 1999:6-7)

11. I asked this question of Smith Jr. and Fromm for a critical reason. Between my initial visit to Calvary Chapel and my return a month later, a significant, symbolic shift had occurred. They had relocated in their big new building. My judgment of the previous tent is that the physical location and accouterments contributed to the Mosaic sense of pilgrimage, which was typical of the counterculture and the early Jesus Movement. I returned to attend the dedication of the new fixed sanctuary, which remains as the worshiping context of the current mother church of the Calvary Chapel denomination. I entered the packed auditorium to find there were no seats available. I sat on the floor, and a deacon immediately approached me informed me that health regulations required that I stand at the back. I complied. No sooner had I shifted, than an attractive, middle class woman, dressed in a good quality pants suit, entered and sat almost exactly in the position I had vacated. The same elder simply smiled, and made no attempt to relocate her. I had arrived dressed in worn jeans, a tee shirt, and no shoes. I wondered then, if the routi-

nization of this charismatic movement had already shifted the community from its previously marginalized status, to a new, gentrified sociology. As postmodernity deconstructs traditional meanings and forms, there may be a need for the church to maintain a pilgrim's status, and consistently, regularly re-radicalize and reposition itself within the culture. This may be a vital issue in the missiology of the church of the future, given the extent and speed of change now globally driven.

12. Di Sabatino recalls: "There was enough to convince me there was something there. You'd get people who are not charismatic, who can't stand charismatics, who think a lot of it as manipulation or psychological mumble jumble and yet they'd tell stories about Lonnie and say, 'Your guess is as good as mine. Hey, I was there and this is what happened.' People who hated Lonnie would tell me [such] stories. So when you start hearing those things, it's not those who surround him, or 'the cult of Lonnie.' It's not those people. It's other people who don't necessarily hold charismatic views. As an historian you have to discern what is 'hype' and certainly there is some, but I don't want to add to that. You get people who are pretty sober, even theologians [who say], 'I was there.'" (Di Sabatino 1999a:22)

13. My observation of surviving Jesus Movement churches is that charismatic, intuitive leaders generally control and shape the revitalized, or new ritual processes in the emerging, social movement. Such a leader in the pattern of a Moses, leading his people to a Promised Land, establishing the monument symbols, and ritual processes, as instruments of worldview framing, pedagogies, strategies, and corporate identity. Because these arise liminally and often without written form and signature of the leader, they become part of the mythology and identity of the movement, and are often perceived at a later date to have naturally arisen from the genius of the community itself. This is rarely so. The most important ritual processes are usually established by one or two significant leaders. For the group to own and personally identify with the movement however, this egalitarian sense of perceived history is important. A wise leader will be concerned about guardianship of the rituals, rather than personal claim to their genesis.

14. It is noteworthy that Paul Boyer's study (1992) in the cultural history of modern American prophecy belief, *When Time Shall Be No More Prophecy Belief in a Modern American Culture*, gives considerable attention to Smith (1992:14, 160, 164, 173, 189, 221-222, 249, 263-264, 269, 314-315, 317, 319, 321, 322, 332-333), and Lindsay (1992:5-7, 10, 126-132, 141, 142, 144, 145, 161-169, 188, 203, 206, 212, 220-223, 245, 251-252, 262-267, 274, 279, 290, 296, 299, 305, 328-335). This award-winning historian of American culture cites few individuals to the extent of Smith and Lindsey, in his examination of the historical influence of millennial prophecy.

15. Bob Marley, (best known for the popularization of Caribbean reggae), as a Rastafarian, "could see the end of Babylon. He saw himself as a prophet warning of impending destruction, [believing] that the end was nigh. He'd been effected by reading *The Late Great Planet Earth*" (Steve Turner 1995:139). Marley concluded it was the "last days. . . . It's the last quarter before the year 2000 and righteousness, the positive way of thinking, must win; good over evil. We're confident of victory" (1995:139). Dylan, shortly after his "born again" experience in 1979, influenced by Lindsey's book, produced two songs, *When You Gonna Wake Up* and *Slow Train Comin'*, which were of strong apocalyptic flavor.

16. T.L Frazier in his book, *A Second Look at the Second Coming. Sorting Through the Speculations* (1999) cites Smith from Smith's own publication, *Future Survival*, (1979) as saying: "From my understanding of biblical prophecies, I'm convinced that the Lord is coming for His church before the end of 1981. I could be wrong, but it's a deep conviction in my heart, and all my plans are predicated upon that belief." It is essential

that I convey to the reader, from a participant's point of view, that the atmosphere was electric and expectant among the Jesus People and especially at Calvary Chapel. Highly existential, apocalyptic hippies were open to anything that made the scriptures immediately relevant. For Smith to declare it as a "deep conviction," had a ring of high probability, or more, for the hearers. This speculative but powerfully attractive expectation was dominant in Smith's preaching. In this author's opinion, it was a very significant factor in domesticating the converted counterculture to conservative politics and mainstream, cultural conformity. An excerpt from Frazier's book on the phenomena of this speculative dating of Christ's return, "Apocalypse Now! Or Maybe Next Year," can be found in the Orthodox journal, *Again* (1999).

17. Preliminary attempts at sociological research concerning the ethical influence of rock 'n' roll music have provided mixed evidence. On the surface, most youth researched indicate that they responded emotionally to the music's sound and rhythm. Others have argued that the very fact respondents confess a lack of cognitive engagement with the ideological content of the song, is *prima facie* evidence of vulnerability to subliminal influences. Californian students on average could not recall the ideology, or meaning, of any of their favorite songs. This has been used by some sociologists to suggest that the students don't take notice of the anti-social lyrics from *Pantera, Nine Inch Nails* or Marilyn Manson. I am convinced that cultural anarchy, promoted by pop music, if not rationally assessed becomes part of the ethical framework of youth, by an unperceived subliminal process. The art form becomes the catalyst, which facilitates the chemistry of rebellion, social experimentation, and moral relativism.

18. As an Australian I am uncharacteristically influenced by the history and methodology of American revivalist culture, having been socialized in a fundamentalist context, which was connected with American revivalism. I listened to the songs with an overwhelming sense of nostalgia, although the lyrics reveal a distinct difference between my own Australian culture and the American culture. The concept of being *welcomed back* to a memory of spiritual enrichment and freedom knows no parallel in Australian history.

19. William G. McLoughlin (1978) in *Revivals, Awakenings, and Reform* has provided a useful summary of four revitalization periods of American culture that have reinforced the "manifest destiny" of the nation. It is this cyclical renewal which possibly has shaped America as "a nation with a soul of a church" (1978:40). Australia in contrast has been described as "a nation with a sunburnt soul." Erling Jorstad (1972b) in *That New Time Religion: The Jesus Revival in America*, draws some parallels between the historic patterns of American religion and the Jesus Movement, but recognizes the radical sociopolitical divergence of many Jesus people from the conservative tradition, as does James David Hunter in *American Evangelicalism: Conservative Religion and the Quandary of Modernity* (1983:46). It is significant that Australia saw many similar manifestation of the Jesus Movement, without the historical precedent of revival experienced in America.

20. The Celtic church employed the arts as a major integrated factor in both mission and ritual process, even ordaining the artist. The cognitive and the affective elements were married in a cultural form that spoke to the heart of the receptor culture. George Hunter III has recently released an excellent assessment of Celtic missiology that is pertinent to the postmodern, cultural context of mission. For further application of Celtic missiology see George G. Hunter III (2000), *The Celtic Way of Evangelism: How Christians Can Reach the West Again*. Pre-modern and postmodern ideas have been interfaced in recent time, as the postmoderns have embraced much of the pre-modern. Neo-Paganism, environmental theology, and holistic worldviews are congruent with a pre-modernity view. Some aspects of pre-modernity as interpreted by postmodernity are compatible

with the early church fathers. Charles Birch (1990), noted Australian biologist, and the first pure scientist to receive the Templeton Prize for contribution to religious and philosophical thought, has embraced the "process theology" of Whitehead and Cobb. In a passionate challenge to modernity's naïve realism (1990) he draws much postmodern argument from the Patristics.

21. Current euphoria concerning the supposed impact of new fundamentalist, apocalyptic, sub-culture movie initiatives is a case in point. The recent theater release of Omega Code, a film dramatizing premillennialist eschatological fantasies, in its first week grossed profits inside the top ten Hollywood performers. Since the movie is franchised through secular theater outlets, the producers easily assumed that this evangelical tool is being viewed extensively by non-believers. A media campaign through Trinity Broadcasting television network successfully engaged thousands of churches in mass congregational attendance's, but there is no guarantee that this too, theologically defective or otherwise, is impacting the wider community. Naive public proclamations concerning its success, and the sensationalist nature of its imagery, may be more alienating than inviting to the unchurched. The adoption of contemporary cultural symbols, even if it attracts new members to the group, does not indicate a penetration of the wider society

22. Street people visit his alternative "church for postmoderns," alongside of "session" musicians, post-yuppie seekers, and Hollywood famed personalities such as Dan Aykroyd. Sunday eve service is in a local nightclub with normal dim-lit bar facilities for the off-the-street visitor. Taylor's band performance is punctuated by open forum for poetry readings, self-revelations, and "no holds barred" responses to contemporary topics. Taylor maintains a very up-to-date knowledge of contemporary literary and arts trends. He has recorded several CDs in contemporary rock and acoustic styles.

23. The theology and methodology of the Movement arose out of differing leadership positions, local client ambiance, and diverse objectives ranging from revivalist hopes of mass conversions, to counterculture resistance to the entire, dominant, cultural matrix. Assessments of Smith's success vary, according to the analysts' worldview and perceived objectives. Certainly Calvary Chapel is a stellar representation of one of the typical forms, but they were at no stage seen by the Movement as the parent body, or the source of Jesus Movement orthodoxy. Significant indigenous leaders were later influenced by Smith, some of them joining Calvary Chapel and abandoning earlier, more radical theology and practice.

Miller (1997) and Peterson (1997) are polarized in their conclusions, but it is noticeable that Miller was not a participant in the Jesus Movement, while Peterson was. Since his unpublished analysis of Calvary Chapel (1996a), Fromm has modified his own position, being highly critical of Miller's analysis (Fromm 1999:32). The more counterculture analysts, including Sparks, Peterson, Sine, and Hirt, were all involved in the early leadership, and have tended to maintain a continuing, counterculture stance on the issues of materialism and social radicalism, associated with the more indigenous forms. Recent conversation between the author and Palosaari revealed that he is a weary, but nevertheless counterculture man, who regards the indigenous movement as communitarian, and anti-establishment, if not mildly anarchist. He bemoans the fact that the "ad-man is the prophet to this era." Peterson, academic and early participant in the Pacific Northwest movement, casts strong doubt on the authenticity of Smith's account of the Jesus Movement. My judgment would be tentatively similar. Smith was not initially involved with the earliest Jesus Movement activists, whose initiatives were lost in the more conservative church growth he rigorously shaped (Peterson 1999).

As an Australian participant I can say definitely, that the Movement in the South Pacific had absolutely no knowledge of Smith when it began. His use of systematic biblical expositions in culturally acceptable forms captivated me during my journey across America, and caused us to establish a similar highly successful Monday evening gathering. These gatherings swiftly grew to over 500 in weekly attendances.

24. Indigenous, counterculture charismatics were able to make connection with trained and experienced sympathizers with access to political, social, and physical resources. An enduring fusion of counterculture freedom and traditional moral frames resulted, as the converts were reaggregated in revitalized, but conservative, new religious movements. Richardson, Stewart, and Simmonds (1979) in Organized Miracles: A Study of a Contemporary, Youth, Communal, Fundamentalist Organization, affirm my findings concerning Calvary Chapel and many other Jesus Movement operations. "These ties with Calvary Chapel may surprise some readers who have been overly impressed with the antiestablishment rhetoric of some groups in the movement. We would suggest that all such claims be taken with a grain of salt, as our experience had led us to the conclusion that there are many ties between most segments of the movement and the "greater society," including the much-maligned 'institutional church' . . . . Other kinds of ties with society have developed over time" (James T. Richardson, Mary W. Stewart and Robert B. Simmonds 1979:38).

CHAPTER 5

The Jesus Movement Seeks the Church – Transfiguration

Stand at the crossways and look; ask for the ancient paths, ask where the good way is . . . . Walk in it, and you shall find rest for your souls. Jeremiah 6:16.

It was a relatively short geographical distance of 400 miles from Calvary Chapel in Costa Mesa, Los Angeles to the Christian World Liberation Front (CWLF) Berkeley California amidst the hip subculture of the San Francisco Bay area. But, these two were worlds apart in theology and sociopolitical leaning.

In 1973, I walked Telegraph Avenue leading onto the Berkeley campus, dressed in my motorcycle leather jacket and jeans. My hair was long, my beard substantial, and my feet were bare. A strange assortment of incongruent subcultures found common cause in the late 1960s in resistance to the system. Even bikers displayed the two finger peace sign, which designated military victory for their father's generation. With its redefinition, came a powerful sense of social "otherness," and tribal solidarity. A tiring and less idealistic rock 'n' roll culture still believed in the Age of Aquarius.

My counterculture appearance led the street people to automatically assume I would be "dealing." Every few paces someone would step out of a doorway and ask me for "dope," "scag," "acid," "speed," or "coke." The memory of the hollowness in the eyes of the addicts is unforgettable. Initially they had celebrated new freedom, and creativity through transcendental meditation, and consciousness altering drugs like acid, grass, and STP. The hollow emptiness that results from heavy abuse of psychedelics gives the onlooker the sense that "the lights are on but no one's home." Making eye contact with these burnt out hippies was like looking into the windows of an empty soul. The "earthly tabernacle" barely survived, but the creative soul had left.

One of many posters on light poles for the length of Telegraph Avenue spoke of the folly of both generations. The plaintive note said, "Dear Suzy, your mummy and daddy still love you. We are searching everywhere for you. If you can come home we will give you a Lincoln, and buy you anything you want"

(Smith and Doney 1987:218). It wasn't a Lincoln she sought in Berkeley. Many parents came to this Mecca of alternative culture, seeking their runaways who left when communication broke down with the "straights."

When I arrived for the first time at Berkeley in 1973, the hippie experiment was in its death throes. Sex, drugs, rock 'n' roll, and utopian politics served as an initial ritual process of liberation from cognitive enslavement. As a structurally alternative society, the counterculture had already failed. Its power to reconfigure values, and reshape institutions in ways that were neither desired nor expected by the straight or alternative cultures is now widely recognized 30 years later. The "boomer" generation did not generally embrace the anti-materialism or the radical politics of the counterculture minority of activists. It did shift ontologically and religiously from the didactic to the mystical, from dualism to holism, from exclusivism to inclusivism, from denominationalism to new religious movements, and from institutionalism to voluntary societies.

Failure to reckon on the savagery of mainstream resistance was frighteningly evident at the Chicago Democratic Convention of 1968. The South Carolina State (1968), Jackson State (1970) and Kent State (1970) killings of students caused some to speak of a pending generational war. Despite the loss of the original hippie euphoria there was still creativity, life, and a surviving interest in new ideas. Human nature's penchant for selfishness, excess and hypocrisy also produced many disillusioned refugees. Disillusionment, a thirst for a New World, and a culture of experimentation attracted many to the Jesus Movement.

Christian World Liberation Front (CWLF) – from Counterculture to Orthodoxy

The Jesus Freaks' belief in "the fall of man" explained failed humanism, while individual conversion provided a manageable miracle-inspiring hope, and the expectation of wider social change (Richardson *et al* 1979:18-19). In this context, CWLF provided a rescue mission and an interactive dialogue between the gospel and Berkeley sub-culture. They were relatively well known in the locality (Wuthnow 1976:34-36).

I watched CWLF founder, Jack Sparks, in action on the Berkeley campus, where he astutely expounded the early chapters of Genesis to a sizable crowd. Dressed in blue jean overalls, he peppered his presentation with localized, counterculture allusions. The casual appearance of the bearded Bible teacher standing on the steps of the Sproul Plaza, teaching from the *Letters to Street Christians* (Two Brothers from Berkeley 1971), the "hip" New Testament version, identified Sparks and his team as an "alternative," rather than part of an "establishment" movement. Openness to dialoguing the text was implied by the use of the term "rap" rather than "study." The desire for a radical alternative to the nuclear family, and the need for community was invoked by Sparks and his followers who referred to themselves as "God's Forever Family" rather than a church.

Sparks was the obvious leader of the group, but he "was no showman" (Heinz 1976a:35). Rather than chaining himself to an external icon, as the flamboyant Arthur Blessitt had done in the Sunset Strip, he carried his cross within him as "a kind of grief for the masses" (1976a:35). I was impressed. Sparks could have passed for a gentle, counterculture, fringe dweller. Although Gallagher (1999) says that, effectively, he was a benevolent dictator who made the significant decisions in general direction and day to day execution, his manner was as a servant, both winsome and open to the groups' ideas. He vigorously taught and lived the Jesus style of suffering servanthood. He won his position of authority by energy, commitment and charisma. Even the groups' Jesus paper, *Right On,* initially owed its energetic direction and its content primarily to him.

It was difficult to ascertain the level of structured program. Time was not of the essence and little fixed structure of operations was apparent. Recent conversations with Sharon Gallagher, an early staffer, confirmed what I felt during my initial experience of the Berkeley group. There seemed to be a constantly changing agenda of activities that ranged from infiltrating a peace march to ministering one on one to the increasing number of homeless or disoriented itinerants. The community houses exhibited a certain solidarity with the human concerns of their non-Christian counterparts, along with an intense desire to "make Christ known" in Berkeley (1976a:9).

The CWLF represented a fusion of the best of a thoughtful evangelical tradition, with a radical counterculture perspective on the state of Western culture. Fundamentalist enthusiasm, generic to Jesus Movement in the Pacific Northwest and in Southern California was balanced by a keen sense of enquiry into the meaning of the localized, and global, social ferment. The meaning of Jesus' life was related to the human context.

Lamin Sanneh (1989) describes three alternate positions the church maintains in its relationship to the non-Christian world around it. The elements of quarantine or separation from the world by an alternative holy community; syncretism or contextualization within the culture of the indigenous group; and thirdly, prophetic confrontation with the cultures' evils are all found in historic religions (1989:39-41).[1] Most groups tend to opt for one of the three at any given time. The CWLF expressed elements of all three positions concurrently and provided sanctuary as an alternative community that was inclusive, and open to the hippies or the churches. The more counterculture aspects of their literature and lifestyle often offended traditional Christians. Yet CWLF critiqued the host counterculture too.

The Berkeley Context

The San Francisco Bay Area has a tradition of radicalism dating back to the appointment of a socialist mayor in 1911 (Glock and Bellah 1976:78), but it was the "Free Speech Movement in the Fall of 1964 that put Berkeley on the political map. It set off a chain of explosions that would affect every major American university by the end of the decade" (1976:78). Bellah links that movement to the Civil Rights Movement, and to the diffusion of counterculture messages which such singers as Joan Baez effectively spread amongst the youth culture. It was in the Haight-Ashbury district of San Francisco, and in Berkeley, that lifestyle experimentation, political confrontation, and spiritual eclecticism were most evident and most concentrated. The nation's attention, whether positive or negative, left wing or right wing, was fixed for a period on the activities of this small geographical area. If the Christian message was to gain credibility on American campuses, Berkeley was surely the right place to set up house.

Glock and Bellah are clear that that the most significant aspects of youth ferment in this area were spiritual rather than political (Glock and Bellah 1976:xiii). If the "abiding impact of the counterculture is most visible in the movements that are essentially countercultural themselves" (1976:xiii), the CWLF was a movement contextualizing itself appropriately in this new religious consciousness. The spiritual values behind the sociopolitical forms were as significant as the political agitation and the social experiment.

The Return of Jesus to the Public Stage

The history of CWLF rises and falls with the religious and political consciousness of the San Francisco Bay area, and the Berkeley Campus of the University of California. The precursor to CWLF was Bill Bright's Campus Crusade for Christ (Campus Crusade) and its attempt to evangelize the campus. Ray Nethery, once Vice-President of Campus Crusade, an early participant in the crusade experiment, had moved into mainstream campus ministries (Nethery 1999). Nethery recruited some of the key people for campus ministry from as far afield as UCLA and Wheaton College, Illinois. They soon radicalized the ministry, opening the doors for the formation of CWLF.

> The organization was just a couple of years old, so I went to UCLA, which was [Bill Bright's] home base and he was just launching out at that point of time, so we did the work at UCLA . . . . I took Josh McDowell when he was a [Wheaton] student out on some evangelistic endeavors . . . . Pete Gillquist came to Christ through a fraternity meeting at the University of Minnesota. We recruited Jon Braun out of that area. (Nethery 1999:2-3)

The birth of CWLF can be traced back to Sparks, an Indiana farm boy turned academic, who became one of Bright's most trusted directors in charge of university ministries. Following marginal connection with church after entering college and the army, Sparks was "truly converted" while he was a math teacher at Lightning Community High School, Franklin Park, Chicago. Through a social visit to Bensonville Bible Church, instigated by his wife, his academic's life was radically rerouted. Sparks' intellect was critical of the fundamentalist sermon but the evidence of love and social integration in the church was remarkable. It set him about reading the Bible from cover to cover. In C.S. Lewis' style, he was confronted by the conclusion that if Christ was the Son of God, full surrender to his purposes was the only logical response.

In 1965 Sparks became a graduate professor of statistical analysis in the Penn State social science department. There he began years of ministry with Campus Crusade, ultimately as full time director. He taught Sunday school at the Christian and Missionary Alliance Church, and oversaw the local Campus Crusade group, which was the largest on the East Coast. Richard Ballew, a key associate in later years, was the Eastern Regional Director and thus became linked with Sparks at Berkeley (Sparks 1999b:3).

Initially representing Campus Crusade, Jack and Esther Sparks, Pat and Kerry Matrisciano, Fred and Jan Dyson, and Weldon and Barbara Hartenburg moved to Berkeley in 1968, throwing themselves into the fray with enthusiasm and a willingness to risk all. The initial vision to evangelize the counterculture came from Matrisciano, a straight but impulsive member, whom Bright felt needed the wisdom and middle-of-the-road balance of Sparks if the project was to work (Gallagher 1999). It was totally unexpected that mild academic Sparks would rapidly embrace a counterculture worldview and take the project far from Campus Crusade's original intention in only one year.

Revolution or Sales Pitch – A Conflict in Methodology

There was no need to rent a crowd in Berkeley; there was one available on call. Some of the edited promotional films and reports of Campus Crusade evangelical outreach were hagiographic. Reports that the crowds that were filmed while listening to a Campus Crusade speaker were indicative of a sympathetic response from the masses were dubious at best.

> Under the aegis of the campaigns slogan, "Solution: Spiritual Revolution," Crusaders carried their message to athletic teams, clubs, fraternities, and sororities, dormitories, student centers, coffee shops, and open-air meetings. Jon Braun [Campus Crusade staffer] recalled, with some amusement, addressing several thousand young people from the steps of the Sproul Hall: "The day before, they [Regents] had dismissed the chancellor of the whole system, and these kids were out there because they thought it was a demonstration against the University. They hadn't come to hear someone preach the gospel. They had relatively little choice . . . . But that is probably the worst experience I have ever had in my life in evangelism." The climax of the blitz came at the end of the week, when Billy Graham addressed a large audience at Berkeley's Greek Theater. On the surface the effort seemed a modest success . . . . The surface however was thin. According to Peter Gillquist [another Campus Crusade staffer] . . . . "We know of only two who really followed through. A second attempt at the 'blitz' strategy had similar results at UCLA." (Martin 1996:94-95)

Campus Crusade claims of major success were in contrast to several on-site staff accounts. They were distressed at the discrepancies between public relations accounts and the realities of the "blitz" at "the peak of the Berkeley cultural revolution."

> Often the claims of those who are in evangelism are far in excess of the reality. The exaggerated claims were just not true. We really appealed to Bill to pull back the video history of the claim, which was filmed, being shown in churches all over the place. It was just embarrassing to me. (Nethery 1999:3)

Gillquist and Braun felt embarrassment, not only at the inflated Campus Crusade publicity exploiting student unrest, but also at the inappropriateness of the methodology and message employed, given the counterculture nature of the Berkeley campus at the time (Martin 1996:91-95). Enthusiastic reports in *Time*

(1971) assumed Campus Crusade activities were an authentic part of the Jesus Movement, though it was listed as a "straight" element (1971:42). Who was, and who wasn't a Jesus Freak was problematic.

In February 1968, some senior Campus Crusade leaders, including several regional directors, began leaving the Crusade, mostly amicably, for a variety of reasons. Gillquist and Braun were early defectors (Gillquist 1992:18). Sparks was the most notable, defecting early 1969. This partly reflected a growing shift in strategic analysis by those who entered as "straight" missionaries, but were culturally transformed by the interchange with the counterculture. Nethery, though sympathetic to the more radical members of the group, never saw himself as countercultural, but he too concluded that the Berkeley culture required a radical contextualization in method and message, that Campus Crusade did not understand, and could not deliver. During the next five years, Campus Crusade dissenters were scattered across the nation's campuses in diverse ministries, but almost all were experimenting with house church, which became crucial in later years.

In April 1969, Sparks' family joined with close friends, Fred Dyson, and Pat Matrisciano and their wives to form the Forever Family commune in Berkeley and shortly thereafter named their organization the Christian World Liberation Front. Their entry into the Berkeley culture was a baptism of fire. Beginning their independent project on campus during a Third World Liberation Front strike, they were spat on by radicals and tear-gassed by police as they carried signs: "It takes guts to follow Jesus, the real revolutionist! Pig [police] state no, anarchy no, Jesus yes! Jesus loves the little pigs, Jesus loves the little students, Why not try Jesus!" (Heinz 1976:36).

Radical Context – Radical Contextualization

The CWLF was never a simple rescue operation like Calvary Chapel. It scarcely could be, if it was to be contextually relevant. Chuck Smith Jr. understands the contrast between Calvary Chapel and CWLF as socially driven.

> Berkeley was not a Costa Mesa social construct. I always felt that what Sparks was doing was more on the edge than we were. They were more socially involved. Part of that was Berkeley. We didn't have student riots. Berkeley is much more urban as opposed to Costa Mesa. I'm just saying that if you take a social scientist and you put it in the context of Berkeley, which is talking about conscience issues, that you are not getting the same dialogue as in Orange County. (Smith Jr. 1999:61-62)[2]

Berkeley developed a unique, eclectic, multicultural libertarianism from a population of academic dissidents, hippies, Vietnam draft dodgers, runaways, Gay Liberation Frontists, street performers, musos, political activists, and even Jesus Freaks. The relationship between the counterculture and CWLF did not occur by "accident," whereby "straight" leaders happened upon the dissenting tribes and were pragmatically drawn into relationship by them, as in Smith's case. The CWLF was an intentional, ideological departure from the start.

The Berkeley context had not only attracted students and hippies. It had attracted the Jesus People, and also some creative, forward thinking "straight" missionaries. The American Baptist Mission Society, in conjunction with the First Baptist Church, Berkeley, launched the Telegraph Avenue Project in the university city (Ford 1972). Some local churches, via support for CWLF, entered into the missionary thrust to reach the counterculture. Walnut Creek Presbyterian Church sponsored a supportive auxiliary, Friends of CWLF (Enroth, Ericson, and Peters 1972:109).

For all of its aggressive initiative in seeking to evangelize students in the Berkeley scene, Campus Crusade had been worlds away from a sympathetic understanding of the core issues which made the Sproul Plaza and Telegraph Avenue a meeting place, and a melting pot for every new idea and lifestyle. The campus was highly politicized, but as Sparks recalls, there existed something of a cross between a carnival and a revolution, a "happening" atmosphere of crazy experimentation and daily expectation.

> The very first day we walked onto the campus, which was noontime, there was a rally on campus and a bit of a riot. Berkeley was called "the noon to five revolution." They would always start with a rally on the Sproul Plaza at noon, and at five o'clock they would quit, because they had to go and watch themselves on TV at night. They'd do all these crazy things during the daytime, and [it was] all over by 5 p.m. (Sparks 1999a:4)

For Sparks, the urgent sense of call to reach the subculture of Berkeley was a dominant compulsion. Sparks' sincerity, his humility, compassion, vision, and sense of urgency were magnetic. In identifying with the hip scene, there really was a need to break all ties with the establishment style of Campus Crusade, which would have been seen clearly as the enemy by the radicals of Berkeley. For Nethery, and several associated defectors, ecclesial issues were central to his decision to leave Campus Crusade in 1968.

> Increasingly I was gaining respect for the church and felt a need to relate to the church. I didn't know quite what to do. I felt I was ruined to return to the church that I had known before Campus Crusade. Not that I didn't respect that, but I just felt I had tasted "new wine," and I could never go back. I remember reading Roland Allen's *Missionary Methods: St. Paul's or Ours* (1962)? He had a phenomenal influence on me. (Nethery 1999:6)

At Berkeley, the methods and philosophy of Campus Crusade were inappropriate, so the Sparks, Matriscianos, and Dysons, created the "alternative" CWLF (Enroth, Ericson, and Peters 1972:102-114; Glock and Bellah 1976:143; Heinz 1976b:143-161; Wuthnow 1976:34-36). CWLF was a genuinely contextual ministry by the end of 1969. In April 1969, after reconnoitering and recruiting, they targeted the radical core of the campus, adopting a Christian strategy, paralleling a campus activist group, the Third World Liberation Front (Heinz 1976a:22). They infiltrated activist meetings and demonstrations, pamphleteering the students with alternative Christian literature, written in Berkeley sociopolitical language. Outdoor preaching or "raps," street theater, and open forum debates were normal communication for the Christian radicals. Unorthodox activities included baptizing new converts in the fountain on the Berkeley mall. They did not ape the faddish aspects of the subculture, but engaged in the worldview struggle of the youth resistance at Berkeley. CWLF was not involved in a charade but came to really share some counterculture values (Martin 1996:94).

They produced Christian comics, a medical handbook, "bust cards" with bail and civil rights information on one side and Jesus on the other. They wrote a new version of the C. S. Lewis satire, "Screwtape Letters" (Lewis 1943), wherein junior devils debated events occurring in People's Park. In a march for peace in San Francisco, they distributed 100,000 leaflets, "out-saturating even the Maoists. They leafleted a conference of industrialists with warnings from the Epistle of James" (Heinz 1976a:43). They provided free drinks for weary activist marchers, dispensed medical care to the strung out, gave food and clothing to the needy, and helped support an agricultural ranch, the Rising Son, in nearby Humboldt County. Jesus communes, Agape, and Pergamos houses emphasized hospitality for the social casualties of the city, served also as respite for transients, rehabilitation for new converts, and training cells for Jesus revolutionaries. The CWLF became known as a prominent group of the Jesus People.

> While the rest of the world looks on in quiet amazement, or with raised eyebrows, the CWLF is busy going about the business of bringing men and women into "the Father's Forever Family." Our judgment is that it has an edge on the other Jesus groups, in terms of intellectual and spiritual maturity. (Enroth et al. 1972:113)

Sparks' leadership reflected a generic form of politically and socially activist faith, which was more typical of England, Australia, and Canada than America (Appendix 4). It espoused a biblically based commitment to a simpler lifestyle, solidarity with the poor, and orthopraxis rather than pure orthodoxy. It was not always understood. Sparks recounted that he had lost considerable financial support from individuals previously aligned with him in the East Coast. His revolutionary style, language, and the leftist-sounding, provocative name, "Liberation Front," cost him the trust of both leaders and friends:

> An old and dear friend from Pennsylvania called me aside this summer and said, "You're cutting yourself off from the good people of America. The way you live and your hairstyle and your dress and the kinds of activities that you're carrying on are cutting you off from the people who are the backbone of this country, and I'm no longer able to support you if you continue that." I said, "I'm sorry I have to disagree with you, but I can't support your stand and I have to continue the way I am." (Kennedy 1971:8)

Sparks believed the counterculture was failing in its bid to transform the culture, but he saw its influence as ongoing. Counterculture idealism was confronted with social realities. The independent, single student eventually had to face the challenges of life in the capitalist's cultural construct of the family.

> There have been a lot of them [radical experiments], many of which have failed; a lot continue. I think there are as many experiments today as ever. In the Christian world there are experiments in community. Mostly they succeed where there is a centering around a family. You ordinarily do not succeed where you have families having to share all their facilities all the time. You have to plan for pri-

vacy for families and you have to have a sensitivity to others' needs. (Sparks 1974a:5)

But it was not social realities that eventually terminated the CWLF. Rather it was theological considerations of the postmodern dilemma that steered most of the foundational leadership in the direction of ancient Orthodoxy. As postmodernity had deconstructed history, defining it as ideologically suspect, the Bible and the history of the church had been overshadowed by an ego-centric gospel that they implicated as central to the ecclesial and theological confusion of denominations and parachurch agencies.

Innovations in Thought and Action

Scarcely any context was more conducive than Berkeley for experimentation in ideas, innovations in sociopolitical strategy and revolutionary angles on age-old issues. Religion became a major subject for deconstruction, revision and synthesis. If Christian faith were to take root in revolutionary soil it would have to look different to the wooden growth of the establishment. If it reflected the "system," it was by definition socially oppressive, spiritually impotent, cognitively sterile and functionally bureaucratic. It was the Jesus that the radicals had never known who CWLF sought to proclaim and emulate.

Jesus as a Revolutionary Role Model

If there was one thing which distinguished the Jesus Movement, it was its determination to focus on Jesus, not on the obfuscations of rationalized doctrine, which often reflected the sociocultural norms of the time rather than the radical humanity of the Master. In Berkeley's hunt for gurus and political revolutionaries Jesus was attractive if the fingers of establishment religion could be prized off his politically betrayed body.

The pretentious and authoritarian nature of political and religious leadership was not only targeted by the counterculture, but was seen by CWLF as contrary to both the teaching and example of Jesus. Jesus became a role model for many who had no time for formal Christianity. Jesus, however much the church mismanaged him, seemed a viable person to lead a revolution. Sparks claimed that Jesus, like Gandhi, carried a mystique of resistance to the establishment, and of communal service among his followers.

> When his disciples were arguing about who was going to be the first among them and what position they were going to occupy in the kingdom, he said: "Look, I've been a servant amongst you." It was apparent that he had been caring for them and serving them in every way. So he says, "I am a servant amongst you and the greatest amongst you shall be the servant of all." At the last meal he had with them, Jesus symbolically washed their feet, again displaying the meaning of leadership. The great Apostle Paul . . . didn't go about looking for people to serve him. He took care of the people who traveled with him; he even worked with his hands to support the people who traveled with him. I think it's pretty clear that the leader serves and cares for [others], rather than expecting people to serve him [or her]. That is the leader in God's calling. (Sparks 1974a:5)

Figure. 5.1 Wanted poster – A Hippie Jesus (Sparks 1971b:11)

ALIAS: THE MESSIAH, SON OF GOD, KING OF KINGS, LORD OF LORDS, PRINCE OF PEACE, ETC.

★ Notorious Leader of an underground liberation movement

★ Wanted for the following charges:

— Practicing medicine, wine-making and food distribution without a license.

— Interfering with businessmen in the Temple.

— Associating with known criminals, radicals, subversives, prostitutes, and street people.

— Claiming to have the authority to make people into God's children.

★ APPEARANCE: Typical hippie type — long hair, beard, robe, sandals, etc.

★ Hangs around slum areas, few rich friends, often sneaks out into the desert.

★ Has a group of disreputable followers, formerly known as "apostles," now called "freemen" (from his saying: "You will know the truth and the Truth will set you free.")

BEWARE — This man is extremely dangerous. His insidiously inflammatory message is particularly dangerous to young people who haven't been taught to ignore him yet. He changes men and claims to set them free.

WARNING: HE IS STILL AT LARGE!

Wanted Poster – The Jesus Outlaw Profile (Sparks 1971b:12)

The CWLF created a "wanted" poster (Figures 5.1, 5.2) displaying Jesus as a long haired radical threatening straight society (Sparks 1971b:10-11). Jesus was many things to many people. One of the early 1970s Jesus albums featured a song entitled *Everybody's* Dressin' Up Jesus. Jesus Movement troubadour, Larry Norman, popularized a folk song, *Outlaw* (1972), which described Jesus as an outlaw leader of "unschooled ruffians," a radical champion of the people, performing poet, miracle worker, and Son of God.

Some analysts missed the purpose of this social movement. Heinz recognizes the focus was Jesus and "making him an issue" (1976a:269-439). To those disoriented by the proliferation of ideologies, Jesus became the "one way" out of both traditionalism, and the new fragmentation. A kaleidoscope of alternative Jesus figures attracted CWLF followers (1976b:149-157). For some, Heinz says, Jesus provided an authentic, alternative lifestyle. For some others, he was a light in the gathering gloom. Many young people saw Jesus as "a love alternative to the hate tripping" of society and politics. For Pedro, Jesus was an anchor ending "pointless wanderings." Jesus was a friend, or a believable social critic. In an experience-centered culture, ecstatic connection with Jesus was the ultimate trip. The strongest image of Jesus, provided by CWLF, was the Jesus who identifies with each one of us, whatever our culture, and whatever our circumstances.

The Gospel According to Berkeley

At the same time as CWLF experimented with alternative lifestyle, it aggressively sought to provide a statement of their gospel in the common vernacular of the sub-culture. CWLF did this by language that was offensive to regular evangelicals but extremely inviting to the counterculture. This adaptation to "Berkeleyese" street language is admirably illustrated in *Letters to Street Christians from Two Brothers in Berkeley* (Two Brothers in Berkeley 1971), a hip version of portions of the New Testament. For an outsider, Berkeleyese ("this world's evil system," "ego-tripping," "vibes," "balling" and "uptight") appeared faddish, inconsequential, and unnecessarily alienating.[3]

These terms were laden with contemporary existential meaning. The fact that it was incomprehensible to "straights" provided a linguistic ritual process whereby counterculture people invited alienation. This reinforced their rejection of the immoral, dehumanizing, dysfunctional, dominant culture of materialism, rationalism, and reductionism. A heightened feeling of glad marginality was felt when employing counterculture language. It created a sense of liminality and alternative creativity. It was not only the words, but also the intimate, folksy, rearrangement of standard words which created an alternative sense of identity. Phrases which were distinctly counterculture in the 1960s, – "cool," "hey man," and "hassle" – have long ago been incorporated into middle class language, particularly in the youth culture, but the countercultural nuance fades with incorporation into popular culture.

Mimicry – Counterculture Tools for Redemptive Purposes

Manifestos were a favorite with left wing students. So Sparks and the CWLF team distributed a manifesto of their own titled *The New Berkeley Liberation*

Program (Appendix 6b) which paralleled the manifesto of the *Third World Liberation Front* (Appendix 6a). Jesus alone could lead the "people of Berkeley, [who] passionately desire personal fulfillment, vital interpersonal relationships, and inner peace." The quest of the student movements would find resolution only if spiritual unity in Jesus was the foundation. CWLF's purpose was told in the first edition of *Right On* (Gallagher 1979b).

> Berkeley can become a revolutionary example throughout the world. We are now under severe attack by the demons of despair, hedonism, and chauvinism. We are being strangled by disruptive and reactionary powers from here to hell.
>
> Our survival depends on our ability to overcome past inadequacies, and to introduce people to a revolutionary program. Jesus Christ will then build a Movement which is both personally humane, and politically sound.
>
> He will enable the people of Berkeley to achieve personal fulfillment; develop compatibility and understanding among groups; and transcend their stifling, ego-centered lifestyles. With him as our leader and liberator we shall resist the devil and his demons, establishing a liberated community in which together we find that he abundantly fills our material and spiritual needs. Under his guidance we will be enabled to develop new forms of democratic participation and new, more godly styles of work and play. In solidarity with others who know Christ, we will permanently challenge the present world system and act as a training center for the liberation of all people on this planet. (Gallagher 1979b:4)

Through the New Berkeley Liberation Program, CWLF pleaded with their non-Christian, radical counterparts to recognize that while CWLF stood in solidarity with them in opposition to the mainframe political culture, the secular alternatives provided neither the power nor the vision for a transformed society:

> Sisters and brothers, unite with Jesus, assist and create, build a revolutionary Berkeley, with your friends, your Lord, your God, form liberation committees, carry out the program, choose the action and do it, set examples and spread the Word. We call for sisters and brothers to form liberation committees to implement his program. Power through the Spirit. All Power through Jesus. (Heinz 1976a:44)

The tone of the document was revolutionary, but the content was weighted towards conservative, evangelical tradition, with an emphasis on personal salvation.

Rediscovering the Mind – the L'Abri Connection

The use of pagan writers to make a contextualized Christian point was not new to Christian tradition, perhaps finding its inspiration first in St. Paul's employment of a love poem to Zeus (Acts 17:27-28; Richardson 1984). But for popular evangelical and Pentecostal culture, the early church model of donning the philosopher's garb was uncommon in the 1950s and early 1960s. Some evangelicals were frustrated that evangelicalism had not provided the tools for engaging in dialogue with the philosophical worldview shift of the dissenting college and graduate culture. American author, Francis Schaeffer opened the cognitive prison door and legitimized the use of modernity reason at the level of popular and graduate apologetics. Schaeffer had no influence on some Jesus Movement groups, but in the network of more radical student and cell church movements, his influence was critical in the early stages of engagement with the counterculture.

A relationship between the counterculture pilgrims and Francis Schaeffer's Swiss educational commune at L'Abri was foundational to his meteoric rise to prominence in some Jesus Movement circles. Englishman Os Guinness and Dutch academic Hans Rookmaker, an Amsterdam Free University Ph.D. in Art and Philosophy, were among the L'Abri mentors. A constant flow of itinerants passed through L'Abri, Switzerland, returning from Katmandu, Amsterdam, and Delhi. They provoked interaction between Schaeffer's conservative evangelicalism and Eastern monism.[4] In the early 1970s, a vigorous discussion surrounded Schaeffer's attack against Transcendental Meditation. He warned the experimental generation that meditation without cognitive content was dangerous; believing it exposed the human mind to spiritual influences which could lead to demonic or psychic distortions. Zen exercises, increasingly popular amongst students, were thus categorized as anti-Christian. Not all Jesus Freaks agreed.

Many Jesus Freaks give testimony to the formative influence of Schaeffer's associates Udo Middleman (audio teaching tapes), (Hans Rookmaaker 1968, 1970, 1971, 1978; Os Guinness 1973, 1994) through books and a voluminous library of audio tapes from L'Abri centers in England, Switzerland and Holland. The L'Abri model of hospitality and a rigorous "guru" and student dialogue provided a pedagogy that was adapted by CWLF, Grace Haven Farm, Mansfield, Ohio, and Xenos, Columbus, Ohio.

> [I thought] we could reproduce L'Abri here [Grace Haven Farm]. I tried that and we did a lot of things before we knew about L'Abri. One of the things that attracted us to it was one of the kids who came drifting through our home asked if we had ever been to L'Abri. I brought it [a book about L'Abri] home and my wife and I read it and said "Good grief, we are doing a lot of these things they're doing even to the fact that our children were basically the same age as Dr. Schaeffer's." (Gordon Walker 1999:11)

In Ohio, Xenos' leaders and Grace Haven Farm drew theological strength from Schaeffer (McCallum 1999a; Nethery 1999; Sparks 1999; Walker 1999). Schaeffer's influence was evident to me through long term relationship with several groups that were affected.[5] Following a visit to Schaeffer's Swiss L'Abri community, Sparks began to "talk of instituting a Christian Counter University to challenge the secular academy" (Enroth, Ericson and Peters (1972:111).[6]

Several Movement leaders – Dennis McCallum, Greg Leffel, Gary DeLashmutt – and some CWLF members also studied at the Jesus Christ Light and Power House, Los Angeles, which began as an alternative academy under the leadership of Hal Lindsey.

> I worked for two years in LA at Light and Power House. That evolved during the period of time I was there. Sparks and Hal Lindsey were part of that. The three of us were instrumental in the founding. It was to bring the presence of teaching and ministry to UCLA and the greater LA area. We'd have a Tuesday night meeting and have a couple of hundred kids in for a talk. There were a lot of Bible studies

that went on which evolved into the Light and Power House to which Gary and Dennis [current leaders of Xenos] went after college. (Nethery 1999:8)

Hal Lindsay's moral behavior and sudden shift to conspicuous consumption following his success with his best seller *The Late Great Planet Earth* (1970) led to disarray.

Underground Literature for the Underground Dissenters

Within three months of launching the CWLF in early 1969, *Right On*, the first Jesus paper, hit the streets to promote dialogue, announce the ubiquitous presence of Jesus, offer succor to the needy, and challenge faiths and lifestyles. A comment attributed to Schaeffer at the beginning of the 1970s was circulating in the underground to the effect that the CWLF was the most creative, contemporary experiment in Christian community and mission, particularly in its *Right On* venture. Upon reading this comment, and reflecting on articles from *Right On*, I added Berkeley in my 1973 American itinerary. I was encouraged to visit the United States by Radical discipleship contacts in the United Kingdom , Jim Punton, and Michael Eastman of Frontier Youth Trust.

This was followed by a highly successful tour of Australia in September and October 1973 by Michael Eastman from United Kingdom and Sparks, from CWLF. Sparks was particularly outstanding when he addressed students and faculty on the radically oriented Monash University.[7] A description of the CWLF and Sparks' role in it, was published in our Australian Jesus paper *Truth and Liberation* (Smith 1973a:10) on the eve of his arrival for our Jesus Family Teach-in.[8]

Right On magazine provided the most contextualized, astute, serious engagement of the evangelical mind with popular culture and the dissenting campus culture. Here was a depth of theological and cultural engagement that was not so evident in most of the other Jesus papers (Figure 5.3). It critiqued contemporary movies, literature, and even the economy of the nation (Heinz 1976a:295). It espoused "the establishment of alternative lifestyles which are based on a new concept of community, and human relationships" (1976a:296).

Being less fundamentalist than many Movement groups, CWLF had developed a revolutionary image. It was this alternative evangelicalism of *Right On* which gained the attention of Heinz (1976a) while working on a sociology project with Robert Bellah and Charles Glock in the Department of Sociology at the Berkeley campus.[9] His research indicated that this "prominent new religious Movement [was] not indebted to the east" (1976a:3). It was a revival of "evangelical Protestantism in the youth culture of the late 1960s, [which] was an advent no social commentators had predicted" (1976a:3). From the street paper *Right On,* the flyers, and from anecdotal data, he presumed they were "not anti-intellectual, did not have flamboyant leadership, and did not take a hard-line fundamentalist approach to evangelism." He was impressed by CWLF's innovative newspaper, the Movement's "intercultural coloration, and its critical attitude towards the American way of life" (Heinz 1976a:3, cf Fig. 5.1).

value of your money is dropping fast, yet it will stand as evidence against you, and eat your flesh like fire. James 5
articles on this page with gratitude from Right On Magazine (C.W.L.F.)

Figure 5.3 An Apocalyptic Critique of Materialism (*Right On* 1974)

Being less fundamentalist than many Movement groups, CWLF developed a revolutionary image. It was this alternative evangelicalism of *Right On* which gained the attention of Heinz (1976a) while working on a sociology project with Robert Bellah and Charles Glock in the Department of Sociology at the Berkeley campus.[9] His research indicated that this "prominent new religious Movement [was] not indebted to the east" (1976a:3). It was a revival of "evangelical Protestantism in the youth culture of the late 1960s, [which] was an advent no social commentators had predicted" (1976a:3). From the street paper *Right On*, the flyers, and from anecdotal data, he presumed they were "not anti-intellectual, did not have flamboyant leadership, and did not take a hard-line fundamentalist approach to evangelism." He was impressed by CWLF's innovative newspaper, the Movement's "intercultural coloration, and its critical attitude towards the American way of life" (Heinz 1976a:3, cf Fig. 5.1).

Right On critically reviewed Jesus music and a wide range of books including *The Study of Suicide* by Alvarez, works by French intellectual Jacques Ellul, R.D. Laing, and a diversity of other authors. *Clockwork Orange, Godspel,*

Slaughter House Five, Crime and Punishment, Bergman's *Cries and Whispers*, and *Brother Sun, Sister Moon*, were some of the significant movies and plays which came under sophisticated critique. In October 1972, *Right On* commenced a regular column entitled "The Radical Christian." This column recognized a need for something beyond the New Left and the Jesus Movement fundamentalism. It accused elements of the Movement of being "anti-intellectual and anti-cultural." *Right On* "believed the Jesus Movement had 'failed' to carry out the implications of being disciples of the Lord of the Universe" (1976a:296). Some of our Australian groups subscribed to *Right On*. We published its best contributions in *Truth and Liberation,* and ran a regular *Christians'* column, serializing their "Berkeleyese" New Testament, *Letters to Street Christians.*

CWLF published literature investigating new religious movements. A careful analysis of exorcism, *Exorcism: How God Counteracts Evil Spirits and Powers* (Sparks 1973) was produced to coincide with the theater release of *The Exorcist*. CWLF gave us permission to print and distribute it in Australian theaters, which we did to great effect.

Pagan Vessels Containing Christian Meanings

A drama and oral interpretation major, Frank, whose family name I have been unable to obtain, having experienced Radical Theater in New York, established a creative tradition in parallel to secular drama on campus. Having met him in the activist days of the movement I was frustrated to find that even Heinz in his comprehensive dissertation on the early days provided no family name or personal details of Frank. Frank saw the secular theater as "a theater of images, which was not serious. It was a rip off. It was obscene, but it was street theater in style" (Heinz 1976a:314). Sparks' long-term dream of street theater became a CWLF feature.

As the early Celts, CWLF was taking the pagan forms and sanctifying them with new meaning, and new purpose. Inclusivism, hospitality, and servant-leadership, became an "alternative" statement in observable form. Communal living was a shared vision of the Christian and non-Christian alike in Berkeley. Sparks believed in examining all lifestyles that are commonly assumed to be right:

> [We need] the hard look to see whether or not it is truly satisfying, truly fulfilling and correct – the kind of life in which one gets a career, goes up the ladder. What we must come to is an examination of whether or not the basis for all that is true, whether or not this is what a Christian ought to be doing. So along with the counterculture groups, I think Christians should be examining the basis for that kind of life.
>
> We at Berkeley have ended up saying we can't buy the old way of ordering our life and we can't buy the counterculture way of ordering our lives. As Christians we simply have to build our lives based upon faith in God, trusting Him to lead us day by day, expecting that at any time along the way He could change the direction of our lives. (Sparks 1974a:2-4)

Central to their mission as followers of Jesus, they discerned elements of incongruity in the counterculture, while simultaneously finding common grounds for co-operation. Sparks recognized risk, but also opportunity:

> The counterculture has failed, that's true, but it has made an impact upon the establishment culture and will continue to do so. This is because it is far from dead. More and more of it is impacting the establishment culture. We as Christians need to build for ourselves, cultures that take on the characteristics of the surrounding culture . . . .We need [also] to pick up specific elements that distinguish us as God's people. (1974a:5)

A Third Way

Despite its Evangelicalism, the focus of CWLF was more than soteriological, as one would expect with a sociologist navigating amidst a counterculture clientele. Di Sabatino (1994) lists CWLF in his taxonomy as a part of the "Jesus People Intelligentsia" (1994:72-74), and challenges the critics' focus on "the emotionally-based, anti-intellectual postures of the majority of the hippie Christians" (1994:72). The Berkeley subcultures were alternative rather than anti-intellectual; Eastern rather than Western; holistic rather than dualistic; relational rather than rationalistic; communal rather than individualist, and spiritual rather than materialistic. This was grounds for authentic Christian dialogue.

During the 1960s threatened "melt down" of Western culture, all previous labels became problematic. Most commentators loosely use the term "fundamentalist" as descriptive of all aspects of the Jesus Movement. The Toronto Institute of Christian Studies unjustifiably referred to Sparks and the CWLF as fundamentalist (Kennedy 1971:7-9). Historic fundamentalism is regressive rather than contextualized, drawing its energy not from a desire to be relevant, but rather to be resistant to changing cultural forces. The counterculture demanded change, not retrogression. CWLF was an evolving movement in an alien culture that it served, loved, and analyzed, along the way to a search for an adequate understanding of community, and ultimately of the church.

Where Calvary Chapel failed to impact the non-traditional elements of the campus (Heinz 1976a:34), CWLF had moved in to live in the culture of dissident protest. While most "straight" ministries viewed the counterculture as a sickness to be healed, the CWLF viewed it as evidence of a "massive erosion of the legitimacy of the American way of life, and a crisis of meaning" (1976a:1). The Berkeley culture's "proliferation of experimental alternatives in dress, living arrangements, politics, and religion," (1976a:1) were viewed as creative, but the counterculture was also recognized as fatally flawed. CWLF affirmed the rejection of the existing order, but also critiqued Berkeley's counterculture which was already proving to be an alternative disaster.

Os Guinness (1973) proposed that against the background of the left and the right of the contemporary political ferment, believers should be a "third race" (Guinness 1994:359-67), and provide an alternative "third way."[10] The ancient *Letter to Diognetes,* circa A.D.150, is worth recalling, as a description of early believers through pagan eyes. It was a much-quoted source of self-identification for the more radical Jesus Freaks.

> The Christians are distinguished from other men neither by country, nor language, nor the customs which they observe. For they neither inhabit cities of their own, nor employ a peculiar form of speech, nor lead a life which is marked out by any singularity . . . .They dwell in their own countries, but simply as sojourners. As citizens, they share in all things with others, and yet endure things as if foreigners. Every foreign land is to them as their native country, and every land of their birth as a land of strangers . . . .They are in the flesh, but they do not live after the flesh. They pass their days on earth, but they are citizens of heaven. They obey the prescribed laws, and at the same time surpass the laws by their lives. They love all men, and are persecuted by all . . . .They are poor, yet make many rich . . . .To sum up all in one word – what the soul is in the body, that are Christians in the world. (Roberts and Donaldson 1867:307-8)

This was not a time of careful, systematic, or tidy thinking. Eclecticism marked believer and nonbeliever alike. Thus Os Guinness, when introducing his chapter on *The Third Race,* (1994:359-367) used the preceding quote from the second century, then followed it by brief entries from the cult mystic Alan Watts, the post Christian existentialist, Albert Camus, and from St. Paul's *Letter to the Corinthians*. An eclectic montage of arts and ideas, ancient and modern, stimulated young activists to confront what had been defined as "the system." In this context CWLF was in search of an alternative evangelicalism.

If the counterculture was defective, the dominant culture was equally unacceptable. The "the third way" (Guinness 1973) was increasingly popular amongst Australian and European Jesus Movements, justifying the radical discipleship claim that the cultural resistance of the Jesus Movement was an authentic counterculture. Christianity's "alternative" status was basically eclipsed by humanism in the twentieth century, but it had been initially countercultural.

> The present erosion of the Christian influence on Western culture brings us close to the removal of the last restraining influences of the Reformation. The striptease of humanism is simply the logic of the Renaissance held in check by the Reformation for four centuries, but now exposed in all the extremes of its consequences. If the struggle of the last 25 years presupposes the tensions and questions of the preceding centuries, it is little wonder that the counterculture is not equal to the task. The Christian faith had a capacity once before to produce a successful counterculture. (Guinness1973:367)

The secular counterculture was a religious movement, but having resisted the "sickness" of the "straight" society, it fell ill itself. It expired far sooner than the popular prognosis had indicated. "The striptease of humanism" (Guinness 1994:17-52) had led the idealistic refugees to a "counterfeit eternity" (1994:237) and an attempted "exit" to Eastern monism (1994:195-232).

Democracy and sensual-liberation were insufficient foundation for restructuring Western culture. The Jesus Movement believed only "one way" was available to transcend the old and new politics. The simplistic belief that Jesus was the "one way" was associated with the sign of the index finger pointed to heaven, but for the radicals, one vital question remained. What do we do about earth? How does the heavenly kingdom manifest itself through the redemptive, serving community on earth? With great difficulty, but with an existential leap of Christian faith and love, we could transcend where rationalism could only sit in modernity's "dust of death" (Guinness 1973).

> It is the hour of the Third Race once again . . . .As Bertrand Russell remarked in one of his more tolerant moods, "The Christian principle, 'Love your enemies [as yourselves]' is good. . . .There is nothing to be said against it except it is too difficult for us to practice precisely." But his emphasis was not strong enough. The Christian life is not difficult; it is impossible. But it is exactly here that humanism leaves off and the Christian life begins.

> That is also why this uniquely "impossible" faith – with a God who is, with an incarnation that is earthy and historical, with a salvation that is at cross-purposes with human nature, with a resurrection that blasts apart the finality of death – is able to provide an alternative to the sifting, settling dust of death, and through a new birth open the way to new life. (Guinness 1973:367)

Belief in a "third way," rejecting the sterility of enlightenment modernity, and the fragmentation of post-modernity, eventually led most of the CWLF leadership back to pre-modern Eastern Orthodoxy.

The Jesus Movement revived the popularity of experiential conversion, addressing the search for transcendence and existential enlightenment. Spiritual conversion, in the explosive and expressive form common to the Jesus Freaks, challenged the loss of the individual's identity, as implied in the Hindu and Buddhist faith, particularly Zen, which attracted many counterculture seekers (Wuthnow 1976, 1978). Transcendental Meditation and other new mysticisms led many from political activism to an internalized, spiritual quest. The more radical element of the Jesus Movement fixed on Christ's incarnational life in a world of real injustice, false religion, and sociopolitical brutality. Being Jesus Freaks implied discipleship, through which the Kingdom of God was embraced, in defiance of structural evil and oppression.

The establishment penchant for judging human beings according to the color of their skin, or external fashions and behavior were targeted by Christian and non-Christian dissenters alike. In the early 1970s the majority of churches were unsympathetic, even hostile toward long-haired males, beards, rock 'n' roll, and blue jeans in the sanctuary. In the mid-1970s the issue of rock 'n' roll music was still vexing. Sparks experienced officialdom's rejection of his unorthodox lifestyle, appearance, and methodology, but he believed any expression that did not violate biblical principle could be used to facilitate the communication of the gospel. He let his hair grow to match an impressive beard. Sparks' response to critics remained firm in defense of contextualization, but he was always gracious to detractors:

> Well I'd talk to them about the distinction between culture and Christianity and I'd really try to communicate a mutual concern. If it's impossible to get through on that level then there is not much I can do and I just go the way God has called me; praying for and loving the brothers and sisters who disagree. (Sparks 1974a:5)

CWLF Evolution of Leadership and Structure

At first appearances the evolution from hippie communalism to authoritarian, sacerdotal orthodoxy which engulfed the senior leadership of CWLF would appear bizarre. Suffering, humble, almost self-denying servitude to the street people of Berkeley had marked Sparks' leadership style. Even his ragged working class clothing bespoke downward mobility rather than academic professionalism. But of course that was radical, Berkeley, intellectual, protest language anyway. The story that follows makes perfect sense as one of several possible responses to the ravages of postmodern deconstructed authority, with its uncertainty, excessive vulnerability and philosophical homelessness.

A Jesus Movement Takes the Long Road Home

Dissatisfied yet creative evangelicals were drawn into the hippie movement as "culture brokers" and "culture advocates" (Van Willigen 1993:109-137). The political activists and alternative subcultures could thus embrace Christianity within the counterculture. The Free Speech movement in Berkeley, and its related ideological commitment to extreme democratization, certainly took its toll on some radical Jesus Movement people, who saw the "priesthood of all believers" and prominent charismatic leadership as incompatible. The cult of the charismatic proclaimer came under increasing attack, almost to the point of mild paranoia. By the mid 1970s some groups had become casualties at the hands of charismatic authoritarians, who evaded communal solidarity by invoking apostolic and prophetic authority. Some leaders, more amenable to collegial and democratic input, were battle worn casualties of social forces not unlike the anarchy and factionalism that plagued the student New Left.

In mainstream America, radical individualism was dominant, and the CWLF mood had been towards the need for community and mutual accountability. The lack of traditional structures to discipline the charismatic energy exposed the weaknesses of their ecclesial models. Nethery, Sparks, Walker, and Gillquist all tell of very early concern over the issue of the "true" church, and the basis of communal authority, well before the rebel breakaway of CWLF.

> December 1965 Christmas vacation, we had a Crusade Conference in Washington DC and Jon Braun, Richard Ballew and I started talking about something really critical. We knew that the name of the game was church and it really came home to us that what Christ had started on this earth was a church and church was where it was. We had to find that Campus Crusade would not in the long run fill the bill, unless Campus Crusade became church. . . .
>
> Campus Crusade was not about to become a church. [Bill Bright] was the leader of Campus Crusade which was bringing people to Christ, which was serving the church. Jon Braun was then the campus coordinator for Campus Crusade. Ray Nethery was a Campus Crusade leader and International Leader and Gordon Walker was the African Director and Midwest Director. (Sparks 1999b:3)

"The Truth (Church) Is Out There" – The Search for an Ecclesiology

Revivals and revitalizations of religion are often marked by an intense desire to "get back" to the true church described in the book of Acts. For some elements of the Jesus Movement, especially the CWLF, this became a consuming passion. Xenos, Columbus, Ohio, through its connection with The Jesus Christ Light and Power House in California, and Grace Haven were involved in consultation and conferencing with the CWLF. Both groups had fleeting connections with fringe groups associated with Watchman Nee, Chinese innovator, and his house church theories.

> There was a lot of theorizing on the early church. The ideology of having a primitive style of church based in houses, led by lay people propagating itself through evangelism and personal discipleship . . . was pretty widespread. We were . . . developing an apologetic that related to a lot of the issues going on in the counterculture. We were more or less adapting the idea of thirst for real love, and the idea of community, to the idea that the Bible is the true source of these things, and that biblical Christianity was the ultimate, radical message. That really was what the counterculture was thirsting for, although they didn't know it.
>
> We never laid a plan to plant a certain type of church. It was always a matter for us to react to opportunities that came up, but we did have a general theology that is very similar to what I believe today in the area of ecclesiology; that there was no reason for Christians in our day [not to] experience the vitality we see in the book of Acts. (McCallum 1999a:5)

The Jesus Movement's interest in the revival of the original model of the church was widespread, from America to Australia, from CWLF in Berkeley to Grace Haven Farm in Ohio. Xenos moved away from the Orthodox model but established a vigorous and highly successful ministry through house churches.

Communalism as an Interim Journey

God's Forever Family (Sparks 1974b), a history of the Berkeley movement, showed why it adopted the concept of a communal and organic view of the church. It began to link the communal search to Orthodoxy, stressing the historic continuity and solidarity of the Christian church from the first century until now. It was a link between contextualized Berkeley Movement and what Sparks and others came to believe was the "historic mother church" (Sparks 1999b).

There was no direct relationship with the traditional structures apart from minority support by some local congregations, so the Movement faced a crisis of care for the numerous converts, many of whom either could not, or would not enter "straight" congregations, even if invited. The traditional church had little understanding of the sub-culture and was in "maintenance" rather than "mission" mode. The Jesus Movement had abandoned all to invade pagan space with the gospel. CWLF was asking what it should do with untutored new believers. There seemed to be no contemporary model of sheep-fold for the new Jesus followers. The parachurch model of discipleship was primarily a functionalist, evangelistic training program. It seemed a far cry from the biblical model. Discipleship was a reorientation of life to follow Jesus' lifestyle. This had more in common with the counterculture's aspirations than formal Christendom.

The communal life of CWLF was not simply a pragmatic response to the casualties of the dissident culture, as the Calvary Chapel communes had been. Nor was it an attempt to restructure the existing church for mission as The Church of the Redeemer, Houston, Texas had done. For CWLF, community was a part of a journey in the direction of ancient church, a respite along the way from Cultural Revolution to a radical transfiguration of ecclesiological forms. Training was not the primary issue. Nurturing and enfolding a new cultural group in a historically valid, sustainable form of church was now paramount. CWLF was the bridge between the group's rejection of fundamentalism and individualism and their embracing of ancient Eastern Orthodoxy (Martin 1996).

> Instead of trying to revise their approach and sales pitch, they began to study the book of Acts, where they rediscovered the importance not just of evangelism, but of the church. "We called ourselves an arm of the church," Gillquist observed, "but we were amputated. We had no real connection to it." We said, "We've got to be church. We can't go out and be hit men for Christ, with no sense of follow-through or permanence or historicity." (Martin 1996:95-96)

Not Church Growth but Church Authentication

The problem was not church planting or church growth but church authentication. Smith had started a new one. Sparks wanted to find the original one and embrace it.

> We were really deeply concerned about one thing – church, and where the people had been in the very center of where the church had been over the centuries, and that sent us back to the beginning . . . .We studied liturgy from the beginning, [particularly] the seven ecumenical letters which were the counsels the whole church had participated in, and we studied the theology of the history [of the church]. (Sparks 1999a:45)

Ray Nethery had Plymouth Brethren roots. Sparks had belonged to several confessions including Methodist and Christian and Missionary Alliance. Walker and Gillquist were Southern Baptists. Despite this diversity, they held in common a passion to make Christ known to the student world, and a growing conviction they must lead the converts into an authentic community of faith.

> Braun and Ballew both resigned over the question of church. I went to Berkeley to start a fellowship of believers; a true Christian community within the context of the street scene and the student scene . . . . and the radical scene in Berkeley, which was volatile at this stage. As you know, at Berkeley we collected an odd assortment of people. We tried three different ways to start church with our group in Berkeley. I mean we were really trying to start church. We started out with our group, which was always meeting on Monday nights. In addition to that we started meeting on Sundays . . . so we started what was a Redeemer King Church in Berkeley. (Nethery 1999:4)

For Sparks, Braun, and Ballew the issue of church was compelling from the mid- 1960s. By 1973 it was an all-consuming focus.

> By 1973 we were back meeting together. Braun, Ballew and Sparks were meeting together every week in King City. I would drive down from Berkeley and up from Goleta and meet in King City and talk theology and ask what was it like in the early church? How did it continue? What were the marks of the early church? Very shortly we were meeting with Walker, Nethery and Berven . . . .We were working out what we were to do and how we would get our understanding of the church. (Gilquist 1999:5)

What began as an investigation of the early church in the Acts of the Apostles soon led to problems of hermeneutics. How could one interpret the meaning of ecclesial forms in Acts without the distortions of modern denominational loyalties? They sought the insights of the Patristics.

> In 1973 we started studying together – five of us – Fr. Jack, Fr. Gillquist, Fr. Braun, Fr. Ballew, and myself spent three years together. We were teaching in the Academy daily and meeting every day up on Fr. Jack's patio, and that was an incredible time of study together. The Academy was actually more of an Academy for us to dig deeply into the early church fathers. There was an enormous amount of study and research that went on by all of us and others – not just us five alone – to try to find out what these early church fathers really teach and preach and believe and how they lived? It was a life changing experience for us. (Walker 1999:4)

In their search they became convinced they were under a divine mandate to restore Jesus Movement converts to the "true church." Pursuing this they formed the New Apostolic Order (NAO).

> By early 1973, Braun, Ballew and I were regularly meeting together. That year NAO was created by the seven ex-Campus Crusade directors, Braun, Ballew, Nethery, Walker, Sparks, Berven, and Gillquist. We had our first meeting of the seven sometime in 1973. (Sparks 1999a:4-6)

The search for apostolic interpretation of the Scriptures was to lead Sparks, and all but one of the NAO leaders, (Nethery) to form the Evangelical Orthodox Church of America (EOCA) in 1977. It was "a phantom search for the perfect church" (Gillquist 1992, ed., 1999:3). The group of house church leaders, having begun with the New Testament model, sought to understand it through the interpretative eyes of the early sub-apostolic church. They came to the conclusion that "the Eastern Orthodox church was the most faithful contemporary parallel" (Di Sabatino 1999a:36). It was "a huge paradigm shift" from individualistic Protestantism recalls Gillquist.

> We believed God was going to bring us to "it" but we weren't sure what "it" was, and until He did, we were willing to take responsibility for what we were doing. There were nights I lay awake all night over that. There were times I thought I was crazy, but we called it the phantom search for the perfect church. To find it in Orthodoxy, it took a year to sort that out in my brain. I didn't think there was any church that looked like the Orthodox Church would look, or vice versa. What did I think? People sitting in a circle singing Jesus hymns? I don't know what I was conceptualizing there. The fact that it was this liturgical and sacramental was . . . [silence as the words hung in the air]. (Gillquist 1999:3)

Discipleship as understood by parachurch agencies was functionalist rather than theological in its purpose. My own research and experience of such agencies – Youth for Christ, Campaigners for Christ, Open Air Campaigners, Inter-Varsity, Gideons International Bible distribution, Evangelical Alliance, and Christian Business Men's Association – supports the group's complaint. Discipling had become the training process by which people were practically taught to evangelize, while the issue of nurture in the church was basically avoided for interdenominational support reasons. One could pursue a discipleship-training program and assume the "discipled" status at the end of completing the course, sometimes after a few months. There was barely any ecclesiology in such courses. The content of the training was often anti-denominational, although officially interdenominational. Critique was often vague concerning issues of authority. To the founders of CWLF, the issue of church as the authority base and the agent for evangelization was germane from the start.

> I said to Jon Braun one day [1967]. . . . "You know what we are? We are reformers. We don't like the church the way it is, and we're trying to figure out what to do about it." Then I thought, "That sounds arrogant." Remember the Bible verses, "The zeal of thy house has eaten me up" (Psalm 69:9, John 2:17). Somewhere we became as attached to our quest for the church as we were in our desire to live for Christ, because we came to see it as his body. I knew if he walked in today I wouldn't say, "There's his head." I'd say, "There's Jesus and he has a body, and that body is the church." As Calvin said [quoting Saint Cyprian] "He who does not have the church for his mother does not have God for his father." We came to believe somewhere along the line that the name of the game had to be church. That was a giant step as opposed to just "knowing Jesus." Knowing Jesus has to be centered in the church. (Gillquist 1999:1)

The New Covenant Apostolic Order (NCAO), embracing approximately 20 churches associated with Sparks, was formed in 1975. The covenant was signed by Ballew, Berven, Braun, Gillquist, Nethery, Sparks, and Walker (Appendix 7).

> There was a "do or die" sense of determination that I found was expressed by every one of the founding leaders of the group. We said to each other, "If we find that all of Christendom does it this way and we are doing it a different way, we will change. We are going to let it judge us. We are not going to judge it. Saint Augustine, Saint Athanasius, and Saint Chrysostom, are they in my church?" Somewhere we did a shift to, "Are we in their church?" We came to the point we were willing to pay any price. It is like the "pearl of great price." Sell everything you've got to obtain it. (Gillquist 1999:1)

For Sparks, the steady journey sounds peaceful and inevitable, perhaps reflecting his temperament, but for some, like Walker, the journey from classic Baptist independence to Orthodox submission was a painful process.

> When it started with me personally was when we were in Grace Haven at Mansfield farm [1969]. . . . I was sitting in this large basement . . .with probably 100 or more kids, if you really packed them in. We were having these worship services, people calling out choruses to sing, sharing precious verses . . . giving thanks; which we loved most. But then we'd get these wild prophecies by people who were drifting through and there were times when I dreaded going in there. . . . I reached the point when I said "We have done our best to form a New Testament

church, using only the New Testament," but not realizing we were really using our non-sacerdotal, iconoclastic, totally-opposed-to-anything-that-had-been-in-existence-for-[more than] 10 year's approach. I realized this was not the kind of church I've been looking for. I'm the author of this church and I don't like it. At that point I was answerable to no one. There was not a soul I was answerable to and I hated that situation. . . . I told my wife, "Something is wrong." I was so upset. (Walker 1999:1)

The house church movement became an entry point to the ancient church for Walker in 1966. After four years at Grace Haven from 1968 to 1972 the Walkers moved to the Nashville area in July 1972 for five and a half years, starting Grace Ministries, "a little corporation" to set up house churches. They went to Franklin, Tennessee in 1977 and slowly moved in the direction of Orthodoxy. Seven small house churches finally combined to become St. Ignatius Orthodox Church. In 1999 I visited the Franklin church in conservative, rural Tennessee and was impressed by the evangelical conviction of priest and people. Despite the incongruity of a small, bustling Orthodox plant in Protestant, fundamentalist, territory, Walker believes it is promising (Walker 1999:3).

In summer 1973 in Dallas, Texas, as the counterculture was winding down, Sparks, Ballew, Braun, Berven, Gillquist, and Walker met with about 70 men who were in process of building what they believed were New Testament house churches. Six of them, who were 40 or older, became the core eldership to research the early church. Sparks investigated worship. Braun chose church history. Ballew took doctrine. Walker chose the biblical text, Berven had pre-Reformation history and Nethery, who resigned in 1978, chose historical research from the Reformation onwards (Gillquist 1992:22-28).

In February 1975, the core group spent a week under rigorous conditions on San Juan Island in Puget Sound off the coast of Seattle (1992:29). Notable was the dogged determination of this group to pursue a journey, the destination of which was a mystery and the path to which was intellectually rigorous and emotionally taxing. Most of them slept on a bare cement floor under cold and damp conditions.

Each gave a report on his findings. They determined that very early in church history, in the apostolic period, the church had established a pattern of worship which divided the gatherings into an "open" liturgy gathering, the Synaxis, and a "closed" Eucharist for members and catechumens under instruction only (Appendix 8). The Eucharist meetings were household size gatherings comprising members who lived within walking distance. At this stage in the development of the movement, there was a transition during which the ancient patterns of Orthodoxy were blending with the preceding house church developments. A "soft Pentecostal" expression of the gifts of knowledge and prophecy were exercised in the Eucharistic household gatherings. As the group moved more deeply into Orthodoxy, this interim shape was abandoned.

A counterculture preference for household-sized, intimate churches was seen as the normative New Testament and early church form by some groups. Watchman Nee, founder of a Chinese house church movement, *Little Flock*, (Edwards 1997:557, McManners 1992:509) impacted some groups including CWLF, Grace Haven Farm, and Xenos. The emphasis upon house churches with high level accountability was a passing phase for CWLF, but has remained a central feature of Xenos.

Same Search – Different Conclusion

While the Berkeley group headed east, others intimately associated with them, including Xenos and Grace Haven Farm, were unsure of the developing rift with the original Jesus Movement vision. Xenos was also intensely committed to the search for the true, biblical, historical model of church, but embraced a house church model rather than taking the Eastern Orthodox route as Sparks and his inner circle finally did.

Sparks and the CWLF team were not alone in their search for what could be called the authentic early church model. During their own particular search they joined some other evangelicals in a "manifesto" release, which became known as "The Chicago Call to Evangelicals" (Weber and Bloesch 1978). They called the divisive, ecclesiologically inadequate schism of Protestant "sects" to a serious search for an Orthodox theology, for creedal integrity, and for historic, apostolic succession.

It was one of many interim steps on the path to Orthodoxy. It lacked the focus of their apostolic order initiative, calling Evangelicals "to find the roots." Sparks did not perceive a solidified response, because "it was too broad" and "didn't make enough heart contact with folks" (Sparks 1999a:45). It synchronized an evangelical search for the biblical truth, a Pentecostal sense of prophetic revelation, and a scholarly determination to unearth the evidence.

> We had a phrase we called "seeing and hearing from God." In John's Gospel it says "Jesus did nothing that He didn't see the Father do" (John 5:19). Our prayer was "Lord let us see and hear from You." We didn't mean by that: divine revelations, "a vision we are going to write, a new book to add to the Scripture" or anything like that; or that we would have infallible guidance and every one who disagreed with us would be wrong. But we knew somewhere out there, there had to be the church and we were asking God to show us where it was. We do believe to this day, and the church does believe the Holy Ghost speaks to her. The safeguard to it is that it happens in counsel, in liturgy. (Gillquist 1999a:2)

Gillquist was appointed in early 1973 as administrator for the historic journey. Each of the core members contributed in significant ways to the "canon" of research findings. Because Gillquist's drive and charisma, and Sparks' scholarship and writing were crucial, place them at the center of a chronology of the unfolding events that led to Orthodoxy. Gillquist's data illustrates the intensity, length, and communality for the development from Campus Crusade to radical CWLF, through house church movement, and finally to full Orthodoxy.

Interviews with foundational members (Gillquist, Sparks and Walker) have been both enlightening and frustrating in their sense of having "arrived" at the end of a long convoluted spiritual and intellectual journey that made historic detail peripheral for them. The liminality and *communitas* of the process overwhelmed the events of their history.[11]

The search for the right church began well before the formation of CWLF. Despite geographical distances this group maintained a tenacious sense of camaraderie and divine guidance. The intellectual focus on historic research with specifically apportioned research tasks and frequent socialization surrounding the enquiry was a process I have rarely seen carried out with such enduring determination.

Berven, according to the rest of the Antiochian Orthodox group, took half of the Santa Cruz Evangelical Orthodox Church of America (EOCA) to form a non-canonical movement, the Orthodox Christian Brothers in the winter of 1978. Walker pastored and reorganized the other half of the Santa Cruz group, bringing them under the EOCA.

> We had all these groups who had been converted through the Jesus Movement who needed to be taken to a safe place amidst the fragmentation, division, and splintering of the evangelical movement. We wanted to take them to the middle of the river of the historic church to a safe place. By 1973, we were on a hard track into the Fathers. This was not a flash in the pan. We had started in the 1960s on a journey to the Fathers of the early church. The Fathers led us to the Orthodox church. We were Orthodox before ever hearing of the Orthodox Church. We wanted desperately to be in that place. We discovered what Rome had done to the Creed when it chose to depart from Orthodoxy. This commenced a process which did not cease until we became Orthodox. (Sparks 1999b:1)

The EOCA appointment of bishops was a necessary, interim responsibility on the way to delivering their congregations to the full authority of Orthodoxy.

> We felt we were doing an apostolic ministry. We, especially Fr. Jon Braun, felt that at times we were exercising a prophetic ministry. He had a way of seeing things and speaking to them that was beyond just preaching. We were never messianic, or thinking we were the center of Christendom. But we felt for the people [God] entrusted to us. If we can't go with the assumption that the gifts of the Holy Spirit are with us, we will never make it. I believe the Holy Spirit was with us and ultimately that resulted in us appointing ourselves as bishops.

> One of the greatest days of my life was when I kissed my bishop's hand and that [interim stage of temporary bishop] was forever in the past. There is a sense in which God graced us to do that for our people, but we knew we weren't graced to do it for the church. We had a few of our guys who didn't come into Orthodoxy because they wanted to still be bishops. Ken Johnson is one of those. (Gillquist 1999:3)

Nethery (1999) was the only defector of the original CWLF group. He disagreed over the shift to Orthodoxy, but still saw the search for the right historic church model as necessary, but he held to the legitimacy of parachurch agencies.

> I think Jack is correct, but I don't think he has the right perspective on the way Campus Crusade pastored itself. It was to be a servant of the church. It wasn't to be the church. It wasn't to develop its own ecclesiology. It was to come alongside of the church and serve the church and feed into the church the people who converted to Christ. (Nethery 1999:4)

Given the best case scenario, could evangelism be independent of ecclesial authority via parachurch agencies that are not answerable to the local church?

I would not want to be party to that. I want to be more answerable to the church; [I want] to be more partnered fully with the church. But when you consider the sleepiness and indifference of the church at times, then you have to respect some of the parachurch organizations that spring up to fill in the gap, even with their glitches. (1999:4)

The nature of the true church was central to a number of cults that were to the far left fringes of the Jesus Movement: The Way International (Lemons 1984); The Local Church and the Children of God (Di Sabatino 1999:17-18; Leming and Smith 1974). The Unification Church (Bryan Wilson 1990:251-266) claimed to be exclusively the true church. The intense and almost cult-like search for the true church was extremely stressful for some, helpful to those who would find resolution in the Orthodox faith, and threatening to health and marriage for most (Martin 1996:6).

Jesus Family Tree – A Personal Observation Movement Pursues Its

During the interim period in 1979, I again visited Sparks and others whom I had previously known at the height of CWLF's movement's phase to investigate what had happened to the movement. By this time, the Evangelical Orthodox Church of America was well established. Sparks had written us concerning the developing crisis between the postmodern model of the radical CWLF and the pre-modern, dramatically different Orthodox development soon after his Australian tour. Much had happened in the few intervening years. Dr. Sparks had become Bishop Jack Sparks, a title subsequently relinquished on entry into the Antiochian Orthodoxy, as its bishops, though not its regular clergy are celibate. In the Berkeley group, there was a sense of weariness, resulting from the free wheeling, charismatic individualism of the Californian culture.

I arrived in crisis from a major split over the question of authority and leadership in our own movement Truth and Liberation Concern (TLC). Rather than exercise the charismatic founders' prerogative by calling the troops to faithfulness and ejecting those who caused division, I chose to quietly exit from leadership, due to my deeply held belief in "suffering servanthood" as the foundation for ecclesial authority, taught by Jesus. "If anyone wants to be first, he must be the very last, and the servant of all" (Mark 9:35).

Following my resignation on November 11, 1982 from the ministry I had founded in 1972, I was bruised and shattered in terms of confidence to lead in the alternative movement in Australia. Bishop Jack placed me with a family whose members had been typical freewheeling Californian "counterculture Freaks." They asked, "Should our children call you Father John, or Bishop John? Bishop Jack has told us that you have been one of the leaders of the Movement in your country." I laughed recalling the struggle over leadership authority I had endured. I was gently, but firmly rebuked.

> You must understand that we were hippies. We know what it is to deny all authority over our lives. We have seen the moral and social damage of the Hollywood superstar mentality and the destructive individualism of Californians. We

do not want our children to grow up in that godless and destructive state. We know nothing about you except that Bishop Jack has told us that you are a man of God, appointed by our Lord and the church to significant leadership in your country. But we have come to believe that irrespective of what you are, the offices and callings of God's church must be taken seriously. We want our children to respond accordingly and be set an example of respect for holy orders. (unknown)

Rather than be recognized as "bishop," I chose "father" for my temporary title. I was sobered with a growing sense of just how radically and thoroughly the new group had embraced the journey to ancient Orthodoxy. It was within this bridging movement of the EOCA that I experienced hospitality the second time, and observed the various public and communal aspects of this new American religious group in search of authentic history, and ritual process. I was granted status to sit in the inner sanctum for days of debate and strategic work with the bishops of the EOCA.

There was a desire to bring undisciplined Californian hippies into a sense of historic ritual process and reverence for the Advent season. It was being proposed that Christmas eve, an all important, final, frenetic day of ritualistic, last minute shopping in the consumer society, be reshaped by the church. Christmas Eve commercial time was to be transformed into sacred time, culminating in an all night vigil, preparatory to the arrival of God's beloved Son. Bishop Sparks was reminded by Bishop Gillquist that this would encroach upon the tradition of Californian, individualistic, nuclear families. Bishop Sparks maintained that even the freewheeling Californians would be in attendance at the bedside for many hours preparatory to the arrival of their own children. "We will remind them of that and call them to honor the birth of God's Son before that of their own earthly children," he said. There was some merriment at the nuanced cunning of Bishop Sparks' suggestion. The radical proposal was unanimously embraced.

At that stage, the morning worship of the New Apostolic Order was broken into two gatherings, in keeping with an ancient tradition of a publicly open service called the Synaxis first, and a closed communion Eucharist to follow (See Appendix 8).[12] Attendees at the second gathering lived within walking distance of their Eucharistic location. The bread and wine were shared with much solemnity amidst ancient liturgical readings and the "soft Pentecostal" exercise of the gifts of the Spirit. A marked sense of communality, and liminality was apparent in these intimate, household, gatherings.

Many Threads in an Iconographic Tapestry

Several quite different biographical threads are woven to create the tapestry of the journey to ancient Orthodoxy. Clark Carlton, a Southern Baptist, James Bernstein, co-founder of Jews for Jesus, Duane Peterson, editor of the prominent Jesus paper *Hollywood Free Paper*, and Vineyard pastors Charles Bell, and Ronald Clausen joined ex-Campus Crusade directors, Braun, Gillquist, Ballew, Walker, and Sparks as Orthodox priests. Michael Harper (1997), highly influential in Britain's charismatic renewal (Pete Ward 1996:119-126) joined a growing number of British Evangelicals and charismatics exiting to the Orthodox faith (Harper 1997; Sparks 1999a).

This coalescence of unlikely converts to Orthodoxy occurred at a time when liturgical Christianity was being challenged by neo-Pentecostalism and new paradigm churches. In the deconstructed religious economy of America and the West in general, old loyalties were (and are) crumbling. The crossover to Catholicism and Orthodoxy from evangelicalism and Pentecostalism reverses the past pattern of defection. Previously the defections were from the two ancient churches to Pentecostal and Fundamentalist folds, following "born again" experience, holiness, and Pentecostal experiences.

Why did some flower children choose to go "home"? Not all went home to Orthodoxy. Some are choosing Catholicism. Patrick Madrid (1994) edits the stories of 11 conversions from Evangelical and Pentecostal Protestantism, to Catholicism including a Campus Crusade college trainee, a staunch Calvinist, and an Assembly of God minister.

Weary of the Road and in Need of a Stable Family

Some forsook the noisiness and clamor of charismatic worship, to find again the still small voice that speaks from silence rather than thunder, lightening, and fire (Bell 1993). Many were deeply disillusioned by the collapse of the Christian, hippie, utopian dream of changing the world. Ancient doctrine, mysterious rituals, and predictable ecclesiastics provided sanctuary and healing.

Others, reminiscent of John Wesley, saw the early church fathers as an essential element of hermeneutics, necessary to develop a fuller interpretation of the biblical text. Sparks described it as a simple progression from the enquiry into the church of Acts to the interpretation of the Patristics, to Antiochian Orthodoxy. Orthodoxy provided a solid resistance to relativism, pluralism, and postmodernity. The inestimable damage done by highly individualist, charismatic leaders, with no answerability to any authority beyond individualized phenomenology, led Walker to seek legitimate, historical authority, and worship.

> I was in charge of the African ministries . . . and I saw Plymouth Brethren and other missionaries and in a lot of homes in West and East Africa, and I came back saying, "If you're going to form another Crusade I'm out of it. What I want really is the church. Myself, I'm going looking for the church." I felt the New Testament could be done [interpreted] with just the New Testament in terms of my ecclesiology. It was not until I had tried as hard as I could try that I gave up on Grace Haven Farm . . . .We knew we were looking for something we didn't have and we thought worship was part of it. (Walker 1999:12)

The Deconstruction of the Charismatic Leader

Within the maturing of the Jesus Movement, many became deeply concerned with the issues of ecclesiology asking: What do we do with all these hippie converts? What authority does charisma represents? The search for authority and historic continuity was an integral part of the search for legitimate identity, particularly since the revitalization phase, being so counterculture and communal, gave rise to accusations of cultism from some secular and church leaders.

There were legitimate and genuine concerns about the unbiblical and socially destructive elements of religious individualism. The sense of history, order, mutuality, and quiet, uncontested authority within Orthodoxy, was extremely inviting to those utopian, charismatic leaders who had been bruised by the experience of community schism, often surrounding conflict over authority. Walker, reviewing major Vineyard churches with which he had been associated, saw that numbers, and popular acclaim of a leader's charismatic wizardry do not provide an ecclesiological basis for authority.

> Worship services we were having were a lot like the Pentecostals, a lot like Vineyard fellowship is right now. . . . [But] It is not the church. It is [only] 20 years old. It is not 2,000 years old. It is not founded on the church of the Apostles. That's what was missing and we didn't even realize it. [Missing was] apostolic succession, true apostolic doctrine grounded on the Trinity and the incarnation and the foundation of the Apostles' Creed which was finally incorporated in the Nicene Creed in its fullness. (Walker 1999:12-13)

In Search of an Enduring Theology in Postmodern Times

Orthodoxy is attractive to some evangelicals because it reflects a social Trinitarian, Eastern view, and a strong Christology. The humanity of Christ and the "mystery" of the Incarnation have been preserved. Paradox and mystery, rather than rationalistic resolution was irresistible. "That's what drew us. That's what caught us. Once we saw that, we said, this is what we've been looking for all this time in our journey, in our stumbling along" (Walker 1999:4). The research was intense and thorough.

Interaction with Eastern philosophy was occurring through the "Spiritual Counterfeits" project of CWLF. Dialogue flourished with kids who had soured on the church because they saw it as holding a strict Cartesian worldview. During the investigation of Eastern monism, did that dialogical interaction of the CWLF with Zen, and other Eastern worldviews prepare the way? Was there a Berkeley worldview connection opening the door to the East in terms of Christian tradition? When interviewed, none of the "Apostolic" seven seemed interested in analyzing the socio-religious drive behind their journey. Walker granted a mild recognition of this cultural element. "I don't know that it [Eastern thought] opened the door. I think it was more like putting salt on food. It may have made it more palatable so to speak. The door that opened for us was the study of the Apostolic Fathers" (Walker 1999:2).

We Simply Heard Him Call

For evangelicals, the intimate sense of divine encounter and God's personalized divine guidance is central. The pilgrims from Berkeley rightly of wrongly believe that Orthodoxy has a strong focus on the human element of Christology and an historical fix on the saints of history. This seems to renew some evangelicals who are weary of the Bultmannian, existential definition of the "faith once delivered." Mystery to the Protestant appears as a concession to the human shortfall of knowledge. Mystery for the Orthodox is embraced along with faith as a comforting rather than frustrating element of reality. Each evangelical convert to Orthodoxy I interviewed testified to the traditional sense of "the Lord's call," but had married it to an anchored historical tradition. The "call" to research into the church fathers was encouraged by Thomas Nelson Publishers.

> I think it was divinely [appointed]; it was providential. Sam Moore, the President [of Thomas Nelson publishers] said he felt he wanted to do that and he heard about Fr. Peter's success about writing books like *Love Is Now* (1978). So he got in touch with [Fr. Peter Gillquist] and hired him as the first Christian book editor they had at Thomas Nelson. One of the earliest projects . . . was to [improve on] a translation they had published years before by Robert Grant, which was an excellent translation of the *Early Church Fathers*, but it was so academic . . . that the average person looks at that and says "forget it." (Walker 1999:4)

Sparks' academic training and warm, relational style of writing had been well established in his counterculture books. The impact of his compelling work on the Patristics was apparent in his colleagues' responses:

> We came up with this concept that this was to be put in one book that laymen could read and get something out of it. Sparks was a natural to do that. He became the editor and wrote these brief introductions to each book and each author of the Apostolic Fathers. We became his committee of proof-readers and that book literally blew my ecclesiastical ship out of the water. I knew I could no longer be a Baptist after I read that; especially the letters of St. Ignatius. It was the *Seven Letters by St. Ignatius* that completely changed my life and I just said "I don't know where we're headed, but I can't be a Baptist anymore." (Walker 1999:5)

The new "apostolic" team came to be rooted in mystery yet so confident in its historic traditions, that it had located itself epistemologically in a pre-modern sense of incarnational certainty:

> St. Ignatius died in the year about 107 as a martyr. He was eaten alive by the lions in Rome. He was the Bishop of Antioch for 40 years. Tradition is [that] he was the little boy in Matthew 18. I first read that in a Protestant commentary when I was teaching at St. Athanasius at Santa Barbara.

> [Metropolitan Philip Saliba] came here to rename and consecrate our building [St. Ignatius]. He said, "You know father, it has been passed down through the Bishops of our Patriarch, that the original St. Ignatius, Antiochian Patriarch, was the one in Matthew 18 that Jesus sat in the midst of the disciples as an object lesson." So I said "Thank you for telling me that." (Walker 1999:5)

Sparks commenced the Academy of Orthodox Theology, in the Spring of 1977. The Movement relocated to Santa Barbara and set about preparing the Academy curriculum, with classes commencing in the fall of 1977. These classes continued on location for 11 years. The EOCA was constituted during the late 1970s, what was to be an interim stage in the journey to full Orthodoxy. A minority of the group have continued as the EOCA, the Indianapolis plant being the most successful, enduring unit.

From the late 1970s to mid the 1980s relationships were developed with leaders of the Orthodox Church of America (OCA). Bishop Dimitri believed that the OCA door would be open to them (Sparks 1999a). Some NAO leaders attended the 1980 Detroit OCA Council. In 1985, several of the EOCA leadership, encouraged by Bishop Maximus of Pittsburgh of the OCA, left for Constantinople. Sparks was unable to attend because of a back condition. On arrival, to their frustration, they found the door was shut to them by the Patriarchy. They were refused audience. Dialogue with the OCA led nowhere, producing neither rejection nor acceptance. At Schmemann's suggestion, they contacted Russian, Greek, and Serbian branches. Gillquist recalls a desperate attempt to escalate the process.

> By 1985 we realized we weren't going anywhere. We've been hanging out for almost a decade with these people, and there's no movement. We don't want to die and not be [fully] Orthodox. So we felt the Lord say to us "Go to Constantinople." We called Bishop Maximos (Greek Orthodox Church) Pittsburgh, January 1985, and he said "I will lead you there. I will go with you. I'll get the Archbishop's blessing." But something happened before we left that talked the Archbishop out of it. He sent me a telegram and it arrived the day after we left for Constantinople. We arrived over there and we got the freeze. We were told that some high official of the Greek Government begged them not to take us because our presence in the Greek Archdiocese would water down their Hellenistic traditions. We don't know whether that's true or not but it would be a plausible explanation. (Gillquist 1999:6)

At first, Sparks recalls there was brokenness and confusion bordering on despair (Sparks 1999a:9). Having cut Reformational, Protestant roots, and risked all to find mother church, she appeared to have withdrawn the "welcome mat" and locked the door. Despair swiftly turned however to dogged determination.

> The Patriarch would not see us. What it did was it put Orthodoxy on notice that we were dead serious. The man who is now Patriarch Bartholomew and another older Archbishop, I think it was Chrystostomus, met with us two days later and we said to them, "We're not going to go away. When you go out to get your newspaper we're going to be at your door. When you go to work we'll be there. When you come home we'll be there. When you put the cat out at night we'll be there. We are not going away." They blinked and we didn't. (Sparks 1999a:6)

The Street Was Right But the Address Was Wrong

It was not to be. While Orthodoxy remained the goal, a different household in that street would welcome them home. Before their abortive journey to Constantinople, Fr. John Bartke had suggested a meeting with the Patriarch of Antioch "out of honor." Gillquist tells the story with characteristic vividness.

> We had an appointment in a few days with the Patriarch of Antioch. I'll never forget the car trip down there. It was Braun, Sparks and myself. Part of us didn't want to go. We just had our butts kicked in Constantinople. Jon Braun said "I'll tell you what we're going to do. I'm going to go in and say, hey Mr. Patriarch. My name's Jon Braun. I would really like to be Orthodox. If you won't take us I'm going to go out and find another Patriarch. I'm not going to worry about kissing hands. I want to have a good time today. I want to be detached." That's just what we needed. We were all stunned by the rejection. (Gillquist 1999:7)

The prior rejection cost a handful of followers, who felt that any Orthodox patriarchy would "clip their wings" and prevent exercise of their gifts. According to both Gillquist and Sparks, the Antiochian Archbishop had only ever urged them to bring more people to Christ, and to plant more churches, rather than seeking to limit their evangelical spirit. They met with Metropolitan Philip and the Patriarch at the Los Angeles Sheraton Hotel, late June 1985. The consultation took about an hour. The Patriarch was most positive and the Metropolitan prophesied swift resolution. Gillquist says:

> When we went to see him, we were under so much pressure. Our people had collected $50,000 to send us to Constantinople and we got back with nothing to report. So we went detached, but it was really enjoyable. It was like night and day to walk in and hear him say, "Welcome brothers". Could it be possible that we three prodigals had just found home? (Gillquist 1999:7)

He requested that they provide a brief history of the EOCA delineating the journey step by step, with a profile on each parish and its pastor, education, congregational size, and facilities. Labor Day of that year was set for finalizing the report. The EOCA Synod of Bishops met in January 1986 to draft a proposal and set March 1986 for discussion of the proposal for parish integration.

> A few of the EOCA groups, including Berven, maintained the EOCA rather than completing the journey to Antiochian Orthodoxy. The Antiochian group believes that their dissent was the result of the Antiochian demand that the status of bishop be relinquished, since Antiochian bishops must be celibate (Sparks 1999b).

Beyond Transformation to Transfiguration

This account of the CWLF journey to Orthodoxy could be described as a study in *transfiguration*. In dictionary terms, transformation and transfiguration conceptually cross over. Both may imply a change in form, in appearance, in structure, in character, and in nature. Transformation however, is often applied by evangelicals to the inner changes which modify outward behavior and symbolic expressions of life, but generally leave the newly transformed believer to go on with business as usual.

When we speak of transfiguration, we allude to concepts. One is of a radical, externally recognizable, visible change in the very nature of how things appear. Secondly, the term has become intimately associated with a spirituality reflecting the supernatural and glorified change in the appearance of Jesus, on the mountain of transfiguration (Matthew 17:1-9). When the disciples saw Jesus transfigured he was recognizable as Jesus, but transfigured before them.

I met the CWLF's leadership at the height of the radical, Berkeley Jesus Movement. Reflecting on the change I found during my second visit, "transfiguration" seems the more appropriate term to apply to the majority of those founding leaders who defected to Orthodoxy. Orthodoxy is so remarkably visual in its piety, and is much more at home with mystical concepts like transfiguration and glorification. These evangelicals are markedly different. They are the same men I met almost three decades ago. They are the same intellectual mentors who encouraged us to experiment with the faith, to seek genuine Christian community, and to hold an ancient faith in a contemporary context.

The same bearded face which was once postmodern, speaks now of a pre-modern, Antiochian Orthodox resistance to fashion by The Right Reverend Father Sparks. The need for cultural differentiation between symbol and meaning is thus illustrated. The bearded face of the Orthodox priest expresses a vastly different world to that of the counterculture professor. Challenge to the existing order of American culture is continued via the Orthodox tradition, even more in contrast to social norms than the counterculture.

> It's hard being Orthodox. It's so un-American. Here we are hierarchical, patriarchal church with discipline. We still kick people out of it if they're heretics, or immoral, which is all the stuff Americans no longer stand for. It's incredible. On the fasting thing we said that if Jesus can suffer for us, the least we can do is to enter into some self discipline to show him that we're grateful. (Gillquist 1999:8)

Everything about them is so changed. For several years, they retreated to a holy mountain with their Lord and with his saints. They descended from the mountain, no less committed to magnifying the person and work of Jesus, but they looked different, they acted differently, and they believed differently. To those who have not ascended that mountain with them, their return is somewhat of a mystery. A growing number of evangelicals are professing a new resolve, stability, mystery, and noncompetitive collegiality. Each recounts the story of a journey during which the icons spoke to them.

I have come to see the shift from the Berkeley radicalism to ancient Orthodoxy as a natural progression, in the revitalization context of the Californian counterculture. Wallace strongly underscores the universal need for ritual process, but isolates it from the supernatural, religious elements of causation, predicting the replacement of the supernaturalistic element with fully adequate secular rituals and symbols in a secular society (Wallace 1966:104-157).

Revitalization begins in counterculture iconoclasm, as a symbolic demonizing of the dysfunctional stress-producing culture. But identity, community and communication require symbols and the routinization of the radical departure. To arrive at a new satisfying, steady state of cultural stasis, the hemorrhage produced by cultural fragmentation must be halted. Revitalization initially increases the cultural stress, but as the new culture is conceived, formulated and communicated a new set of rituals and social forms are embraced. The new equilibrium is different from the former state, but it is always a synthesis of that which is conceived as worthy from the past and appropriate from the present. CWLF are in this sense a copy book example of the journey from social alienation, or liminality, to transformational reaggregation in a surprising new form. The fusion of Pentecostal vision, cultural resistance, ritual process, evangelical zeal and sacerdotal Orthodoxy is one of the least expected, but extraordinarily innovative fusions in cultural history. Fr. Sparks remarked upon reading the following analysis, that despite his lack of interest in sociohistorical causes, he found the list reasonable, even compelling, if not conclusive:

1. The Berkeley journey led to the East. The mood at every level was away from Western traditions. The Eastern Church, with its sense of mystery, of art, and of meditation was naturally more attractive than the Catholic alternative.

2. The search for community was intense for Berkeley pagans and Jesus Freaks. Protestant communal orders had rarely endured, but the Berkeley seekers came to believe that communalism had been a mark of mission and contemplation in the Eastern tradition. Their fixation with Orthodoxy seemed to divert them temporarily from the arguably greater tradition of monastic mission in Celtic and other Catholic movements.

3. While rejection of constituted authority marked the counterculture, its frenetic search for gurus and radical mentors led many Christians and non-Christians to authoritarian groups. The rejection of the existing order was a thinly veiled search for valid authority. Orthodoxy provided the sense of authority not based on dangerously authoritarian, charismatic individuals, but on tradition, ritual and synodical order.

4. The marriage of sensuality and spirituality had long been a dilemma for fundamentalist Protestants. The grace and art of Orthodoxy is reflective of a tradition which celebrates beauty and holiness, united in form and meaning.

5. The Orthodox tradition supplies iconography as a sensual aid to contemplation and transcendent meditation. The search for the mystery of life, in silence and visual art, was an enquiry to which many of the Jesus Movement members related.

6. Postmodernity's rejection of modernity's rationalism led to pre-modern roots, rather than nostalgia. If the Enlightenment had failed and postmodernity had only achieved the fracturing, and discrediting of the dominant modernity paradigm, going forward could only be an extension of existing failure. The only way forward was backwards to sure foundations. The interest in tribal lore, neo-pagan tradition, ancient Buddhist, and Hindu traditions reflected a widespread counterculture propensity to go "back to the future."

7. Symbolism, ritual process, and unconventional vestments were as much a mark of the counterculture as was the iconoclasm of its political protests. Ritual process was reintroduced to a youth culture whose adolescence was above all else, marked by deprivation of tribal, ritual processes. Orthodoxy provides a way to be incorporated into a new definition of humanity, a historic continuity of human identity, while providing a sense of communal incorporation transcending, yet embracing space and time.

8. In a peculiar defiance of the established order, the counterculture sought to express its liminality and reaggregation to a new communal consciousness, by distinctives of dress, decorum, and ritual. In defiance of social convention hippies grew long hair, Hari Krishna devotees shaved it off. Rock concert attendees took off their clothes, while hippie girls wore long granny dresses. Ancient signs were desacralized, only to become sacred in a new order – the military victory sign of the two-finger V form became the anti-war peace sign, and the cross of Christianity became the crow's foot of peace protesters. What other expression of Christian tradition could deliver a more symbolic, social defiance than the ancient church of the exotic East, with its rituals and premodern traditions?

9. A longing for community ran parallel to a desire for personal freedom. Orthodoxy offered "koinonia" in the ancient Spirit, through devotion and mysticism. The fellowship with millenniums of saints, staring beatifically from every aspect of Orthodox building interiors, provided a sense of cosmic closure on all the 1960s turmoil.

10. A desire to make time stand still in the frantic experimentalism and religious diversification of the American west coast was seen in the posters of that era: *Stop the world I want to get off* or *Tune in, turn on and drop out.* Crystal Gayle sang, *Slow Down, You Move Too Fast. You've Got to Make the Morning Last.* Jesus was *The Bridge over Troubled Waters.* A poster declared *He is the Still Point of a Turning World.* Orthodoxy slowed the pace of change and decay, taking cultural anarchists out of the modernity-postmodernity maelstrom, into the arms of the enduring, unflappable saints of God.

The journey was not an emotional, mindless response to sociological determinism. They made a radical, startling series of cognitive and lifestyle changes. They could have made different ones. Their context had created powerful forces for radical change, including many alternatives they chose to ignore. Gilquist admits they were in danger of a vastly different conclusion, had events turned in a different direction.

> I want to write a tract "Looking for a good nondenominational church?" That's what we are – the church that existed 1,500 years before there were denominations. I think we had to drop out of organized Christianity to make this journey. We would meet together and come up with what the Fathers were teaching on this matter. We would have been kicked out of every church we were ever in, if we believed *that* inside their church. "Well you guys are following little known people like Athanasius and St. Chrysostom," [they would say]. Give me a break. They [the Saints] follow the Scriptures. That's why we follow them. We were only accountable to each other, which was also a risky thing. I think had we not gone Orthodox, ultimately we would have been a cult. You can't do the things we were trying to do without the grace and the Holy Spirit in the church, that mystical thing which is in Orthodoxy. (Gillquist 1999:4-5)

Even so, the choices would have been as variable in their possibilities as were the sociocultural drivers that helped shape the momentous change. In hindsight, they view it as the hand of God, and of Mother Church.

The CWLF was perhaps one of the most marginal of the Jesus movement groups. They most assuredly left the traditional church, while focusing on the search for the "true" church and an ecclesiology to sustain their converts against the ravages of postmodernity. Having set up a resistance Movement against the counterfeits of secularism and institutional religion, they concluded the future belongs to the past. As modernity unravels in the free fall of postmodernity, mere nostalgia for a dysfunctional, recent past is simply a delay in the realization of the inadequacy of rationalism and naive realism. To rebuild on the constantly shifting sands of subjective revisionism, is to betray the flock to even greater insecurity. When you are lost, it is time to return home with the prodigal sons and daughters of history. Since postmodernity is but the adolescent progeny of a dysfunctional modern parent, the secular rebels of Berkeley rightly analyzed the failure of their parents, but had no substantial *modus operandi* for a liberated future. Like the prodigal in a pigsty of his own making, many weary Jesus Freaks simply set off for home. To the CWLF it was insufficient to go back to the "good old days" of fundamentalism. The only path was to go back to the historic roots of the faith.

The Reformation was both the seedbed of liberation and the breeding ground for sectarianism, radical individualism, and utilitarian materialism. Go home where nothing has changed, where the confusion is resolved, and the ecclesial family life is tried and proven. The most consistent conviction held by all the converted radicals to Orthodoxy that I interviewed was the overwhelming sense of having "come home" at last.[13]

Francis Schaeffer's son Frankie moved to Greek Orthodoxy, surprising evangelicals, particularly given his rather maverick and outspoken individualism concerning art and the church. After relocating to Massachusetts he was christmated [consecrated] December 16, 1990 in the Greek Orthodox community. He describes his shift as "the culmination of a rather long personal odyssey which took me from the heart of evangelical Protestant 'denominationalism' into the historic church" (Frankie Schaeffer 1997:60).[14] His story is included in Evangelical Orthodoxy's Journal *Again,* founded by Berven, published by Peter Gilquist, now embraced by AOC with Metropolitan Philip as the overseer.

Gillquist, nurtured by the cultural conditioning of the Southern Baptist Church and Dallas Theological Seminary, forsook the independent, congregational model, to embrace submission and ancient liturgy. To this aggressively evangelistic soul, it felt like home. He recalls, "I said to Jon Braun, 'If they make me the assistant sensor loader for council liturgies, I'm still going to go in.' I look back and I just grin. To come home; the joy of it all was so incredible" (1999:5).

Sparks started his journey from Berkeley to ancient Antioch in the mid-1960s. It was a long, exhausting pilgrimage, from traditional denominationalism to para-church, to independent house church planting. Finally he fell into the arms of the most ancient, continuing ecclesia of Jesus' sacramental saints. He came "home" to give his senior years to translating the works of the church Fathers and the Septuagint version of the Apocrypha. He spoke tenderly, almost sentimentally of *Coming Home: Why Protestant Clergy are Becoming Orthodox* (Gillquist, ed. 1992), his favorite book, recounting the stories of clergy-convert journeys to Orthodoxy. Pondering the convoluted journey and the arrival at this adoptive home he smiled, recalling others who had followed in the way.

Fr. Seraphim Bell received his BA from Oral Roberts University and his Ph.D. from Aberdeen University in Scotland. He took his Vineyard congregation with him when he was ordained to the Orthodox priesthood on June 13, 1993.

> The journey to Orthodoxy has not been an easy one. It has come with trial and tribulation. However, as the psalmist says, "We went through fire and through water, but you brought us out to rich fulfillment" (Psalm 66:12). My congregation and I have experienced a sense of the fullness of Christ's church that we had never known before. We give thanks to God for His grace in leading us home – and we unhesitatingly invite other evangelicals and charismatics to join us. (Bell 1993:55)

To some thoughtful evangelicals and post-Pentecostals, mother church no longer appears as a safe and nurturing bosom. She is a diverse, bustling market place that may care today, but be replaced tomorrow. An intentional search for a nurturing ecclesial mother led Sparks and 40 colleagues (Chandler 1975:34) neither in the direction of modernity, nor postmodernity, but premodernity. The rationalism and reductionism of modernity had become a nightmare. Liberalism had torn up the foundations of the "faith once delivered" (Sparks 1999a:14). The deconstruction of all that is authoritative was seen as profane. Orthodoxy is an ecclesial home in a world hostile to grace and order.

For some who did not make the journey with Sparks, Orthodoxy was remote from the contextual task to which they felt called. Thirty CWLF staffers battled on, retooling for the less exotic, more cynical, more materialistic 1980s and 1990s. Upon termination in 1975, Sparks requested the name CWLF be withdrawn, as the continuing group did not reflect the direction of its founders. The remaining group called themselves the Berkeley Christian Coalition. Some ministries continued under other names. *Right On* Jesus paper became *Radix*, edited by Sharon Gallagher, an original member of the *Right On* team and the CWLF community. The *Androclean Outlook,* begun by Sparks in *Right On* earlier, is continued almost three decades later in *Radix*. New College Berkeley (previously a street university, Crucible), and the Christian Counterfeits ministry remain a testimony to an enduring commitment born of courage, determination and dissent, when the length of a man's hair, the color of one's politics, and the extent of one's social conformity determined the status of one's Christianity. Gone are the days of grandiose people's fronts and utopian dreams. Exotic faiths, pluralism and cultural diversity are no longer a creative adrenaline, but simply normative realities. Sharon Gallagher recalled:

> Following a journey to L'Abri, Sparks desired to commence a free university or street level university. This eventuated under the name Crucible and was given leadership by Bernard Adeney. It was Bernie who wrote the "Position Paper of Dissent" at the time of the division of the CWLF Movement. [Both Bernie and Sharon continued with the original ministry, renamed Berkeley Christian Coalition]. Crucible continued after the division under the name New College, Berkeley, and is still operating today. (Gallagher 1999:1)

The break from CWLF was extremely painful Gallagher recalls (2000). Further divisions plagued attempts to maintain a radical model of house church and communalism under the new Berkeley Christian Coalition, led by original member Bill Squires. Sparks' very strong charisma was patriarchal and for many like Gallagher, he really was a major father figure. While Sparks never appeared to be a demagogue, he was a strong control agent and his gracious patriarchal style caused his followers to feel considerable fear of displeasing him in anything they did (Gallagher 2000:1). One split, the Bartimaeus Community, rescued by John Hirt of Australia's House of the New World, and academic dissenter Ched Meyers, set its membership standards high, demanding commitment and local residence for all members (Gallagher 1999:1). They have valiantly sought to hold a line of socio-political revolt, sometimes sharing prison cells for their civil disobedience in commitment to antinuclear, and anti-armaments' convictions (Hirt 1998:195-198).

Both Californian models, Calvary Chapel and CWLF pursued faith with sincerity and endurance, reflecting centripetal and centrifugal aspects of Christ's mission to the world. "Go ye" and "come unto me" are both invitations of Christ to humanity. There is a community bearing his name to be nurtured, embraced, and perpetuated – a home with a welcome mat of grace, and love for whomsoever. There is a strong historic link between this chapter and the next, in which I will describe some typical Australian variations of the movement. CWLF was the most influential of all the American groups during the fledgling days of development in Australia.

Events in Berkeley were bewildering for many in Australia who had experienced the ministry and warm persona of Jack Sparks during his visit to the Australian Jesus Movement. CWLF seemed to be the one movement in the United States which most reflected the radical and socially transforming understanding of Jesus, the counterculture prophet-God. *Right On* was read almost as enthusiastically as our own publications and its articles borrowed frequently for republication in *Free Slave*, and *Truth and Liberation*.

Having shared the radical vision of the Berkeley brethren initially, the Australians did not follow in the sacerdotal paths of their former radical friends, but battled on as the social calm-down of the 1980s approached. The permanent imprint of the Australian Jesus People remains in the revitalization of a new Christian culture of indigenous theology and evangelism, but the movement largely failed to routinize early enough to establish the church plants of the relative grandeur of Calvary Chapel or Vineyard in the United States. Some of the cultural reasons for the Australian Movement's radical worldview, its meteoric rise to success, and its substantial collapse after 20 years of impressive influence will be explored in Chapter 6.

Notes

1. The first position is that of quarantine (Sanneh 1989:39), in which the church retreats from the world in self protection, viewing it as alien and likely to pervert or pollute the purity of the gospel stream. This attitude is often expressed in communal groups that set up alternative societies under the rule of God.

The second, and according to Sanneh, the most normative pattern for the church to successfully propagate the gospel is a form a syncretism (1989:39-40), whereby the truth of the gospel finds new expression in cultural forms familiar to the pagans, but open to reinterpretation in terms of the truth of the gospel. One might assume that the current contextualization position in the gospel and culture debate involves the investigation of the syncretistic form. Conservative Protestant missiologists such as David Hesselgrave (Hesselgrave and Rommen 1992) seem dominated by fear of concessions to syncretism.

For other Protestant mainstream missiologists, such as Dr. Darrell Whiteman, in "Contextualization: The Theory, the Gap, the Challenge" (1997), contextualization in an essential element of the gospel purpose to illuminate the message of a receptor-oriented God of love – an essential if the local church is to be an indigenous expression of a biblical faith. Similarly, recent Catholic missiologists such as Robert Schreiter, in "Enculturation of Faith or Identification with Culture" (Schreiter 1994) are careful to preserve original Christian meanings in the interchange of form, while recognizing the essential of incarnational application to culture.

The third position Sanneh describes as prophetic (1989:40-41), in which the church vigorously confronts the demonic and the ungodly in the secular world round about. Very rarely does one ever observe churches or movements that have a balance of these in even tension. It could be argued that some of the missional Catholic orders come close. CWLF earnestly sought to maintain orthodoxy in essential theology with a radical application to the socio-political frame of mission to Berkeley. In my opinion, they alternated between each of the paradigms according to context, theological statement, and pragmatism.

2. The Los Angeles Jesus Movement took a different direction. With the strong fundamentalist, soft Pentecostal Smith as the primary agent in routinizing the converted hippies, the Jesus Movement conformed to the conservative influence of Costa Mesa culture (Wind and Lewis 1994a:665-67).

3. While the hip language may not connect with a reader who has never associated with the particular subculture it represents, it should be possible to sense some of the Berkeley nuances through the following extract. I have chosen this particular example from The Second Letter to Street Christians because it emphasizes central tenants of the more radical position of the CWLF. It presents a countercultural, revitalization attitude of rejection of the whole cultural matrix, in its employment of such terms as "ego tripping world system," and "the evil world system itself." The phrase "whole plastic bag" hints at the anti-materialistic aspect of the original Jesus Freaks, who seriously embraced this aspect of the counterculture. Terms such as "brothers and sisters," and "God has really laid a heavy love on us," reflect the centrality of the love ethic, and the communitarism which was apparent across a wide range of Jesus people groups, as seen in the following street paraphrase of the First Epistle of John:

"Dig it! God has really laid a heavy love on us! He calls us His children and we are! The world system doesn't recognize that we're His children, because it doesn't know Him. Right on, brothers and sisters, we are God's children even though we're a long way from being what He's going to make us. Don't get hooked on the ego-tripping world system. Anybody who loves that system, doesn't really love God. For this whole gig – the craze for sex, the desire to love everything that looks good, and the false security of believing you can take care of yourself – doesn't come from our Father but from the evil world system itself. That world system is going to be gone some day and along with it, all desire for what it has to offer; but anyone who follows God's plan for his life will live forever. "Dig it! This whole plastic bag is exactly what Jesus liberated us from" (Two Brothers from Berkeley 1971:205-206).

4. Monism proposes that there is only one reality; the infinite divine essence is identical with nature, and the separation of substance from the spiritual realm is a false dichotomy. Monism is an integral part of Hindu and Buddhist thinking. This appealed to the young rebels for several reasons. It challenged the status quo. It carried the mystique of the East; it was pre-modern wisdom. It seemed capable of challenging not just the actions of reductionist science, but the very reality base on which all of its assumptions rested. It was novel and it was being embraced by that ubiquitous counterculture icon, the rock and folk musician.

One of the most enduring memories of working in the counterculture as a Jesus Freak, was the commonality of experimentation with Eastern philosophy and practice. Right On and Truth and Liberation consistently published articles interacting with Eastern groups and Eastern philosophy (See Truth and Liberation: "Truth Sunnies, 'Comparative Religions in a Nutshell.'" Vol. 1(2):8; "Krishna or Christ." Vol.1(5)13-14; "Divine or demonic? The Guru Maharaja Ji." Vol.2(2)6,7; "Up from Zen." Vol.2(3)7,9.

From an evangelical and Western point of view, Guinness (1973) described the new fascination with Eastern philosophy amongst students in a chapter entitled "The East, No Exit" (1973:195-233). He particularly critiqued the weaknesses of monism. This is not to suggest that Western dualism is without its own inherent weaknesses. The loss of unity and organic understanding of the nature of the universe led many students to embrace pop Eastern concepts. In accepting the proposition that "unity alone is real, then what is the world of diversity or the phenomenal external universe as we know it (1973:215)? Only by the denial of the phenomenal world could the illusion be maintained. Guinness seeks to explore the relationship between monism and personality, and monism and reality, claiming that in their attempt to exit from the immoralities and incongruities of rationalistic, dualistic, Western society, the students of the 1960s had bought into a different set of incongruities and sins against God and humanity.

5. Jesus Movement analysts by the early 1970s recognized a connection between Schaeffer and the Jesus Movement (Enroth, Ericson, and Peters 1972:77, 111). Nethery found stabilizing help at L'Abri in Switzerland, returning to work at Grace Haven Farm as a L'Abri type, experimental stop-off for young people. Schaeffer contributed to Britain's Greenbelt Festivals' Christ and culture debate. Greenbelt made the theological issue of Christ and culture central in the choice of performing artists, seminar speakers, and topics for presentation. In contrast, Smith's mentors were conservative Bible teachers, Arthur Pink, Martin Lloyd Jones, G. Campbell Morgan, and William Newel, none of whom provide a modern or postmodern apologetic (Fromm 1999:58).

6. The Crucible (later developed into the New College, Berkeley), a street university, was formed and led by Bernie Adeney (1995), a recognized scholar in crosscultural ethics and a missionary to Indonesia.

7. In September 1973, Sparks with Michael Eastman of Britain's Frontier Youth Trust, came to Australia for a highly successful ministry tour associated with our group and a number of other groups, concentrating on university campuses. Sparks' skill at making the text winsome and relevant to the non-Christian students was abundantly evident as he spoke on the campus of Monash University, Melbourne. This university had been Australia's hot bed of radical dissent and the location of the historic initiatives in invitro-fertilization. While the great calm-down on campus had probably begun, there was still negativity and hostility towards the establishment, including conservative Christianity. Dr. Jack Sparks as we knew him then expounded the Book of Ecclesiastes as the gospel to secular humanity. He was challenged by a popular character calling himself The Wizard (The Wiz). Donned in a cultic black cloak, wearing a tall, peaked, witches hat, he frequently engaged visiting speakers in dialogue. His sharpness of wit, facility with language, and remarkably extensive knowledge base equipped him to deconstruct, if not humiliate almost all comers. Sparks responded with gracious repartee, wit, and social scientific acumen, such that the crowd basically saw the event as a draw. Berkeley's Sproul Plaza had provided Sparks with a graduate school education in contextualized rhetoric and oratory. He had learnt well. Many were motivated to further spiritual enquiry, not simply by his ability, but by the grace and warmth of his responses.

8. The following entry was published in our Australian Jesus Paper following my return from visit to Calvary Chapel, CWLF, the Church of the Redeemer and other Jesus Movement communities: "CWLF is an organization of evangelical Christians with a unique ministry to the street people of Berkeley and the students of the University of California campus. It was one of the first groups identified as Jesus People and Jesus Freaks by the press. In July 1969 the organization began an underground newspaper

called Right On, the first and, many observers feel, the best Jesus paper. Employing the hip vernacular of the street people, the paper brings the revolutionary message of Jesus Christ to a population of radicals, activists, dopers, and ordinary university students. [These] subcultures were overlooked and even scorned by many churches and straight Christians. The activities of CWLF include an extensive literature ministry including pamphlets, tracts, leaflets and comic books, as well as manuals like a freshman orientation handbook designed for students, and a medical handbook that details basic first aid techniques, and discusses how to plan a nutritious diet on a shoestring budget. All of the literature contains the same simple message of the gospel of Jesus conveyed in the hip language so familiar to members of the youth culture" (John Smith 1973a:10).

9. Donald John Heinz has provided an extraordinary investigation into the CWLF, covering the period of foundation until the organizational beginning of the journey to Orthodoxy. The research resulted from a discussion group of faculty and students from the Department of Sociology at the University of California, Berkeley, in the Graduate Theological Union program. Robert Bellah and Charles Glock came together with the students and directed the project, which was part of a general research into the new religious consciousness spawned in the San Francisco area. Heinz, though not a convert to the values of CWLF, was a sympathetic participant observer. His examination of Right On and some of the other CWLF ministries is detailed and extensive in its probing of the CWLF motivation. More than any other academic I have read, he grasps the essential fact that such groups were determined above all else, to make an alternative Jesus known to the restless, revolutionary seekers of the counterculture. His dissertation was produced in 1976 for the Graduate Theological Union of the University of California, Berkeley.

9. Donald John Heinz has provided an extraordinary investigation into the CWLF, covering the period of foundation until the organizational beginning of the journey to Orthodoxy. The research resulted from a discussion group of faculty and students from the Department of Sociology at the University of California, Berkeley, in the Graduate Theological Union program. Robert Bellah and Charles Glock came together with the students and directed the project, which was part of a general research into the new religious consciousness spawned in the San Francisco area. Heinz, though not a convert to the values of CWLF, was a sympathetic participant observer. His examination of Right On and some of the other CWLF ministries is detailed and extensive in its probing of the CWLF motivation. More than any other academic I have read, he grasps the essential fact that such groups were determined above all else, to make an alternative Jesus known to the restless, revolutionary seekers of the counterculture. His dissertation was produced in 1976 for the Graduate Theological Union of the University of California, Berkeley.

10. British socio-political Christian journal Third Way commenced publication in Guinness's home country, England, in part as the result of the widespread fascination with the "third way" concept. This was in line with much of the later content of CWLF's underground, alternative Jesus Paper, Right On, and Radix, which has continued the tradition since the division of CWLF, and the reforming of the non-Orthodox members, under the name of The Berkeley Christian Coalition.

11. In seeking to understand the sense of absolute finality expressed by each of the CWLF converts to Orthodoxy, I found the ritual process theories of Van Gennep (1960) and Victor Turner (1969) most helpful. The founders of the Evangelical Orthodox Church of America (EOCA) began in a strongly structured ministry under the leadership of Bill Bright of Campus Crusade. The time from 1968 to 1998 until their final acceptance by the Antiochian Orthodox Church (AOC) was psychologically and socially a lengthy "sweat lodge" period of extreme liminality. Almost a decade was spent in the anti-structural activities of Berkeley, of house church planting and rejection of the main-

stream ecclesiological homes, which had nurtured them into adulthood. Even the EOCA period was a liminal state in that it was not classic Pentecostal, Conservative Evangelical, Liberal Protestant nor even fully Orthodox. During the lengthy period of anti-structural pilgrimage, one senses a profound development of communitas between the pilgrims – a sense of irretrievable separation from the previous institutional securities as a major factor in the profound and affective bonding. It is not surprising therefore that the final resolution of reaggregation into Orthodoxy has been marked by a sense of humility and hierarchical closure. The sets of serial terms developed by Van Gennep of separation, marginality, and reaggregation – or in reference to spatial transitions, preliminal, liminal, and post liminal – reflect accurately what I observe as the ritual process and psychosocial outcomes of their journey.

12. The Synaxis was highly ritualized, deeply moving, ancient and processional, but open to all. After the public Synaxis, the congregation dispersed and only catechumens in preparation for membership, and full members attended the Eucharistic gatherings, which were held in the homes of the leaders.

13. A weakness to my research of the Orthodox converts from CWLF has been the lack of responses from the women of Orthodoxy. The wives of interviewees have been present on several occasions, contributing occasionally. The little they have said seems on the surface to parallel the resolution expressed by their spouses. The response to patriarchy in a postmodern, feminist society seems less obviously stressful in Orthodoxy than Catholicism, but for me it is an argument from silence, not from any valid research.

14. I had an opportunity to spend many hours of conversation with Frankie Schaeffer during the European Christian Artist's seminar in Holland, 1994, at which we were both presenters. He publicly dismissed the evangelicalism of his father, asserting that the only true godliness lay in the example of unknown monks, who lived in secluded, monastic commitment to the faith. He believes evangelicalism is fatally flawed, by the fact that its leaders must project themselves into media consciousness, publicizing their exploits and expertise to justify the support of the evangelical community, for the economic underwriting of their ministries. He continues to pursue his interest in screen writing, film directing and writing.

CHAPTER 6

The Jesus Movement in Australia – Radicalizing the Church

"He will not falter or be discouraged until he establishes justice on the earth." "Thy Kingdom come on earth." Isaiah 42:4; Matthew 6:10.

Bewildering, rapid, and extensive change has been a sociological constant since the last world war. Serious social dysfunction and widespread upheaval in values, worldview, and institutions occurred during the period between the 1950s and the 1970s. In reaction, revitalization movements challenged the existing situation, seeking to establish alternative, more satisfying cultures. Differing responses to disorienting change and associated cultural disintegration were variables within the occurrence of revitalization movements during the 1960s and 1970s.

For some individuals and social groups, the reduction of culture stress could only be achieved by the resolution of perceived anomalies, including perceived socially destructive elements of technological society, the spiritual barrenness of scientific rationalism, and the divisiveness of social injustice. Most Australian Jesus People chose a socially activist engagement, rather than a pietistic retreat in the face of cultural instability and loss of personal identity. This chapter will focus on the popular responses typical of the Australian Jesus Movement. But allow me first to put this more sociopolitical approach in a wider context of the North American "alternative" groups.

Revivalism, familiar to North Americans, concerned itself with the individual's salvation, often disengaging from worldly affairs. Revitalization, on the other hand, while disassociating with perceived dysfunction of society, attempts to establish an alternative culture in this world, rather than the next, or as in the case of the Reformation, to overthrow the existing order. McLoughlan (1978) has distinguished between the two forms of religious movement, showing the major awakenings of the United States to be culture informing and transforming revitalizations. I believe this study of the Australian Jesus Movement will demonstrate that its occurrence was a clear attempt to confront and revitalize a culture that has no tradition of either revivals or awakenings on a large scale.

As previously established, revitalization is a process whereby persons through a social movement seek to resolve cultural conflict and create a more satisfying and comprehensible social order. Native American attempts to rescue their tribes from total cultural collapse first drew the attention of Wallace, providing the data from which the theory of revitalization was derived. Colonialism had destroyed Amerindian cultural integrity, stability and unity, through government policies of conquest, land acquisition and forced assimilation (Pflüg 1998:27-33). Their culture was based on a spiritual, mystical relationship with nature, a cohesive communal identity, tribal, consensual decision-making, a code of reciprocity, and an agricultural and hunter-gatherer economy. The loss of relationship to tribal lands, the forced dependency upon a cash economy, and the relocation of communal members to a nuclear rather than extended family context, had devastating impact on individual and communal stability.

The demise of the tribal culture was primarily related to unjust and genocidal policies and actions of white colonialist government. The well-meaning attempts of missionaries to assimilate the people into a European form of a Christian lifestyle exacerbated the deteriorating situation. Conversely, some elements of Christian influence may have also provided a cultural bridge for Native Americans to revitalize their culture by the innovative synthesis of traditional values and rituals in a new historical context (Martin 1999; Pflüg 1998: 50, 101, 239, 248-249; Wallace 1952:155-160).

In the opinion of revitalization movement leaders of Native American cultures in the Great Lakes region, revitalization required radical responses to the causes of the cultural collapse, not only the symptoms of it (Pflüg 1998). Social and political compliance for the sake of physical survival became untenable for some groups. Peace for them would not be the absence of conflict but the reign of justice and restoration of traditional culture. It was felt by many in the Native American cultures that the restoration of cultural stability and health could only be achieved by a social order that addressed and acted upon the causes of their alienation. Compliance with the dominant sociopolitical hegemony could only lead to further social disorder. Radical revitalization was the chosen path. Only counterculture resistance and the repositioning of traditional values in a new social configuration could provide the way to both individual and communal healing.

This was clearly also the view of another alienated "tribe" in recent American history, when Roszak wrote his counterculture manifesto for the youthful dissidents of the 1960s and 1970s in *The Making of a Counterculture* (1968) and *Where the Wasteland Ends* (1972c). Many dissidents of the 1960s concluded that the widespread alienation in their culture was the consequence of a dysfunctional social and political order. Only by radical departure from the materialistic social norms, and by the re-establishment of communal values, spirituality and a compassionate ethic, could the individual find a healthy fulfilling existence and society be saved from imminent collapse. The option of a separate cultural entity of the Amerindian type was hardly feasible for the techno-urban defectors of the 1960s, although some communes briefly sought the alternative of radical rejection and total departure from the dominant culture in lifestyle and ideology.

Some Christian groups of the 1960s revitalization movement emphasized personal salvation, spiritual peace and a new network of support for mutually assuring faith. If Calvary Chapel represented the former scenario of personal salvation, the Australian movement distinctly pursued a radical concept of the kingdom of God on earth. In this chapter I will provide a case study of that alternative movement.

Alternative movements sometimes sought to challenge the entire external world, to make it congruent with radical values of justice and equality for all. All the groups I have researched sought to address cultural distortion and to create a more satisfying culture for their adherents. While all followed a similar processual revitalization path as described by Wallace (1966:158-163), the methods and outcomes were markedly different in expectation and social consequence for each group.

In most American groups the renewal was less obviously theological or ideological in focus. Calvary Chapel had constructed a well-positioned lifeboat with all modern conveniences in expectation of the immanent return of Jesus, and the sinking of the cultural "Titanic." Jesus did not return as swiftly as Pastor Chuck Smith prophesied. Still apocalypse fixated, they made peace with Southern California's radical individualism and conspicuous consumption, establishing a church that fitted their baby boomer clients. Some movements grappled with modernity's failing rationalism, convinced that the marketplace of ideas had to be invaded if the society was to be revitalized. This was preferable to merely providing lifeboats to rescue the casualties of a distorted culture. As we saw in the previous chapter, Berkeley's Christian World Liberation Front initially adopted this focus, but later abandoned it in search of the original church, leaving a few of the early visionaries to struggled on in the restructured Berkeley Christian Coalition.

Worldviews were in a state of creative flux in the Jesus Movement. Reliance on "charismatic or "prophetic" leaders, rather than formalized statements of faith, or traditional routines, allowed for swift, comprehensive revisions of faith and practice. There has been a tendency to label groups according to their initial worldviews. To understand new movements this is inadvisable during early stages. Some Jesus People groups, founded by naïve-realists (Hiebert 1994),[1] developed sophisticated, critical-realist insights by interaction with the counter-culture, and by communally driven self-theologizing that sought to explain the gospel to the local culture.[2]

Shiloh Youth Ministries is a good sample of this analytical problem. Sociologists (Richardson, Stewart, and Simmonds 1979) described the Shiloh movement, one of the most indigenous of the hippie, Christian movements, as a "contemporary, youth, communal, and *fundamentalist* organization" [my emphasis]. The use of *fundamentalist* as descriptive of this group is problematic as the authors admit (1979:17). By the conclusion of the research by Richardson, Stewart and Simmonds, Shiloh was developing sophisticated apologetics on environment and justice issues, quite contrary to the politically conservative tradition of historic fundamentalism (Peterson 1990a:105).[3]

In 1978, Shiloh's Study Center in Dexter, Oregon, became a conference center and school. In 1981 it became a retreat center to promote "caring community," and to "teach and equip believers to creatively and effectively encounter the challenges that modern secularism thrusts upon biblical faith."[4] A pattern of critical education in holistic discipleship and social action became normative in many such groups. Traditional moral values and radical social resistance were synthesized in a non-fundamentalist form typical of revitalization innovation. Like Shiloh, the Australian movement was neither revivalist nor fundamentalist, but certainly radically traditionalist, and clearly countercultural.

In seeking to understand the conservative radicalism of the movement, I found Melissa Pflüg's (1998) ethnographic description of Native American "traditional" values, specifically in the context of revitalization, an enlightening parallel to the radical conservatism of the Australian Jesus Movement. The Jesus People returned to tribal-traditional rather than fundamentalist values, drawing on the communal values of the first century communal tradition of the church, as the Quakers, Anabaptists and Mennonites had done in previous North American renewals.

These values were grounded in the social vision of *The Acts of the Apostles*, through primitive Christian rituals (baptism, foot-washing), socialism, and rituals of *communitas*,[5] an intense existential sense of community typical of revitalization (Turner 1969:96-97; Pflüg 1998:231-233). Pflüg in the previously cited passage provides a convincing rationale for the connection between ritual processes of socioreligious activism, political resistance, social transformation, and *communitas*. According to Pflüg, the Odawah essentially understood "religiousness as fundamentally action oriented and future looking, as it was always concerned with social transformation" (Pflüg 1998:231).

The Jesus People in Australia clearly followed such a pattern. They became convinced that the ancient tradition of Jesus had been hijacked and suppressed by a materialistic, Western, colonialist, counterfeit that could only be overcome by a "Jesus revolution." True religion could no longer rest secure in the safety of orthodoxy but must embrace orthopraxy, the activism of an incarnate, world-transforming God in Christ. Jesus' ethical code of pacifism, love, and communal itinerancy with his disciples bound them in a sense of revitalized identity and counterculture challenge to the dominant, troubled culture. At the core of this revitalization was the embrace of ancient, traditional paths to cultural renewal, rather than a defensive, twentieth century fundamentalism.

As the original obsession with the expected "soon return" of Jesus gave way to a realistic sense of responsibility for the environment and the social order, long term strategies emerged to address ongoing distortions within the culture. The apocalyptic mood was maintained, but the millenarian focus was replaced by a moral apocalypticism, reminiscent of Old Testament prophets, Amos, Jeremiah and Micah (Koch 1982, 1983). Rather than escape via the pre-millennial "rapture" in the face of apocalyptic doom, morally driven, sociopolitical action was preferred. In Australia, the American obsession with the "rapture" rather than cultural revitalization was derisively referred to as an "eschatological relax-a-tab."[6]

I am not suggesting that Australia alone produced intellectually and socially activist Jesus People. Ohio's Xenos remains as an American example of intellectual challenge to secularism, but they have not pursued the sociopolitical implications of the gospel, nor have they adapted to postmodern thinking as most groups did in Australia. They have maintained a theological rather than prophetic vigil, having sustained a strong evangelical apologetic. They continue to fight the battle with distinctly rational tools. Their corporate mind is alive and engaging. The philosophical ground around them has moved to postmodernity, but despite their Schaeffer-style of argumentation, they are still attracting significant numbers of students, from the postmodern, Ohio State University campus. Unlike CWLF, Xenos has not developed a clearly counterculture perspective on political issues, but has maintained the alternative savor of a new religious movement.

Many within the overall movement embraced more distinctly "alternative" social views, with a strong intellectual engagement of the wider culture. Some contemporary, radical discipleship authors and scholars in America were leaders and pioneers in the Jesus Movement, or experienced their theological formation in the activist phase of the Movement. Examples include Joel Green, formerly of Asbury Theological Seminary and now at Fuller Seminary,[7] Ched Myers, a sociopolitical exegete (1990),[8] David Badstone of Central American Missions Partners,[9] Bernard T. Adeney, author of *Strange Virtues: Ethics in a Multicultural World.* (1995),[10] Tom Sine, futurologist, social critic, and author of numerous books on practical discipleship,[11] and Wes Granberg Michaelson, one time Chief Legislative Aide to Senator Mark Hatfield, who was intimately associated with Shiloh and *The Other Side* publication. In the early 1980s, Michaelson was teaching ecological theology at Shiloh[12] and had become Research associate for the Reformed Church in America in Environmental and Global Resources. He eventually rose to the highest position of leadership in the Reformed Church of America.

In searching for examples of the more radical form of the Jesus Movement, exemplifying a commitment to public discourse and mission in counterculture confrontation of the dominant culture, I have found that Australia provides some of the best samples. Impressive ideological and activist, counterculture activity by American Jesus People existed, but it was less typical than in the South Pacific. For a clear example of the Jesus Movement as a dissenting counterculture, attempting to revitalize the culture, the Australian groups provide an excellent case study.

Australian Jesus People in Dissent

Scholars, whose typologies have focussed primarily on America, have largely ignored the unique features of the Australian revitalization. Di Sabatino's annotated bibliography (1999a), though comprehensive, contains no citations for the

Australian Jesus Movement. Attention is given to Europe, and to the United Kingdom.

> However, the Jesus People were not confined to America, or even North America, by any means, and their presence in other countries, especially Western European nations, dates back to almost the beginning of their recognized existence in America, and it is probably there, particularly in Britain that they continue in their most "unadulterated" form today. (Di Sabatino 1999a:10)

The advisory editor of this bibliography series,[13] an Australian academic, does not confine the Movement to America in his introduction to Di Sabatino's contribution, but he makes no mention of the considerable Jesus Movement activity in Australia. John Painter (1997)[14] sheds some light on the lack of recognition of the Jesus Movement in Australia. As a sympathetic outsider, he suggests that the Movement was highly visible, but not recognized by the generic term "Jesus Movement." Jesus People were known by ministry and commune names.[15] To avoid identification as an American, colonialist, implant, leaders de-emphasized ties with the American Movement, despite deep camaraderie between many Australian and American leaders and communities.

In Australia, the Jesus Movement developed a high public profile by its activism and outspokenness on issues of justice for Aborigines, youth, women, and the unemployed. Socioeconomic critique was an integral element of its evangelistic witness. Many Australian Jesus People viewed civil disobedience, demonstrations, and illegal street marches as necessary in defiance of "Caesar." Most expressions of the Australian movement were focused on worldview, on social engagement, and vigorous resistance to the secular powers and institutions. Australians tend to ask, "What are your relationships and commitments?" rather than, "What are your beliefs?" or, "What do you feel?" This confrontational edge marks the controversial style of the Australian movement leadership. None displayed it more than John Hirt, founder of the House of the New World.

> Concerning my sociopolitical and critical hermeneutical "edge" – I direct the reader to the "Australian" differentia. To that "strong social consciousness which has always been a characteristic of Australian writing." Hence 'the lively social conscience which flourishes in the Australian society, appears in its writing as an important aspect of the pattern of radicalism" (T. Inglis Moore [1971]). Therefore, if at times my writing sounds "committed," it is meant to be so. I make no pretence that it is not. I have not wanted to write an "objective" work. I neither wanted to, nor could. There is nothing neutral about the kingdom quest of Jesus. There never was when it was first done, or written about. And there never will be either. Unable to outdistance the kingdom's liberative bias, I take sides; I confess it, and I do not withdraw from it. Those who recoil from this confession, bear scrutiny concerning their own biblical endeavors. We do well to remember that nothing is composed in a neutral environment – including academic, sociopolitical theology. (Hirt 1998:2)

This politically aligned, activist evangelicalism fused a clear advocacy for the marginalized, with a theological apologetic for justice, even though strategies, methods, and theological traditions varied considerably. Common cause for justice arose from a variety of traditions and meanings, but activism, intellectual engagements and compassion bonded a diverse group of new religious movements from the beginning. The movement, as in the Native American revitalization groups, was based on the revitalization premise that the existing system was not amenable to the people's needs, but in need of substantial transformation. The contents of the major Australian Jesus papers reveal a consistent belief that a cultural crisis had occurred requiring substantial overhaul and replacement.

During the "heady" days of anti-Vietnam War Protest, Melbourne's Monash University was a hotbed of academic and student dissent. The Jesus Movement group, Truth and Liberation Concern invaded the Campus in 1973, enthusiastically supported by the widest range of student groups – the Catholic Newman Society, the Lutheran Students, the Evangelical Union, the Student Christian Movement, and some activist secular groups. The student journal supplied a full page of academic staff and administration names in support of the two-week mission. Such was the eclectic spirit of enquiry amongst students that the counterculture foray attracted capacity crowds to midday meetings held in the largest lecture theatre. Many were turned away. Presentations were deliberately provocative and anti-establishment. Topics included: "Stop Believing and Start Doubting;" "God is Dead, Marx is Dead and I'm not Feeling too good Myself;" "Who am I in your Brave New World;" "I'm not my Brother's Keeper – I'm My Brother's Brother;" "Jesus the Revolutionary."

Lectures focusing on anti-war, Christian socialist and counterculture propositions attracted a great number of young Marxists. Half way through one address, a small group of Satanists broke into the theatre in an attempt to break up the meeting. Instantly a group of Marxists, who had increasingly entered into friendly dialogue with radical Christians, leapt to their feet and physically threw the interjectors out of the theatre to the applause of the crowd. An academic remarked that the Christian initiative had aroused more interest and enthusiasm on the campus than any other program.

A similar mission on the Adelaide campus attracted a couple thousand students for an open-air presentation on the Barr-Smith lawns. Such was the remarkable spirit of protest, enquiry, and exchange of ideas that the Australian Jesus Movement embraced the dissent gladly, in common cause with Marxists, Anarchists, feminists, environmentalists, peace activists, and seeking pilgrims, all proclaiming the expected demise of the culture.

A Seed from Afar – Mutated and Nurtured in Foreign Soil

Historic timing, geographical isolation, and contrasting biographies of the leadership [16] shaped the Australian expressions differently from the American movement. Australia saw many varied expressions of the Jesus Movement, including some elements similar to those in America. In clear contrast however, the dominant forms were less fundamentalist, more socially activist, and theologically sophisticated, reflecting the popular culture. Apart from the Children of God, little of extremist, cultist behavior occurred in Australia. Critics sometimes supposed communalism and aggressive youthful radicalism could produce cults.

The tragic Jim Jones event in Guyana in 1978 cast a shadow over many counterculture groups

The American Connection

Modern communications enabled interaction between Australian groups and their American brethren, but no visits from American leaders gave rise to the developments in Australia, as in the United Kingdom. Unlike the European and British Movements, Australian groups were indigenous plants, but global communications guaranteed that once the American Movement was subject to media interest, its presence and message was felt abroad, even before the public media frenzy of 1972. Europe, being geographically closer to America, experienced considerably more influence by American leaders. Some initiatives in the United Kingdom were triggered by visits from American Jesus People. Street preachers and musicians – notably Blessitt, Palosaari, Pulkingham, and Norman – helped shape it there (Pete Ward 1996:80-104).

Australian leaders made select visits to America on fact-finding missions, to meet with other "tribal" leaders, to form alliances, and compare strategies. Some visited, or corresponded with "alternative" groups and leaders, particularly Berkeley's CWLF, Church of the Redeemer, Post-American (Sojourners), and some of the more radical expressions in the Pacific Northwest. John Hirt, a major inspirational force in Australia, spent considerable time in the Berkeley context, building relationships with radical Catholic and Baptist Liberation theology advocates while pursuing graduate studies.

American influence was significant but not initiating or defining. It was more selectively filtered and controlled, and occurred on indigenous terms. The globalization of media accelerated the growth of the Australian Jesus Movement. The "underground" press started in America amidst the political ferment on university campuses, facilitated by the new technology of offset printing, becoming a global student obsession.

The counterculture was evangelistic, spreading a message of peace, communalism, spirituality, and environmentalism, by all means. The Australian Jesus Freaks adopted the culturally popular underground press which was employed by street evangelists and Jesus communes in the publication of *The Free Paper*; *Coming Home*; *Focus*; *Free Slave*; *Rap*; *Sydney Town Express*; *Tell*; *Theos Sun*; *Truth & Liberation*; *Dayspring*.

In 1973, strategically chosen visitors were invited to expand the local, conceptual framework, specifically: Dr. Jack Sparks,[17] theological analyst Os Guinness,[18] and Michael Eastman of Britain's Frontier Youth Trust. At the popular level, musician Barry McGuire[19] made several visits and was greatly appreciated in the 1970s and 1980s. Musician Larry Norman made several visits beginning in 1975 (See Figure 6.1). Arthur Blessitt came much later. These three had less local influence than teaching visitors.

Global-local cross-pollination influenced young, radical Christians through grass roots itinerancy during early development. Foreign impact on Australian groups occurred incidentally through these grass roots connections. Interaction with counterculture youths on pilgrimage from Asia and Europe was common.

Many converts returned from Francis Schaeffer's L'Abri community in Switzerland (E. Schaeffer 1969). Schaeffer's Ashram style engagement was instrumental in converting disillusioned pilgrims, ending their search for gurus in exotic lands.

Several leaders of the Australian Movement visited L'Abri, whose literature and audiotapes were influential early in the Australian Movement's development. Dutch academic, Hans Rookmaaker (1968, 1970, 1978, 1986) and Oxford trained Os Guinness (1973), associates of L'Abri, had more influence as the Movement progressed.

Schaeffer's return to his fundamentalist roots in epistemology and social conservatism eventually caused many of the Movement leaders in Australia to look for mentoring in the direction of young evangelicals (Quebedeaux 1974) like Jim Wallace and Jim Punton. Liberation theologians and missiologists – evangelical Protestants (Guillermo Cook; Orlando Costas), and Catholics, both liberation theologians (Gustavo Gutierrez; Jose Miranda) – and devotional activist Henri Nouwen, were significant influences on the Movement's approach to theology and methodology. An immense thirst for knowledge created an eclectic openness to any authors, or preachers, whose content was culturally relevant, ethically compelling, intellectually stimulating, and socially innovative.

Despite the relative independence of the Australian Jesus Movement, similarities existed. American writers uniformly link the phenomenon to revivalist antecedents.[20] Its impact on Australia and the United Kingdom, being devoid of such precedents, requires further explanation. Similarities may point to the pervasive influence of America on other English speaking cultures. Or they may be seen as simultaneous expressions of postmodern, psycho-religious deconstruction, or perhaps the impact of globalization and accompanying cultural synthesis. Anthropologically, universal elements of human religiosity may have been expressed in the Jesus Movement response to secularism and urbanization, irrespective of variations in socioreligious tradition. The processual similarities are consistent with classic revitalization responses to similar distress over cultural distortions that marked other Western cultures globally at that time.

I believe however that Australian variations in theology and cultural interplay require further explanation. The Australian experience was consistently different in its interaction with secular culture. No prior precedent of revivalism of the North American genre existed in the Australian historical consciousness. Quite different local influences would seem to be causal of the variations in belief and practice in this instance. How significant then were the local, cultural and historical influences, and what were those sociocultural variables?

The Sociocultural and Ethnohistorical Context

The profoundly formative influences of foundational history of younger democracies like America, Canada, New Zealand and Australia are not immediately

Figure 6.1 Larry Norman 1974 – Loved in Australia for his Counterculture Style.

obvious. But as the twig is bent, so the tree grows. Early national history often shapes the character and institutions of a people. The Revolutionary and Civil Wars and the First Evangelical Awakening were powerful influences in the shaping of America's constitution and national identity. Her frontier experience shaped the religious consciousness that arose out of the Second Evangelical Awakening (Ellwood 1973:24-44; McLoughlin 1978:44-66, 131-140). Since several scholars have strongly emphasized the significance of historical religious precedents in the study of the movement in the United States, it seems vitally important to provide the reader with a similar historical analysis of the quite different background which gave rise to the Australian variations of the movement. Without this the revivalist antecedents commonly related to the rise of this revitalization in North America may be mistakenly assumed to have relevance to the movement universally, and therefore to Australia in particular.

The Significance of Australia's Peculiar, Historical Antecedents

Without historical perspective, meaningful cultural analysis and interpretive conclusions are at best naive, and incomplete. The difference between American and Australian history is fundamental to an understanding of their contrast in national religious consciousness. The theological framing of their respective worldviews is deeply rooted in their histories. In comparing Australian and American religious formation, there has been an "underestimation of the historical, theological content of much American religiosity" (Mol 1985:186).

> I think that the peculiar, peaceful symbiosis of aggressive secularization and religiosity in American society has its origin much further back in the pre-industrial, but culture-creating era of American history. The Great Awakening in the eighteenth century, and the fervent religion of earlier periods made for the Americanization and therefore vitalization of European religious forms. It also led to the inevitable profanation or secularization of American society once the charismatic phase had become irrelevant for the now self-propelling cultural forces ... [A]t any rate the similarities between the religious scene in England and Australia and the dissimilarities between Australia and America make sense only in terms of some such historical argument. After all, unlike America, Australia has never had anything like this religious fervency dissolving it from the Old World heritage. (Mol 1985:186)

The sources of Australia's peculiar characteristics, including its dominant form of secularism, were the obsession of Manning Clark (1968, 1976, 1980, 1987), arguably the nation's most prestigious and controversial historian. He framed his historical analysis around the long-term consequences of the nation's birth, brutal colonial infancy, and insecure, anti-British adolescence. An agnostic for much of his life, and a Catholic convert from nominal Anglicanism in his final days, his sensitive accounts of Australia's history became very influential in the lives of the Movement leadership. While searching for an authentic Australian expression of the Movement, history became the consort of theology and missiology. Australian Jesus Movement owed much of their self-theologizing and understanding of indigenous mission to the popularization of Clark's history in the 1970s. The Movement in Australia was birthed during an intense, adolescent rejection of mother England's cultural apron strings. The rejection of American influence was also a major aspect of the contemporary revolt.

The tyranny of distance. The isolation of the island continent had produced a unique, markedly different flora and fauna from Europe and America, including the earth's only monotremes,[21] the platypus and the echidna. The natural history is paradigmatic of the effect of historical isolation during the nation's Anglo-Australian cultural formation. Its indigenous peoples, cut off from the rest of the world for between 40,000 and 60,000 years, survived as possibly the oldest extant culture on earth.[22] Isolation is assumed to be a significant factor in the formation of our national traits. Prominent historian, Geoffrey Blainey (1983) shaped his analysis around this factor, in his work on Australia's unique experience, *The Tyranny of Distance: How Distance Shaped Australia's History*. Historian, John Ramsland (1987) saw it as the formative element of consciousness in the social structures of the Manning Valley, New South Wales.

Geographic and sociopolitical isolation conspired with the brutal convict system and climate related hardships to create a tradition of rugged independence and stoicism, expressed in the colloquial language of Australians even today. When bushranger [outlaw] Ned Kelly, a poor Irish immigrant was hung in the Melbourne Jail, his final words, "And now it comes to this. Such is Life," became the folk symbol for the national character. The more affable phrase, "She'll be right mate," became the modern expression of valor in the face of defeat, rather than a positive assurance of expected success.[23]

A case of cosmic orphanhood and homelessness. A stoic and sardonic attitude toward life was rooted in Australia's Colonial beginnings. The founding of the Penal Colony (1788) was brutal, debauched, and untimely. The American Revolution closed the doors to England's dispatches of convicts from overpopulated prisons to her colonies in Virginia. Visionary citizens, embracing a charter for independence and freedom, did not found Australia's church in contrast to America. Government appointed the Church of England as a moral gatekeeper for the aristocracy, declaring judgement on convicts that were herded into compulsory chapel services. The Governor appointed Anglican chaplains as magistrates, who were renowned for their Calvinist harshness metered out to convicts, which included Christian social activists, and Irish rebels, petty thieves, and the genuinely dangerous criminals. Petty crime against the properties of the rich, or the celebration of Catholic mass in Ireland could result in deportation. Australia's clergy-magistrates sat as judge and jury in the court of morality, and superintended up to 300 brutal lashings at a time, by the cat o' nine tails.

George Loveless, Methodist lay preacher and founder of the British Trade Union Movement, served seven years of chained slavery in Tasmania for the civil disobedience of organizing a strike by disenfranchised farm laborers.[24] It finally destroyed Loveless' faith in the institution of the church (R. Davies 1963:130).

> Good God, what hypocrisy and deceit is here manifested! The most cruel, the most unjust, the most atrocious deeds are committed and carried on under the cloak of religion! .... Those hypocrites who pretend to be so scrupulous, that

rather than submit to have their most holy religion endangered, they . . . are some of the first to separate man and wife, to send some to banishment, and others to the Poor-law prisons; to oppress the fatherless and the widow. From all such religion as this, "Good Lord, deliver us!" (John Smith 1989:12)

As an agent of the State, the establishment Anglican Church participated in the reign of cruelty and abandon, thus provoking an anticlericalism and negativity towards organized religion, which remains a national characteristic. The second half of the nineteenth century saw the abandonment of the Anglican magistrate system. A diversified role beyond that of moral enforcer had always existed for the church, but the public image of the church hierarchy lingered on, encouraging the growth of free churches. Despite dehumanizing beginnings, and the growth of nominalism and secularism, the church has exercised a good, powerful influence as a minority, establishment movement.[25] Major contribution to socialization had been made in rural districts, where a Methodist Church could be found in virtually every town. Methodism had expressed solidarity with Unionism and issues of justice, but the patrimony of government granted to Anglicanism had alienated the masses from that bastion of privilege through its moralist subservience to the agenda of the privileged. Despite its aggressive open-air evangelism, the Salvation Army was an exception to Australia's view of institutionalized religion, because of its street level work, and tireless service among the poor. Australia was to become a prime example of successful democracy, but without the religious meanings of America.[26] Little of legislative import was generated by religious sentiment in Australia. Australians, resentful towards the British parent, inherited and finally controlled the family farm but were jealous of American independence. There was no antipodean revolution. Australians have tended to resent secular or religious authority ever since, but they rarely revolt.

The English occupation of Australia in 1788 occurred more than a century after European and English settlers had arrived in North America. The timing, at the end of the eighteenth century, was at the high point of European rationalism and deism. Popular Australian poets, novelists, and statesmen of the first 100 years, unlike their American counterparts, were mostly agnostics and atheists. The literary "greats" typified by novelist Marcus Clarke, and poets Adam Lindsay Gordon, Henry Kendall, and Henry Lawson, were people who had accepted scientific rationalism as spelling inevitable death to religious credibility.

Amongst the middle class and educated, the literary tradition of Australia showed that deism had triumphed, leaving little trace of God's presence on the Australian landscape. Hans Mol (1971, 1985), prominent Australian analyst of Australian religion, observes that there has always been a vigorous minority committed to the life of the church, but lacking a major role in the nation's intellectual formation. "With the exception of major historians, most of the writers on Australian society moved in circles where religion was not important" (Mol 1971:x). In contrast, the enduring influence of Puritan, and Congregationalist Christianity was established early in America.[27]

The formative voices of Australian culture were lost somewhere between a painful, post-Christian death, and a difficult pre-Christian birth. Australia's popular thinkers were desperately transitional men, languishing between unbelief in an unsustainable past, and faith in an unknown future. Some sought analgesic escape from painful non-belief. Marcus Clarke was an opium addict; Lawson, Gordon, and Kendall were alcoholics. Wounded by the horror of convict history, and the barrenness of the bush, they felt a God-forsakenness in the marrow of their colonial bones. Their writings were courageous dismissals of God, full of wistful anguish, caught somewhere between the ghost of a belief in the Fatherhood of God, and stoic, courageous, enlightenment agnosticism. This sense of cosmic abandonment and spiritual vertigo appears early in the writings of Australia's favorite sons. Manning Clark described the nineteenth century period of cultural development as the era of *The Kingdom of Nothingness* (1978:271-31).

<u>Rural myths and urban realities</u>. Australia has been one of the most urbanized nations on earth since European occupation, with more than 80 percent of its population in six cities; but its identity myths are obtained from rural tradition. The best known of these myths is "mateship." The intense sense of male camaraderie in war, in times of rural crisis, sports, and in economic hard times, seemed to be collapsing in the 1960s. Despite Australia boasted a tradition of egalitarianism, but its carefree materialism, rugged individualism, and pragmatic secularism seemed to be an unlikely social glue to bond the young democracy as a spiritual community. D.H. Lawrence was critical of Australian society in his novel *Kangaroo* (Lawrence 1923). He characterized the national consciousness as crass, adrift, and without a core of meaning and identity.

> The bulk of Australians don't care about Australia. . . . And why don't they? Because they care about nothing at all, neither on earth below, or in heaven above. They just blankly don't care about anything, and they live in defiance, a sort of slovenly defiance of care of any sort, human or inhuman, good or bad. If they've got one belief left, now the war's safely over, it's a dull, rock-bottom belief in obstinately not caring, not caring about anything. (Lawrence 1923:72)

To outsider Lawrence, as to many European migrants, the lack of meaning was bewildering. Thus his mythical migrant declares alienation in the far country.

> He felt broken off from his fellow men. He felt broken off from the England he had belonged to. The ties were gone. He was loose like a single timber of some wrecked ship, drifting over the face of the earth . . . . He was broken apart; apart he would remain. (1923:287)

Barren soil breeds a barren soul.[28] Australians are an enigma – self reliant, independent, hospitable, and pioneering, but rarely religious. The pioneers of the culture "knew no more about the clergyman's beliefs, than the cleric knew about the all-important horse craft on the cattle station" (Manning Clark 1978:271). The spiritual dearth, making Australia one of the most secular nations on earth, is traceable to a period when post-Christian "nothingness" replaced the centering vision of the Kingdom of God.

The struggles of Australian writers reflect the Australian popular consciousness. It is helpful for non-Australian's to read of the secular despair of Australia's authors. Popular poet, Henry Lawson, thought a different god to that of established religion would see the best in humanity, judging with mercy and removing the advantages of class prejudice. His poems, "Second Class Wait Here!," "Saint Peter" and "The Good Samaritan," held hope for a "fairer go" beyond "the Great Divide." Lamentably, the official, religious dogma bore closer resemblance to the law of the Pharisees, than to the Christ-like, redemptive cry in the heart of this great Australian socialist.

A nation in search of a meaning and a soul. From the 1970s, cultural stresses created an intense search for meaning and identity in Australian culture. At the conclusion of the 1980s, Australian biologist Charles Birch (1990) called mechanistic Australians to reject their materialism in favor of "meaning" and "purpose."[29] It became popular to research the "lack of meaning in the land of plenty," (John Smith 1989) by historical analysis of the Australian consciousness. The contribution of the Jesus Movement to the renewal of Australian church and society was in the context of an unprecedented wave of national enquiry into our identity. In America, the 1970s were years of recovering from social upheaval, cultural repositioning, and redefining of the nation's identity and spiritual heritage (Hunter 1983:46; Jorstad 1990:4-10; Roof 1993, 1999; Tipton 1984; Wuthnow 1998). In Australia during the 1970s, it appeared as if the nation was seeking the first dawn of spiritual meaning.

In search of indigeneity – advance Australia where? Overwhelmed by an optimistic belief that humankind was on the verge of a great social, evolutionary leap forward, the sustaining foundations of English, religious tradition were further weakened. The comparative cultural positioning of the church in Australian society had always been in stark contrast to America. I am impressed by Robert Ellwood's argument that "the United States does not have the [European] model of a single state church, thoroughly intertwined with the history and culture of the land, but rather has long been, to a degree virtually unequaled anywhere else, religiously pluralistic. The United States is the only major country in the world largely populated by religious dissenters from some state church or another" (Ellwood 2000:224). Thus religious pluralism, dissent and voluntarism are seen historically as foundational and patriotic, thus facilitating periodic religious revitalization.

Although the Australia church had been legally separated from affairs of the State and the judiciary in the colony, a tradition of establishment links to major denominations made the birth of new movements difficult. Churches had been established along ethnic lines.[30] Government granted denominations specific geographical regions over which the particular denomination held exclusive rights for Aboriginal missions. The Australian experience of church for the majority of its people was not expressive of revolutionary innovation, but rather of establishment conformity. Most Australian Prime Ministers have been the products of private denominational schools.

Not by law but by cultural precedent, restricted religious trade was the Australian norm until the emergence of the Jesus Movement and the Charismatic Movement in the 1960s and 1970s. Fierce opposition to new movements as "sheep-stealers" delayed the birth of indigenous churches. Australians, conditioned by a history of European and British migrant-based denominationalism, viewed Pentecostals, and even respectable holiness and revivalist American groups, suspiciously.[31] Since World War II, voices had been raised, occasionally calling for the indigenization of the church. During Sir Alan Walker's Mission to the Nation he preached extensively in secular locations, with an Australian accent in style and content. His was one of the early voices to call for a peculiarly Australian, religious consciousness and for an Australian expression of church.

> Australia needs a truly Australian church. The Christian faith will not reach the hearts of the Australian people unless it is interpreted in the light of our own national consciousness and social situation. Only a fully indigenous church will be able to respond to the unfolding moral and spiritual demands of the nation . . . The task of Christian thinkers is to come to grips with the distinctive problems and characteristics of Australian consciousness. (Alan Walker 1972:1)

It is significant that these sentiments appeared as editorial comment for a respectable mainstream research bulletin, *St. Mark's Review*.

> Is there an authentically Australian expression of religion? Is it Christian, and if so, how are we to recognize it and affirm it. . . .Is Christianity in the literal sense of the word, "ecumenical," transcultural, or non-cultural; or is it to be made up of different, but complementary expressions of the Christian faith, each shaped by the "cultural" experience in which it is at present located. (Walker 1972:1)

Debates raged during the 1970s "gospel and culture" enquiry, as to whether Australia was Christian or post-Christian.[32] Peter Kaldor (1987), Uniting Church Board of Mission researcher, expressed the Australian missional dilemma well:

> Churches in Australia have given little thought to the cultural appropriateness of their ministries. Yet if the same people were to work for a foreign culture overseas, it would be perfectly natural to encourage local leadership and to establish patterns of church life and ministry that were culturally appropriate. In the missionary fields in our own backyards the principles are no less important and must be rediscovered. (Kaldor 1987:219)

For Australians the land of faith is a foreign country. Only when religion delivers service detached from religious propositions, as in the ministry of the Salvation Army, is it seen as a patriotic expression of the culture.

> In Australia, faith had to be practical or it was not real; otherwise it was contemptuous and the butt of amusement. As the bushman and their "Outback" songs in scorn put it: "parsons and preachers are all a mere joke." Religion had always historically been viewed as being in cahoots with officialdom, and therefore the enemy of common folk. Our Australian history with justified hostility named the clergy as, "these batterers upon effete superstitions, these cringes to wealth, these despises of the poor, these prosperous Judas's." As far as we could see the traditional Australian view of the Clergy was right: too many Australian Ministers spoke with "plumb in the mouth sounds" and tried to act as posh "poms." Thus cast, they were representatives of a Christianity more at home among the "gentry" than the common folk. There were some rare exceptions (mostly among the Catholics), but basically they were "a bunch of well meaning, but tolerably harmless men who had perfected the art of tea drinking and biscuit-nibbling and little more." (Hirt 2000:182)

The establishment church previously appointed as the sanctifier of the meritocracy was now challenged to be relevant to the masses. When the Jesus Movement hit the headlines in Australia, God was far removed and irrelevant to the average Australian. The nation was secular, and the church was a subculture that rarely appeared in the media to address issues other than sexual deviation, gambling, and alcohol abuse. Alarmed at the Church's distance from the popular culture, clerics began to experiment.

In 1981, David Millikan, a scholar and media presenter released *The Sunburnt Soul* in book and TV documentary form. Millikan's contribution was well publicized and ably promoted the gospel and culture debate.[33] A central Millikan tenet that Australians were as religious as Americans, but expressed their spirituality in a secularized form of mateship in the pub, was welcomed by anti-clerical secularists, but was not convincing to many who were involved in market place evangelism. Most were inclined towards Bishop Bruce Wilson's (1983) belief that Australia was post-Christian and irreligious. During the 1980s the search for an Australian theology and mission strategy was a popular and an academic pursuit (Breward 1988; Garvin 1987; Harris, Hind, and Millikan 1982; Kaldor 1987; Malone 1988; Smith 1989; Wilson 1983).

"Gum leaf theology" became popular by the end of the 1970s, indicative of populist moves to contextualize the gospel. Socially conservative Anglicans took the message in culturally relevant form to pub and workplace (Hannaford 1985). Even the traditionalist Lutherans began to contextualize theology, liturgy, imagery, and hymnology (Habel and Hart 1983).[34] The Jesus Movement led the way in indigenous theology and contextual methodology, or at least fanned the flickering flame of denominational interest in cultural relevance. The innovative genius of the youthful movement drew some applause and co-operation from previously defensive denominations. By the 1980s, a new denominational attitude was evident in the acceptance of a new paradigm of church planting. Lutheran, Anglican, Uniting Church, and even Catholic journals began reporting the activities of the Jesus Movement in a positive vein.[35] Religious deregulation, foundational to American democracy, was at last emerging in Australia at the conclusion of the twentieth century. The Jesus Movement became the harbinger of a new springtime of experimentation.

The Timing of the Nation's Soul

Whatever the broader cultural patterns of a nation, the initiatives of new social movements are driven by contemporary, social imperatives, by popular consciousness at the time, and by political opportunities that facilitate successful innovations. Local and global forces promote or conflict with attempted change.

The global context – searching for independence. Australia's links with America were deeply rooted in shared war camaraderie in the First and Second World Wars, the Korean War, and finally in Vietnam. In the 1960s a weakening of pro-American attitudes was evident during President Johnson's visit in 1967. By 1972 Australians overwhelmingly wanted their own foreign policy, popular culture, and faith.[36]

Local context – it's time for a change. A comparison of American political and religious event timelines reveals a significant difference in the positioning of the relative revitalization phases. The American Jesus Movement was at the height of national attention when the counterculture was in recession and a conservative Richard Nixon was at the height of political ascendancy. In contrast, Australia was entering a socialist period of political consciousness and radical legislative change. Gough Whitlam's socialist Labor party regained office, after 23 years in the political wilderness (1972), as conservative Nixon was elected to office for a second term in the same year.[37]

Some Jesus Movement groups actively campaigned for Whitlam, while warning that a lack of a transcendent foundation would undermine good socialist ideals (John Smith 1973b:6). During a wave of nationalism identity and destiny became central themes in both popular and high culture. The political climate spawned new movements. The traditionally conservative, older generation clashed with a younger generation of idealists over our involvement in Vietnam.[38] The mood was ripe for innovation. A counterculture faith was well positioned for success.

The 1960s phenomena were made for television. Australians were exposed to the same disturbing television images and journalistic critiques of Western culture, destabilizing society, and leading to the troubled decade from the mid 1960s to mid 1970. The symbolic dissidence of long hair and counterculture dress had spread to our country, raising the ire of institutional church and educational institutions. Students were suspended from school for hair length, clothing, and protest insignias. Bible teachers taught that "long hair" is a "disgrace" to a man (1 Corinthians 11:14). Marijuana and psychedelics had also created dysfunction amongst Australian youths. Nimbin, a large counterculture community, drew "drop outs" to a morally free "love in" zone in a lush, tropical "Eden" on the New South Wales coast. Cultural distortion was met by a wave of alternative hope for change, even religious change. In this psychic and intellectual flux the Jesus Movement arose, indigenous, antiestablishment and euphoric, to surf the wave of new consciousness in a previously barren, secularist, anti-church culture.

A Brief Taxonomy of Australian Jesus Movement Groups

Minor variations were as numerous as the number of groups, but a clear pattern emerged along a continuum from parachurch outreach programs to radical house church communes. New movements were evangelizing, teaching, creating rehabilitation centers and sometimes planting alternative churches. House churches, radical communities, rehabilitation houses and discipling, evangelizing, parachurch movements proliferated, several examples of which shall be described later in this chapter.

Radical, Intentional Communities

Communes provided free space for subversion, for dropping out of the parent's world, and for connecting with a visionary tribe of Christian revolutionaries. The communities were not for perfecting the saints for the soon return of Jesus. Nor were they re-socializing units to equip new converts for re-adaptation to the mainstream Protestant work ethic or conformity to its institutional values. They were discipling, training centers to equip Christian, counterculture activists, preparing them to engage the powers in a struggle for justice and peace so that God's will be done on earth.[39] Pilgrims could crash for a night, or embrace a permanent commitment to the revolution in an atmosphere of heady love and ecstatic hope.

Rescue and Rehabilitation Houses

Some communities focused on refugees from confusing worldviews, destructive lifestyles, and shattered illusions. Free accommodation was offered to the homeless, the dysfunctional, the drug abused, and the single mother. They cared for, and rehabilitated the homeless, the unemployed, the drug dependent, the criminal, even pedophiles, in a communal care model. Often called halfway houses, these were a Christian initiative, years ahead of state and church institutional responses to youth homelessness.

House Churches

It is needful to differentiate between cell, or home groups and house churches. The house church movement sought intimacy, accountability and a family sense of the body of Christ, believing the early church probably sustained healthy community in units not much greater than an extended family size of a dozen or twenty members. House churches were household sized congregations that embraced all elements of church in the downsized unit. Baptisms, communion, evangelism and social welfare were generated or maintained in home groups led by trained pastors. Sometimes cell church life was supplemented by larger gatherings of several communes or home groups for Bible teaching or inspirational "raps."

While some groups established communes operating their ecclesial life on a small group basis, most found that their worship attracted larger numbers. This, combined with a growth rate vastly out-weighing the capacity to train sufficient house church leaders, tended to produce larger groups meeting for worship and instruction. Many communal groups moved their focus in and out of ministry, intentional community, church, and radical training cells. Some became independent churches embracing all elements of church life, but often denying denominational status. Some began as outreach but were forced to embrace the responsibility of church, to disciple and nurture the converts.

The development of a cellular model of churches was by no means restricted to those defecting from their denominational roots. Running parallel to the new movements and in fellowship with them, house churches and communal discipleship groups arose at the edge of denominations. It was within the historic denominations that house churches based on a radical model of New Testament ecclesia were pioneered by dissenting scholars within the church fold (Banks 1990, 1994; Banks and Banks 1998).[40]

> Other Christians, influenced by the New Testament models of the house church, have moved away from the historic churches to create small and intimate fellowships, where the whole body of believers could exercise their gifts. While this Movement has not developed the momentum of the British house church networks, it has had some very strong leadership and the capacity to learn, because of the influence of people like Dr. Robert Banks,[41] a former Anglican academic, who has become a parachurch leader of national and international stature. (Breward 1988:80)

Banks and others within the establishment felt common cause with the Jesus People in the search for a more faithful and culturally enriching model of church. Jesus Movement festivals and teach-ins (Figure 6.2) embraced such denominational rebels for their own educational purposes. "Straight" churches sometimes resourced and embraced Jesus Movement churches that had denominational links for fear of losing their visionary youth some of whom found the Jesus Movement a context for creative experimentation.

Freedom in ministry was sometimes denied them by conservative local churches, so these semi-independent groups began to fulfill all the requirements of a church, basically outside denominational structures, protocols or authority lines. The House of the Gentle Bunyip developed such a local congregation that was independent but linked to the Baptist Union.

Parachurch and New Church Agencies for Outreach

Culturally accessible centers and pop-culture accouterments were spawned all over the country. A variety of "lighthouses of hope" – Jesus Light and Power House, Jacob's Ladder, Agape House, Koinonia, Fusion Centers, Theos coffee shops, the Salt and Light Company, and numerous other drop in centers, coffee shops, and overnight accommodation centers – were strewn across the cultural seascape. They provided a network for shipwrecked hippies, dissidents, and wanderers. Empathy, life experience, unconditional love, 24-hour-a-day availability, and the stabilizing authority of shared biblical faith worked wonders for thousands of marginalized youth.

Some units were purely for contact and outreach. Others ran the full gamut of ministries, from outreach to rehabilitation to alternative church community. God's House, The House of the New World, the House of Freedom, TLC, and The Glebe Zoo were typical of these. The movement produced and nurtured many creative musicians, performing artists, and proclaimers for mission. Jesus Centers provided 24-hour counseling and practical help for those in crisis, attracting those alienated from the welfare provisions of both Church and State. Ministering centers defied local ordinances and served as flophouses for accommodating wandering dropouts. Thousands of lasting converts were introduced to faith and to radical church.

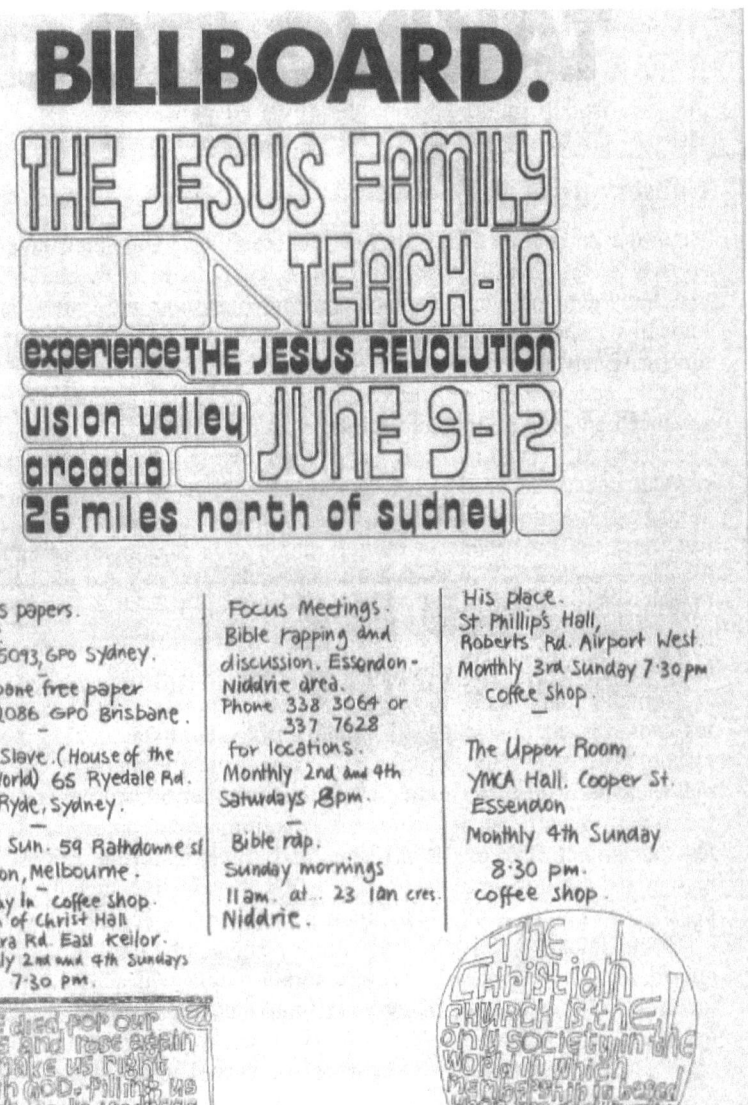

Figure 6.2. Billboard Announcing a Joint Jesus Movement/Church Teach-In (1974)

These centers provided a rich tapestry of redemptive stories to captivate visitors, who soon would be adding their own conversion accounts of the power of Jesus.

Conservatives and Subversives

In the Australian Movement the counterculture Christian flavor was almost entirely birthed and sustained not by indigenous hippies, but by evangelicals who had "gone native." The leaders of the Australian movement had been theologically trained, were children of the manse, and in most cases respected pastorss or Christian workers prior to dropping out in serious protest. They paralleled the secular reality of middle class kids rejecting parents, career, economic advancement, and traditional values.

Parachurch agencies were developed by new Jesus Movement churches without due consideration for ecclesiastic authority. As a leadership that was almost entirely comprised of ex-conservatives who had defected and gone native, they felt a nagging uncertainty about their legitimacy as an extension of historic church. For the child of the manse the sense of marginalization and dubious legitimacy was acute. By what authority did we operate in the denominational hegemony of an Australian church that had never known the American experience of religious deregulation? Were we only parachurch?

A plenary address by Howard Snyder at the Lausanne Congress in 1974, using material for his books, *The Problem of Wineskins* (1975), and book *The Community of the King* (Synder 1977) was critically important for Jesus Movement leaders who were invited at the last minute to attend. From that point on we came to regard our new churches as legitimate and our ministries no more or less parachurch than the departments and ministries of the historic church. We recognized our own organizations as *new* wineskins in which the liberating gospel wine was made available to a new generation neglected by the *old* church.

Soon, fundamentalists, conservative Festival of Light moral crusaders, and neo-Pentecostal evangelists found common cause with radical movements, for the purpose of embracing a new era of making Jesus a cultural issue throughout the land. Some denominational leaders joined with counterculture leaders who were establishing competitive new religious movements through previous denominational connections. The social marginalization of the church in an increasingly adversarial, secular culture aligned "strange bedfellows." Necessity birthed innovation, creating new networks and deregulating religious forms.

Perhaps more remarkable than any other relationship was the relationship between Catholic charismatics and Jesus Movement communities. Bitter conflicts between Anglicanism and the priest-less Irish convicts of the first 12 years of colonialism had forged inter-faith hostilities.[42] Jesus Freaks and Protestant Charismatics bypassed the conflict. They were welcomed in Catholic schools, teaching students how to transcend nominalism through "new birth," and the "power of the Spirit."

There were almost as many varieties of local forms as individual organizations, but virtually all innovations arose as one of three archetypal groups. I have therefore chosen to examine three Movements more closely – Theos Ministries, the House of the New World, and Truth and Liberation Concern/Care and Communication Concern (TLC, CCC) – as they represent the dominant themes, cultural innovations, and missional forms of the movement in Australia. My arbitrary choice ignores some outstanding, surviving ministries such as Fusion.[43]

Theos Evangelism and Training – Market Place Encounters

Theos team members typified the dissenting children of the evangelical establishment, who never quite left their ecclesiological homes, but made their mainstream, evangelical, parents and church leaders nervous, though tentatively enthusiastic over their innovative effectiveness. Many of those rebels of yesteryear are today's leaders in the church. Their target audience was the "pagan" youth of Australia.

History

Theos Youth Ministries started in 1968 as a coffee shop at a Scripture Union (SU) Beach Mission at Wilson's Promontory, Victoria. It grew in two years to 11 coffeehouses or "drop in" centers at holiday resorts, with 300 team members. Founded by John U'ren[44] These Youth Ministry sponsored a variety of initiatives, embracing a "common sociopolitical, biblical mix" (U'ren 1999:4).

> Rugged, not so academic, street wise, questioning if not anti establishment, these volunteers were questioning SU's style and were contributing new energy and creativity. Street Theatre, a large tent at the huge Woodstock style, Sunbury Rock Festival with God's Squad and other agencies uncovered a new "frontier." All these new volunteers were asking for training, so courses were designed. (U'ren 2000:12)

The radical house movement was producing an impressive number of indigenous musicians and proclaimers for mission. The Jesus Movement's activist emphasis produced a frantic level of activities, creating a felt need for training and education. John U'ren was the pivotal figure in facilitating joint projects and relationships between groups. Jointly sponsored Teach ins and training camps brought together the full range of Jesus Movement groups for inspiration, national strategy, and spiritual formation. Having access to SU's traditional resources benefited all groups.

Typical of all Jesus Movement groups, rock music, dramas, art, street theatre, and films were accouterments to touch the nerve of the vibrant youth. Some evangelical churches and SU itself were worried about the direction in which this cultural contextualization was taking the Movement.

> Theos was growing into more a movement or an organism of subversives rather than an organization. It stayed within the SU movement and is still there but now much reduced. Over the years there have been a number of year-round Theos

centers established. Staffing these and getting ongoing funding has always been difficult. (U'ren 1999:12-13)

John U'ren joined SU staff in 1974, but there were some SU traditionalists who had reservations from the start. "Theos friendships with radicals like Athol Gill, John Smith, John Hirt, David Wilson, and others made SU traditionalists nervous" (U'ren 2000:13-14). Those were days of both exhilarating successes in communication with youth and severe conflict with the old order of leadership.

Biographical Tracks

In each movement account I will emphasize the significant role of founding leaders, firstly because in the Australian context the strengths and foibles of the founders are intimately linked with the successes and failures of the respective movements. Secondly, movement theory has noted the significance of leaders in the formation of movements, the development of strategies and worldview, and the sustainability of the group (Jasper 1999; McAdam 1988, 1989, 1999).

John U'ren, now in his sixties, with a background of traditional, evangelical conservatism, was one of the more mature leaders of the youth movement. A father, business-man, and active lay worker in Methodism and later in the Uniting Church of Australia, U'ren's commitment to unchurched youth led him to a lifetime of experimentation and the championing of youth causes.

Worldview framing. Influenced from its inception by the work of Francis Schaeffer, the Jesus Movement saw the issue of worldview (Kraft 1979:53-63; Whiteman 1983:478) as central to the task of counterculture revitalization. We understood the power of the cultural institutions and social arrangements to fix the worldview of the people. We saw our task in part to invade the marketplace of ideas on campus and in the popular media with an alternative worldview to that of secularism, materialism and radical individualism. If the culture was at a point of dysfunction and collapse then its worldview had to be challenged and overthrown.

It was axiomatic that revitalization could not be sourced from within the corrupted system, but from forgotten traditions and the creative fringes of freedom. Third World and alternative views were sought. Some leaders became truth sleuths, searching in the mines of past treasures and seeking wisdom from other cultures and from the dissenting edge of Western culture. Though largely self-taught, the movement leaders had access to a few academic radicals and with their help developed a keen eye for relevant literature on culture and mission. Closely aligned to Smith and Hirt, John U'ren was a tireless collector of books and articles which fueled the fires of discontent with the system and hope for its overthrow. U'ren has been a primary resource of inspiration and relevant data for mission, being a voracious reader who constantly passes on new publications to key leaders. He shared his sources of theology and missiology. If Hirt was theologically oriented, U'ren was socioreligiously oriented. His closest friend in the mission to radicalize the church was Athol Gill, founder of the House of the Gentle Bunyip.

Significance of U'ren's role. U'ren was atypical of Jesus Movement leadership in that he was a serviceable public lecturer, but lacked the charismatic fire of most of the leaders. His organizational advocacy skills and connections to the establishment made him an invaluable friend and counterbalance to more incendiary leaders of the Movement. Without fanfare or fair recognition, he brought to birth a groundbreaking movement of contextualized gospel outreach, through astute deployment of SU's resources, to train and commission youth activists in the Theos movement. He tirelessly acted as a mediator between the radical movement and the establishment, and brokered relationships between competitive elements within the Jesus Movement itself. He was committed to facilitating others in a self-effacing manner, uncharacteristic of most movemental visionaries.

Purpose of the Theos Program

The purpose of Theos was not ecclesiological or even primarily theological, although the movement was cerebrally active amongst un-churched youth in their attempts to make sense of a swiftly changing society. Theos was dedicated to the task of pre-evangelism. In an excessively secular culture the church had failed to establish the networks of positive relationships with the youth culture, which was largely ignorant of doctrine or faith experience. By relocating the discussion to the familiar context of rock concerts, festivals, coffee shops, and beaches, Theos was a familiar and favored presence, making the Christian message user-friendly. A folksy style, contemporary communication, and well-trained youth presenters were the hallmark of the movement.

Local Cultural Innovations

Theos Sun. Theos Sun described in its masthead as, "An Australian Jesus Paper for SU Victoria," was aimed at a younger audience of high school students, providing up to date news on Jesus People happenings, pop culture issues, testimonies of converts, and youth social issues.[45]

> Theos Sun Newspaper was first launched in 1973. It finished publishing in 1978. Twenty to forty thousand issues were printed three to four times a year and distributed to youth groups, schools, youth workers, and churches. Primarily the paper was an evangelistic tool that gave Theos the vehicle for evangelism and also to dialogue about sociopolitical issues. Theos was established to reach young people outside the church. It also was attempting to respond to the rather superficial evangelical climate that was coming out of the [American] Jesus Movement with its "one way" Jesus signs and mimicking of Coca Cola advertisements declaring "Jesus is enjoyable, taste and see," and "Jesus is the real thing." (U'ren 1999:12)

The newspaper was distributed by the Theos team, often traveling in a psychedelic bus, which became a favorite innovation with youth in city and country towns.

> Theos Mobile Jesus Bus went to the rescue in country and suburbs. Theos' ministry bus outfitted a double-decker, ex-Sydney commuter bus, with sound and video equipment, converting it into a coffee shop, entertainment center, and pre-evangelistic, mobile meeting-house. Brightly colored with typical psychedelic captions, it traveled with a team on weekends to outer suburbs that had become

spiritual deserts and social disaster areas. Urban planning had been overlooked or was haphazard with a distinct lack of facilities for the new flood of baby boomer youth. The bus went to such suburbs and to regional country local shows, events, schools, and carnivals throughout Victoria. In many cases churches and agencies asked for the bus and its team to assist in local outreach. (U'ren 1999:12)

The Master's Workshop. The need arose for an alternative training unit to bypass traditional communications and theological hindrances to relevant ministry. The Master's Workshop thus grew out of the energy and creativity that had through Theos engulfed the once conservative, traditional SU. It was established in 1974 by U'ren, under the direction of Peter Corney. Peter Corney was an Anglican priest whose vitality and support of the emerging youth Movement attracted a team around him, some with full-time honorary roles and some working on the tent-maker principle of self-support.

The curriculum and in-service training was prepared and designed to attract these new Christians who were seeking an alternative to the status quo, and an alternative to the prevailing philosophy of materialism, and greed. In keeping with the popular youth counterculture, many young people viewed their parents' church and social lives as prime targets for biblical critique. They wanted to challenge the existing values and practice, and to seek alternatives both ideologically and practically.[46]

Master's Workshop became more a "working-out-from," or "sending-out-to" headquarters, rather than a drop-in center. It described itself in each course flyer: as a "Training Center for members of the Jesus Family."

> The Master's Workshop is a training house, a center for nurturing and equipping Christians. . . . It is a center for radical study (radical in the sense of RADIX = THE ROOT). For the Christian this means being biblical. It is our aim to help Christians think through an alternative life style that is RADICALLY Christian, and to resist being tamed and molded by the prevailing culture. The workshop is also a resource center for Christian workers in the youth and student scene. We have a musician's register and a broad-sheet bank. We provide consultative service for those operating Christian coffeehouses and drop-in centers.[47]

Graduates traveled around Australia and overseas to be stimulated by new ideas and models of contextualized ministry. The Master's Workshop developed the Christian Volunteer Course which required participants to give up a year to train and serve in a "Christian Peace Corps," a "scheme to bring together ordinary but pressing human needs and the people to meet them in a central directory for "opportunities for service." Christian Volunteer Course was also seen as "a means for people to experiment with alternative vocational styles." Theos and the Master's Workshop colluded in frontier ministry within the traditionally conservative, older support base. Peter Corney left the Master's Workshop in 1976 to take up the Vicar's position at St. Hilarys Kew, creating a highly successful youth oriented parish. Christian Volunteer Course closed in 1986.

Ecumenical happenings. The descriptive language of the public gathering adapted to the shift from cognitive to affective language. The conference became a "teach-in." The camp meeting became a "happening." Public gatherings for proclamation or worship were "festivals (Fests)." Facilitated by U'ren, the

Master's Workshop was a catalyst to bring major Jesus Movement players together, to mount several Jesus Movement public initiatives financed by some traditional but risk-taking sponsors. These events did much to unite the many new movements and communities with interested traditional churches.

Possibly the most significant "happening" facilitated by the Theos Movement, drawing on considerable "old world" resources and connections, was the Kairos gathering in the national capital, Canberra, in 1973.[48] The event saw a huge gathering of Jesus people surrounding the Parliament House of Australia, joined by the heads of churches, bishops, clergy, leaders, Members of Parliament, and ordinary, everyday Australians.[49] Public proclamation, singing, and performing arts invaded the streets, and shopping. Outreach was developed in an atmosphere of celebration and inclusion, rather than the traditional "them and us" style of Christian propagandizing. The march around Parliament was a ground breaking strategy. A concluding prayer vigil by hand-holding youths completely surrounding the Parliament complex had the emotional feel of the 1960s hippies surrounding the Pentagon to levitate it. Kairos made the front pages of the national press. One hundred thousand Jesus newspapers, jointly produced and printed by the *Theos Sun* team, announced "Kairos: Australia's Moment."

Partnerships and relationships were established that last to this day, because of Kairos, the Jesus Family Teach-Ins, Servants in a Strange Land (justice and peace training), Toward 2000 leadership conferences, and Strength to Love camp meetings. These annual, weekend, live-in camp meetings were supplemented by monthly "after church" radical expository evenings, called Prophets Pulpit [still operating]. Established by U'ren, Smith, and Gill after a pub "buzz session," these expositions still maintain the radical theological tradition and form a strategic connection between the aging "hippie" mentors and generation X.

Political Opportunity

Theos seized the sociological mood of the hour. The interest in "speakeasy" contexts in coffee shops and open festivals was well exploited by Theos and Fusion, a youth movement initiated in the 1960s by Mal Garvin (See endnote 39). Youth flooded the coffee shops and open-air festival events mounted by its trained youth workers. Theos was extremely mobile, appearing wherever a youth social "happening" could be found, with a non-confrontational, entertaining accessibility. As the times have changed, so has the continuing Theos organization. Theos continues to operate primarily as an organization ministering to vacationing youth. The movemental aspects have long passed. Routinization has resulted in the establishment of a well-organized, pre-evangelistic outreach program for SU but it is no longer at the dissenting edge of the culture. The founding radicals have moved on.

The House of the New World – Communal Counterculture Subversives

The House of the New World was the archetype of radical, intentional communities, found in most Australian states. The founder, John Hirt, was a 28 year old, single, Baptist pastor who was "dissatisfied with traditional forms of ministry" (Hirt 2000:1). He remains an incendiary champion of the poor and marginalized, and a fearless opponent of exploitive economic and political forces. A creative strategist and powerful orator, Hirt can gain and hold a crowd on the street or campus.

History

The House of the New World was commenced in April 1970. It grew initially from five committed young Christians, who were university students or graduates, certainly making the group a-typical of the overall movement. "With a few solid committed Christian friends" Hirt established a "counterculture center" in Sydney for training "pilgrims of the impossible," providing sanctuary for the "no-hopers" of society, and proclaiming and dialoguing a radical gospel with University students, high school students, and "so-called ordinary people" (2000:1).

The House developed many symbols of alternative beliefs and practices. "Seeds of Liberation" shop provided books, seedlings, seeds, health information, recipes, candles, crafts, wall hangings, tapestries, and posters. Special events included literary readings nights, pottery groups, and social justice awareness nights. Films were critiqued culturally and theologically "as part of the heady ethos that flowed from the search for a counterculture alternative" (Hirt 2000:2).

> These meetings mainly revolved around a coffeehouse every Saturday night and an open discussion group called "awareness night" every Tuesday night. From these small beginnings the house started to attract more and more earnest seekers after truth and assistance. Our central working team grew to eleven workers and was supported by trained teams of committed young adults – people we had put through a one night a week course for 26 weeks team training, involving issues like pastoral care, drug counseling, biblical, political and theological study. For most of its nine-and-a-half years the House of the New World saw on average of over 350 people come through its doors every week. (Hirt 1999:2)

Unlike traditional, religious meeting places, Jesus centers frequently housed people off the street, whose problems ranged from the psychiatric histories to practical need for a bed. Many came out of curiosity but stayed for rehabilitation and discipling. The House of the New World was a counterculture house that grew beyond Sydney into a collegiate network of alternative, discipling communities in Adelaide, Melbourne, Canberra, and Brisbane. The House lasted for nine and a half years before it was destroyed from within due to "power and ego battles" (Hirt 2000:2). No verifiable statistical information is available as records were lost at the time of the dissolution. The House of the New World arose at a significant period for both church and society.

The House was a center for discipleship training, set up as an alternative faith center alongside a quite inward looking, conservative, staid and sterile church. Both streams of evangelical and liberal traditions were in a deep rut. It was at the time when the counterculture, "alternative lifestyle" Movement was emerging in Australia. Alongside this Cultural Revolution the peace movement was growing in reaction to the Vietnam War. Palm Sunday marches had a fresh rush of revolutionary enthusiasm! Marxism became an explored, legitimate alternative. The peace and counterculture movements blended into a larger movement. Symbols, dress styles, images, and non-conforming reactions or behaviors expressed protest against the "Establishment." Their philosophy and counter- establishment protest was expressed in art, posters, and graffiti on their vans, cars, and homes, and supported by alternative hairstyles and nil use of cosmetics. (U'ren 1999:1)

Political opportunity, social accessibility, and the peculiar popularity for maverick and unorthodox leadership coalesced. The biographical details of prophet-leaders may be as significant as the cultural context. The significance of the actors' influence on the movement's outcomes is apparent in this story.

Biographical Tracks

The indisputable founder/leader was John Hirt. Hirt earned his Ph.D. in philosophical theology, and religious studies, at the University of Sydney, graduating in November 1998. Following graduation, he has been a Minister of the Word in the Uniting Church of Australia (UCA) and its chaplain to the Sydney University, despite Baptist ordination, and strong Anabaptist convictions.

Hirt's role in the House of the New World. There is no doubt that Hirt's role was that of a "prophetic energizer and pastoral visionary" (Hirt 2000:3). Hirt held a radical "New Left" approach to democratization and grass roots leadership. He appeared not to covet even elected authority for himself; he could not help but become leader in the eyes of the team and the clients. Hirt's incendiary rhetoric, passionate vision, and sympathetic comradeship inevitably attracted a crowd and a following.

> I guess I would have to say that I was in Weberian terms both a charismatic personality and the charismatic leader who started a vision and the house. I have always found it hard to talk about [my role] since I don't like people who talk about themselves overly much. But if I don't talk about what I did, I guess the stories of what others did will not really get the mention and the notice that they deserve. At the outset, it should be understood that I could only do what I did because of the good support that I had from a few close friends who, when others betrayed me, were there still as good friends. . . . Any profile I had always seemed to intimidate those who wanted more recognition, and acted in corrosive ways upon the egos of those small minded people, who in my view never really understood the loneliness of my calling – of my solitary life. (Hirt 2000:2-3)

The cost of a demanding social and spiritual, counterculture vision, accompanied by an enigmatic, evolving, but ill-defined approach to authority structures, took its toll on Hirt years later.

> It has to be sadly said that my role as leader was never really accepted by a lobbying group within the house's executive of eleven. My role necessitated a constant moving among the "troops." For one year that I can remember I never spent

more than one night in the same house. I was constantly on the move – on speaking engagements, in high schools, universities and among church and political groups and among our many affiliated community households. For more than 18 months I remember I never had a night off and for several years I lived on five dollars a week, sleeping in the basement on a fold up plastic banana bed. Eventually I did move into a comfortable, shared community house, where I was nurtured and cared for in ways for which I will be forever grateful. The loyalty of close friends and that close accompaniment of Jesus kept me going. All of this took its toll and within three years of the house's commencement I had gotten ill – physically rundown with serious stomach ulcers (which I still carry). For all of this, I would do it all again – tomorrow. (Hirt 2000:3)

John Hirt married a talented American, Carol Rowley, who he met in radical Christian feminist circles while involved with the Californian, radical Christian peace movement. Even family responsibilities scarcely tamed his passion and self-sacrificing lifestyle. Economic disaster and social opposition to his uncompromising political commitment to the poor has been countered by the strength and creativity of his wife and the support of his children. "Costly discipleship" was the heroic, self-defining lifestyle, leading to many similar stories of great expectation and great cost to the emotional and family life of the pioneers. Conversations with many early activists during research for this project however, consistently evoked the idealization of the foundational days.

<u>Worldview framing</u>. Hirt, a prominent Australian leader in the most theologically, and politically radical network, received his spiritual formation primarily from dissenting American mentors. The theological and political influences of the last 30 years were shaped by relationships, and mentoring from key Liberation Theology scholars (Hirt 1998:iii).[50] Through involvement in American civil disobedience on behalf of the poor, the environment, world peace, and Central American victims of American policies, Hirt developed into a determined, seasoned, astute social activist.

Purpose of the House of the New World Movement

Whereas many American Jesus Movement groups began as theologically minimalist rescue operations to "save" the alienated refugees of the counterculture, the House of the New World began as an expression of middleclass youth's desire to rediscover the radical meaning of the gospel. Describing themselves as "pilgrims of the impossible" with a dream "to take God's revelation in Jesus Christ seriously," Hirt and his team took their cue from the sixteenth century Anabaptist movement (Hirt 1998:177). Hirt's core evangelicalism was evident in his emphasis on grace. Christ's call to "follow me" was "a grace filled invitation to follow on the road" (1998:177). Primary mentor, Athol Gill, taught that "following Jesus must never be reduced to work, by which we seek to gain God's approval. Discipleship is an act of grace. It is our joyous response to Jesus – who he is and what he does" (1998:177). The purpose of the community was established by its theology, from which grew its counterculture attitude toward Church and State.

> It was our contention that the institutional church had almost successfully strangled Jesus in its ecclesiastical foliage. We wanted to be free to find the boldness and fidelity of Jesus' quest again – the un-church-tainted Jesus. Our faith search was for the Jesus whom the "little people" loved, who poured himself out for the marginalized and disenfranchised, the Jesus who was prepared to do whatever must be done to bring the lowly and broken into the immediacy of God's mercy and forgiveness. (Hirt 1998:180)

Hirt and his followers accused the church of "cultural insularity and reactionary politics" and "the deification of self-orbiting, ecclesiastical cultural patterns" (Hirt 1998:181). Hirt's Movement embraced "the early churches unabashed contempt for everything in their culture which stood contrary to the Lordship of Jesus" (Hirt 1998:183). In summary, Hirt's vision was that of a seamless garment of action-reflection, of critique, and communal engagement.

> We were most concerned to be about a form of evangelism that was both profoundly private and public. Discipleship formation as we understood it had to contain the necessary biblical components of deep personal faith with relevant and prophetic public acts of Christian truth-telling and praxis. Evangelism for us had to contain the necessary pastoral components of real Christian charity and care, especially for the underprivileged, the broken, and those not normally welcomed into middle-class expressions of Christianity. We sought in fact, to be a rampart of the kingdom of God in the world. . . . .There was a deep desire to intellectually reach out into the world and engage it in meaningful ways. This meant for us different forms of culture critique and ideology analysis regarding contemporary art forms, current intellectualism, prevailing political issues and theological engagements relevant to Christian faith making sense, in a world dominated by militarism, racism and materialism. (Hirt 1998:2)

With a "few crude symbols of faith and hope," (1998:181) with a revolutionary rhetoric, new songs, redemptive political action, and an intentional community they sought a "spiritual, theological reconstruction that could bring the intellectual, and activist worlds back together" (Hirt 1998:181).

Local Culture Innovations

While some innovations, such as Jesus Papers and Jesus rock music were generic to the Movement in the Northern and Southern Hemispheres, local initiatives took on distinctive, indigenous content and styles. Some other innovations such as The Master's Workshop/Scripture Union), God's Squad Motorcycle Club (Truth and Liberation Concern), and the School of the Prophets (House of the New World) appear to have been unique to the Australian movement in the 1970s. The innovations of the Australian Movement were particularized in the context of the Australian social history, and tended to be driven by theological presuppositions before pragmatics, in counterculture defiance of a generally pragmatic Australian culture.

Communalism. The House of the New World communalism fused ideological and practical elements. The House of the New World and associated groups took advantage of the philosophical and theological sympathies of youth towards radical alternatives in politics and lifestyle. The nature of the Kingdom of God was to them communal in intent, and survival was contingent upon unity and pooled resources. Their biblical study led them to the conviction that communal living was the resource whereby the early Christian communities functioned, survived, and overthrew the existing order of demonic Roman imperialism.

> And then it has to be said that we were forced into community because of economic necessity. Alone we could not survive; alone and independent of each other's financial resources we just couldn't make it. So, we asked all of the sympathizers to pledge weekly amounts of support, from one to ten dollars. The remarkable element here is that our support came from students and normal church people. We never had in the whole life of the house major financial backers. We never had bankrolled wealthy Christians funding us. We were just too anticapitalist, and anti "prosperity gospel" to ever draw their support. So, our communalism was motivated from our biblical, ideological commitments and the result of pragmatic necessity. (Hirt 2000:3)

The House of the New World was primarily an intentional community movement based on ideology, mission, and strategy.

Media impact. Religious and secular media, print, and electronic, gave considerable attention to several of the Jesus Movement leaders. *Vogue* fashion magazine (Gartner 1973:86, 87) featured the House of the New World. An outreach radio "talk-back" program called "Hirt Line" played Christian rock music and drew many calls for help during two and a half years of operation. Hirt was "anchorman" for a late night, current affairs TV program on Sydney's channel 9.

Drama groups. "In order to prophetically witness in the street, the teams gathered performers who acted out gospel messages and political parables" (Hirt 2000:3) with deliberately provocative, sociopolitical implications. Hirt was a natural "rabble rouser" who would leap upon fountains, statues, campus forums, or any place conducive to crowd gathering, with guitar in hand and a folksy, engaging stump oratory. Musicians, participants in communal life and "confrontation drama teams" performed in public forums, high schools, churches, and universities – "any place they could get a hearing." (Hirt 2000:3)

Christian Board Riders. Today many Christian surfer groups exist, including Christian Surfers and Christian Board Riders, but at the time of its founding the surfer subculture was anathema to Christians and to the average parent. They feared the "sex, drugs, rock 'n' roll and "beach bum" image of this dissenting youth culture" (Hirt 2000:4).

> This group was actually in existence before the house began. I had started it about three years before. It soon found that the house was a good place for its meetings. From this one Christian surfing group grew over 200 other surfing groups – none of the surfing groups currently in existence (to my knowledge), has ever had the theological, ecological or political concerns of the original group. (Hirt 2000:4)

Hirt, not satisfied to merely evangelize the culture, sought to engage the "close to the earth" dissenting proclivities of the early surf movement in environmental, radically responsible discipleship.

Free Slave Jesus paper. *Free Slave*, self conscious as a "home grown brain," was possibly the most cerebral, overtly sociopolitical Jesus paper in the world, and the most ethnocentric in Australia. Birthed in the "Slave Quarters" of the

House of the New World, and jointly produced by the House of the New World and Brisbane's sister community, the House of Freedom declared on its masthead: "Periodically Inspired. Jesus is Lord. A Voice of the Christian Counterculture." Its articles reveal its radicalized theology, college and graduate level interests and sociopolitical agendas.[51]

The School of the Prophets. The School of the Prophets (SOPS) was an internship course, modeled on the Paulo Freire (1970) praxis method of experiential learning. It was a small theological school primarily based on the theology of Dr. Athol Gill, a New Testament theologian in Brisbane. SOPS attracted young, thinking, passionate participants, who explored the radical teaching of Jesus. From this method of learning and the ethos of community living, the label "radical discipleship" emerged, and became the defining concept that drove their mission. SOPS was founded to facilitate the original vision and impetus of the House in its calling to radical discipleship.[52]

> This group received extra training and mentoring beyond the normal team training of six months. The school of the prophets was a one-year intense course of hard work without financial support or promise. This faithful company was the backbone of the House. Many have gone on to do remarkable things in their lives, working for the Kingdom [of God] in "theo-political" arenas of life, both locally and internationally, from University academics to social workers among the poor and broken. (U'ren 1999:7)

David Batstone and Ched Myers of America were two interns from the House of the New World, and the House of Freedom before returning to America, where they have become significant intellectuals in theological education. Although the influence of Dr. Thorwald Lorenzen (1995) was significant, the impact of Dr. Athol Gill on Hirt, SOPS, and the wider movement, through his writings, and theological lecturing cannot be over emphasized.[53] Gill, a New Testament scholar, was a major theological influence in the House of Freedom, the House of the New Word, and the House of the Gentle Bunyip. Until his death in 1992, he lived in community with his family in the radical "Bunyip" community, in stark contrast to his seminary colleagues at Whitley College, Melbourne.

> His passionate emphasis was that evangelicals had for too long treated the Gospels as [primarily] descriptive. Gill argued that conservative theologians accepted Paul's writings as prescriptive and the gospel writers as descriptive. Gill's claim that the gospels were prescriptive meant that when Jesus proclaimed the reign of the Kingdom of God, he was therefore sociopolitical. The Sermon on the Mount was nearer in some aspects to Marx's writings than to conservative theologian's sermons, claimed Gill. (U'ren 1999:6-7)

The Movement developed as a "prophetic voice" of lament and concern over injustice. The outcast and the marginalized were the agenda for Jesus People ministries. Such a theology did not frighten the students, who were attracted by the integrity of the call to follow in the way of Jesus, but Gill's claim that the core business of Jesus was the poor and marginalized, provoked hostility in his denomination.

Self-theologizing. Paul Hiebert (1994:88-94) proposes that critical contextualization is essential to the development of an indigenous movement. Robert Schreiter (1985:16-21) observes that theology is now developing outside the control of professional theologians. Through Liberation Theology's action-reflection hermeneutic, and the development of grass roots community attempts at self-understanding, local prophets and poets are redefining the role of the Christian community. The phenomenological examination of local culture, to which Hiebert (1994:88) refers, was combined with a praxis application of the Scriptures that led to a critical analysis of Australian and global, sociopolitical norms. An Evangelical version of action-reflection hermeneutics drove much of the Australian Jesus Movement's indigenous theology and practice. The House of the New World developed a particularly aggressive and inspiring form of self-theologizing,[54] borrowing from the Third World, but applying the method to local issues of justice and peace.

Outcomes and Impact on Church and Secular Culture

Hirt, as activist as ever, now in the context of denominational, university chaplaincy, describes what happened to his communal dream:

> The House of the New World is closed now. It fell apart from the inside. Nothing from the outside had the power to bring the House down. Our failure was both calamitous and unremarkable. The crippling neurosis that brought our company undone was not new. The shadow of ourselves overwhelmed us. Too many "sought to do what was right in their own eyes" (Judges 17:6). . . and yes, we had our "Absalom(s) in the gate" (cf. II Samuel 15:2-6). In our failure, the myth of what we thought we had become could not match the reality of what we were. Having defeated ourselves, we had no positive response to the question posed by a brother past: "Will our inward power of resistance be strong enough, and our honesty with ourselves remorseless enough, for us to find our way back to simplicity and straightforwardness?" Our hope turning to darkness was almost past. And to lose hope is to go close to losing the virtues of faith and love. Our dream could not long endure without these three strengths together. Finally, through all the jealously and bickering, our faith and love became as imperiled as our hope. And although our band did not capitulate without a passionate struggle, too many lives were sore wounded, and we had grown weary in body and heart. Being so distressed, we were no longer close to each other, and so not brave enough to face the changes in our lives that the vision called forth. Many wondered why we could not go on, but we could not, and others said they knew something so sacramental could never last. (Hirt 1998:187-188)

The ultimate outcomes were not so bleak. To my knowledge, none of the heroic dreamers of the movement have abandoned the cause, but rather have retooled and relocated. They work in a new social, and religious contexts, still to live by the principles of a radical Christ. Athol Gill has gone to his reward. Badstone and Myers maintain the radical faith in America and frequently in international conferences. The secondary leaders are now mostly in denominational ministries.

Truth and Liberation/Care and Communication – A Missional Community

Many local "lighthouse" initiatives resulted from Jesus Movement discipling or evangelizing. Incendiary prophets, poets, musicians and political activists, whose popular culture style sparked interest in places hitherto resistant to religious penetration, lit fires throughout the land. The author founded such a missional Movement, which is the final Australian example of the Jesus Movement investigated in this enquiry.

History

Truth and Liberation Concern was founded in 1972 by the author and his wife, as a counterculture, activist movement. As unpredictable as the social upheavals of the 1960s had been, the gestalt that transformed conservative evangelicals like Hirt, U'ren and me into radicals was even more incomprehensible at the time.

> It was hard to believe that just a few years earlier I had stood in a pulpit, the shortness of my haircut leaving my ears open to the breeze, dressed in a somber suit of conservative cut. During my message I had delivered a stinging diatribe against the black American civil rights leader Martin Luther King. I claimed he was a dangerous communist bent on the breakdown of American society. I believed it. Yet here I was, covered in badges bearing hip Christian slogans, looking like a well fed Rasputin in black leather and hanging around at night in a small-town high street with a group of people generally regarded as the scum of the earth. (Smith and Doney 1987:7)

The 1960s had ended in America with Richard Nixon triumphant. In Australia the euphoric sense of cultural revolution was in the ascendancy as it was on the wane in America. It was an age of freedom and questioning like we had never experienced before. Yet it had almost passed me by. I had discovered *The Beatles* and *Crosby, Stills, Nash and Young* as they were about to disband. Having been challenged as a teacher by New Left colleagues in the Wonthaggi High School staff room, and disturbed adolescents in class, I was found wanting. I was determined that if my faith meant anything, it had to address the events and cultural distortions of that era. I left teaching, convinced the educational system was as dysfunctional as the culture in general, with memories of teenagers in depression and confusion at the hands of conflicting fundamentalist parents and cynical, hedonist, New Left teachers. Teenagers were engulfed in a cultural war zone.

Employment with a highly respected evangelistic agency, Campaigners for Christ concluded in my dismissal, ostensibly for dangerously Pentecostal leanings, increasingly hippie appearance, and pop culture leanings. Defiant attendance at the Sunbury Pop festival amidst blatant sex, drugs, and rock 'n' roll was the final, intolerable behavior in the eyes of my conservative employers, whose even more conservative patrons were threatening withdrawal of support. During the two years with Campaigners a gestalt shift occurred. I made contact with Jesus People abroad and commenced a joint Australia-Spokane, Washington, street level, tabloid Jesus paper.

> In 1971, [in cooperation with the Jesus Freaks in Spokane, Washington], we had produced our first edition [of an underground paper] under the modest title, *Truth*. It was self-consciously hard-hitting and alternative, published in time for Christmas. The front cover displayed an image of the crucified Christ, with the headline, *Happy Birthday, Jesus* (Figure 6.3). It caused quite a stir in the Christian community. But more importantly, it made people look hard at what the birth of Jesus really heralded. We distributed 5,000 copies free in the streets. [It reached a circulation of 35,000 within two years]. (Smith and Doney 1987:144)

A fresh examination of Jesus under the searchlight of the wider cultural revolution revealed a disturbing gospel that was urgent, upsetting, and simultaneously political, social, and personal. The Bible was no longer a hitching post, but a signpost directing me on to a more compassionate reality. Australian journalist, Max Harris, wrote, "Christians are a dim, ego-tripping minority who are dead set on telling everybody why they ought to become Christians, instead of finding out why they aren't."[55] In this spirit, though pre-empting the Harris critique, I determined to vacate the sanctuary and reposition my self-education and mission in the streets and youth hangouts, possibly for life.

Coffee shops, poolrooms, university forums, and rock concerts were the place of dislocation, reorientation, and transformation. They were prime cultural locations. Hippies, bikers, street kids, and all sorts would descend on the coffee shop, most of them equipped with an honest spirit of enquiry, and a readiness to grapple with the big questions of the universe. We would often have raging debates about war, peace, life, death, faith, and the meaning of everything, lasting into the early hours of the morning.

It is difficult to provide an orderly description of the transformation and chaotic change in life-style, cultural ambiance, and networks of friendship, simply because it was not a planned journey, but rather a liberating shipwreck of an old world, and the discovery of an exotic island, by an unprepared castaway. An overwhelming sense of religious call, combined with an adrenaline-driven, social adventurism is a potent mix. For my wife Glena the gestalt shift was as bewildering as it was exhilarating for me.

> Now she was faced with this wild-eyed hairy radical whose sermons were beginning to touch more and more on politics and social issues. He was grooving on Bob Dylan and Crosby, Stills, Nash, and Young, reading Timothy Leary, and wearing Levis. It was no wonder she said to me in tears one day, "I don't even know who you are any more. You're not the same man I married. It's not that I don't believe in you, or that I doubt you. I just don't understand the changes." (Smith and Doney 1987:129)

Figure 6.3 Happy Birthday Jesus – The Controversy Begins
(Truth and Liberation 1971)

We were swept along by a sense of miraculous, divine call. We journeyed in an atmosphere of the extreme liminality of revolutionary ideas. We metamorphosed in the company of a subculture of open, questioning, searching, experimenting young people, who were in search of a message and a guru. There was a clear sense of mission objectives, but the organizational developments and initiatives were dynamic, situational, and rarely planned long in advance. We flew in liminal space. Freshly dismissed from respectable religious service, we were a young couple with three children, a mortgage, and no visible means of support. The first edition of the Jesus paper had received an overwhelming response from the street level and the college/university scene. Dropping out to join the counterculture was easy, but financial survival was tenuous.

> We had some immediate difficulties to face. We already had the second edition of the paper pasted up and ready to go, but no money to get it printed. I could have used some of the three months salary [provided by Campaigners for Christ upon my dismissal] but I'd given an undertaking that I would only use the money for my family and myself. We needed 450 dollars. Glena said, "I believe God's with us in this, go ahead and publish it. You won't have to pay the bill for a month." But I wasn't so sure. I had absolutely no support from any outside source that could finance either the paper, or anything else. And in 1972, four hundred and fifty dollars was a lot of money. But Glena was firm. She made me send it to the printers. Later that same day, two checks arrived in the post. They exactly covered the amount we needed. They came from two anonymous Adelaide University students who knew nothing of our circumstances, but just felt they ought to send us some money. (Smith and Doney 1987:149)

Living on the edge was both a necessary education to empathize with footloose and pilgrimaging youth, and a liminal experience that inspired adventure, creativity, experimentation, and faith. It was a lifestyle of creative uncertainty.

> There was one fortnight when we received just one dollar. We started eating our way through the contents of our cupboards. It was getting scary. On the way to speak at a high school, I stopped by the side of the road and prayed, "God, I don't care if I have to eat grass, but I can't expect my family to do that. Please do something. Show me this isn't some mad venture of my own, but that you're with me – that this is right."
>
> When I got home, Glena met me at the door with a big smile. She was holding a fat envelope in her hand. It had been dropped in earlier that day by a group of Christian students from Monash University. Knowing how little students had to spare, Glena said, "I'm not going to open it; I'm scared it will be single dollar bills." It wasn't. They'd collected one hundred and twenty dollars. It covered the month's mortgage repayment and food. It was quite amazing in its timeliness. (Smith and Doney 1987:150,151)

The naming of a movement is socially significant, and like most Jesus Movement groups, names and ministry concepts emerged co-incidentally and inspirationally.

> Then one day, Glena and I were reading the Bible when we came across that simple but beautiful statement by Jesus, "You will know the truth and the truth

will [liberate] set you free." Now, the word "liberation" was very big at the time, both in revolutionary and Christian movements. Since liberation meant freedom, we decided to change the paper's name to Truth and Liberation. We needed a name to call the trust we had to set up to receive any funds we were sent for my ministry. And so struck were we by the concept, that we decided to call ourselves Truth and Liberation Concern or TLC, "Tender, Loving Care." It might sound a bit dated now, but it meant a great deal to us at the time. (Smith and Doney 1987:150)

A following had not been sought but our home was often packed for those seeking subversive teaching and dialogue. Through the Jesus Paper and public proclamation, word was out that Jesus was invading Australia as he had done in California. Formalizing and stabilizing a fast growing and popular movement is like laying an egg on a moving escalator. In a sense nothing was normal. Time and space were simultaneously both sacred and profane, a seamless garment of divine encounter.

At one stage more than 35,000 people had our home address. We were printing that many copies of our paper *Truth and Liberation* and it was going to acid heads, freak communities, motorcycle gangs and prisons, as well as to anyone walking the street who was prepared to accept a copy. And the only address on it was our own home. So anyone who felt like looking us up knew where we were. The people who tended to get hold of the paper were often very mobile and therefore news of what we was doing spread throughout the underground network. We had all sorts of desperate, searching men and women turn up on our doorstep.

One guy decided he wanted to come and see us, so he rode his Harley (which had no seat) all the way down from northern Queensland. He made the journey of around 1,500 miles, sitting on the frame. Of course you make someone like that welcome, organize a place they can stay and spend time finding out what there needs are and why they've come all this way. This is an extravagant example, but multiply these chance visitors by hundreds and you'll get a picture of our life. (Smith and Doney 1987:176)

Given the radical understanding of community that the Christian counterculture embraced, it was essential to either provide a crash pad, commune, or open one's own family space to the hordes of wanderers typical of that era.

After Lyndal was born, we made contact with a really derelict biker and brought him home; an enormous, lanky guy with jeans so filthy they could probably have been registered as a germ warfare factory. I can still see Glena's face frozen with alarm as he swooped down and picked up our new baby, enfolding her in his massive arms. But his battered, hardened face softened and melted as he looked at Lyndal, and Glena breathed an inward sigh of relief. Guys like these gave us a lot of surprises. Their appearance was so often deceptive. Children can be an amazing communication bridge between hostile adults. (Smith and Doney 1987:178,179)

Our domestic situation was under extreme stress. Glena's health was at risk, and there seemed to be no let-up in the demands of an increasing clientele. Through friends from our past Methodist connection, an old house in Bayswater, Melbourne on a large block became available, and a "drop in" cum communal pad, administration, and teaching center evolved, five minutes from our home in Boronia.

> The house was used 24 hours a day. This was the great period of the dropout. In the warmer months of the year, young, disaffected Australians would drift around the country, carrying with them the barest minimum required for survival. Word got around, both through our paper and the formidable underground network, that "Truth and Lib" or "TLC" as we came to be known, was a place where you could usually crash out for the night. The old house was dubbed "The Jesus Light and Power House" and received some amusingly addressed mail to the "Jesus Gas and Fuel Company." [(Smith and Doney 1987:181)

That house became the location of thousands of life transforming encounters, some of which were bizarre. One "acid head" swore, long after he was tripping, that he had seen an eight-foot hairy spider with salivating fangs, next to his bed. Some of these guys had no real means of discerning fantasy from reality. Many of the people we had to deal with were in various states of psychological and emotional disrepair. Acid took a disastrous toll on burned-out minds in those years. We had more than one university psychology major that dropped out of their studies after overdoing psychedelics. Many came with the feeling that we were the only people they knew who would understand what they had gone through and were prepared to give the time to help.

One of the extraordinary factors in the foundational days was the breakdown of traditional social networks. Graduate students and illiterate street kids, contemplative and criminals, Buddhists and Christians, the sane and the insane met in an atmosphere of *communitas*, not as strangers but as part of a rediscovered human family.

> I particularly remember Smelly John [name changed]. He was one of those bikers who took immense pride in wearing his "originals." It used to be common practice in the bike world never to wash your Levis. You bought one pair of jeans and wore them constantly, unwashed, until they rotted. In some clubs it was the custom to urinate on another's Levis as part of some peculiar initiation rite, or even to rub blood into the denim. Add to that liberal doses of oil, grease and other nameless substances, and before long these originals got to be pretty gross. (Smith and Doney 1987:183,184)

> I can recall another guy, 'Chopper,' who used to hang around the place, and whose jeans were so far gone he had to staple them together every time he put them on. He had no zipper at the front and held himself together with a giant safety pin. He would sit in the front row during our Bible study sucking noisily on a huge, slimy, filthy dummy [pacifier]. (Smith and Doney 1987:184)

In such a context, with unpaid, untrained volunteers for staff, daily routines are anything but routine. We were a young movement with inexperienced and unqualified volunteers. Sometimes their inexperience meant that they couldn't handle these crises and primary leaders would be called out of our beds to deal with the situation.

> On another occasion, one of the people we were working with who had a drinking problem as well as smoking a lot of dope, threatened to take his own life. He was swallowing pills from a bottle in one hand and waving a hatchet in the other.

He claimed he would cut anyone down who tried to stop him. It was all very melodramatic but ultimately futile, since once the pills had taken effect he would have passed out and we would have sent him straight to hospital to be pumped out. But our alarmed volunteers hadn't the experience to realize this. We really threw people in at the deep end and asked them to deal with situations that would perplex professionals. They did brilliantly, considering the circumstances. The same man came up to me one evening after hearing me preach, and handed me a semi-automatic rifle with 500 rounds of ammunition. He told me he had found a first-floor room in Collins Street, which faced a busy thoroughfare, in the heart of Melbourne. From there he had planned to fire into the crowds and see how many people he could get before the police got him. I can't tell whether he meant to do it or not perhaps this was another of his grand gestures. [Long term evidence supports the genuine nature of his claim]. But the rifle was real enough to send a shiver through me and to make me thank God that his work in that man's life had prevented the possibility of a number of deaths. This gentleman went on to establish a successful drug rehabilitation center. (Smith and Doney 1987:185)

One evening, at the conclusion of a Bible teaching a businessman came to the front to seek conversion, accompanied by some gang members who handed in a medieval-type mace, a hatchet, and five switchblades. One lad had deteriorated so far that our staff found him injecting barbiturates into his penis. He had collapsed all his major blood vessels through heroin injections. He could no longer operate as a dealer to meet the expense of heavy addiction, so he sought brief relief by injecting analgesics under his skin. The result was a hideous crop of large red sores all over his body. He could scarcely walk as cellular degradation in the soles of his feet had taken a terrible toll.

Our ministry was not only to the poor or dysfunctional. One son of a rich and prominent businessman on the Gold Coast said, with tears in his eyes, "My Mum and Dad can send me to the Bahamas for a holiday, but I don't know if they love me and I have no idea who I am." This common encounter with meaningless materialism, typical of the Australian culture, provoked our movement to position ourselves with the counterculture in its critique of capitalist society.

> This brought us to the attention of the chief psychiatrist of a State Children's Court. This man, a Sri Lankan by birth, called me in and asked me about the nature of our work. I began defensively, not wanting to sound like an irrational Christian, dispensing cheap spiritual solutions to deep social and emotional problems. But he stopped me. He said, "You don't have to defend yourself to me. I'm not a Westerner, I'm not a materialist like most of you Australians. I'm observing in this country a breakdown in the culture that is so severe, that if you can't reverse it by finding some kind of foundation, then you are finished. You are a civilization that is dying from within. Don't be tender about the faith aspect of your work. The kids who are coming to these courts are often in a frightening state of disrepair. They get younger and their problems get worse year by year. So serious is their state of breakdown, the only person who can help them now is an evangelist." He wasn't a Christian. He was probably Hindu. But he understood that there are spiritual causes to social problems as well as psychological and environmental ones. We were agreeing that if you tackled all three cause in an integrated way, then people were able to change. (Smith and Doney 1987:228)

We wore a badge with two arrows facing each other with the words "Christian Counter Culture." We believed that true Christianity stood in clear opposition to the materialistic "bigger, brighter, better" syndrome. We believed and still do that to follow Christ is to be in conflict with violence, indifference and selfishness. I used to wear a sticker on my helmet that came from John Hirt's House of the New World in Sydney. It said, "Break the hate habit, love your neighbor." The Australian Jesus Movement initially was as active in serving the marginalized as it was in making converts.

In Australia our groups were both welfare and advocacy centered. A 16-year-old girl ran from one of our school seminars crying, "I've got to have a changed life. It's got to be different." She had been raped repeatedly by her father, her brother, and even her grandfather. Her mother was lesbian and she fled home into the arms of a man who, with his two sons, took her in – only to find they too were to use her for personal pleasure. The devastation of such kids is almost terminal except for a massive cleansing and affirmation of a spiritual dimension. There simply are not enough people who care to be involved in long term, emotionally exhausting, and even dangerous intervention and care. "Hey Jesus loves you, here's a Bible to read," is a totally inadequate response. With the breakdown of family life and the glorification of violence and power in our cultures, it will be much worse before it is better. Thus we geared up for a crusade of love and justice.

The establishment, whether adults against children, men against women, rich against poor, had formed a self-protective conspiracy. We were determined to break the code of silence. We soon discovered the public exposures of crooked lawyers, corrupt doctors dealing drugs, criminal accountants and inhumane functionaries in the Government departments were often deserved. We believed there were too many professionals making themselves fat and famous on the backs of the poor. Corruption and cynicism thrived amongst intelligent and supposedly compassionate elites. We declared verbal war on the abuse of privilege, power and status. Professions, politicians and business CEOs, appeared too protective of one another. Who would speak for their hapless clients?

> I remember our discovery of a deserted, urban, aboriginal wife, who had lived for weeks on dry Cornflakes. She had applied for welfare for herself and her children. The Government officer sent to investigate accused her of being a black whore. He accused her of having a husband in the cupboard. Dehumanized and humiliated, she slammed the door in his face. She ran into the shower fully clothed, and screamed as the water poured over her. She vowed never to seek help again, even if she starved. It was a privilege to be able to help her. The poor and weak are dependent on the wealthy, the powerful and the articulate to speak for them, but they get precious little help. The services such people get from doctors, lawyers and social workers are too often inadequate. Those who suffer don't have the confidence or the clout, and they don't know the system well enough, to demand satisfaction.

> Poor one-parent families often get a raw deal. These are the modern equivalent of the widows and fatherless that the Bible constantly commands God's people to protect. One woman we looked after for a while illustrates starkly the predicament of such people. Her wrists looked like crossword puzzles, they had been

> slashed so many times. The court understandably removed her children because she could no longer cope. Under our care she recovered substantially, but the courts wouldn't budge on their judgement. After many attempts to get her kids back, she broke down again and attempted suicide, and was placed with a psychiatrist. At the start of one of her half-hour sessions he asked if she'd mind if he rang his colleague. After a 25-minute conversation setting up a weekend's golf, he then put the phone down and said, 'Well, I see we only have five minutes left. Never mind. Have you still got some of the tablets I prescribed last week?' If you're weak and vulnerable, it's difficult to know how to respond. Someone in the psychiatrist's position holds all the cards. This woman went home and, in despair, she slashed her wrists – again. (Smith and Doney 1987:234)

As with the House of the New World, our ministry developed as a praxis response of a radical theology forged in the daily experience of human crisis. We had no intention of reinventing the wheel by starting a new denomination, but the weight of human need and the success of contextualized communication eventually necessitated the formation of a community of faith. People started coming in hundreds. I had started the studies to give some strength and biblical education to the staff and in-circle supporters.

In the summer of 1974 numbers peaked at over 500 people sitting outside with their pillows and blankets, hungry for relevant truth. And though this was straight Bible teaching, every night more people would ask how they could become believers. We would end up talking to them until one and two in the morning. This gave us an extra problem. What were we going to do with all these new Christians? We tried to feed them into churches around the city, but many kids felt alienated and uncomfortable because they were unused to church, and in some cases they were made to feel unwelcome. Many of them didn't bother. Monday night was their church and they didn't want to go elsewhere. My American investigative trip convinced me of the need for our own church.

> I discussed this question with local churchmen, a number of whom admitted that if we started sending all these people their way, they wouldn't be able to cope with the influx, or the culture. So we agreed that in order to meet the needs of these people, we had better form ourselves into a church, with all the proper sacraments of baptism communion, and marriage. My days of more formal pastoral experience in the Methodist circuit were now to become very useful. (Smith and Doney 1987:221)

Thus we began as a local community and national outreach which developed into a church plant, as the result of evangelistic success and denominational tardiness to accept counterculture converts. It was a movement that combined Methodist circuit-riding evangelism (on Harleys rather than horses), a quest for authentic communal living, and a fierce commitment to social justice. TLC's teams crisscrossed the nation on mission until 1982 when leadership struggles in the inner circle severely tore the fabric, and reduced the impact and breadth of mission for several years. The author, with several key ministry leaders, and most of the foundational arms of the ministry, reconstituted as Care and Communication Concern (CCC) and St. Martin's Community Churches. CCC operates in almost all fields of its original Jesus Movement endeavor, and some more recent initiatives.[56] TLC continues as a stable, creative, local community.

Aggressive social activism, through media, proclamation, and involvement in marches, sit-ins, and social advocacy, gave the movement a heroic, popular profile. Some struggling mainstream churches joined forces with the Jesus people, enlisting their street-wise, popular culture witness to assist local initiatives. Very secular crowds were bought within the sound of the Church's message for the first time. Thousands of schools and colleges were invaded drawing capacity crowds to hear relevant and provocative explanations of Jesus' teachings.

Biographical Tracks

The author's background was that of a conservative evangelical, Methodist, clergy family, mostly serving in rural centers. During adolescent years, American fundamentalist material from Bob Jones University, John Rice's *Sword of the Lord*, and the John Birch Society was influential. The social righteousness of the Methodist tradition was in conflict with the racism of 1960s fundamentalism.

At the end of the 1960s, while concurrently a high school teacher and a Methodist pastor, my relationship with senior high school students as class teacher during the week and as pastor, friend and youth worker on weekends exposed the inadequacy of my evangelical tradition. The worldview and methodology was inappropriate to identify with or communicate with the emerging generation. At the end of the decade I responded to a call from Campaigners for Christ to become a youth evangelist and teacher. In February 1972, my employment with Campaigners was terminated after a theological paradigm shift in worldview, political allegiances, and ministry focus. Once dismissed, Jesus Movement leadership occurred naturally and swiftly. Responsive youth audiences encouraged and accelerated the rate of change in both ideas and methodology. The alienation from traditional roots was a liminal experience which led to intense reflection on the state of marginalized peoples.

During two all-night, college student prayer meetings, the author received Pentecostal style prophecies announcing, "I send you as an apostle to the Gentiles, not to the Jews." The conflict between the Jews and Gentiles in Acts and the Pauline epistles, became the paradigmatic basis for abandoning traditional ways and embracing the "gentile," marginal youth. Explosive youth responses to ministry catapulted the author into the Jesus Movement. The initial shift away from extreme right wing, establishment politics and theology, did not occur through a process of slow acculturation, but as a "Damascus Road" experience (Acts 9:1-19). It was an overnight shift from the establishment to the margins (Kirsten Hill 1987; Matthews 1991:33; Moreton 1992:8).

Worldview framing. Influences on the author's worldview were many and varied. Francis Schaeffer provided a bridge to a more reasoned evangelicalism, leading eventually to the dissenting fringe of the Anabaptist tradition and eventually to the Latin liberationists. Once the door was open to new paradigms, relationships with other radical Jesus Movement communities encouraged a rapid rate of growth towards an activist, Christian counterculture lifestyle. Gill, Hirt, and U'ren were part of the journey of theological and social change. A Methodist style of social application of the gospel to contemporary poverty and injustice was also a significant element. Evangelical faith survived the journey but in a more Christocentric and radical form.

Purpose of the Movement

TLC was a synthesis of several elements of the Christian counterculture combining a strong sense of evangelistic and social mission. TLC released an explanatory leaflet which was typical of the times, expressing the "on the road" pilgrim search for an alternative Christianity.

> Sometime about mid 1972, a handful of concerned brothers and sisters began to break out of traditional cultural containment in response to a growing compassion for the alienated of our society, and in light of our Master's own life style of care for the little people. But it led to more than a few compassionate acts to one or two sub-culture groups. In company with many other Christian counterculture halfway houses, study cells and ministries, we began the long hard trek back to seek a New Testament, compassionate, Christ-like life style. We are still trekking. Christ we know, but to extricate ourselves from the insensitive, unchristian materialism, which has even engulfed some of mid century western Christianity, is to swim against the tide. (John Smith 1974b:1)

As a revitalization movement we saw the "system" as doomed. Persisting in pervasive cultural misery would lead to "the ultimate destruction of society (if not the whole world)" (Wallace 1966:160). In *Truth and Liberation*, in bold upper-case type we said, "The system is evil and a rip off! The system is materialistic! The system is opposed to God. He who lives for himself cannot please God. We have watched this country die long enough. To live is Christ. To love is Christian."

Dissent and alternative life style were part of the perceived gospel. We particularly targeted the futility of consumerism and an identity based on ownership and corporate power. A taped address by Francis Schaeffer provoked us to choose anti-materialism as the theme for an edition of *Truth and Liberation*. Materialism was the passionate focus of the attack on society in text and graphic (Figure 6.4). Truth and Liberation Concern was part of the "Christian Counterculture."

> Our community is an attempt to be a genuine expression of an alternative life style rather than the normal Australian materialistic selfishness. We consider it our responsibility to pursue the implications of Jesus' teachings into every area of our lives and to come to grips with the pressing political, social, and economic questions and problems, which are facing all of us in 20th century Western civilization. (John Smith 1974b:2).

Figure 6.4 Materialism – This is Where It All Ends
(Truth and Liberation 1973)

In typical revitalization style we demonized "the system" (Wallace 1966:159, 1956:270). A cover of *Truth and Liberation* (1974) depicted the world as a sad faced globe in melt-down condition, with band aids and sutures marking the futile attempt to heal the environmental disaster symbolized by smoke stacks and toppling oil derricks (Figure 6.5). Beneath the cartoon image was written: "You are the orphans of an age of no tomorrows" (Joan Baez); "Today even the survival of humanity is a utopian hope" (Norman O. Brown); "Nature has let us down, God seems to have left the receiver off the hook, and time is running out" (Arthur Koestler); "The whole creation groaneth and travaileth in pain together until now". . ."[She] shall be delivered from the bondage of corruption, into the glorious liberty of the children of God" (Paul, Romans 8: 22, 23). A classic attempt was made to reinvent early Christianity as the path to renewal.

> As a group of Christians, we are trying to show that a lifestyle patterned on the example of Jesus Christ and maintained by daily relationship with His Spirit gives real hope to people who have seen through the falseness, foolishness, and emptiness of the world system. We are trying to show that where there was alienation, there is love; where there was bitterness, there is warmth; where there was guilt, there is real forgiveness; where there was emptiness, there can be meaning; and where there was destruction and death, there is now healing and life. (John Smith 1974b:4)

Despite the elements of apocalyptic radicalism, the historic catholicity of the church was recognized.

Truth and Liberation Concern had rejected the popular term "parachurch," defining itself as a church movement but maintaining love and respect for historic denominational forms.

> Quite a few of us had no former contact with any type of Christian living, but we realize that we are a part of the wider Christian church and we are in no way antagonistic or opposed to the more "established" church groups. We have developed into a community in response to the deep and continuous need to care for the new people coming amongst us. (John Smith 1974b:2)

Possibly TLC's was the most overtly evangelistic of the Australian movements. A belief that the middle class church had ignored youth's search for relevant faith led TLC to pursue its evangelism outside the usual safe havens of traditional mission.

> One of our deep concerns is for those people who traditionally have not been familiar with the established church and we genuinely aim to reach out in love, to such people. . . . Amongst us, we have people who have come out of the heavy drug situation, people from broken families, people who have been active in the outlaw motor cycle scene, people who used to be alcoholics. (John Smith 1974b:2,3)

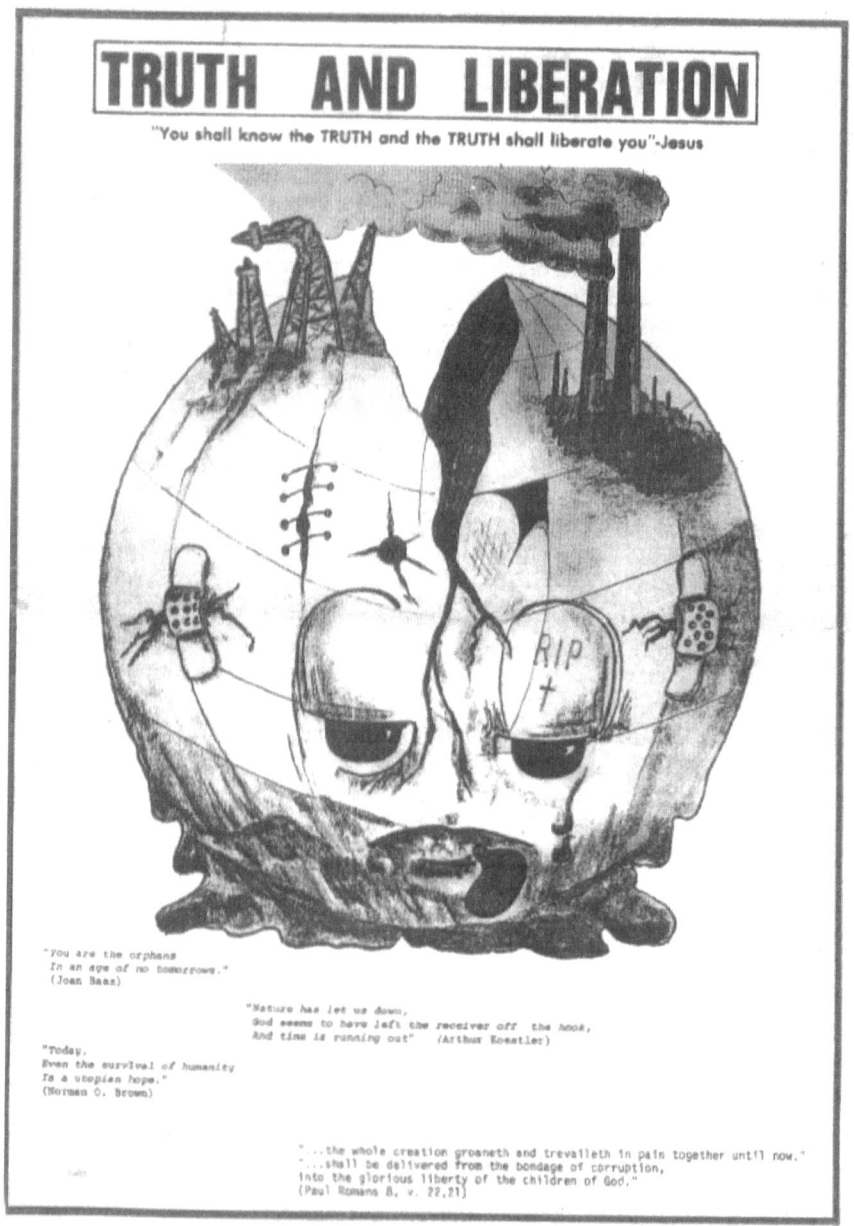

Figure 6.5 The Sad World Awaiting Liberation (*Truth and Liberation* 1974)

The call to conversion was traditional but the consequences of the "new birth" included social engagement. A dual model of civil disobedience, and civil responsibility, was deeply ingrained in the Australian movement, challenging the Richardson, Stewart, and Simmond (1979:271-274) conclusion that Jesus Movement "conversion" was typically conversion to a new group, and thus implied a fundamentalist withdrawal from engagement with the world at large. The recognition of switched allegiance holds true, but the withdrawal concept does not. Evangelism, advocacy, and culture brokerage ebbed and flowed into each other. To become friends of the marginalized or poor inevitably meant alienation from one's own abusive culture. It also led to advocacy and civil disobedience when law enforcement stepped beyond reasonable bounds.

Local Cultural Innovations

The Jesus Movement, typical of revitalizations, was highly innovative in its pre-routinization stage, as it developed its strategies for political orientation, recruitment, cultural transformation, growth and survival (Wallace 1956:274-275; 1966:160-162, 209-212). Having separated from main stream institutions and intellectual propositions, the Movement sometimes had to reinvent the wheel, or at least the model, in order to communicate with a dissenting clientele, and even to survive in a fast moving context.

Truth and Liberation Jesus paper. In 1971, while still with Campaigners for Christ, the author launched the Jesus paper, *Truth*, as an extra-curricular initiative. Its theological and social departures from conventional evangelicalism, created tension with Campaigners for Christ, and an attempt was made to "buy it out." Changed to *Truth and Liberation*, it became a "periodically inspired," 12 page, underground tabloid, with a peak circulation of 35,000. It reached thousands of youth with no previous connection to the church. Many were dramatically converted to Christian faith and embraced a socially radical view of Christianity. *Truth and Liberation* combined the socio-political elements of *Free Slave*, with the news of Jesus people happenings and attempts to contextualize the gospel in the Australian culture.[57] It dealt with world issues, other religions (Zen, Buddhism, and Divine Light Mission), and counterculture issues – materialism, the environment, indigenous rights, critiques of the Jesus Movement's theological inadequacies, popular culture, rock music, and movies. Teaching cassettes, drop-in houses, outreach centers, and mega-events were advertised. Comics, dramatic event photos, and cartoons attracted visually oriented youth.

God's Squad Christian motorcycle club. Although God's Squad became prominent nationally as a ministry of TLC and Care and CCC, the initial seed was sown in Sydney in late 1969.[58] It was possibly the first missional, Christian motorcycle club in the world to be linked with the Jesus Movement. The Sydney beginnings were perhaps a general sign of secularizing influences on evangelical outreach. They sought to evangelize their bike-riding friends with a mainstream, fundamentalist missiology. The complicated story of the Sydney chapter's demise and the considerably revised form of the Squad after the Melbourne-Sydney synthesis in 1972, is told in the author's autobiography (Smith and Doney 1987). With a distinctly radical theology and integration into the holistic mission of TLC, it was an integral part of the Jesus Movement.

The rate of conversion in the biker scene is low compared to other alternative groups like the 1960s hippies. The marked difference in response between the two cultures is consistent with Rogers' theories of "the diffusion of innovations" (Rogers 1995). The bikers form a closed culture. Bikers have found an alternative, clearly defined, ritualistic brotherhood that provides considerable fulfillment. In spite of this, God's Squad has succeeded in representing the New Testament Jesus, as the object of marginalization and assassination, which endears him to some bikers. Dedication of children, marriages, and funerals are the most dynamic entry points into relationships with this very closed subculture.

It has been an enduring, well-publicized product of the Jesus Movement (Fig 6.6). In the United Kingdom every "outlaw" club has invited God's Squad to their "invitation only" gatherings in the inner sanctum of their clubs' headquarters. The president of God's squad has officiated at a wedding and a funeral representing two warring clubs within months of each other. The conflict resulted in several deaths, one of which initiated the request for pastoral leadership at the funeral. The other club requested God's Squad to officiate at a marriage service. Crossing the line in such cases is virtually unheard of except in the experience of our ministry.

School – The only place where you meet everyone. Under the banner of Christian Option, and later Values for Life, student outreach began in 1971, addressing student groups, primarily in class time, in seminars and forums. Over 4,000 government, religious, and independent secondary schools, and primary schools have experienced these seminars. It is possibly the most significant element of TLC/CCC's impact on the nation. There is no other social location where almost all of a generation can be met for dialogue, instruction, and long-term cultural formation. We often bluntly reminded students that tomorrow's homeless, pedophile, divorcee, suicide, corporation success, and Prime Minister are all sitting together in one place for that brief time. School was potentially the locale for the most comprehensive database for knowledge of youth attitudes.[59] Our counterculture presenters were culturally acceptable to the teenagers, but were a professionally trained, morally conservative, stabilizing influence at a time of cultural distortion. We were thus attractive to parents, teachers, and students alike.

We used contemporary communication, providing stand up comics and popular musical presentations, but the most significant element was our aggressive, well-researched, confrontational critique of the society's state of being. New communication aids were devised. The most useful was a "React Card" which did not require a student's personal details, enabling frank responses, no matter how outrageous. Space was provided for questions that they always wished to ask. The choice was available to leave details for later pastoral help. School administrations rejoiced that "at-risk" youth were thus found and helped. Kaldor and Kaldor (1988) wrote an independent assessment for the Uniting Church Board of Mission (1988:53-54).[60]

The 'bikies' who preach love

JOHN SMITH

The last of a series by NEIL JILLETT

JOHN Smith describes himself as he was four years ago: "the very conventional, short-back-and-sides son of a Methodist minister and very strong in the Christian faith."

Now, at 31, he is even stronger in the faith. He's also mad keen on motor-cycles and spends much of his time with bikies (a term he doesn't find offensive).

With his ponytail hair, torn jeans, floral shirt and high boots, he looks a bit of a lair. But it is generally agreed among the various groups in the Jesus movement, and by outsiders sympathetic to the movement's work, that John Smith is its most successful and dynamic leader.

Mr Smith, a Queenslander who taught social studies in Victorian schools, was troubled that his conservative evangelical faith did not equip him to deal with life and its problems. He was disturbed that humanists — whom he tends to despise as sexual libertines — occasionally seemed to have the right answers.

Teaching

After abandoning teaching and working for two years with a Billy Graham - style evangelical troupe, he found himself simultaneously falling in love with motor bikes and radically revising the expression of his faith.

Now he is in charge of a Jesus movement group whose names are as flamboyant as his personality.

The group operates under the general title of the Truth and Liberation Concern. Its headquarters are called the Jesus Light and Power House. The group's members, as they vroom-vroom through the suburbs and countryside in an effort to bring other bikies and Jesus together, call themselves God's Squad.

The bikes are useful tools for propagating the faith. They attract hordes of kids when God's Squad turns up on one of its many visits (by invitation only) to hold discussions and services at schools (state and independent) and churches (of all denominations).

Like most Jesus people, Mr Smith thinks the established churches have largely failed to persuade Australians that the only way to live is by the standards of practical Christianity (sharing, caring and loving). But he is grateful for any help these "failures" offer.

The Power House, a battered weatherboard in North Bayswater, is owned by the Methodist Church, which is selling it at a bargain price to an Anglican doctor who has promised to give it to the Truth and Liberation Concern.

The Power House is not concerned only with bikies. Anyone can drop in and expect help, practical or spiritual. The rooms are stacked with tape-recordings and equipped with earphones so that visitors can quickly tune into a reading from the Bible, some friendly advice on how to kick the drug habit, or a talk on what to do if their marriage has fallen apart.

Mr Smith admits that, just as the established churches (as he views the scene) are failing to attract the young to Christianity, the Truth and Liberation Concern has not established strong contact with people out of their teens and 20s.

But he says the fact that he and some of his colleagues are family men heading towards middle age should help to correct this fault.

Morals

The generation gap is already being bridged by the Festival of Light (FOL), according to its Victorian chairman, Dutch-born businessman Dirk Bakker. He says its 1300 supporters include people of all ages.

The FOL is not, strictly speaking, part of the Jesus movement, because its basis seems to be in a form of the Christian ethic, not in Christian faith. As Mr Bakker, a Baptist, says, FOL people are united by moral tone rather than by theological doctrine.

Hard-core Jesus people cannot be united by both.

The FOL has assorted clergy on its committees, but they act as links with, rather than representatives of, the main denominations.

Like its branches in other states, the FOL here is an offshoot of the organisation founded by British anti-porn campaigners Lord Longford, Mary Whitehouse and Malcolm Muggeridge.

The common factor between the Jesus movement and the FOL is that both are basically groups of Christians who have announced their readiness to defend "Christian standards" in what they see as a society set on the slippery slope to moral bankruptcy.

Critical

Young Jesus people and the FOL share a horror of "R" films and books, Gay Liberation and other manifestations of what most of us used to call moral laxity, and some of the humanist pronouncements of the Federal Attorney-General, Senator Murphy.

But the Jesus people often implicitly and sometimes explicitly criticise the FOL as too narrow and negative and not sufficiently concerned with other "un-Christian" aspects of our society, particularly some of the practices of big business and the political parties.

Because it has avoided most of the freaky excesses of the Jesus movement in America, the movement here appears to have the cautious approval of conservative clergy and church-goers — when they have tried to understand its aims and spirit.

But they also fear it could get out of hand, that it could become socially disruptive and undermine, especially among young people, the authority of the established churches.

Figure 6.6 The Bikies Who Preach Love (The [Melbourne] Herald, 1975)

On a mobile mission from God. The wandering charismatic model of blitzing the unchurched culture was married to an "alternative" theology for the Australian culture. God's Squad and the Values for Life teams were an integral part of wider missions. Over three decades indigenous preachers were learning the art of popular oratory "on the road." Outlaw bikers became evangelists to private girls' schools!

Our movement preached a revised evangelical code throughout the land (Wallace 1966:160), which combined "a promise of individual salvation" and "cultural salvation for the society" (1966:160). Like Methodism's Wesleys (Ellwood 1973:39), we called vigorously for a conversion to the poor and to scriptural justice throughout the land. The promise of a transformed social order, linked to the values of Jesus' Beatitudes (Matthew 5:3-16; Luke 6:20-26) had great appeal during the socialist surge in Australian society at that time. Conversely we warned of peril with respect to the existing order (Wallace 1966:161). While our critique of the establishment was sometimes strident, the "straight" church, as the society in general, was so concerned about the condition of their drug-using, protesting and itinerant teenagers, that the church both liberal and conservative often called upon us and financed ecumenical outreaches of significant, city-wide dimensions. Our radical social focus endeared us to students, radicals, the media and the secular society in general. Our revised code and new mazeway (Wallace 1956b:270-273; 1966:161) synthesized traditional Christian elements with shifts in emphasis and consciousness within the psychedelic culture (Ellwood 1973:11-23), thus attracting many converts from the cultural fringe of the counterculture.

Our strong biblical, intensification of moral norms through the rituals of Jesus rock concerts, proclamation and alter calls in public rallies (Wallace 1966:130-135) attracted even those who were disturbed by hippie appearance, street language and social radicalism (Cf. Ellwood 1973:x and Richardson, Stewart, and Simmonds 1979:20-21, 38). On occasions, tent missions in parks or arenas were underwritten by dissenting, older church members, when local churches feared involvement.

Our outreach missions exhibited two features that distinguished them from most evangelistic "crusades." Firstly we nuanced and refocused the message according to the sociocultural realities of the nation and local culture. Whereas our biblical training was a textual focus, our evangelism was a contextual one (Kaldor and Kaldor 1988:58). No traditional hymns or "churchie" aspects of culture were included in our youth rallies. The music was not only popular in form, but included secular content. In New Zealand, the *Challenge Weekly* (Francis 1991) recognized that part of the genius of the Jesus Movement was a cultural "chameleon" style ability to reach hitherto "unreachable groups" by being a part of the culture. We were preaching to the Gentiles, while the rest of the church was still preaching to the Jews. We embraced the "revival" tradition but recognized how far away the audience starts from (1988:58-59). *Alive*, claims this method "revolutionized Christian outreach in Australia" (Atkinson 1999:22).

Through an aggressive popular culture approach to itinerant outreach, vigorous advocacy for the marginalized, and frequent appearances in the electronic media, the Movement developed a popular profile. Outreach by Methodist style itinerant preaching in cities and country towns was assisted by Harley Davidson-riding members of God's Squad. Free publicity was provided by a constant release of print and electronic media from a positive secular media. The media highlight of God's Squad's Harley riding evangelists appearing on streets, in every local pub and bar, became a symbol of working class camaraderie for many who never darkened the door of a church.

The second significant innovation was the concept of "a peoples' church on wheels" (*The Herald*, 1972; Colleen 1982), invading every cultural ghetto. We targeted very specific subcultures, meeting them on their territory – the poor in the housing project, the Aboriginal by the campfire and in the urban ghetto, the student on the campus, the musician at a gig, the average guy in the pub, the homeless in the street. In the words of General Booth "We do not fish in other peoples waters. . . . Out of the gutters we will pick up our converts" (Railton 1912:77). Meetings dealing with specific cultural issues were arranged. Police, psychiatrist, doctors, voluntary health providers, lawyers, the unemployed, and homeless, indigenous peoples, youth groups, city hall officials, educators, politicians, sports and service clubs, arts and crafts groups, bike clubs, women's groups, country associations, parents, singles, and a host of others were addressed separately. After the evangelistic rally, God's Squad motorcycle riding members scattered throughout local clubs and pubs till the early hours of the morning, interacting on a friendship basis, demonstrating that Jesus is truly a "friend of publicans and sinners" (Matthew 9:10, 11:19; Mark 2:15-16; Luke 5:30, 15:1).

The Jesus Light and Power House. The movement outgrew the original facility and built an adobe complex, debt free, through the combined labor of the congregation. It was in traditional, colonial Australian architectural style, with an auditorium seating close to 1,000. It was the largest adobe brick structure in the Southern Hemisphere. The communal aspects of the project, including the rehabilitation effect on the lives of some recovering alcoholic craftsmen, stimulated public discussion concerning the advantage of owner-builder projects. Such was the interest aroused, that the author was asked to contribute a chapter to an Australian Broadcasting Commission volume, *The Home Building Experience* (Archer 1985:114-127).

Worship, counseling, Bible studies, concerts, crafts, and conferences occurred. In this facility many ministries were nurtured. TLC established its own media operation at the Jesus Light and Power House, supplying books and records, and a cassette library of thousands of tapes on Christian and secular issues. Leather goods were made and sold at non-exploitative prices. Jesus Movement iconography bonded and ritualized our camaraderie. Horseshoe nail crosses, leather carved fish (representing catacomb, underground Christianity), and leather Bible covers were favorites.

Set in beautiful relaxed Australian bush, Montrose House provided a place for young Christians to learn to live in community. It offered emergency accommodation for homeless teenagers, deserted wives, single mothers, and even criminals.

Outcomes and Impact on Church and Secular Culture

Unlike some elements of the movement which sought to create a satisfactory Christian culture of security and stability for their members, thus revitalizing previously distressed and confused casualties of the 1960s cultural upheaval, our declared intention had always been to create a revolution in both church and state. Perhaps there is some irony in the fact that our reputation for effective itinerant influence across the nation conceals the fact that our own communal experiment suffered severely as a consequence. The revitalization effect upon the wider culture may have been far-reaching and more pervasive than that of Calvary Chapel on the American secular culture. However, the establishment of an impressive, localized steady state by Chuck Smith and his followers, through primary, residential attention given to organization during the routinization phase underscores the principles of revitalization survival delineated by Wallace (1956b:275).

The impact of our movement on the church culture has been such that many churches now embrace many radical elements of our theology, and ministry. Although denominational alternatives now abound, and the counterculture attractiveness of the group has waned, a robust and respected mission to the nation remains.

Media impact. The ministry gained much public attention, being the subject of well over 800 journal and newspaper articles in French, German, Dutch, British, New Zealand, and Australian national and local publications. Making Jesus news in the media market was an intentional strategy – and we succeeded. It was not an engagement for the sake of self-advertisement, though as an ancillary element, it created a highly successful product awareness campaign. Jesus belongs to the people, not to the archbishops or the religious bureaucracies. From rock music to talk shows the media were the eyes, ears, and mouth of the popular culture. It was our desire by every means to make Jesus known which motivated our media exploitation.

Our controversial positioning in the culture enhanced our media relationship (de Salis 1989:2; Kevin Murphy 1987:42-43; Stannard and Molloy 1984:34-36). The media reported on the substantive issues as well as the sensational aspects of long haired hippie Christians riding Harley Davidson motorcycles onto university and high school campuses (Brolly 1991; Coutts 1981; Hannagan 1990; MacPherson 1989:11). Outspokenness, combined with fringe appearance and Jesus Movement enthusiasm, opened many doors to communication with media. Youth alienation and suicide, indigenous land rights, racial and gender equality, poverty, and homelessness were issues that were central to an emerging social consciousness.

Added public exposure was provided by media engagements through print, television and 60 second public service radio announcements concerning sociocultural, and ethical issues. These are still produced for daily transmission over more than 100 stations, in the capital cities, major rural cities, and in the United Kingdom, Europe, Pakistan, and some African countries.

Self-theologizing. What was true of Hirt's movement applies also to TLC/CCC, except that the development of theology was perhaps more literally "on the road" and less structured, apart from weekly expository sessions. Team discussions on Gnosticism would likely occur in a pub after a conversation with a modern Gnostic on campus. "Doing the text" became the key to self-theologizing, taking the text to the field of action, and testing the theory in missional context.

> Several Jesus Movement leaders, including U'ren, Smith, Hirt, and Gill attended the 1974 Lausanne Congress, benefiting from interaction with other evangelical dissenters. Delegates at the Congress discovered that the Lausanne Declaration had been pre-written before the Congress and was going to be presented as a "fait accompli." In spite of the powerful input that came from the developing world delegates on behalf of the poor, the Declaration was still to be presented.... Several Australians (Gill, theologian, communal pioneer, author of *Life on the Road*, (1989), U'ren, Hirt, and Smith) initiated an alternative response, joining forces with like-minded pioneers from the United Kingdom, the United States, and Latin America. (U'ren 1999:16,17)[61]

Ian Breward (1988), church historian for the Melbourne College of Divinity, wrote of the impact of the innovative 1970s, observing that by the end of the 1980s the church had at least begun to relocate its presence, its message, and its cultural shape. Breward views the shift from parachurch movement to church planting apostolate as a positive progression related to the Movement, as exemplified in the author's group.

> Smith's "Truth and Liberation Concern" was a fascinating example of a church which grew out of compassion for the broken. Smith has since founded Care and Communication Concern based at St. Martin's Community Church since 1984. Whether such groups will become indigenous churches in their own right, growing through the crisis of losing their first generation leadership remains to be seen. But they give the lie to the claim that Australian Christians have not produced any homegrown churches. (Breward 1988:80)

It is symbolic of a new day that Jesus Movement authors' texts, challenging both the secular and church cultures are now widely embraced (John Smith 1989 and Garvin 1987). Catholics, Protestants, liberals, evangelicals, and Pentecostals use these texts.

Conclusions

This chapter has sought to illustrate the revitalization focus of the Australian movement in particular, as a distinct contrast to traditional revivalism. The Australian movement experienced large numbers of individual conversions to Christian faith and discipleship, but it rejected the "lifeboat theology" of nineteenth century D. L. Moody's revivalism. It understood itself to be living in a culture that was beyond mere analgesic need and in the final throes of collapse. It did not wish to abandon the Titanic, but to radically rebuild it. The theology, sociology, and strategy of the three major movements I have described was that of counterculture, prophetic challenge to the existing order, but also a call to transformational reconstruction. It was a movement to create communities as samples of the "New World" of the Kingdom of God, on earth as in heaven; to provide liberation from racial, class, and gender tyrannies in the name of Jesus.

I have sought to establish the notable differences between the Australian Movement and the Movement in the United States, and to suggest reasons for its more counterculture expression. Equally notable are the consistent similarities in the early stages, the charismatic leadership, and process of development, even when the ideological conclusions varied. It is the consistent processual details of this diverse movement that points to a social scientific explanation. Revitalization appears to most adequately explain the causation and formation and development of the whole Jesus Movement. It is useful then to revisit Wallace's theory and compare his, and Pflüg's Amerindian finding with those of this research of the Jesus Movement. This will be the focus of the next chapter as we return to reassess the whole movement in terms of revitalization theory.

Notes

1. For a detailed description of these epistemological terms, "naïve-realist" and "critical-realist" see *Myths, Models, and Paradigms: A Comparative Study in Science and Religion*, Ian G Barbour, 1974. For a missiological application of these epistemologies, which is obviously pertinent to a mission centered movement such as the Jesus Movement, see Paul Hiebert's *Anthropological Reflections on Missiological Issues*, 1994, particularly the sections, "Epistemological Foundations for Science and Theology," Pp. 19-34, and "The Missiological Implications of an Epistemological Shift," Pp. 35-51

2. For a description of the "self-theologization" process, see Paul Hiebert 1985, *Anthropological Insights for Missionaries*. Pp. 195-196, 215-219.

3. Early in its development, typical of the indigenous groups of Jesus people, most Shiloh members did not vote as they had abandoned hope in the system, but by the time Jimmy Carter was elected his supporters overwhelmingly outvoted those for Gerald Ford by 83% of Shiloh voters. By then only 17% of their members failed to vote because of despair of the political system or theological disregard for voting (Peterson 1990a:105). By 1980, when all had left the collapsed Shiloh movement, only 9% were indifferent to voting, but the considerable majority was sympathetic to Reagan rather than Carter. In 1988 half the former members could not support any of the candidates. Of those who were voting participators, more preferred Jesse Jackson, than George Bush, although half the voting respondents supported Pat Robertson. Peterson's surveys revealed that most ex-Shiloh members claim to be conservative but 68% are pacifists, who since departure from Shiloh have been influenced by the Anabaptist tradition through John Howard Yoder, Clarence Jordon, Ronald Sider and *Sojourners* magazine (Peterson 1990a:109-114). All of this indicates the diversity rather than conformity of the more indigenous movements, in contrast to the consistent conservatism of the Calvary Chapel members as indicated by Miller's similar survey (Miller 1997:118-120, 209-210, 242). Certainly Shiloh could not be categorized as classic fundamentalist in its sociopolitical proclivities.

4. As quoted in an undated pamphlet produced for public relations information by Shiloh.

5. The anthropological perspective of Victor Turner (1969) has popularized the term *communitas*. Following the experience of acute *liminality* individuals experience an intense sense of existential and timeless connection to each other, as they are re-aggregated in a new social arrangement, usually following a stressful ritual process. While the common term community embraces structural elements of the new arrangement, the intensity, intimacy, mystery and existential bonding experienced is not necessarily inherent in the concept of community. Turner chooses the Latin term *communitas* rather than community, "to distinguish this modality of social relationship from the 'area of common living. It is rather a matter of giving recognition to an essential generic and human bond, without which there could be no society" (Turner 1969:96-97).

6. In Australia "relaxatab," initially a brand name for a chemical relaxant, became generic slang for escapist analgesics. The premillennial eschatology popularized by Dallas Theological Seminary, and later by Hal Lindsay's *Late Great Planet Earth* (1970) and Chuck Smith's popular preaching, was common to some of the evangelically influenced Jesus Movement leaders in Australia at the beginning. It emphasizes the miraculous removal of the faithful from the earth (the "Rapture") prior to a period of universal social and moral collapse, (the "Great Tribulation"). True believers thus tend to abandon the social order, entrench themselves in the evangelical subculture, and remain fascinated and fixated by popular preachers who adroitly interpret world events in terms of literalist, and historicist interpretations of obscure biblical texts. Their emphasis on activism and revitalization caused most Australians to abandon the popular American emphasis, in the belief that the hope of the "Rapture" had become a moral analgesic, causing the abandonment of the biblical obligation to engage in sociopolitical activism.

7. Dr. Joel Green of Asbury Theological Seminary served on the faculty of New College, Berkeley, (originally known as the Crucible), an innovative street university begun in the radical days of the CWLF by Bernard Adeney, author of *Strange Virtues*: *Ethics in a Multicultural World* (1995). CWLF became the Berkeley Christian Coalition when Dr. Jack Sparks and most of the foundational leadership embraced Orthodoxy to form the New Covenant Apostolic Order. Bill Squires, a foundational member of CWLF, took over the leadership of the continuing group, assisted by Sharon Gallagher and David Gill as continuing editors of *Right On*, renamed *Radix*. Green recalls the Berkeley experiences were formative in his theological development and commitment.

8. Ched Myers is the author of the critically acclaimed sociopolitical exegesis, *Binding the Strong Man: A Political Reading of Mark's Story of Jesus* (1990). The significance of Myers to current theology and biblical research is attested to by the fact that his Markan exegesis is highly recommended by a breadth of scholars and activists including Daniel Berrigan, Walter Wink, Norman K. Gottwald, and Richard A. Horsley. On the back cover recommendations, Walter Wink goes so far as to describe this work on Mark as "quite simply, the most important commentary on a book of Scripture since Barth's Romans." This socio-literary exegesis supplies compelling evidence of the complexity and commitment generated intellectually and socially in the liminal space of the radical Jesus Movement, of which Myers was an active participant while an intern in the Australian School of the Prophets. Myers has also provided a scholarly, but activist, social critique of contemporary American culture, calling for a radical relocation of Christian discipleship, squarely in the face of America's imperial context. (See Ched Myers, (1994), *Who Will Roll Away the Stone*: *Discipleship Queries for First World Christians*). Typically, in a chapter in that volume, ("I Will Ask You a Question: Interrogatory Theology"), he calls for a theology which refuses to rationalize social reality. (For a further

contribution on this subject, see also his contribution in *Theology without Foundations: Religious Practice and the Future of Theological Truth* (Hauerwas, Murphy, and Nation, Eds. 1994: 91–116). For many like Myers, who began their discipleship and their careers in a movement which was berthed in the secular world, rather than the institutional church, following Jesus must always be a radical engagement with society at large.

9. David Badstone is another American activist and member of the radical discipleship group associated with the American West Coast, and with the communal movements of Dr. John Hirt and Dr. Athol Gill, who established The School of the Prophets in Australia, (SOPS) based on a Paulo Friere model of pedagogy. Badstone has been for some years a leader in the Central American Missions Partners group (CAMP), which during the troubled 1980s ferried many concerned evangelicals into Central America, to view for themselves the nature of conflict and oppression, and America's role in the interests of its national security. A journey to Central America under sponsorship of CAMP by the author was a disturbing and life changing experience. Evangelical scholar, Guillermo Cook spent a day deprogramming the mostly North American delegation, which had seen refugees, war casualties, and met with rebel leaders in El Salvador, and Sandinista cabinet members in Nicaragua. Dr. Howard Synder, of Asbury Theological Seminary, shared part of the journey. A similar experience was life transforming for mega rock group icon, Bono Vox of *U2*. He has remained a tireless campaigner for Third World Human Rights ever since a journey to Central America with Badstone in the 1980s. This commitment has broadened to a well-publicized leadership in the Jubilee campaign to forgive international debt burdens on Third World nations. A conversation between the author and President Reagan's pastor revealed that he had similarly been "converted" by a CAMP visit, and had sought to influence the President towards a change of policy regarding his support for the Contras. Badstone has recently stepped into the role of editor of *Sojourners*, which was founded by Jim Wallace.

10. Bernard Adeney led the radical street university project known as the Crucible, which became Berkeley's New College. Adeney spent some years in Indonesia as a missionary to the Muslim population.

11. The author has a long-term friendship and association with Tom Sine, who has frequently visited Australia and New Zealand. He has had considerable impact on our own post-Jesus Movement groups, particularly with respect to a radical application of discipleship to lifestyle and socioeconomics. His works call upon a wide experience of observing and interviewing creative leaders around the world, particularly those who are genuinely grappling with postmodernity. His support of coalitions of younger leaders emerging in the alternative churches has endeared him to post-modern radicals.

12. Reference from the advertising leaflet entitled "Earthkeeping: A Biblical View of Environmental Stewardship." The conference was held at the Shiloh Study Center, March 19 and 20, 1982. The program included a "Mars Hill Forum" at the University of Oregon and a talk show on KBMC, 94.5FM.

13. Dr. G. E. Gorman, advisory editor of the Bibliographies and Indexes of Religious Studies series, is from Australia's Charles Sturt University, in the Riverina region of southwestern New South Wales.

14. Dr. John Painter, Professor of Theology at St. Mark's National Theological Center, Charles Sturt University, is an academic currently involved in a new national research initiative which is seeking to establish an indigenous outlook on Australian church history and the contextualization of biblical studies and theology. John Painter has taught New Testament Studies in England, South Africa, and Australia. A member of Stadium Novi Testament Societas, he has authored *The Quest for the Messiah* (second edition 1993), *Theology as Hermeneutics* (1987) *and Mark's Gospel New Testament Readings*

(1997). John Painter is also a colleague and close friend of Thorwald Lorenzen, a major influence upon the radical Anabaptist Jesus Movement communities led by Dr. John Hirt and Dr. Athol Gill. Previously a professor of biblical studies at the Baptist Theological Seminary, Ruschlikon, Switzerland during its more radical days, Lorenzen is now the Baptist pastor of Canberra Baptist Church.

15. Some well known groups and ministries were: Truth and Liberation Concern, The House of the New World, The House of the Gentle Bunyip, God's House, The House of the Rock, The Abode of the Gentle Toad, Jacob's Ladder, Christian Option, Theos Coffee Shops, Values for Life, God's Squad Motor Cycle Club, and The Resurrection Community.

16. Most of the Australian leaders, despite radical counterculture commitment and appearance, were conservative evangelicals who experienced swift paradigm shifts and embraced the dissenting culture as visionaries and strategists as well as evangelists, communal organizers, and pastor-teachers. Hirt was an ordained Baptist pastor; Smith (the author of this dissertation) was a Methodist pastor and national itinerant evangelist as well as the son of a Methodist minister, and a third generation preacher. Gill was an ordained Baptist and professor of New Testament in both Baptist and Uniting Church seminaries. U'ren was a well-known member of a prominent Methodist dynasty, the brother of a Methodist missionary who became Victorian Moderator of the Uniting Church of Australia. He was for some years also the director of Scripture Union, a century-old, British youth organization, from the stable of InterVarsity, or Evangelical Unions, as they are locally known on university campuses. In South Australia, the most prominent leaders were Methodist (later Uniting Church) clergy and youth workers and a charismatic Lutheran pastor who developed a substantial ministry assisted by youth workers and folk singers.

17. Jack Sparks endeared himself to the Australian Movement as a gentle radical whose persona was Old World and exceedingly gracious. His position on issues of culture and American imperialism was very counterculture. As the left line of politics was in the ascendancy in Australia, while in distinct retreat in America, the timing of his coming was excellent. His presentations on Australia's major campuses to large audiences of secular and even anti-Christian students were exceptionally successful. His swift shift to Orthodoxy was a shock to most, but his profound concern with community and ecclesiology in retrospect was congruent with his journey. His literary contributions, *Letters to Street Christians* (1975) and *God's Forever Family* (1974), were a significant contribution to counterculture Christian growth. *Right On*, Sparks' original brainchild and the first of the American Jesus papers, was far more suited to the Australian Jesus Movement in content and style. Prophetic, satirical articles, cartoons, and astute critique of contemporary literature and performing arts had great appeal to the senior high and college students, which were a major network of Jesus Movement supporters.

18. Os Guinness played a significant role in framing the worldview of many Australian Jesus people. *Dust of Death* (1973) was available on audiocassette, and relatively uneducated, but deeply committed young converts typically listened to the material many times. Constant dialogue over such material developed an interactive self-theologization, which came up from the grass roots simultaneously with more formal studies and reflections. *In Two Minds*, a later contribution from Guinness on the subject of the pathology and theology of doubt was also significant for the growth of many members of the community. A tape entitled "The Responsibility of Knowledge" is still circulating and being enthusiastically reflected upon amongst the new, postmodern generation members of the community. Guinness' later works, *The Gravedigger File* (1983), *The American Hour, No God But God* (1992), and *Fit Bodies Fat Minds* (1994), have had less impact, partly

because Guinness' tendency towards much more right wing politics has not appealed to some. Guinness has retained a strong modernity frame of reference, while an attempt to reframe the issues in more postmodern epistemology appeals to many of the contemporary, earnest inquirers into contextual theology.

19. McGuire continues to sing in the folk style of the early Jesus Movement days, despite the discouragement of souring experiences with a market driven Contemporary Christian Music industry (CCM). By his account, record companies have exploited his naivete towards material things and left him with no control or income from his earlier music. His hippie simplicity in presentation was electrifying. The author's many conversations with him over the years have revealed a level of disillusionment with the culture's move away from the simplicity and anti-materialism of earlier days. Still living on the edge, Barry has regrouped with Terry Talbot, brother of Franciscan convert, John Michael Talbot.

20. Although Australia lacked America's revivalist tradition within the religious culture, a small fundamentalist, "in-house" obsession with the concept stimulated invitations to American visitors such as Edwin Orr during the 1960s, telling Australians of American and Welsh revivals as the way to national renewal.

21. Monotremes are mammals, which lay eggs but suckle the young at the breast upon hatching. The platypus of Australia and the echidnas (spiny ant-eaters) of Australia and New Guinea are the only living examples of this animal. Evolutionists regard these two mammals as a long surviving links between reptilian and mammalian developments. The isolation of Australia and the absence of carnivores, with the exception of the recently migrated dingo from Southeast Asia, are believed to be the cause of their survival.

22. Their interaction with the invaders has been marked by bewilderment on both sides; the indigenes were culturally in far greater contrast to the Euro-Australian invaders than the comparable Native American cultures were to the Euro-American colonialists.

23. In contrast to America, our national celebration of identity and character is Anzac Day, commemorating our worst military defeat. The English command sent the flower of Australia's youth into certain defeat, against entrenched Turks, at Gallipoli, during World War I. Anzac Day (Australian and New Zealand Army Corps) reinforces the stoic sense that "it matters not if we win, but how we play the game." The noble, stoic embrace of defeat is axiomatic to being traditional Australian. Poet henry Kendall wrote, "Life is mostly froth and bubble; Two things stand like stone – Kindness in another's trouble; Courage in your own."

24. Loveless was immortalized as a leader of the "Tollpuddle Martyrs" (Crowley 1980:472-473; Clark 1968:294-295; John Smith 1989:14-15). Symptomatic of ecclesiastic complicity in colonial injustice was the disregard for the plight of his family, by Loveless' English, Wesleyan Church after his transportation.

25. The Catholics were disallowed official priestly presence for the first dozen years, their only leadership representatives being Irish, clerical convicts. Catholicism became a significant force amongst the poor and working classes, in social service, education and ameliorating faith being highly represented by the poor, the marginalized, and the working class. Through extensive educational institutions, abundant social welfare, numerous inner city missions, and urban development, the church, Catholic, and Protestant, was eventually rehabilitated as an establishment benefactor, rather than a democratic popular movement as in the America's experience.

26. South Australia granted women political suffrage in 1894 and acceptance in the National Parliament in 1902 (Crowley 1980:443), 26 years and 18 years respectively, before America's Nineteenth Amendment (1919), (enacted in January 1920) granted female suffrage to United States female citizens.

27. Within a decade of the Declaration of Independence (1776), the Methodist Episcopal Church was established (1784) and was to have a profound influence in the frontier development. The Founding Fathers from Washington to Jefferson waxed eloquent concerning the religious foundations for the new nation, while warning against religious hegemonies connected to political powers.

28. The rural history of struggle with marginal climates and vast distances, and the urban beginnings of a convict system, seemed to have centered the soul in a materialistic survival mode, as D.H. Lawrence saw it: "Look at [them] – they're awfully nice, but they've got no inside to them. They're hollow. How are you going to build on such hollow stalks? They may well call them cornstalks. They're marvelous and manly and independent and all that, outside. But inside, they are not. When they're quite alone, they don't exist . . . .They've just gone hollow . . . . Everything is outward – like hollow stalks of corn. All that struggle with bush and water and whatnot, all the mad struggle with the material necessities and conveniences – the inside soul just withers and goes into the outside, and they're all just lusty robust stalks of people . . . . They've no soul to bargain about . . . . They're nice. But they haven't got the last everlasting bit of soul, solitary soul, which makes a man himself" (Lawrence 1923:146-147).

29. Birch is a process theologian, Australia's most celebrated biologist, and the first scientist to win the Templeton Prize for religion.

30. Most European immigrants and Irish convicts and immigrants were Catholic. The Scots were Presbyterian; the Germans were Lutheran; the Scandinavians and Dutch were usually Reformed. At the margins of social respectability Methodists and Baptists drew their traditions from England rather than America.

31. The Christian and Missionary Alliance, Nazarenes, and Wesleyans – have found difficulty in gaining acceptance, and were denied counselor status by the local Billy Graham organizers of the 1956 crusade. The Graham Crusade in 1956 resulted in notable church growth and a remarkable increase in Bible College and seminary applications, but by the late 1960s the established church was in serious decline.

32. Some of us doubted it had ever been Christian in any substantial sense. It had reflected some of the deist tendencies of Wesley's England at the time of Captain Cook's "discovery" of the "Great Southland of the Holy Spirit," as the Spanish had speculatively labeled this mysterious land. The author and some other activists preferred to call it a pre-Christian country awaiting the liberating message of an indigenized form of the gospel.

33. A Fuller Seminary Ph.D. in philosophical theology, Millikan seriously examined the unique Australian land-based identity, sardonic humor, and native skepticism. He probed the Australian spirit of anti-intellectualism, skepticism, and secularism, calling all Christians to embrace the Australian tradition of egalitarianism (1982). He was associated also with *Zadok*, a socioreligious journal to promote well-researched discussion about the interface of religion and culture in Australia, making a unique and enduring contribution.

34. One theologian employed a prominent Australian artist Pro Hart to provide Australian rural images for a nativity account. Jesus was thus born in a nearby wool shed on a sheep station, surrounded by kangaroos and bandicoots, because "there was no room in the pub." Lutheran folk singer Leigh Newton produced an album, *Christmas in the Scrub*, contextualizing the birth narrative amidst Australian gum trees with the "laughing jackass" bird, or Australian kookaburra joining the angels in praise of the new born "baby in the straw." The Christian lead singer of the pub band *Glass Canoe* (a euphemism for a glass of beer) re-imaged Jesus' baptism so that a kookaburra rather than a dove descended. The voice from heaven says in very "outback" jargon: "This is my little 'tacker'

and I reckon he's just all right." Some found this colloquial approach offensive, but for many of the un-churched it was immediately gripping, convincing "Aussie pagans" that the message was more culturally believable.

35. The following are samples of positive coverage of our Movement by Methodist and later, Uniting Church, Anglican, Lutheran, and interdenominational press.

Interdenominational press: *Together*, "A Friend of Jesus Today. John Smith, Leader of God's Squad," 1979.

On Being, a popular national interdenominational journal spanning parachurch, evangelical, and Pentecostal cultures, gave feature length coverage to our own movement on several occasions: "Mustering Australia's Lost Sheep, 1980, 7(2 [March]):4-8; "God Cares." 1982a, 9(6):4-8; "The Common People Heard Him Gladly," 1982b, 9(6[July]):5-11; "Why John Smith Went to Prison," 1989a, 16(9[September]:22-24; "The Australian Connection," 1989b, 16(October):20-22.

Even the major fundamentalist national journal *New Life*, though critical of the street language and social gospel tones of the Movement, consistently and even enthusiastically supported some of the Jesus Movement initiatives: "John Smith's Four Weeks Overseas . . . . Huge Media Coverage in London," 1987a, September 10; "Fourth Melbourne Prayer Breakfast . . . . John Smith Focuses on the Nation – and Presents the Gospel!" 1987b, December 10; "John Smith to Minister on the East Coast of the US," 1988a, April 21; "Christianity or Humanism? – Lively Debate at Melbourne's La Trobe University" 1988b, October 13; "Good on You Smithie," Bob Thomas, 1989, August 1.

In New Zealand, where the Movement was relatively significant alongside the extraordinary impact of the Charismatic Movement, the popular evangelical, soft-Pentecostal journal, *The Challenge Weekly*, ran feature length articles about our Australian ministries. See for example Vic Francis' article, "Christians [are] 'like Pharisees.'" 1991, 49(1):17ff; "Chameleon Evangelist Speaks to 'Unreachable' Groups: Changing His Colors to Suit His Environment," 1991, 4(2):24ff.

Uniting Church: *Uniting*, "Behind the Bikie Image, a Message for Life." 1984; "20th Century Wesley, Aussie Style." Paul Ainsworth, CWN Series 1986, September 12.

Anglican Press: *Church Scene*, "Outreach: Go Out and Do It," 1985, May 30; *Church News*, "Christianity or Humanism? Debate at La Trobe University." December, 1988; Muriel Porter, "John Smith – Australian Evangelist." *Australian Ministry*, 1991, August: 12-15; and Lutheran Press:

Lutheran: "Squad in Melbourne." *Encounter for Lutheran Youth*, Neville Lienert, 1972, December: 2-3.

Few accounts of the Australian Jesus Movement have ever been published by insiders, Ron Ellis, a Youth for Christ director in Geelong, published a light-weight, enthusiastic account early in its development, entitled, *Jesus Revolution Down-Under* (1972). More scholarly but brief analysis, including historical material was provided by Uniting Church historian Ian Breward in *Australia: The Most Godless Place Under Heaven* (1988), and by Uniting Church sociologists Peter and Sue Kaldor in *Where the River Flows: Sharing the Gospel in a Changing Australia* (1988). These were released in the late 1980s, but failed in the author's opinion to fully recognize the Movement's significance in the acceleration of indigenous religious forms, and the surge in church planting initiatives.

36. In the market place the United States always seemed to do it better and a love-hate jealousy was standard fare for Australians because of America's sheer numerical capacity to dominate the market. In the 1950s, a preacher with an American accent always seemed more authoritative if not mesmerizing. By the 1970s an American accent created suspicion rather than positive intrigue amongst the first wave of postmoderns.

Independence from America's influence was not the only adolescent national obsession. The collapse of the Whitlam government via the antiquated power of the Queen's representative, the Governor General, was to inflame nationalism and promote a smoldering passion for a Republic, which remains a contentious issue today.

37. On December 2, 1972, Gough Whitlam was elected Prime Minister, partly on the basis of his vigorous opposition to the Vietnam War, with his call for a more truly indigenous political stance, whereby Australians could cease being subservient to American interests. This was a significant element in the change of Australia's political landscape. Whitlam reflected the idealism of the counterculture and engaged in positive face to face dialogue with dissident youth. This was in contrast to the establishment brutality of the Kent State government response under Richard Nixon's parallel administration. After a lengthy period of long and bitter conflict between the Left and the Right, Whitlam, a highly charismatic, rhetorically brilliant, Fabian socialist, emerged as a nationally popular, alternative leader. He was committed to education reform, social egalitarianism, aboriginal rights, and structural revolution in the interests of a new humanitarian society. His vision of a just and humane society appeared in stark contrast to the establishment. Young Australians flocked to his New Left politic. Australia was a joint participator with America in South Vietnam to fight against the North Vietnamese's communist insurgence. A deep nationalist resentment by many idealistic youth, conflicted with an historic, Australian subservience to American foreign policy.

38. A conspiratorial atmosphere developed, fueling a youth resistance to the old order. In the 1980s it was revealed that Australia's famous Methodist cleric and innovator, Sir Alan Walker's had been under surveillance in the early 1970s. His involvement in anti Vietnam War marches and his Methodist socialism, had provoked ASIO, Australia's equivalent of the CIA, to compile on him, one of the largest files held on any Australian.

39. The House of the New World, (Sydney); The Abode of the Friendly Toad (Adelaide); The House of the Rock (Adelaide); The House of Freedom (Brisbane); the Jesus Light and Power House (Melbourne); Resurrection Community (Melbourne), and a host of others were a network of centers for intentional, Christian subversion, with shared philosophies and programs. There appears to have been an alternative Jesus family in every major city and rural center.

40. While Jesus People groups found inspiration and understanding often through the praxis model of action-reflection in the market place engagement of evangelism, social protest and care, they supplemented their education by engaging radical scholars from the established church. Dr. Robert Banks and his wife Julia were favorites, particularly amongst the alternative communities in Canberra and New South Wales. Os Guinness had given a lecture against "giantism" in Western culture at a Jesus Happening. This lecture influenced many philosophically towards the house church model for which Robert and Julie Banks were the best known Australian exponents.

41. Banks is still committed to the development of an alternative model for the Australian church, having written extensively on what he believes to be the normative early church model of house gatherings. He served as a Professor at Fuller Seminary, Pasadena, CA for some years, co-authoring materials with his highly competent wife Julia. He returned to Australia for the final stages of his wife's terminal illness, and is now involved in a renewed gospel and culture academic enquiry in Australia. Several house churches following Banks' model continue, particularly in New South Wales. Banks has produced several texts on the cellular nature of the New Testament Church. See *The Church Comes Home: Building Community and Mission Through Home Churches* (1998); *Going to Church in the First Century: An Eyewitness Account* (1990); *Paul's Idea of Community: The Early House Churches in Their Cultural Setting* (1994).

42. In the 1850s conflict over the rights of Catholics to enculturate their constituents by their educational tradition provoked rivalry that eventually delivered state education to secularism, legislated as "free, value free, and secular." In the 1970s the historic hostility between Catholics and Protestants, particularly evangelical Protestants began to break down. While researching I was surprised to discover that the song claimed by the Jesus Movement as its theme song, "They'll Know We Are Christians by Our Love," was created by a charismatic Catholic community in Ann Arbor, Michigan, in 1966. It was a favorite hymn amongst Jesus Freaks very early in the Movement, indicative of a crossover between the Catholic charismatic communities and the early counterculture Jesus Freak communes. It swiftly found its way to us through the underground network of the Movement.

43. Fusion, developed by Mal Garvin prior to the Jesus Movement, was interactive with the Jesus Freaks and remains a major contributor to inter-church evangelism, social critique, and support of the marginalized. John U'ren, a participant observer of a comprehensive representation of Australian Jesus Movement groups, has provided the following concise, brief sketch of Mal Garvin and his work.

"Fusion has now established itself as an ordaining body, its staff having had a long record [of ministry] in five states of Australia and many cities and towns. Starting as a coffeehouse in Hornsby, New South Wales in the early 70s under the name Teen Crusaders, it has spread around Australia as a youth movement. It adopted the name Fusion in the mid-1970s. Garvin, one of its founders and now its Chief Executive Officer, has experimented with many models of community, not claiming Fusion to be a worshipping congregation. The Jewish kibbutz idea was one of their experiments although they have explored many. Their target has primarily been youth and in particular youth in crisis situations. Rehabilitation with education has been their main platform. Fusion today is still going strongly in a small town Poatina, Tasmania. [They established in Poatina] a major community outreach center, where team training takes place. Cottage industries, a motel, and small mini cars are available for hire. Their industries [support] the program costs [subsidized by] government grants money. Houses in the village are available for purchase and occupants are required to participate in the community life and ministry. Fusion runs an accredited TAFE [Technical and Further Education] level youth diploma course, plus courses on personal development and leadership. It is the key promoter and initiator of the Aussie Awaking program that for 10 years until 2001, united churches throughout Australia to march on Easter Sunday, claiming Easter as the critical Christian event. Fusion has also linked to the 2000 AD event/strategy and gained international recognition. Overseas it seems to be understood by the other 2000 AD participants, that Garvin has the whole Australian church united behind the 2000 AD Beyond event, but only a small part of the evangelical church and parachurch agencies have identified with the 2000 AD idea" (U'ren 1999:5-6).

44. See endnote 13 for a brief resume of U'ren's background and role in the Movement.

45. Subjects in 1973 included: "Is the Future a Bummer? School's Nearly Out;" "Jesus in the Schools;" "Things Have Changed for Barry McGuire – a Testimony." (McGuire became a central figure in the counterculture when his rendition of Eve of Destruction became a major hit, and a focus for media bans across America in 1965); "Ambition and Materialism;" "The Difference Between Life and Death;" "Forever Family Pty. Ltd.;" "Jesus People Arrested;" "The Jesus Busline;" "Footballer Becomes Christian;" "The Jesus Way Is It;" "Nature is the Art of God;" "Stop Truth Decay – Read the Bible Now."

46. The following courses for the three term year of 1974 give an idea of the biblical, strategic, alternative nature of the MW agenda: "Print Workshop" (for training in writing techniques, research methods, layout and production of off-set printing of broad-sheets, tracts and tabloid Jesus papers); An expository Study of Galations;" Screen Printing Workshop;" "Creative Listening;" "Stage 2 of Counseling Course;" "Introduction to the Christian Faith;" "An expository Study of II Corinthians;" "A Theology of Community;" "The Ethical Implications of the Old Testament"; "Preaching and Public Speaking"; "Child Psychology and Communicating the Christian Faith to Children;" "An Introduction to Piano Accordian;" Personal evangelism in the coffee house;" "Studying and Teaching the Bible;" "New Horizons for Contemporary Women (Women's Liberation, Feminine Mystique, Suburban Loneliness etc);" "Cooking for Large Numbers."

47. From the 1974 Master's Workshop course flyer, Spring (Term III).

48. Kairos, a Greek word denoting a special time or occasion, was particularly inspiring as a concept for the youth event. The Prime Minister, Gough Whitlam had convincingly won the election a few months before, on a platform of social justice and renewal. His political slogan was "It's Time" [for a change]. The Movement was euphoric in its Jesus lifestyle commitment to revitalization. The Australian Movement tended towards postmillennialism, holding that it was the age of Jesus rather than the Age of Aquarius. In Australia the Movement rode on a wave of optimism, believing a new era of interest in justice and spiritual values was on the rise. In contrast the American Movement was a lifeboat for the drifting, disillusioned, counterculture casualties, in a period of left-wing decline and division.

49. The Kairos 73 Canberra event (1973) was a huge "gathering" of youth that surrounded the Parliament House of Australia, Canberra, with the heads of churches, bishops, clergy, leaders, and Members of Parliament. Ordinary everyday Australians marched around Parliament House finishing with a prayer vigil for the nation. A "Jesus Family Teach-In" preceded the busing of 450 young people from Victoria, plus another 1,500 from around Australia to Canberra for the "Kairos 73" demonstration, just after the Federal election in 1972. It became the first of many Christian demonstrations in the national capital and in other cities annually, during Easter season.

The Kairos event made the front pages of newspapers around Australia. 100,000 tabloid newspapers Kairos 73, were distributed. Kairos 73, a single issue tabloid, was produced jointly for the national demonstration of Jesus People by The Free Paper (Brisbane), Coming Home (Perth), Focus; Rap; Sydney Town Express; Tell (Sydney); Theos Sun and Truth and Liberation (Melbourne). It announced: "Kairos is a Greek way of saying "It's time." A Greek way of saying "It's God's time for Australia." The following article headings appeared in Kairos: "An Open Letter to the Hon. E.G. Whitlam [Prime Minister] M.P. Parliament House, Canberra, A.C.T. [Australian Capital Territory] 2600." From The Jesus Family P. 3; "For you Mr. Churchman, it's about Bikies and Such" P. 4; "Jesus in the Streets" P. 5; "Quo Vadus Australia?" Pp. 6-7; "The Games People Play" P. 8; "Educated for What? Come Home Wendy" P. 9; "Jesus People Directory" P. 10; "The Jesus Way Is It" P. 10; "Sex and Society" P. 11; a new day rises . . . proclaiming liberty to the captives, recovery of sight to the blind, freedom to the crushed and broken hearted" P. 12.

In the House of the New World's, Free Slave report of Kairos, a full page photograph showed "Jesus Freaks," heads bowed, gathered under a roughly constructed cross, on the steps outside the floodlit Parliament House, for an all night prayer vigil. It bore the caption, " 'O Australia, Australia . . . how often would I have gathered your children together as a hen gathers her brood under her wings – and you would not' – Jesus." Another page showed a traffic policeman, arms akimbo looking at a continuous line of Jesus Freaks holding hands as they surrounded the Parliament building to pray. Over his mystified head a thought balloon contained a question mark.

50. Influential mentors included Dr. Robert, and Sydney McAfee Brown (Berkeley Graduate Theological Union and Pacific School of Theology); Dr. Jorge, and Janice Pixley, (Liberation Theology study group at the National University of Mexico); Dr. Jose Miranda, Dr. William, and Mary Herzog; Dr. Thorwald, and Jill Lorenzen (International Baptist Seminary, Zurich, Switzerland); Dr. Athol Gill (Baptist Theological Seminary, Melbourne, Australia). John Hirt worked actively with Phil Berrigan, Liz Macalister, and Fr. Daniel Berrigan S. J.

51. The following sample article headings provide a sense of this counterculture student agenda: Vol. 2, No. 3 Issue 8, (January 1974, Easter – Anzac Day); "Remember" (A highly peace-activist, critical analysis of Remembrance Day, the equivalent of Memorial Day in the US) P. 1; "Why Slaves Labor – How Easter and Anzac Got Mixed Up" P. 2; "The Exorcist - Review" P. 3; "Quadrophenia" The Who P. 3; "Why Bother with the Resurrection" Pp. 4-5; "Occulture" The Counterculture: Revolution or Reiteration" P. 6.

Vol. 2 No. 4 Issue 9 (November 74); "Working for the Man: a Critique of the Work Ethic" Pp. 1, 7; "Letter to Miss America: Critique of Christian Women in Beauty Contests" P. 2; "Images of Progress: You Can't Get There from Here, but Who Wants to Go: Urban Planning" P.3; "A Response to Lausanne: a Radical Alternative Statement" Pp. 4-5; "Occultism" P. 6; "Countering the Rip-offs" P. 7; "A Cartoon reply to Nietzsche" P. 8. Vol. 3 No. 1 Issue 10 (1975); "The Radical Kingdom" P. 2; "Cosmic Voyager: Episode 2001: Cartoon" Pp. 4-5; "In Numbers too Big to Ignore: House of the New World Involvement in Women's Day March" P. 6.

52. "Radical Discipleship" became the descriptive and prescriptive label for the style and content of the commitment of many of Australia's Jesus People. Its origins at the local level are uncertain, but the author assumes it to have arisen through Hirt's interaction with radical leaders while in America. John Hirt claims to have initiated its use for the self-description of our form of Christian discipleship in the Australian Movement and I find no reason to dispute his claim. For a more detailed theological understanding of the House of the New World definition of Radical Discipleship see Hirt's Ph.D. Dissertation, "Radical Discipleship: Towards the Theology and Sociopolitical Implications" 1998, School of Studies in Religion, The University of Sydney.

53. Dr. Athol Gill as an activist as well as an academic, was a key figure in the founding of the House of Freedom in 1973. Gill, an ordained Baptist minister who received his doctorate in New Testament at Ruchlikon, Switzerland, was lecturer in theology at the Queensland Baptist Theological College in the early 1970s. There he attracted students who were seeking to interpret his theology of radical discipleship. For a period, after conflict with conservatives in the Baptist Seminary, he served in King's College, the Queensland Uniting Church seminary. He later relocated to Melbourne, where he became Professor of New Testament at Whitley College. This is the undergraduate and graduate Baptist facility in the Melbourne College of Divinity coalition of denominational seminaries, adjunct to Melbourne University. There his influence was profound, developing a radical theological, urban renewal tradition despite early opposition from a strong fundamentalist lobby in the denomination. Many dedicated urban radicals have been supplied for a changing Baptist ministry context through the influence of Gill and those associated with his House of the Gentle Bunyip community. His published works include Life on the Road: The Gospel Basis for a Messianic Lifestyle (1989); Discipleship Studies (1978); The Fringes of Freedom: Following Jesus, Living Together, Working for Justice (1990). His influence on many of the Movement's leaders including Hirt,

U'ren, and Smith, was as great as any other contributor to the debate on applied and contextualized Christianity.

54. Self-theologizing is seen by Paul Hiebert (See Anthropological Reflections on Missiological Issues 1994) as an integral part of true contextualization. If the meanings of the gospel are not re-interpreted in the local reality, even if the forms of colonialist mission are expressed by local symbols, a truly indigenous form has not been developed. The desire to establish a local identity for the faith in Australia made the Jesus Movement sympathetic to the action-reflection model of theological development. The investigation of global alternative movements inspired local applications where the issues of self-determination were generic. Mutual understanding was established between marginalized people around the globe. The School Of the Prophets program reflected the global-local relationship central to Robert J. Schreiter's (1997) enquiry into theological synthesis, syncretism, the rise of a "new catholicity," and the tension between globally-driven, cultural homogenization and local particularism (See Schreiter 1997 The New Catholicity: Theology Between the Global and the Local). The School of the Prophets was locally driven, but drew extensively on the resources of key liberation theologians for assistance in developing its hermeneutical tools for local, cultural critique. Many of its participants and instructors embarked on investigative tours of Central America at the height of the civil wars in El Salvador, Guatemala, and Nicaragua, forging lifelong bonds between radical Australian Evangelicals and Catholic liberationists. My own group likewise developed such bonds and on monthly basis for many years we have provided preachers and worship leaders for a local, Catholic, El Salvadoran refugee church. Some of our number learnt Spanish to facilitate ministry in this Catholic context.

55. While I am confident of the accuracy of this quote from a carefully preserved, personal record of quotable quotes filed over a lifetime, it was collated before the invaluable education in graduate citation essentials. Max Harris is a well-known Australian socio-cultural commentator, whose commentaries, like many of his genre of Australian critics, are insightful if somewhat acerbic. I believe this quote comes from either the Melbourne daily, The Age or the national, weekly journal, The Bulletin, somewhere between the mid-1970s and 1980s.

56. Christian Option in schools and universities, God's Squad Motorcycle Club outreach to bikers and fringe-dwellers, and the charismatic, evangelistic/apostolic mission teams, with their audio tape ministry, continued with CCC. Church plants became known as St. Martins Community Churches, named after the Anglican building rented for the first plant in Carlton, inner city suburb of Melbourne, Australia. According to the story/legend of the early church St. Martin of the Fields, he was a soldier turned pacifist, and of a social justice and welfare practitioner. He seemed to be an appropriate icon for the theology and practice of our movement.

57. Typical contents as found in Vol. 2, 2 (1974) were: "Now Time 74 comes to Sydney" – announcing the visit of Fuller Theological Seminary's David Hubbard P.2; "Editors Vibes." (Thoughts on current affairs and issues in the Movement) P.2; "God's House" (A report on Another Jesus Movement ministry) P. 3; "Resource Center tapes" P. 3; "In School" – reports of Jesus visiting schools" P. 4; "W[estern] A[ustralia] Gets Involved" P. 5; "A Story from the Sixties." (The conversion story of Barry McGuire, Singer of Eve of Destruction Pp. 6-7); "Notes from the Music Scene. What's the Score?" P. 6; "A Critical Analysis of the Jesus Revolution" Os Guinness Pp. 8-9; "Profile on Dr. Jack Sparks and Michael Eastman: a special Jesus Family Teach-in" P.10; "Cassettes" 10; "Materialism: This is Where it Ends." (This anti-materialism article by Francis Schaefer was the cover story, accompanied as the cover picture of a wrecked car yard full of crushed vehicles piled one upon the other) P. 11; "Letters to Street Christians" P. 12;

"Mixed Vibes" – Readers Comments Pp. 12-13; Comic: A radically revised, hip version of " Four Spiritual Laws" Pp. 14-15. On the back page was a cartoon picture of a buzzard, sitting on the Bible, clasping it shut, with a Papal ring on one claw.

58. John Hirt, whose interests sub-culturally lay in the surf rather than on the open highway, supported the group to which the author was originally chaplain, and later founder of a restructured group. It began independent of the House of the New World, but found a meeting place and encouragement from the community center there. The Sydney Squad folded soon after a reshaped and re-envisioned chapter was formed in Melbourne, later re-forming a chapter in Sydney and several other centers in Australia and abroad, continuing to the present time. This initiative was formed for outreach to one of the most marginalized groups, the motorcycle fraternity, particularly of the "outlaw" and "loner" variety. God's Squad has adopted the culture of the outlaw scene except for those elements that are clearly immoral. The Squad embraced the biker pattern of lengthy, preparatory ritual process before investing "colors," whereas most Christian motorcycle clubs do not require an apprenticeship, and colors can be purchased rather than "earned."

59. When a senior research fellow of the Australian Council for Educational Research undertook a Federal Government sponsored evaluation of methodology, content, and measurable outcomes, he confessed to difficulty in maintaining objectivity. He recounted asking himself, "How could anyone fail to respond to the experience of one of these seminars" (Withers 1997:60). He concluded:

"They are powerful strategies, educationally and ethically respectable, and they stick. Put quite simply, every young person needs them – the more, who get the contact, the better for the country. And the less it will have to spend later, I believe, in coping with the homeless, disaffected, and juvenile, and cleaning up after the suicides. Yes, I think it's that good" (1997:61). Professor of Education, Brian Hill (1991) (Appendix 11) of Murdoch University, Western Australia, spoke of the program's "significant ability to evoke genuine responses from people of a wide age range" (1991).

60. In 1982, over a period of eight months, we ran half-day seminars in every Government and private high school in Adelaide and communicated on all university and college campuses, under the banner of God Cares. Hundreds of other youth events including bush dances, retreats, youth rallies, concerts, and parent nights, assisted by considerable media attention, established a model and a foundation for a permanent, religious education program for South Australia. Australia's major Christian journal, On Being (now Alive), gave the project massive coverage On Being (1982). Embraced by the heads of churches, new curriculum, seminar programs, and chaplains became a permanent reality in the South Australian schools. South Australia had been the most secular state during the previous decade.

61. U'ren, Hirt, Gill, and Smith worked with notable contributors Jim Punton of Frontier Youth Trust, UK; Jim Wallis of Sojourners community and journal; Ron Sider Rich Christians in an Age of Hunger (1977); John Howard Yoder The Politics of Jesus (1972). Latin America Fraternity of radical evangelicals joined forces through Peruvian theologian Samuel Escobar, and Rene Padilla Mission Between the Times (1985); Padilla editor of The New Face of Evangelism (1976). The alternative covenant was entitled "Theology Implications of Radical Discipleship." (J. D. Douglas, ed. 1974:1294-1296). Written collectively, the alternative Lausanne Covenant was given the blessing of John Stott in the plenary session, and was included at the back of the Lausanne report, Let the World Hear His Voice (J. D. Douglas, ed. 1974).

CHAPTER 7

Communalism for Empowerment – A Modernity Response

The Church of the Redeemer (Episcopal), Houston, Texas: Coming Home to Community

The third model of Jesus Movement revitalization may be called an enlivened tradition, wherein mainstream congregations embraced elements of the Jesus Movement, while maintaining their historic connections. They provided the means and an established ecclesiology to embrace and nurture the movemental insights, under the umbrella of traditional denominationalism. A significant handful of historic churches interacted with, or provided support for the street and campus ministries of Jesus Movement groups.

Hollywood Presbyterian Church established a positive and nurturing relationship with the hippies and non-churched youth early in its development (Enroth, Ericson and Peters 1972:145-147), as did Open Bible Church, Concord, Massachusetts. The Church of the Blessed Sacrament, Seattle, and according to Plowman (1971:16-18), many other Catholic churches were influenced by the Movement.[1] The nearest to a theme song for the Jesus Movement was a hymn from a Catholic charismatic community in Ann Arbor, Michigan. As far abroad as Australia the sense of *communitas* was palpable during the singing of this Trinitarian, communitarian, theme song:[2]

We are one in the Spirit; we are one in the Lord,

And we pray that our unity may one day be restored.

And they'll know we are Christians by our love, by our love (X2).

In Canada, where the Jesus Movement was evident "in all ten provinces" (Di Sabatino 1999:8), some prominent congregations followed suite (Di Sabatino 1994:65-71). Relationships between churches and radical youth ranged from provision of resources or co-operation in ministry, to revolution of congregational structures.[3]

The level of interaction between the minority of sympathetic, denominational churches and the Jesus Movement varied considerably. Some threw in their lot completely with the Movement; others offered ancillary support or released staff to the missionary task alongside of the Jesus freaks. Some took on board principle elements of the Movement and restructured their own congregational life. The Church of the Redeemer (Redeemer), Houston, Texas, reflected the latter model, by embracing communitarianism and a congregational movement into the highways and byways in charismatic mission, to the neighborhood and beyond.

I have entitled this "A Modernity Response" because it was contained within the basic framework of the historic Episcopal Church while adopting some elements of the Jesus Movement and neo-Pentecostalism (Poloma 1982:11-21). In the CWLF, the relationship with the counterculture led evangelical leaders to pre-modern Orthodoxy to totally reshape theology and form such that the end product was unrecognizable. Calvary Chapel (CC) forsook its denominational connections, crafted a postmodern, affective fusion of fundamentalism, soft Pentecostalism, and popular culture.

Experiencing the Pew with a View (of the Street) — A Visit to Houston

One of the defining aspects of the Jesus Movement, in common with the hippie counterculture, was the quest for tribal identity and community. This religious quest, added to the fact of itinerancy and anti materialism, gave rise to hundreds of communal experiments across America and abroad. It was a surprise however, in the Christian counterculture to hear that a prosperous group of Episcopalians had virtually turned their church life into a communal experiment.

On the eve of my leaving for America in the summer of 1973, a prominent Baptist church, which was intensely interested in radical community in Dallas, Melbourne, suggested that I visit Redeemer and report back to them.[4]

When I arrived at Redeemer, it became obvious that they and the Jesus Movement shared common ground, despite Redeemer's Episcopal ecclesiology. The socioeconomic level of the average participant in this renewal movement was a far cry from street people and the hippies of New York or California. The church was missional in its focus with 500 to 600 members in approximately 40 households. People, whose socioeconomic and educational background ranged from Ph.D. scholars to refugees from the street (Pulkingham 1973), lived in communal households. The social breadth and personal diversity embraced by Redeemer's new communal kinship is revealed in Pulkingham's account of the community's ministry, *They Left Their Nets* (1973).

Freedom of form, emotional ecstasy in worship, and a charismatic emphasis on healing and miracles, blended with a strong measure of Episcopalian quietism. My first night was a dramatic introduction to the community. I had some idea of what to expect, having seen a film about this community while in Australia, but it was far beyond my expectations as I recorded in my autobiography (Smith and Doney 1987).

> The people here held in beautiful balance the richness of a structured liturgy with the freedom of the Holy Spirit. There was a definite pattern to their services, yet there was always space for people in the congregation to make their own spontaneous contribution to worship. I felt enriched as a result.
>
> A remarkable event took place on my first evening here and it concerned my son, Paul. Paul had begun to suffer badly from asthma from the age of three. He had a number of allergies to which the asthma was connected. He would often contract bronchitis at the same time and had been hospitalized on eight occasions already. And we didn't know how to handle it. He had been through a number of close calls before in oxygen tents
>
> That evening, I went to one of their [Friday night healing] services. I was quietly soaking up the gentle atmosphere when I was stricken by total panic. What if Paul had a bad asthma attack? My itinerary had been vague and my wife, Glena had no phone number for me. What if he died? It was something I had feared several times before. Now for some reason I felt a chill of dread creep over me.
>
> In the midst of this fog, I heard one of the church's elders speaking. She said, 'There is someone here tonight from the other side of the world. He is from thousands of miles away and his son has asthma.'
>
> I can't remember her precise words, but she mentioned his age, which was correct and said that he was undergoing an attack at that moment. 'Your heart is filled with fear and God has told me to ask you to come up for prayer,' she continued. I was completely stunned. No one in this church knew me. And yet what she had said was so specific, she had to be talking about me. Still dazed I made my way to the front of the church.
>
> The woman welcomed me, prayed for me and then for Paul. I returned to my seat. And then she added, 'I don't have a verse of Scripture for you, but I believe God wants me to give you this verse of a hymn. "Peace, perfect peace, with loved ones far away. In Jesus' keeping you are safe, and they . . .."'
>
> I found when I phoned home that Glena was staying with her family in Queensland at that time and Paul did have a serious asthma attack. But because she was home, Glena's brother-in-law was nearby. A sufferer from asthma himself, he was able to pass on techniques that could control Paul's attacks. Paul has never needed to go back to hospital with his problem since. (Smith and Doney 1987:218-220)

The central issue within Redeemer at that time was the issue of community for mission as an essential statement of the gospel. Many elements common to renewal all over the country were evident in its life and mission. Its worship was a fusion of the grace and order of the Episcopal tradition, with a joyous, childlike, emotional freedom, and an expectation typical of the Jesus Movement and the early Charismatic Movement.

I have observed and recorded carefully the worship lyrics and performance of many congregations in neo-Pentecostal and new paradigm churches and noted that the "first person" is dominant in the lyrics. The body language and worship activity reflects the gathering of a large number of individuals, each intensely aware and focused on his or her own personalized relationship with the divine. This was not what I observed in those days at the Redeemer. Rather than a sense of "me-ness," there was an acute sense of "us-ness." The leadership, the body language, and the lyrics were far more expressive of the early Jesus Movement than of the current neo-Pentecostal movement. When the accent is on the communal experience, the worship lyrics are typically expressed in plurality, as in early Jesus Movement songs,[5] many of which have resurfaced in recent times in the singular mode rather than the original communal expression. The original emphasized the plurality of worship.

The more recent versions frequently replace "we" with "I":

Heavenly father we appreciate you.

Heavenly father we appreciate you.

We love you, adore you

We bow down before you

Heavenly father we appreciate you.

At the heart of Redeemer was the conviction that the church could not fulfill its mission or express the fullness of its redemption through Christ unless it laid aside radical individualism and associated materialism. In common with JPUSA in Chicago, their communes required the full surrender of one's family and social life to other brothers and sisters in the faith. To be a bona fide participant in the full life of the Christian community, one needed to enter into a covenantal relationship and truly belong to one of the communities.

These communities comprised several families and the incorporation of some unattached singles as surrogate "family" members. Economically, they operated by the rule of the common purse. Even young teenagers who wished to go surfing would have to negotiate the use of common property. The North College household to which I was assigned as a guest was overseen by John and Margo Farra, who were both part of the governing body of the church. There was an unusual level of peaceable relationship, deep love, and visionary enthusiasm shared by community members from the youngest to the oldest.

John Farra was an attorney and with his wife Margo, jointly led the household with all members surrendering their possessions and the economic control of their lives to the communal experiment. To them, it was not an experiment but obedience to a supernatural vision, initially coming through the Pulkinghams. The charismatic gifts of prophesy, "word of knowledge," and "interpreted" glossolalia was an integral part of the decision making. Lengthy, reasoned, and vulnerable interchange occurred between the leaders. If it meant extending the discussion for weeks, rather than coercing or bypassing a member's disquiet, so be it. The dissenter was regarded as possibly the aberrant voice of the Spirit to the group.

I cannot recall any reason for freedom of access afforded me at Redeemer. In the midst of a periodic reassessment of the entire communal infrastructure, I was invited to attend several days of internal leadership discussion and decision-making concerning the community. More than 500 people were living in community at the time.

For days there was intense discussion concerning each household and the individuals within it. It was proposed that if relationships were not operating well, or persons within the community were not growing in grace and fellowship, that the household membership be redistributed. The concept of disturbing and rearranging so many families in relocation was, at the time, beyond my comprehension.

I watched the group patiently seek to break a deadlock for hours through prayer and charismata, as they searched for divine affirmation or denial of the dissenting opinion. This was followed by frank and open evaluation of possible psychological causes, or even childhood experiences, which could have sourced the disquiet. Corporate consensus as the basis for discerning divine guidance was firmly in place at that time in the Redeemer community.

I have not observed such a level of consensual vulnerability in the decision making process anywhere since the days spent in that governing body. Consensus, and the necessity of arriving at a decision on the basis of "it seemed good to us and to the Holy Ghost," (Acts 15:28 KJV), was the order of the day. Only in the context of an unusual level of *communitas* (sacred community, comradeship, and mutuality) (Turner 1969:44-165), could such an operation succeed.

The central tenet to my understanding was that community was viewed not as an option, but as a divinely appointed necessity. The ultimate purpose of this drastic rearrangement of the churches' social and cultural agenda was mission to the world and restoration of New Testament church (Pulkingham 1980:28-53). There was a mood of experimentation and of luminal eagerness to discover where the Spirit might lead. The founder of the community, Graham Pulkingham, explains this expectant openness to change I experienced there in a collation of papers appropriately titled *Renewal, An Emerging Pattern* (1980).

> We must ever be open to the fresh leading of the Spirit, and we must ever be open to hear and see what the world is doing as well. We must not be closed in upon our national identity our culture, or ourselves if God is to have a people who in history, in this fast changing world, will demonstrate the judgment of His word upon it. The church must enliven God's word in the terms of its own day.
>
> For these reasons, I see this subject of 'the shape of the church to come' to be so massive. Who knows what the world will look like in 50 years time? One would have to be more than a prophet. Our world is changing rapidly, in three to five year increments. And in some respects, especially economically and politically, it is changing annually or twice annually. As the church in a world experiencing major, radical changes in its institutions, we need a prophetic command, a vision if you will, of what God is presently doing throughout creation. We must be sensitive to God's Spirit concerning such matters as denominational structures, nuc-

lear family system, racial/cultural tensions within our societies, growing new 'one world' nationalism. We must be open to accept changes in church institutions, in family, in society, in the world, as we know it. (Pulkingham 1980:35)

No single element of community life stood in isolation from any other. The level of mutual expectation was stimulated by shared life through abandoned commitment. In the rich tradition of communistic societies (Nordhoff 1960) it was evident that costly personal commitment, accompanying a worldview belief in the essential nature of community was foundational. Nordhoff asserted that "men cannot play at communism. It is not amateur work. It requires patience, submission, and self-sacrifice often in little matters where self-sacrifice is peculiarly irksome . . . . "Bear ye one another's burdens" might well be written over the gates of every commune. (Kanter 1972:61)

My arrival coincided with great excitement among Redeemer's congregation concerning the missional fruits of their communitarianism. They had committed themselves to the cultural transformation of a depressed inner city school, whose teachers and pupils were hostile, conflicting, and dispirited.

The physical environment was blitzed and reflective of social hostility and student anarchy. The communal members committed themselves to refurbishing the rooms, fixing broken walls and redecorating the school with artistic flare.

The school population returned from summer vacation to find an environment which declared 'You are cared for; you have dignity and a future.' Letters from a revitalized staff and student body brought tears to many eyes in the church, as children's testimonies to the remarkable transformation were read to the people. Many members of the community became involved in urban culture brokerage and advocacy.

The Redeemer community had seriously engaged in an attempt to reframe evangelical theology and missiology in terms of social trinitarianism and a radical ecclesiology. In common with some Jesus Movement groups, traditional forms gave way to methods reflecting the "priesthood of believers" in a demonstration of the kingdom of God. The church needed to believe differently to undergird a shift in lifestyle and organization. The Redeemer community evangelized visitors like myself with strong communal rhetoric, declaring intentional community to be "good news" or "gospel" to a lonely, materialistic, and divorce-ridden society.

I had experienced "power encounters" in both the Jesus Movement and classical Pentecostal circles, but usually where this was a significant part of a community's experience, the primary focus of the group was upon public meetings for prayer and healing. At Redeemer in the early 1970s, there was a remarkable blending of gentle Anglican piety, Pentecostal power encounters demonstrated by apparent exorcisms, physical healings, and emotional. This was not a community developed by standard evangelism. It appeared to bypass the classic evangelical/liberal conflict, leaping directly into a faith, which did not require cognitive proofs for verification.

There was an artistic beauty to all that was happening and expressions of a creative spirit occurred at every sensory level. In contrast, evangelicals have no idea of the spiritual, sensual nature of the employment of incense in worship.

The cheese, wine and grapes, which are the precursor of the ancient Tannebre preparation for Good Friday in Easter celebration, even incorporate taste. There were colorful, stylistic, creative banners, liturgical dancing, replete with colored streamers weaving patterns in the air as the dances swirled to a refreshing variety of musical forms and instrumentation, in the midst of traditional High church, Episcopalian symbols.

Everywhere there were stories of unusual life transformations and confirmations of divine encouragement and instruction. The gifts of the Spirit celebrated within Pentecostal and Charismatic circles were in evidence, but exercised with a quiet almost artistic dignity. The Eucharist was available daily.

My liturgical conditioning had primarily been in the Methodist church where communion was held monthly or quarterly. I had been introduced to the Plymouth Brethren tradition through my wife, where "the Lord's table" was central to worship on the "first day of the week" with no formal liturgy or sacerdotal expressions.

At Redeemer, for the first time in my life, I found myself eagerly looking forward to a daily Eucharistic celebration, which combined the artistic grandeur of High church Anglicanism, the emotional energy of Pentecostalism, the holiness of Methodist revivalism, in an atmosphere of quietist Brethren expectation of the moving of the Lord's presence. The traditional, colorful vestments of High church revealed the Episcopal aspect of daily Euchatist, but the serving priests demonstrated shared brotherhood and sisterhood, in humble equality and communal love.

A Short History of an Episcopal Experiment

A number of historic, liberal, denominational churches, operating by the modern paradigm, embraced the creative energy of the Movement. Redeemer is an example of this interchange whereby an historic, modernity model of ecclesiology embraced the affective faith and creativity of the Movement, inside of the existing traditional structure.

Rather than abandoning the relationship with the mother denomination as CC had done, some denominational churches experienced a transformation of existing congregational life and theology by the interchange. In common with social movements, religious renewals, or even local congregational transformations, the changes at Redeemer began with the conversion of the primary actors on the stage.

When the Pulkinghams faced the full import of their relocation of ministry to the dispirited, dying, urban parish in Houston, they concluded they had neither the gift nor the empowerment to meet the challenge. Graham Pulkingham literally walked the streets and opened his eyes to the urban crisis described later in this chapter. Houston's inner city at the time was regarded as an endangered species.

Pulkingham "longed to go the University of Chicago to do graduate work in anthropology so he could understand where it all fits. It was this interest in understanding the world and his interest in anthropology which caused him to sense while in Houston, that Christianity ought not to be made safe and secure" (Pulkingham 1999:1). His initial attempts to build bridges with local angry urban youths met with escalating hostility and vandalism against the church properties.

Although he was by his own confession a soft liberal and certainly neither an Evangelical nor a Pentecostal, he sought out a notarized religious leader who had earned a reputation as a mover and shaker amongst angry urban youth. David Wilkerson, an unorthodox Assemblies of God pastor had invaded the youth gangs of New York City and spread the story in a best selling autobiography (Wilkerson 1963). Pulkingham attributes the transformation of his ministry and of the languishing urban parish to a meeting with Wilkerson.

In 1964 I had only heard of The Cross and the Switchblade but its author's fame reached my ears and from the sound of things Dave Wilkerson was familiar with the fellowship of Christ's sufferings. We met in August at his Brooklyn headquarters in an encounter that was one of three crucial stages in shaping the future of my ministry. He prayed for me. In my eyes his credibility before God was not to be impeached, and when he prayed a spiritual baptism descended without fanfare and infused my life with long-awaited powers. It was not simply a matter of ecstasy during his prayer that caused me to claim a special work of grace over and above salvation, a "baptism with the Spirit."

The several months of baptism and suffering that finally led me into the New York experience, and the astonishing months of baptism with power following it, were far more cogent in commending Jesus' own baptism than was ecstasy. In fact, the gospel record seems not to emphasize ecstasy as an intrinsic mark of Jesus' ministry; and it was that very thing – His ministry, or the empowering source of it – I was in search of it when everything else failed in Houston . . .. Suffering, ecstasy, power.

They all happened to me dramatically during 1964 and all of them continue to be an intimate part of my pilgrimage with Jesus. But none of the three is of greater significance than the others . . .. Redeemer could never have found renewal as it later developed had not spiritual gifts been foremost in my expectations after returning from New York.

I earnestly sought their effect in ministry, even to the point of being willing for Pentecostal excesses to be unleashed. Let them run wild if they would. What did it matter? I had resolute faith in the God of my visions, being assured that a loving community could tame even the most ardent enthusiasts and harness them for the work of renewal. Prophecy engendered faith, and faith brought forth works of power . . .. Each unpredictable day became a fresh new adventure. (Pulkingham 1973:15-16)

Both Betty and Graham Pulkingham were transformed through the charismatic experience and over the next few months that transformation was spread to a core of parish members whose worldview, vision of life, and sociological understanding of the human environment, were radically changed. This was the spark, which ultimately lit fires from Texas to Denver to Pittsburgh and across the world to New Zealand, Australia, England, and Scotland. A group called Redeemer for Mission gathered together 50-60 people and formed three traveling troupes to spread the message of the gospel and of a radical new communitarian method of being church.

Margaret Poloma (1982), in a sociological analysis of the neo-Pentecostal Charismatic movement, regards Redeemer as a classic example of the emerging impact of the Charismatic movement on historic churches. She provides a thumbnail sketch of developments which resulted in two decades of complex and diverse developments arising from the initial spark of charismatic conversion.

Over the next few years, the Redeemer in Houston was transformed. Parish members often left comfortable suburban homes to cast their lots with the poor surrounding their church. Sharing their lives and resources, they combined their efforts to serve residents of this area in Houston. In describing the history of the community, Schiffmayer (1979:1) notes its move from being "a dead parish in a decaying neighborhood" to being a "lively congregation of 800 today."

He attributes this growth to the evolution of a concern for the needy, the open manifestation of gifts of the Spirit, and a structured leadership that shares the responsibilities with the rector. It has not only served the community in Houston, but Redeemer has sent out leaders to other communities in different parts of the world. (Poloma 1982:143)

Central to the mission and *koinonia* of Redeemer was the intimacy and shared vision nurtured in a redefinition and formation of communal leadership. From the base of localized revitalization, three teams were trained and commissioned to bring the discoveries of the Houston community to the attention of the church and society across America and around the world. Communities at home and abroad were founded in fellowship with Redeemer.

Evangelism through creative music and demonstration of communal love, demonstration of healing faith and folk proclamation of the story of Jesus' influence on Redeemer congregants obtained a responsive ear around the Western world. The traveling group, known as the Fisherfolk, won hearts and minds by a blend of charismatic spirituality, creative arts, and commitment to the alienated and poor. A time-line of the rise and fall of this remarkable revitalization of an inner city parish reveals an intense, socially redemptive but highly vulnerable model (See Appendix 12).

Location and Social Timing

The Houston of the 1960s was not likely territory for a thriving Episcopal ministry. The location of Redeemer, initially named Eastwood Community Church, was the site 30 years before for a communion, which served a substantially middle-class community in Houston's East End. Demographics had radically changed and by the time Graham Pulkingham accepted the invitation to become rector of this rundown cause, "the face of Houston's East End was pocked and scarred by three generations of onward development and growth" (Pulkingham 1972:19). The population had increased twenty fold in just over half a century and the previously white domination was challenged by pockets of poor urban African-Americans and an ever-increasing number of Mexican Americans.

During the 1950s the black community, living in squalor, began moving out from the edge of the central business district as the Hispanics moved in. Pulkingham describes the diminishing white population as a "pie shaped segment, isolated between a wedge of black inhabitants" to the south and "encroaching Latins to the north east" (Pulkingham 1972:19).

At the bite of that piece of pie, stands the Episcopal Redeemer. "An unwitting symbol of changeless wealth, it was cornered by poverty in a segment of the city that was surrounded on every side except south by a population in flux . . . then in its abandonment, the parish neighborhood was becoming tawdry and unkempt. (1972:20-21)

Pulkingham's description is of a location in urban crisis, common to many cities around the world in an era of urban disintegration. The poor whites were "frightened geese before a barking dog" (1972:21) because of their race and implied culpability in the face of Hispanic and black urban poverty all around.

The location becomes significant to the story as the declining and depressed nature of the congregation stripped church members of any subcultural comfort zone for retreat from their context of urban disintegration. To this was added a new component of hippies and other youth itinerants during the latter part of the 1960s.

The counterculture was still alive in Houston in 1973, when the Divine Light Mission (Guru Maharaja Ji) hosted their Millennium '73, bringing devotees from all over the world to Houston's Astrodome (Glock and Bellah 1976:63). Redeemer's context of mission from the 1960's on was the multicultural and religiously plural heartland of a Texan city. The social geography of the area impressed itself upon the 37-year-old rector (Pulkingham 1972:19-21) as he surveyed the streets of his new appointment.

This in turn was to send him to another location of urban conflict, New York City to seek advice from David Wilkerson. What began as a consequence of the renewal of this priest, diffused as his congregants responded to an urban mission vision, which in turn impacted housing, schools and other sociogeographic elements of the city.

The Coalescence of the Charismatic and Jesus Movements

During the 1960s, Burns (1990) asserts, "several million Americans engaged in making history. They acted beyond the usual bounds of citizenship to change social practices. Many aspired to create a new society. In the process they transformed their own lives. If they did not realize their dreams, they did shape the future" . . . (1990:11).

Many movemental theorists researching the 1960s make no mention of the Charismatic Movement or the Jesus Movement. Some reputable scholars (Glock and Bellah 1976, Wuthnow 1976, Roof 1993, Wind and Lewis 1994, Poloma 1982) have recognized that these movements were social movements expressive of the sociohistorical developments of that time. As with all social movements during their liminal, developmental stages, clear definition of the borders between them is difficult.

Case histories may reveal the connections, mutual influences, and common grounds and coalescence of these separate but related movements. The combined and highly interactive influences of these two movements on Redeemer are a worthwhile source of ethnographic data for researching the roots of modern communitarian movements. It is no co-incidence that I found myself at Redeemer on an investigation of the Jesus Movement, with no personal connections to Episcopalian or Anglican churches, apart from the dynamic interplay between charismatic congregations and the Jesus Movement.

As previously stated in the early stages of awareness the traditional Evangelical and Pentecostal churches were usually hostile towards the movement or at best affirmative from a distance. Liberal, traditional Catholic, and mainstream Protestant churches which had experienced the fresh winds of the Charismatic Movement were enthusiastically open to fellowship and joint evangelistic and worship enterprises.

They embraced the Jesus Movement rituals and communications innovations, and even accepted the socially "deviant" elements of communitarianism, soft socialism and prophetic denunciation of our parents' capitalist socioeconomic. It is justifiable for the Redeemer experiment to be seen as an eclectic fusion of elements, which had free interplay between the two movements.

Pete Ward (1996) provides an illustration of the significance of this coalescence of the Charismatic Movement and Jesus Movements, in the British context. The Charismatic Movement (Poloma 1982) had taken root in the historic denominations a decade earlier than the Jesus Movement. Ward maintains that, in Britain very little alternative Jesus Movement activity occurred in the form of new denominations, or Jesus People communes, its influence being felt in the traditional churches and religious institutions.

One enduring exception is the Jesus People Army still operating in England. The interactive influence of both the Charismatic and Jesus Movements on the Evangelical community was profound, pervasive and enduring. It diffused substantially throughout the churches via the fellowship and cooperation between the two movements.

If a continuum of the typologies of the Movement were drawn it would begin as the deviant, cult movements such as Children of God and The Way International at one extreme and extend to the denominational synthesis represented by Houston's counterculture communitarian congregation at the other end.

Redeemer's people offered a variety of interpretations of the relationship between the movements. Some saw it in terms of worldwide renewal. Some saw the local changes as linked to the Charismatic Movement's invasion of the Anglican, Episcopal, and Catholic churches.

Some saw it as the simple consequence of the biographical events pertaining to their rector's spiritual journey. Some saw it as closely related to the Jesus Movement, while others viewed it as part of a wider renewal of the Spirit in American culture. Several leaders of the Houston renewal said that contact with hippies and the Jesus Movement was primary in the development of community and mission at the Redeemer (Pulkingham 1999, Farra 1999, Newman 1999, and Woodruff 1999).

Movements towards intentional community based on the unity of the Spirit and New Testament Pentecostal *koinonia*, were all part of the 1960s religious and social upheaval. Ward concludes that Redeemer's outreach and its innovative worship team, the Fisherfolk, were part of the Charismatic Movement rather than the Jesus Movement. But he sees these two forces as converging inside the traditional British churches, in a way, which rarely happened in America.

Redeemer was one exception to the general rule. The containment of the Jesus Movement and its Pentecostal elements, as a renewal within the church, carried within it "a conservative ethos which was itself a reaction to the youth culture of the 1960s" (Ward 1996:199). The Charismatic Movement molded some of the youth culture forms of the Jesus Movement, mollifying the more antistructural tendencies of the youthful rebellion.

> In both the United States and Britain young people were embracing hippie style and behavior in increasing numbers. Charismatic renewal 'created a Christian version of the counterculture." It is in the discovery of a new freedom of expression in worship that parallels between the movement and youth culture is seen most clearly. Michael Harper, one of the early leaders of the movement in Britain, places great emphasis on the liberty brought about by renewal in the Spirit. "One of the clearest marks of a true outpouring of the Spirit is the free and spontaneous worship which those affected offer to God, sometimes for hours on end. (Ward 1996:119)

The highly publicized images of young Jesus people worshiping in their communes, or en-masse at seaside baptisms, softened the attitudes of many traditional worshipers towards the undisciplined and unkempt rebelliousness of the Jesus people. The radical shift of charismatics from traditional forms to congregationally driven, free worship, had prepared them to accept other aspects of unorthodox behavior by the youth. The old Pentecostals and fundamentalists had believed "you can either play gospel for Jesus, or blues for the devil," but the charismatics readily embraced contemporary folk and dance arts. This facilitated an early alliance between Jesus freaks and many Charismatic churches.

The interface between the Charismatic Movement and the indigenous Jesus Movement is difficult to define. Without the prior softening of religious attitudes through the Charismatic Movement, the Jesus Movement, with its glossolalia and prophetic style, would never have been accepted as an authentic revival. It is equally arguable that the Jesus Movement as a popular, cultural movement influenced the Christian culture towards more individualistic, therapeutic, antiestablishment, and charismatic forms (Miller 1997:20-22).

In Redeemer's mission focus, there were specific connections to elements of the Jesus Movement. Consultation with Wilkerson led the rector to a charismatic experience and swiftly thence to a communitarian mission, opening a way for more direct contact with counterculture youth. Wilkerson's relationship with the Jesus Movement was mercurial. At times he capitalized on it, confessing his inner struggle or "square reaction to these long haired, bare-footed, guitar-carrying, weirdly dressed hippies." Wilkerson viewed the Jesus Revolution as both good and bad (1971:59-69), but he had a clear, passionate love for the kids at the edge of society which was transmitted to Graham and Betty Pulkingham. The connection became more direct as the renewed community felt the local presence of counterculture kids.

Betty Pulkingham (1999), Bill Farra (1999) (an original elder and planter of the continuing community near Pittsburgh) and Grover Newman (1999) (a founding elder of their Denver, Colorado community) attributed the 1970's focus of Redeemer's mission substantially to the impact of an unusual visit from afar:

> The Redeemer had a visit from Victoria Booth Demerest, a descendant of William and Catherine Booth's daughter [the Marechale, who set up the work of the Salvation Army in France]. There was a division in the Booth family concerning speaking in tongues. This great-granddaughter, Victoria Booth-Demerest [a charismatic], was connected to the Left Bank Parish through marriage to an Episcopalian Priest. Through this connection,[6] she visited the Redeemer in 1968 and had lunch at the Rectory.
>
> She looked like a hippie; dressed with the beads and all the other counterculture paraphernalia. There was a flow of counterculture hippies from the West Coast [via California] to the East Coast that had made Houston, Texas, a stop off point. Victoria Booth Demerest challenged the Redeemer concerning the appalling fact that the church was not reaching this flow of hippie kids.
>
> There were some attempts to reach them, notably the Southern Baptists [as an exception to the rule]. On the strength of this challenge, Mimi Farra commenced a coffee shop outreach called the Way In. While this outreach connected with some hippies, it primarily connected with youth groups who were challenged in their mission. All the arts, music and performing arts found their place in the Way In. Eventually the creativity of this group infiltrated worship at Redeemer.
>
> There was a deep liturgical renewal through which the young people both hippies and "straights" became involved in the communal houses. Troubled youth from the streets became involved and the church attracted more and more youth both "straights" and counterculture. Out of this, the Fishermen incorporated were formed, though they were named Fisherfolk in England. (Farra 1999:1)

The Contemporary Mood of Communal Experimentation

Capturing the youth mood of the hour, a core of Redeemer members became convinced of the missional need for intentional community. While biographical events appear to have propelled the vicar and his congregation towards radical renewal, the drastic shift arose in a broader geographical and historical context. Their community was one of many. Its peculiarities arose at a local and biographical intersection with powerful cultural influences:

> The Christian community's movement flourished in the 1960s and 1970s, along with parallel moments for civil rights, war resistance, and the environment. Individualism was "out," love was "in," and community founders were local celebrities - at least for a while. Christian intentional communities were riding the waves

of a much broader cultural movement that also included the birth of many secular intentional communities. The manifest flaws of society all called for a new radical synthesis. (Janzen 1996:48)

Testimonies from communal members centered on a charismatic call, more than any search for self-actualization. Beyond Tipton's (1984) understanding of the search for moral meaning in 1960s, there is a long communal tradition in America (Nordhoff 1960) as an expression of spiritual idealism, particularly during times of social upheaval and national identity crisis. "Between the Revolutionary and Civil Wars (approximately 1780-1860), almost 100 known utopian communities were founded" (Kanter 1972:61). The cultural sources for millenarian and utopian communities during the revival of the 1960s deserve much more attention, although theoretical investigation of the tension between American radical individualism and the search for community has been researched well by Etzioni (1993) and Rosabeth (1972).[7]

The Postmodern Shift from the Intellect to the Heart

There is continuing debate as to whether the Jesus Movement and the Charismatic Movement are the first popular, postmodern response within the Christian tradition. As Miller (1997) has noted, "Western philosophy of religion has been dominated by Enlightenment thought, which prescribed rationality and scientific empiricism as the basis for all explorations of truth" (1997:22). For at least the last two centuries, Miller I believe rightly asserts, "mainstream religion had become a disembodied, cerebral matter" (1997:22).

Roszak, as a popular counterculture academic of that period, inspired youthful rebellion against rationalism, scientific reductionism and the technocracy's depersonalization (1972). His trenchant attack on the reductionism of modern scientism was congruent with the primitivism of the Jesus Movement and of the Charismatic Movement, which was beginning to invade traditional fundamentalism and evangelicalism.

While not denying the significance of cognitive belief systems, postmodern evangelicals such as Tom Sine (1999) refers to the "right brain, left brain" paradigm in reference to the paradigm shift, which he believes was launched by the Cultural Revolution of the 1960s. "The Jesus freaks were very much into right brain, very much into the arts [and into] relationships. They didn't always do relationships well. They were a precursor to postmodern culture; much more on the right side, much less rationalistic, controlled, directed" (Sine 1999:8).

The Charismatic and Jesus Movements claimed that the Spirit of God had leap-frogged them from the traditional, cognitively laden, religious worldview to a new, nonlinear level of thought. They thus felt no obligation to "conform to the norms of logic and rational discourse" (Miller 1997:23). Prophesy, healing, exorcism, ecstatic praise, and affective worship dominated both movements, bypassing traditional rational discourse.

Critical attacks against Freud and increasing acceptance of Jungian psychology were undermining the dominant paradigm of empiricism in popular psychology. Contact with a wide range of Charismatic, denominational churches, has led me to conclude that a balance is more often struck between the cognitive and the affective elements of religion where the charismatic element is modified by historic theology and tradition inside denominationalism.

The Charismatic Movement and the Jesus Movement paralleled to each other, though the Jesus Movement was a later phenomenon. They converged in some traditional denominational settings. While CC represented a deconstruction of the previous denominational model, some historic churches sought to embrace the postmodern accouterments inside their traditional, modern, ecclesial structures. At Houston, modernity models of ecclesiology embraced elements of a postmodern epistemology.

Leadership and Organization

The 40 households operated with one family placed in charge of each household by the seven or eight elders elected by the church. The eldership gave direction from outside, though at least some of them were themselves living in a communal household. John and Margo Farra were elders of the whole church and led the North College household where I stayed. The elders had direct access to every household, weekly meeting. According to Grover Newman, "this worked well and the life of the communities was well regulated" (1999:1). The shared leadership model developed by Graham Pulkingham promoted a communal truth despite the pervasive influence of his charisma.

> Graham Pulkingham was the visionary who gave us an understanding of the body of Christ. He humanized the priesthood. Graham had the last word because he had emphasis on the Word. Sometimes we would stay almost all night to resolve difficulties and differences. Sometimes 2 a.m. – 3 a.m. in the morning, Graham would get a word from the Lord, which we knew was the proper conclusion [but] I never felt disenfranchised because I didn't have a collar. (Newman 1999:1)

For a decade, the shared vision, charismatic energy, emphasis on redemptive love, and strategic mission was highly successful at home and abroad. Late in the 1970s Lovelace reported that Redeemer was a thriving community.

> The congregation appears to be thriving on this kingdom-centered approach. Some members have turned down promotions in their ordinary vocations in order to remain with the community and carry on its work. The ideal of the church as a servant people to heal and help the world, often articulated in non-Evangelical circles. They usually lacked the dynamic necessary to bring it to realization, beginning to operate almost automatically in this congregation as it was knit together in community and filled with the Holy Spirit. The result is a working model of a balanced ministry of love expressed both in evangelism and social action. (Lovelace 1979:228)

When the primary leadership departed on mission, the new leadership became more controlling and was influenced by the Shepherding Movement from Fort Lauderdale, Florida.[8] The sister community in Colorado was impacted by the Jonestown massacre following the revelations of that communal disaster. A psychiatrist visited the Colorado community following counsel with a client.

The local TV showed images of Jonestown while the newscaster talked about the Denver Community of Celebration (Newman 1999:2).

The stress caused a reassessment of the role and function of leadership. There was a measure of leadership fallout, resulting in Grover returning from Denver to Houston, where the church leadership withdrew from its previously close relationship with the communal houses. "There were many young people involved in the community, but at this stage the Redeemer withdrew from giving direction and the youth were left to their own devices" according to Newman (1999:2).

With the Denver community's leadership depleted the group weakened and folded in 1985. The Houston community, which was birthed in 1965, was nigh unto death by the late 1970s, although its family of intentional communities expanded in other places into the 1980s (Appendix 12). Bill Farrer reports that it "became very embarrassing." Farrer believes the "intense community model was not sustainable by the parish model of leadership, believing a more ratified basis of relationships under a religious order [is more conducive] to intentional community" (Farrer 2000:1).

Innovation in Organization and Ministry

Tipton (1984) emphasizes the 1960s search for individualism in the context of American utilitarianism and "work ethic" Protestantism (1984:6-14), but those of us who participated in those movements embraced the strongest rejection of utilitarian individualism.

The search for self-actualization demonstrated the law of diminishing returns. The unity of human beings expressed in the monism of the counterculture found a Jesus Movement response in the charismatic unity of the Spirit. Thus many of the Movement's groups became involved in communitarian experiments, not as a self-actualizing therapy, nor solely as a missional tool.

It was an expression of the belief that the individual could never find his or her ground of being or destiny except in the context of real community. This, as much as liberty in worship, became the common ground between the more indigenous expression of the Jesus Movement youth and the Redeemer community.

Tipton regards such alternative communities arising out of the 1960s as a reaction against the loss of moral meaning in the social context of post-war America. Thus religious groups "as a class, reconstitute community as the context of personal and social identity" (Tipton 1984:238). There is a lingering functionalism in such an interpretation. It is difficult for the non-participant, social scientist to explain the nature of such a radical departure from the dominant cultural paradigm of the nuclear family, when the participants were in fact socially well satisfied with their world at the time of departure.

The central aspect of the Redeemer was its communitarian experiment. The charismatic aspects of the church's life were in common with many churches. The Friday night healing services I observed were more ordered and communally structured than the traditional Pentecostal forms, which center in a gifted charismatic healer. Though more therapeutic and communal at Houston, such gatherings were common to other charismatic groups.

Here the communal households were not only a pragmatic response, but they expressed a fundamental understanding of theology and witness to the world. Pulkingham says, "[I] t was the call of God, not the call of wearied flesh: Only 33 caught a vision of the source of power and stayed to share it. They left their homes, their possessions, their jobs - some left their suffering and despair - because a loving voice had whispered, 'Come, follow Me'" (Pulkingham 1973:13).

> Within three years it grew to such a size that by its gentle takeover an Episcopal parish ended one era of life and entered another. Then the parish became the community – a charismatic servant community whose influence now extends around the world . . . .. It was not a "church" community established by a bishop, vestry or ordained minister. It was a community called forth by prophetic visions and established by the authority of our radical commitment to one another in love; we found no occasion or need for a covenant agreement or for a charter or for rules. The authority of our life together - love - was the rule by which we lived; love of the brethren belonged more and more to our peace. (Pulkingham 1973:25)

The combination of the Jesus Movement style and radical communitarism was rare within a denominational tradition. This radicalism was in a "high culture" context. The pioneers were affluent and well positioned people, not countercultural hippies. Hundreds of persons of power and privilege turned their back on traditional American family life for the sake of obedience to a perceived calling and a commitment to mission.

While recent attention has been given to the missional focus of Celtic, common purse communities, little appears to have been done on the significance of modern revivalist communities for the purpose of challenging the dominant culture in a centrifugal action of mission. Charles J. Mellis' contribution to the Jesus Movement enquiry, titled *Committed Communities: Fresh Streams for World Mission* (Mellis 1976) is also descriptive of the nature and purpose of the Redeemer community. They were early denominational innovators in combining communalism with mission to the world.

They took their cue from the sociology of similar movements emerging in the 1960s, and their theological justification from the early church's example. Lay pastor, Bill Farra whose commitment to social justice and racial reconciliation remains central, leads the remaining community in Pennsylvania. That community has embraced a democratized adaptation of the order of St. Benedict as a centering discipline (Appendix 14).

Neighborhood Renewal

For Redeemer members, community renewal was the aim, embracing evangelism, celebration, and building self-esteem of depressed urban school children. Confronting demonic forces, and facilitating recovery for addicted persons was Kingdom of God business. Ministering the baptism of the Holy Spirit to the powerless, advocating for racial minorities, caring for Mexican "wetbacks," and rebuilding tired and dilapidated buildings, was integrated in an ambitious program of personal, spiritual, and social transformation (Woodruff 1999:1)

The local Lantrip Elementary School was at the center of the community, and was transformed by the input of the church. "Although the nature of the community is now quite different, the local church continues today to work with that school. Likewise at Aliquitta in Pennsylvania, the later Redeemer plant there embraced a strong emphasis on healing of the body and of racial and social divisions within the society" (Pulkingham 1999:1). Bodily healing fell short of a gospel of community. The church had to be the unifying presence of Christ in the context of every social ill.

> When Pulkingham took up his appointment as vicar of the Redeemer in inner city Houston, Texas, he was immediately struck by the deep social and spiritual needs of the young people in his area. His first move was to open up the church building to some of these young people, but he felt powerless to help them. In Gathered for Power he tells how he sought out Wilkerson in New York and eventually came into a new experience of the Spirit. Back in the parish in Houston a community of people renewed in the Spirit began to grow. People became committed to moving back into the inner-city area round the church and a series of programs to help the poor in the local community was initiated. The result of renewal was a transformed church which was 'charismatic in ministry, corporate in life and leadership, sacrificial in loving service and Eucharistic to its core – a flavor not possible until the parish and the community had become one.' (Darnell 1996:122)

Pulkingham's conviction and teaching was that the task of social renewal via the Kingdom of God was not possible without a reordering of our corporate lives in community, around the central figure of Jesus. Jesus would reward such obedience to the principals of the Kingdom with the outpouring of the enabling visionary power of the Holy Spirit. Gathering together in radical community for the purpose of changing the world was not solely a Christian contribution.

An expression of a counterculture, non-Christian model related to me by the founder of The Farm, in Tennessee, is reminiscent of the process which emerged among Jesus Movement and charismatic groups. Gaskin's eclectic spiritual community embraced communitarianism for holistic reasons also:

> The dysfunctional culture didn't enlighten us – it alienated us. Hippies and rock 'n' roll, acid, and eastern teachers enlightened us. So it was always enlightenment, and then if you were going to talk about enlightenment, you had to talk about right livelihood and vocation. You couldn't have your life deny your beliefs. That's really hard to do by yourself. You need to have some people with you to do it and so it just became a natural part of the burst of spirit that we wanted to live together and that we had our ways and we didn't want to be bothered with other ways. (Gaskin 1999:1)

Redeemer believed a communitarian model alone could establish the renewal of the kingdom of God. My own sensitivities were greatly stirred during my time at Redeemer where the preaching of community took on all the urgency and idealistic expectation of the gospel. For Redeemer member's personal salvation, the ministry of the Holy Spirit, social responsibility, and communal living were a seamless garment. Loveless (1979) captures the centrality of communalism in this holistic program.

> Following an experience of new in filling with the Holy Spirit, the pastor, Graham Pulkingham, began to observe and promote a community-gathering process within his congregation in which individuals and families began to band together in close groups for nurture and prayer. Many moved into one section of urban Houston so they could be together and in some instances set up communal households. Part of this process of gathering was an inevitable shift of the center of gravity of personal concern in each family, so that the kingdom of God and not personal success became the dominant factor in decisions and outlook. Gradually a strategy of congregational mission and ministry was unveiled; the church was to pour itself out in meeting the needs of its local community, both in evangelism and in works of social compassion. (Lovelace 1979:228)

Redeemer became a model for community love and compassionate mission, giving rise to similar innovations at the Community of Celebration Denver, the Church of the Messiah Detroit, and St. Paul's Episcopal Church, Darien (Poloma 1982:144). It also sensed a strong calling to educate the world church concerning community, Christian love, charismatic worship, and charismatic social action. Until the mid 1980s it appeared to work well.

Mobilizing the Congregation for Mission

Although it has already been implied, it needs to be specifically noted that Redeemer became "a church for hire." Because of the deep sense of communality, developed via a mission centered bonding of their communities, they were able for a time to combat the denominational tradition of clergy verses laity in mission.

The sense of social contract was so great that professional people subjected career advancements, geographical preferences, and materialistic possibilities to a vigorous truly missional church. To be part of the church and to enjoy the benefits of communal support and fellowship, one had to partake in the unity of purpose, driven by a sense of corporate divine call.

Thus, as with a number of Jesus Movement groups in the 1960s and 1970s, wandering charismatics did not travel alone, but like the Pied Piper of old were surrounded by those who wished to partake in the music of a divine tune. As many as one hundred members of the congregation would move to a new location, blitzing a community with the demonstration of their commuted love and miracle working faith. It was a team effort interactively stimulating faith and vision among the participants and surprising receptor audiences with the weight of their exuberant communal presentations.

The Fisherfolk, Liturgy, Art, and Dance

The communitarian culture provided an evident sense of corporate vision and focus, as well as emotional and social support for those engaged in mission ventures. In one sense, no aspect was unique if viewed in isolation. Pentecostal emphasis on the Spirit and on religious emotional experience was standard. High-church liturgy as contemplative aid to religious experience was an Episcopal norm.

Folk art and folk music abounded in the Jesus Movement. It was not the invention of a revolutionary new form, but the creative reconfiguration of existing forms in a fresh presentation, which was innovative. The therapeutic and experiential influence of the Pulkinghams brought about a new emphasis on charismatic worship, the gifts of the Spirit, and the ethic of love in community.

Ward (1996) says a link between the Jesus Movement kids and the adult evangelicals was forged as the consequence of the fact that "charismatic worship was the place where evangelicals tapped into the wider youth culture and started to 'express themselves.'" In prayer and song, people were encouraged to lay bare their feelings for God (1996:120). Ward notes that, through this innovation, "the body also suddenly became important in worship." Even in the restrained British culture, "congregations began to embrace each other with hugs and hugging" (1996:120).

Liturgical dance became more than a spectator sport as individuals who felt inspired seemed to forget where they were and readily express their ecstasy by dancing in the services. In charismatic Anglican and Catholic circles, as well as amongst the Jesus people, a new generation embraced not just a postmodern oral culture, but also a visual culture.

Creative banners (with bright and stylistic decoration) declared hope, community, mission and a love depicted by images of Jesus, the ever present dove of the Holy Spirit, the flames of Pentecostal fire and the pouring forth of living waters. Ward observed that through this innovation they developed "a folk feel to worship" as a "reaction to the movement within the wider culture." In the midst of a fragmented society, people failed to find a "communal identity and so began to manufacture their own. This produced a renewed and engaging Christian subculture" (1996:125).

In the United Kingdom youth response brought together 3,000 young people at a fine arts seminar in 1972 (1996:121), which linked Judy McKenzie and Stuart Henderson, performing artists now familiar to many who have been associated with the United Kingdom's evangelical scene. According to Ward, this event was "a melting pot where the Jesus Movement, the Charismatic Movement, and later issues of simple lifestyle and involvement in urban ministry were to mingle together" (Ward 1996:121). Ward's sequential summary of events, which led coincidentally to radical community, affective worship, and urban mission, reflects what I concluded during my investigation of Redeemer.

Betty Pulkingham waxed eloquent regarding a song from the Episcopal Hymnal entitled *They Cast Their Nets,* which includes the phrase *such happy fisher folk.* The song speaks of the ministry to the world being "strife clothed." It speaks of the peace of God in the midst of the cost of discipleship. Initially the Fishermen Incorporation, a group of missioners, was renamed by "accident" in England as Fisherfolk. "One evening, in the township of Chorleywood in South England, a young man being somewhat confused as to how to introduce the signing and preaching group, said, 'Welcome young people. I introduce to you the Fisherfolk.' The name stuck." (Pulkingham 1999:2)

It was "while on the Isle of Cumbrae off the coast of Scotland, listening to the rocking rhythm of the waves," that Betty Pulkingham had a revelation as to the meaning and shape of the Fisherfolk ministry (1999:2). The Fisherfolk traveled the globe, promoting charismatic worship and communitarian attitudes in the worldwide Anglican Communion. The influence on generations of British Evangelicals was pervasive and enduring according to Ward. It impacted the highly influential Baptist, David Watson, the Anglican Charismatic leader Michael Harper, and the Pentecostal prophetess Jean Darnell (Ward 1996:119-133).

> In the early 1970s Pulkingham came to Britain, first touring with the music group the Fisherfolk and later establishing the Community of the Celebration, which was eventually to link with the group at Post Green. Graham's wife Betty was the creative force behind the evolution of the worship at the Redeemer. With her background in choral music it was soon recognized that worship was a "charisma" given to Betty. Under her guidance an approach to music evolved which embraced a variety of musical styles and was also devoted to charismatic worship.
>
> This type of worship was much appreciated in England. Graham Pulkingham, and in particular the Fisherfolk, significantly influenced the ministry of David and Anne Watson at St. Michael's, Belfry in York. Anne was inspired by the shared community life of the church in Houston and in time a number of community houses were also established in York. David was . . . enamored with the songs of the Fisherfolk. (1996:123)

In the United Kingdom, the impact of the Jesus Movement and the Charismatic Movement is evident particularly within of its recent current hymnody. Except for the black churches, the UK antipathy towards US emotionalism is legendary, but the Fisherfolk found a ready response to their unique blend of Anglican, charismatic warmth.

> Through the marvelous ministry of the Fisherfolk we learned the combination of dignity and joy, depth and simplicity, quality and gentleness, spiritual sensitivity and artistic skill. Countless people today are hurting, often because of the pain of broken relationships; but through gentleness of worship the Spirit of God can touch and heal those inner wounds. (Watson 1983:3)

Ward reports that the sweet reasonableness of the Anglican charismatics crossed class lines to reach the emotionally restrained upper echelons of the culture.

> It is in worship led by the group from the Redeemer that we start to see the paradox of charismatic renewal in England. It is strange that a movement, which at heart is a response to a need for experience and self-expression, should be so mild and reasonable. In part this is explained by the origins of those who were first affected within the Church.
>
> Those from the mainstream denominations who were attracted to charismatic renewal were from solidly upper middle-class professional backgrounds; Michael Harper was curate at All Souls, Langham Place, David Watson and David Ma-

cInnes were both products of Bash camps, while Tom and Faith Lees were titled gentry. They shared a clear desire to seek God in new ways but on the whole this was done to the accompaniment of the reassuringly conservative Sound of Living Waters.

Betty Pulkingham forged a fruitful working relationship with well known Charismatic Jeanne Harper to produce worship hymnals, Fresh Sounds, and Sounds of Living Waters with a "remarkably broad range of music (Ward 1996:123).

Betty Pulkingham believes the second major contribution made by the Redeemer and particularly the Fisherfolk, was that of liturgical formation. While they brought spiritual vitality to many within the Episcopal movement they also brought a renewal form of liturgical formation to the free churches. Many Baptists and others, who previously disdained fixed liturgical forms, found a new strength and form in the creative, artistic, charismatic renewal of dance and worship music. This liturgical formation enabled Evangelicals and Pentecostals to internalize the Christian message in prayer and worship in a new way.

The short history of some modern groups had robbed them of connection to the larger family setting of the history of mother church. Redeemer brought together the best of ancient liturgy with a solid theological core and an affective Pentecostal freedom. Pentecostal sentiment was given deeper form, as well as meaning, because of its connectedness to a long history back to the Church fathers. The missional commitment and involvement of a substantial number of the congregation added further to the living expression of mission.

A Global Parish for Reeducation and Innovation

Betty Pulkingham believes that the Houston movement reintroduced an old agrarian model of the ministering Christian household. In mission around the world, Redeemer sought to provide alternative patterns for living, which would counter the atomization of modern society, enrich relationships, and combat loneliness. It provided an extended family for the growing number of child victims of divorce, and economic based distraction of parents from quality and quantity time with the family.

In the Redeemer, healthy peer groups were developed for adolescents. Comfort and companionship was provided for divorcees. A 24-hour a day loving instruction and psychological reinforcement was at hand for those ravaged by substance abuse. Betty Pulkingham is still attracted by this model.

> In this alternative model was a largess, a maturing that enabled people to see beyond the nuclear family. Just as my country grandparents would take in the wayward and provide therapy for the sojourner, so these Christian households were available for the refugees of urbanization, for the single parent, for the alienated adolescent or the searching wanderer. (Pulkingham 1999:3)

She believes the influence of community living for the youth was good. Her youngest son is a jazz musician, attending an Episcopal Church, which has an excellent blend of black and white congregants. He teaches guitar and has a strong sense of communal commitment (Pulkingham 1999:3).

The Redeemer congregants and leaders regarded their communal discoveries as a gospel statement, which placed upon them a responsibility to leave their nets and tell the world the good news. They sought to offer their very best gifts to the world. The church did not exist for them as a spiritual retirement village but a training ground to prepare for battle against the forces of selfishness and marginalization. It may be they paid a high price, as the balance between the centripetal and the centrifugal elements of the gospel was not maintained.

> As the focus turned worldwide and away from the neighborhood, the cream of leadership was trained and sent out. Ministry teams initially went out from The Way In. . . . Pulkingham used the image of cream on the milk and said that the cream needed to be skimmed off the top so that more cream could rise up to the surface. But of course if you take all the cream there isn't any more to rise. (Woodruff 1999:1)

Redeemer enthusiastically evangelized churches globally with the good news of the extension of the family of God in a new social communitarianism. Eventually internal scandals, authoritarian patterns in some households, and a depletion of competent leadership broke the essential link between the global mission and the local, worshiping, and congregational leadership.

From Euphoria to Disillusionment

The early power of communal mission was remarkable. Despite the resources and the traditional assets for organization, Redeemer suffered the demise of its communal dream, possibly due to some of the forces, which collapsed a number of key Jesus Movement indigenous groups.

> It is estimated that in the 1970s there were about 1,000 Christian communities across the United States. The influence of these communities was phenomenal; many of them served as wellsprings of renewal within Christian circles. Up until 1975, almost all the music sung by charismatic communities and churches came out of the Word of God and the Redeemer communities. By the millennium, we thought, much of American Christianity would look like our social experiment. (Duin 1996:52)

Julia Duin, having belonged to Oregon and Houston communities, has continued to monitor the general decline of such movements. She is highly critical of the leadership, theology, and practice of the Redeemer, but states it was "fabulously successful" and was responsible for "spreading charismatic renewal in communities such as Reba Place, Evanston, Illinois and Word of God, Ann Abor, Michigan" (Duin 1996:54). Most of these communities are no more.

> That was 21 years ago. Of all the communities that lasted into the 1980s, several of the larger ones have collapsed or splintered in the past three years [1993-1996]. Word of God, the largest community with 3,000 adults and children, split into factions in 1990.
>
> Ralph Martin, their principal leader and internationally known Catholic charismatic renewal leader, has spent much of his time since then seeking repentance

and amends for the wrongs perpetrated by this community over its twenty year history.

> Reba Place Fellowship, a community with roots in the Mennonite-Anabaptist tradition survives in a much smaller form today. Sojourner's Community in Washington, DC founded in the early 1970s, . . . lost three-quarters of its members in just the last few years. With the possible exception of JPUSA, most Christian communities that began in the 1960s and 1970s, the peak period of their growth, have met with disaster. (Duin 1996:52)

Duin focuses on authority and submission in charismatic renewal and speaks strongly of male hegemony and hostility towards the nuclear family. She strongly implies Redeemer members were unaware of "the strange theology behind their famous community" (1996:54). Many Redeemer members disagree.

It is true that Redeemer's founder, morally flawed as were Jesus Movement leaders Frisbee, Parks, Palosaari, and Herrin, moved on to Denver in 1972 after exposure of homosexual affairs with congregational members revealed in 1990 (1996:52). He remained priest on leave until 1975 to become Provost of Scottish Cathedral Millport, Isle of Cumbry. He returned to Redeemer 1980-1982 as assistant priest, and then relocated to South England, Post Green Community Lythchettminsler, and Dorset from 1983-1984. (Newman 2,000:1).

My research raises questions about Duin's assumptions. Duin assumes in *Communities Journal of Co-operative Living* (1996) that the collapse of Redeemer resulted from the immoral behavior of its leader (1996:54) and from the defective philosophy and practice of the community with respect to theories of authority and submission (1996:51-55).

It is too easy to attribute the collapse of communities to the failure of leadership, to inadequate philosophies of community, to male driven authoritarianism, or to inadequate organizational skills. The coincidental collapse of many groups during the 1980s suggests a broad trend, which points to more wide-ranging cultural factors.

Several elders, including Betty Pulkingham, are united in the recognition that there had been some disappointing moral lapses within the community, but all of them stressed the enduring blessings that had resulted from Pulkingham's ministry. They recognized that even the biblical accounts reveal highly charismatic but often deeply flawed characters used by God for the long-term benefit of humanity. They stressed that Pulkingham had taken several steps back from the usual authority exercised by the senior priest in an Anglican community, and had facilitated and encouraged not only the power sharing of men, but also of women within the community.

Pulkingham's shift to a more global ministry and his consequent departure from resident leadership at Redeemer in 1972 parallels the slow disintegration of the local community bereft of its foundational, inspirational leader. The communal dream appears, however, to have evaporated for more reasons than the removal of the dreamer. The assumption that the energy and focus was not sustainable without the charismatic leader may contain an element of truth, but such a conclusion again misses the broader social factors.

The survival of radical experiments in cultural innovation is somewhat akin to the survival rate of salmon seeking to reproduce against the current of a river of floodtide. As with the salmon, the determined effort to swim against the tide and regenerate a new generation may result in the demise of those who supply the fertile egg. Some great ideas hatch and matured. Many fail the birthing process and some are destroyed long after their life shows form and promise against the odds.

The surprising outcome of this congregational revitalization and experimentation with community is that this most resourced of the Charismatic Jesus Movement attempts was relatively short-lived (1965-1985). Nothing formally remains in Houston of the radical Episcopal communitarianism. In 1998, the Community of Celebration in Britain dissolved, but at the time of this research, some members are still fostering their relationship with the continuing Community of Celebration in the Pittsburgh diocese, Pennsylvania, where the tradition is small but alive and reassessing the original vision. This community is currently involved in a reexamination of their history and the revision of their calling in a radically changed socio-religious environment.

In the meantime, the creative legacy of Redeemer in styles of liturgical, charismatic praise and evangelical outreach in the worldwide Anglican-Episcopal community lives on. When asked about the rise and fall of communitarian life in Houston, Colorado, England, and Scotland, Betty Pulkingham said, "Community is a God given structure but it is very fragile. It needs the space to grow, in up and down experiences and requires an environment that is conducive to this" (Pulkingham 1999:3).

There were pressures from within. Redeemer did not embrace community for community's sake but community for missions' sake. Betty Pulkingham is not negative about the experiment. She points out that there was an outpouring of the Holy Spirit, which facilitated the radical experiment. There was an interest in community during the counterculture period, which encouraged experimentation.

There was at times a Pentecostal congregational resistance from some who did not want to pursue an Orthodox heritage but "it was that heritage which acted as a stabilizing and balancing aspect" (Pulkingham 1999:3) to a very liminal experiment. In the midst of the radical innovations, the church remained always true to Episcopal polity.

The period immediately following the Jonestown massacre of the Jim Jones' group was an intense psychological low. Many came to fear and doubt the communal model, but according to Betty Pulkingham, it was a time that helped the community sort out what is genuine and what is cult (Pulkingham 1999:3).

John Farra and Grover Newman experienced conflict, which ended with Newman peaceably departing from the community at Denver. Newman now believes he should have stayed to battle it out. Farra left his wife Margo Farra in Denver in 1985 and returned to Houston. Margo, a strong and visionary elder in earlier days died of cancer in 1989.

Despite a traumatic withdrawal over leadership conflict in the Denver community in which he was a foundational elder, Newman still warmly remembers community, as an extended family for which there is no substitute:

> There is a vacancy in human experience, which cannot be filled without a broader sense of family. When you give up all together, there is an element of fellowship unknown elsewhere. There is a sense of mutual dependence.
>
> When the Pulkinghams left with other team members, it left a dilution of membership. I would do it again. I'm a virtual expert on community but there is none. I feel some sense of loss to that extent. There is great benefit resulting from community closeness and care. (Newman 1999:1)

If he had his time over, he would have excluded some people from the community (Newman 1999:1). "One of the problems is the aging process whereby people grow older and life's experiences take people away. The only time I ever saw a functioning example of a biblical body of Christ was in Redeemer. I miss the depth of fellowship of former days [aged seventy now]." He would have "liked to have stayed in Denver" (Newman 1999:2).

The demise of this charismatic movement may have resulted from giving too much. Too many left for England and Denver, such that the place was gutted. A sizable proportion of the congregation left to plant other communities, instruct churches in the process, and fulfill renewal ministries through the Fisherfolk project.

The weakness to this pattern was that too many of the cream of leadership were taken out of the basic group, thus weakening the foundations and eventually leading to the breakdown of the communal experiment. The principle of "skimming the cream from the top for mission" that Pulkingham employed (Woodruff 1999) becomes the law of diminishing returns, if new cream is not brought to the vat at a commensurate rate. It was not simply the numbers but the strategic removal of the most capable and charismatic members en masse which left the base to less capable leadership who embraced a more authoritarian order.

There is a formidable conflict between current global capitalism and attempts at radical communion and theology. Joe Peterson, sociologist and experienced communal experimenter in personal conversation, strongly affirmed that various economic elements had as much to do with the collapse of the outstanding communal experiment with which he was associated as any other factor. An examination of the hippie experiment at The Farm, Tennessee, reveals a similar economic capitulation for the sake of survival. (See Appendix 17).

The "fallenness" of humanity expressed in radical selfishness appears problematical when one attempts to establish "common purse" community. Times changed and with the shift away from 1960s radical anti-materialism, the people's priorities changed. As Newman observed, "It is very difficult to have community without poverty" (1999:1).

Economics are a significant factor in the collapse of some utopian communities, both Christian (Shiloh) and hippie forms (See Appendix 17). "Conspicuous consumption," rather than voluntary poverty or downward mobility, became the order of the day by the 1980s. The complication of family and the needs of a different generation of young people rent the fabric of communal idealism. As the surrounding culture changed, and the radical hippie alternative culture died, there was a change in attitude.

In contrast to the high culture experiment in Houston, JPUSA, one of the most vulnerable of all communitarian experiments, without the support of historic tradition and the availability of trained personnel and denominational material resources, continues in Chicago after 26 years. After tenuous beginnings, threatened by dysfunctional founders, the next generation of JPUSA regrouped in the face of imminent collapse and built enduring structures for relationships and mission. This indigenous communitarian experiment, having succeeded on its own, has however felt the need to enter the historic flow of the Christian church, becoming a religious order of the Swedish Covenant church.

Whether the Houston experiment was a failure or not is problematical. Consistently the participants look back on the former days as unparalleled in fulfillment and significance, feeling the culture has lost its way, but believing the creativity of Redeemer has left an enduring impact on the Western church, as far a field as the United Kingdom and Australia. Even those who express criticism of elements of the project (Duin 1996; Ward 1996) confirm this.

Joe Peterson (1996), with experience of 32 years in intentional communities, finds fault with classic evaluations of success or failure based purely on materialistic and geographical criteria:

> Yet Christian communities by and large do last, at least in the "faithfulness" of their believers, if not as geographical entities. Many of the people I have lived with in Christian community over the past 26 years are still around and still vital in their faith, even though the geography of their community experience has adjusted in some cases many times over. I consider these colleagues "my community" as much as I do the people I happen to live with presently. Community, at least for Christians, is more a heartbeat than geography. (Peterson 1996:50)

David Janzen (1996), after undertaking wide-ranging surveys of Christian communities, suggests that the demise of many communities is more of a statement about the "corruption of our minds" and of "our civic life by the current social ethic" (1996:49). He sees the renewal of history by God as a minority operation from the grass roots such as occurred in the 1960s and 1970s.

John Wagner (1996), another scholar investigating current communal experiments is even more direct in his criticism of social evaluative methodology:

> In the scholarly literature as well as in ordinary conversation, the discussion of "utopias," "communes," "alternative societies," or other intentional communities is frequently accompanied by judgments concerning the "success" or "failure" of these ventures. The legitimacy of such judgments seems to be taken for granted, even though few historians and social scientists would entertain similar questions about the "success" of San Francisco or of a village in New Guinea.
>
> This is not to say that such judgments are philosophically invalid – indeed, some have argued that normative judgments ought to occupy a more respected place in the study of human cultures. All the same, the concepts of social success and social failure are by no means an established part of historical, anthropological, or sociological scholarship. Unless the terms "success" and "failure" are carefully defined, their use may lead to confusion or even to deliberate obfuscation

Unfortunately, many discussions of community "success" beg important questions. Although such discussions may appear logical and persuasive on the surface, they often employ undefined, poorly defined, or shifting criteria of success. Even when the criteria are defined, the appropriateness of the particular choice of criteria is rarely defined, nor is the existence of other logically defensible criteria usually acknowledged.

The question begging becomes compounded if an author proposes, for example, to "explain" why it is that "communes always fail." Such an argument indirectly assert that (1) there exists a single, known set of criteria by which it is possible to judge decisively the success of a communal society, and that (2) according to such criteria, all or most of the communes of the past have failed. (Wagner 1996:50)

Wagner has provided a seven-point evaluation of communal success (Appendix 13), reminding us that success is a multi-faceted affair. A project may have failed abysmally by one criterion and succeeded admirably by another.

Betty Pulkingham believes "None of it got wasted. It's all being used in the kingdom somehow. There is a lot to be thankful for. I believe in the divine recycling process. God doesn't waste anything" (Pulkingham 1999:3). She still believes in the communal ideal, that:

There is a need to show that living life together is a sign to the world; [it] is durable and viable, and needs to be presented. It was not a failure. It's a continuum. It was born of life. Therefore it didn't cease to have life. It didn't loose its life. We are living souls and we go on. The locale, the shape, the form may change but it was born of life, and it will burst out again (Pulkingham 1999:3).

There is substantial evidence in talking to the aging pioneers of Redeemer's communal-liturgical-charismatic innovations that, at least for them, it was the highlight of lives well spent in diffusing faith, love, and hope. Newman misses the Houston community and says there are some benefits of closeness and care, which remain as a legacy. I also discovered a strong theology and social attachment to the concept of the body of Christ being organic, relational, and communal rather than simply functional as often found in congregational membership (Newman 1999:2).

Some may ask why I have included a traditional congregation in the research of the Jesus Movement. It varies in a number of respects. It emerges inside the traditional structure. It is not strictly speaking a youth movement. Many of the aspects, which bear similarity to the classic Jesus Movement, emerged midstream in its history. In summary, we need to recognize:

1. The heights of both the Denominational Charismatic and the Counterculture Jesus movements historically coincide.
2. There was considerable interplay between Redeemer and Jesus Movement personnel, including the author.
3. Significant players moved in and out of Redeemer and many Jesus Movement groups, including the Fort Lauderdale Shepherding leaders. Both shared a revitalization dream rather than a traditionalist lifeboat theology whereby souls were simply to be saved and secured for hea-

ven.
4. The dominant leadership model for both movements was that of charismatic, prophetic innovators.
5. As expressed earlier in the text, Redeemer rose and fell with the birth and death of the youth driven culture of idealism.
6. As the radicals in Redeemer and the Jesus Movement in general faced shifts in the economy of their family life, the experiments diminished in their popular appeal.
7. Both were strongly committed to intentional community. It is not surprising therefore that communities *Journal of Cooperative Living* (1996), when dedicating an issue to the rise and fall of Christian communities, includes Redeemer, Shiloh, and other Jesus Movement communes in their enquiry. Testimonies to the interaction between Redeemer and the other communities are found in this *Journal*.
8. Both surfed a brief wave of secular revolution. Individualism was out; love was in. In the face of the proposed manifest failure of the nuclear family, both groups sought alternatives. At that stage, serial monogamy as an escape route for Christians was inconceivable.
9. Direct connections with the counterculture and the Jesus Movement is a well-attested fact of Redeemer's history. Some elements such as the connection at the beginning with the street ministry of David Wilkerson certainly opened the doors to a culture unattractive to older Christians. The impact of the distinctly hippie styled Demarest-Booth became a direct link to marginalized youth.
10. If CC is to be seen as a Jesus Movement outcome, certainly Redeemer must be seen at the very least as an interactive response to the Movement. I would suggest that the Charismatic Movement in the denominations as distinct from Pentecostalism and neo-Pentecostalism, was an adult response to the same social phenomena as created the revolutionary youth expression we call "The Jesus Movement." They are at least close cousins.
11. The basis of the collapse of Redeemer as a communitarian experiment remarkably parallels a repetitive pattern in similar Jesus Movement youth communes. Both suffered from serious relational failures on the part of prophetic leaders. Both were injured by relationship to radical shepherding authoritarian teachers from Florida. Both saw their fortunes rise and fall with the wider cultural shifts from idealism to individualism. Both were bought to grief by the changing needs of their maturing families. Both suffered initial adulation by the media and later persecution by media from the time of the Jonestown massacre. Both grew weary of the demands of a frenetic mission to the wider world. As Janzen (1996) observes, both Movements were based on "daily love, hidden service, and humble forgiveness" (1996:48-49). When exposed to TV cameras and effusive print media affirmation, the glory "gave way to pride, attention seeking and competition" (1996:48-49).

12. At least in my personal experience, such denominational charismatic and Jesus Movement communities interacted and publicly affirmed each other's ministries as part of the same movement of Jesus.
13. Both were centered in the human life and healing ministry of Jesus. We used to say, "the Jesus Movement is just Jesus moving."
14. Redeemer shared the same vision of centrifugal mission, urban revitalization, liturgical, missional experimentalism, prophetic proclamation, intense emotional Koinonia, and the prophetic proclamation of the gospel in the marketplace.
15. Finally, aging participants (I have interviewed many) from Redeemer, and the youthful Jesus Movement groups, consistently hold to the belief that despite some cognitive dissonance and relational scars from that hyperactive era of their lives, no alternative has been found as fulfilling.

All over the world, continuing effective ministries, which may bear little structural resemblance of Redeemer and the Jesus communes, nevertheless bear testimony that both movements have left behind a transforming legacy.

In the next chapter, I will look into the tension between tradition and innovation in this Revitalization movement. Along the way to the future, the movement discovered the past, and gained some interesting fellow travellers along the way.

Notes

1 The experimentation with liturgical dance, folk mass, and open hospitality in the Catholic Church may have contributed to an earlier acceptance of change by more radical priests, and acceptance of the hippie seekers or new converts. The commitment of politically activist clergy, such as the Berrigan brothers, may have delivered credibility not afforded the generally right wing, conservative evangelicals and Pentecostals.

During a lengthy interview with one of the early Jews for Jesus members, whose ministry has been centered in liturgical and interpretive dance, the issue of church rejection aroused strong emotional recall in her. Her Jewish heritage made her suspicious of all churches, but upon conversion she was surprised to find strong rejection from Pentecostals, but support from Catholic charismatics.

"Because I come from a non Church background, I don't have a personal involvement, or personal awareness of what things ecumenically were like, because I don't come from that scene. To me, all Christians and Catholics were the people who persecuted us. They were all one thing. So when I got saved, I assumed they were all the same thing, but I found out differently afterwards. I think the Catholic Church went through its own changes that were more countercultural in the late sixties, with their folk masses. I had friends that were Catholic . . . because the whole Catholic Church was more into social action and social justice than most churches."

Australian Baptist Jesus Movement leader John Hirt, had a relationship with the Berrigan brothers, who were vilified and even imprisoned for their forthright, Catholic resistance to militarism in general, as well as the Vietnam War in particular. Folk masses became, for many, readjusted as ritual processes for celebrating freedom and solidarity with the poor, against the dominant paradigm of the industrial military complex. The Jesus Movement in Australia has borrowed from some of these sources for liturgy, see A.H. Matthias Zahniser *Symbol and Ceremony. Making Disciples Across Cultures*. (Monrovia, CA:MARC, 1997) Pp. 183-210, particularly Pp. 201-206. Revolutionary a Cappella worship music is still popular in the radical arm of the movement, the following being a favorite:

> We're gonna keep on moving forward (three times),
> Never turning back" (two times).
> We're gonna teach our children justice,
> Never turning back.
> We're gonna speak the truth to power,
> Never turning back.
> We're gonna take our stand together,
> Never turning back.

2 Di Sabatino, a Canadian by citizenship and birth, described considerable interactive relationship between some Canadian churches and the Jesus Movement. He recalls that it was a typically untidy, dynamic and divisive revitalization: "The preacher there has a family steeped in the Canadian Pentecostal Church named Jim McAlister. Anybody I talked to who loved him. Benny Hinn came from there. He was one of the Shekinah dancers. There were two groups there; there were the cerebral who wanted to learn about the gospel and then the Pentecostal charismatics with a real Messianic, Judaic sway. They were big on prophecy.

A Prophecy came down in 1972 that one of the worship leaders who were a phenomenal violinist was going to play on the mountain when Jesus touched down. So they all got together and went to Israel because this prophecy was going to be fulfilled. It split the church. It was ridiculous. How do you stop that? People would get very emotional.

These preachers would come in and say something and these people would go off on it. You'd get into these little groups and I talked to people who were trying to talk people out of it by saying 'this is not sober. It's devastating. It is wrong.' You couldn't talk Benny out of that. I don't know whether he went to Israel, but he was into the Messianic [group]. I talked to people who knew him and he loved God with all his heart, but he's one of the most gullible people you ever met.

He was in Toronto for all of his formative years. At the Toronto Catacombs this Anglican minister in downtown Toronto enjoyed the vibrancy of these kids and let them use his church to worship. [There are] all sorts of little stories. J.F. Packer said it was amazing what he saw in Toronto Thursday nights, with 2,000 kids "praising the Lord" (Di Sabatino 1999:9)

3 One of the earliest contacts our Australian group, Truth and Liberation made with the Movement internationally was with The Catacombs in Toronto. In the second edition of our Jesus paper we published a thoughtful article, "Jesus People, For Thinking People," which was strongly counterculture, criticizing the established church but equally noting the hypocrisy and powerlessness of radical politics to revitalize Western culture, or liberate the individual.

An accompanying article by Jesus freak Rush Greenslade and *Christianity Today's* Edward Plowman announced, "A Great Awakening? Revival in Canada," told of several Bible colleges and denominational groups canceling annual events to join in revival type events. More than 3,000,000 were said to have "jammed the Civic Center" and thousands filled the city's largest sanctuary, belonging to the United Church of Canada. With the article a letter from Candy Waldron of The House of Life reported a Jesus paper circulation of 50,000 and a baptism of over 50 young people at her local church.

Clearly there were gains for the traditional church, which was willing to host the Christian element of the Cultural Revolution. Cheltenham Anglican Church, a previously upper middle class sedate Melbourne suburban cause, opened its doors to the Jesus freaks early in the development of the Australian movement. The consequences could only be described as a Cultural Revolution.

Alternative youth flooded into the church and encouraged by a very well spoken vicar (who has since become a bishop) they revolutionized the form of the Anglican Evensong Service. Spontaneously, with no prior warning, a Jesus freak would leap to his or her feet at any point of the service, plunging the index finger into the air as the "One Way" Jesus sign crying in a loud voice, "Attitude Check!" The Jesus freaks and many fascinated regulars would jump to their feet and in reply call out "Praise the Lord!" It became the liturgy, which created a liminal tension increasing the sense of expectation and attentiveness in the congregation. The church grew substantially and in turn, provided the gospel and discipleship for many lonely youth drawn by the growing reputation of the church as a Jesus people sanctuary.

4 Dallas shortly thereafter became one of the few denominational units in Australia to totally radicalize its congregational and church life by embracing a full communitarian, shared purse lifestyle. This operated for many years, suffered under a cloud of accusation concerning sexual misconduct on the part of the leadership, but reshaped and continues today to minister in one of the most needy satellite suburbs of Melbourne.

5 Although few of the leaders would have understood the term social trinitarianism, the intense searching of the Scriptures in a socially communal context led many of the groups to a far more Eastern orthodox rather than Continental Calvinist understanding of theology. Although there were some "Jesus Only" groups, most were very Trinitarian and the following song is typical of the theology expressed in Jesus Movement hymnology.

We are one in the Spirit; we are one in the Lord (repeat)
And we pray that our unity will one day be restored
And they'll know we are Christians by our love, by our love (repeat)

We will walk with each other; we will walk hand in hand (repeat)
And together we'll spread the news that God is in our land
And they'll know we are Christians by our love, by our love (repeat)

We will work with each other; we will work side by side (repeat)
And we'll guard each one's dignity, and save each one's pride
And they'll know we are Christians by our love, by our love (repeat)

All praise to the Father, from whom all blessings come
And all praise to Christ Jesus God's only Son
And all praise to the Spirit who makes us one
And they'll know we are Christians by our love, by our love (repeat)

This style of social Trinitarian thought was more congruent with Orthodox, Episcopalian and Catholic liturgical developments than the more Calvinist evangelicalism. Rather than following a Continental, hierarchical understanding of the economy of the Godhead, many Jesus people embraced a more egalitarian social gospel from the example of the Trinity.

6 Victoria Booth-Demarest was the granddaughter of the founders of the Salvation Army, William and Catherine Booth. Her connection with the Episcopal Church was not through her husband but through her daughter who was married to an Episcopalian. Victoria Booth-Demarest was the daughter of Catherine and William Booth's eldest daughter, Catherine Booth [Jr.]. Catherine Jr. was one of 10 siblings, five boys and five girls. Known for her pioneering evangelism and social work in France and throughout Europe as the Marechale, (The Marshall), she also earned the name "the Heavenly Witch" for her uncanny spirituality and capacity to "read" peoples' characters on initial contact. She married the Reverend Arthur Sydney Clibborn, to become Catherine Booth-Clibborn.

She had a fall out with the Salvation Army after her mother's death but pursued a lengthy unorthodox and highly fruitful, evangelistic career in her own right. Her daughter, Victoria Booth-Demarest, married a Presbyterian Minister, Agnew Demarest. Victoria Booth-Demarest was born in Paris in 1892, married and came to America in 1918, died in 1983. She was a fiery evangelist, spoke to a crowd of 20,000 in Europe on one occasion, and spoke German, French, and Dutch.

She and her husband wrote many gospel songs and published several hymnals. She wrote at least nine books beginning with *The Lily* in 1917. This was followed by *Broken Lives* (1924), *The Holy Spirit* (1927), *Shade of His Hand* (A book of consolation, 1941, 1963), *What I Saw in Europe* (1953), *King David* (1964), *Alive and Running* (Devotions for active people, 1976), *A Violin a Lily and You* (1976). Her last book, *God, Women and Ministry* (St Petersburg, Florida: Sacred Arts International with Valkyrie Press, Inc., 1978) is an aggressive confrontation of racism, snobbery and prejudice against female equality. She is listed in *Who's Who in America*, as an author and musician.

Her connection with Houston was through her daughter, also named Victoria, who married Claxton Monro, an Episcopalian who was a priest at St. Stephen's, Houston, a short distance from the Redeemer. In 1954 Munro launched the Lay Witness Movement in the American Episcopalian Church, writing two primary books for the movement (*Witnessing Laymen Make Living Christians* and *The Story-Telling Handbook*), after working as an assistant to Samuel Shoemaker for two and a half years. Claxton and Victoria Booth-Monro served at St. Stephen's Episcopal, Houston, from 1950 to 1981 when Claxton retired. It was during the visit by Victoria Booth Demarest to her daughter, that she preached twice at the Redeemer as a result of which, the Redeemer community was moved to open their coffee shop ministry. At the end of the 1960s, about the time of her mother's visit to St Stephen's and Redeemer, her daughter Victoria and Claxton Monro also launched an evening coffee shop service at St Stephens. This ran successfully from 1969 to 1980.

According to Victoria Booth-Monro's daughter, Mary McGregor, her parent's coffee shop attracted 200-300 young people each Sunday night when hippies, 'druggies' and youth in general sat on the floor. A combination of secular and religious folk and soft rock music was enjoyed between 7-10 p.m. and her father Claxton insisted on a presentation of the gospel in this largely non-church Jesus people atmosphere. She informed me in 2,000, that her mother is now 80; her father died in 1991.

Victoria Booth-Demarest's granddaughter is currently in a strategic leadership position, training Church planters and outreach workers for the Episcopal Church in Texas. In this period of the centrality of church planting and discipling, rather than the old model of itinerant evangelism, the continuing saga of the Booth family is worthy of consideration. Several communications with the most significant leadership of the Redeemer Renewal, have affirmed extraordinary, long term consequences from just two preaching by the then aging itinerant 68 year-old counterculture evangelist." She had a passion for the counterculture kids, which she diffused through conventional congregations by her hip appearance and prophetic challenges from the pulpit.

7 Despite the apparent demise of the majority of intentional communities, a thriving network of continuing communal movements exists and one of the clearinghouses for information, reflection, and analysis of a wide variety of communities is the Fellowship for Intentional Communities (Route 1, Box 155, Rutledge, MO 63563). This group publishes a quarterly journal called *Communities Journal of Cooperative Living.* Joe V. Peterson, a sociologist who has spent the majority of his adult life either associated with or participating in radical communities has access to a very large repository of research data. A number of his contributions are listed in this dissertation's References Cited. At one stage he was an elder at The House of Elijah, a Jesus People Commune in Yakima, Washington and later administrator for Shiloh, which arguably was the largest communal group in the history of the US. Peterson produced a fascinating thesis for his Master's Degree on the rise and fall of the Shiloh group. He informs me that one of the best scholarly works is *Organized Miracle: A Study of a Contemporary, Youth, Communal, Fundamentalist Organization* by James T. Richardson, Mary W. Stewart, and Robert B. Simmonds (New Brunswick, New Jersey: Transaction Books, 1979).

8 Throughout this dissertation I have referred to the influence of this small group of aggressive Pentecostal-Charismatic preachers whose influence at the edge of the Jesus Movement and the Charismatic Movement has been strongly evident, not only in the US but in New Zealand, Australia, and Britain. The following analysis by Duin "Authority and Submission in Christian Community" is in my opinion, fairly accurate (In the quarterly journal *Communities Journal of Cooperative Living*, Fall 1996, Issue #92, Pp. 51-55. Contact Route 1, Box 155, Rutledge, MO 63563).

Although the Florida-based Christian Growth Ministries group did not form an intentional community as such, their teachers visited the Word of God community in the early 1970s, conferred with its leaders, and wrote articles for its magazine, *New Covenant.* Discipleship concepts also made their way into the Redeemer community in the mid-1970s through an elder who had personal ties to Christian Growth Ministries leaders.

What is not generally known is the part that Watchman Nee, a Christian teacher in China, had played in creating charismatic authoritarianism. Nee had tremendous influence on the renewal, as Jesus People and charismatics alike avidly read his books in the mid-1970s. Nee's 1948 book, *Spiritual Authority,* systematized not as important as obedience. Thus, if there is a conflict between what you feel God is telling you and what an elder is telling you, ignore the former to obey the latter. The way to experience spiritual victory is to submit to whatever human spiritual authority figure has a revelation from God about you, which is considered more accurate than what God may be saying to you directly.

This whole scheme of leadership was made even more popular in Christian circles outside of the charismatics and intentional communities through inspirational Christian public speakers. Taught to thousands at a time in mass gatherings, the message of the virtues of the "chain of command" spread to countless individual Christians. This authority concept created havoc in many Christian communities, especially in the Word of God community. In 1976, men who were full members of the community wore white cloth vests or "mantles" at community meetings, symbolizing headship. The women covered their hair with waist-length white veils, symbolizing submission. The mantles and veils eventually went by the wayside, but in their place husbands were taught to make up a weekly schedule for their wives to follow at home. Husbands were never to do the dishes, clean the house or change diapers, coach their wives during childbirth, or perform other "feminizing" activities. Women were supposed to rein in their emotions so as not to use them to manipulate their husbands. Such rulings were a major reason for the breakup of Word of God in 1990."

CHAPTER 8

Back to the Future – An Enduring Catholic Paradigm

Go post a lookout and have him report what he sees .... And the lookout shouted, "Babylon has fallen, has fallen." Isaiah 21:6, 9.

It may seem to be a late imposition to look now at the theoretical framework used for the interpretation of my research material in greater depth, but in so doing we employ an accepted model for qualitative analysis (Rudestam and Newton 1992:36-41, 56). Any method of presentation is for the purpose of "making sense of the data in ways that will facilitate continuing, unfolding of the enquiry and second, lead to a maximal understanding . . . of the phenomenon being observed" (Lincoln and Guba 1985:224).

To determine whether the theory of revitalization fits the conclusions of this enquiry, the Jesus Movement must first be described so that its social texture is felt freely and the underlying forces are understood, before confident conclusions are drawn by the researcher and reader. A brief outline of the theory was supplied in the introduction, but more detailed reflection is appropriate now, after immersing the reader in the findings of the ethnography and history of the Jesus Movement. The validity of using the theory makes more sense after familiarity with the research findings.

This chapter will expand on the process of revitalization, and propose more directly that the 1960s-1970s social movement researched in this dissertation is an example of that which was spoken of by Wallace in his phenomenological examination of another, yet related, occurrence of a revitalization among Native Americans. In both instances a people group sought to innovate culturally for survival in the midst of a perceived collapse of the surrounding culture. It will be argued firstly that despite the pre-1960s dating of the theory, it is an enduring paradigm, relevant to the more postmodern occurrence of the 1960s counterculture.

It will also be proposed that despite the Native American cultural context of the original theory, it is applicable to the predominantly white, Euro-American movements of the counterculture and to its Jesus Movement expression. Significant parallels exist between Native American revitalization and the Jesus Movement under examination in this enquiry. This dissertation concludes that the data gathered in researching the Jesus Movement supports revitalization as an enduring theory capable of the broad historical and cultural application proposed by Wallace.

For revitalization to be a reasonable lens through which to view analytically the phenomenon of the Jesus Movement there must be clear, analogous parallels between the Native American and non-Native American experience. Though the movements may not be similar in historic timing, origin, or structure, they are remarkably similar in function. For the purpose of demonstrating the similarities of purpose and function of these social movements, the ethnographic work of Melissa Pflüg (1998) has been invaluable. She has applied revitalization theory to the recent history of the Odawa people in a finely detailed manner, which I found evocative in the comparison I sought between the revitalization of native and postmodern groups. It is one of several ethnographies that could be used as a parallel, but is a particularly appropriate account for comparison with the counterculture movements of the 1960s.

Finally, I wish to show that the socio-historical prerequisites for revitalization, and the classic process or outcomes of revitalization are observable in both the historic timing and ethnographic detail of the Jesus Movement. The Jesus Movement occurred at an historical period suited to revitalization. Its reason for existence, *modus operandi,* and developmental form give the appearance of a revitalization movement.

Revitalization as Transformational Religion

Throughout history, the rise and fall, success and failure of religious movements has significantly influenced cultural renewal and transformation. Historic changes caused by scientific modernity, reactionary postmodernity, and globalization have not eclipsed the universal phenomenon of new religious movements, which usually occur in times of major cultural vertigo.[1] The ubiquitous nature of religion suggests that it fulfills universal needs for meaning, community, and transcendence. Thus, in times of social disintegration and culture stress, when the stabilizing traditions and institutions fail to answer life's major questions, innovative new religious movements often occur.[2]

Arising out of stressful periods of social angst, new religious movements follow consistent patterns of growth and incorporation. "Major cultural-system innovations" Wallace observed, "are characterized by a uniform process" (Wallace 1956b:264). Triggered by pervasive stress and culture distortion, they sometimes become positive forces for innovation and renewal of cultures, which are changed substantially in the process. Wallace observes that not all, but "many such movements are religious in character" (1956b:270). Almost all his examples are intensely religious movements (1956b:264-268; 1966:30).

The Communist Movement is a secular exception (Wallace 1966:210), but such "non-supernaturally rationalized" movements nevertheless display distinctly religious phenomena to attract a following (1966:262). Communism embraced charismatic "sacred" figures (Marx and Lenin), a system of ritual processes (mass communal gatherings), "sacred' symbols (hammer and sickle), "sacred" places (Lenin's tomb, Red Square), and sacred texts (the works of Lenin, Marx, and Engels). Dialectical materialism and utopianism formed a secular eschatology.

Revitalization theory concerns itself with those movements which are a "deliberate, organized, effort by members of a society to construct a more satisfying culture" (Wallace 1956b:265, cf. Hiebert 1983:389). Such "conscious organized efforts to perpetuate a culture [or develop an alternative culture] can arise only when a society becomes conscious that there are cultures other than its own, and the existence of its own culture is threatened" (Linton 1943:240). Thus, the revitalization paradigm was derived from an anthropological analysis of Native American cultures that were under threat of extinction due to the effects of colonization. The tragic disintegration of Native American culture since European invasion, and subsequent movements to revive the corporate identity and cultural cohesion of the dispirited people provided ethnohistoric data for the anthropologist to interpret (Ferraro 1998:299).

An Enduring Catholic Paradigm

Though predating popular postmodernism, revitalization (Wallace 1952, 1955, 1956a, 1957a, 1958b, 1966, 1969) remains an enduring and adaptive paradigm. As a synthesis of ethnohistory and social psychology, it seeks explanation for individual and mass psychological responses to periods of inordinate culture stress. Wallace's interest in "theories of human behavior in extreme situations" (1955), and "mental illness, biology, and culture" (1972) gave rise to a psychological anthropology rich in ethnohistorical perspective.

Although the theory was derived from studies of preliterate and homogeneous groups, Wallace believes revitalization movements occur in many part of the world, in diverse cultures and throughout history. It is likely that most of us have at some stage experienced or observed some aspect of the revitalization process (Hiebert 1983:394; Martin 1999:1). History records many deliberate efforts to innovate continuously over a substantial period of time, in contexts as variant as the Industrial Revolution, and "probably also the Neolithic and Urban Revolutions" (Wallace 1980:485).

Wallace views the "revitalization models as being a special case of paradigm development" beyond standard typologies, and useful in "culture-historical analysis," as an aid in analysis of "the conditions under which domains of culture become susceptible to paradigmatic change" (1980:485). It has been broadly applied to everything from local culture to urban planning. Such a model is ideal for analysis of the 1960s cultural revolution. Some scholars define a revitalization movement in the strict context of "primitive peoples," as a call "to a return to traditional practices, customs and beliefs after the partial erosion of such practices through contact with more modernized cultures" (Williams 1989:241).

Others observe that "the general configuration can be applied to American history" to the Puritan Awakening (1610-1640), the First Evangelical Awakening (1730-1760), and the Second Evangelical Awakening (1800-1830). The theory of revitalization is applied to Puritan, Methodist, and Baptist Awakenings (Marty 1976; McLoughlin 1978; Wuthnow 1987). Wuthnow applies the paradigm to socialist and Christian Millenarian movements, while differentiating between ideological revolutions and revitalization movements (Wuthnow 1987:223-240). Few theoretical models are as frequently employed in the discussion of religious movements as the revitalization paradigm (Marty 1976: 156-157; McLoughlin 1978:10-24; Miller 1997:26; Rogers 1995:399-400; Snyder 1997:48-54, 267-270; Williams 1989:17-18, 105, 108-109, 112-114, 144, 232).

It is important to reiterate the significance of the revitalization theory despite the passage of time since its conception. As an anthropological paradigm it appears in the literature of that domain more frequently than in social movement literature. In the field of anthropology, the paradigm shows no recent sign of a decline in status (Ember and Ember 1999; Ferraro 1998; Turner and Bruner 1986). The only criticisms of which I am aware is that the theory has been misunderstood and limited to studies of tribal peoples by some scholars (Joel Martin 1999; Kraft 1996a). Secondly, it has been proposed that Wallace has failed to expand the model in the context of ideological rather than social and psychological conflict (Klass 1995:152). Klass believes Wallace's observations need to be taken "a short distant further" since his "formula is not invariable. Sometimes the repertoire is simplified, and sometimes two sets of fundamentally different and even conflicting assumptions, beliefs, and practices continue to be exhibited, not only in the same cultural system, but even in the same application." (1995:147).

This dissertation supports a stable tradition of revitalization theory in its chosen field of missiology (Eugene Nida 1990:256-257; Paul Hiebert 1983; Kraft 1996; Tippett 1979; Whiteman 1983). Tippett employs the revitalization principle in his field of expertise in Melanesian studies, applying it to the Marching Rule in the Solomon Islands. Anthropologist and missiologist Darrell Whiteman extensively develops the work of Tippett concerning the Melanesian Marching Rule, providing a periodization breakdown of the five stages of revitalization with respect to Melanesian renewal (1983:273-275).

I have sought to apply Victor Turner's theories concerning the creative power of liminality in ritual process to the innovative and countercultural developments in revitalization. Following the conclusion of the application of this theory to the Jesus Movement revitalization, I discovered a similar application in one of Tippet's unpublished papers concerning the effects of liminality and marginalization on the Melanesian revitalization movement, in *The Liminal Years: Selected Essays 1943-1976.*

The lack of rebuttal in recent sociological, movemental literature is as significant as the paucity of its specific mention. Recent social theorists have clearly accepted the model as a "given" concept in social theory (Marx and McAdam 1994; Peter Williams 1989). More important is the general acceptance of cultural stress as a cause of the initiation of social movements and the revival of the application of Weber's charismatic leader motif which is also incorporated in Wallace's description of the revitalization process. As noted in Chapter 2 and this chapter, considerable commentary on the significance of charismatic figures in the articulation and popularization of a movement's code and mission by such charismatics complies with Wallace's conclusions concerning the stages of revitalization. Colin Campbell (1996) has however strongly criticized contemporary sociology for its lack of recognition of Weber's emphasis on individualistic action because of sociology's obsession with situationalism. While the term revitalization (sometimes synonymous with revolution in social movement literature) may not occur often, conceptually its dynamics remain in social theory.

The application of revitalization theory to the Jesus Movement provides a test case beyond the usual ethnographies of non-European tribal movements. While several scholars have assumed the Reformation and the Evangelical Awakenings of the eighteenth and nineteenth centuries were revitalizations, obviously no leaders or participants are available for ethnographic interview to assess them fully.

Since revitalization is an unscheduled social response to specific cultural dysfunction, it occurs less commonly than other forms of social movement. It naturally receives less attention than other more rationally birthed forms. The significance of revitalization lies in its intuitive nature and its capacity for a brief period to promote rapid systems innovation. Because the innovative period is short-lived, the process provides a brief time for scholarly investigation. Its unscheduled appearance and rapid internal change through routinization further complicates examination and verification.

Ample time has passed since the 1960s – 1970s revitalization for objective analysis, yet it is a sufficiently recent occurrence to enable extensive interviews with many who were involved. This dissertation primarily seeks to identify the nature and causation of the Jesus Movement, but in doing so, it adds to considerable available evidence for the validity of the theory, beyond the context of tribal movements.

Revitalization –
A Synthesis of Tradition and Radical Adaptation

McLoughlin (1978) uses revitalization to differentiate between revivalism as a movement to convert individuals, and religious gestalt shifts (1978:xiii, 8-9) that "provide alternative strategies . . .to cope with the broad necessities of social change" (1978:10). Revitalization is a "grand overall design" which is "suitable to the various regional, class, color, ethnic, or educational groups within the nation," when confronting "jarring disjunction between norms and experience, old beliefs and new realities, dying patterns, and new realities" (McLoughlin

1978:10). McLoughlin views the religious transformation of the last several decades as the "Fourth Evangelical Awakening" (1978:11, 211).

While seeking to make converts, the Jesus Movement sought to organize the new believers in a concerted effort to revolutionize society and the church. The attempted synthesis of alternative religious consciousness with previous forms of communalism, and "back to the earth," pre-technology rituals, suggests that the movements that emerged from the 1960s were a revitalization rather than a revival.

New religions movements spring up to create a new social order. The syncretism of traditional values with new social conditions provides a reordered, integrated universe for the citizens. Elements of simplification, accommodation, and innovation combine (Klass 1995:147) to re-establish cultural order, cohesion, confidence, and personal fulfillment. Revitalization has been employed as paradigmatic for understanding the nature of religious conversion, as a macro cultural concept, with a micro application to the field of the psychology of religion (Rambo 1993:23-26). It also provides new impetus for the ongoing debate concerning Weber's concept of charismatic authority and routinization (Weber 1964:363-373, 1968:48-65, 180-181). Wallace applied the paradigm "in a truly catholic manner" (Martin 1999:1), "to movements as broad and complex as the rise of Christianity, Islam, Buddhism, or Wesleyan Methodism" (1978:10).

Researchers increasingly recognize the synthesis occurring in revitalization is deliberate, and the resultant cultural renascence seeks to provide a more satisfying culture (Martin 1999:3-6). Recent scholarship, "comfortable with ambiguity, and drawn to hybridize," recognizes the "creative ways native men and women appropriated, used, reinterpreted, modified, and reinvented Christianity, and the multiple ways they connected, and continue to connect Christianity to their own traditions" (1999:4). The significant root, *vitalization* reflects renewed vitality resulting from innovative systems, ritual processes, and adaptive worldviews. At first sight, revitalization movements may appear to be conservative, and backward looking, but critics of the New England awakening (1798-1808) later observed that, rather than being "out of step with the times," the "revitalization movement had created new mechanisms, and opened old mazeways for religious growth and organization" (McLoughlin 1978:111).

While religion is normally a conservative force in culture, revitalization provides an explanation for the consistent historic incidence of religion as a culturally transformational force (Ferraro 1998:298-203). The strength of the model for interpreting my data is that it provides explanations that are applicable in the context of premodern, modern, and postmodern epistemologies. Revitalization occurs when confidence in stabilizing institutions wanes, ethical and relational guidelines for personal, social, political and economic behavior become confusing, impractical, inconsistent, and destructive of social cohesion and personal fulfillment on a wide scale.

Critical to revitalization is the widespread experience of such high levels of stress and strain that conventional religion and politics cannot hold the society together. Cultural stress and distortion are the common thread, and the response is an intentional focus on the replacement of the existing dysfunctional matrix with a new gestalt. The loss of self-esteem, sustainable meanings, and social cohesion for an increasing number of individuals places them under intolerable stress. Disillusionment, disorganization, and disturbing social indicators such as substance abuse, violence, suicide, and familial disintegration result from the ineffectual responses of central institutions.

Joel Martin, in his excellent presentation to the American Anthropological Association (1999), reaffirmed the durability of the revitalization concept, while calling for a broader application and interpretation of the model. The universal acceptance of this model as "normative in the cultural debate amongst anthropologists" (Lett 1987:291), has established revitalization as paradigmatic in the investigation of cultural crisis, innovation, and rapid change. To Martin, the concept is so central to cultural research that *revitalization is to Anthropology what paradigm was to the history of science* (1999:2). Wallace clearly saw it as a paradigm model (Wallace 1980:485). For almost a half-century revitalization theory has maintained its credibility.

Though revitalization is an enlightening concept, it is problematic, partly because it may appear to reflect a desperate, conservative, backward looking and nativistic response to the impact of progress on primitive culture. Sometimes social historians have robbed *revitalization* of the rich, intended meaning of its creator (Martin 1999:1).

> The "re" in "revitalization" is problematic; it encouraged interpreters to think of these movements as somehow backward looking. "Revitalization" privileges plots that detail how beleaguered peoples sought to restore a lost wholeness and resurrect a cultural past, and/or to regress psychologically, to reverse history, and to return things to the way they were before colonialism. Revitalization, unfortunately, too easily blends with deprivation theory and notions of "nativism" to authorize chrono-political discounting of indigenous movements. Revitalization, in sum, encouraged interpreters to overlook the novelty, creativity, and modernity of these movements. (Martin 1999:2)

Martin suggests that *vitalization* is a necessary concept to rescue revitalization from being described in merely fundamentalist and reactionary terms. A recurring view of scholarship is that the attempts to revitalize the culture during the 1960s were fundamentalist, simplistic, and troglodytic, rather than innovative and recreative (Richardson, Stewart, and Simmonds 1979).[3]

The concept of "mazeways [as] mental images of self, society, and culture through which values operate in maintaining social order" (Marty 1976:157), provides a key to the process. When the real world no longer approximates to the mazeway interpretation received by acculturation, chronic stress develops. If the inconsistent mazeway is not adapted, the actual cultural realities changed, or a passive, satisfying alternative sub-culture found, cultural disintegration escalates. "When the social fabric deteriorates sufficiently, revitalization movements are likely to appear in an effort to bring about a more satisfying society. Some movements call for a return to the better days of the past; others seek to establish a completely new social order" (Ferraro 1998:299). Revitalization occurs when "there are too many elements present in the cultural 'solution,' when behavior is minimally predictable and approaches randomness" (Wallace 1966:214). It becomes necessary for cultural solidarity to "eliminate some behavioral elements and to codify the residue" (1966:214).

The innovative genius of revitalizers is seen in their capacity to reintroduce powerful dynamics of the past, or utopian visions for the future, while also accepting critical, contemporary realities. All revitalization movements begin with a counterculture rejection of a dysfunctional culture, believed to be creating widespread stress. But the genius is not found in simple rejection of the present, or nostalgic reclaiming of the past, but in a fusion and reconfiguration of widely different cultural elements.

Common Ground –
Native Americans and the 1960s Counterculture

I investigated revitalization theory as a tool for explanation of the counterculture revolution of the 1960s, and specifically, the Jesus Movement. I became convinced of significant parallels between the Handsome Lake story, the revitalization of the Odawa people in the Great Lakes region, and some movements of the 1960s and 1970s. The social consequences of cultural alienation led the Native American communities to alcoholism, the collapse of traditional family structures, inactivity, and widespread emotional depression.

By the end of the 1960s social disaffection The Euro-American tribal counterparts in the counterculture experienced widespread substance abuse, rejection of traditional family structures and mores, and often disengagement from either the workforce, or previously enrolled academic training. Apart from location and racial characteristics, it is hard to differentiate between a burnt-out, unemployed hippie smoking dope, and a dispirited Native American sitting amidst empty beer cans.

Severely conflicting worldviews existed concurrently in the cultural mazeways of Western culture. This contributed to cultural distortion and to the resultant innovations when stress levels reached a critical point. If there is an anthropological word that most describes the marginality of both Native American and 1960s counterculture dissidents, it is *liminality*. The term liminality (Victor Turner 1969:166-172) is used frequently to indicate a state of "in-betweenness," uncertainty, or suspension from supporting structures. Derived from the Latin root *limen*, "doorway, gateway or threshold" (Pflüg 1998), "chasm, or margin" (Lee 1995:153-154, 155), liminality is deliberately instigated in tribal groups, by extreme social and physical processes, as the initiating act of culturally bonding, ritual processes. When liminality is the unexpected and unscheduled result of social dysfunction, it may occur as a negative or culturally destructive liminality. In such cases citizens may fall into a chasm of disorientation, rather than entering a door of creative synthesis and renewal.

Marginality was inevitable for Native Americans, but the intensification of it by rejection of white support mechanisms is shown by Melissa Pflüg (1998) to have been part of a deliberate process. Thus, the door was opened for a reaggregation to a new identity and a sense of unifying *communitas* (see endnote 7) which was essential to the creation of solidarity. Since individual and social identity was a prime casualty of cultural dysfunction, a drastic measure was required to cleanse the people of destructive associations before a new identity could be forged from traditional myths and rituals, and new commitments to a purified lifestyle.

It may be argued that the hippies and the Jesus People experienced a self-imposed exile from mainstream culture, but it would be easy to overlook the extent of their symbolic protest through ritual clothing, social forms (communes and rock concerts), and ritual processes (public song and dance, meditation, experimental drug use). It is clear that intensified marginalization and liminality was savored by these groups as a psycho-spiritual path to cleansing from the establishment, entry to creative space, and the bonding communitas of a new identity.

Stress – The Mother of Invention

The experience of marginality and stress, particularly if experienced in subcultural solidarity, can be a motivational process initiating revitalization whereby participants react creatively to extreme psychological liminality. Intuitive, prophetic leaders birth unrehearsed ritual processes, so that that disorientation is employed as a motivational doorway to cultural renewal. Melissa Pflüg repeatedly notes that the disconcerting liminality created by colonialist disturbance of the Native American culture was the stimulus that gave rise to innovative rebellion and creative synthesis, leading to a new steady state (Pflüg 1998:59-60).[4] For the Odawa social marginalization through colonialism provided motivation and an "Open Door [that] embodied a way to empowerment" (1998:59). Millennia ago, the devastation of Jewish slavery lead to the rise of a Hebrew prophet (Moses), who instigated a journey to the "Promised Land," replete with a new identity, solidarity, and ritualized processes of cultural renewal.

The Odawa prophets led their people from individual marginality to tribal solidarity, collective identity and reintegrated community. The social crisis provoked by white, colonialist policies was a threat to identity, meaning and cultural survival. Revitalization was born as "the prophetic leaders reinterpreted and reapplied rituals and mythic themes to reintegrate communities and overcome threats of divisiveness" (1998:65). Liminality provoked the reconstitution of myth and ritual that was synthesized in the changed cultural reality of post-colonialism.

Different Enemy, Similar Strategies

For the counterculture, it was not colonialism but the technocratic redefinition of humanity that produced spiritual alienation and social disintegration (Roszak 1995:2-41). The speed and extent of cultural changes in techno-urban society had disoriented the hippie dissidents of the 1960s. Technology profoundly impacted family traditions through the invention of the oral contraceptive (1951), new youth independence via the automobile, and changing mores promoted by a liberalizing electronic media. The sociopolitical tensions of the Cold War era, the ecological crisis, the impact of multiculturalism on traditional religious institutions, and the divisiveness of Vietnam War conscription produced a profound identity crisis in the academy and the youth culture. This was of such dimensions that anthropologist Margaret Mead described the result as a generation gap, equivalent to a cultural Grand Canyon (Mead 1978:xvi-xx). Faced with a failing counterculture revolt, many youths sought identity, social solidarity, and a renewed meaning to their lives through the revitalizing efforts of the Jesus Movement. This movement sought to redefine youth by a reintegration to a new identity and social order, through the beliefs, rituals, and communal associations of a counterculture Christianity.

Pflüg's thorough description of the difference between the "traditionalists" and the conformists in Odawa revitalization sheds much light on the discussion regarding fundamentalism and the Jesus movement groups (1998:15-36). Both the counterculture and the Odawa the loss of a meaning to make sense of life had undermined personal and group identity. Both groups recognized the alienation of materialistic dependency and sought through ritual and lifestyle to mount resistance to the market forces of the dominant culture. They intuitively sought to synthesize a ritual processes whereby meaning and identity could be re-established in a confusing, pluralistic world. A rite of passage through a socio-religious revolt was sought by both.

Jesus Freaks, like the adaptive Odawa, were not merely reactionary but creative in their attempt to synthesize ancient tradition and new cultural realities. Thus they were radical conservatives, seeking to preserve an identity under siege by technology, while looking forward to a revolutionary new order and reconstituted identity. They revived ancient symbols and myths of first century Christianity in synchronism with the protesting pop-culture of their times. The peace symbol – two fingers raised in v-form – was replaced by the "one-way" raised forefinger. The ancient catacomb symbol of the fish wedded solidarity in faith to a sense of social rejection and resistance to materialism. The Jesus pop concert and Christian arts festivals revived the spirit of the traditional camp meetings of the nineteenth century Awakening (McLoughlin 1978:208). During past popular religious renewals, open air or camp meetings were marked by indigenous hymns and intuitive, motivating oratory; time was of little import as spiritual fervor overwhelmed all else. Mass emotion and locally populist new forms of religious expression gave a sense of a "new thing" while affirming the roots of religious tradition and the birth of the faith. Revised concepts, new goals, and new means were created from a synthesis of primitive Christian concepts, counterculture forms and communal means. While hippies surrounded the Pentagon in a hand holding ritual of pagan exorcism, the Jesus Freaks in Australia surrounded the parliament in a hand holding prayer vigil.

Initially Jesus people itinerancy, typified by Street Level, Spirit of Elijah, Highway Missionary Society, Shiloh, JPUSA, TLC, and Arthur Blessitt (synchronous with hippie mobility), communal living (House of the New World, JPUSA, Street Level, Calvary Chapel) and counterculture rebellion (CWLF, House of the New World, and TLC) were socially threatening. Even the Pentecostals felt the Jesus Freaks were out of control. Following the respectable 1950s, their affective, demonstrative, religious fervor in the late 1960s was viewed as unhealthy. But, the unbridled ecstasy and prophetic energy of the Jesus Movement revived the historic patterns of social and emotional forms from previous Evangelical Awakenings, lead by marginalized, itinerant preachers in camp meetings. Lay leadership, popular music forms and charismatic prophets had been the mark of previous revitalizations.

In the Native American and counterculture movements the desire for peaceful retreat from culturally destructive institutions was sometimes mixed with establishment resistance resulting in violence. The social violence enacted against the dominant culture by disaffected Native Americans cannot be attributed simplistically to the effect of alcohol or innately violent tendencies. It also must be seen in the context of violations suffered at the hands of the dominant culture. So, it was with the counterculture.

The violence of the Chicago police at the Democratic Convention in 1968, law enforcement's violent responses at Kent State in 1970, and on other campuses, contributed to the increase in public hostility.[5] The history of America's institutionalized violence from the frontier to Wounded Knee, to segregation, slavery, black lynching, and massacre in Mai Lai, set the stage for violent reactions of the Weathermen and the Black Panthers. The Jesus Movement suffered verbal hostility, notably from fundamentalists, Pentecostals (Wilkerson 1971:41-69), and cult deprogrammers, but it was remarkably free of physical opposition. In response, even the more radical elements of the Jesus People embraced symbols and rituals that highlighted the centrality of the pacifist tradition of historic movements such as Anabaptists, which highlighted Jesus as the Prince of Peace.

Depressed isolation, an analgesic lifestyle (substance abuse), and counter violence against the system could deliver no satisfying, stable, alternative society to the dying Native American tribes. Nor could that recipe provide triumph for the disillusioned hippie counterculture. The intuitive Seneca prophet, Handsome Lake, opened the door to a third way for his followers (Wallace 1966:31). This was the emergence of neither total capitulation, nor unwinable resistance to the dominant culture. Instead, the prophet, armed with the compelling magnetism of charisma, and the declaration of a divine revelation and vision, led his people to a productive New Way. It was something *old* and something *new*, creating a new social stability out of the dreams of the past and visions for the future.

Pervasive social disorganization, disillusionment, and disorientation experienced by a failed hippie counterculture opened the door of opportunity to Arthur Blessitt, Lonnie Frisbee, Jim Palosaari, Linda Meisner, John Higgins, Jack Sparks, John Hirt, and a host of other Jesus Movement incendiary prophets of both doom and hope.

Similar to the marginization of Native Americans from mainstream values and way of life, the sense of alienation from the dominant culture was vigorously expressed by the counterculture of the 1960s. Jesus People shared a rejection of the existing order but their proclamation of an alternative, holistic Third Way was more than a revivalist lifeboat. It was not simply an *escape from* but a *rebirth to* the Kingdom of God.

That the dominant values emphasis and institutional supports were viewed by the Christian and secular counterculture as dysfunctional, alien to social cohesion and threatening to the survival of human happiness is evident in the titles and contents of many books during the 1960s and 1970s. Roszak (1972c) described the end result of materialism, scientific reductionism, desacralization of nature, and atomized individualism as a desert wasteland. Drawing on the bleak prophesies of the Revelation of St. John and the art of William Blake, he asserted that "we have not stumbled into the arms of Gog and Magog; we have *progressed* there" (1972c:xx). Typical of revitalizing prophets, he proclaimed, "It is the energy of religious renewal that will generate the next politics, and perhaps the final radicalism of our society" (1972c:cover jacket). The popularity of the apocalyptic *The Late Great Planet Earth* (Lindsay 1970) revealed a parallel sense of impending doom amongst the Jesus People.

It is worth noting that at a global level, the current stress and disorientation resulting from the September 11 terrorist act against the United States and the collapse of the centrality of the nation states has promoted the role of apocalyptic Islamic and Christian worldviews in corporate identity. Philip Jenkins (2002) claims "The twenty-first century will be regarded by future historians as a century in which religion replaced ideology as the prime animating and destructive force in human affairs" (2002:55). It appears that the role of prophetic and apocalyptic religion as the initiator of rapid change and innovation is unlikely to disappear in the face of globalization.

The Native Americans believed the collapse of traditional values, community and unifying tradition had occurred at the behest of colonialism (Pflüg 1998). The counterculture believed scientific materialism had torn the fabric of human brotherhood and sisterhood, destroyed the sacred connection with nature, and devastated the tribal unity of humanity. Some hippie leaders recognized distinct parallels between the Native American story of the destruction of their cohesive culture at the hands of the United States political structures and their own counterculture struggle (Gaskin 1981:195-199). Both Native American and counterculture dissenters lamented the devastation of personal and social identity as the work of a failed cultural elite.

Rock group *Kansas* described the ontological crisis in a song declaring "*All we are is dust in the wind.*" *Supertramp's Logical Song* topped the charts with the plaintive cry, "Please tell me who I am." Both Native Americans and counterculture tribes believed the fragmentation of communal values was a primary source of personal anomie. Thus for Christian and secularist alike, for both Native Americans and hippies and even some mainline congregations, a return to communal living became an article of faith and survival (Mellis 1976). The need to defy the mainstream model of the nuclear family was deeply felt as a principle of revitalization, and vigorously preached by most of the Jesus Movement prophets with whom the author was familiar, particularly in the Australian movement.

The research data of Chapters 3-6, shows that communalism was a dominant social phenomenon in the Jesus Movement, specifically as a stress relieving, radical departure from the perceived disintegration of human solidarity due to cultural collapse. Communalism, though not essential to revitalization, is often symptomatic of it. The loss of personal and corporate identity may drive the sufferers towards tribalism, religious *communitas* through communalism in an attempt to create a socially less stressed support system. Communalism is also a symbolic condemnation of the individualism perceived to have caused painful anomie.

Dave and Nita Jackson (1974) released *Living Together in a World Falling Apart*, linking the hope of revitalization to the adoption of communal living. Sparks (1974a) reflected the CWLF commitment to this social alternative, as did Pulkingham (1972) in the Church of the Redeemer. The most influential Jesus Movement groups invariably experimented with communal models. Shiloh (Peterson 1990a, 1990b, 1996a, 1996b); Street Level (Di Sabatino 1994); JPUSA (Bozeman 1990); CWLF (Heinz 1976a) maintained communes as a resistance movement to the destructive elements of individualism, and as a model for revitalizing their corporate life. In North America (Borowski 1984; Hiley Ward 1972); Britain (Pete Ward 1996); Australia (Hirt 1998) communal departures from the suburban nuclear family were embraced in the hope of revitalizing a fragmented and stressed culture (Hillendahl 1996:39-41; Janzen 1996).

Revitalization movements seek to simplify and focus the culture in the midst of bewildering complexity. Back to basics, particularly traditional values and ritual processes became the theme for both Native American and counterculture revitalization. Simple lifestyle movements abounded in the 1960s cultural revolution. Counterculture movements spoke often of back to the earth and grass roots principles (Fike 1998; Gaskin 1981, 1999). Many counterculture Christians embraced the simple lifestyle/back to nature model, adding the stewardship of God's earth, and the redirection of its resources to renewal of the planet and its inhabitants to their rationale for their commitment (Diana Christian 1996:20-23).

The typical pattern of the prophet receiving a divine revelation and vision which attracts a following of disaffected citizens is also a distinct parallel. This applies whether the prophet was the Native American's Handsome Lake (Wallace 1966:31-33, 211-213); Tecumseh (Pflüg 1998:59-61); and Tenskwatawa (Pflüg 1998:59-61); or the Jesus People's Lonnie Frisbee, Jim Palosaari, or Arthur Blessitt. The complicated process of reviving, reshaping, and reinventing moral codes, ritual processes, and symbols to enforce them, is apparent in the Jesus Movement, and the native revitalization of the Iroquois. It is no mere coincidence that the Jesus Movement groups embraced tribal ways, embracing itinerant or nomadic patterns of life, invoking tribal images and dreams, and reviving ancient Christian, ritual processes. At times they took biblical names to create a tribal sense of identity (Shiloh, Jacob's Ladder, House of Elijah, Spirit of Elijah) for the group, or the communal arrangement in which they lived (Peterson 1999a:8).

Given the extent, speed, and counterculture nature of the initial forms of the Jesus Movement as a part of the broader cultural revolution, the revitalization paradigm is most suited as a key to understanding. Wallace's theory is congruent with the pattern of the Movement's sociohistoric development. The Jesus Freaks, like those of the broader counterculture, were seeking social transformation, rather than mere reform of the existing order. Though drawing on biblical assumptions, rather than the monastic fusion of Western and Eastern thought of the counterculture, the Jesus People found common cause with their secular counterparts, in an attempt to overthrow a defective, materialistic worldview, which was wanting in moral meaning and ontological strength.[6]

The Rocky Road to Revitalization

Wallace groups several movements – nativistic, messianic, revivalist, millenarian, utopian, and revolutionary and charismatic movements with separatist churches and cargo cults – as revitalizations (Wallace 1966:163-165). Several of these forms were seen in the Jesus Movement. "Moses" Berg and Linda Meisner evidenced messianic convictions; definite millenarian tendencies were common in movements such as Calvary Chapel. New York's Forever Family was a separatist, cult church that even separated along generational lines, claiming people over 30 were carnal and spiritually dangerous (Traill 1978). Some groups were decidedly Utopian, especially those of the more Left Wing, activist, radical discipleship movement in Australia.

The least common form was the nativistic movement, in keeping with Wallace's proposal that in revitalizations "initial doctrinal formulations emphasize love, co-operation, understanding." Only as opposition stiffens do they expel invaders and become more nativistic (1956b:278). As Handsome Lake had sought accommodation of cultures rather than expulsion, in the intuitive understanding of survival needs, so the Jesus People increasingly built bridges with the traditional churches, preferring to accept and integrate the gifts and resources of "straight" sympathizers, whether they joined, or assisted from the margins.

In their variant forms of revitalization (Wallace 1956b:275-276), some identified with revival of the ancient traditions – Calvary Chapel promoted the ancient *communitas*[7] in the Spirit from Acts Chapter 2. The importation of foreign, cultural elements, such as Marxism and utopianism was common among some radical Jesus Movement groups. Utopian promise of a new day was particularly evident amongst the communities of the House of the New World genre. Variations were the consequence of both sociocultural and psychological factors (Wallace 1956b:275; 1966:34-35), as I have sought to underscore in the description of the Australian groups. They shared common ground as "major cultural-system innovations are characterized by a uniform process" (1956b:264). In response to cultural developments during the 1950s and 1960s there was a uniform, "processual order," from "steady state" to "serious cultural distortion." Historical periodization provides evidence of the necessary precursors to revitalization.

As proposed by Wallace, religious and secular means are both adopted by such movements. The political and organizational, "secular" elements tend to emerge as necessitated by organizational demands for routinization (1956b: 277-278). This shift, from vision to political engagement with institutions, resources, and media occurred in every Jesus Movement group investigated. All groups experienced the initial three stages of conception, communication, and organization, and even entered the fourth phase of adaptation as required by Wallace to rate as revitalization movements (1956b:278-279), but several failed to survive the late routinization stage.

At this point it is necessary to see if the socially destructive conditions necessary to trigger revitalization existed at the time of the appearance of the Jesus Movement. Whether the process and order of events is consistent with the model of revitalization must also be established. The process moves from steady state, to increasing stress, leading to cultural distortion. This provokes revitalization attempts to reduce the stress levels, ultimately leading to a resolution in a new steady state. Because the Jesus Movement was a revitalization second wave in response to a highly stressed, faltering counterculture, periodization is made more difficult than is already the case in an inevitably arbitrary choice of historic timing. I will therefore seek to indicate the time lag between the Christian and the general counterculture.

1. Steady State 1945–1955

Wallace asserts that the process occurs only after the departure of a culture from a normal, steady state in which citizens find satisfactory values and social cohesion in the existing cultural matrix. Australian culture ran parallel to the United States in its experience of public discontent, occurrence of a counterculture, and some revitalization, but I shall use the more globally known story of the United States to make my paradigmatic point.

Initially, a culture is able to cope with the minority of dissatisfied citizens, "who dwell on the fringes of society. The level of stress and social deviance is manageable through corrective institutions and social restraint" (Wallace 1966:158). Following World War II, celebration, prosperity, and the reaffirmation of traditional values marked the period of reconstruction. America, spared the devastation served on European cities, experienced the period of the "happy days." The experience of widespread prosperity amongst the middle class, the growth of comfortable suburban housing, the proliferation of modern conveniences, and the prosperity of Protestant churches gave the impression of a great leap forward. Church attendance was at an all time high.

2. Increased Individual Stress 1956–1962

Sometimes a culture begins to lose its way, passing through a period when "increasingly large numbers of individuals are placed under what is to them intolerable stress, by the failure of the system to accommodate their needs" (Wallace 1966:159). War, social disintegration, worldview shifts, and many other factors may contribute to a loss of cultural equilibrium. "Anomie and disillusionment become widespread as the culture is perceived to be disorganized; crime, illness, and individualistic asocial responses increase sharply in frequency" (1966:159). The following sketch of 1950s history will illustrate the arbitrary nature of the periodization.

That the underlying stress reached a new level of significance in 1956 is impossible to prove, but I have chosen 1956 as a significant year of developing race tension, which was to engulf the nation in the following decade. In the period between the 1954 "Brown vs. Brown" Supreme Court decision to desegregate, Rosa Parks' much publicized 1955 initiation of the Montgomery bus boycott, and the Supreme Court's decision to desegregate public transport, the dominant white culture must have wondered where it would end.

Despite the increasing prosperity, the growth of the middle class, multiplied suburban, home ownership and the wonders of new technology, all was not well at several levels of the culture by the mid-1950s. Beneath the apparent unity, patriotism, prosperity, and comforting faith, currents of developing discontent and cultural stress were evident. The institutions, traditional belief in manifest destiny (McLoughlin 1978:105-106), and the ability of technology to provide a New World of unprecedented pleasure and security strengthened the culture to cope with a growing minority of intellectual and social dissidents. The definition of "increased individual stress" is highly subjective, and the choice of social indicators and significant events is debatable.

Few social historians have investigated the 1950s and 1960s with such passion and awareness of both "high" and "popular" culture as Robert Ellwood (1994, 1997, and 2000). The Korean War began in 1950 (Latourette 1964:724). The Algar Hiss spy trial ended, and the revelation of charges against atomic scientist Klaus Fuchs and the Rosenberg accomplices resulted in their execution. The enemy was not abroad but at home. Robert Ellwood's choice of 1950 as the "crossroads of American religious life" is compelling (Ellwood 2000). He concludes the 1950s were a river "flowing towards a valley of decision" (Ellwood 1997:227) – "quiet and confident" but "troubled" (1997:227-236).

The beginning of the new decade saw the peaking of the flood of GI Bill college graduates, a gestating force for later cultural change (Ellwood 2000:15-17). Brown vs. Board of Education was yet four years away, but young Martin Luther King was being deeply stirred in a seminary lecture by Mordecai Johnson extolling the nonviolent resistance of India's Gandhi. Malcolm X had converted to the Black Muslims. Intellectually the foundations for broader dissent were being laid. The beatniks were gathering in 1950, as Alan Watts (1950) released *The Supreme Identity*, serving early notice of the coming fusion of Christian mysticism, Taoism and Zen from the 1960s dissent to the present (Ellwood 1987, 2000; Wuthnow 1976, 1978). L. Ron Hubbard's (1950) Church of Scientology text, *Dianetics* joined the 1950 *New York Times* best seller list, alongside Immanuel Velikovsky's (1950) *Worlds in Collision*.

It was a year marked by a gathering cultural conflict between establishment Protestantism and increasingly influential and outspoken Catholicism that would culminate in the 1960 presidential election of J. F. Kennedy. Pope Pius XXIII declared "1950 as the decisive year for communists, Jews, dissidents, schismatics, pagans, sinners, and atheists to come back to forgiveness and reconciliation" (Ellwood 2000:145). As prosperity increased, government assisted education and churches flourished, but racial, religious and social dissent was on the rise.

Awareness of inappropriate and unsustainable cultural mores in sexual, religious and racial contexts emerged in the early 1950s. Cultural dysfunction began to proliferate, due to both the inadequacy of worldview and the alienation of people from society's institutions. A critical mass of disenchanted individuals was building, as modern media revealed the dark realities of racial oppression in "the land of the free."

The ugly conflict of the McCarthy investigations pointed the finger of accusation at the sacred institutions of church and state, suggesting that communists abounded in state departments, historic denominations, and in the entertainment industry. Anti-Communist publications highlighted the contrast between establishment liberal Protestantism with its penchant for peace activism, and the growing Catholic and fundamentalist identification with American, conservative patriotism.

The level of gathering fear is indicated by the fact that "one in ten Americans said they knew somebody who acted suspiciously enough to make them think he might be a communist" (Ellwood 1997:140). The stalemate and ultimate compromise-defeat of allied troops against the North Korean invader promoted the domino theory of the spread of "yellow communism" throughout Asia. Revelations of institutional sins – particularly the injustices of Southern law enforcement and courts, the arms race, and Government, anti-democratic meddling in Guatemala on behalf of the American Fruit Company – was undermining public confidence in the integrity of the system (Ellwood 1997:103-138). The government and conservatives nearby Guatemala had became a purported beachhead for communist destruction of the American way of life but interference with her internal politics was anti-democratic hypocrisy to the growing ranks of socialist sympathizers (1997:128-130).

The first post-war atomic bomb tests were on Bikini Atoll in 1946. The first hydrogen bomb had been tested at Einewetok, November 1, 1952. But, the first Soviet hydrogen-bomb test in August 1953, followed by a United States test on Bikini Atoll, five times more destructive than the 1952 device, provoked growing fear of an arms race with incalculable possibilities for global destruction. Thus emerged such cultural products as the private bomb shelter, as well as a plethora of books and movies projecting the end of the world or the appearance of dangerous genetic mutations. Accounts of the indigenous people of Bikini suffering radiation burns fired the imagination of fearful citizens. Talk of the cobalt and nitrogen bomb possibilities rendered trust in the proliferation of bomb shelters virtually obsolete. By the end of the 1950s, novels and movies created an apocalyptic scenario for the planet. I personally remember the sense of helplessness in the face of inevitable doom, which accompanied the reading of Neville Shute's 1957 novel *On the Beach*. The film version (1959) was particularly poignant for Australian dissenters as they read of the last survivors of a global atomic holocaust awaiting death on a Sydney beach. The atomic age potentially challenged conventional moral values and even humanities' survival (Ellwood 1997:125-128).

If science had undermined or discredited the basis for faith in the "sacred text" as the exclusive and divinely inspired "truth," the nuclear age was challenging faith in a scientific gospel. Many of my generation were fixated in horror by the now famous photograph of the Bikini Atoll test, and our Jesus Papers carried a reflection on this madness as "reverse creation" (Figure 7.1). World War III would not take very long it seemed, but that was cold comfort.

Revelations of pesticide damage to the environment provoked anger and growing fear of an ecological "silent spring" (Carson 1962). Neo-orthodoxy and existentialism challenged conventional religious worldviews of both conservatives and liberals. The "leap of faith" undermined biblical fundamentalists and "worldly" liberals. The secular city challenged the assumed relevance of the historic religious establishment in all of its forms. The popularization of psychology accelerated the shift from dogmatic, cognitive religion to affective faith, in search of an identity free of institutionalism.

Television and an investigative press revealed the ugliness of institutional racism, judicial criminality, and military brutality. Within a decade the camera had become the instrument of the Cultural Revolution.

Internally all was not well. Rising crime rate, particularly amongst rebel youth, by whom traditional family authority was being questioned, had by 1954 caused a growing sense of middle class powerlessness and hopelessness (Ellwood 1997:144). In 1956 white-collar jobs replaced blue-collar jobs as the dominant production mode of employment. Class conflict increasingly divided left and right in academy and workplace. Weary alienation from institutions and the fear of a depersonalizing mass society were evident in William H.Whyte, Jr.'s *The Organization Man* (1956), and David Riesman's *The Lonely Crowd* (1997:153-157).

3. Serious Cultural Distortion 1963-1970

The third phase, according to Wallace, is a period of serious cultural distortion (1956b:266-267), when many are lost in a maze of dissonance between individual expectations and the culture's contrary performance. The search for a new cognitive map, and the abandonment of hope in the "system," creates apathy, hostility, and psychosocial disorder on a wide scale. Previously sustaining familial traditions break down, and disregard for officialdom, patriotism and institutions provokes denigration of the system. A critical mass of defectors becomes open to charismatic figures that offer a path to a satisfying new culture.

From the mid 1950s "all hell broke loose" in American culture. Beginning with the 1954, May 17, Supreme Court outlawing of school segregation in Brown vs. Board of Education, an irreversible process of Cultural Revolution began. In 1955 Rosa Parks was arrested for refusing to give up her seat on a bus to a white man in Montgomery, Alabama. November 13, 1956 the Supreme Court banned segregated seating on Montgomery buses. August 29, 1957 Congress passed the first Civil Rights Act since reconstruction. A turbulent 1960s decade appeared inevitable.

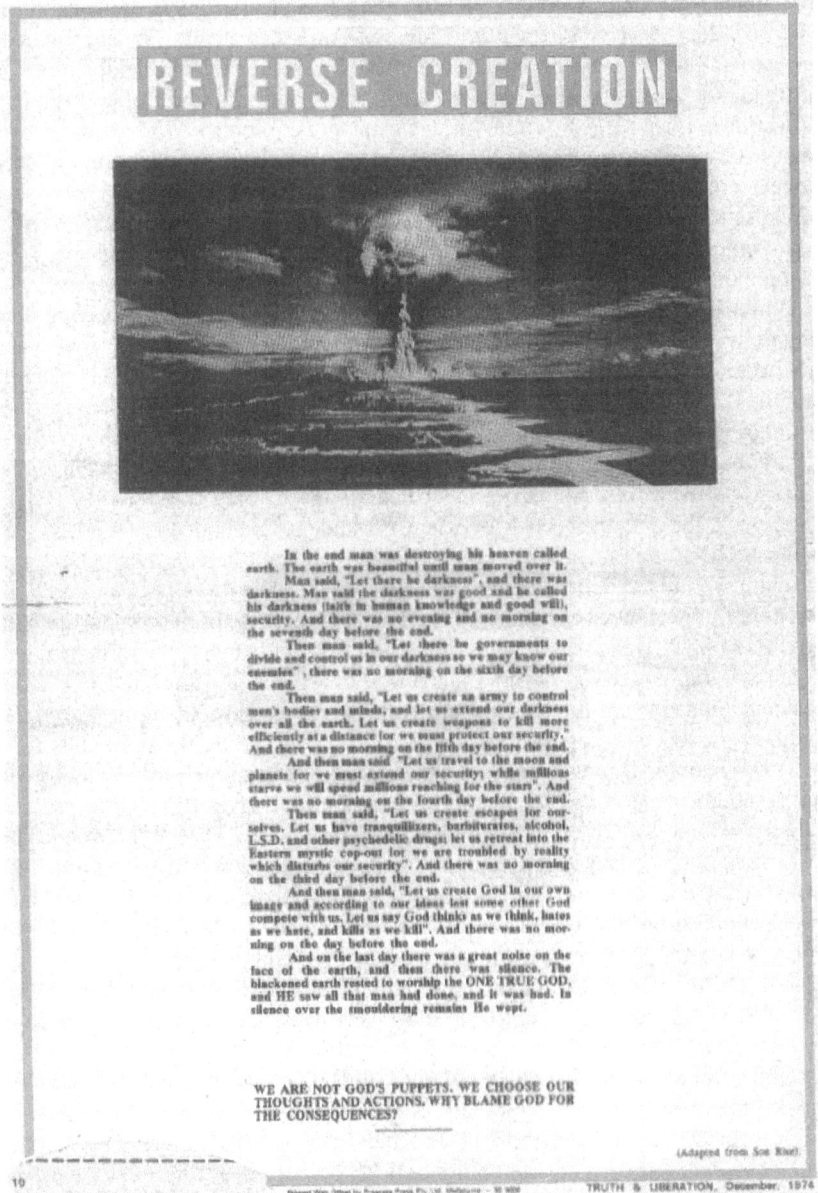

Figure 7.1 Bikini Atoll Atomic Test – Reverse Creation
(*Truth and Liberation* 1974)

With the election of John F. Kennedy as President in 1960 both euphoric hope and deep despair gripped and divided American hearts. When Kennedy was assassinated in 1963 the nation mourned. In 1963 peaceful demonstrators in Birmingham, Alabama were met by angry white citizens and police brutality. Dr. Martin Luther King Jr. wrote his *Letter from Birmingham Jail* during subsequent incarceration. Images of the attack dogs terrorizing women and children elicited international sympathy and support for the civil rights movement. For me, those images eventually buried social conservatism. Medgar Evers, NAACP field secretary was murdered June 12, 1964, at the doorstep of his Jackson, Mississippi home.

On August 28, 250,000 Americans gathered at the Lincoln Memorial to hear King deliver his immortal *I Have a Dream* oration. On September 15, four black girls were brutally murdered when a bomb exploded in 16th Street Baptist Church, Birmingham, Alabama. This shook even moderate white segregationists, and escalated the decline of white supremacy. Freedom's Summer voter registration marches raised the hopes of desegregationists but three civil rights workers involved were murdered (McAdam 1988). During the 1964–1965 academic year, the Free Speech Movement of student rebels at the University of California, Berkeley Campus challenged their academic institutions. There was a growing optimistic belief that the old order would collapse.

The turmoil of the second half of the 1960s was of significant proportions. In 1965 Malcolm X was assassinated; the Selma to Montgomery march began, and white civil rights activist Viola Liuzzo was murdered by the Ku Klux Klan. President Johnson sent the first ground combat troops to Vietnam on March 26. Congress passed the Voting Rights Act of 1965. In Watts, Los Angeles riots killed 189 people. This was the first wave of a devastating period of widespread civil disobedience and violence across the nation, in a civil disturbance producing riots in over 100 cities through to July 1968. In 1967 Detroit experienced a week of race riots. Eldridge Cleaver (1967) released *Soul on Ice,* his diatribe against white society. The 1967 Six Day War created a groundswell of eschatological expectation that Christ's return was imminent, as Jerusalem was united under Jewish rule for the first time since the birth of Christianity.

In 1968, the dizzy fantasy of the "Summer of Love," first human "Be-In," held in San Francisco's Golden Gate Park, was overshadowed by the Vietcong Tet Offensive catching the Nixon Administration by surprise. Police officers shot indiscriminately into a crowd of black students at South Carolina State College, killing three, and the Democratic National Convention erupted in violence and protest. On April 3, Martin Luther King Jr. gave his poignant *I've been to the Mountaintop* speech in Memphis, only to be shot dead the next day. This sparked the worst single day of 1960s rioting during the following week, in 125 major cities, as deep despair struck those committed to racial justice. President Johnson signed The Fair Housing Act – The Civil Rights Act of 1968, but devastation was to follow with the assassination of Robert F. Kennedy.

Student revolution occurred in the University of Paris in 1968, and spread throughout France, further provoking the dissent of students in America. Less significant, but symptomatic of the cultural fracturing, feminists boycotted the

Miss America Pageant in Atlantic City, lugging "freedom trash cans," in which they dumped "symbols of female enslavement," high heeled shoes, kitchen detergent, girdles, and bras. Attempting to re-ignite the dying embers of the hippie dream, 400,000 gathered for the Woodstock Festival, Bethel, New York in 1969, but when bad drugs and violence marred the Altamonte follow-up concert in 1970, Lennon lamented that the dream had ended.

The new decade saw the continuation of cultural distortion, as the revelation that President Nixon had lied concerning the American bombing of Cambodia sparked off protests across American universities. Police fired into a woman's dorm at Jackson State University, Mississippi, killing two black students and wounding 30. Four students were killed when National guardsmen opened fire on protesting students at Kent State University, Ohio. In Denver, Colorado segregationists dynamited one third of the school buses. The level of disaffection with the existing culture led many to avoid the stress by dropping out of society. Increased risk-taking behaviors, violence, and conflicts between various groups in the society – parents and children, citizens and law enforcement, students and faculty – was symptomatic of severe cultural fragmentation. In 1968, Abbie Hoffman, a hippie leader who earned a five-year prison term for conspiracy against the state, released *Revolution for the Hell of It.*

The arts – performing, literary, and visual – were the nerve ends of the soul of the body politic. It is difficult for those who did not participate in that era to realize the cultural dynamic of a song such as Dylan's "The Times, They are a Changin," or the moral rage provoked in millions of youth worldwide by Dylan's "Masters of War." After the Kent State shootings, Crosby, Stills, Nash, and Young penned an angry song of protest, "Tin Soldiers and Nixon Coming, We're Finally on Our Own," evoking passionate responses from youth, which talked seriously of a generational war. Some felt that the older generation and the political structures were so recalcitrant that no revolutionary changes to the culture could occur. They would kill their own unarmed children rather than admit to shame or countenance change.

"By the late 1960s, the love and peace generation had been transformed into the drug and violence generation" (Stuessy 1990:169). What had begun as a communal movement was in disarray by the end of the 1960s. The generation that had hoped to "change the world, rearrange the world" now turned inward to find personal spiritual fulfillment and enlightenment.

Simon and Garfunkle's release, "The Sounds of Silence," reflected the shift from drugs to spiritual meditation and the influence of Eastern Monism on the musical scene (Stuessy1990:197-198). Swami Prabhupada formed the International Society for Krishna Consciousness. In 1966 John Lennon announced the Beatles were more popular than Jesus. In reaction angry preachers promoted monster bon fires, burning *Beatles* discs across America. John Lennon constructed lyrics based on Timothy Leary's version of the *Tibetan Book of the Dead* (1964). George Harrison, prior to recording the *Sergeant Pepper* album, spent six weeks with Indian Ravi Shankar learning Sitar, and spirituality.

Swami Prabhupada launched a major publicity campaign targeting disillusioned drug experimenters, offering drug free "highs" through meditation and higher consciousness. Two months after the release of *Sergeant Pepper*, *The Beatles* linked up with Maharishi Mahesh Yogi, the founder of The Spiritual Regeneration Movement. Harrison visited Haight-Ashbury, and shocked by what he saw of lost and addicted kids on the streets, publicly abandoned his belief in psychedelic drugs and called for a meditation alternative.

In 1967, Swami Prabhupada developed a vision for rock music as a popularizer of Krishna Consciousness. January 27, he appeared on stage with the *Grateful Dead, Big Brother and the Holding Company, and Jefferson Airplane*, for a Mantra Rock Dance to raise finance for a local temple. In 1968, *The Beatles* announced they were giving up drugs to find a better way in transcendence and spirituality, through the meditation practices of the Maharishi. They traveled to Rishikesh, India to study Hinduism and meditation. Over some months, one by one they returned disillusioned (Stuessy 1990:130,138). Pete Townsend of *The Who* stated "The only escape from World problems is in meditation." From 1969 onward, Meher Baba, India Guru claiming Deity, informed the work of Townsend. Harrison publicly declared his continuing commitment to Krishna Consciousness calling a concert audience to join in a Krishna mantra.

The breakdown, suicide, and relational chaos of the rock and folk icons during this period contributed to youth disillusionment, ultimately encouraging thousands to embrace Jesus as the only way. Roger "Syd" Barrett left *Pink Floyd* mentally vegetated by substance abuse (Stuessy 1990:301). Brian Jones of the *Rolling Stones* died in a substance abuse context (1990:163). Marianne Faithful attempted suicide (1990:163). In 1970 Cass Elliot of *The Mammas and the Papas* died and John and Michelle Phillips divorced (1990:197). Two of the big three rock 'n' roll rebel icons, Janis Joplin, and Jim Hendricks died and the third, Jim Morrison, died the following year. All were aged 27. Jim Hendricks died of an overdose, possibly as an act of suicide (1990:253). His final song, written on the eve of his death, was laced with references to Jesus and spiritual searching. Janis Joplin died of a heroin overdose (1990:246). The following year Jim Morrison, the genius of *The Doors*, died officially of a heart attack induced by a long period of substance abuse (1990:251). "In 1968 the FBI reported 61,843 state marijuana arrests, a 98% increase over 1966" (Obst 1977:222). By 1971 it was estimated that five million Americans had experimented with psychedelic drugs. The carnage continued well beyond the 1960s. In 1978 Keith Moon of *The Who* died obviously from extended self abuse and drug abuse (Steussy 1990:282).

In the 1960s the rock "live in" concert became a religious institution and ritual process in the attempted revitalization of culture. In 1969 on the Isle of Wight 200,000 met to hear Bob Dylan and 500,000 met in upstate New York for the Woodstock Festival (Jasper 1975:68). Yoko and John Lennon released the single album "Give Peace a Chance" (Stuessy 1990:138), Timothy Leary published *The Politics of Ecstasy* (1968), and Paul McCartney hinted at the imminent breakup of *The Beatles*. John Lennon responded angrily in public, but it was apparent that the Beatles were each going their separate ways. The group collapsed. *The Beatles* released "All You Need is Love." It had been more than just a worldwide popular song. It was a desperate heart cry of a generation, which was beginning to unravel through drugs and promiscuity. It is significant that for many I have interviewed, *The Beatles* were a fundamental icon of revolutionary hope. Some have shared that the breakup of *The Beatles* was to them a mortal wound to the soul that led to Christian conversion (Carothers 1999:3-6). Lennon released "My Sweet Lord," with its haunting religious pluralism, embracing both Christian and Hindu (Krishna) worship terms as *Crosby, Stills, Nash, and Young* split up (Stuessy 1990:138-340).

Religiously, we experienced "liturgical and artistic experimentation," the "new morality in *The Secular City*" (Cox 1965), and "theologians who wanted to be *Honest to God*, but ended with *The Death of God*" (Marty1976:93). "Evangelicalism and Fundamentalism tied themselves to the discredited, conservative, Republican cause in the Barry Goldwater campaign of 1964, and seemed to have been compromised thereby" (1976:89). Fundamentalism and evangelicalism expanded their influence while mainline denominations lost ground though, despite attempts to popularize the faith for the secular city (Handy 1984:185; James Hunter 1983:41-101; Stark and Glock 1968:204-224; Wuthnow 1998:28-94). Exotic and esoteric spirituality increasingly captured the minds of youth (Johnson 1971; Wuthnow 1976, 1978, 1998:52-84).

Mainstream, traditional faiths, long the staple of American society, were under challenge from within and without. A new wave of religious deregulation was appearing:

> The characteristic book-titles about Protestantism in this period were: The Gathering Storm in the Churches; To Comfort and to Challenge: A Dilemma of the Contemporary Church; The Prophetic Clergy; The Jesus Revolution; The Evangelical Renaissance; and, best known, the already mentioned Why Conservative Churches Are Growing. The prophetic clergy had been dispersed or were in disarray; the Jesus revolution led to Evangelical prosperity. Harold E. Quinley, as he watched the prophetic clergy dwindle, saw chiefly "the continuing lay backlash," "a spiritual revival," "liberal losses," and "retrenchment and decentralization." (Marty 1976:92-93)

Precious symbols of the culture were desecrated. The flag was burned. The traditional cross was replaced by a broken "crow's foot" peace sign, rumored to be satanic. The victory V sign of World War II became the peace sign of the anti-war draft dodger. Tidiness, neatness, self-control and the Protestant commitment to self-control and industry, gave way to long hair, rock music, public nudity in the much acclaimed "Hair" production, counterculture clothing, and intentional unemployment (Illich 1977).[8] Pagan and Eastern chants accompanied the surrounding of the Pentagon by hippies for whom the exorcism of the military center was thought necessary. Respected institutions were the object of suspicion, derision, and even violence. The military, the CIA, the FBI, and the police were maligned for racism, the napalming of women and children in Vietnam and complicity in foreign dictatorships. University administrators, professors, governors, mayors, parents, church leaders, were subject to youth derision.

Even the Presidency, the apex of American stability, was vilified. The reactionary forces on the other side were assassinating student protestors in the interests of maintaining the system. Abandoning traditional sanctions, investigative journalism fanned the flames of popular disaffection with images of war and protest. Severe ontological distortion occurred as the nation briefly lost its sense of "manifest destiny." The ill-fated Vietnam engagement stripped the nation of its honor at home and abroad, as Americans cursed their own country in public.

Science hailed conquests in a space race, beginning with Russia's Sputnik in 1957, and America's humiliating "flopnik" of the same year, reaching its climax in the American moon landing on July 21, 1969 (Unger and Unger 1998:304-313). Such scientific success in space only highlighted the social failure of the culture to cope with issues of war, poverty, racism, and crime on earth. Science delivered a New World of safe promiscuity via the pill in 1960, but shadowed the planet with the mushroom cloud of apocalyptic fear during the Cuban missile crisis of 1962 (1998:250-256).

Mores and beliefs previously assumed impregnable gave way to pluralism and the new morality. Homosexuality, sexual experimentation, divorce, and pagan sensuality were rehabilitated, to become normative within a few decades. God died and resurrected in multiple, pagan, or polytheistic manifestations. Popular culture was enslaved permanently by the market, as the commodification of human experience and global culture triumphed. A hippie generation called its parents to walk a mile in the stranger's moccasins, and multiculturalism ensued. Old values were called into question, in an almost frantic search for new, more integrated values central to a youthful quest. Thousands "dropped out" to experiment with exotic lifestyles and beliefs.

Traditional answers were insufficient, and the reformulation of a new mazeway was inevitable. A communal consciousness reflected the desire to challenge "the system," as the counterculture hippies and Jesus Freaks alike, disdainfully labeled the "straight" world of their parents. Fundamentalists built their walls higher to preserve the culture, while many of their children shared common concerns with their secular counterparts. They reconfigured the faith of their fathers in affective, anti-materialist, communitarian, and socially inclusive terms. Was there evidence of Wallace's revitalization process in response to such psychohistorical turmoil?

4. Revitalization – 1963 to 1970 (Counterculture); 1968 to 1978 (Jesus Movement)

Distortion and revitalization occur in tandem, the renewal overlapping the disintegration. I have struggled long to decide approximate dates for this period, concluding that the death of J. F. Kennedy was both the darkest hour and the fountainhead of escalating protest and determination for idealists, dissenters and prophetic dreamers. In 1963 Bob Dylan popularized "The times they are A-changin,'" serving notice of a minority, mostly youthful intent to take over the culture and redeem it. Cultural distortion continued into the 1970s, but the hopes of the counterculture to change the world were fading by the late 1960s as politics, revolutionary arts, free love, psychedelic drugs, and transcendental meditation had all failed to rescue the dissenters from stress and disillusionment. It is the finding of this investigation that the Jesus Movement revitalization begins at the same time that the wider counterculture disintegrates. The revitalization periodization therefore overlaps.

Revitalization may be inversely proportionate to the collapse of the culture. The distortions of the 1960s facilitated an aggressive confrontation and penetration of the culture by a movement seeking to overthrow the existing order. Martin Marty said the period from 1965 to 1975 was an era marked by "social activism, radical theological experimentation, religious identifications with the New Frontier and the Great Society," and "dissent against increasing involvement in Southeast Asia" (1976:93).

During this fourth phase of revitalization, a movement responds to the crisis by the establishment of its own alternative order, in lively conflict and some synthesis with the wider culture (Wallace 1956b:270-275). This may be a period in which the movement is established in a parallel culture, forging its own separate identity, or is absorbed in existing forms, re-envisioning, or revitalizing the wider culture. Revitalizations are usually religious in nature, as dissenters seek new beliefs through charismatic leaders, who lead the movement through a process of re-envisioning and reconstruction.

The failure of the first wave of counterculture rebellion led to deeper despair, opening the door to a grass roots, Christian, revitalization movement, led by many newly enlightened casualties of failed politics and religion towards the end of the 1960s. The movement was prophet-led, consistent with revitalization theory. The initial movement towards revitalization had not been Christian, but it was an intensely spiritual response, fusing Catholic mysticism, esoteric Gnosticism, Eastern religion, paganism, spiritualism, and New Age environmentalism (Wuthnow 1976, 1978).

The concentration of this enquiry is upon the Jesus Movement and thus we must ask specifically if the Jesus Movement followed the revitalization pattern proposed by Wallace in style and substance? Several clearly observable elements evident during the revitalization phase are noted by Wallace (1966:158, 159-162). We will now examine these and compare them with the development of the Jesus Movement.

It appears such movements always begin with charismatic visionaries, which we will first consider. Such leaders must provide guidance and inspire colleagues to lead the movement through the formulation of a new mazeway, or code as the basis for a less stressful, more satisfying culture. Communication by various means is critical as the movement seeks to attract followers and resources. Since the reduction of stress is necessary if the movement is to succeed, organization of innovative chaos into a functional, financially stable program must occur early in the process. The movement must adapt swiftly to changing conditions internally and in the wider culture during early development and it must redirect energy from innovation to maintenance. Thus the basis for a less stressful social arrangement is established so that the process of routinization achieves a predictable routine for survival and social stability. We shall now consider the Jesus Movement in terms of this processual description.

<u>Prophetic, visionary leadership</u>. Prophetic or charismatic leaders are the starting point in Wallace's description. The issue of charismatic leadership is a

contentious but necessary focus in this enquiry, as previously stated in Chapter 3. Both success and failure in the Jesus Movement repeatedly were related to the style, strategy, strengths and character weaknesses of the founding figures, or the ability of powerful missionaries, who capitalized on the charisma of the founders. Such missionaries often supplemented founders, providing the routinizing skills necessary for the consolidation and survival of new religious movements.

No movement without a prime mover. Creative individuals rather than general movements initiate major cultural innovations (Barnett 1953; Melton 1999:7; Whiteman 1984:56, 57). Wallace's adaptation of Weber's concept of charismatic authority underscores the importance of biography in understanding social movements.[9] The Jesus Movement's pattern of leadership and growth was dominated by highly charismatic figures as described in Chapter 3. The dominance of charismatic founder-leaders has become a prominent issue in recent social movement theory (Melucci 1996a:332-347; Stewart, Smith, and Denton 1994:89-109). The impact of leadership upon framing of a group's worldview (Jasper 1997:171), and on recruitment and strategy development (1997:80, 287-289, 330-331) is more freely recognized in current attempts to empirically ground leadership concepts in social theory.

In search of leadership and a following to the Promised Land. Melucci (1996a) revisiting Weber's definition of charisma asserts that despite its profane transfer "from the religious arena to the sphere of politics," it remains "a central component in the great transformation of modern societies" (1996a:336). Leadership paradigm shifts are sometimes micro-revitalizations (Rambo 1993:24-25), which through the persuasion of rhetorical power attract (1993:84-85), cement, and clarify explicit ideological frames, (Jasper 1997:171) direction, and strategies (1997:45-46, 151).[10]

Major cultural differences arising from historical and social contexts are an integral part of biographical tracks.[11] The fact that most Australian Jesus Movement leaders were cross-cultural missionaries, with traditional, but evolving evangelical backgrounds is significant.[12] Ideological formation in a modernity frame was an influential element for these leaders, but most were theologically self-educated.[13] The personal biographical elements of leadership were critical to doctrinal formulations.

Political opportunity was a formative influence in the emergence of leadership, but leadership responses varied. The less substantial influence of fundamentalism on the Australian leaders facilitated more interactions with Catholic Charismatics and liberationists. Since no manifest destiny construct existed in the Australian mind, typically counterculture elements received more affirmation, as the nation was in search of an historic identity. In Australia the search for a soul, hitherto ill defined by its history, projected our rebel persona as that of pioneers of the national ontological quest.

Wallace notes that hallucinatory visions by one individual, often apocalyptic or communal in their projections, provide the focus for mass movement, gestalt shifts, similar to an individual's ecstatic conversion or *new birth* (1966:334-35). The method by which the Jesus Movement leaders fulfilled a prophetic role

(Weber 1964:358-406) and the extent to which they adhered to, or deviated from orthodox, historic Christianity, varied, but the pattern of the prophetic leader was uniform. Chuck Smith, Palosaari, Higgins, Parks, Meisner, Peterson, Sparks, and Frisbee, typically all claimed some form of Pentecostal or prophetic revelation as part of their call and vision to commence Jesus Movement leadership. John Hirt was typical of some less Pentecostal style of leaders, who nevertheless, as recorded in Chapter 6, saw themselves in terms of Weber's charismatic visionaries. The apocalyptic, communal, revitalization theme was never far from any of the early leaders. Sparks, Smith, Palosaari, Meisner, McGuire, Parks, Peterson, Hirt, and Gill, were archetypal in this regard.

Revitalization prophets experience a microcosmic revitalization of their own, which dramatically transforms and reinterprets the meaning of their own life and calling. Such personalities are unlike the normal pattern of the gifted leader who overseers established religious organizations. Weber's definition of the charismatic authority of the prophet (Weber 1968:252-267)[14] is congruent with Wallace's descriptive analysis of revitalization movement initiators. Such a bearer of charisma is one "who by virtue of his [her] mission proclaims a religious doctrine or divine commandment" (1968:253).

<u>Weber and charisma</u>. Weber's concept of "charismatic authority" provides insight into both the strengths and weaknesses of the movement's prophets. They emerged from native counterculture ranks and sometimes from dissenting Pentecostal and evangelical ranks. Often bicultural "straits" stabilized the chaotic energy of the Movement. The incapacity of modernity to even contemplate supernaturalism precludes all possibility of going beyond phenomenology to spiritual cause and process. Divine call is explicit in the charismatic leader's proclamation to followers and implicit in the resultant authority structure. Weber identifies the social significance of such charisma, not in its cause, but in the effect upon the disciples (Weber 1964:359). Weber describes the prophetic charismatic as typical of the inspirational leadership of new movements. His charismatic or prophetic leadership model and descriptive typology of the same are both useful and controversial (Weber 1958:245-252, 1964:358-392, 1968).[15]

Power over the followers is by virtue of the vision, personal gifts, the attraction of the new mazeway, the skills of organization of the leader, and the trust of the inner circle of supportive leaders. Charismatic "authentication" is by manifestation of power, by extraordinary rhetorical presentation, and by projection of a sense of divine call.

> Wallace puts forth as the third stage of the revitalization movement the appearance of a prophet who personally undergoes a traumatic religious experience that epitomizes the crisis of the culture. Often such prophets have hallucinatory visions or dreams (for them it is as real as any physical experience) in which they directly confront the deity. From that confrontation they receive (or have revealed to them) new formulations of divine law. (McLoughlin 1978:16)

While such language reduces the rich dramatic and personal texture one observes in the life and leadership of Martin Luther King, Handsome Lake, or a Chuck Smith, the basic details are consistent with revitalization movement leadership from Africa to Australia. The charismatic leader with a vision of a new mazeway promotes a new, integrated explanation of life. Usually such prophetic, charismatic leaders, like Handsome Lake, are recipients of "supernatural" visions from a divine source. The visionaries, orators, and prophets, rather than warriors, administrators, and lawmakers, are the initiators of revitalization, both Native American and European.

Clifford Trafzer laments that "except for a handful of experts, most notably anthropologists, scholars, and laymen have expressed little interest in understanding prophets" in the Native American context (Trafzer 1986:ix).[16] "Without some understanding of the significance of prophets [in] religions" (1986:xiv) there can be little understanding of cultural revitalization. Chapter 3 emphasized the significance of the charismatic prophets for this reason. The centrality of the charismatic founders of the 1960s, 1970s, Jesus Movement is consistent with the Wallace typology and certainly normative in the Jesus Movement.

In tracing the journey of prominent Jesus Movement groups we should ask whether the biographical information of the leaders' worldview developments was as significant as regional or sociopolitical contexts. The dominant influence of culture on the leaders is indisputable, but there are a great variety of possible leadership responses to cultural realities, requiring volitional responses that determine direction, strategy, networking, and even worldview development.

Calvary Chapel's success in its routinization of the initial counterculture energy is attributed consistently by participants to the personal style of Smith, his communication skills, and his distinct strategies for growth. Sometimes however, cultural forces beyond the power of leaders to predict, or exploit, may have as much influence to shape a movement.[17] Several failed Jesus Movement prophetic founders have recalled their inability to counter the negative effect of the Jonestown massacre on public attitudes towards communal experimentation.

While the ego strength of such leaders may call into question some of their agendas, Melissa Pflüg (1998) provides valuable insight into the dynamics of the prophet's perceived calling in the revitalization of the Odawa. The revitalizationists, she maintains, possessed exceptional understanding of the "moral gifts of ritual" (1998:61). Their "careers and works echo the centrality of the healing and regenerative power of enacting the interconnected ethics of generosity (personating), life giving (gifting) and wisdom (empowering)" (1998:61).

Whether charismatic figures are driven by perceptions of impending disaster, which sensitize them to a search for divine encounter, or whether the visionary call initiates such intense apocalypticism, varies in my observation of such leaders. Melissa Pflüg theorizes that revitalizationists are driven by "ethical duty during a major cultural transition" and also by the "relational nature of identity" (1998:61). Perhaps this explains the centrality of such figures, that have extraordinary ability to bond disciples to themselves, and also to a moral vision expressed in some form of communalism. The importance of central control by the visionary may thus be rooted in the nature and intensity of his or her understanding of relational significance, in an historic moment of imminent cultural collapse. This is an alternative to the tendency of Wallace to view the prophetic mind as a psychosomatic ego disorder.

Throughout their lives, each of these revitalizationists acted to empower himself and thereby strengthen the people . . . .. Thus the revitalizationists' claims of having been appointed or selected to lead after ritual communications with the "Great Spirit," "Creator," or "Master of Life" can be put in a new light. Perhaps none of these leaders actually accepted a personal identity defined by ethical acts of giving as a means of constructively addressing the social disruption by others. (Pflüg1998:62)

My research indicates most of the charismatic leaders of the Jesus Movement recount distinct, supernatural, prophetic callings in one form or another as the initial basis for their program and the authority to parent their following.[18] A minority of those who exercised charismatic leadership did not emphasize the personal, divine encounter, or manifest the healing and prophetic gifts. Nevertheless, they were authoritative in proclamation, and attracted strong followings characteristic of such movement leaders.[19] Pflüg suggests some leaders were driven to the divine in response to intuitive concern in the face of imminent cultural collapse. They operated from an understanding that:

> The crisis was a threat to identity; the challenge was to restructure identity; the solution was to rework ritual and myth. The prophetic leaders worked to restore and establish right and ethical relationships by maintaining and reinforcing identity through ritual acts, to reconstitute tradition and myths, define "a people" and therefore a reintegrated group with renewed purpose. The prophetic leaders reinterpreted and applied rituals and mythic themes to reintegrate communities and overcome threats of divisiveness and liminality. (Pflüg 1998:64)

To varying degrees, all these elements occurred in the recent Jesus Movement. Lonnie Frisbee was a sign prophet whose demonstration of healing and miracle power attracted thousands of followers and the initial attention of both Smith and Wimber. John Hirt became the prophet of socio-revolutionary action. While Jesus marches to celebrate the faith or protest the agenda of gays or abortionists are now part of Christian tradition, the revitalization marches embraced issues of desegregation, the release of Nelson Mandela from prison, and the state of the planet's ecology.

Followers of such prophets "crystallized around charismaticaly gifted individuals, who either through miracles, or through exemplary life, through 'economic' release (from the world) . . . sought to legitimate themselves as guarantors of the (messianic) hope of redemption" (Stegemann and Stegemann 1999:163). While the miracle workers "represented one answer to individual distress, then the prophetic-charismatic movements developed a liberation concept, as it were, for the internal and external distress of the entire people" (1999:163). The biblical pattern indicates that the charisma of apostle, evangelist, and prophet are bestowed upon individuals (Romans 12:4-9; 1 Corinthians 12:4, 11:12:28-13:3, 14:1-40; Ephesians 2:20-21, 4:11-14; Hebrews 2:4) who in turn are meant to be servants committed to building up the communal group. In modern, traditional circles, the terms "apostolic" and "prophetic" (Snyder 1977:87-96) came to be applied to communities (Hunter 1992:142-171, 107-116).

The Jesus Movement vigorously debated the validity of the prophetic and apostolic calling in the 1970s. Some concluded apostles had historically been those who had a supernatural, direct commission from Jesus independent of the religious community.[20] The significance of itinerant, charismatic proclaimers, as apostolic authority figures within the Jesus Movement remains a contentious issue.[21] Conflict between leaders in Xenos reflected this tension (Leffel 1997:59-74; McCallum 1999b:1).[22] The values, self-definition, and the sense of vocation in inspirational leaders, is an interactive component in which the actor plays a leading role on the cultural stage. The meanings, which source and motivate human beings to lead others, or to follow leaders, are multi-layered.[23] For Weber, teachers, philosophers, and legislators are of a different order.

> What primarily differentiates such figures from the prophets is their lack of that vital emotional preaching which is distinctively of prophecy, regardless of whether this is disseminated by the spoken word, the pamphlet, or any other type of literary [or performing arts] composition . . . . The enterprise of the prophet is closer to that of the popular orator (*demagogue*) or political publicist than to that of the teacher. (Weber 1968:260, 261)

His typology of authority remains useful for my purposes. However, I conflict with Weber on two minor applications of his theory. He states that Jesus, as a classic charismatic, "was not interested in social reform as such,"[24] unlike the standard Hebrew prophets (Weber 1968:258), and that "Wesley [is] to be distinguished from the category of [charismatic] prophets" because he did "not claim to be offering a substantially new revelation" (1968:261).[25] Following their inception movements sometimes take on a life of their own, particularly since the Civil Rights era of the 1960s, manifesting less evidence of the prominent charismatic leader.[26]

Elements of Reformation and Restructuring

Wallace proposes that a healthy relationship between the individual and society necessitates "every person in society to maintain a mental image of the society and its culture, as well as his (her) body and behavioral regularities, in order to act in ways to reduce stress at all levels of the system" (Wallace 1956b:266). Our mental image of the external and internal world, or mazeway, embraces perceptions of self, society, and the physical environment. A mazeway is maintained by each individual, and "can be manipulated by self and others in order to minimize stress" (1956b:266). Under intolerable social stress people are exceptionally open to the influence of leaders who envisage a new understanding of a new society. Mazeway reformulation to reduce stress initiates revitalization, if concurrently engaging sufficient individuals (1956b:276).

Revitalization must fulfill certain non-sequential elements of transformation and regulation of its energy to reach the final destination of a new and stable, alternative culture. Wallace observed the following elements or aspects of progress. First is the formulation of a new worldview, or code of beliefs. Second is a well-developed means of inspirational and popular communication to believers and potential believers. Third is the formation of adequate organizational structures, lines of command, responsibilities, and realistic expectations. The fourth element is a period of reassessment and adaptation to both internal and external needs of a changing group and context, the management of opposition, and the resolution of ambiguities in belief and lifestyle within the group. The formation of a new cultural reality, a secure, less stressful, alternative is the fifth element. Finally, the routinization of the creative energy such that predictability reduces the uncertainty which promotes stress is the sixth and possibly most critical factor. I shall now reflect on these factors in greater detail.

1. Mazeway reformulation of a new code. In the presence of widespread dissatisfaction with existing mazeways, a prophet encodes the vision of a new society. This blueprint for a new society is created by a process called "mazeway reformulation" (Wallace 1966:270). This process is intensely visionary and religious, and also "abrupt and dramatic, usually occurring as a moment of insight, a brief period of realization of relationships and opportunities" (1966:270). For the dream to be fulfilled, the movement must proceed beyond initial prophetic excitement, through a process establishing core values, communication networks, organizational stability, adaptation to sociopolitical realities, and the establishment of manageable routines and community expectations (1966;158-162). Innovation must give way substantially to maintenance of a new cultural matrix.

The role of the charismatic leader does not end with the initiation of a movement. Usually a visionary leader continues to shape the beliefs and methods of the new movement, particularly the content and form of communication typical of the group and indicative of the group's self-definition, aims and objectives. One of the most notable aspects of Wallace's revitalization model (1972:507-509) is his descriptive typology of communication during the "mazeways reformalising" of a movement's worldview.

He uses Weber's concept of charismatic leadership, but calls for a more *interactionist concept* between leaders and followers whereby "the catalytic function is to convert latent solidarity into active ritual and political action" (Horsley 1994:141). Weber's ambiguity as to whether the charisma lies in the visionary, or the power attributed to the leader by the followers, is shared by Horsely and Wallace (Horsley 1994; Wallace 1966:273).

> For Weber, charismatic leadership is based on the emotional form of community relationship. He says there is no such thing as appointment or dismissal of a charismatic leader, and no career, hierarchy or promotion. Rather, there is simply a call to follow and obey, to mission and duty. The charismatic leader has no salary or benefice, but lives by voluntary gift. More conventional forms of leadership, such as traditional (e.g. inherited or ordained) and rational (e.g. institutional or constitutional) authority, are despised by those party to charismatic leadership. Frequently but not always, a charismatic leader claims fresh or even divine revelation of truth, and this helps form the basis of his or her authority. Charismatic leaders are prophets, in Weber's terminology (1965:46-79), rather than priests, the latter being functionaries who administer and promote established religions or systems. (Muston 2001:8)

Wallace claims that "with a few exceptions, every religious revitalization movement with which I am acquainted has been originally conceived in one, or several hallucinatory visions, by a single individual" (Wallace 1956a: 270). The dream or vision results from the appearance of a supernatural being. Wallace's extreme secularism, and his interest in the phenomenon from a psychological standpoint, caused him to view such experiences as a form of psychiatric abnormality. There are however, less dramatic forms of "divine revelation" that produce vision and charismatic authority.

With the renewed interest in Weber's typology, several other definitions and descriptions of charismatic leadership have emerged. B. Wilson recognizes a form of prophecy that is inspired, authoritative and forthtelling, rather than foretelling (B. Wilson 1975:118). Andrain and Apter (1995) see the magnetism of such leaders as attracted by their search for "self esteem, empowerment, and solidarity with a collective cause" (1995:289), because the leader articulates "transformative values in a conflict riven environment," challenging "both traditional and bureaucratic authority" (1995:286). Such charismatic leaders link the disciples' personal identity quest to critical events and priorities during a period of rapid change.

The leader's ability to interpret the times and engage followers in bonding political action is part of the powerful charisma. Particularly where people feel powerless, as they do during a time of extreme cultural distortion, the bold challenge to conventional values, and established elites that is projected by the charismatic, builds a communal sense of dignity and power (Andrain and Apter 1995:292). Leaders in the Australian Jesus Movement who proposed political as well as eternal salvation particularly reflect this form of leadership. Their embodiment of the shared values of dissident youth gave the Jesus Movement charismatics' initial power.

Yukl (1998) approaches charisma from a psychoanalytical standpoint. Burns prefers to see movemental leaders and founders as transformational, rather than charismatic, in their capacity to elevate a mutual following "to higher levels of morality and motivation" (Yukl 1998:20). Bass (1985) stresses the strong emotion, which arouses a following, and the identification of that following with the ideals and needs of the group. Tichy and Devanna see revitalization leaders as visionaries and change agents who have exceptional trust in their own intuition as motivators and mobilizers and who display analytical thinking, sensitivity, to people's needs and a capacity to articulate values (Tichy and Devanna 1986:122-124). It is the skill of projecting a vision with simplicity and appeal, in a specific cultural context that is paramount.

Risk taking in ideologically and socially challenging contexts provides a testing ground for the fast growing and changing movement. Conger and Kanungo (1998) note characteristic behaviors of charismatic leaders. They exhibit substantial visionary departure from the social norms, personal risk taking, economic and status self sacrifice, unconventional strategies, accurate prophecies and projections, self confidence, personal power and initiative, and a social attitude of broad disenchantment with the existing cultural order (Conger and Kanungo 1998:76-77, 80, 86-87).

These qualities were consistently the mark of every movement leader I have known, and those I have researched through the eyes of their disciples. The possible exception is the element of self-confidence. Where leaders such as Hirt,

Sparks, and the author sometimes expressed self-doubt and insecurity, the prophetic call and vision overrode the deficit of self-esteem shortfall, providing an appearance of confidence in crisis situations and public speaking.

Melucci underscores the "leader-constituency" element of leadership in social movements, seeing the charismatic power vested in "a form of interaction, in which each of the actors involved makes a specific investment, therewith achieving specific advantages" (Melucci 1996a:333). This aligns with revitalization theory in that the relationship only lasts while leader and follower find the cost of radical departure from the previously cultural state is advantageous. If the high tensile experience of revitalization does not deliver a more satisfying culture expediently, the movement soon collapses. The final dissolution of Palosaari's Street Level is an example.

Melucci, again consistent with Wallace, notes that charismatic leaders survive only if objectives are defined, structures, and cohesive of the movement are maintained, and the support base is mobilized towards the movement's goals as the identity of the group is maintained and reinforced (Melucci 1996a:339-341). A recent Masters degree thesis by an Australian has examined this author's leadership as a charismatic and transformational leader of an Australian revitalization movement, noting that the Australian groups afford classic examples of transformational, revitalization leadership.[27]

It is not only an issue of self-perception or style, but also an issue of ideological framing, albeit through perceived revelation. To the prophet comes:

> [A] unified view of the world derived from a consciously integrated and meaningful attitude towards life. To the prophet, both the life of [hu]mankind and the world, both cosmic and social events, have a certain and coherent meaning. To this meaning the conduct of [hu]mankind must be oriented if it is to bring salvation, for only in relation to this meaning does life obtain a unified and significant pattern. (Weber 1968:266)

The message of the Jesus Movement departed from the liberal and the fundamentalist tradition. The prophetic figures identified a popular belief that the system in all its forms, was "ego-tripping," materialistic, exclusive, and ignorant of impending collapse of "this world's system," a term used frequently in a derogatory fashion in CWLF's *Letters to Street Christians* (Sparks 1971a). The hippie Christian not only mounted revivals to convert sinners to personal salvation; but also promoted an apocalyptic call for radical departure from the existing, unworkable system. Hiley Ward (1972) has clearly indicated departures from mainstream denominations in direction, theology, and social association. He distances the Jesus Freaks from classic fundamentalism (1972:154-167), accurately predicting that Jesus Movement groups would be a laboratory for a new form of religious leadership (1972:40-73), and the creative edge of new social responsibility (1972:74-83).

Robert Johnson (1971) recognized a new far more existential vision of God had resulted from the overall consciousness revolution. Ellwood's early assessment of the Jesus Movement (1973) placed it in a vulnerable proximity to organized evangelicalism, unlikely to survive the end of the drug culture, and more likely to be absorbed into a more youth oriented, renewed evangelicalism. His more recent contribution (Ellwood 1994) reviewed the counterculture period as a postmodern religious configuration

Wallace notes that the prophetic authors of the new code of values and conduct are also the primary communicators of it in the revitalization stage (1966:160). This was clearly the case in the Jesus Movement. The visionary leaders generated new codes and worldview adaptations clearly before they introduced new symbols and ritual processes.

Wallace sees religion as expressing the primary human need for ritual rather than ultimate meaning (1966:104-157). In the 1960s, Wallace even predicted the imminent supplanting of religious ritual by scientifically devised rational alternatives (1966:268-270). The significance of ritual is unassailable, but its underlying meaning, purpose and significance does not become as easily apparent to the outsider.[28] Jesus Movement groups initially appeared iconoclastic in their anti-structural, anti-establishment forms, yet the evidence of reworking myth and ritual abounded. Every Jesus Movement group with which I am familiar – and they are many, from six different countries – began highly critical of the "dead" rituals of denominationalism and of high culture society. Jesus Papers sported cartoons pillaring denominational ministers and priests in their clerical garb, carrying miters, and wearing ecclestical headgear.

Revitalization movements seek to simplify the cultural codes for a confused citizenry in times of cultural complexity. The Jesus Movement clearly sought to do this. However, in keeping with the universal human need for symbols and rituals as vehicles of meaning and social solidarity, it proliferated its own symbols and forms, borrowing ancient rituals, adapting traditional symbols, and creating new ones representing a changed social order.

The raised finger in a "One Way – Jesus," sign was a psychological bonding symbol as surely as the two-finger victory sign was to counterculture hippies. Following in the ways of the counterculture, Jesus People demonstrated en mass and developed their own distinctive clothing styles, replete with many religious symbols including "the cross" and the ancient sign of the fish. The reintroduction of these symbols however, was distinctly radical, the fish being reintroduced as a sign of the marginization of the faithful in the catacombs, in defiance and rebellion against the pagan power of Rome. The ocean baptisms, the rock festivals, the communal lifestyles, the handholding, candle-bearing demonstrations were high ritualistic activities.[29]

No more clear example of this revitalization journey can be found than that of CWLF, Chapter 5, which journeyed from anti-ritualistic fundamentalism to radical Jesus Movement, and finally to possibly the most ritual laden tradition on earth, that of full Orthodoxy. CWLF's conversion to Orthodoxy was a natural expression of the anti-structure journey from liminality to reworked ritual and reintegrated symbolism.

Wallace sees a progressive function of both the charismatic leader and the new group (1966:160-162). The first is the "formulation of a code" which the prophet introduces. The content of the message delivered often breaths destruction and judgement on the old world order, calls for a radical conversion to a new morality, and the establishment of a transformed social arrangement which may be communal, utopian, or missional. Examples of each abounded in the Jesus Movement.[30] The apocalyptic element was apparent whether in the prophetic teachings of Smith, or in the politicized, socialist, utopian Christianity of Hirt. Stegman and Stegman (1999), in their social history of the first century Jesus Movement, describe revitalization elements congruent with Wallace, and remarkably similar to the late twentieth century counterpart. Prophetic-charismatic movements, marked by protest against socio-economic and religio-political chaos, gave rise to millenarian movements, sign-prophet-charismatic and revolutionary movements (Stegman and Stegman 1999:162-192). They also gave rise to non-violent resistance and mass protests (1999:171-172).

2. Communication. Communication is primary, whether by intense personal engagement, mass exhortation, literature distribution, performing arts, music or winsome and engaging conversation (Wallace 1956b:270-273; 1966:160-161). All these elements, particularly aggressive one-on-one witnessing, the Jesus rock concerts, and charismatic preaching attracted thousands to Calvary Chapel. Street Level and TLC made great use of Jesus street papers. In Berkley, CWLF excelled in the distribution of engaging literature dedicated to cultural and political critique from a Jesus standpoint and one-on-one personal evangelism after public demonstrations or proclamations. In most groups the impact of day-after-day dialogue in the intimacy of communal life was a powerfully converting force which was not obvious to outsiders.

It is arguable that revitalization operates on a different basis to standard organizations. In normal situations personal friendships and one-on-one conversational evangelism appear to be more significant in the conversion process than public proclamation by preachers, according to current church growth theorists (Gibbs 2000:172-176). The capacity of "larger than life" charismatic prophets to attract followers during the usually brief period of cultural renewal seems to depart from the norm. Weber views the charismatic's power to gather converts as a special case (1968:253-255). Standard reformers, teachers, ethicists, and even social reformers fall short of the required power to persuade (Weber 1968:261).

"What primarily differentiates such figures from the prophets is their lack of that vital emotional preaching which is distinctive of prophecy, regardless of whether this is disseminated by the spoken word, the written word, the pamphlet [as with Jesus papers], or any other form of communication (1968:261). The enterprise, Weber proposes, is "closer to that of the popular orator (*demagogue*) . . . ." (1968:261). In this respect the relationship of Native American prophets, preachers of the Awakenings of the 18th and 19th centuries, and the Jesus Movement popular communicators represent the revitalization prophet rather than the astute organizational strategist. Some who began as "crowd gatherers" move on to train others in a rich tapestry of roles in multi-strategy evangelism.

During the innovative phase of the Jesus Movement communication was a "seamless garment" of public discourse, pamphleteering, interpersonal dialogue between believing and non-believing freaks, creative and entertaining performing arts with a clear purpose, and numerous acts of social solidarity in loving care and free accommodation. It would be unwise to form a hierarchy from the variety of communication forms, but the public communication of the message via popular culture art forms and "folksey" and earnest styles of discourse were highly impacting in the early years. It was not uncommon for TLC to hold a packed hall of un-churched adolescents and early twenty-year-olds for two hours of rock music, followed by a passionate, hour-long proclamation. Not only did audiences stay for the duration, but seekers for faith and participation in social justice engagement would remain for another hour of counsel and instruction. In rural districts audiences sometimes outnumbered the official population of the town. It is noteworthy however that the same preachers who gathered and influenced the masses during the revitalization phase are still useful communicators but often far from the mega-influences they were. The location of the communication, whether personal dialogue on campus with fellow students, rock singing in the local park, was sometimes as significant as the quality of presentation. The message was repositioned from the sanctuary to the street.

The Jesus Movement leaders filled a vacuum at the time, developing communication strategies in a process of discovery along the road. While inventing some new forms, they mostly rediscovered, or intuited age-old principles of indigenous method and incarnational lifestyle. The centrality of the prophetic, public proclamation, in balance with intimate friendship and intense personal discussion was a standard method for Jesus Freaks. They hit the streets daily with their leaders, engaged the masses in conversation and returned to their communes for debriefing, training, testimony, sharing, and strategizing. The interplay between leader and the followers was complex and interactive. The popular diffusion by charismatic envisioning which marked the movement was remarkable, occurring during a period of increasing secularization.

A significant element of movement growth is that of evangelistic "communication" of the code, the vision, and the "goal culture," which in this case were predominately young students, counterculture dissidents, and anyone who did not like the world as it was. Evangelical fervor as a mark of revitalization (Wallace 1956b:272) was overwhelmingly evident in the Jesus Movement. As described in Chapter 3, the Jesus people took to the highways and byways in an itinerant frenzy paralleled by few movements other than Methodism. The intense, prophetic, inspirational communication was directed to both potential converts and to the perceived enemies of a better society. The perceived enemies of a better society came under prophetic denunciation. Apocalyptic, inspirational rhetoric is a significant element in the revitalization period. During a period of many media exposures of the Jesus Movement, itinerant charismatics, Frisbee, Palosaari, Meisner, Parks, Blessitt, and many others exemplified the revitalization phase.

By promising a New World of personal fulfillment through conversion to the group and its ideals, and an eschatological hope of things to come, the message provided new status, social security, and communal purpose. The centrality of the prophetic, public proclamation in balance with visionary sharing with the faithful is sometimes under–stressed by movemental theorists. Wallace's understanding of this element is most appropriate to the style of the evangelical proclaimers of the Jesus Movement.

Current social movement theorists are recognizing the significance of rhetoric and mass communication in promoting new movements (Jasper 1997:161-162, 273-274; Melucci 1996:225-228; Stewart, Smith, and Denton 1994:47-57, 131-138; Touraine 1977:290-294). The ability to articulate and communicate a movement's message in an arresting, gripping manner, is an essential element of charismatic leadership (Conger 1989:72-92; Conger and Kanunga 1998:172-187). The use of electronic and print media, particularly the exploitation of visual images by astute leaders, was a significant factor in gaining converts. A sense of communal power and influence, and the engagement of external political and economic support links, enhanced the distinct identity of disciples. It is claimed that Chuck Smith possessed a legendary intuition and a clear policy of exploiting media, which in the Californian sub-culture attracted thousands in early movement years (Wind and Lewis 1994a:687).

The Australian Movement established a popular persona that endeared it to multitudes of teenagers through extensive, positive, electronic, and print media. Blessitt and Palosaari made much use of the media, as did Parks, Sparks, Higgins, and Hirt. The offset printing revolution made possible cheaply produced street papers easily distributed by a multitude of Jesus Freaks. Lack of top-heavy establishment organization enabled charismatic leaders to release up to the minute, sensational material, at a popular culture level, unimpeded by editorial committees. *The Hollywood Free Paper* reached half a million circulation. Our own publication reached a high point of 35,000. Our research indicated four or five individuals often read one copy. Rock concerts were ready media platforms for the charismatic leaders to get their message out to the pop culture.

The nature of the charismatic and prophetic gift facilitates populist rhetoric. Elements of contextualized communication now familiar to the academic community were often picked up along the road by leaders, filling a vacuum at the time, synthesizing rather than inventing old principles of indigenization in method and lifestyle. Perhaps it was not so much the genius of discovery as the power of popular, "diffusion of innovation" (Rogers 1995), which marked the Movement in its communication.

3. Organization. The swift growth rate of the disciples, who bring with them an intense expectation of a changed order beyond rhetoric, creates an expedient pressure for organization. The intensity and diversity of the communal experience requires swift and astute administration to reduce relational stress. The charismatic leader chooses true believers as co-leaders, often autocratically and sometimes collegially. The leader must manage a balancing act between establishment resistance and popular acclaim. As people are converted and join the movement as followers, those closest to the prophetic figure as his close disciples become the leaders. These later become more involved in the maturing and constant reshaping of the message and the institutionalizing of leadership roles. Loyalty to the leader transcends the significance of skills or prior experiences (Wallace 1956b:273-274; 1966:161). Issues of dogma, authority structures, accountability, resources management, opposition, media management, public relations, daily and long-term scheduling, strategies, and instigation of new programs emerge early.

Organizational chaos often marks the beginnings of revitalization. The more successful the movement, the more chaotic the organization, and the more difficult it becomes for one person to administer all elements. The development of programs, the refocusing and contextualizing of the code, the development of strategy, the use of media, pastoring of the flock, the training of leaders, handling of opposition, exploitation of political opportunity, and the development of sustaining financial structures, constitute a formidable agenda for any one person.

The fact that so many obviously charismatic founders in the Jesus Movement made shipwreck of highly successful movements was sometimes an indication of the enormity of the organizational task. Despite extraordinary capacity to initially create a community of willing, self-sacrificing, almost fanatical disciples who were willing to live in a strict, shared purse community and travel around the world on a beggar's income, Jim Palosaari failed to establish an enduring movement. My informants spoke in mythical proportions of his charisma.

Despite frightening dysfunction in his character, they all lament the loss of the magic they initially experienced. Today Palosaari is simply an employee of a fund raising consortium. Similar stories can be told of several of the most charismatic founders. Some of the most capable are now in regular pastoral ministry. U'ren and Hirt work for the Australian Uniting Church; Higgins is one of Chuck Smith's pastors; Peterson is employed by the Military and the University of Washington. Parks is in secular work, and Sparks is submitted to the hierarchy of the Orthodox Church. Pederson is an Orthodox Priest. Some movements have survived – Calvary Chapel, JPUSA, TLC, and CCC– but in every case, the charismatic founders passed through stressful organization and routinization, after the heyday of recruitment and legendary visions.

Charismatic authority, often viewed as dangerous because of its non-rational, non–legal basis, centers initially in the prophet as the final authority in defining the message but as routinization occurs, it becomes shared and ultimately legal-rational. The disciples increasingly become the full-time staff and help formulate policy. "The tri-cornered relationship between the formulators, the disciples, and the mass followers is given an authoritarian structure – even without the formalities of older or bureaucratic structure – by the charismatic quality of the formulator's image" (Wallace 1966:161).

The rate at which this transfer of power occurs varies considerably. Thirty years after its birth, Calvary Chapel is still ruled by the benevolent dictatorship of Chuck Smith, who still signs all the checks and rules the policy, décor, and programs. At the other extreme, the CWLF leadership now submits to the sacerdotal authority of the Orthodox hierarchy. Melton (1996) says that the founders of new religious movements eventually reach a point where growth denies the primary leaders general access to followers. Rapid change occurs, and despite the initial centrality of the leader, the vision must be transferred to others and the responsibility to organize and stabilize must be shared. Although revitalization movements begin with a top-heavy influence of charismatic founders, the natural process of necessary restructuring for survival appears to rectify the overdependence on the leader. Once the group achieves a good measure of routinization and organization, and the group survives for the leader's natural lifetime, the new movement is usually permanent (Melton 1996:96).

4. Adaptation. During this period of revitalization, modification of belief, policy, and practice occurs. External opposition becomes both an asset to draw disaffected citizens to the radical cause, and a threat to the survival of a low resourced and marginalized movement. The prophetic leader superintends the modification of belief and practice. Synthesis and increasing pragmatism is inevitable as the movement adapts to the social realities of the wider culture, and the pastoral needs of the followers (Wallace 1956b:274-275; 1966:161-162). Wallace notes that the new movement during revitalization struggles with both internal and external elements (1966:161-162). While a revolutionary movement, the group naturally evokes mythical proportions of heroism and villainy. New movements require opposition to attract adventurous souls and achieve public notoriety as a distinct alternative to the system. Extreme, unresolved conflict, or powerful external forces might eventually destroy the movement, if compensations for members are less than the cost of membership. Since desire for reduction of bad stress attracts followers, increasing their stress creates disillusionment and defection. Thus constant adaptation to political realities without, and strategic formation of adaptive strategies within, marks this period.

The growing need for resolution of mazeway ambiguities, particularly those that are highlighted by critics, is necessary to keep the reputation attractive to potential converts, and to reassure the followers of the prophet's mazeway alternative. Calvary Chapel's adaptations were highly successful, repositioning the Movement for the post-counterculture generation of Californian, consumerist, and baby boomer adults. Shiloh on the other hand held to a radical communalism that brought the full force of the Internal Revenue Service against them following the Jonestown scandal. The failure to adapt to capitalist realities destroyed the largest communitarian movement in American history.

5. Cultural Transformation. Notable transformation of the psychosocial state of the followers must occur if the movement is to survive to the steady state stage. With a new order established, a more satisfying culture is developed. Extensive cultural changes liberate followers to embark on organized projects, sometimes with an inflated expectation to achieve wider political, social, and economic reform" (Wallace 1956b:275; 1966:162). At this stage, "some projects fail – not through any deficiency in conception or execution, but because circumstances make defeat inevitable" (1956b:273).

"The revitalization, if successful, will be attended by a drastic decline in quasi-pathological, individual symptoms of anomie, and by the disappearance of cultural distortions" (Wallace 1966:162). Wallace assumes that movemental success includes "internal social conformity," implying that organizational survival and "a successful economic system," are primary. In this respect Street Level failed, but Calvary Chapel and JPUSA, though poles apart in their attitude to consumerism, have thrived till now.

If the purpose of revitalization is the reduction of culture-destroying stress, then Calvary Chapel Movement and JPUSA may have been the most successful of all. The level of membership satisfaction and smooth organization found in both groups is outstanding. The irony is that for this to have occurred, the period Wallace describes in terms of adaptation was successful for Calvary Chapel movement because it basically abandoned its original counterculture stance, and embraced the new fusion of Californian spirituality and conspicuous consumption. As revitalization it was a success. From a prophetic point of view it may have abandoned the message that once attracted dissenting youth culture.

If a movement does not establish its own comfort zone and provide a localized satisfactory culture, and even fails to organizationally survive, but has left a notable impact on the wider cultural configuration to this end, in my opinion it may still be considered to be successful. If the wider culture accepts major elements of the dissenting minority's revised worldview, even if that counterculture fails to establish a distinctly new institutional form in its own right, it is surely arguable by Wallace's own premise, that a new steady state is formed around altered mazeways. The movement has thus been largely responsible as a catalyst for a perceived reduction in stress and the formulation of a more satisfying general culture.

6. Routinization. Social realities require the innovative, revolutionary movement ultimately to focus on maintenance. The single student radical becomes a parent, and the needs of family compete with revolutionary dreams. Appropriate administrative and legislative forms must be devised to meet the diversity of disciple's needs and the changing mission. Long term survival is now the focus and innovation wanes.

Maintenance proportionately increases. New ritual processes and social contracts are developed to perpetuate the historical myth, replacing original iconoclasm and stabilizing the vision. The survival of the prophetic visionary is not guaranteed, and a legal-rational basis for transfer of power from the prophet to the followers becomes a concern. Normalization of beliefs and practices becomes inevitable "with the mere passage of time" (Wallace 1956b:275). The timing and extent of routinization is in tension with charismatic, prophetic authority (Weber 1964, 1968), but failure at this point appears to spell death for even the most creative revitalization movements. Conflict is inherent in the process of routinization (Weber 1968:48-65). Charismatic authority is "sharply opposed both to rational, and particularly bureaucratic authority, and to traditional authority, whether in its patriarchal, patrimonial, or any other form" (1968:51). Charismatic innovation is inversely proportionate to the extent of routinization.[31]

The more successful the movement, the earlier this conflict will arise, and the more critical is its management for survival. The emphasis eventually shifts from innovation and freedom, to maintenance and responsibility. Possibly no issue was more vexing for the Jesus Movement. Wallace notes (1966:162) that in religious movements the code must be reworked as growth occurs, and the identity of the movement imprinted in the public consciousness through retelling the story, by creating myths and rituals for the reconfigured culture. Those expressions of the Jesus Movement which have survived have a strong sense of their history, well developed ritual processes which synthesize traditional forms, primitive Christian mythology and contemporary pop culture expressions of faith and *communitas* (See Endnote 7).

A discouraging proportion of the Movements failed to survive the transfer of leadership power, not because of the natural death of the leader but because of internal conflict over dysfunctional leadership. Inadequate clarification of role and status, or failure to adapt to changing circumstances or social environment may prevent revitalization of the group. Sometimes the failure of the leaders to replace the tension ridden old culture with a revitalized, stress relieved alternative, in a time frame which does not undermine the followers' expectations, created terminal internal conflict.

It is notable that only a small minority of the hundreds of American, intentional community movements with which I am familiar have survived, despite in some cases, massive initial success, as in the instance of Shiloh Youth Ministries, Spirit of Elijah, Street Level, and the House of the New World. In Australia, of the scores of revitalization expressions in the 1970s, only three have institutionally survived (TLC, CCC, and Fusion). It appears that benevolent dictatorship as exhibited by Smith has worked well in the routinization of Calvary Chapel, where the leader has remained close to base, and made maintenance of his leaders a top priority from the earliest days. The critical significance of routinization, organization, and institutional change is a central issue to social movement theory (McAdam, McCarthy, and Zald 1996:211-214).

A critical factor appears to be the rate and timing of routinization. If vigorously pursued too early, the charismatic innovation and genius is lost, and the movement simply becomes an institution. If pursued too late, as occurred I believe in our TLC Movement in Australia, the sheer unregulated energy self-destructs the movement as leadership conflict develops. When routines are not established clearly, and the basis of social control is not clarified, authority conflicts, ideological and tactical fragmentation produce stresses at a level that causes followers to defect. Initially it is accepted that a break with existing order will be stressful. Some stress may even create a new sense of meaning and purpose in the followers, but prolonged stress and a delay in fulfillment of the vision for change becomes intolerable for some disciples. It is not worth the cost of commitment, if the charismatic's utopian promises are not realized in a time frame congruent with the mazeways of the disciples. Extremely mission focused groups in the Movement tended to fare badly at the level of pastoral care of their own people, as illustrated by Street Level, Spirit of Elijah, and TLC.

In contrast to standard organizations, breaking with a revitalization movement has ontological implications recognized by Wallace. Such is the supernatural sense of expectation that departing members feel heightened disillusionment, and fear that they are characterized as traitors rather than simply agents of alternative, free choice. Disillusionment is inversely proportionate to utopian illusion. The absolute nature of the call and vision may predispose the group to regard such departures as spiritual divorce. The enduring anger, pain, alienation, and even rejection of faith which has accompanied collapse of such groups as Street Level, Shiloh, the House of the New World, and TLC is a negative corollary of the movement's revitalization power.

My research and personal experience indicates that when the process has ended, activists are often left bewildered, and disillusioned, if not embittered (McAdam 1988, 1989, 1999). Many of their ideas have become main stream, while they, in their failed attempts at institutional transformation, have seen their earlier political influence wane, or evaporate. The majority of the culture experienced a great calm-down due to the successful revitalization attempt to produce a less stressful culture. Stress and tension had been the fuel of almost pathological counterculture energy, but ultimately it takes a severe toll if the relief from stress which motivated the disciples is too long in coming.

The transition from charismatic leadership to routinization has been fatal for many groups. Some of the more socially activist, radical Christian groups, most of which did not survive, had tended more towards a socialist, or even mildly anarchist model of authority, reflective of the secular, politically left-oriented groups. This eventually destroyed them from within. John Hirt lamented, "We cannibalized ourselves."

Most of the high impact movements of the 1960s and 1970s have either ceased operation, as Shiloh, Spirit of Elijah, the Jesus Army, and the Highway Missionary Society, or metamorphosed beyond recognition, in the case of CWLF's move to Orthodoxy. Xenos and Calvary Chapel have institutionalized well and are stable for the foreseeable future, but their significance to the consciousness and values revolution previously documented, is not as apparent as that of some movements which have not survived. Most seem to have failed because of economic collapse, failed routinization, excessive opposition, and failure to adapt to new cultural realities.

The New Steady State

Routinization ushers in a new steady state. All tensions are not resolved, but the critical stresses are reduced to a manageable level, restricted again to a minority of individuals at the fringes. The acceptance and institutionalization of a reordered culture leads to this new steady state. People in general can cope again with their stresses and find a meaningful existence. The new steady state is very different from the previous one. Values have changed. New rituals and social forms have appeared. Wallace notes that "changes in the value structure of the culture may lay the basis for long, continuing changes in other areas" (Wallace 1966:163).

> A new Gestalt is in operation, for the members of the revitalized group and the host and/or neighboring cultures . . . [T]he Movement has been institutionalized. The neighboring cultures had a new Gestalt. I have spoken not only of the establishing of the New Religions on the landscape and in the description of the landscape but also of their "suffusive" character. Western religionists meditate; "secular man" thinks there may be something to astrology; collegians follow the Indians back to nature and tribe; Catholic liturgists adopt what they can from black revitalization religions. The episode may have passed, but the New Religion, even in "steady state," had changed the religious map, opened a new vista and made new options available to the subsequent generation. (Marty 1976:156)

This appears to have been the outcome of the process for North America since the 1980s, although much potential for stress remains. Previously incompatible theologies and alliances have emerged. Distinctly separate, easily identified colors of the religious spectrum of the rainbow of possibilities are fused into a new light, synthesizing many continuum possibilities. The whole spectrum comes together in a new perspective, such that it is possible to be at once, a Pentecostal, a Catholic, and a sacerdotal liberationist. *Hollywood Free Paper* founder, Duane Peterson, is now an evangelical, street-working, social justice oriented, Orthodox priest.

Summary –
Common Cause for Ancient and Modern Cultures

This chapter sought to describe in more details the principles and process of revitalization. It could be seen as a dated theory created before the popular shift to a postmodern epistemology. True, it was developed for description of homogeneous, indigenous cultures seeking survival from the effects of nineteenth century colonialism and its aftermath. In reply to such possible criticism, this chapter argued for its breadth of application, and catalogued the wide acceptance and engagement of the theory in more recent research, in a diverse range of inquiries. The research and conclusions of this project further support its continuing value as a movemental paradigm.

If the theory is truly paradigmatic, one would expect that despite local differences of culture, and historic details as to causes of culture threatening dysfunction, revitalization in the Native American and postmodern, techno-urban society would manifest similar dynamics and share similar cultural causality, ontological pathology, and processual development. This chapter sought to provide representative, though far from exhaustive evidence that in both cases the cultures faced culture degradation in sufficient proportion to deteriorate severely their social cohesion, meaning and fulfillment.

In both instances a psychosocial state of anomie, epistemological uncertainty and social conflict caused the groups to abandon hope in the cultural matrix and its institutions. The research supports the proposition that widespread decay of cultural stability occurred during the 1950s and 1960s, typical of conditions that precede and stimulate revitalization. The Jesus Movement, as part of the 1960s and 1970s cultural response to stressful times, followed the processual development route described by Wallace. The Movement's historic timing related to the disintegration, social upheaval and settling down of the culture as a revitalization incidence.

Initially classic prophetic leaders, whose success and failure depended upon the extent to which they followed the process Wallace described, initiated the movement. Encoding and transmitting a new mazeway, organizing and regulating the followers, dealing with opposition, exploiting political and physical resources and routinizing the functions of the movement in stable organization and economic security was the process that established some revitalization operations in a steady state of stable, enduring organization. For some groups the dynamics that produced innovative success initially were the cause of their demise. The seduction of popular acceptance produced an activism, which was blind to the need for organization and routinization.

A need remains for a final chapter to reflect upon the journey of enquiry from theoretical and practical perspectives, to apply the findings to current mission to society, and to suggest further research into aspects to which this dissertation has only alluded.

Notes

1. Melton (1996:85) reports that the religious movement incidence in America has expanded from 17 groups in 1790 to more than 2000 at the beginning of the new millennium. Hiebert says "contemporary religious history is to a large extent, the history of the rise and growth of new religious movements and messianic cults," embracing over 6000 in Africa and "thousands of cargo cults and prophetic movements" in New Guinea, Oceania, Japan, and the Philippines (Hiebert 1983:388-399).

2. Discussion continues as to whether virtually all religions are the result of human responses to periods of cultural stress (Ember and Ember 1999:285; Stark 1996a:78; Wallace 1966:30). The primacy of ultimate meanings of life and death, and the search for values and justice for human contentment and identity, belong rightly in the socio-religious rather than the scientific domain (Stark 1996b:428-433).

3. Martin also proposes that prejudice in the social science field against Christian, colonialist missions, further restricted a full understanding of the innovative, rather than merely nativistic, or culturally adaptive elements of revitalization amongst Native American tribes responding to the surrounding Western culture. The myth of primitive harmony (Edgerton 1992) has caused analysts to downgrade the genius of revitalization, which reconfigures a new cultural steady state, via an innovative marriage of traditional values and symbols with new rituals and meanings, survivable despite contemporary, cultural hegemonies.

4. See Melissa Pflüg 1998:59-60, 64, 68, 123, 133, 139, 189, 232-233, 235, 236, 240-241, 243, 245, and 247, 250.

5. Perhaps more recent medical evidence of the violent effect of extended marijuana use would help explain why the movement that began in peace activism, had by the end of the 1960s begun to manifest itself in violence among tribal-like dissenters in the dying days of the Haight Ashbury experiment.

6. Many scholars have recognized an enduring influence of 1960s movements on the overall secular and religious cultural configuration (Ellwood 1994; Glock and Bellah 1976; Guinness 1994; James Hunter 1983; Jorstad 1972b, 1990; Miller 1997; Roof 1993; Tipton 1982; and Wuthnow 1976, 1998). The Jesus Movement has been often viewed separately as a fundamentalist response, exploiting the genuine revolution rather than being an integral expression of the overall movement of the 1960s. Its notoriety via the press did not occur until the 1970s. Thus it has not been sufficiently examined, or understood, despite its pervasively influential impact on both mission and ecclesiology. This movement reflected a radical contextualization and application of the Christian message to a revitalization gestalt.

7. As previously noted in Chapter 6, Endnote 5, Victor Turner (1969) has popularized the term *communitas*. Following the experience of acute liminality individuals experience an intense sense of existential and timeless connection to each other, as they are re-aggregated in a new social arrangement, usually following stressful rituals. The common

term community embraces structural elements of the new arrangement, but the intensity, intimacy, mystery and existential bonding experienced in *communitas* is not necessarily inherent in the concept of community. Turner chooses the Latin term *communitas* rather than community, "to distinguish this modality of social relationship from the 'area of common living.' It is rather a matter of giving recognition to an essential generic and human bond without which there could be *no* society" (Turner 1969:96-97).

With specific reference to the common experience professed by both hippies and the counterculture Christian groups, I find Turner extraordinarily insightful as an outsider, but astute observer. Turner notes "The values of *communitas* are strikingly present in the literature and behavior of what came to be known as the 'beat generation,' who were succeeded by the 'hippies' . . . who 'opt out' of the status-bound social order and acquire the stigmata of the lowly, dressing like 'bums,' itinerant in their habits, 'folk' in their music tastes, and menial in the casual employment they undertake. They stress personal relationships rather than social obligations, and regard sexuality as a polymophic instrument of a immediate *communitas* rather than as the basis for an enduring structural social tie" (1969:112-123). Turner further speaks of the "hippie emphasis on spontaneity, immediacy, and 'existence' [that] throws into relief one of the ways in which *communitas* contrasts with structure" (1969:113). Turner notes that *communitas* is experienced particularly during life crises during the passage from one structural status to another. It "may be accompanied by a strong sentiment of 'human kindness,' a sense of the generic social bond between all members of society – even in some cases transcending tribal or national boundaries" (1969:116). He speaks of this state as sometimes producing a "permanent condition of sacred single 'outsiderhood' (1969:116). *Communitas* may be existential or spontaneous – "approximately what the hippies today would call 'a happening'," or "normative or ideological" (1969:132). He sees parallels between Gandhi's "holy poor," the poverty of the original Franciscans, and the chosen marginality of simple lifestyle hippies.

The choice of structural inferiority appears to create *communitas* (1969:133). Role playing and ritual process may be deliberately used to stimulate *communitas*, which "is richly charged with affects, mainly pleasurable ones" (1969:139). There is an apocalyptic form of *communitas* which is produced as a bond between those who share apocalyptic mythology, theology, or ideology, including millenarianism (1969:153). With the exception of the sexual aspect of the counterculture, the Jesus Movement shared to a remarkable extent the sense of intentional marginality, liminality, and *communitas*. The sense of mystical union and the transcendence of time and space I observed and experienced in the early days of the Movement were palpable. Something of this extreme, affective, mystical union, maybe observed in the early media photography of Jesus Movement worship, in which mutual ecstasy was apparent in the faces of dancing, hand-holding, Christian hippies.

Jung Young Lee (1995) makes much of Turner's theory, underscoring the creative power of marginality to create a New Testament *communitas of liminality and love*. He believes that the *communitas* reflected in the pentecostal community of the first century is only experienced by a choice of anti-materialistic, social marginality (1995:149-170). This was certainly a stance held by the early Jesus People, and to my observation the ecstatic and existential sense of *communitas* which marked the movement waned as the counterculture, marginal, anti-materialist commitment gave way to mainstream acceptance and the return to middle class values. The charismatic experience familiar to Pentecostalism appears to revive this phenomenon. Ritual processes in worship, youth festivals and special events such as baptism also create a temporary form of *communitas*.

8. By the late 1970s Ivan Illich had released *The Right to Useful Unemployment and its Professional Enemies* (1977) in explanation of the abandonment of the Protestant work ethic by disillusioned youth.

9. Miller 1997:26; Rogers 1995:399-400; Weber 1964:363-373, 1968:48-65, 80, 138, 144, 180-181; and Peter Williams 1989:17, 18, 69, 105, 108-109, 112, 114, 144, 232, 241.

10. A typology of Jesus Movements based on biographical histories of leaders, and subsequent styles, as well as membership biographies, could provide crucial insights into successes and failures of respective movements (Jasper 1997:64-68, 172-178, 240-241, 319).

11. The biographical tracts of influential movement leaders have recently been seen as a significant element in the human interaction with dominant cultural themes. Personal nuance and development of particular mazeways may hinge on intellectually or socially traumatic, isolated events in a leader's life. My own influence in the movement's social conscience was considerably influenced by one such, apparently random, traumatic encounter with a civil rights supporter. One confrontation at the conclusion of a public presentation triggered a permanent intellectual and moral reversal for the author, from a classic racist frame to civil rights commitment.

12. John Hirt (House of the Gentle Bunyip), John Smith (Truth and Liberation Concern and Care and Communication Concern), John U'ren (Theos), David Wilson (God's House), Mal Garvin (Fusion), and Fuzz Kitto (Koinonia) are examples from the Australian movement covered in this dissertation.

13 . With the exception of Dr. Athol Gill (House of Freedom and House of the Gentle Bunyip) not one Australian Jesus Movement leader had a graduate education, though a few had (undergraduate) college degrees. A personal sense of inadequacy in this regard was a driving force in the biographies of us all. Considerable ministry in secondary schools, colleges, and universities placed pressure on activists to keep abreast of both secular and theological literature. Most became avid readers and researchers, subscribing to professional and scholarly journals. The pursuit of a more analytical rather than fundamentalist response to emerging, postmodern, cultural distortions, caused most of our Australian Movements to identify early with the CWLF and Xenos genre of the American Movement. Added to this, was the seminal influence of a small group of academics such as Gill in Australia, Padilla in Latin America, and McAfee Brown in the United States.

14. Weber (1958:245-252, 1964:358-392, 1968) pioneered the concept of "charismatic leadership" and his descriptive typology has endured despite some opposition. Perhaps it would be advisable to explore the processes and meanings behind charisma, rather than seeing it as epiphenomenal to the movemental issue. I find the eclectic combination of the theories of Weber, Barnett, and Victor Turner congruent with the central place of charismatic leaders, at least in the foundational and inspirational stages of revitalization. Horsley also recognizes Weber's concept of charismatic leadership but calls for a more "interactionist concept," between leaders and followers, whereby "the catalytic function is to convert latent solidarity into active ritual and political action" (Horsley 1994:141).

15. Rodney Stark is somewhat dismissive of Weber, claiming "discussions of charisma did not move beyond definitional and descriptive statements and said nothing about the causes of charisma" (Stark 1996a: 24). Stark says little of the charismatic role of Paul the apostle in the Gentile, Jesus Movement revitalization of the first century, except to quote him as a commentator on certain ideas and processes of Christianity's meteoric rise (1996a:108-109).

16. Trafzer attributes this to "cultural bias and intellectual ethnocentrism that has prevented an understanding of native religions, prophecies, and spiritual movements" (1986:ix). The missiological concentration of scholars on the more pragmatic Chuck Smith, John Wimber, and the second generation megachurch leaders of the Jesus Movement, is to the neglect of such initiating prophets as Frisbee, Higgins, Blessitt, and Palosaari. This may indicate a similar ignorance concerning the nature and significance of Weber and Wallace's prophets in American, white, cultural revitalization, and in the more inclusive Pentecostal phenomenon.

17. The "big picture" impact of media images and the co-incidental cultural metamorphosis in the general society may be decisive in setting the strategies and tone of the movement. Movement leaders however interact with cultural realities in a variety of ways which may prejudice or promote the movement's survival. Marked variations of opinion, life choices, and worldview may occur between siblings who have been subject to almost identical cultural influences. This may be partly explained in terms of psychology, biochemicallly driven variations in temperament, relative positioning in the family, or cultural influences via diverse peer group experiences. Differing mazeway and life style choices however remain as variables that may be triggered by isolated events, which set a biographical path of remarkable consequence for the individual and for the development of social movements. In the Jesus Movement, political leanings of both leadership and disciples varied. Lifestyle variations were evident between sedentary and itinerant ministry participants. The philosophical flavor, the evangelistic content, discipleship materials, ritual processes of the groups and the educational background of members also varied considerably.

18. This is clearly the case with Blessitt and his lone ministry. Other examples are; Frisbee and Smith (Calvary Chapel), Higgins and Peterson (Shiloh), Hoyt (Upper Streams and House of Judah), Meisner (God's Army and Children of God), Palosaari (Street Level), Parks (Spirit of Elijah and Truth), Pederson (Hollywood Free Paper), Pulkingham (Church of the Redeemer), Wimber (Vineyard), Wise (The House of Acts), and Gillquist (CWLF/New Apostolic Order).

19. These would appear to include Nethery, (Grace Haven Farm), Hirt (House of the New World), Gill (House of Freedom and House of the Gentle Bunyip), Sparks (CWLF), and McCallum (Xenos).

20. Whether churches, rather than individuals, can be prophetic or apostolic, or whether the "prophetic" and "apostolic" element can be sustained within a community without the stimulation and vision of the resident or visiting prophetic and apostolic voice and charisma remains debatable. In Peter Wagner's new paradigm church plant stories, *The New Apostolic Churches* (1998) "apostolic" is "a pattern" in church growth movements (Wagner 1998:17). To establish the "apostolic" definition he draws on the phenomenology of the African Independent Churches, the Chinese house churches, the Latin American grassroots or "base community" churches and the modern charismatic movement. There are arguably more differences than similarities between the indigenous African churches, Chinese house church movements, and the new paradigm Western churches. The prophetic nature of some indigenous African movement founders is more congruent with some of the Jesus Movement groups. The mega-church movement has also reinterpreted these early Christian designations applying to an emerging sociological shape. The biblical and historical designation of prophet and apostle is far more closely aligned with Weber's description of "charismatic" prophet-leaders. The wandering charismatics of the Jesus Movement era are far more typical of such a calling than the next generation of mega church leaders, whose concentration is primarily upon the contextual shaping and managing of single, local congregations. This is not to denigrate the new

style of leadership and innovation represented by such prominent figures as Bill Hybels and Ralph Moore.

21. The Jesus Movement debate concerning the relative significance of charismatics, both itinerant and sedentary, to the later development of new communities of faith, and mega church congregations was long and divisive. In Australia the founding fathers of the communities were eventually designated as "one amongst equals," which term was indecisive and only intensified conflict over the authority of founding prophets to decide policy or action on behalf of the group. The charismatic, innovative skills that bond followers to extraordinary, inspirational leaders seem to militate against routinization and healthy communal regulation. Max Weber's phenomenological observation that charismatic authority is inversely proportionate to legal-rational authority is pertinent to this issue (Weber 1964:358-366).

Dennis McCallum concedes grudgingly that the leadership of Xenos, a well-routinized Jesus Movement plant in Columbus, OH, was the fruit of the visionary leadership, despite an initial theology of more community-based authority. Greg Leffel, an early young leader of Xenos, still believes that ecclesial form and movemental methodology is of greater importance than the gift of the charismatic in achieving the transformation of society (Leffel 1997:59-74 cf. McCallum 1999b:1). Many effective Jesus Movements groups divided or collapsed following conflicting views over the extent of authority vested in the founder-apostle, or in the community itself.

22. The author's position is one of synthesis, being unwilling to mollify or neutralize one position by the other. The timing, pace, extent, and manner in which the vision and authority are passed on from prophets, and apostles to the wider group is critical and depends on many variables. These must include the social nature of the group, the task and vision of the people, the sociopolitical context, the depth and extent of gift within the group and the underlying ideological framework to which participants adhere.

23. Albrow (1990) interprets Weber as distinguishing at least eight settings for the meanings from which an individual's leadership is driven (1990:211). For Weber, meaning arises from:

1. The actor's intended meaning
2. The meaning to the other person
3. The meaning on average
4. The meaning in terms of a dogmatic system
5. The meaning in ideal-typical terms
6. The meaning as discovered by social scientist/historian
7. The meaning to self
8. Institutionalized meaning (1990:211)

24. The argument for Jesus' direct social intention, and even revolutionary challenge in teaching and practice is contentious, but well established as a reasonable theory by the textual and interpretive works of numerous biblical scholars (Gill 1989; Gottwald and Horsley 1993; Ched Myers 1990, 1994a, and 1994b; Myers, Dennis, and Nangle 1997; Miranda 1977; Theissen 1978); theologians (Robert Brown 1984; Comblin 1998; Gutierrez 1973; Tesfai 1994); missiologists (G. Cook 1985; Costas 1974, 1982). Church historians (Snyder 1991; Yoder 1972) have added their findings to this body of opinion.

25. Weber's assessment of Wesley, with historic hindsight is open to question also. While Wesley may not have directly claimed a new revelation in the sense that founders of the Mormons or the Pentecostal movement have done, his theology and practice in the social context of 18th century England, radically challenged the deist developments of

the Enlightenment and the determinism of continental Calvinism. Vilification of Wesley and his followers as "enthusiasts" was accompanied by attempts on their lives on numerous occasions, such was the sense of threat to the existing order as perceived by some leaders of his day. Anglican clergy, who viewed him as a heretic promoted vigorous opposition, even encouraging street brawlers to break up open-air meetings. Certainly he recorded in his journals experiences of the Spirit and of revelation congruent with Weber's "prophet" motif, including an event in Fetter's Lane which modern Pentecostal have claimed was an experience of Pentecostal anointing accompanied by speaking in tongues. Recent scholarship concerning Wesley has questioned the traditional view that he was a Tory reformer rather than a revolutionary. John Wesley's understanding of stewardship as the redistribution of wealth (Jennings 1990:97-117) and his "demystification of wealth" (1990: 29-46) though pre-Marxist would disturb the dominant western cultures if comprehended and enacted by any political leader today. His position on slavery, with its accompanying trenchant rejection of market force arguments in defense of that "execrable trade in human flesh" (1990: 85) is a critical issue. His declared conviction that civil disobedience was a Christian necessity "notwithstanding ten thousand laws, right is right" and that "there is an essential difference between justice and injustice" (1990: 83-85) which legislation cannot change, was remarkably close to the contentions of the counterculture civil disobedience charters of the 1960s. The visionary control of Wesley over his movement, his counterculture stance against both church and state, combined with his "vital emotional preaching [and publishing] which is distinctive of prophecy" (Weber 1968:260-261) place him firmly in the tradition of the charismatic leader. His movement is also within the perimeters of historic revitalization movements. The remarkable aspect of Wesley was his ability to routinize what historians have described as a chaotic first few years into a dynamic structure and accountability formation which gave rise to the descriptive name "Methodist." The author's Jesus Movement group derived much of its radicalism, social activism, market place model of preaching from the example and teachings of Wesley and his Methodist teams.

26. In such movements as the Feminist Movement, the Animal Rights Movement, and the Anti-Nuclear Movement, incendiary prophets made vital contributions to ideology, political strategy, and the public perception of their cause. The charismatic authority paradigm of Weber's typology does not entirely coincide with all of the 1960s and 1970s counterculture movements, which were of a deconstructed, postmodern genre. The beginnings of such movements still manifested the initiating presence of visionaries whose oratory and apocalyptic style reflects the phenomenon of charismatic visionaries which Weber noted was widely evident across cultures and historic eras, being found in Hebrew, Christian, Zoroastrian, and Greek cultures (Weber 1968:255-257).

27. "John Smith, A Charismatic and Transformational Leader." Philip B. Muston (2001), MA. Thesis, The School of International, Cultural, and Community Studies, Edith Cowan University, Perth, Western Australia. The author is a graduate of the University of Melbourne and Nottingham University, United Kingdom. This thesis has been well researched, having the advantage of being written by one who has observed the author of this dissertation over 30 years, first as a youthful student, then as a professional journalist, and later as a mature Episcopal priest. Muston carried out extensive interviews with admirers, past and present staffs, detractors, disillusioned defectors from the movement, the founder's parents, spouse, and associates spanning 40 years. While sympathetic, it is critical and thorough. As far as I am aware it is the first such academic enquiry into the substance and style of a recent revitalization leader, particularly with respect to Weber's charismatic typology. The issues of relationship to the discipleship community,

the psychosomatic aspects of charismatic style, and the question of the necessity of hallucinatory visions as a prerequisite of revitalization leadership, are all well considered.

28. While Pflüg in my opinion reflects the same functionalist weakness as Wallace in the identification of myth and ritual as the central human need, I believe myth and ritual is a secondary function to ontology, epistemology, and spirituality. The revitalization theme remains pertinent however, in both nativistic and postmodern contexts. The "chicken and the egg" controversy denies the importance of neither chicken nor egg, irrespective of which comes first. The conclusions do however seriously effect our interpretation of religion and the nature of reality. That ritual process is universally crucial in human experience of religion and socialization is beyond question. See Victor Turner, *The Ritual Process: Structure and Anti-Structure* (1969), and in *The Anthropology of Experience,* Victor Turner, and Edward M. Bruner, eds. (1986).

29. For an archetypal account of the journey from iconoclasm to ritual process in the Jesus Movement, the reader would do well to read the final chapter of A. H. Matthias Zahniser's *Symbol and Ceremony* (1997). In this text he provides considerable detail of the many ritual processes employed by my own group, Care and Communication Concern, and explores the reasons for their development.

30. Literally thousands of alternative communes developed, as described in accounts of Calvary Chapel, Shiloh, and the House of the New World. Their names were often indicative of their philosophy and focus. Some were missional and therapeutic, and somewhat utopian as in the case of Shiloh and the Church of the Redeemer. The theological and social emphasis of the many movements varied considerably, often changing substantially according to the chronology of their development. Some groups that initially embraced utopian dreams turned to a therapeutic emphasis, or to spiritual mysticism in later disillusionment. My community was always rather Methodist in its strong sense of evangelical mission. John Hirt's community was a therapeutic center, a subversive, "alternative" utopian cell, a missional base, and an Anabaptist enclave.

31. The method by which the leaders fulfilled a prophetic and apostolic calling and the extent to which leaders adhered, or deviated from orthodox, historic Christianity requires further analysis. It is critical to uncover the dynamics of the shift from high energy, acute vision, and counterculture activism to the stage of routinization (Wallace 1966:161-163; Weber 1947:363-372).

CHAPTER 9

The Jesus People Movement – Revitalization and Mission

*Multitudes, multitudes in the Valley of Decision,
For the day of the Lord is near in the Valley of Decision.* Joel 3:14.

This book provides a history and analysis of the Jesus Movement and an enquiry into its significance for theoretical understanding and missiological implications. As an historical documentation of the Movement it is representative rather than comprehensive. It has however provided sufficient detail of varied and contrasting forms of the Movement to provide the basis for a reasonable hypothesis as to its causation, nature, and application to present and future society.

Common Cause

The data revealed considerable diversity of leadership styles, belief systems, and organizational forms. Despite this diversity, shared elements of context, purpose, and process formed a unifying pattern in the Christian element of the 1960s counterculture. Numerous localized expressions shared central themes, similar social causation, and parallel cultural processes despite widely varied geographical incidence and diverse outcomes. This fact indicates that there are social scientific explanations beyond the personal agendas of the initiators and participants. The numerous local expressions together form a unity of purpose and process and thus represent a definable social phenomenon. Chapter 8 served to demonstrate that revitalization theory is a specially suited lens through which to examine the Movement. Some distinct elements and applications of revitalization became apparent during this investigation of the Jesus Movement as an example of revitalization.

Predictable but Unexpected

Revitalization theory was devised by a social scientist whose personal bias was secularist. He believed that supernaturalism was on the way out in the 1950s and 1960s yet his research pointed to a social process typical of new religious movements in times of cultural upheaval. The counterculture movement of the 1960s and 1970s was a surprise to most theorists, particularly because of the movement's radically spiritual orientation at a time of rising secularism. Heinz remarks that the evangelical movement amongst youth was even less expected being "an advent no social commentators had predicted" (1976a: 3). In retrospect however, the cultural outcomes of that era were predictable, if analysts had speculated on the historic incidence of religious revitalization responses to other times and situations of extreme culture stress and social anomie.

Perhaps the possibility of a widespread religious response to the cultural malaise was obscured by the secularism which held sway amongst academicians before the influence of more sympathetic sociologists such as Bainbridge, Finke, and Stark (Bainbridge 1997; Finke and Stark 1997; Stark 1996a; 1997). The early signs of religious revitalization may have been eclipsed by the confident belief that secularism had triumphed. Temporarily blinded by the wizardry of science and technology, the cultural analysts failed to take seriously the growing spiritual angst among the minority culture of academic dissidents, popular culture artists, and counterculture youth. As we have seen in this enquiry, the genius of revitalization is its capacity to revive lost or dismissed tradition in synthesis with contemporary cultural reality. In times of cultural distress we would do well to keep a lookout for new revitalization movements that interact creatively with escalating spiritual hunger and reestablish languishing ethical norms in a new cultural configuration.

Flight from Stressful Times

The Vietnam War generation felt alienated by an older generation that provided neither motivating hope nor appropriate cultural responses to the crisis. The absence of hope in the youth culture and the loss of respect for traditional leadership and traditional ideology led French social analyst Jacques Ellul (1973) to describe the era as a time of deeply felt social abandonment. My research of counterculture literature, analysis of the pop culture, and interviews with scores of participants revealed a uniform perception by a significant body of citizens that Western culture was a culture *in extremis*. Many at the time viewed the world as "falling apart" (Jackson and Jackson 1974), in a philosophical, relational, and technological wasteland (Roszak 1972a, 1972c). Thus a plethora of counterculture attempts to reduce the level of stressful anxiety was born, finding final expression in the youthful search for Jesus as a culture transformer.

Revitalization Principles Elicited from the Research

The Jesus Movement shared elements of the counterculture's spiritual rebellion in its longing for relationship, a soulful faith, and an escape from the stress of greed, racism, class, and war. But its message had wider appeal. Many baby boomers suffering suburban alienation (Ellwood 1997:155) were open to the celebrating, love-oriented Jesus People. As Jesus Freaks discovered their lost Jesus family in receptive churches, their contagious, simple, relational faith and communications innovations were diffused throughout many traditional churches and new church plants. Behind the almost child-like faith and optimism of the Jesus Freaks lay an unscheduled revolution of thought and lifestyle that had resulted from social forces few of the participants recognized, or even thought to analyze. In retrospect, they may be seen as the consequence of those forces, but they were also culture changing, intelligent participants in an intentional movement to transform their dysfunctional society.

The Significance of Social Movements

As a power for cultural change in periods of crisis, social movements at times appear to succeed over and above normal processes of enculturation. While many movements and revitalization attempts fail, some succeed in substantially changing the culture. Social movements really do matter (Giugni, McAdam, and Tilly 1999). My findings suggest that of all forms of social movement, revitalization movements hold the most promise for widespread cultural renewal in times of extreme cultural malaise. It is my hope that this book will make some small contribution to the ongoing research into charismatic leaders, new religious movements, innovation, and principles of movement initiation and organization. This may be especially important at a time when a new generation is manifesting signs of stress and discontent with current social realities. During the period of research and writing, forays into the youth festival movement have revealed a renewed desire for a more holistic and communitarian experience amongst festival attendees.

Routinization – A Crucial Element of Revitalization

Further reflection on the critical success or failure of groups to intentionally modify the movement's innovative momentum by routinization may seem repetitious, following considerable treatment in Chapter 8, but the data indicates that this is possibly the most critical factor for survival in revitalization movements. If revitalization attracts followers initially because of the hope for the change it engenders and promises, it disillusions followers terminally when chaos, unaccountability, confused lines of authority, and poor communication create intolerable stress within the movement itself. If innovation outstrips stable management and overstresses the participants, then internal division and membership hemorrhage is inevitable.

Forewarned and Forearmed

Revitalization theory emphasizes the normality of culture change, under specific, abnormal conditions. Wallace contends that many revitalization attempts occur, but a minority survives (1966:30). The high attrition rate of the counterculture Christian groups is consistent with this observation. The picture painted in the previous chapters is one of creative chaos, magnificent achievements, some lasting successes, but too often of tragic disintegration. It is difficult to routinize and organize such chaotic energy to establish a stable, reconstituted steady state.

Most of the leaders of the Jesus Movement lacked both formal education and extended experience in leadership and organizational formation. "To be forewarned is to be forearmed." Revitalization theory provides invaluable data for future movements to consider at critical stages of their development. This research provides valuable clues to survival for such social movements, for the good of the over-all culture.

All major Australian groups either folded, or suffered serious setbacks at some stage, after astonishing success in the early years. During the period of attempted routinization, as illustrated in Chapter 6, internal failure rather than external opposition undermined survival. This weakness limited their ultimate impact and resulted in considerable psychological and relational damage to dispirited leaders and followers. Having begun with illusions of revolutionary success, they experienced disillusionment due to their failure to profit organizationally from their initial impact on the culture and from the resultant popular support.

If our Australian movement had been aware of revitalization processes, and had acquired understanding of the assets and deficits of charismatic leadership as explained by Weber and Wallace, the outcomes might have been vastly different. Knowledge of revitalization theory would have been invaluable for many leaders, whose charisma was not matched by knowledge, or training in movement theory, administration, and principles of leadership. If leadership had been aware of Wallace's revitalization process during the height of the Jesus Movement, predictably changes in its development could have occurred. Tensions developed within the Movement not only through personality flaws and ideological differences, but also from predictable cultural forces, though personal conflicts were often blamed exclusively.

Had the theoretical understanding of the causes and processes inherent in revitalization been common knowledge at the leadership level of the Jesus Movement, many disappointing failures might have been avoided. Leaders might have recognized those counterculture tendencies that created suspicion of organization and resistance to routinization. Resources, including creative personnel, should have been proportioned in a better strategy for long-term survival. Better balance could have been achieved between the inspiration of the masses to catch the counterculture vision of cultural renewal and the employment of facilitators and pastors to establish permanent, local units. Ministries could have balanced the elements of inward and outward journeys to avoid loss of personnel through stress. More concentration should have been given to planting stable communities, and to training pastors rather than proliferating wandering charismatics.

They might have embraced stabilizing ritual processes earlier. Truth and Liberation established stabilizing ritual processes much more intentionally after major division and regrouping in 1983. The threat of diminishing innovation and loss of vision often causes charismatics to fear organization and accountability, but such leaders could research ways and means periodically to revitalize the organization, to keep the communities they established missional in focus, but stable and less stressed.

Herein lies an all-important principle of revitalization. Arguably, the most successful group, Calvary Chapel, made the stability of the movement a top priority. Other West Coast groups – Shiloh, Highway Missionary Society, and Spirit of Elijah – blazed like innovative comets: they grew rapidly, experimenting and itinerating, but self-destructing within a decade. They failed to stabilize and routinize for economic and structural survival. In any culture the economic aspect is significantly integrated functionally with ideology, relationships and technology. There are inescapable economic aspects of survival. Without adequate resources and organizational maintenance of those resources the greatest visionary cannot lead a movement for long.

Visionaries who are essential to inspire people movements are not always adept at maintaining them. Weber noted that disregard for material things and willingness to labor without reward is typical of the prophet or true charismatic. He further identifies the charismatic's tendency towards avoidance of the "profane", the disregard often for daily routine, and an antipathy of the charismatic towards rationalist solutions to problems (Weber 1964:358-363). While rhetoric, native cunning and even miracles may gain initial supporters for the revitalization visionary, economic and resource failure will soon scatter the disillusioned followers.

Few leaders combine all the insights and abilities to sustain a fast growing movement for very long. The biblical paradigm of the functioning body, with many members contributing to the wellbeing of all is a significant statement concerning routinization. The case studies previously provided indicate the absolute necessity of structure, organization, accountability, routinization and shared responsibility in new movements if they are to survive beyond the initial euphoria, and certainly if they are to maintain a second generation leadership. My research underscores the fundamental significance of the processual order of revitalization. Unless the ministries closely followed the process outlined by Wallace (see Chapters 1 and 7), they did not achieve full revitalization status or outcomes. This is not only a theoretical perspective, but a pragmatic one also.

Marginalization and Innovation

The elements of social disorientation and marginalization are critical not only to the deterioration of the culture, but also to its possible renewal. Necessity is still the mother of invention. The innovative period of the Jesus Movement revitalization affirms the relevance of Victor Turner's (1969) model of ritual process in the journey to renewal and reintegration. The significance of cultural alienation, leading to a process of liminality, creativity, and re-aggregation to a new synthesis was dominant in the experience of the Jesus Freaks. As indicated in Chapter 8, this was a critical factor in the experience of counterculture *communitas*. Highly ritualized processes achieved the path through a liminal doorway into a new social synthesis of traditional values and revolutionary community, supporting the synthesis of the Wallace and Turner models.

The Brief Door of Opportunity

Wallace emphasized the short duration of possible entry through the doorway to revitalization. Within a few years of the initial outburst of creative energy, the chaotic nature of revitalization necessitates rapid refocus on organization and maintenance of the movement. In every group investigated, my research revealed a frantic pace of change in ideas and social experimentation during a relatively brief period. Almost all the major innovations of CWLF were in place within a year of its creation, including Right On, the Spiritual Counterfeits project, and pamphleteering during peace protests. Older institutions, advancing by legal-rational processes, take much longer to innovate. Their capacity to experimentally seize the brief moment of opportunity is severely limited by the sustaining processes of routine, tradition, and bureaucracy. Revitalization movements experiment at great risk under stress, providing a social laboratory of innovations, which should be visited by institutions that are losing creative initiative.

Identity, Meaning, and the Simplification of Social Complexity

Both Pflüg (1998) and Wallace (1966) note that personal meaning and identity are closely related to shared meanings (1998:35-65) and group identity (1998:15-36). When the group feels oppressed by alien forces, creating marginalization and social dysfunction, it seeks renewed meaning and identity through the revitalization process (1998:240-254). In the 1960s Western societies faced racial tensions, the Vietnam War controversy, rapid techno-urban change, scientific reductionism, ecological crisis, and soulless materialism.

A disaffected proportion of the culture sought to form an alternative society that would deliver meaningful identity and tribal relationships. It was not surprising therefore that the Jesus Movement emphasized experience above objective knowledge, ethics above theology, relationships above institutions, eschatology beyond history.

The Jesus Freaks sought, as the Odawa had done, to find a way to create a "contemporary narrative – mapping a 'New World,' a transformed status and the way things should be" (Pflüg 1998:10). They created movemental and communal names reflecting this dream – the House of the New World, the House of Freedom, the Christian World Liberation Front, The Jesus Family, God's Forever Family, Agape (Love) House, Love Inn, Resurrection Community, and Shiloh (" . . . until Shiloh come; and unto him shall the gathering of *the people* be" Genesis 49:10).

The tribalism of the hippies and the communalism of both hippies and Jesus Freaks reflected a crisis in existential meaning, identity, and ethical relationships for counterculture youth. The traditional path of the Odawa to a renewed Amerindian community was a similar quest. We may apply Pflüg's description of the Odawa prophets to the Jesus Movement. "The prophetic leaders reinterpreted and reapplied rituals and mythic themes to reintegrate communities and overcome threats of divisiveness and liminality. In so doing they not only reconstructed tradition but also carved a collective identity" (Pflüg 1998:64). The

Jesus People were bound together in tribal communality as Jesus Freaks, creating a sense of personal power and identity. The Jesus Movement was a quest for both individual and collective identity, and a search for meaning to make sense of a culture that increasingly failed to deliver either through its fragmenting mazeways or disintegrating social contract.

The Vexing Role of Leadership in Revitalization

Tension and pain over leadership power accompanied the evolution, organization, and routinization of most groups. No issue was more vexing than that of the basis of authority and the position of the charismatic founders. Significant charismatic personalities who broke with traditional institutions and social codes were found in the Jesus Movement units I investigated.

Leaders of less Pentecostal groups – CWLF, Xenos, and most of the Australian groups – made less of prophetic revelations in the authentication of their inspirational and visionary roles. Even so, the less Pentecostal examples – Sparks, McCallum, Gillquist, and Hirt – exhibited a supernatural sense of divine calling to the specific task of radical revitalization. This "calling" did not prevent conflict over authority and accountability. Even the teaching of "servanthood as the basis of authority" did not change human nature or the sociology of the movements. Some followers set out to make the authorities suffer

All the Jesus Movement groups shared a similar period of high stress over the authority of their founders once the initial creative excitement was over and routinization became necessary. This occurred irrespective of location, religious background, or level of theological sophistication of leadership and followers. In some cases, severe accusations were leveled against founders. Joe Peterson (1996b, 1988) has provided an excellent analysis of the demise of Shiloh surrounding the removal of the charismatic founder, John Higgins, which severely fractured the group. Ohio's Xenos suffered a severe split over leadership style, but unlike Shiloh, it survived and consolidated through the experience.

The most radical of the groups in terms of anti-materialistic, Jesus-centered communalism, JPUSA, has maintained collegial leadership and despite the downgrading of dominant charismatics they have a continuing "prophetic" voice. They routinized and organized early, and held to a well-developed code of faith and practice. They survive and thrive despite the shift in the general culture to conspicuous consumption. They continue to itinerate for the gospel but have not duplicated their ministry elsewhere.

Calvary Chapel established a smooth and enduring pattern of survival and spectacular reproduction of its ministry, but not without conflict and the departure of Wimber, Frisbee, and others. As early as my visit in 1974, some members were distressed at Chuck Smith's "benevolent dictatorship." Even the gentle, unassuming Jack Sparks was criticized for inordinate influence over decision-making in CWLF. He expressed personal pain concerning conflict between himself and some other leaders in a letter he sent to close friends around the world at the time of his departure from CWLF to create the Evangelical Orthodox Church of America on February 15, 1979.

In Australia, tension concerning the nature of power and authority vested in founders of the Jesus Movement led to diverse ideological frameworks. These ranged from democracy to "Christian anarchy" amongst the Anabaptist groups, the House of the Gentle Bunyip, and the House of Freedom. Conflicts over basis of authority resulted in the severe division of TLC. This tension also collapsed the House of the New World. The House of Freedom members claimed that they were "Christian anarchists."

In every case I investigated, the question of authority and the rights and responsibilities of the founders was a stressful and divisive issue. Research into the phenomenon of charismatic leadership will remain a challenge for those who analyze modern new religious movements and for those who seek to initiate new causes.

Revitalization movements require a counterculture vision, a focal point for the movement. The need for uncomplicated, rapid innovation, which is unimpeded by the slower, legal-rational requirements of committees, and precedent, invites prophetic, decisive leadership. The "felt need" for the abandonment of failed, dissatisfying social forms prepares the unhappy citizens for a natural bonding to charismatic, prophesying, activist leaders. Equally, if the dream is to be owned by the followers and the chaotic counterculture phase replaced by a culturally satisfying, predictable, orderly alternative, the role of the leader eventually must change. The transition phase appears to be consistently problematic. My hope is that this preliminary examination of recent revitalization will promote a more thorough enquiry into the inherent strengths and weaknesses of revitalization leadership.

With the help of a strong militarily trained colleague, Pastors Romaine and Smith established a clear line of command, a recognizable theological core, well run administration, and worship and missional routines following the innovations of the early Frisbee years. They, in contrast to many other failed groups, created a balance between innovation, movement, and stable, stress-reducing predictability.

During the twentieth century, the place of prophet and apostle in church planting and growth often was ignored before the rise of the Jesus Movement and the Charismatic Movement. Some scholars have underscored the vital importance of the prophet over the warrior, or the administrator, in Amerindian revitalization (Trafzer 1973). Some have recently emphasized the charismatic prophet (Horsley 1994, 1999; Stegemann and Stegemann 1999) as essential to the founding of Christianity. The secular enquiry into charismatic leadership in managerial theory has advanced significantly in the last couple of decades (Conger 1989; Conger and Kanungo 1998; Tichy and Devanna 1986).

The danger of hubris during the early days of fast, popular growth, parallels the positive significance of an exciting, visionary, innovative prophet as the inspiration for a committed following. Does revitalization attract certain dysfunctional individuals whose psychological abnormalities are functionally useful in times of social collapse? Are the dysfunctions which are sometimes characteristic of charismatic prophets amenable to change, or avoidable with foresight and strategic management? Are revitalization leaders created from ordinary personalities through the extreme stress of counterculture resistance? Do the historic conditions that stimulate revitalization create the charismatic persona, or is it latent and thus thrust to prominence by prevailing social conditions? It does appear that a combination of latent gift, opportunism, and culturally constructed awareness combine to raise innovative leaders in times of acute demand for innovation. From a religious perspective, what is the nature of the charismatic leader's call, and how do we authenticate it? Is leadership the primary cause of failure in the case studies, or was failure inevitable for many groups caused by sociocultural elements beyond local prediction or control?

Research Projects – Unfinished Business

Some aspects of this enquiry remain unsatisfactory because of brief or partial treatment. The Australian movement, being so far from the American tradition of revivalism and largely ignored in the standard Jesus Movement histories and analysis deserves greater attention. The usual development of revitalization moves away from initial countercultural, prophetic tendencies, but the Australian groups that have survived have retained a fair element of the "radical discipleship" model. The strengths and weaknesses of this are worthy of analysis. As a participant for 30 years this author is unsuited for the task of an independent history of the Australian Movement.

The vexing problem of routinization in revitalization is given preliminary attention in this work but much more detailed analysis of the process is necessary. A book specifically examining the process as embraced or resisted, in both successful and failed Jesus Movement units could yield needed insights for future movements.

The Jesus Movement dwelt close to the edge of Pentecostal and Charismatic movements. Perhaps the power of Pentecostal Movement locally and globally has been its development of a "micro" revitalization model. The megachurches appear to evidence a pattern similar to a localized revitalization. Research of these highly successful models, as possible revitalizations, is appropriate given the unprecedented global growth of the Pentecostal Movement in a period of global war, pestilence, and political dissatisfaction.

Revitalization leadership appears as complex as routinization, perhaps because the central role of the leader may equally facilitate or hinder the process. The nature, weaknesses, and strengths of charismatic leadership specifically within revitalization would provide an excellent basis for another book. The relationship of the prophetic visionary to the process of revitalization would be a sufficient challenge to research.

Finally, postmodernity purports to challenge many previously sacred models and concepts of belief and structure. This book was already too broad in scope and too diverse in research to allow for a postmodern analysis of revitalization. Will the loss of faith in the "big stories" of religion, science and politics undermine public confidence in social movements; or are such movements, even recent ones, forming on a non-ideological basis? It is high time for revitalization and postmodernity to dialogue in a book.

Missional Implications for Consideration

The counterculture of the 1960s was hostile toward all institutions, including institutional religion. Stagnation and complication of philosophy and function was a cause of culture stress during the 1960s. The institutional church approach complicated the issues and equivocated on issues of everyday values. While its ideological position was inclusive, it tended to derive its support from the high culture, rather than the popular culture. The Jesus Movement provided a simple, but ethically demanding message that appealed to the idealism and straightforwardness of youth. Some movement groups failed to establish lasting communities of faith, but in terms of penetrating the pop culture they were singularly successful.

Will the Church Fail Next Time?

Investigation of the movement's history, on three continents in northern, southern, eastern and western hemispheres, confirmed that during the first few years of revitalization, the established church was sometimes ignorant of the spiritual search on street and campus. The church was initially critical, or hostile to the peculiar appearance and behavior of the counterculture innovators.[1]

During our attendance at the Sunbury Rock Festival in 1971, my wife Glena spent many hours in conversation with counterculture groups and individuals. She was shocked at the volume of drink and drugs consumed, and by the completely casual attitude towards sex, but she warmed immediately to the openness of the counterculture. Glena was overwhelmed by the numbers of kids who had only the vaguest sense of direction in their lives, and no real belief, or framework in which to live.

As previously recounted, in the early hours of the morning she sat on the hillside reading her Bible and reflecting on the prophecy of Joel, which seemed existentially rather than exegetically, to sum up everything we had experienced that weekend. Tears streaming down her face, she read to me, "Multitudes, multitudes in the valley of decision" (See Figure 8.1). She looked across this sea of people and said, "John, here *they* are. But where is the church?"

Just Being There, for a Start

We both understood why we were there, because the church plainly was not, apart from a few old Salvation Army officers and the growing tribe of Jesus Freaks. But the church was not there, and despite improvements in communication, seeker sensitive services and market compatible growth strategies, the majority of evangelistic activity is still centered in the refurbished chapel, rather that the market place of popular culture.

The non-seeker, sensitive or otherwise, will not ever be at our upbeat, church based presentations. It remains for the church to live its message in the unfamiliar and disconcerting places of public intercourse and discourse. It bears repeating that church is meant to be "in the world, but not of it," but today it is "of the world but not in it."

When the physical location of the church building complex is the context of evangelization (even if the buildings are modernized and user-friendly), it will not engage the non-church culture comprehensively. Rather the church must adopt St. Paul's evangelistic strategy (Acts 17:17-21) by boldly repositioning itself in the market place and the academy to make friends of sinners as Jesus did. It is argued by some scholars that congregations averaging no more than twenty orchestrated the long-term triumph of Christianity in the Roman world (Strom 2000:173-181). They mobilized believers to invade the external world by conversation, compassion, and courtesy to all.

To the market place and centers of urban chaos they went, understanding the Master's commission as a call for disciples to *go* to the world rather than provide entertainment to bring the sinners *to* the church. This does not deny the excellent work done for "fringe" people by innovative megachurches. In fact it is possible to combine the concept of a locally relevant program in a modern building complex, with a mobilization of members to "be there" in the market place, but the "sanctuary complex" appears to dominate the agenda of the church's program at an exorbitant resource cost. If for instance $50 million used in building extensions were directed towards an army of young visionaries released to invade the bars, clubs, and other youth gathering points to build conversational bases for evangelization, would the impact on the resistant element of the culture be greater?

If our feet are familiar only to the sanctuary's carpets, rather than the dusty paths of cultural mobility, public discourse, and popular culture, it can only be expected that the majority of the unbelievers, and alternative believers, will remain unfamiliar with the mobile, revitalizing Savior. The Jesus Movement recaptured the boldness and invasive spirit of the first century tradition, and repositioned the ancient Pentecostal tradition of mission squarely in the context of a dysfunctional pop culture. When the Jesus Movement burst upon the pop culture scene in the 1960s the church released minimal resource, too little, too late, towards the revitalization opportunity. If the resources of traditional faith had been redirected early to aid the Spirit's revitalization activity, it is likely that a much greater proportion of that generation, mostly now unseen in the sanctuary, would have been attracted and employed in a transformation of secular culture.

Retracing the steps of the under-resourced but innovative Jesus Freaks provides a convincing case for a personnel-based strategy rather than a facility and program based agenda for renewing the culture. As previously noted, the problem of the counterculture evangelists was never one of successfully engaging and converting the opposition or the indifferent. The failure of many Jesus

Figure 8.1 Multitudes in the Valley of Decision – Rock 'n' Preach. Kaniva, Australia 1974

Movement groups was their inability to understand and cope with the stress of organization and routinization – an area well understood by the resource rich, traditional church. Perhaps the lesson here is to bring together the marginal, creative and often unmanageable and outrageous innovators, and the experienced CEOs of the establishment, on an equal playing field. This was substantially the secret of Calvary Chapel's success.

Don't Drag Your Feet

Since the window of opportunity remains open only briefly, a church that is committed to navel-gazing in the sanctuary remains unlikely to engage the popular culture in its time of brief openness through revitalization. Cultural chaos is the provocateur of cultural transformation. The church must keep watch for the moment of transformational likelihood. Rather than sounding the retreat during times of moral, social and political confusion and distress, the church must abandon the fortress and take to the streets. Join the revolution, and influence the outcomes. Leave the fold and seek the sheep, for in many historic strongholds of faith there is proportionately one sheep left in the fold to 99 outside the fold.

As the sun set on the counterculture in the mid-1970s, major denominations such as the Southern Baptists in the United States, and the ecumenical forums of England and Australia warmed toward the young rebels. They sometimes provided resources and personnel, cross-cultural communication opportunities, and political connections. John 'Uren, as described in chapter 6 was a master of strategy during the revitalization in Australia, connecting the radical young activists to political opportunity and to the resources of denominational and Government. The stimulating opposition had been a source of creative energy in the beginning of revitalization; the belated support of outside sympathizers was a factor of economic survival for some Jesus People, as too few churches opened their hearts and resources to hippie converts in time. The majority of churches missed the door of opportunity.

The AIDS crisis provides an illustration of a vital principle. The shift in world consciousness was swift and comprehensive. The church may have lost the initiative as it debated the proposition of the "plague" as a divine judgment and philosophized as the Greek sophists had done in the face of another comprehensive plague during the birth of Christianity (Stark 1996a:79-88). Then according to Stark, the revitalization movement that was the early church led the way and powerfully impacted the Roman world. The debate over the ethics of condoms and clean needles for drug users gave the impression the church was opportunist when it finally declared that Jesus loves AIDS victims. The leadership of the fight against AIDS is clearly a secular force, while the church has been eclipsed and relegated to the less culturally impacting role of mercy and care "after the fact." Thus by delaying until the territory was "safe" the church failed to be at the vanguard of opportunity to impact the popular culture. Similarly, it had initially debated hair length and rock music in the face of the hippie counterculture's search for faith.

In a dangerous and dramatic time of permanent global flux, the 21st century beckons the church to be bold, immediate, and activist. Social movements with a short shelf life, producing sub-cultural, people movement coalitions of mutual protestors, are a likely outcome of current globalization. Such groups usually comprise the unevangelized and their homogeneity provides the visionary church with a special window of opportunity.

What's in it for the Church?

Even by default, in the long term the denominations, or local churches, may have been the chief benefactors of the Jesus Movement, as their superior resources purchased the inspiring innovations of the street evangelists. This provided them with the tools to make considerable gains in growth (Reid 1991, 1995). During my research I have come to the conviction that the missing link between the period of church abandonment of popular culture in the 1960s, and the current interest in a missional focus for the church is the pioneering work of the largely forgotten apostles and prophets of the counterculture. It could have produced much greater outcomes in terms of penetrating the wider society at a time when there was greater sympathy in popular culture and the media towards Jesus and His young revolutionaries. In those days, even the *Doobie Brothers* were singing, "Jesus is just alright with me."

The most telling moments in the advance of the church are when it is movemental. It is then that it influences the culture. Fostering such movements is of paramount significance even if they are short-lived revitalizations. If resources had been available at the height of the tribal search for faith and community, the spiritual jungle of current pluralism may have claimed less wandering souls. My advice to the church is to be on the lookout for revitalization movements and to get on board before the gate of opportunity closes. Better still, the church should see itself in terms of revitalization rather than institutionalization, ever on the lookout for those prophets and apostles who by calling blaze the trail to better times.

The initial resistance and failure of the church to respond positively was significant, given the short period of revitalization available. By the time the Movement was recognized and embraced, the extreme stress period was in decline. As a participator and observer I felt deeply disappointed that the cultural changes in my traditional evangelical friends came too late to surf the wave of youth's intense search. It is symptomatic that worshipping Jesus People were singing, "Bridge Over Troubled Waters" almost as soon as the song hit the charts. Churches were adopting it as a paradigm of Jesus' care years later, when the popular culture had left it behind. From a missional standpoint, the church must be on the lookout for signs of revitalization and enter the cultural crisis at street level early, if it is to influence the culture rather than only save individual souls.

Profit while the Rush Is On

Social Movements deliver significant numbers of conversions during indigenous revitalization. If numbers of conversions is a significant issue, we should note that subcultural-tribal mass conversion is an outcome of popular revitalizations, for a brief period of heightened cultural tension. Such renewal periods not only deliver numbers, they deliver previously non-existing networks for future growth in less dramatic times. A young, countercultural, student-musician finds common cause with a 60 year-old, suburban housewife, across traditional age and social boundaries, when peace movement activism calls both of them to a Washington "sit-in" at the Pentagon. Later imprisonment for civil disobedience binds them together in a sense of transcendent meaning and *communitas* bordering on the dynamic experience of the New Testament church. If such people are to find the faith adequate for their journey towards liberated humanity, the church must be there and be involved. Revitalizations are a unique entry point for renewal of both the church and the world.

When a church lives at risk and makes friends with the dissenting fringe it taps the resources of network remote to traditional evangelism. One of the marks of the Jesus Movement was its penetration of subcultures not usually available to main stream church. The radical ambiance of the movement attracted political activists, environmentalists, and the marginalized seeking social justice. New networks were incorporated in the faith. It is during such brief times of cultural upheaval that the church often loses the opportunity. Much could be attained by a liaison between resource rich churches and creative movements at the early stages of revitalization's rapid innovation. Self- preservation, a natural reaction of institutions in times of change, often prevents the church from its potentially most fruitful advance.

The Magic of Marginality

Taking the message to the margins is not only a mission strategy from the standpoint of converting the outsider, but equally it is a model for recreating and re-focussing the church itself. The power of marginal status to create innovative alternatives and promote subcultural *communitas* is seen "through a glass darkly" by those who dwell in the centers of power and tradition. Counterculture engagement in the revitalization process creates radical disassociation and liminality. This is pivotal to the experimentation and innovation which the church must find if it will be relevant in a swiftly changing, cultural context. What began as an intuitive, socially driven journey to the margins of the youth culture has become a firm intellectual construct of theology and social science. Visionary, prophetic insight is established on the margins where there is nothing to lose and everything to gain by experimentation and openness to truth. It is no coincidence that the "whistle-blowing prophet" Ezekiel was taken beyond the city walls to hear the voice of God (Ezekiel 3:22).

Culturally we are increasingly dependent for survival upon our access to the brokers of the culture (Rifkin 2000:140), yet even the market strategy of the power elite recognizes the creativity in the "otherness" of subcultures and alien societies. Designer label companies spend millions of dollars to send cultural sleuths in search of creative ideas in ghettoes and alternative cultures (2000:173-177).

When bonds to traditional masters are broken the spirit of revolution becomes possible. It is the focus of our age to find comfort and to reduce stress, yet it is in the extremity of inordinate stress that we discover creative alternatives. The church, if she is to be creative, must embrace the creative conflict of ideas, the clash of cultures, and the sound of dissent amidst the din of conformity. The closer to Jesus the saints position themselves, the more marginal their voice sounds to the trunk-like conformity of state and church. As a strategy, the church should invest substantial resources in the risky, but promising contexts of dissent and divine dissatisfaction. Cultural stress is an invitation to creative engagement, rather than defensive retreat.

Revitalization rather than incremental change is the preferred model for the church in times of popular alienation. As one particular form of social movement, revitalization is remarkable in its capacity to be a bridge between liberal and conservative prejudice, and to synthesize popular dissent and conservative values. The Jesus People fused traditional and radical elements for survival. Even as their master had demonstrated 2000 years before, to be socially inclusive is compatible with intensifying values and beliefs. The renewal of societies under stress requires a synthesis of the historic past and contemporary reality. Perhaps the analogy of tree rings is an appropriate paradigm. Some years ago, my family was asked by a neighbor to chop down and remove a magnificent Australian silky oak tree at the margin of our property, grown from seeds I had collected from the bush. My son cut it down with a chainsaw while the family watched and bemoaned its removal. Only the stump remained. We had a brief argument about the age of the tree. It was settled by counting the annual rings of the tree on the remaining stump. A good dendrologist could not only calculate the age of the tree from the number of rings but also from the width of each ring, which were good or drought years. Its history is recorded in the "dead" rings.

The life however, is vested in the tenuous, most recent growth of the outer ring. If a two-inch slice, half an inch deep is cut around the circumference of the tree, the tree will die. The life and future of the tree is the last, half-inch-thick bark. If ring-barked, the sap which provides life to the branches and leaves is cut off and the tree dies.

Here I perceive an analogy of the church – institutional and movemental. The majority of the tree is what some people call the "dead wood" of its traditions, protocols, liturgies, history, and biography. Much of what some see as the "dead wood" of history, tradition, and ritual process, is the transmission of ancient wisdom and accumulation of redemptive stories. Meanings and concepts cannot be preserved and transmitted without symbol and ritual. It is peculiar that postmodernity sometimes demotes history while elevating the significance of story. The transmission of the text and of the story is a matter of history, and institutions, intellectual and religious, provide a basis for the synthesis of the old and the new in revitalization. Without that trunk or the rings of its history, its tradition, its core, the fragile life on the edge could not survive.

How tenuous and fragile are the growing edge of the tree and the future life of the church! If one strips the creative, marginal, outer edge of the life of the church, you have something like first century Judaism, which Jesus typified in terms of death (Matthew 23:27). Despite the rich heritage of history, ritual process, and redemptive story, the tree of life had been ring-barked. The religious form bore no fruit and provided only a vista of desolation. For those who ignored the tenuous life offered by counterculture prophets there could only be desolation (Matthew 23:37-38). The future of the tree is always vested in the vulnerable outer edge.

Life is at the margins, not at the position of control, or tradition. Perhaps that is why Jesus mostly worked at the margins. Life is marginal. No matter how successful yesterday was, one year on and it is a dead ring of the tree. Yet, without the "dead" rings of the church there is no body of intellectual continuity, no redemptive history from which revitalizing revolutionaries may draw their models, and reshape the present cultural realities. Somehow, we must maintain that central core of history and tradition, while promoting life on the edge. Revitalization periods provide an uncommon *kairos* moment for the church, if she will take the risk of faith. At such historic moments, she walks with Christ outside the gate of convention, creating a synthesis of prophetic experimentalism, and tried and proven values of tradition, structure, and organization.

Concluding Challenge

In the words of the peace activist song of the 1960s, "When will we ever learn?" It is my tenuous hope that such studies as this will provide another ring of history from which a new generation may forge analytical and practical wisdom. Like the prophets and apostles of the 1960s and 1970s, we can create a fusion of counterculture rejection of dysfunctional elements of the culture, and rich traditions, ritual processes and timeless values of a creative past.

It was known as the Jesus Movement because it was infatuated, intrigued, overwhelmed, and revolutionized by an historic and mystical engagement with the Galilean prophet. The desire of the CWLF to make Jesus an issue in Berkeley, amidst a plethora of emotive issues at the time, is what the movement was about. He alone seemed credible, or capable of leading a revolution of transformational proportions. It was a Jesus movement. It was all about Jesus – prophet, sage, itinerant hippie, unemployed wanderer, whistleblower against organized tyranny, friend of the outcast, mystic, Eastern guru, psychic healer, lover of lilies in the field, rejected genius, revolutionary, storyteller, winemaker, liberator of children and women, and an outlaw "with a band of unschooled ruffians" (Norman 1972). In the midst of revitalization chaos we called him the "still point in a turning world." Jesus was the ultimate culture stress-reliever.

I doubt much has changed since then. Jesus is still good conversation if you can get the religionist's hands off his throat long enough to let him to speak for himself. Even the Muslims, the Buddhists, and the Australian agnostics have time for him. The passionate drive to make Jesus the topic of liberating conversation was possibly the simplest, yet most profound of the principles of missiology successfully employed across cultural diversity by the Jesus Freaks. If the church would be a revitalizing, alternative movement, penetrating and renewing the culture, it must recover the principle of centering in the most arguable, most believable, most inviting, most adaptable, most imaginative, most compelling reason for the outsider to believe. The church is always at its best when it is a revitalization Jesus Movement.

Notes

1. The following testimonial from sociologist Joe Peterson is typical of many stories of initial conflict and confusion between the hippie believers and established churches:

"It didn't take me long to sober up and realize that some people experience Jesus, and some people just follow the routine, and there's terrific judgmentalism. There was terrific persecution going on in the Jesus Movement from other Christians; many hassles; and lots of competition. Christians organized to try to drive us out of town. One time later I went to a meeting for Bill Glass. A couple of pastors know me. An Assembly of God pastor sitting in front of me stands up and says, 'How are we going to get these young people out of that House of Elijah?' Everyone who knew me just went stoned faced. I did not say anything. Nobody responded. He then sat down. Things went on like this frequently. [There were] all kinds of attempts to get rid of us; constant criticism. I was even offered money to be bought off by other members of churches. If I would leave and take the people with me, they would give me money and pay for a way out of town; all kinds of things. Not only that, but Billy came one time to see me. He had just come back from Alaska and he had on gold nugget watches and jade rings, and he offers me money if I would join his group. He would put these people to work. 'You wouldn't have to work another day in your life Joe.' He was a real estate agent before he got the Jesus People going. All kinds of stuff like that would happen. It just drove me into the Bible. Then Carl Parks and his people were very helpful at that time."

"There were pastors who were supportive of us. The Stone Church, a big Assembly of God in town – Dale Carpenter the pastor at one time, told off his elders who were complaining about the Jesus people coming to the church. It was a big charismatic church so it was easy to go in and wave our hands at the altar. We didn't know any better. He said he would quit if they did not allow us in the church. In another church, a Methodist African Episcopal combination kind of church, people had complained that some of the Jesus people had shown up in jeans and sweat shirts, and he was up there preaching God loves you no matter what you're wearing. He whipped off his robe and he had on his jeans and sweatshirt."

"The conservative Baptist pastor called me a couple of times saying how much he admired what we were doing, and it was something he would have liked to have done, but he couldn't. He could not let anybody know and he could not talk to me in public, or let anyone see him with me. So then, there was ostracism and I don't blame them.

There was accusation we were stealing kids out of their churches, but we did not have any of their kids. They were all migrants. We were drug users and things like that [they claimed]. We joined the evangelicals. We joined the association of churches. We went to church and did all kinds of things and would not be a church like the one [you] go to church on Sundays. We would not do that. We told people if you want to go to church, you can go to church. It is not about church. Our church cannot go to you. You are church 'Where two or three are gathered in My Name.' We wrote our own songs because nobody knew the Christian songs. Sometimes we would take hymnals and write our own music to it because we could not read music. We would be very amused when we would go to church and hear how these songs really sounded. When we played our versions, we were accused of being demonic."

"One time I was speaking at a big coffeehouse and the staff all became Christians in one night. They had me come back a few nights later and the place was packed with over 100 people. [There were] two women standing by the back door clutching their bibles. They came up to me and said "Joseph, we know you are of the devil because you use certain phrases. I spoke in hip street language and I used *Letters to Street Christians* at that time King James was still a struggle. The *Living Bible* had just come out. They told me they thought I was of the devil. The major reason was because they had been teaching the Bible to the young people for 20 years and never got that attention, so the only reason I got that kind of attention was because it was of the devil."

"They said they felt they should pray for me. I could always use prayer so they proceeded to cast out the demon of 'mesmerization' and stuff like that. They got a hold of several of our people and it got pretty bizarre. Many bizarre things happened. It was very, very intense and in many ways, very unpleasant." (Peterson 1999a:10-12).

APPENDIX 1

A Time Line for Developments during the 1960s and 1970s with Significant Political, Popular Music Culture, and Jesus Movement Events

Introduction

This is an alignment of popular culture and music events of the post-World War II counterculture period, which nurtured, or provoked a revolution amongst youth in the non-Christian youth culture. Synchronized with that I have added details of the Christian subculture that became known as the Jesus Movement.

Several issues emerge when noting the timing of the Jesus Movement. It appears during the splintering and disintegrating stage of the counterculture, as drugs and violence compromise it. The first haven for the counterculture, as the storm develops, is that of alternative religions, particularly Eastern beliefs. The Jesus Movement surfs on a growing wave of spirituality from other sources.

It is also notable that the decline of the Jesus Movement as a major force begins soon after the shift from counterculture values to a market driven culture again. Once the Cold War has ended and the scandals of Watergate and Spiro Agnew are gone, the force of the youthful rebellion dissipates. The inevitable domestication, which comes with career and family, further erodes any cohesive resistance to consumerism and radical individualism. The communal experiment is thus abandoned by all but a few dedicated, spiritually focused groups, not all Christian in orientation.

The importance of the violent and tragic events of the 1960s and early 1970s is reflected in the music of the times. The relationship between Eastern gurus and many of the most popular rock and folk singers during the 1960s is now well documented, but its significance may not have been fully realized by many scholars. The relationship between the popular culture, particularly music, and the spread of a reconfigured worldview that embraced elements of Eastern philosophy, is subject matter for another dissertation.

A series of steps led to the final period of deep disillusionment, producing for a brief period an exceptional openness to an indigenous Movement of evangelical faith amongst hippies. This was assisted worldwide by the radical relocation and worldview shift of some slightly older, evangelical leaders. During the earlier period from the mid-1950s to the mid-1960s there was not only a widespread rejection of previous cultural norms in such areas as civil rights, but there was also an optimistic sense that the old order would collapse. It is difficult for those who were not counterculture or civil rights' activists in that era, to realize the emotional and cultural dynamic of a song such as Dylan's *The Times They Are a Changin'*, or the moral rage provoked in millions of youth worldwide as they listened to Dylan's *Master's of War*. Some of us as young evangelicals, without abandoning our biblical framework, were more motivated to mission by some of the music of our contemporaries than any other factor. It was literally life changing.

The involvement of key music figures in the use of transcendental drugs to open spiritual doors of consciousness, and the later shift of some of them towards meditation, and other Eastern practices to the same end, made a big impact. It is possible to understand the timing of the rise of the Jesus Movement, basically in response to the disenchantment of the counterculture, without pondering both the political and popular cultural events coincidentally.

By the end of the 1960s the counterculture, which had begun as a more communal movement, was in disarray and the generation that had hoped to "change the world, rearrange the world" (Crosby, Stills, Nash, and Young 1970a) now turned inward, seeking to find personal spiritual fulfillment and enlightenment. Some believe that the *Beatles* release of the simple love song *Hey Jude* in 1968, was a declaration that the generation was giving up the search for truth and spirituality. It was returning to the same old romanticism, which had already failed in the 1950s. The counterculture generation found a voice for their protest and a comfort for their anguish in the music more than any other place.

It is important to compare the musical developments and the personal tragedy in the lives of the human icons of that period, with the political events which gave rise to the youthful, cultural insurrection, as exemplified in their life and music. After the Kent State shootings, Crosby, Stills, Nash, and Young produced their angry song of protest by declaring *Tin soldiers and Nixon coming; We're finally on our own*. This song, *Ohio*, evoked passionate responses from many of the youth, which were talking seriously of the possibility of a generational war. It was felt by some that the older generation and the political structures were so recalcitrant, that no revolutionary changes to the culture could occur. They would kill their own unarmed children rather than admit to shame, or countenance change. It was the musical troubadours in both the secular counterculture and the Jesus Movement, who very often carried the wishes, the anguish, and the ideology of that affective generation.

Andrew Fletcher in 1703 said, "Give me the making of the songs of a nation and I care not who makes the laws" (Stuessy 1990:393). Ethnomusicologist Alan Merriam observed, "The importance of music, as judged by the sheer ubiquity of its presence, is enormous . . . . There is probably no other human cultural activity which is so all-pervasive and which reaches into, shapes, and often controls so much of human behavior" (Merriam 1964:218). Century's earlier Martin Luther had said, "Music is one of the greatest gifts God has given us; it is divine and therefore Satan is its enemy. For with its aid, many dire temptations are overcome; the devil does not stay where music is" (1990:394). In no place was the evidence of the cultural reconfiguration of values more evident during the 1960s than in the popular music of the youth. The lyrics and commitments of musicians underwent drastic and swift transformation by the end of the 1970s. Stuessy reflects the cultural change that impacted the popular music styles, with the insight of a musicologist:

> Society fragmented into hundreds of subcategories of self-interest groups. The relative simplicity of the old demographics - male and female, youth and adult, black and white, lower, middle, and upper class - fragmented into a complex array of demographic clusters. The sellers of products and services responded accordingly. A specially designed product or service was made available for each mini category within the society. As John Naisbitt wrote in *Megatrends*, we moved from an "either/or" society to a "multiple option" society. Naisbitt points out that the automobile industry offered 752 different models, including 126 different "subcompacts"; there were over 200 brands of cigarettes; a store in Manhattan specialized in light bulbs, offering 2,500 different types. By the end of the decade, instead of three television networks, cable systems offered the viewer over forty choices. Grocers offered not just mustard but everything from peanut mustard to all-natural, salt-free, Arizona champagne mustard" (Naisbitt 1982: 241). There were magazines for every conceivable mini group; the bookstores were stuffed with self-help books on everything from diets to how to make a million dollars.
>
> By the end of the decade a new self-orientation had begun to grow as the focus turned toward self-realization and self-fulfillment. People wanted to "find themselves" and explore their own consciousness, to learn "who they were." With the tragedies of 1969 to 1971, this trend became dominant. The attitude became one of "to hell with society, I must take care of me." Students from the 1970s were less concerned with world peace and racial equality, and more concerned with acquiring the skill needed to get a job and make money. As a by-product of this withdrawal process and the new "me-ism," there seemed to be a reaction against the heavy complexities of the 1960s. Many youth of the 1970s were tired of the heavy issues, the obscure texts, and the intricate complexities of 1960s rock. Instead of the experimentation of the Beatles and the sophistication of jazz rock and art rock, many went "back to the basics" and embraced the simpler styles of disco, country-oriented rock, and hard rock. (Stuessy 1990:302-303)

The communitarian and utopian dreams took on a sentimental wistfulness, replacing the strident commitment to social change, which had emerged in the protest songs of the 1960s. Now youth may have extended the rebellion of the generation gap, but as one wit put it to me, "We rebelled, but we knew what we were rebelling against. These kids just rebel for the sake of it." The evolution from idealism to disillusionment, to Eastern mysticism, to fragmented individualism, is apparent in the following time line.

Unless otherwise stated the information concerning music events and chronology have been obtained from Bob Dylan (Bob Dylan: *The Very Best* 1993, and *Bob Dylan's greatest Hits* Vol. 3, 1994); Bernie Howitt (*Rock Through History: Understanding the Modern World through Rock and Roll 1950s to 1980s* 2nd edition, 1994); John Smith and Alan Harvey (*Searching for Satisfaction*, 1996); Joe Stuessy (*Rock and Roll – Its History and Stylistic Development*, 1990); Steve Turner (*Hungry for Heaven*, 1995). Details of Black Civil Rights are from Charles M. Christian (*Black Saga: The African American Experience: A Chronology*, 1995). Historical details unless stated otherwise are obtained from Obst and Kingsbury (1977); and Unger and Unger (*The Times Were A-Changin'*, 1998).

Entries concerning music, arts, and pop culture are listed in different type face and font size, to underscore the significance of popular culture in promoting revitalization attempts:

A Time Line of Secular and Jesus Movement Events

Font Details

Standard Times New Roman font = General political and social events
Larger Helvetica font = Popular culture – history and biographical details.
Times New Roman bold = Jesus Movement and related religious, historical details

1954   May 17: Supreme Court outlaws school segregation in Brown vs. Board of Education

1955   Rosa Parks arrested for refusing to give up her seat on a bus to a white man in Montgomery, AL.

1956   November 13: Supreme Court bans segregated seating on Montgomery buses.

1957   Little Richard quits rock to go to Bible College, returns later to rock, finally quits in 1977 to become an evangelist in the Universal Remnant Church of God.

August 29: Congress passes first Civil Rights Act since reconstruction.

1958 **Jack Sparks later leader of the Christian World Liberation Front, (CWLF) Berkeley, CA is converted to active Christian faith.**

May 17: Between 15,000-30,000 Americans, mostly black, convene on the steps of the Lincoln Memorial in Washington DC to pray and demonstrate for the black voting rights act being debated by politicians

1959 **Peter Gillquist (later colleague of Sparks) makes a firm commitment to Christ at the University of Minnesota Fraternity Bible study run by Campus Crusade for Christ (Campus Crusade).**

Gordon and Mary Sue Walker, graduates from Southwestern Theological Seminary, Fort Worth, TX, have pastored several churches, and have a heart for evangelism. They contact Gillquist about joining Campus Crusade. They later become colleagues of Sparks and Gillquist, and co-workers of the Grace Haven alternative community in OH.

1960 A thousand black college students protest against segregation in Montgomery.

94% of the South's black students are in segregated schools.

In Philadelphia, 400 Black ministers lead a boycott against Sun Oil, Gulf Oil, Pepsi Cola and Tastee Baking, obtaining the hire of 600 Blacks for middle and higher administrative and managerial jobs.

Timothy Leary discovers the therapeutic use of psychedelics.

Peter Gillquist meets Dick Ballew and a number of men with whom he "would spend the rest of my life" at a Campus Crusade conference in Twin Cities. Gillquist joins Campus Crusade at Southern Methodist University, Dallas, TX, while enrolled at Dallas Theological Seminary.

February 16: Lunch-counter sit-ins spread to 15 cities in five Southern states.

February 1: A wave of sit-ins begins in Greensboro NC started by black college students.

February 13: France becomes the fourth nation to explode an atomic bomb.

376   Appendix 1

        The Student Non-Violent Coordinating Committee is founded.

        March 5: Elvis **Presley is discharged from the Army**.

        March 15: Police arrest more than 350 students during Orangeburg, South Carolina lunch-counter protests.

        April 9: FDA approves first public sales of birth-control pills.

        April 10: US nuclear submarine completes a round-the-world voyage.

        April 21: Race riots break out in Mississippi.

        June 12: **Roy Orbison's** *Only the Lonely* **enters the Top 100 songs**.

        June 30: Belgium's grant of independence to the Congo leads to power struggle among black factions

        July 31: The Nation of Islam calls for a Black State.

        August 19: Russia sentences U2 pilot Gary Powers to 10 years jail for espionage

        September 26: The first of four TV debates between Kennedy and Nixon is aired.

1960   October 12: Russia's Krushchev pounds the table with his shoe at the UN 25 anniversary resulting in pandemonium and adjournment of the session.

        October 17: Four national chain stores announce integration of lunch counters in 112 Southern cities.

        October 26: Kennedy secures Martin Luther King's jail's release after his Atlanta sit-in arrest.

        Nov. 8: Kennedy narrowly defeats Nixon in the closest presidential election since 1884. A catholic occupies the White House for the first time.

        December 2: Pope John XXIII meets the Archbishop of Canterbury for the first time since the Catholic/Anglican split in 1534.

1961   **Jack Sparks, while a faculty member of Colorado State College**

(now The University of Northern Colorado) meets Ballew, who requests that Sparks become a Campus Crusade faculty sponsor. They will be involved in the Berkeley radical Jesus Movement group, CWLF in the early 1970s, moving to Antiochian Orthodoxy a decade later.

Gillquist begins work in Chicago, IL recruiting Wheaten College students to develop Campus Crusade ministry at the Northwestern University.

February 21: **The National Council of Churches approves artificial birth control in family planning**

Race riots break out in Mississippi and the University of Georgia.

A Japanese Zen master, who arrived in the San Francisco Bay area in 1958, sets up the Pacific Zen Center. (Between 1965 and 1966 the number of students at the center doubled).

March 1: President Kennedy creates the Peace Corps.

March 5: Alan Shepherd becomes the first American in space.

March 13: Freedom Rides begin to test discrimination in public facilities, having left Washington DC to march south on March 4.

March 17: US launch the unsuccessful attack against Castro's Cuba.

March 21: US military aid sent into Laos

April 17: The Bay of Pigs; unsuccessful US attack against Castro's Cuba.

1961 May 1: Gary Powers in US U2 spy plane is shot down by the Soviets.

May 1: To *Kill a Mocking Bird* wins the Pulitzer Price.

May 20: Four hundred National Guardmembers battle white citizens in Montgomery, who are reacting to Federal government enforcement of integration.

May 30: CIA-financed assassins kill Dominican Republic dictator Tryillo.

June 5: The Supreme Court orders Communist organizations to

register.

June 16: Russian dancer Rudolph Nurveyeu defects at the Paris airport.

June 18: Ben E. King's *Stand by Me* tops Rhythm and Blues chart.

July 2: Author Ernest Hemingway suicides.

August 10: The Justice Department drops its 27-year-old ban on importing the Paris edition of Henry Miller's *Tropic of Cancer*.

August 13: East Germany closes the Berlin border and begins building the Berlin Wall.

September 1: Russia resumes atmospheric nuclear testing, breaking a three-year moratorium.

September 18: UN Secretary General Dag Hammarskjöld dies in a plane crash during a Congo peace mission.

October 6: J.F. Kennedy pledges nuclear fallout protection for every American in view of Soviet A-bomb testing.

October 23: A Sino/Soviet split surfaces when China's Chou En-Lai walks out of a Communist World Congress in Moscow.

December 11: Kennedy sends the first combat-level troops, 400 helicopter crewmen to South Vietnam.

December 20: Reports show 2,000 US Military advisers and technicians are in South Vietnam.

1962 Two black churches are incinerated by white supremacists in Sasser, GA.

Bob Dylan declares the answer is *Blowin' in the Wind*, asking disturbing questions about war and freedom:
How many times must the cannon balls fly before they're forevermore banned?
How many times must a man look up, before he can see the sky?
How many years must one may have before he can hear people cry
How many deaths will it take 'til he knows too many people have

died?
How many years can some people exist before they're allowed to be free?
How many times can a man turn his head pretending he doesn't see?
The answer my friend, is blowin' in the wind (Dylan 1993:17-19).

January 29: Nuclear Test Ban talks in Geneva between US, USSR, and Britain collapse after three years

April 25: US resume atmospheric nuclear testing despite widespread protest.

June 11-15: The Students for a Democratic Society hold their national convention at Port Huron.

June 25: **The Supreme Court bans prayer in schools.**

July: The Telstar satellite relays the first live telecast continent to continent

August 5: **Pop Icon Marilyn Monroe dies under suspicious circumstances.**

September 27: **Dylan earns his first** *New York Times* **review.**

October 1: James Meredith enrolls as the first black at University of Mississippi s.

October 15: US pilots in Vietnam shoot first despite orders to fire only in defense.

October 18: The Nobel Prize honors the discovery of the DNA double helix.

October 20: **Peter, Paul, and Mary led the LP charts.**

October 23: Kennedy orders the blockade of Cuba in the Russian Missile crisis.

November 5: *Silent Spring* by Rachel Carlson tops the non-fiction best seller list and causes pesticide uproar.

December 31: Reports indicate 11,000 US military advisers and technicians are aiding South Vietnam.

1963 Long before Margaret Mead (1971) pens her famous anthropological reflections on the nature of the generation gap, Dylan releases *The Times, They are A-Changin'* (Dylan 1993:110-111) indicating an astute understanding of the extent and nature of the cross-generational conflict.

Dylan prophesies, *It's a Hard Rain's A'gonna Fall* (1993:28-30).

Timothy Leary becomes begins lecturing theological students and enlisting them in sacramental use of "acid" (LSD) to create mystical, transcendent experiences.

April 12: Peaceful demonstrators in Birmingham, AL are met by angry white citizens and police brutality. Photographs of the attack dogs terrorizing women and children elicit national sympathy and support for the Civil Rights Movement.

April 16: Martin Luther King Jr. writes his *Letter from Birmingham Jail* on toilet paper and note pad sheets while incarcerated there.

May 27: Harvard fires Richard Alpert for his LSD experiments and dismisses Timothy Leary at the semester's end.

June 12: NAACP field secretary, Medgar Evers is murdered on the doorstep of his Jackson, Mississippi home by a leading white segregationist (Christian 1995:417).

June 17: First woman in space is Russian Valentina Tereshkova.

June 20: California courts label Lenny Bruce a narcotic's addict.

June 26: J.F.Kennedy makes his "Ich bin ein Berliner" Berlin Wall speech.

June 29: Peter, Paul, and Mary make Dylan's "Blowin' in the Wind" a commercial success.

July 26-29: The Newport Folk Festival crowd hails Bob Dylan, Joan Baez, Pete Seeger, and Phil Ochs.

August 28: A quarter of a million Americans march on Washington DC in a civil rights' protest. They gather at the Lincoln Memorial and hear Martin Luther King Jr. deliver his immortal *I Have a Dream* oration.

	September 15: A bomb is set off in the Sixteenth Street Baptist Church, Birmingham, Alabama kills four young black girls.
	Blacks boycott Chicago schools.
	November 2: South Vietnam's President Ngo Dinh Diem is killed in a coup.
1963	November 20: American Military personnel in Vietnam number 16,800.
	November 22: J.F. Kennedy is assassinated in Dallas.
	November 29: Lyndon B. Johnson is sworn in as President of the United States.
	December 4: The Ecumenical Council votes to permit the use of the vernacular in Catholic Mass.
1964	During the 1964-1965 academic year, the Free Speech Movement of student rebels arose at the University of California, Berkeley campus
	Brian Wilson of the *Beach Boys* takes acid and says "I saw God and it just blew my mind."
	Dylan releases arguably the most savagely antiwar song of all time where he accuses the military leaders in *Masters of War* (Dylan 1993:68-69) of hypocrisy, soulless materialism, and exploitation of youth.
	January 29: The anti-nuclear film *Dr. Strangelove* is released.
	February 7: *The Beatles arrive* at New York, appear on the Ed Sullivan Show and all rating figures are smashed. Beatle mania hits the US. Until May 2 they will hold No. 1 single and album positions in the US charts – they hold the first five spots on US charts on April 14.
	February 25: Cassius Clay adopts the Muslim Faith, becoming Muhammad Ali.
	May 24: First issue of LA Free Press sparks off an underground newspaper trend.
	June 1: The *Rolling Stones make* their first American appearance.

Freedom's Summer, voter registration marches occur.

August 4: The dead bodies of three civil rights workers involved in the voter registration are found murdered in Mississippi.

October 14: M.L. King Jr. Wins the Nobel Peace Prize.

October 16: China explodes its first atomic bomb.

November 1: Ray Charles is arrested on narcotic charges.

December 3: The Berkeley Free Speech Movement ends with 796 arrests.

1965

December 11: Soul music's "great" Sam Cooke is shot dead. Bob Dylan releases his anti materialistic song *Like a Rolling Stone*.

Simon and Garfunkle release *The Sounds of Silence* album reflecting the influence of Eastern monism on the musical scene.

Harvey Cox releases his book *The Secular City*.

January 2: M.L. King makes Selma, Al the focus for voting rights.

February 7: President Johnson orders the first sustained bombing of North Vietnam.

February 21: Malcolm X is assassinated.

March 7: The Selma to Montgomery Civil Rights march begins.

March 8: President Johnson sends the first ground combat troops of 27,000 to Vietnam.

March 21: The National Guard is employed to protect the Freedom March.

March 26: The Ku Klux Klan murders white civil rights activist Viola Liuzzo.

Spring: Mick Jagger and the *Rolling Stones*, release *I Can't Get No Satisfaction* (1990:159). By July 10 it leads the charts.

June 3: Edward White is the first United States astronaut to walk in space.

June 14-18: Arrest 856 people during voting protests in Jackson's Mississippi.

July 9: Congress passes Voting Rights Act of 1965. Signed by LBJ August 6.

July 21: In the Vietnam conflict, 503 have died.

July 25: Bob Dylan outrages his followers by abandoning his acoustic guitar for the electric guitar.

August 11: In Watts, Los Angeles, riots kill 189 people and begin a civil disturbance, which produces riots in over 100 cities through to July 1968.

Fall: **Campus Crusade decide to "crack" Notre Dame University, South Bend, IN, with an evangelistic blitz.**

September: Swami Prabhupada forms the International Society for Krishna Consciousness.

1965 September 25: Barry McGuire (later to be converted to Christ) is No. one on the charts with the critical song *Eve of Destruction.*

October15-16: Weekend antiwar protests occur in 40 cities.

November 18: Americans who have died in Vietnam combat now number 1095.

December 4: US troops in Vietnam number 170,000.

1966 During 1966 and 1967, LSD transformed the rock 'n' roll scene (Steve Turner 1995:51-61, 70-82; Os Guinness 1994:236-273).

By the late 1960s, the love-and-peace generation has been transformed into the drug-and-violence generation (Stuessy 1990:169).

John Lennon constructs lyrics based on Timothy Leary's version of the *Tibetan Book of the Dead.*

George Harrison of *The Beatles* just prior to recording *Sergeant*

Pepper spends six weeks with Indian Ravi Shankar at his home, learning Sitar, and spirituality.

Swami Prabhupada launches a major publicity campaign targeting disillusioned drug experimenters, offering drug free "highs" through meditation and higher consciousness.

Mike Pinder of the *Moody Blues* claims "In ten years time we're going to be singing hymns."

Spring: Mick Jagger and the *Rolling Stones* release *I Can't Get No Satisfaction* (1990:159).

April 8: *Time* cover asks "Is God Dead?"

April 18: Masters and Johnson shatter public perceptions of sexual behavior.

April 21: Vietnam combat toll is 3,047.

Summer is a turning point for the future CWLF – Orthodox leaders. Jon Braun, Dick Ballew, Jim Craddock, Robert Andrews, and Peter Gillquist covenant to meet at 6 a.m. for breakfast every morning in San Bernardino, California. Gordon Walker and Ken Berven often join them to study the New Testament.

1966 **Campus Crusade staffers create "student mobilization" groups on campuses based on the New Testament church pattern of community, commitment, and teamwork. They stopped short of baptism and the celebration of communion, but are innocently on a collision course with Campus Crusade.**

Ecclesiology becomes more and more central as they desire to organize converts into New Testament style units of fellowship and discipleship. Intense study of the book of Acts is occurring.

Great response is occurring for Christian outreach during the school year 1966-1967 at Notre Dame University.

July 12-15: Chicago black riot.

July 14: Eight Chicago student nurses murdered.

July 15-22: Brooklyn blacks riot.

July 18: Cleveland blacks riot.

July 28-29: Baltimore erupts in violence.

August 5: John Lennon claims *The Beatles* are more popular than Jesus.
Angry preachers promote monster bon fires, burning *Beatles* albums across America.

September 19: Timothy Leary proclaims LSD the Sacrament of his new religion.

September 20: George Harrison goes to India.

November 8: California elects Ronald Reagan as Governor.

December 22: US toll in Vietnam is 6,407.

1967 Between 1967 and 1972 over 800 Jesus communal houses are established.

Converted "acid head" Ted Wise, his wife Liz, and four other Jesus communal members open a small storefront mission to the street, in the Haight-Ashbury district of San Francisco. This is possibly the first Jesus Movement ministry. Independently converted hippies themselves, they are soon joined by other counterculture converts with a sense of intense mission to the freaks of southern California. Several couples, believing literally in the Acts story of the primitive Church, sell all they have and adopt communal lifestyles.

Lonnie Frisbee, soon to become the "pied piper" of Los Angeles, is converted and begins ministry to hippies around the beaches of the southern Californian coast. He later is embraced by Chuck Smith, Pentecostal pastor-teacher, and is instrumental in seeing a small congregation, Calvary Chapel explode in numbers. Thousands of counterculture youth are led to faith by Frisbee, and incorporated in the new style church by the teaching of Smith in a giant circus tent.

Tony and Susan Alamo begin a ministry to addicts and hippies forming the Alamo Christian Foundation

The "Summer of Love," first human Be-In" is held in San Francisco's Golden Gate Park. It called the "last hurrah of hippiedom" by Di Sabatino (1999:7).

This is also the year when anti-war sentiment propelled 400,000 protestors, many publicly burning their draft cards, to march from New York's Central Park to the United Nations building in defiance.

Thurgood Marshall is appointed as the first black associate justice of the US Supreme Court.

The "Berkeley Blitz" is carried out by Campus Crusade as an evangelistic initiative on Berkeley campus under the slogan "Solution: Spiritual Revolution" involving Gillquist, Braun, and Sparks.

Gillquist and Braun have a seminal discussion on their passion to reform the existing church.

Swami Prabhupada develops a vision for rock music as a popularizer of Krishna Consciousness.

McCartney tells "people" his eyes have been opened to the existence of God.

1967   *The Beatles*, Donovan, and *Beach Boy's* Mike Love, go to the Maharishi's 15 acre Ashram in India for lectures and intense meditation experiences.

Richard Furray of the *Richard Furray Band* joins Steven Stills, Neil Young, and Dewey Martin to form *Buffalo Springfield*.

January 27: He appears on stage with the *Grateful Dead, Big Brother* and the *Holding Company,* and *Jefferson Airplane* for a Mantra Rock Dance to raise finance for a local temple.

George Harrison of *The Beatles* visits Haight-Ashbury. He is shocked by what he sees of lost and addicted kids on the streets and he abandons his belief in psychedelic drugs.

Pete Townsend of *The Who* states, "The only escape from World problems is in meditation."

February: **Kent Philpott, Seminary student with Beatnik background enters the Haight-Ashbury with a mission to the hippies.**

February 12: Eldridge Cleaver releases *Soul on Ice*.

February: The *Beatles* announce they are giving up drugs to find a better way to transcendence and spirituality, through the meditation practices of the Maharishi. They travel to Rishikesh, India to study Hinduism and meditation. Over some months, one by one they return disillusioned.

March 29: *The Beatles* record the emotive song *I just need somebody to love. I get by with a little help from my friends.*

April 15: Spring Mobe's New York demonstration draws 100,000.

April 28: Mohammed Ali is stripped of boxing titles for refusing Army induction.

May 13: 70,000 supporters of the military parade in New York.

June 2: Two months after the release of *Sergeant Pepper* the *Beatles* link up with Maharishi Mahesh Yogi, the founder of The Spiritual Regeneration Movement. The cover of the album heralds the spiritual eclecticism and childlike humor of the counterculture. Crowd of 87 faces and images includes Dylan, Gandhi, guru Sri Yukteswar Giri, Alesister Crowley, Edgar Allen Poe, Aldous Huxley, Dylan Thomas, Tony Curtis, Karl Marx, Marlin Brando, Oscar Wilde, Shirley Temple, Albert Einstein H.G.Wells, Sonny Liston, and Sri Lahiri Mahasaya, a television, a Mexican candlestick, and garden gnome.

1967   June 5: The Six Day War begins between Israel and the Arab nations.

The Jews recapture Jerusalem, raising the prophetic tension of many that believes Christ's return to be immanent.

John Smith and his finance Glena Walker are at Melbourne Bible Institute, Australia, very sociopolitically conservative and like the majority of the students, are convinced the end of the world is nigh and Jesus' return will prevent their longed-for marriage.

June 19: Paul McCartney admits LSD use.

June 28: Mick Jagger and Keith Richard jailed after drug arrest

July 11: Newark NJ riots leave 26 dead.

July 24: Detroit experiences a week of devastating race riots; 43 die.

September 7: US Troops in Vietnam number 464,000.

October 3: Woody Guthrie dies at 55.

October 22: Anti-war marchers storm the Pentagon.

November: *The Beatles* release *All You Need is Love* [*Magical Mystery Tour*] which becomes more than just a worldwide popular sing. It becomes an almost prophetically desperate heart cry of a generation that is beginning to unravel through drugs and promiscuity. It is significant that for many I have interviewed, the *Beatles* were a fundamental icon of revolutionary hope. Some have shared that the breakup of *The Beatles* was to them as a mortal wound to the soul (Carthorse 1999:3-6).

November 8: November 8: John Lennon divorces Cynthia

November 9: The first issue of *Rolling Stone* is published.

1968 Historian Charles Kaiser described this year as "the moment when all of the nation's impulses towards violence, idealism, diversity and disorder peaked to produce the greatest possible hope – and the worst possible despair" (Kaiser 1988).

Campus riots or revolts come to Crisis point as 300 colleges and universities face demonstrations, strikes, administration building takeovers or suspension of classes (Gitlin 1987).

Police Officers shoot indiscriminately into a crowd of black students at South Carolina State College, killing three.

The Black Power Movement ends. Former Congressman Adam Clayton Powell, Jr., urges Californian College students to "begin a Black Revolution."
Black students do a sit-in protest on Boston's University Campus taking over the administration building.

Sharon Tate is brutally murdered by the drug crazed Manson "Family" and much media attention to the grizzly affair raises the anxiety of the nation.

Roger "Syd" Barrett leaves *Pink Floyd* mentally vegetated by substance abuse (Stuessy 1990:301).

Furry joins *with Stills, Crosby, and Nash* in Poco (Stuessy 1990:201). Later, Furry becomes converted through the Jesus Freaks (1990:191-192) and has for many years 1967 been a still somewhat counterculture style pastor in a church associated with Smith's Calvary Chapel).

Paul Simon pens the now famous line from *Mrs. Robinson; Jesus loves you more than you will know w*hich becomes part of the sound track for *The Graduate* movie.

Crosby, Stills, Nash, and Young release *Chicago*, in which they call the youth of America to "Please come to Chicago" to demonstrate against the political Convention, assuring all that *We can change the world; [We can] rearrange the world.*

At that time it was reported by investigators there were 110 counterculture papers in Canada and the United States, and 23 in Europe which belonged to the Underground Press Syndicate. A further 200 papers claimed sympathy with the counterculture press. The Berkeley *Oracle* had a local circulation of 100,000 at that time (Jasper 1975:125).

According to Tony Jasper (1975:125) "there were at least fifty Jesus papers published in the United States [by the end of 1968], put together by groups of [mostly] young people with no relation to any establishment organization."

1968   The Children of God, later known as the Family of Love was formed as an extreme communal Jesus Movement cult by David Brant Berg, a one time minister in the Christian and Missionary Alliance who "went native" in terms of extreme rejection of all the "world's systems" (Deborah Davis 1984).

The most publicized Jesus Freak, Arthur Blessitt, self-proclaimed minister to Los Angeles' Sunset Strip, opens up his Christian nightclub, His Place.

Ramparts magazine releases an early report on the hippies and the beginning of the Jesus Movement.

The House of Elijah 1968-1979 commences in Yakima, WA. Within a year it comes under the leadership of Joe Peterson.

Lonnie and Connie Frisbee join Chuck Smith in what becomes a Movement of over 1,000 church plants in America and as far afield as Australia. He falls out after some years, finding Smith too conventional [October 71]. Briefly, Frisbee joins John and Jackie Higgins to form a commune, the House of Miracles in Costa Mesa CA.

Higgins, converted in 1966 by reading the Bible as a hippie, to disprove it, experiences a vision, which becomes Shiloh Youth Revival Centers, Inc. (1968-1989). According to Peterson (1999), this becomes the largest communitarian Movement in the history of the United States. Communes numbering 178 are established in 30 States between 1968 and 1978. Higgins is later forced out of leadership of his movement by his board. He rejoins Smith and becomes a pastor of a New Mexico plant of Calvary Chapel.

January 30: The Vietcong Tet Offensive surprises the Administration.

February: Gillquist hears "a still small voice saying 'I want you to leave.'" He phones Braun to say, "I'm through." Braun replies, "So am I" (Gillquist 1992:18). A variety of issues cause "scores of us to leave Campus Crusade. The parachurch wind had gone out of my sails. Above all, we wanted to be a New Testament church" (1992:17).

Gillquist mails his resignation and "the exodus" begins (1992:18). Sparks and a Campus Crusade team begin taking the Christian message in the radical atmosphere of the Berkeley campus and the street culture of Telegraph Avenue.

March 10: Gallup Polls finds 49% feel US troops in Vietnam are a mistake.

March 14: combat deaths number 19,670.

April 3: Martin Luther King Jr. gives his famous *I've Been to the Mountaintop* speech in Memphis.

1968   April 4: King is assassinated.

April 5: The worst single day of 1960s rioting occurs extending to April 15. Black Panther, Bobby Hutton is killed and Chicago's Mayor Daley orders "shoot to kill arsonists."

April 11: L.B. Johnson signs The Fair Housing Act – The Civil Rights Act of 1968.

April 23-30: Columbia University taken over by students.

May 10-11: student revolution occurs in the University of Paris and spreads throughout France.

May 17: The "Catonsville Nine," led by the Berrigan brothers, burn draft files.

June 6: Robert F. Kennedy is assassinated.

June 14: Dr. Benjamin Spock is convicted of conspiracy to counsel draft dodgers.

July: **Brian Jones of** *The Rolling Stones* **dies in a substance abuse context (Stuessy 1990: 163).**

August 1: 541,000 troops in Vietnam.

August 8: Nixon and Agnew nominated amidst riots in Miami FL.

August 20: The Soviets invade Czechoslovakia, crushing the revolution for democracy.

August 26: FBI reports 61,843 marijuana arrests, a 98% increase in two years.

August 28: The 1968 Democratic National Convention in Chicago erupts in violence in protest as Humphrey and Muskie is nominated.

September 7: **Feminists boycott the Miss America Pageant in Atlantic City, lugging "freedom ashcan" in which they dump "symbols of female enslavement; high heeled shoes, kitchen detergent, girdles, and bras**

October 16: DNA decoders win the Nobel Prize

October 17: Two United States runners are expelled from the Olympics for their Black Power salutes during the medal presentation ceremony.

November 1: The U.S. has dropped more bombs on North Vietnam than in all of World War II.

1969   Marianne Faithful attempts suicide (Stuessy 1990:163).

200,000 meet on the Isle of Wight to hear Bob Dylan (Jasper

1975:70).

Yoko and John Lennon release the single album *Give Peace a Chance* (1990:138).

From 1969 onward, Meher Baba, Indian Guru claiming Deity informs the work of Townsend of the *Who*.

Newsweek estimates astrology has 10 million fully committed adherents (Wuthnow 1978:46).

American Baptist Convention chooses its first black leader.

Walker, having worked for Campus Crusade on Ohio State, Kent State, University of North Carolina, and other schools, as well as serving as Coordinator of African Ministries, leaves Campus Crusade to form Grace Haven Farm in Mansfield, OH. He and his wife Sue minister to many Jesus Freaks. Several attempts are made by members to start house churches.
Nethery feels called to this project at Grace Haven Farm. Nethery and Walker break rank with para church tradition, and begin baptizing and holding communion in the winter.

Dunaways start a similar community in Anchorage, AK.
The Ballews start a living room church in Atlanta, GA.
Ballews and the Brauns go to Santa Barbara, CA to join former colleagues of the Campus Crusade group from the University of California, Santa Barbara campus (UCSB). They are now close to the Sparks.

Gillquists shift to Memphis State University TN as fundraisers.

The *Hollywood Free Paper* is founded by Duane Pederson (now also an Antiochian Orthodox priest), eventually peaking at a 500,000 copy edition, although over a million copies were produced for events at the Hollywood Rose Bowl (Heinz 1976a:298).

After the breakup of *The Beatles*, George Harrison told a British newspaper that he now believed "music should be used for the perception of God, not jitterbugging" (*Rolling Stone* December 2001). He was to be a spiritual pilgrim until his death in 2001. His release of *My Sweet Lord*, with its chorus of *Hallelujah* and Hare Krishna, revealed the spiritual syncretism and mysticism that marked the rest of his days.

Cass Elliot of *The Mammas and the Papas* dies and John and Michelle Phillips divorce (Stuessy 1990:197).

1969   Simon and Garfunkle release *Bridge over Troubled Waters*.

Meher Baba's face appears on the cover of *Rolling Stone* magazine.

Timothy Leary publishes *The Politics of Ecstasy*.

Paul McCartney hints at the imminent breakup of the Beatles.

John Lennon responds angrily in public and it becomes apparent that *The Beatles* are each going their separate ways. *The Beatles'* film *Let it Be* is released (Stuessy 1990:138).

The collapse of the group has occurred. Lennon releases *My Sweet Lord* with its haunting religious pluralism embracing both Christian and Hindu (Krishna) worship terms.

Anthropologist Margaret Mead publishes her last book, *Culture and Commitment*, a sympathetic analysis of the youthful rebellion, calling it the "generation gap."

Hans Rookmaaker associated with Francis Schaeffer's L'Abri ministries and later with Berkeley's CWLF, releases *Modern Art and the Death of a Culture*.

February 12: The National Guard moves onto the University of Wisconsin campus after black studies protest.

April 3: U.S combat toll in Vietnam surpasses the Korean War toll at 33,641.

April: **Sparks and colleagues leave Campus Crusade to form Christian World Liberation Front (CWLF) on the Berkeley campus and create an off campus house church. Sparks is a radicalized ex-professor of statistical analysis in the behavioral science department of Penn State University.**

Sparks publishes *Right On* street paper in an attempt to make Jesus an issue in the midst of issue-oriented Berkeley. Berkeley's underground Jesus newspaper, *Right On*, is one of the first street-level Jesus Papers. It includes an article by newly elected Senator Mark Hatfield. Creative street theatre, communal houses, and teaching cells attract students to the Movement – which survives today as the Berkeley Christian Coalition.

Right On introduces the concept of a "third way" neither establishment nor radical, to propagate an alternative to left and right politics. In November, the sixth edition is the first to be numbered and the seventh edition is the first to be dated. December 15, the eighth edition reveals CWLF as the publisher. It gives Jesus people testimonies, announces rock concerts, and critiques rival religious movements such as Transcendental Meditation, Krishna, and the Occult. The ninth edition January 1970 introduced the editors.

1969   The *Peoples' Medical Handbook* is published by CWLF. The *Last Whole Earth Catalogue* praises the publication.

The *Wanted* poster of Jesus as a Revolutionary, used in following decades by many radical movements, is released by CWLF but not being copyrighted, it has been extensively used without recognition of its creative source.

April 11: Harvard University students strike to back black studies and end ROTC demands.

April 19: Black students take over the student union at Cornell University. They demand an end to racism and a separate black college

April 29: President Nixon's American invasion of Cambodia sparks off protests across American universities.

May 4: Four students killed when National guardsmen open fire on protesting students at Kent State University, OH.

August 15-17: At Bethel, New York 500,000 gathers for the Woodstock Festival (Jasper 1975:68).

September 18: Jimi Hendricks dies (aged 27) of an overdose, possibly as an act of suicide (1990:253). His final song, written on the eve of his death, is laced with references to Jesus and a spiritual search.

September18: Jimi Hendricks dies (aged 27) of an over dose, possibly as an act of suicide (1990:197). His final song, written on the eve of his death, is laced with references to Jesus and a spiritual search.

September 28: *The Beatles'* song "Hey Jude" tops the charts.

October 4: Janis Joplin dies of a heroin overdose (Stuessy 1990:246) aged 27.

November 9: Chicago street gangs form the Rainbow alliance.

November 12: Lt. Calley is charged with the My Lai massacre.

December 4: Police kill Black Panthers Hampton and Clark.

December 8: Charles Manson and four followers indicted for the Tate-La Bianca murders.

1970   Over 30% of America's college and university campuses experience disruption and protest, mostly peaceful, but burning and bombing of buildings also occurred on 30 campuses. The backlash begins to become violent

Crosby, Stills, Nash, and Young release their angry indictment of the Kent State event and the system's violence, singing *Tin soldiers and Nixon coming. We're finally on our own.*
(John Smith remembers vividly, conversations in which youth were seriously entertaining the purchase of arms to protect themselves against their parent's generation, saying, "Our parents will kill us before they will let us change the "system" of their materialistic politics").

The national Urban Coalition is formed by religious, business, labor, and civil leaders to focus national attention on problems and solutions for blacks in cities.

During the early fall of the school year some schools are closed because of violent racial conflicts. In Pontiac, Michigan, racial conflict leaves four whites, and two blacks wounded from gunshots. Snipers and arsonists are active in Henderson, North Carolina and violence spreads from a downtown school to the streets resulting in hundreds of arrests.

In Denver CO, segregationists dynamite about one third of the school buses.

During this year a significant number of black leaders are elected to a variety of positions in federal and local government and civil posts:

Clifton Wharfton Jr. to the presidency of Michigan State University; ten black members to the Atlanta, GA, legislature; Charles Rangel to the New York's Eighteenth Congressional District; Kenneth Gibson as the Mayor of Newark, NJ; James McGee as mayor of Dayton, OH; Dr. Hugh Scott as superintendent of Washington DC schools; Ronald V. Dellums, Parren Mitchell, and Ralph H. Metcalf to Congress.

Right On issues student polls as a contact methodology on Berkeley campus.

The House of the New World commences as a radical counterculture Christian movement in Sydney, Australia as an experiment in communalism, training in subversive faith, and ministry to students and "surfies."

Xenos, Columbus, OH begins in the form of a loose coalition of Jesus houses. More structured teaching begins the following year. Xenos continues as a mega-church sized operation today, based on a house church model with combined houses for teaching. Mission work is established in several overseas countries, and an outstanding teaching base has been established.

Carl Parks founds The Voice of Elijah ministries in Spokane, WA with *Truth* Jesus Paper as a highly successful underground communication.

1970   A popular Westcoast band, *Wilson McKinley* are converted through Linda Meisner and soon after join Parks.

Jews for Jesus commences under the leadership of Moishe Rosen, attracting many counterculture Jewish students who were hostile about their parents' materialism. A vigorous and astute pamphlet ministry is carried out on the University of California, Berkeley campus.

Arthur Blessitt announces his call to "blitz the nation for Jesus Christ," and commences his now famous cross carrying pilgrimages, beginning a 3,500-mile journey from Los Angeles to Washington DC. He begins soon after, to pilgrimage through Europe and has considerable Jesus Movement impacts on England and Scotland.

Hal Lindsey, an early prime teacher in an alternative Californian Jesus Movement academy, publishes *Late Great Planet Earth* which captures both the eschatological mood of Pentecostals, evangelicals, and Jesus Freaks and the apocalyptic "whole earth" ecology of the counterculture. It quickly becomes a best seller. After enormous notoriety and economic success he defects from the movement, divorces and marries a student with whom he had an affair. He has become a mainstream, neo-Pentecostal, eschatology and investment "guru" and television presenter in recent years.

February 18: The Chicago Seven are acquitted of conspiracy to incite riot at the 1968 Chicago Democratic Convention.

March 3: In Lamar, South Carolina, tear gas and riot clubs were used to disperse white wielding base ball bats and ax handles against blacks being integrated into a previously all-white school. State troopers made no attempt to arrest offenders despite injury to children.

May 14: Police fire into women's dorm at Jackson State University, killing two black students and wounding 30 others. Over 75 schools are closed for the rest of the year.

June: *Right On* Vol. 1.17 is said to come from the Catacombs of Berkeley with no mention of CWLF.

July: Some northern cities see racial riots over housing unemployment and crime.

September 11: The IRS revokes tax-exemption status of five all-white private academies in Mississippi when they refused to enroll black students.

September 29: Egypt's President Nasser dies.

November 26: Simon and Garfunkle split up.

1971 Jesus is *Time* magazine's "Man of the Year."

It is estimated 5,000,000 Americans have experimented with psychedelic drugs by 1971

Crosby, Stills, Nash, and Young split up. (They reunite summer 1974 in an "on and off again" pattern, usually coming together around political events such as the Anti-nuclear Musicians United for Safe Energy demonstrations in 1979 and the Survival Sunday Concert in 1980). (Stuessy 1990:340).

The second Isle of Wight concert features Joan Baez, Joni

Mitchell, *The Doors*, Jimmy Hendricks, the *Who*, *Sly and the Family Stone*, Jethro Tull, Miles Davis, Emerson, Lake and Palmer, and *The Moody Blues* (Jasper 1975:71).

Arthur Blessitt, hippie, cross carrying preacher releases his book *Turned onto Jesus* (Blessitt and Wagner 1971).

The Jesus Liberation Front, British equivalent of Berkeley's CWLF communal Movement is established in Hemel Hempstead, England.

Sly Stone of *Sly and the Family Stone* having become "eccentric, unpredictable and irresponsible . . . by an extreme fondness for cocaine" consistently arrives late or does not appear at all for major concerts and in Chicago, causes a riot by his nonappearance. The late 1971 album *There's a Riot Going On*, No. 1 on the charts, "carried ironic implications" (Stuessy 1990:344).

Rice, one of the creators of *Jesus Christ Superstar* reports to a British rock paper, *Sounds*, that if *Superstar* had been written five years earlier "it would have disappeared without a trace" (1975:35).

Jim Palosaari, an actor who had dropped out and became a counterculture protestor, was converted and trained by Linda Meisner in the Jesus People Army. He and his wife Sue found Street Level Ministry and a commune in Milwaukee, Wisconsin. Much attention is given to the Milwaukee Jesus People by the Wisconsin media for the next year.

Billy Graham releases a sympathetic analysis of the Jesus Movement entitled *The Jesus Generation*.

Melbourne Jesus People begins publishing a joint issue of Washington's State Jesus paper *Truth*, with Australian content included.

1971 **Sparks and a colleague publish *Letters to Street Christians*, a version of New Testament Epistles in the distinctive sub-cultural counterculture idiom of the Berkeley street people.**

Right On publishes a tribute to Malcolm X stating "America has failed the black man by not following the teaching of the revolutionary Savior Jesus Christ."

The Reverend Jesse Jackson forms People United to Save Humanity (PUSH).

Six Ku Klux Klan members are arrested in Pontiac, Michigan, for bombing ten school buses.

Race riots occur in Wilmington, North Carolina; Brownsville, New York City; Chattanooga, TN; Jacksonville, FA; and Columbus, GA.

On May 21: the National Guard is required to quell the riots in Chattanooga, TN. when more than four hundred arrests are made.

Black unemployment remains twice that of whites. In urban contexts 32 percent of black youths are unemployed

Erhard Seminars Training (EST) personal transformation programs begin growing to a network of 300 paid employees, 25,000 volunteers in 29 cities and 270,000persons trained a decade later. The program applies self-help, positive thinking, Zen, Gestalt psychology, self-hypnosis, and Mind Dynamics (Tipton 1982).

Guitarist John McLaughlin, prominent British blues and jazz player, converts to the teachings of Sri Chinmoy to explore a new form of spiritual
music after being unimpressed by a childhood in the Church of Scotland.

July 3: Jim Morrison, the genius of *The Doors* dies officially of a heart attack, induced by a long period of substance abuse (Stuessy1990:251)

February: **During a driving snowstorm at midnight, Walker baptized 26 people in an icy pond (including Greg Leffel who would later become a key house church leader in the Xenos fellowship).**

February 9: Jack and Betty Cheetham, freelance photographers' do a story for *Look* magazine and are converted in the process (Palms 1972:14).

1972   **Enroth, Ericson, and Peters release a comprehensive survey and analysis of the Jesus Movement, *The Story of the Jesus People*: *A Factual Survey.***

January: Sunbury Pop Festival, Australia's equivalent of Woodstock occurs on the outskirts of Melbourne. The farmer, like his counterpart in the America for the Woodstock Festival, offers his property to the young people. Some years later he is converted to the Christian faith.

January: **The author is dismissed from his evangelistic post on returning from the festival, allegedly because drugs and sex, and rock 'n' roll mark such festivals so they "are not a suitable place for a young evangelist to be."**

Truth and Liberation Concern (TLC) as an outreach to youth and the counterculture begins in Melbourne, Australia.

Linked to TLC, the Melbourne chapter of God's Squad is formed with an integrated, contextual, and multifaceted mission focus from high school students to biker outlaw clubs.

The Jesus Movement, as a counterculture Movement in Australia, surfs on a wave of popular national sentiment, being a partner in promoting utopian change, in contrast to a rescue operation at the end of a failing experiment in America. The euphoria is short lived, but the indigenous Australian movement has established its reputation in the mainstream of the culture.

Due to cultural differences, Australia's Jesus paper *Truth* breaks official ties with Carl Parks *Truth*, to produce an indigenous paper. Due to legal conflict with a soft porn, Fleet Street style paper of the same name, our Jesus paper is named after the Jesus Movement ministry *Truth and Liberation*.

Clay Ford tells a first hand story of Christian ministry amongst the street people of Berkeley, *Jesus and the Street People: A First Hand Report from Berkeley.*

Palosaari pulls out of Wisconsin and travels Europe and Great Britain with his rock opera, *Lonesome Stone*, which has considerable impact in England, being partly the catalyst for Greenbelt Festivals, which have continued successfully to draw thousands every year from 1974 to 2002.

Converted through Palosaari, Glenn and Wendy Kaiser blues-rock musicians of considerable talent, break with Palosaari over his irregular behavior and promiscuity to form Jesus People USA

(JPUSA) in Chicago, IL. This ministry to freaks, fringe people, the homeless, and just about anybody else resides in shared-purse communal arrangement to this day.

Aretha Franklin popularizes *Amazing Grace*.

1972 Richard M. Nixon is re-elected President of the United States, increasing the sense of despair and failure amongst the disintegrating counterculture.

Gillquist quits work at Memphis State and returns to freelance writing.

Explo 72 is organized by Campus Crusade in an attempt to capture the Jesus Movement energy and bring it under a mainframe evangelical influence. Some Jesus People view this as the final demise of the movement, as the "Establishment began to take over and routinize the previously counterculture, underground movement, domesticating and making political conservative Evangelicals of previously radical Jesus Freaks (Witherington 2000; Peterson 1999).

Walkers leave Grace Haven Farm and move to an old farmhouse in a remote area in Tennessee.

Eighty thousand delegates attend the weeklong training and inspiration "fest." The *Dallas Morning News* reported that 180,000 attended the final Jesus Music Festival (Eshelman and Rohrer 1972:iii).

June: *Right On* has 2,000 individual subscriptions, with 10,000 bulk orders per month. Free distribution accounts for most copies. Ten vending machines are set up in the San Francisco Bay area.

July: Walkers shift to Nashville, TN and begin teaching some cell groups until early 1978 naming their project Grace Ministries embracing seven house churches which eventually combined to become an Orthodox community.

November 5: *New York Times* believes between 25 Jesus Movement groups are publishing 50 fairly stable monthlies including *Right On*.

By the end of 1972 the Watergate scandal has eclipsed the Jesus Movement as a phenomenon in the media.

December 2: Gough Whitlam, an ardent Fabian Socialist, became Prime Minister, partly on the basis of his vigorous opposition to the Vietnam War, with his call for a more truly indigenous political stance, whereby Australians could cease being subservient to American interests. This was a significant element in the change of Australia's political landscape. Whitlam reflected the idealism of the counterculture and engaged in positive, face to face dialogue with dissident youth. This was in contrast to the establishment brutality of the Kent State government response under Richard Nixon's parallel administration.

1973 Bob Dylan releases one of the most enduring and popular of all folk rock songs ever written *Knockin' on Heaven's Door* (Dylan 1993:54-55).

February: ***Right On*** **is distributing between 15,000-20,000 copies monthly.**

February 22: Israel shoots down a Libyan commercial plane.

February 27: Native Americans occupy the town of Wounded Knee in protest against government treatment of Native Americans.

Summer: **several of the ex-Campus Crusade leaders who are experimenting with new church model leaders meet while in Dallas for a Christian Publisher's Convention. "Old troops" gather together to establish a network of those involved in building New Testament style churches. During these meetings, seventy men, 50 of whom Ballew claims were Ex-Campus Crusade staff workers (Ballew 1997:14) share, fight, teach, and eat together. An informal network is formed for those who are establishing what they believe to be New Testament house churches. They share a sense of loneliness and tiredness.**

A few months later, a group meets at Sparks' Berkeley home. Six are chosen, who are 40 years of age or older, and appointed as elders. They are Sparks, Braun, Ballew, Berven, Nethery, and Walker. Gillquist is added later as the seventh.

The New Covenant Apostolic Order (NCAO) (Appendix 9) is formed as an umbrella for about 19 churches. Under this authority, Braun, and Ballew found a house church in 1973 at Isle of Vista, CA.

This core group (NCAO) agrees to meet for a week every quarter

and provide the oversight of a network of house churches. At this conference, they divide areas of study between them. Sparks is to investigate worship; Braun to examine church history; Ballew looks at doctrine; Walker examines biblical textual evidence; Berven looks at pre-Reformation history and doctrine; Nethery examines the same from the Reformation to the present. Gillquist is appointed as administrator.

Fall: Braun holds a mini conference on the history of the church at Grace Haven Farm at which members from Xenos are in attendance.

A house church cell linked to the Sparks, Braun, and Gillquist movement is commenced at Eagle River, AL. It later becomes an Antiochian Orthodox Church when the wider group is chrismated.

London's Wembley Stadium hosts *Spree'73* Jesus culture event, attracting 11,000 delegates for a weekend of popular culture.

1973   The Children of God cult goes to United Kingdom, establishing its first commune in Bromley, southeast London.

Ron, "Pig Pen" McKernan of the *Grateful Dead* dies at 27.

Larry Norman, Jesus Movement troubadour visits England (again).

The House of Freedom, a radical community associated with Sydney's House of the New World, commences in Brisbane, Australia.

Theos Sun Jesus paper is launched in Melbourne, Australia and later nationally. It becomes a very popular Jesus paper, much used in coffee shops and schools.

September 11: General Pinochet seizes control of Chili in a bloody coup.

October 9: Elvis and Pricilla Presley are divorced.

October 10: Spiro Agnew resigns as Vice President because of corruption charges.

1974   Britain's Greenbelt Festival, the first major Jesus festival in the UK is held (Jasper 1975:180).

40,000 Christian youth meet for a festival in Taize, France, calling for the complete renewal of the church (1975:181).

During Kairos '74, thousands of mostly young people flood Canberra, the national capital of Australia, to march, and surround parliament for prayer, demonstrate for Jesus, and meet in strategic study groups.

JPUSA, Chicago embraces plurality of leadership.

Christian bookshops ban a Larry Norman album across America because of its jacket cover and because his songs pose problems and questions without giving definitive answers (1975:181).

The Vietnam War ends.

Harrison of *The Beatles* declares his continuing commitment to Krishna Consciousness calling a concert audience to join in a Krishna Mantra.

The world release of *Jesus Christ, Superstar* occurs.

August 9: Richard M. Nixon resigns the Presidency following the Watergate scandal.

1974 The Master's Workshop, a radical training center for Jesus People in Melbourne Australia, is established by Theos Movement by John U'ren and Peter Corney.

Jacob's Ladder, a typical Jesus Movement commune, center for training, outreach, is commenced in Adelaide, Australia.

The House of the Rock began as a Jesus Movement community with emphasis on care of homeless and disoriented youth in Adelaide, Australia.

Koinonia, a Jesus house and ministry began in Port Lincoln, Australia.

A major conference is held again at Grace Haven Farm, with the group of seven declaring that as a group God has given them a prophetic and apostolic authority to lead the groups on to the "true church." They call for submission to their leadership and some groups, including Xenos, hold their council to consider the implications. Xenos soon decides not to pursue relationship with the NCOA.

Sparks move in late 1974 to the University of California, Santa Barbara campus as the hippie era dies down. Sparks publishes *God's Forever Family* (1974) anecdotally telling the story of CWLF's beginnings and its search for authentic true church community.

1975　The group meet at a cabin on San Juan Island in Puget Sound. Reports are given concerning early church worship, separating the Synaxis from the Eucharist (Appendix 7). Examination of the writings of Justin Martyr, Hippolytus, the Didache, Polycarp, Clement of Rome, Ignatius of Antioch, and Athanasius, leads them to believe in the liturgical nature of worship in the early church.

By mid 1975 they come to the conclusion that the church is sacramental, worship is liturgical, and church government is hierarchical. They form an Episcopal structure embracing bishops, presbyters, deacons and laity under an umbrella organization called the New Covenant Apostolic Order (NCAO) (Appendix 9). They seek to establish churches with 12 characteristics (Appendix 8).

There are revelations of previous FBI and CIA spying on black leaders through wiretapping and background investigations

WGPR-TV, in Detroit becomes the first black-owned television station.

The Voting Rights Act of 1975 abolishes literacy requirements for voting.

Joseph W. Hatcher becomes the first black state supreme court Justice (Florida).

1976　Jimmy Carter wins the presidential election, and appoints many black judges.

Newsweek names 1976 as the "Year of the Evangelicals."

The Highway Missionary Society (1976-1988) is formed associated with Shiloh and The House of Elijah.

"CWLF mail began to look more Orthodox" according to Orthodox reviewers (Gillquist 1992:128)

1977 August 16: Elvis Presley is found dead at home.

Black Consciousness leader Steve Biko dies in police custody in South Africa.

Sparks distributed preliminary study papers which, according to Fr. Alexander Schmemann, the Dean of St. Valdamir's Seminary, New York were Orthodox. Fr. John Bartke, converted as a high school junior in 1969 in one of Sparks' Bible study groups in Berkeley, is now Orthodox.

St. Athanasius Orthodox Christian Academy opened in Santa Barbara with an initial faculty core of Sparks, Ballew, Braun, and Tom Webster.

Fr. Schmemann calls Bishop Dimitri, a Southern Baptist convert to Orthodoxy, concerning this group of "evangelical Christians who appear to be discovering the Orthodox Church."

Spring: Bishop Dimitri, phones Fr. Ted Wojcik of St. Innocent Orthodox Church in LA requesting he visit the Santa Barbara group. He contacts Sparks at the newly formed Academy of Orthodox Theology and visits Sparks and Ballew at the Academy.

The Academy of Orthodox Theology later becomes St. Ignatius Academy, a community of scholars to research Orthodoxy, translate documents, and train students.

The New Covenant Apostolic Order (NCAO) forms Conciliar Press and begins the quarterly publication of *Again*. Ken Berven launches *Again* magazine, which continues now under the Antiochian Orthodox authority.

Right On street paper becomes *Radix* (Gallagher 1979:2).

The Redeemer's drop-in center, Way In, in Houston, TX, closes. The group became turned in on itself in the second half of the 1970s, parallel basically to the folding of the Jesus Movement influence in the district. "It was a sign of the times that it was created and it was a sign of the times that it collapsed" (Jeannie Woodruff 1999:1).

1978 Keith Moon of *The Who* dies obviously from the extended self abuse and drug abuse (Stuessy 1990:282).

Bob Dylan attends a Bible study cell group in Larry Norman's home (Steve Turner 1988:170).

Theos Sun, Melbourne, Australia Jesus Paper ends publication. Koinonia, South Australia community and outreach closes down.

Sparks' *The Apostolic Fathers* is published (Sparks 1978).

Bishop Dimitri visits the Santa Barbara Evangelical Orthodox academy.

A group of the leadership attends St. Innocent Orthodox Church Holy Week.

Later a group visit St. Vladimir's Seminary, NY and are warmly welcomed by Metropolitan Theodosius, the head of the Orthodox Church of America (OCA) and professors Alexander Schmemann, John Meyendorff, Thomas Hopko, Paul Lazar, and Veselin Kesich

February: **Nethery resigns from the apostolic group predicting that if they keep moving in the direction they are pursuing, they will finally become fully Orthodox. Although this is denied at the time, in retrospect, Gillquist recalls that from 1977 to 1987, much time was spent getting to know the Orthodox Church.**

Margaret Mead reissues a revised version of her work on 1960s generational conflict, maintaining her 1971 edition had, if anything, underestimated the enormity of the Generation Gap, a phenomenon "that had never occurred simultaneously ['world-wide'] before and on such a scale." She asserted the "gap" was in fact "as deep as the Grand Canyon and parallel with the Pacific Ocean," and that there would never again be a generation again "like ourselves." (Mead 1978:xix).

November 18: Jim Jones and his community are lost in a mass suicide in Guyana.

Many informants I interviewed remember this event as a deathblow to an already struggling communal movement. The American government, previously soft towards genuine communal experiments, begins to use the Internal Revenue Service to collapse common purse communities. This method eventually destroys the largest movement, Higgins Shiloh communities. Church of the Redeemer informant's claim the fear of cult leaders as a result of Jonestown swiftly undermined leadership and was a part of the

collapse of their communal experiment.

1978 In Australia, Rev. Ted Noffs, a controversial but popular Uniting Church worker amongst King's Cross addicts, writes extensively in the *Sydney Morning Herald*, concerning the danger of such sects, naming the author of this document as a possible cult leader and God's Squad as a possible dangerous cult. Soon after this internal conflict concerning leadership and authority begins a disintegrating process which splits our movement in half and stems the flow of success and creativity for some years.

1979 The House of Elijah closes operations.

Bob Dylan turns to the Christian message and releases *Slow Train Coming* (Dylan 1979; Stuessy 1990:191-192). In 1983 he appeared to have left that emphasis with the release of *Infidels* (1990:191).

By the end of the 1970s the direction of rock music is reflecting the cynicism about political and idealistic commitment, turning rather to personal fulfillment. Tragedy led eventually to directionless such that musicologist Stuessy describes the 1970s as the decade of "non direction" (1990:301).

February: **The group forms the Evangelical Orthodox Church of America (EOCA), establishing a Synod of Bishops and embracing Eastern Orthodoxy. It is decided that discernment of the truth and the will of God for the church are to be Conciliar being found through their church councils, whether they be local, regional or ecumenical.**

The Abode of the Friendly Toad is commenced in Adelaide, South Australia as a radical outreach café, community, and training center.

1980 Ronald Reagan is elected to the presidency and the great calm down begins as national pride, patriotism and old values are popularly championed by the new administration.

The threat of Russia is diminished in the face of Reagan's confident stand against the traditional enemy.

Jacob's House and Servants Community, Adelaide, South Australia, folds.

The House of the Rock, Adelaide, South Australia, ceases operation.

Melbourne's Master's Workshop closes its doors.

1985   January: At the Synod of EOCA, Walker proposes a direct approach to request entrance into the Eastern Orthodox community.

April: Fr. John Bartke of St. Michael's Antiochian Orthodox Church recommends they have an audience with the Patriarch of Antioch, Ignatius IV, while he is visiting Los Angeles in June-July with Metropolitan Philip.

June: A group goes to Constantinople, Turkey. Audience with the Patriarch is refused. After heated interchange and debate, they return to America. Deeply depressed, they consider abandoning the quest for acceptance by the Orthodox Church, but believing such action to be a forsaking of the faith and the church, they regroup. Having been rebuffed by the Orthodox Church in America, they decide to petition the Patriarch of Antioch, Ignatius IV.

Metropolitan Philip grants them audience and they (Braun, Ballew, and Gillquist) have audience for an hour with the Patriarch Ignatius and Metropolitan Philip. Metropolitan Philip requests the EOCA Synod of bishops make a draft proposal.

1986   March: The EOCA and Metropolitan Philip exchange draft proposals. Following a day of discussion, a joint proposal *Preliminary Agreement between Metropolitan Philip and Bishop Peter Gillquist* is agreed upon.

June: Four bishops of the Synod of the EOCA elect to step away from the EOCA in its determination to be received into the Orthodox Church.   They choose to continue building the EOCA.

September: Synod meets in New York with Metropolitan Philip Saliba. Fourteen Synod members of the EOCA (one dissenter) embracing seventeen parishes and 2,000 members from Alaska to Atlanta elected upon invitation to enter the Antiochian Orthodox Church (AOC).

1987   February 15: "Sixty new priests and deacons and 200 new Evangelical Orthodox faithful join the ranks of holy Orthodoxy at the St. Nicholas Antiochian Orthodox Cathedral of Los Angeles.

"Brothers and sisters in Christ, welcome home," says Metropolitan Philip Saliba. Over 500 more people are chrismated three days later.

March: **EOCA parishes, including three EOCA bishops from Jackson, MI; Memphis, TN; parishes in Ottawa, Saskatoon, and Borden in Canada follow by the end of the month.**

April: **Parishes Anchorage and Eagle River, AK and two parishes in Seattle, WA, embrace Orthodoxy. Within a few months, new missions begin in Fargo, ND; Salt Lake City, UT; East Lansing, MI; Bloomington, IN; Beaver Falls, PA; Wheaton, IL. The Antiochian Evangelical Orthodox Mission (AEOM) is commissioned to bring full Orthodox faith to North America.**

1988   The Highway Missionary Society ceases operation

1989   Shiloh Youth Revival Centers close after a decade of conflict with the IRS.

As Dylan enters the 1990s he releases *Political World* , stating:
We live in a political world
Love don't have any place
We're living in times when men commit crimes
And crimes don't have a face
He goes on to say that in this political world:
Wisdom is thrown into jail . . . rots in a cell, misguided as hell, leaving no one to pick up a trail. In this world . . . mercy walks the plank and *courage is a thing of the past . . . children are unwanted . . . and peace is not welcomed at all* (Dylan 1993:76-83).

A new postmodern cynicism, an atomized search for personal pleasure and fulfillment, and a diverse popular culture with fewer universal icons have replaced the idealism of the 1960s and 1970s. Perhaps again bob Dylan expresses the tone of the culture in a recent song that confesses, "I used to care, but things have changed."

1990   December 16: **Frank Schaeffer, son of L'Abri's Francis Schaeffer, is chrismated into the Greek Orthodox Church.**

1991   Senior pastor Charles Fox of Family Christian Fellowship, a Calvary Chapel affiliate in Placerville, CA reads *Becoming Orthodox* by Gillquist (1989).

1993	June 12: **Vineyard Christian Fellowship San Jose, CA becomes Orthodox.**
1994	Thomas Nelson Publishes the *Orthodox Study Bible* ed. Fr. Jack Sparks.
1995	Ex-Calvary Chapel Pastor Andrew Fox, with a number of his congregation are baptized and chrismated into the Antiochian Orthodox Church at Ben Lomond, CA. A month later, he is ordained into the ministry.
1996	The House of the Gentle Bunyip, Melbourne Australia, the most enduring communal, radical discipleship group in Australia closes its operation. Most of its leaders go to Baptist pastorates or to Baptist academic posts in Baptist.
1998	The House of Freedom, Brisbane, Australia closes its operation.

APPENDIX 2 (A)

Calvary Chapel

Basic Sunday Morning Worship Service and Meeting Style

        Greeting and prayer by Smith
        Congregational hymn
        Prayer by one of the associate pastors
        Announcement of activities for the coming week
        Offering
        Congregational hymn(s)
        Reading of Scripture (Smith reads the first and all odd-numbered verses; the congregation reads the even verses in unison)
        Sermon by Smith (an exposition of the Scripture text)
        Benediction ("The Lord bless you and keep you . . ." sung responsively)
        Smith moves down the aisle to the entrance to greet congregants informally.

Bible study is central, given in a folksy, literalist style of verse-by-verse exegesis. Simplicity with linguistic and conceptual accessibility to the masses is attached to "a common sense realism" (Balmer and Todd 1994:681). Evening meetings and Bible studies are preceded by lengthy praise and worship singing. The members flow with what appears to "be Spirit led" spontaneity of choice and style of song. The congregation knows the songs and songbooks are only used on Sunday morning when more traditional hymns are mixed with contemporary songs. The early style of Jesus rock/folk music is still a lingering presence. Songs are strung together by gentle explanation, devotional snippets, or the change of key through the strumming of guitars. Leadership is distinctly male, and the men tend to lead the music score with women often providing a "counterpoint, a kind of musical embroidery that adds an unmistakable sweetness to the rendition" (Balmer and Todd 1994:683). There is a modified Pentecostalism, in which the emotional freedom is restrained from excesses, demonstrating a mid-position between classical Evangelical emphasis on truth and Pentecostal overemphasis on emotional experience. No sacraments are observed in the Sunday morning services. Charismatic gifts are restricted to small groups. Communion is held on a weeknight, baptisms are held irregularly in the Pacific Ocean. [Adapted from a Sunday Bulletin, the author's recollections, and those of Balmer and Todd (1994:679-685) more recently].

Appendix 2 (B)

Calvary Chapel Programs

Sunday:
Junior High Fellowship (x3)
High School Fellowship (x3)
Spanish Service
Deaf Fellowship
Children's Special Education
Arabic Service
Children's Deaf Ministry
Korean Service (x2)
College and Career Prayer Meeting

Monday:
Women's Intercessory Prayer Group
Working Women's Joyful Life Bible Study
Proverbs Class for Men
Bible Study (Chuck Smith)

Tuesday:
Prayer Breakfast
Musicians' Fellowship
High School Mothers' Prayer Meeting
Music Ministry Bible Study
Bible Study
Men's Fellowship
50-plus [age group] Bible Study

Wednesday:
Men's Prayer Breakfast
Noon Bible Study
Korean Fellowship
Junior High

[Many cell groups and house fellowships target particular issues]

College and Career
High School
Becoming Disciples (for new believers)
Adult Study in Psalms
Arabic Study

New Spirit/Alcohol and Drug Recovery
Single Parents' Fellowship
Believers' Fellowship

Thursday:
Spanish Women's Bible Study
Bible Study
Adult Fellowship
Singles' Prayer Meeting
Bible Study and Communion (Smith)
Children's Special Education

Friday:
Women's Joyful Life Bible Study
Singles' Group
Missions Fellowship
Spanish Study
Messianic Jewish Fellowship
Prison Fellowship

Saturday:
Men's Prayer Breakfast
Korean Prayer Meeting
Women's Prayer Meeting
High School Girl's Bible Study
Physically Disabled Fellowship
Elders Pray for the Sick and Needs

A list compiled from three Sunday bulletins: May 10, 1987, May 17, 1987, July 30, 1989 (Balmer and Todd 1994:686)

APPENDIX 3

Calvary Chapel –
Four Winds Doctrinal Foundations

Summary Editorial Introduction

There is no published document for the mother church in Santa Ana. The informality and freedom of the movement expresses itself in the independent choice of various Calvary Chapel units. They do as they will regarding this, so long as they do not depart from the basic teachings and political position of Chuck Smith and the mother church. Balmer and Todd (1994:689) were told by several pastors that "'If someone ordained by Calvary Chapel should espouse ideas – theological, political or social – that deviate from the positions staked out by Smith, he would doubtless be called to account for his views.' Bob Haag, one of the pastors at Calvary Chapel, said Smith would very likely talk to the person in an attempt to point out his errors. Although there seems to be no formal mechanism for ouster, Calvary Chapel has exercised a kind of 'dis-fellowship' that resembles expulsion." Chuck Fromm informed me [the author] that expulsion is rather along primitive, tribal lines in that the offender is virtually placed outside the village and dis-fellowshiped. For example, "the offender's name might simply disappear from previous listings of Calvary Chapel associates" (Fromm 1999). Although I have not heard any official statement, I would assume from the statistics given by Miller (1997:222-223) on the political positioning of Calvary Chapel's pastors, membership in the Democratic party would be somewhat alienating for a pastor. Eldership and pastoral positions are exclusively male prerogatives. A feminist position would certainly not be countenanced. Membership is extremely fluid and basically controlled by the level of social acceptance of the congregant as a form of cultural reward or punishment for views expounded.

Fundamental issues are:

1. The inerrancy of Scripture and basic Trinitarian theology and Christology.
2. Proscription of alcohol, tobacco and extra marital sexual relationships. (The high level of divorce amongst Californian Charismatics and Pentecostals is said to be modifying attitudes on divorce by emphasizing grace and forgiveness but not sanction).
3. Total intolerance of homosexuality.
4. A "pro-life" position in the strongest terms. In 1990, twenty-six members of the congregation at Costa Mesa were serving jail sentences for having disrupted abortion clinics (Balmer and Todd 1994:685).
5. Belief in the Premillennial Return of Christ.
6. A "soft"-Pentecostal belief in the spiritual gifts of the Holy Spirit, including healing and speaking in tongues, but the belief that love rather than "supernatural gifts" is the evidence of the Holy Spirit's power in the individual and the church.

The Four Winds Calvary Chapel on the Internet under the Calvary Chapel Logo released the following Doctrinal Statement. Although it can not be taken as a formal document on behalf of the denomination it is congruent with the Calvary Chapel literature and the research of Balmer and Todd, Di Sabatino, and the author. Emphasis in the text is as received, to reflect the intent of the group.

Doctrinal Statement of Four Winds Calvary Chapel

> Ephesians 4:3-6 . . . endeavoring to keep the unity of the Spirit in the bond of peace. There is one body and one Spirit, just as you were called in one hope of your calling; one Lord, one faith, one baptism; one God and Father of all, who is above all, and through all, and in you all.

JESUS IS LORD!!

CALVARY CHAPEL FOUR WINDS HOLDS TO THE FOLLOWING DOCTRINAL TRUTHS. CCFW BELIEVES . . .

* In one God, eternally existent in three separate persons, Father, Son, and Holy Spirit.

* That God, the Father, is personal, transcendent, and sovereign in relation to all His creation.

* That Jesus Christ, is fully God and fully man, born of a virgin, lived a sinless life, provided atonement for our sins by His substitutionary death on the cross, was bodily resurrected by the power of the Holy Spirit, ascended to the right hand of God, the Father, and ever lives to make intercession for us.

* That after Jesus ascended to heaven, He poured out His Holy Spirit on the believers in Jerusalem, enabling them to fulfill His command to preach the gospel to the entire world, an obligation shared by all believers today.

* That all people are by nature sinful (failing to live the life that God desires for us), separated from God because of our sin, and personally responsible for our own sin and destined for eternal judgment.

* That salvation comes as a result of God's grace and the drawing power of the Holy Spirit, salvation is effective when a person receives Jesus Christ as Lord and Savior; trusting Jesus Christ alone to save him and repents (turns away) from his sinful life to serve God.

* That immediately upon salvation (born-again), the Holy Spirit indwells that person, sealing him for eternal life. Personal sins are forgiven (past, present, and future), and the forgiven person becomes a child of God.

* That the gifts of the Holy Spirit, as mentioned in Scripture, are valid for each believer today and are to be exercised in love and within.

Scriptural Guidelines for the Edification of the Body of Christ

* In the inerrancy of Scripture, that the entire Bible is the inspired, infallible word of God.

* That the Bible (the word of God), under the power of the Holy Spirit, has the ability to change a person's life and bring the believer to maturity in Jesus Christ.

* That the church will be raptured (taken up to heaven) into the presence of Jesus Christ before the tribulation period and the second coming of Christ, with all His saints to rule on earth, will be personal pre-millennial, and visible.

Contrary to what may be happening in the church at-large today, CCFW rejects

1. The belief that a Christian can be demon-possessed.

2. Any teaching that limits Jesus' atoning work on the cross, and that people are elected to go to hell. Rather, anyone who wills to come to Christ may do so.

3. The "positive confession" teaching of the word of faith movement.

4. Man-made predictions or writings that supersede Scripture.

5. Incorporation of humanistic and secular psychology into biblical teaching.

6. An over-emphasis of spiritual gifts-experiential and emotional signs and wonders to the exclusion of biblical teaching.

7. Any person or teaching that would turn believers away from the Lord Jesus and cause division within the body of Christ.

* In our worship services the focus is on a personal relationship with God through worship, prayer, and the teaching of the Word of God.
Speaking in tongues and prophecy is not encouraged during the worship service because we believe the Holy Spirit will not interrupt Himself and distract from the teaching of the Word of God.

* God's love for us, as demonstrated through Jesus Christ, should motivate a believer to Godly living, heartfelt worship, committed service, diligent study of God's Word, regular fellowship, and participation in adult baptism by immersion, and the Lord's supper.

http://www.calvarychapel.org/fourwinds/DOCTRINAL.html

APPENDIX 4

Elements of Style and Substance in Radical Jesus Movement Leadership

This analysis of the CWLF leadership is generic, not just particularized:

1. The leaders of the more cerebral end of the movement such as CWLF had at some stage been fundamentalist, strongly Bible-based preachers, or teachers, prior to personal radical worldview shifts during the 1960s.

2. Francis Schaeffer who legitimized apologetics and proposed a gospel capable of addressing the secular modernity culture initially influenced their leaders. Many hippie converts went to his Swiss community at L'Abri.

3. Most were at least a decade older than the disciples, but such leaders embraced a revised evangelicalism which Michael Quebordeaux typified as *The Young Evangelicals* (Quebedeaux 1974) of the Berkeley movement (Di Sabatino 1999:63). This revised evangelicalism was a "Third way" between the anti-intellectualism of fundamentalism and the rationalism of liberalism, providing a balance between discipleship evangelism [and social responsibility]. They forged an intellectual apologetic within the counterculture.

4. Their modus operandi involved more than analysis of the counterculture and more than Christian propaganda adapted to hippie culture. They were disenchanted with conservative responses to student issues of social, political, and religious import. Most went "native," sharing the counterculture's gestalt shift, abandoning society's institutions, and rejecting the rationalistic, materialistic, and individualistic philosophies of the mainstream. They were converts as well as cross-cultural missionaries.

5. They held common cause with the counterculture concerning civil rights, ecology, communalism, peace activism, and the need for a more affective rather than cognitive religious experience. The right to protest and the necessity to be culturally inclusive was a deeply felt belief, not just a communication ploy.

6. While a few leaders involved in the Jesus Movement may have later embraced Liberation Theology too uncritically (Newman 1990), most embraced a balanced action-reflection hermeneutic, but found themselves somewhat alienated from both the traditional church and the political revolutionaries.

7. They felt partially marginalized from the counterculture due to its excessive monism and rejection of all authoritative frameworks. Accusations of "counter revolutionary" subversion were leveled at Christian radicals who were the marginalized of the marginalized.

APPENDIX 5

Christian World Liberation Front, New Berkeley Liberation Program

The people of Berkeley passionately desire personal fulfillment, vital interpersonal relationships, and inner peace.

1. Jesus Christ will free all who come to him from bondage to the crippled self, the maimed world, and the scheming devil.

2. He will enable all who come to Him to develop their inner talents, abilities and resources to the fullest.

3. He will turn the schools into training grounds for liberation of the inner self.

4. He will destroy the powers that bind us as we turn to Him, the only One who truly serves the people.

5. He will provide for the full liberation of men and women as a necessary part of the revolutionary process of building His family.

6. He will take responsibility for basic human needs.

7. He will make drugs obsolete.

8. He will bring a new spirit of concern and cooperation among people who turn to Him and trust Him for moment by moment direction.

9. He will continue to show His concern for the poor and oppressed people of the world.

10. He will eliminate fear of tyrannical forces and powers.

11. He will create a soulful Christianity in Berkeley.

12. He will govern perfectly.

13. He will unite Berkeley Christians with others throughout the world to demonstrate His alternative to the present world system in all of its manifold manifestations.

Sisters and brothers, unite with Jesus, assist and create, build a revolutionary Berkeley, with your friends, your Lord, your God, form liberation committees, carry out the program, choose the action and do it, set examples and spread the Word.

We call for sisters and brothers to form liberation committees to implement His program. POWER THROUGH THE SPIRIT. ALL POWER THROUGH JESUS (Heinz 1976a:44).

APPENDIX 6

Berkeley Liberation Program

1. We will make Telegraph Avenue and the South Campus a strategic free territory for revolution.

2. We will create our revolutionary culture everywhere.

3. We will turn the schools into training grounds for liberators.

4. We will destroy the university unless it serves the people.

5. We will struggle for the full liberation of women as a necessary part of the revolutionary process.

6. We will take command responsibility for basic human needs.

7. We will protect and expand our drug culture.

8. We will break the power of the landlords and provide beautiful housing for everyone.

9. We will tax the corporations, not the working people.

10. We will defend ourselves against law and order.

11. We will create a soulful socialism in Berkeley.

APPENDIX 7

New Covenant Apostolic Order

Being convinced it is the will of God the Father, the Son, and the Holy Spirit and because we are living in a time of great need for a new expression of the church, in continuity with biblical, apostolic and catholic tradition, we the undersigned are establishing the NEW COVENANT APOSTOLIC ORDER.

We are NEW COVENANT because we believe the new covenant promise is for the church today. God through the Holy Spirit does indeed write His law upon the hearts of His people, those who live under the government and reign of the Lord Jesus Christ.

We are APOSTOLIC because the service and authority of Apostleship is necessary today to lead the church to live under Christ's reign. Apostleship is a gift to the church required throughout its history. God has called us to this ministry.

We are an ORDER because we as one among other such groups of people are called to serve the Lord in His church. Such orders have strong historic precedence. We are committed to the goals, characteristics, organization and doctrinal statements herein set forth.

GOALS

1. To build, as workers under God, the CHURCH OF THE NEW COVENANT, a communion of churches whose people experience the Lordship of Christ, are committed to each other in this life, and look forward to the hope, the ultimate establishment of the Kingdom of God.

2. To build churches, culturally and locally oriented, in which the people share community and are cared for under the Lordship of Christ by a serving, indigenous leadership.

3. To strive for catholicity in our relationships with other existing churches and communions of churches.

CHARACTERISTICS

Churches raised up by this apostolic order and joining the Church of the New Covenant are called especially to the following concerns:

1. <u>Grace:</u> Our God deals with us according to His gracious loving character. We are grateful recipients of this grace and are called to reflect it in this world.

2. <u>True Community:</u> These congregations of people are to be committed to God and to each other, being truly involved in all aspects of each other's lives.

3. <u>Vision:</u> We are committed to a vision of the raising up of churches reflecting the Kingdom of God and expressing the church catholic. These churches are called to be the salt of the earth and to be light shining in the darkness of a fallen world. Each church is called within its own local and cultural setting to be a living demonstration of the blessing and order of God's reign in contrast to the confusion and anarchy of Satan in a rebel world.

4. <u>An Authoritative, Serving Leadership:</u> The government of each church is carried out by an eldership (ideally plural) devoted to serving the congregation. These elders have authority under God, and the people are committed to their serving leadership.

5. <u>Care:</u> These congregations are called to look after the needs of their people in all areas of their lives, including financial, emotional, intellectual, spiritual, and vocational.

6. <u>Seeing and Hearing from God:</u> One consequence of the new covenant is the baptism in the Holy Spirit enabling God's people to see and hear from Him. As Christians walk in obedience to the Spirit, they should expect God to communicate with them. The church is responsible to determine when God has in fact spoken and to obey accordingly.

7. <u>Good Works:</u> Faith without works is dead. Each congregation is committed to putting love into action individually and collectively. This includes preaching the Gospel to the poor and care for the sick, the poverty-stricken, and people afflicted with other troubles.

8. Godliness: Human beings are responsible for their conduct. The words and works of the citizens of God's Kingdom are to be in obedience to their King. We are committed to living lives of love, moral purity, truth, kindness, justice, goodness and those other characteristics to which God calls His people.

9. Orthodox Theology: We teach and hold to those doctrines which have their base in Scripture, are in keeping with the formulations of the early councils of the church catholic, and have been commonly held by all communions of orthodox believers. We are not interested in new or novel doctrines.

10. Worship: The heart of worship is praise and thanksgiving. These churches joyfully and regularly gather at the throne of God to worship the Father, the Son and he Holy Spirit. Each member is encouraged to participate.

11. The Hope: We look forward to the Second Advent of Christ, the King, and participation forever in the Kingdom which He will one day fully establish.

12. Catholicity: The church is divided. That is not the ideal of God. We long for the church to return to a state of unity which will show the world that He is Lord.

ORGANIZATION

ELDERS

Ideally, each of the churches is governed by plural eldership. These elders are ordained by the apostolic workers with the agreement of the people of the church.

Initial identification of a potential elder comes from the Holy Spirit through persons in the church and/or through the apostolic workers. In any case there must be apostolic recognition of the elders. Elders are responsible for the care and government of the church. They are responsible to see that the church is taught correct doctrine in all spheres of life.

DEACONS

Deacons are chosen to serve the church by the agreement of the elders and the people. Deacons are responsible for the care of the physical need of the church and its people. They work under the leadership of the elders.

PRESBYTERY

Within local areas the churches are served and united by a presbytery of all of the elders of those churches. This presbytery concerns itself with:

1. The unity of its churches.

2. The guardianship of apostolic doctrine.

3. The supply of gifts and ministry to its churches which have need of assistance.

4. The local care of young men and women preparing for the work of ministry.

REGIONAL APOSTOLIC COUNCIL

All of the presbyteries in a larger defined area are served and ministered to by a Regional Apostolic Council. This council, composed of members of the New Covenant Apostolic Order, will give itself to:

1. Raising up churches of the nature already defined.

2. Establishing these churches under the Lordship of Christ and seeing to it that they are grounded in the application of sound doctrine to the lives of the people.

3. Discovering, ordaining, overseeing, and training elders and workers.

4. Providing examples in simplicity of lifestyle, in practice of Christian community, in submission to the leadership established by God and in commitment to the church locally and universally.

5. Setting up education and training for the preparation of the people for service and ministry.

GENERAL APOSTOLIC COUNCIL

The New Covenant Apostolic Order is served and led by a General Apostolic Council presently made up of Dick Ballew, Ken Berven, Jon Braun, Peter Gillquist, Ray Nethery, Jack Sparks and Gordon Walker. All members of this council share the aforementioned goals. They will give themselves primarily to the raising up of churches, to prayer and ministry of the Word, to apostolic doctrine, to the oversight of regional apostolic councils, and to the publishing of literature which will build up the church.

GENERAL ASSEMBLY

Overall authority in the church and in the apostolic order is vested in the General Assembly of the Church of the New Covenant. This General Assembly is presently composed of all the elders of all the churches and the members of the New Covenant Apostolic Order. As the churches multiply, and the numbers become unwieldy, the presbyteries will choose representative elders to serve on the General Assembly. The General Assembly will meet annually and as necessity requires.

PERTINENT DOCTRINE

We embrace as foundational to proper theological definition and true belief in this century (as in previous Christian centuries) three creeds which are catholic in their acceptance and recognition:

The Apostles Creed: We believe in God the Father Almighty, maker of heaven and earth, and in Jesus Christ His only Son, our Lord who was conceived by the Holy Ghost, born of the virgin Mary, suffered under Pontius Pilate, was crucified dead and buried; He descended into hell; the third day He rose again from the dead; He ascended into heaven and sitteth at the right hand of God the Father Almighty; from thence He shall come to judge the quick and the dead. I believe in the Holy Ghost, the holy catholic church, the communion of saints, the forgiveness of sins, the resurrection of the dead, and life everlasting.

The Nicene Creed: We believe in one God the Father all-sovereign, maker of all things visible and invisible; and in one Lord Jesus Christ, the Son of God, begotten of the Father, only-begotten, that is, of the substance of the Father, God of God, Light of Light, True God of True God, begotten not made, of one substance with the Father, through whom all things were made, things in heaven and things on the earth; who for us men and for our salvation came down and was made flesh, and became man, suffered, and rose on the third day, ascended into the heavens, is coming to judge living and dead. And in the Holy Spirit. And those that say, 'There was when he was not,' and 'Before he was begotten he was not,' and that, 'He came into being from what-is-not,' or those that allege, that the Son of God is 'of another substance or essence' or 'created', or 'changeable,' or 'alterable,' these the Catholic and Apostolic Church anathematizes.

The Chalcedonian Creed: Therefore, following the holy Fathers, we all with one accord teach men to acknowledge one and the same Son, our Lord Jesus Christ, at once complete in Godhead and complete in manhood, truly God and truly man, consisting also of a reasonable soul and body; of one substance with the Father as regards his Godhead, and at the same time of one substance with us as regards his manhood; like us in all respects, apart from sin; as regards his Godhead, begotten of the Father before the ages but yet as regards his manhood begotten, for us men and for our salvation, of Mary the virgin, the God-bearer; one and the same Christ, Son, Lord, Only-begotten, recognized in two natures, without confusion, without change, without division, without separation; the distinction of natures being in no way annulled by the union, but rather the characteristics of each nature being preserved and coming together to form one person and substance, not as parted or separated into two persons, but one and the same Son and Only-begotten God the Word, Lord Jesus Christ; even as the prophets from earliest times spoke of him, and our Lord Jesus Christ himself taught us, and the creed of the Fathers has handed down to us.

2. Because of the loss of truth in the church, in our time, we feel there are certain matters which require attention from a doctrinal standpoint. The creation, the personalness of God the Word of God and eschatology are a few. At this writing we have not completed a definitive statement of our view of the Scripture because of its pressing importance to those reading this document.

<u>The Scripture:</u> is the only authoritative, God-breathed, infallible record given by God to humanity; it is revelation and it is unique. Scripture as interpreted by the agreement of the church universal is the only authoritative source of doctrine.

We the undersigned commend this statement of direction and organization to the churches which we serve. We are fully aware that this document is preliminary work. We are eagerly open to anything God may say through anyone in any of our churches. We request that this document be considered and that any suggestions come via the elders to a meeting for all of our elders from all of our churches at Grace Haven, June 28-July 1, 1976.

[Signed: Ballew, Berven, Braun, Gillquist, Nethery, Spark, and Walker].

APPENDIX 8

Early Church Worship Routine

Following the reception of research reports on the form and function of the early church and its modes of gathering, worship and instruction, it was concluded by the seven elders of the New Covenant Apostolic Order (NCAO) that the early church was sacramental, and worship was liturgical. They also concluded the form of gathering early in church development separated the service into an open and closed form. The Synaxis was open to all. The Eucharist was preserved for members and catechumens (applicants in training and under instruction for admission to church membership. The basic routine of these gatherings were as follows:

Synaxis

Greeting and response
Hymns, interspersed with
Readings from Scripture, the "Apostles' Memoirs"
The Homily
Dismissal of those not in the Church

Eucharist

Greeting and response
Intercessory Prayers
Offertory – of bread and wine
Consecration of Gifts
Communion
Giving of Thanks
Benediction
(Gillquist 1990:31)

APPENDIX 9

New Covenant Apostolic Order's Ideal Church Characteristics

By mid 1975 the coalition of ex-Campus Crusade Directors, involved in a variety of ministries around America including CWLF, Grace Haven Farm and a growing number of house church units, come to the conclusion that the church is sacramental, worship is liturgical, and church government is hierarchical. They formed an Episcopal structure embracing bishops, presbyters, deacons and laity under an umbrella organization called the New Covenant Apostolic Order (NCAO).

They sought to establish churches with twelve characteristics:

1. Grace
2. True community
3. Vision
4. Authoritative, serving leadership
5. Care
6. Seeing and hearing from God
7. Good works
8. Godliness
9. Orthodox theology
10. Worship
11. The Blessed Hope
12. Catholicity

APPENDIX 10

Preliminary Agreement Between Metropolitan Philip and Bishop Peter Gillquist, clearing a path to entry by individuals and churches of the Evangelical Orthodox Church of America [EOCA] to enter into the Antiochian Orthodox Church [AOC].

1. Expression of hope for full union in the near future.
2. The union will require some modifications of attitudes on both sides. It will be necessary for us to solve the problem of married episcopates. This will be worked through at a future meeting between the Metropolitan and the Synod of the Evangelical Orthodox Church.
3. Upon the chrismation and/or ordination of those who are willing and meet the requirements, a relationship can be set up bringing the Evangelical Orthodox Church into the Antiochian Archdiocese.
4. The structure that is now the Evangelical Orthodox Church will continue its mission of preaching Orthodoxy to the American public.
5. Under the Metropolitan, the new body will be headed by a Council under its president.
6. The Metropolitan will appoint an acceptable liaison officer to work with the headquarters of what is now the Evangelical Orthodox Church. The officer will advise and answer questions that the Council may have and after a given period, his office will be closed.
7. A committee of theologians to whom the Council can refer theological and liturgical problems will be appointed by the Metropolitan.
8. The new structure will follow the financial system now enforced in the Archdiocese and will report quarterly to the Archdiocese on its financial status and growth or decline.
9. The new structure in the Archdiocese will establish internal liturgical uniformity acceptable to all in consultation with the Committee of Theologians.

POSTSCRIPT

It is important to reiterate the significance of the revitalization theory despite the passage of time since its conception. As an anthropological paradigm it appears in the literature of that domain more frequently than in social movement literature. In the field of anthropology, the paradigm shows no recent sign of a decline in status (Ember and Ember 1999; Ferraro 1998; Turner and Bruner 1986). The only criticisms of which I am aware is that the theory has been misunderstood and limited to studies of tribal peoples by some scholars (Joel Martin 1999; Kraft 1996a). Secondly, it has been proposed that Wallace has failed to expand the model in the context of ideological rather than psychological and social conflict (Klass 1995:152). Klass believes Wallace's observations need to be taken "a short distant further" since his "formula is not invariable. Sometimes the repertoire is simplified, and sometimes two sets of fundamentally different and even conflicting assumptions, beliefs, and practices continue to be exhibited, not only in the same cultural system, but even in the same application." (1995:147).

This dissertation supports a stable tradition of revitalization theory in its chosen field of missiology (Eugene Nida 1990:256-257; Paul Hiebert 1983; Kraft 1996; Tippett 1979; Whiteman 1983). Tippett employs the revitalization principle in his field of expertise of Melanesian studies applying it to the Marching Rule in the Solomon Islands. Anthropologist and missiologists Darrell Whiteman extensively develops the work of Tippett concerning the Melanesian Marching Rule, providing a periodization breakdown of the five stages of revitalization with respect to Melanesian renewal (1983:273-275). I have sought to apply Victor Turner's theories concerning the creative power of liminality in ritual process to the innovative and countercultural developments in revitalization. Following the conclusion of the development of this theory to the Jesus Movement revitalization, I discovered a similar application in one of Tippet's unpublished papers concerning the effects of liminality and marginalization on the Melanesian revitalization movement in *The Liminal Years: Selected Essays 1943-1976*.

The lack of rebuttal in recent movemental literature is as significant as the paucity of its specific mention. Recent social theorists have clearly accepted the model as a "given" concept in social theory (Marx and McAdam 1994; Peter Williams 1989). More important is the general acceptance of cultural stress as a cause of the initiation of social movements and the revival of the application of Weber's charismatic leader motif also incorporated in Wallace's description of the revitalization process. As noted in Chapter 2 considerable commentary on the significance of charismatic figures in the articulation and popularization of a movement's code and mission by such charismatics affirms Wallace's conclusions concerning the stages of revitalization. Colin Campbell (1996) has however strongly criticized contemporary sociology for its lack of recognition of

Weber's emphasis on individualistic action because of sociology's obsession with situationalism. While the term revitalization (sometimes synonymous with revolution in recent social movement literature) may not occur frequently, conceptually its dynamics remain in accepted social theory.

The application of revitalization theory to the Jesus Movement provides a test case beyond the usual ethnographies of non-European tribal movements. While several scholars have assumed the Reformation and the Evangelical Awakenings of the eighteenth and nineteenth centuries were revitalizations, obviously no leaders or participants are available for interview to assess those movements adequately.

Since revitalization is an unscheduled social response to specific cultural dysfunction, it occurs less commonly than other forms of social movement. It naturally receives less attention than other more rationally birthed forms. The significance of revitalization lies in its intuitive nature and its capacity for a brief period to promote rapid systems innovation. Because the innovative period is short-lived, the process provides a brief time for scholarly investigation. Its unscheduled appearance and rapid internal change through routinization further complicates examination and verification.

Ample time has passed since the 1960s – 1970s revitalization for objective analysis, yet it is a sufficiently recent occurrence to enable extensive interviews with many who were involved at the time. This dissertation primarily seeks to identify the nature and causation of the Jesus Movement, but in doing so, it adds to considerable evidence for the validity of the theory beyond the context of tribal movements.

Furthermore, the evidence of massive impact on the Jesus Movement is becoming more and more obvious. At the first Revitalization colloquium at Asbury Theological Seminary in 2009, the number of delegates who as academics and specialists were either participants or converts of the Movement was remarkable. Dr. Robert Tuttle reflected on his experience at Fuller theological Seminary, noting that at one stage the majority of students at the seminary were similarly part of the revitalization. One young, delegate at the ATS conference, now a frontier worker with the urban poor told me of his parents' were converts and participants in the movement, communally caring for hippies and addicts. He reported that forty of the converts resulting from their Jesus People ministry as just one family are now in Christian ministry.

Far more importantly than the encouragement of past glories however is the application of the lessons to be learnt from the incendiary, visionary, but apparently short-lived Revitalization Movement, to the 21st century Christian witness to a globalized and troubled context. I would underscore two vital issues. The first is the failure of any Twentieth Century efforts to lastingly produce a steady state of reduced cultural stress in Western cultures. Martin Seligman's epidemiological research into clinical depression provides disturbing evidence of a tenfold increase since the end of World War II. The shift in each decade has been to a younger demography, such that it is now common for primary school children to require professional psychological or psychiatric help for this illness. Seligman's research strongly suggests that clinical depression is culturally induced as the consequence of inadequate worldview, the collapse of appropriate institutional support, and the isolation of the individual from organic and social, communitarian solidarity.

Most of the indicators posited by Wallace are again prevalent in our postmodern societies. Issues of pre-emptive war, citizen violence, breakdown of consensus concerning familial tradition, and rampant materialism have returned with a vengeance since the days of communalism, simple lifestyle experimentation and peace activism. The same signs of dangerous cultural distortion are on the increase again. The cavalier, dangerous and unconscionable behavior of the corporate world and the world of television preachers would make Gordon Gecko reconsider the proposition that *greed is good.*

The Jesus Movement above all else sought to follow Jesus' teachings and even the style of His inclusive love and socially defiant deconstruction of the world of the Scribe and the Pharisee. They exuded a childlike naïveté strangely reflective of Jesus own teaching concerning the faith of a child. They loved the lilies of the field without desiring to own and franchise them at inflated prices. They saw the solidarity of humanity based on a common divine ancestry that denied ego-tripping class, economic war on the two-thirds world. They asked how we could logically *kill people who kill people, to prove killing people is wrong*. They saw peace not as a technique but as a reality grounded in the politics of Jesus, so effectively employed by Gandhi, Martin Luther King and St Francies.

My contention is that the agenda of the counterculture movement of the Jesus People is as relevant and critically significant now as it was then. At the beginning of the 1970s, we claimed *Jesus Freaks are ecology freaks.* Ministries such as Shiloh in the USA and all of the major Australian expressions of the Movement were publically committed to environmentalism. Somehow most of the essential messages of love, of resistance to materialism and radical individualism and of non-violent resistance have not merely been muted – they have been reversed in a return to conspicuous acquisitiveness, self-esteem obsession, aggressive nationalism and voluntary association rather than an intimate, mutual, communal relationship nurtured by Church as a holy institution.

They were not really freaks in the conventional sense. The rest of the world is freaky and continues to based on assumptions that are self-evident failures. Pre-modern, modern, postmodern emerging after postmodern – whatever the shifting of the sociological or philosophical sands the enduring message of Jesus needs to be understood and embraced in real life. When I recall those remarkably renewing days. I find myself both alarmed and reassured by the substantially naïve, childlike simplicity and literalness with which the hippies initially responded to an untutored reading of the gospel text. I am alarmed that the establishment so quickly convinced them that they should no longer take seriously the radical message of Mark six, as beautifully interpreted in the *Message* translation:

He sent them off with these instructions: 'Don't think you need a lot of extra equipment for this. You are the equipment. No special appeals for funds. Keep it simple.' And no luxury inns.

He gave them authority and power to deal with the evil opposition…right and left they sent the demons packing…

Then they were on the road. They preached with joyful urgency that life can be radically different, they brought wellness to the sick, anointing their bodies, healing their spirits (6: 6-13).

That is what we really believed back then. My prayer is that we might believe it again. Perhaps this all-too-inadequate history and analysis can add to the growing sense of interest and even tentative excitement surrounding the possibility of revitalization in our time, and without national or socio-cultural borders.

REFERENCES CITED

Adams, Robert Lynn, and Robert Jon Fox
    1972   "Mainlining Jesus: The New Trip." *Society* 9(2):50-56.

Adeney, Bernard T.
    1995   *Strange Virtues: Ethics in a Multicultural World.* Downers Grove, IL: InterVarsity Press.

Adler, Moshe
    1974   "Alienation and Jewish Jesus Freaks." *Judaism* 23(Summer):287-297.

Ahlstrom, Sydney E.
    1972   *A Religious History of the American People.* New Haven, CT: Yale University Press.

Ainsworth, Paul
    1991 "20th Century Wesley, Aussie Style." *CWN Series* September 12. London: Greenbelt Festivals.

Albrow, Martin
    1990   *Max Weber's Construction of Social Theory.* New York: St.Martin's Press.

Allen, Roland
    1962[1912] *Missionary Methods: St. Paul's or Ours.* Grand Rapids, MI: Eerdmans.

Altizer, Thomas J.J.
    1961   *Oriental Mysticism and Eschatology.* Philadelphia, PA: Westminster Press.
    1964   "Nirvana and the kingdom of God." *New Theology* No 1:50f. New York: MacMillan.

Amin, Samir, Giovanni Arrighi, and Andre Gunder Frank

1990 *Transforming the Revolution.* New York: Monthly Review Press.

Ammerman, Nancy Tatom
1997 *Congregation and Community.* New Brunswick, NJ: Rutgers University Press.

Anderson, Joanne
1986 "Child Suicide Causes Complex." *The Sun Living Supplement.* November 11:1.

Anderson, Terry
1971 *Movement and the Sixties: Protest in America Greensboro to Wounded Knee.* Oxford, UK: Oxford University Press.

Andrain, Charles F., and David Ernest Apter
1995 *Political Protest and Social Change.* Basingstoke, U.K: Macmillan.

Annett, Stephen, ed.
1976 *The Many Ways of Being: A Guide to Spiritual Groups and Growth Centers in Britain.* London, UK: Abacus.

Archer, John
1985 *The Home Building Experience: John Archer Talks to Owner Builders.* Sydney, Australia: Australian Broadcasting Corporation.

Arweck, Elizabeth, and Peter Clarke
1997 *New Religious Movements in Western Europe: An Annotated Bibliography.* Westport, CT: Greenwood Press.

Askew, Thomas A., and Peter W. Spellman
1984 *The Churches and the American Experience: Ideals and Institutions.* Grand Rapids, MI: Baker Book House.

Atkinson, Alison
1999 "World Shakers." *Alive* (December 1999/January 2000):16-22.

Baez, Joan
1971 "The Hitchhiker's Song." *Blessed Are.* New York: Vanguard Recording Society.

Bainbridge, William Sims
1980 "Client and Audience Cults in America." *Sociological Analysis* 41:199-214.
1980 "Sectarian Tension." *Review of Religious Research* (December 1980): 105-124.
1981 "The 'Consciousness Reformation' Reconsidered." *Journal for the Scientific Study of Religion* 20:1-16.
1982 "Shaker Demographics 1840-1900: An Example of the Use of US Census Enumeration Schedules." *Journal for the Scientific Study of Religion* 21(4):352-365.
1984a "Formal Explanation of Religion: A Progress Report." *Sociological Analysis* 45(2):145-158.

1984b "Religious Insanity in America: The Official Nineteenth-Century Theory." *Sociological Analysis* 45(3):223-240.
1989 "The Religious Ecology of Deviance." *American Sociological Review* 54(4):288-295.
1990 "Explaining the Church Member Rate." *Social Forces* 68(4):1287-1296.
1997 *The Sociology of Religious Movements.* New York: Rutledge.

Bainbridge, William Sims, and Rodney Stark
1963 "On Church and Sect." *American Sociological Review* 28:539.
1979 "Cult Formation: Three Compatible Models." *Sociological Analysis* 40:283-295.
1980 "Client and Audience Cults in America." *Sociological Analysis* 41:199-214.

Baker, Paul
1979 *Why Should the Devil Have All the Good Music?* Waco, TX: Word Books.
1985 *Contemporary Christian Music: Where It Came From, What It Is, Where It's Going?* Westchester, IL: Crossways Books.

Ballew, Richard
n.d. *Coming in From the Cold.* Mt. Hermon, CA: Conciliar Press.
1997 "The Early Years: Grace and Truth." *Again* 20(1):13-15. Ben Lomond, CA: Conciliar Press.

Balmer, Randall
1989 *Mine Eyes Have Seen the Glory: A Journey into the Evangelical Sub-culture in America.* Chicago, IL: University of Chicago Press.

Balmer, Randall, and Jesse T. Todd, Jr.
1994 "Calvary Chapel, Costa Mesa, California." In *American Congregations.* Vol. 1. *Portraits of Twelve Religious Communities.* James P. Wind, and James W. Lewis, eds. Pp. 663-698. Chicago, IL: University of Chicago Press.

Balswick, Jack
1974 "The Jesus People Movement: A Sociological Analysis." *Journal of Social Issues* 30:23-42.

Banks, Robert
1999 *Going to Church in the First Century: An Eyewitness Account.* Beaumont, TX: Christian Press.
1994 *Paul's Idea of Community: The Early House Churches in Their Cultural Setting.* Revised edition. Peabody, MA: Hendrickson.

Banks, Robert, and Julia Banks

1998 *The Church Comes Home.* Peabody, MA: Hendrickson Publishers Inc.
Barbour, Ian G.
   1974 *Myths, Models, and Paradigms: A Comparative Study in Science and Religion.* New York: Harper & Row
Barker, Eileen
   1989 *New Religious Movements: A Practical Introduction.* London, UK: Her Majesty's Stationary Office.
Barrett, David B., and Todd M. Johnson
   2001 *World Christian Trends AD 30-AD 2200: Interpreting the Annual Christian Megacensus.* Pasadena, CA: William Carey Library.
Barnett, Homer G.
   1953 *Innovation: the Basis of Cultural Change.* New York: McGraw-Hill.
Bass, B.M.
   1985 *Leadership and Performance Beyond Expectations.* New York: The Free Press.
Bastien, Brian
   1970 "Hollywood Blvd. – One Way." *Christianity Today* 14(2):328.
Batstone, David
   1992 "Jesus, Apocalyptic, and World Transformation." *Theology Today* (October):383ff.
Beaudoin, Tom
   1998 *Virtual Faith: The Irreverent Spiritual Quest of Generation X.* San Francisco, CA: Jossey-Bass Inc.
Beaumont, Rosina
   1989 "God Squad Leader Socks It to Society." *The Sunday Tasmania. Living – Religion* June 25:4.
Bell, Daniel
   1995 *The Cultural Contradictions of Capitalism.* Revised edition. New York: Basic Books.
   1996 Bell, Father Seraphim [Charles]
   1993 "O Lord, Establish This Vineyard." *Again* 16(2):52-55. Ben Lomond, CA: Conciliar Press.
Bellah, Mike
   1988 *Baby Boom Believers in the 90s.* Wheaton, IL: Tyndale House.
Bellah, Robert
   1982 "Preface" in *Getting Saved from the Sixties.* Stephen N.Tipton. Pp. 13-16. Berkeley, CA: University of California Press.

Berger, Peter L., and Thomas Luckman
   1966 *The Social Construction of Reality: A Treatise in the Sociology of Knowledge* New York: Doubleday.

Berkey, R.F.
    1972   "Jesus and Jesus People." *Christian Century* 89:336-338.

Best, Bruce
    1985   "The Archbishop's Mission." *The Age* September 3:11.

Bibby, Reginald W.
    1987   *Fragmented Gods: The Poverty and Potential of Religion in Canada.* Toronto, Canada: Irwin Publishing.
    1990   *Mosaic Madness: Pluralism without a Cause.* Toronto, Canada: Stoddart.
    1995   *The Bibby Report: Social Trends Canadian Style.* Toronto, Canada: Stoddart.

Bibby, Reginald W., and Donald C. Posterski
    1985   *The Emerging Generation: An Inside Look at Canada's Teenagers.* Toronto, Canada: Irwin Publishing.
    1992   *Teen Trends: A Nation in Motion.* Toronto, Canada: Stoddart Publishing.

Birch, Charles
    1990   *On Purpose.* Kensington, Australia: New South Wales University Press.

Blainey, Geoffrey Norman
    1983 [1966]   *The Tyranny of Distance: How Distance Shaped Australia'sHistory.* South Melbourne, Australia: Sun Books.

Blessitt, Arthur
    1972   *Tell the World: A Jesus People Manual.* Tiptree, Essex, UK: Lakeland.
    1999   Telephone interview by John Smith. December 1.

Blessitt, Arthur, and Walter Wagner
    1971   *Turned on to Jesus.* London, UK: Word Books.

Bloom, Allan
    1987   *The Closing of the American Mind.* New York: Simon and Schuster.

Boeth, Margaret, Mayo Mohs, and Richard Ostling
    1971   "The New Rebel Cry: Jesus is Coming." *Time* June 21:1,38-49.

Bonhoeffer, Dietrich
    1959   *The Cost of Discipleship.* London, UK: SCM Press.

Borowski, Karol
    1984   *Attempting an Alternative Society: A Sociological Study of a Selected Communal – Revitalization Movement in the United States.* Norwood, PA: Norwood Editions.

Boyer, Paul
    1992   *When Time Shall Be No More: Prophecy Belief in Modern American Culture.* Cambridge, MA: Belknap Press of Harvard University Press.

Bozeman, John M.
    1990   "Jesus People USA: An Examination of an Urban Communitarian Religious Group." MA thesis, Tallahassee, FL: Florida State University.

Braun, Jon E.
    1997   "The Early Years: Parachurch to Church." *Again* 20(1):10-12. Ben Lomond, CA: Conciliar Press.

Breit, Liz
    1989   "Pastors Arrested at Gunpoint in the Philippines. Two on Human Rights Mission Landed in Jail." *Knox News* August 1:8.

Breward, Ian
    1988   *Australia: "The Most Godless Place Under Heaven?"* Melbourne College of Divinity Bicentennial Lectures. Melbourne, Australia: Beacon Hill Books.

Brolly, Mark
    1989   "'Left' Link Can Mean Death, Say Pastors." *The Age* July 25:19.
    1991   "Biker Sends Boys on the Highway to Heaven." *The Age* July 24:16.

Brown, Norman O.
    1968   *Life Against Death.* London, UK: Sphere Books.

Brown, Patricia
    1971   "Who Are the Jesus People." *Yakima Valley Sun* February 25:16.
    1976   "House of Elijah: A Part of Yakima for Six Years." *Yakima Valley Sun* September 30:3.

Brown, Robert McAfee
    1984   *Unexpected News: Reading the Bible with Third World Eyes.* Philadelphia, PA: The Westminster Press.

Buhl, Achim
    1999   E-mail communication with John Smith. July 9. Internet: achim.buehl@stud-mail.uni-wuerzburg.de

Burns, J.M.
    1978   *Leadership.* New York: Harper and Row.

Burger, Peter, and Brigitte Burger
    1971   "The Eve of the Bluing of America." *The New York Times* February 15:7.

Burgess, Harold
    2000   Personal interview by John Smith. February 29.

Burns, Mary-Violet
    1971   "Prophets in God-Rock." *Home Missions* June-July:47-52.

Burns, Stewart
    1990   *Social Movements of the 1960s: Searching for Democracy.* New York: Twayne.

Cahill, Tim
    1973a   "Infiltrating the Jesus Army Part I." *Rolling Stone* June 7:42-50.
    1973b   "Infiltrating the Jesus Army Part II." *Rolling Stone* June 21:50-60.

Camera, Dom Helder
    1971   *Revolution through Peace.* New York: Harper & Row.

Campbell, Colin
    1996   *The Myth of Social Action.* Cambridge, UK: Cambridge University Press.

Campbell, Gordon
    1989   "John Rides on for a Better Way." *The News* January 30:12.

Carlson, Betty
    1970   *An Unhurried Chase to L'Abri.* Wheaton, IL: Tyndale House Publishers.

Carothers, Lisa
    1999   Personal interview by John Smith. June 16.

Carson, Rachel
    1962   *Silent Spring.* Boston, MA: Houghton Mifflin.

Caudill, Charles C.
    1974   Correspondence. May 16. New York: Department of the Airforce.

Chandler, Russell
    1971   "Top '71 Religious News: World Revival." *Christianity Today* 16:322-323.

Cheetham, Jack, and Betty Cheetham
    1971   "The Jesus Movement is upon us." *Look* 9(2):15-21.

Christian, Diana Leafe
    1996   "Finding 'Ecotopia.'" *Communities: Journal for Cooperative Living.* 92(Fall):20-23.

Christian, Charles M.
    1995   *Black Saga: The African American Experience: A Chronology.* Boston, MA: Houghton Mifflin.

Church News
    1988   "Christianity or Humanism? Debate at La Trobe University." December:n.p.

Church Scene
    1986   "'Outreach: Go Out and Do It'." May 30:n.p.

Clark, Charles Manning Hope
    1968   *A History of Australia.* Vol. 2. *New South Wales and Van Diemen's Land 1822-1838.* John Sands Pty. Ltd., Artarmon, Australia: Melbourne University Press.
    1976   *A Discovery of Australia: 1976 Boyer Lectures.* Melbourne: Australian Broadcasting Commission.

  1980 *Occasional Writings and Speeches.* Melbourne, Australia: Montana/Collins.
  1987 *A History of Australia.* Vol. 6. London, UK: Oxford University Press.
Clark, Stephen B.
  1972 *Building Christian Communities: Strategies for Renewing the Church.* Notre Dame, IN: Ave Maria Press.
Clarke, Jan
  1989 "God Squad 'Bikies' Denied Hotel Entry." *Ballarat News*:n.d., n.p.
Clarke, Marcus
  1874 "His Natural Life." *Victorian Review* n.d., n.p.
Cleaver, Eldridge
  1967 *Soul on Ice.* New York: McGraw-Hill.
Clecak, Peter
  1983 *America's Quest for the Ideal Self: Dissent and Fulfillment in the 60s and 70s.* New York: Oxford University Press.
Collins, Dan, and Nelly Greisen
  1998 "First Love. Contemporary Christian Music Pioneers." Compact Disc 1, Track 1, Newport NPD 1605. Newbury Park, CA: Newport Records.
Coltier, Alain
  1986 "John Smith: Le Sermon Sur La Moto." *Societé* November 5. N.p.
  1989 " Moto Les Nouveaux Durs a Cuir." *LÈquipe Magazine* April 8:51, 55.
Comblin, Jose
  1998 *Called for Freedom: The Changing Context of Liberation Theology.* Maryknoll, NY: Orbis Books.
Commonweal
  1972 "Jesus People." 97:44-46.
Conger, J. A.
  1989 *The Charismatic Leader: Behind the Mystique of Exceptional Leadership.* San Francisco, CA: Jossey-Bass.
Conger, J.A., and Rabindra N. Kanungo
  1998 *Charismatic Leadership in Organisations.* Thousand Oaks, CA: Sage Publications Inc.
Conway, Ronald
  1971 *The Great Australian Stupor.* Melbourne, Australia: Sun Books.
  1978 *Land of the Long Weekend.* Melbourne, Australia: Sun Books.
Cook, Guillermo
  1985 *The Expectation of the Poor: Latin American Basic Ecclesial Communities in Protestant Perspective.* Maryknoll, NY: Orbis.

Cook, Margie
    1991   "The Church Today: Losing the Edge in the Message Business." *Bulletin* January 15:18-22.

Corry, Geoffrey
    1973a   "Is There a Jesus Movement in Britain? An Interim Personal Report by Corry, Field Officer of the British Council of Churches Youth Department." Spring. Sixty-second Meeting of the British Council of Churches.
    1973b   *Jesus Bubble or Jesus Revolution: The Growth of Jesus Communes in Britain and Ireland.* London, UK: British Council of Churches Youth Department.
    1973c   "The Jesus People." *Christian Herald* May 25:17.

Costas, Orlando E.
    1974   *The Church and its Mission: A Shattering Critique from the Third World.* Wheaton, IL: Tyndale House
    1982   *Christ Outside the Gate: Mission Beyond Christendom.* Maryknoll, NY: Orbis Books.

Coutts, Di
    1981   "Padre-turned-bikie is Setting a Hot Pace on Campus. The God's Squad Hits the Trail." *The Australian* July 15:5.

Cox, Harvey
    1965   *The Secular City.* New York: Macmillan.
    1995   *Fire from Heaven: The Rise of Pentecostal Spirituality and the Reshaping of Religion in the Twenty-first Century.* Reading, MA: Adison-Wesley Publishing.

Creswell, John W.
    1994   *Research Design: Qualitative & Quantitative Approaches.* Thousand Oaks, CA: Sage.

Crews, Ron
    1999   Personal interview by John Smith. May 30.

Cronin
    1984a   *A Camp-Fire Yarn: Henry Lawson Complete Works. 1885-1900.* Vol. 1:48.
    1984b   *A Fantasy of Man: Henry Lawson Complete Works 1901-1922* (2):201.

Crosby, David, Stephen Stills, Graham Nash, and Neil Young
    1970a   *Chicago*, all from the album *4 Way Street*. Atlantic Records (digitally remastered).
    1970b   *Find the Cost of Freedom.* From *4 Way Street*. Atlantic Records.
    1970c   *Ohio.* From *4 Way Street*. Atlantic Records.
    1970d   *Southern Man.* From *4 Way Street*. Atlantic Records.
    1970e   *Teach Your Children Well.* From *4 Way Street*. Atlantic Records.

1970f   *Love the One You're With*. From *4 Way Street*. Atlantic Records.

Croskery, R.
1971   "The Jesus Revolution Is On." *Congregationalist*. November 8:2.

Crowley, Frank
1980   *Colonial Australia 1875-1900: A Documentary History of Australia*. Vol. 3. West Melbourne, Australia: Thomas Nelson.

Cullmann, Oscar
1970   *Jesus and the Revolutionaries*. New York: Harper & Row.

Darnovsky, Marcy, Barbara Epstein, and Richard Flasks
1995   *Cultural Politics and Social Movements*. Philadelphia, PA: Temple University Press.

Davies, Margedd
1974   "Bikies with the Bible." *The Sun* August 26:49.

Davies, Rupert E.
1963   *Methodism*. Westminster, London, UK: Epworth Press.

Davis, Deborah
1984   *The Children of God: The Inside Story by the Daughter of the Founder, Moses David Berg*. Hants, UK: Marshall Morgan & Scott.

Davis, John
1995   "Bikie Preacher Slams Abandonment of Young." *Toowoomba Chronicle* May 4:4.

Davis, Nanette J., and Clarice Stasz
1990   *Social Control of Deviance: A Critical Perspective*. New York: McGraw-Hill.

Davis, Rex
1978   *Locusts and Wild Honey: The Charismatic Renewal and the Ecumenical Movement*. Geneva, Switzerland: World Council of Churches.
1996   "Charismatic Renewal: Impressions from a World Survey." *Study Encounter* 11(4):1-13.

De Flevokrant
1987   "John Smith: 'Onze Generatie Verziekt de Volgende'." August 23:4.

Dean, James, performer
1955   *Rebel without a Cause*. Burbank, CA: Warner Brothers Pictures.

Demian, Richard
1986   "Teen Suicides Shock Report." *Daily Mirror,* Sydney October 28:1-2.

de Salis, Simon
1989   "An Evangelist with the Common Touch." *The Sunday Examiner* July 2:2.

Didion, Joan
    1968   *Slouching towards Bethlehem.* New York: Farrar, Straus & Giroux.

Di Sabatino, David
    1994   "Jesus People Movement. Counterculture Revival and Evangelical Renewal." MA thesis, McMaster University. Hamilton, Ontario, Canada.
    1995   Letter from Di Sabatino to Steve Turner, reflecting upon Turner's critique of Jesus rock artists and Larry Norman in particular. August 27.
    1996   "Obituary to Frank Durkin." Internet:sabbi@the-wire.com.
    1997   "From Counterculture Experientialist to Pentecostal Evangelist: Lonnie Frisbee's Influence upon Evangelism." Cognate Essay presented to Queens University.
    1999a   *The Jesus People Movement: An Annotated Bibliography and General Resource.* Westport, CT: Greenwood Press.
    1999b   Personal interview by John Smith. September 15.
    1999c   "Lonnie Frisbee: A Modern Day Samson." *The Quest for the Radical Middle.* Bill Jackson. Appendix 3, Pp. 381-396. Capetown, South Africa: Vineyard International Publishing.
    1999d   Telephone interview by John Smith. November 18.
    1999e   Internet communication with John Smith. November 19. Internet:sabbi@the-wire.com.
    1999f   "The Flame of Renewal: the Music of the Jesus Movement and Its Influence. *Worship Leader* July-August:22-27.

Disher, Paul
    1991   "God's Squad. The Men and Their Movement." *Tilt* 1(11):33-34.

Dodd, Carley H.
    1998   *Dynamics of Intercultural Communication.* 5th edition. Boston, MA: McGraw Hill.

Donohue, John W.
    1973   "High on Jesus." *America* August 4:66-67.

Donald, John
    1976a   "Jesus in Berkeley." Ph.D. dissertation, Graduate Theological Union, Berkeley, CA.
    1976b   "The Christian World Liberation Front." *The New Religious Consciousness.* Charles Y. Glock, and Robert N. Bellah, eds. Pp. 143-162. Berkeley, CA: University of California Press.

Donovan, John J.
    1972   "Religious Revivalism as Counterculture." *Spiritual Life* 18:47-57.

Douglas, James Dixon, ed.
    1974   *Let the Earth Hear His Voice: Official Reference Volume: Papers and Responses: International Congress on World Evangelization.* Minneapolis, MN: World Wide Publications.

Douglas, Mary
    1978   *Natural Symbols: Explorations in Cosmology with a New Introduction.* London, UK: Rutledge.

Dowling, Levi H.
    1972 [1935]   *The Aquarian Gospel of Jesus Christ: The Philosophical and Practical Basis of the Religion of the Aquarian Age of the World.* Transcribed from the Akashic Records by Levi. Santa Monica, CA: DeVorss and Co. Publishers.

Druin, Toby
    1971   "Echoes of the Movement." *Home Missions* (June-July):43-46.

Duin, Julia
    1996   "Authority and Submission in Christian Community." *Communities Journal of Cooperative Living.* 92 (Fall):51-55. Box 115, Rutledge, MO: 63563: Fellowship for Intentional Community.

Dunaway, Barbara
    1997   "Grace Community Church – Alaska." *Again* 20(1):20-23. Ben Lomond, CA: Conciliar Press.

Durkeim, Emile
    1951   *Suicide: A Study in Sociological Interpretation.* Glencoe, IL: Free Press.

Dylan, Bob
    1979   *Slow Train Coming.* Burbank, CA: Amigo Studios/Special Rider Music.
    1972   *Bob Dylan: The Very Best.* New York: Amsco School Publications.
    1994   *Bob Dylan's Greatest Hits.* Vol. 3. New York: Columbia.
    1997   *The Concise Bob Dylan.* London, UK: Wise.

Eckersley, Richard
    1988   *Casualties of Change: The Predicament of Youth in Australia. An Analysis of the Social and Psychological Problems Faced by Young People in Australia.* Carlton South, Australia: Australia's Commission for the Future Ltd.
    1992   *Apocalypse? No! Youth and the Challenge to Change: Bringing Youth, Science, and Society Together in the New Millennium.* Carlton South, Australia: Australia's Commission for the Future Ltd.

Edgerton, Robert B.
    1992   *Sick Societies: Challenging the Myth of Primitive Harmony.* New York: The Free Press.

Edwards, Darren
    1984   "In the World of Hell on Wheels. God's Squad Spreads Gospel." *Sunday Observer* October 14:4.

Edwards, David L.
    1997   *Christianity: The First Two Thousand Years.* Maryknoll, NY:Orbis Books.

Eister, Allay W.
    1973   "Quasi-groups and New Religious Movements: Some Theoretical Considerations and Some Empirical Findings." *Focus on US Bibliography.* Pp. 435-449.

Eliade, Mircea
    1958   *Rites and Symbols of Initiation: The Mysteries of Birth and Rebirth.* New York: Harper & Row.
    1963a   *Myth and Reality.* New York: Harper Torchbooks.
    1963b   *Patterns in Comparative Religion.* New York: Meridian Books.
    1987[1957]   *The Sacred and the Profane: The Nature of Religion.* San Diego, CA: Harcourt Brace & Company.

Eller, Vernard
    1973   "Lesson of Valparaiso." *Brethren Life and Thought* 17(2):101-108.
    1973b   *The Simple Life: The Christian Stance toward Possessions.* Grand Rapids, MI: Eerdmans.

Ellis, Ron
    1972   *Jesus Revolution Down-Under.* Geelong, Australia: Hilltop Press.

Ellul, Jacques
    1954   *La Technique ou l'enjue du siècle.* Paris: Librarie Armand Colin.
    1964   *The Technological Society.* Toronto: Vintage Books/Random House.
    1973   *Hope in Time of Abandonment.* New York: Seabury Press.
    1976   *The Ethics of Freedom.* Grand Rapids, MI: William B. Eerdmans.

Ellwood, Robert S., Jr.
    1976   *One Way: The Jesus Movement and Its Meaning.* Englewood Cliffs, New Jersey: Prentice-Hall.
    1979   *Alternative Altars: Unconventional and Eastern Spirituality in America.* Chicago: IL: Chicago: The University of Chicago Press.
    1994   *The 60s Spiritual Awakening: American Religion Moving from Modern to Postmodern.* New Brunswick, NJ: Rutgers University Press.

1997   *The Cross and the Grail: Esoteric Christianity for the 21st Century.* Wheaton, IL: Quest Books. The Theosophical Publishing House.

1998   Review of *The 60s Spiritual Awakening: American Religion Moving from Modern to Postmodern* by the author, Robert Ellwood on internet: Ellwood for amazon.com (Kirkus Reviews, May 15 1994).

2000   *1950: Crossroads of American Religious Life.* Louisville, KY: Westminster John Knox Press.

Ellwood, Robert S., Jr., ed.
1987   *Zen in American Life and Letters*, ed. Malibu, CA: Undena.

Ember, Carol R., and Melvin Ember
1993   *Cultural Anthropology.* 7th edition. Upper Saddle River, NJ: Prentice Hall.

1999   *Cultural Anthropology.* 9th edition. Upper Saddle River, NJ: Prentice Hall.

Emerson, Robert M., Rachel I. Fretz, and Linda L. Shaw
1995   *Writing Ethnographic Field Notes.* Chicago, IL: University of Chicago Press.

Enroth, Ronald M.
1973   "Where Have All the Jesus People Gone?" *Eternity* (October):14-17, 28.

1983   "The Christian Counterculture. " *Christianity in America: A Handbook.* Mark A. Noll, et al., eds. Pp. 469-473. Grand Rapids, MI: William B. Eerdmans.

Enroth, Ronald M., Edward E. Ericson, Jr., and C. Breckinridge Peters
1972   *The Jesus People: Old Time Religion in the Age of Aquarius.* Grand Rapids, MI: William B. Eerdmans.

Etzioni, Amitai
1993   *The Spirit of Community: The Reinvention of American Society.* New York: Simon & Schuster.

Etzioni-Halevy, Eva
1985   *The Knowledge Elite and the Failure of Prophecy.* Boston, MA: George Allen and Unwin.

Evans, Peter
1997   *The Concise Bob Dylan: The Music and Complete Lyrics for Forty-nine Dylan Songs.* London, UK: Wise.

Eyerman, Ron, and Andrew Jamison
1998   *Music and Social Movements: Mobilizing Traditions in the Twentieth Century.* Cambridge, U.K: Cambridge University Press.

Farra, Bill
1999   Telephone interview by John Smith. December 20.

Ferraro, Gary
    1998   *Cultural Anthropology*. 3rd edition. Belmont, CA: Wadsworth Publishing Company.
    2000   *Cultural Anthropology*. 4th edition. Belmont, CA: Wadsworth Publishing Company.

Fike, Robert, ed.
    1998   *Voices from the Farm: Adventures in Community Living*. Summertown, TN.: Book Publishing Company.

Finke, Roger, and Rodney Stark
    1997   *The Churching of America 1776-1990: Winners and Losers in our Religious Economy*. New Brunswick, NJ: Rutgers University Press.

Fishman, Samuel Z.
    1973   "Jewish Jesus Freaks." *The Jewish Digest* 18(7[April]):1-3.

Ford, William Clayton, Jr.
    1972   *Jesus and the Street People: A First Hand Report from Berkeley*. New York: Harper & Row.

Forever Family
    1999   Forever Family archives. Internet: http://www.angelfire.com/mocobu/images. See also www.angelfire.com/nm/cobu/gen.html.

Foss, Daniel A., and Ralph Larkin
    1986   *A New Theory of Social Movements: Critical Perspectives in Social Theory Series*. South Hadley, MA: Bergin & Garvey.

Francis, Vic
    1991   "Chameleon Evangelist speaks to 'Unreachable' Groups Changing His Colors to Suit His Environment." *Challenge Weekly* [New Zealand] January 24:6.

Freire, Paulo
    1970   *Pedagogy of the Oppressed*. New York: Herder and Herder.

Friedenberg, Edgar Z.
    1959   *The Vanishing Adolescent*. New York: Dell Publishing.

Fromm, Charles E.
    1983   "New Song: The Sound of Spiritual Awakening." Paper presented to Oxford Reading and Research Conference. July. Oxford, UK.
    1996a   "The Jesus Movement Revival." Term paper presented for "MH 521 in History and Theology of Evangelical Awakenings." May 25. School of World Mission, Fuller Theological Seminary, Pasadena, CA.
    1996b   "Maranatha and The Kingdom of God. MT 520 Biblical Foundation of Mission." School of World Mission, Fuller Theological Seminary, Pasadena, CA.
    1999   Personal interview by John Smith. August 23.

Fry, Peter, and Malcolm Long
    1977   *Beyond the Mechanical Mind.* Sydney, Australia: The Australian Broadcasting Commission.
Fukuyama, Francis
    1992   *The End of History and the Last Man.* New York: Free Press.
    1999   *The Great Disruption: Human Nature and the Reconstitution of Social Order.* New York: Free Press.
Gallagher, Sharon
    1979a   "From *Right On* to *Radix*: A Short History." *Radix* (July, August):3-4.
    1979b   "New Berkeley Liberation Program." *Radix* (July, August):4.
    1999   Telephone interview by John Smith. December 14.
    2000   Telephone interview by John Smith. February 9.
Gartner, Suzanne
    1973   "God's Squad Talks to Young Bikies Who're in the Jesus Movement." *Vogue Australia.* December/January:86-87.
Garvin, Mal
    1987   *Us Aussies.* Sale, Australia: Greenwood/Gordon.
Gaskin, Stephen
    1981   *Rendered Infamous: A Book of Political Reality.* Summertown TN: The Book Publishing Company.
    1999   Personal interview by John Smith. April 10.
Gaskin, Stephen, and the Farm Band
    1974   *Hey Beatnik! This is the Farm Book.* Summertown, TN: The Book Publishing Company.
Gasset, Jose Ortegay
    1971   *The Mission of the University.* New York: Norton.
Geertz, Clifford
    1973   *The Interpretation of Cultures.* New York: Basic Books.
Gelwick, R.L.
    1972   "Will Jesus Revolution Revive Anti-Semitism?" *Christian Century* 89:545-548.
Gerlach, Luther, and Virginia Hine
    1970   *People Power & Change: Movements of Social Transformation.* New York: Bobbs-Merrill.
Gibbs, Eddie
    2000   *Church Next: Quantum Changes in How We Do Ministry.* Downer's Grove, IL: InterVarsity Press.
Gill, Athol
    1978   *Discipleship Studies.* Sydney, Australia: Australian Council of Churches.
    1989   *Life on the Road: The Gospel Basis for a Messianic Lifestyle.* Homebush West, Australia: Anzea.

1990 *The Fringes of Freedom: Following Jesus, Living Together, Working for Justice.* Homebush West, Australia: Lancer Books.

Gillquist, Peter
1972 *Love is Now.* Grand Rapids, MI: Zondervan.
1974 *Let's Quit Fighting About the Holy Spirit.* Grand Rapids, MI: Zondervan.
1979 *The Physical Side of Being Spiritual.* Grand Rapids, MI: Zondervan.
1992 *Becoming Orthodox: A Journey to the Ancient Christian Faith.* Brentwood, TN: Wolgemuth & Hyatt Publishers.
1993 *The Orthodox Study Bible.* General edition. Peter Gillquist, Nashville, TN: Thomas Nelson.
1997 "Our Ten Years in Orthodoxy." *Again* 20(1):41-43. Ben Lomond, CA: Conciliar Press.
1999 Personal interview by John Smith. May 5.

Gillquist, Peter, ed.
1992 *Coming Home: Why Protestant Clergy Are Becoming Orthodox.*
Ben Lomond, CA: Conciliar Press.

Ginsberg, Allen
1963 *Village Voice Reader.* New York: Black Cat Books.

Girard, Chuck
1971 "Welcome Back." *Love Song.* Dunamis Music BMI.

Gish, Arthur G.
1973 *Beyond the Rat Race.* Scottsdale, PA: Herald Press.

Gitlin, Tod
1987 *The Sixties: Years of Hope Days of Rage.* New York: Bantam Books.

Giugni, Marco, Doug McAdam, and Charles Tilly, eds.
1999 *How Social Movements Matter.* Minneapolis, MN: University of Minnesota Press.

Glock, Charles Y., and Robert N. Bellah, eds.
1976 *The New Religious Consciousness.* Berkeley, CA: University of California Press.

Goodman, Paul
1962 *Compulsory Mis-education and the Community of Scholars.* New York: Random House.
1972 *Growing up Absurd.* New York: Random House.

Gordon, David F.
1974 "The Jesus People: An Identity Synthesis." *Urban Life and Culture* 3(2[Jul]):159-179.
1984 "The Role of the Local Social Context in Social Movement Accommodation: A Case Study of Two Jesus People Groups."

Journal for the Scientific Study of Religion 23(December 4):381-395.

Gosney, Jim
 1979 "House of Elijah. Closing after Acceptance Was Won." *Yakima Herald-Republic*. September 15:n.p.

Gottschalk, Earl C., Jr.
 1971 "Hip Culture Discovers a New Trip: Fervent Foot Stompn' Religion." *Wall Street Journal* March 2:1.

Gottwald, Norman K. and Richard A. Horsley, eds.
 1993 *The Bible and Liberation: Political and Social Hermeneutics*. Revised edition. Maryknoll, NY: Orbis Books.

Graham, Billy
 1971 *The Jesus Generation*. London, UK: Hodder & Stoughton.

Graham, Stephen R.,
 1989 "Hal Lindsey," *Twentieth-century Shapers of American Popular Religion*, Charles H. Lippy, ed. Pp. 249-250. Westport, CT: Greenwood Press.

Gray, Bill
 1972 "God's Squad Leader Says: Get Moving." *Age* October 18:7.

Graybill, Larry
 1972 "The Jesus Movement: Its Common Tenets and Its Word to Brethren." *Brethren Life and Thought* 17(Summer):149.

Greco, Anna
 1987 "God's Angel." *The Herald* June 10:25.

Green, Joel
 2000 Personal interview by John Smith. January 4.

Grenz, Stanley J.
 2000 *A Primer on Postmodernism*. Grand Rapids, MI: William B. Eerdmans.

Grindal, Bruce
 n.d. "Comparative Questions for the Interpretation of Religious Lives and Religious Groups." Tallahassee, FL: Florida State University Department of Anthropology.

Gross, Paul R., and Norman Levitt,
 1994 *Higher Superstition: The Academic Left and its Quarrels with Science*. Baltimore, MD: The Johns Hopkins University Press.

Guder, Darrell L. ed.
 1998 *Missional Church: A Vision for the Sending of the Church in North America*. Grand Rapids, MI: William B. Eerdmans.

Guinness, Os
 1973 *The Dust of Death: A Critique of Western Culture*. Downers Grove, IL: InterVarsity.
 1983 *The Gravedigger File: Secret Papers on the Subversion of the Modern Church*. London, UK: Hodder & Staunton.

1994[1973] *The Dust of Death: The Sixties and How It Changed America Forever.* Revised edition, Wheaton, IL: Crossways Books.

Guinness, Os, and John Seel, eds.
- 1992 *No God but God: Breaking With the Idols of Our Age.* Chicago, IL: Moody Press.

Guralnick, Peter
- 1994 *Last Train to Memphis: The Rise of Elvis Presley.* Boston, MA: Little, Brown and Company.

Gutiérrez, Gustavo
- 1973 *A Theology of Liberation.* Maryknoll, New York: Orbis.

Habel, N., and P. Hart
- 1983 *The Man with the Bushy Red Beard.* Sydney, Australia: Collins.

Hamilton, Michael S.
- 1999 "The Triumph of the Praise Songs. How Guitars beat Out the Organ in the Worship Wars." *Christianity Today* 43(8[July 12]):28-35.

Hancock, Sir Keith
- 1973 *Today, Yesterday, and Tomorrow.* ABC Boyer Lectures. Sydney: Australian Broadcasting Commission.

Handy, Robert T.
- 1984 *A Christian America: Protestant Hopes and Historic Realities.* 2nd edition. New York: Oxford University Press.

Hannaford, J.
- 1985 *Under a Southern Cross.* Adelaide, Australia: Tabor.

Hannagan, Sue
- 1990 "John Smith Spreads 'Universal Message'." *Northern Argus* August 11:3.

Harder, Mary White
- 1974 "Sex Roles in the Jesus Movement." *Social Compass* 21(3):345-353.

Harder, Mary White, James T. Richardson, and R.B. Simmonds
- 1975 "Jesus People." *Psychology Today* December: 45-50, 110-113.

Hargrove, Barbara
- 1980 *Religion for a Dislocated Generation.* Valley Forge, PA: Judson Press.

Harper, Michael
- 1973 *A New Way of Living.* Plainfield, NJ: Logos International.
- 1997 *A Faith Fulfilled: Why Are Christians Across Great Britain Embracing Orthodoxy?* Ben Lomond, CA: Conciliar Press.

Harpur, Tom
- 1971a "Today's Generation Needs a New Brand of Minister." *Toronto Star* May 8:61.

1971b   "Many Young Hitchhikers are on a Religious Quest." *Toronto Star* August 7:89.
1971c   "Turning on with Jesus: Fad or True Revival." *Toronto Star* August 28:81.
1971d   "Jesus People May Bring About a New Reformation." *Toronto Star* December 4:93.
1972   "Fervent Teenagers Say: Isn't Jesus Wonderful!" *Toronto Star* February 19:85.
1974   "Jesus People Blend into the 'Straight' Churches." *Toronto Star* May 11:4.

Hasselquist, Helene
1971   "House of Miracles." *Lutheran Standard* 11(November 2):12-13.

Hauerwas, Stanley, Nancey Murphy, and Mark Nation, eds.
1994   *Theology without Foundations: Religious Practice and the Future of Theological Truth*. Nashville, TN: Abingdon Press.

Haughey, John C.
1990   *The Faith That Does Justice: Examining the Christian Sources for Social Change*. New York: Paulist Press.

Havens, Richie
1971   *The Richie Havens Collection*. CD album sleeve: RCD 20036, Salem, MA: Ryko/Rydodisc.
1994   *Richie Havens Cuts to the Chase*. Rhino Records Inc. R2 71735.

Hayward, Douglas James
1997   *Vernacular Christianity among the Mulia Dani: An Ethnography of Religious Belief among the Western Dani of Irian Jaya, Indonesia*. Lanham, MD: American Society of Missiology and University Press of America.

Headley, Ian
2000   Personal interview by John Smith. January 5.

Heelas, Paul
2001   *The New Age Movement: The Celebration of the Self and the Sacralization of Modernity*. Oxford, UK: Blackwell.

Heinz, Donald
1976a   "Jesus in Berkeley," Ph.D. dissertation, Graduate Theological Union, Berkeley, CA.
1976b   "The Christian World Liberation Front." *The New Religious Consciousness*, Charles Y. Glock, and Robert N. Bellah, eds. Pp. 143-161. Berkeley, CA.

Henderson, Stewart
1984   *Greenbelt since the Beginning: The Last Ten Years*. Ipswich, UK: Last Minute.

Hengel, Martin
1971   *Was Jesus a Revolutionary?* Philadelphia, PA: Fortress Press.

Hesse, Hermann
    1951   *Siddhartha.* New York: New Directions.
    1963   *Steppenwolf.* New York: Holt, Rinehart & Winston.
    1968   *The Journey to the East.* New York: Farrer, Straus & Giroux.

Hesselgrave, David J., and Edward Rommen.
    1989   *Contextualization: Meanings, Methods, and Models.* 2nd edition. Grand Rapids, MI: Baker Book House.

Heuvel, Albert van den.
    1972   "The Jesus People: an Ecumenical Challenge." *Ecumenical Courier* 31(1):4-5.

Hiebert, Paul G.
    1983   *Cultural Anthropology.* Grand Rapids, MI: Baker Book House.
    1985   *Anthropological Insights for Missionaries.* Grand Rapids, MI: Baker Book House.
    1991   *Anthropological Reflections on Missiological Issues.* Grand Rapids, MI: Baker Book House.

Hiebert, Paul, G., and Eloise Hiebert Meneses
    1995   *Incarnational Ministry: Planting Churches in Band, Tribal, Peasant, and Urban Societies.* Grand Rapids, MI: Baker Books.

Hill, Barry
    1985   "Zealot in the Cause of Reason." *The Age, Saturday Extra* March 2:4.

Hill, Brian
    1991   Correspondence to Hill. Also included as appendix 2 in *Values Education in Australian Schools.* 1997, Graham Withers, Australia: Council for Education Research.

Hill, Kirsten
    1987   "Bikie Preacher Takes Beliefs to the Streets." *The Sun* December 12:25.

Hillendahl, Lou
    1996   "A Community of Counsellor Pioneers." *Communities: Journal of Cooperative Living* 92(Fall):39-41.

Hirt, John
    2000   Recorded phone interview by John Smith. May 3.
    2002   "Radical Discipleship: Towards the Theology and Sociopolitical Implications." Ph.D. dissertation. School of Studies in Religion. University of Sydney, Australia.

Hoffman, Abbie
    1968   *Revolution for the Hell of It.* New York: The Dial Press.

Hollenweger, Walter J.
    1997   *Pentecostalism: Origins and Developments Worldwide.* Peabody, MA: Hendrickson Publishers, Inc.

Horsley, Richard A.
    1994   *Sociology and the Jesus Movement.* New York: The Continuum.

Horsley, Richard A., with John S. Hanson
    1999   *Bandits, Prophets, and Messiahs: Popular Movements in the Time of Jesus.* Harrisburg, PA: Trinity Press International.

Horton, Gerald
    1975   "Book Review." *New York Times.* December 13:1.

Houtart, Francois, ed.
    1974   "New Religious Movements in the USA." *Social Compass* 21 (March):227-244.

Howard, Jane
    1971   "The Groovy Christians of Rye. New York." *Life* May 14:78-86.

Howitt, Bernie
    1994   *Rock through History: Understanding the Modern World through Rock and Roll: 1950s to 1990s.* 2nd edition. Melbourne, Australia: Longman Cheshire.

Hubbard, L. Ron
    1950   *Dianetics: The Modern Science of Mental Health: a Handbook of Diabetic Therapy.* New York: Hermitage House.

Hunsberger, George R.
    1998   *Bearing the Witness of the Spirit: Lesslie Newbigin's Theology of Cultural Plurality.* Grand Rapids, MI: William B. Eerdmans.

Hunsberger George R., and Craig Van Gelder, eds.
    1996   *The Church between Gospel and Culture: The Emerging Mission in North America.* Grand Rapids, MI: William B. Eerdmans.

Hunt, Dave, and Ta McMahon
    1988   *America, The Sorcerer's New Apprentice: The Rise of New Age Shamanism.* Eugene, OR: Harvest House.

Hunter, George G., III
    1987   *To Spread the Power: Church Growth in the Wesleyan Spirit.* Nashville, TN: Abingdon.
    1992   *How to Reach Secular People.* Nashville, TN: Abingdon.
    1996   *Church for the Unchurched.* Nashville, TN: Abingdon.
    2000   *The Celtic Way of Evangelism: How Christians Can Reach the West Again.* Nashville, TN: Abingdon.

Hunter, James Davison
    1983   *American Evangelicalism: Conservative Religion and the Quandary of Modernity.* New Brunswick, NJ: Rutgers University Press.

Huxley, Aldous
    1954   *The Doors of Perception.* London, UK: Chatto and Windus.

Illich, Denisovich Ivan
    1971   *De-schooling Society*. New York: Harper & Row.
    1977   *The Right to Useful Unemployment and its Professional Enemies*. London: Marion Boyars.

Ison, Colleen
    1982   "Inside a Powerhouse of Faith: A Church takes to the Road." *Ringwood-Croydon Mail* October 13:n.p.

Jackson, Bill
    1999   *The Quest for the Radical Middle: A History of the Vineyard*. Cape Town, South Africa: Vineyard International Publishing.

Jackson, Dave, and Neta Jackson
    1974   *Living Together in a World Falling Apart*. Carol Stream, IL: Creation House

Jacobsen, Cardell K., and Thomas J. Pilarzyk
    1972   "Faith, Freaks, and Fanaticism: Notes on the Growth and Development of the Milwaukee Jesus People." Paper read at the annual meeting of the Society for the Scientific Study of Religion, Boston, MA.
    1974   "Croissance, Developement et fin d'une Sect Conversioniste." *Social Compass* 21:255-268.

Janzen, David
    1996a   *Fire, Salt, and Peace: Intentional Christian Communities Alive in North America*. Evanston, IL: Shalom Mission Communities.
    1996b   "Where Have All the (Seventies) Communities Gone?" *Communities Journal of Cooperative Living* Fall 92:48-50. Rutledge, MO: Fellowship for Intentional Community.

Jasper, James M.
    1997   *The Art of Moral Protest: Culture, Biography, and Creativity in Social Movements*. Chicago, IL: The University of Chicago Press.

Jasper, Tony
    1971   *Jesus in a Pop Culture*. Glasgow, UK: Fontana Books.

Jenkins, Philip
    2002   "The Next Christianity." *The Atlantic Monthly* 290 (3[October]):55.

Jennings, Theodore W. Jr.
    1990   *Good News to the Poor: John Wesley's Evangelical Economics*. Nashville, TN: Abingdon Press.

Johnson, Robert L.
    1971   *Counter Culture and the Vision of God*. Minneapolis, MN: Augsburg.

Jones, Caroline
    1990   *The Search for Meaning*. Crowes Nest, Australia: ABC/Collins Dove.

Jones, General David C., Commander in Chief
    1974   Correspondence to Mr. Peter Holmes, Dio Gloria Trust, Bromley, Kent UK. May 9. New York: Department of the Airforce, United States Airforce in Europe.

Jordan, Clarence
    1968   *The Cotton Patch Version of Paul's Epistles: A Modern Translation with a Southern Accent, Fervent, Earthy, and Rich in Humor.* Clinton, NJ: New Win Publishing Inc.
    1969   *The Cotton Patch Version of Luke and Acts.* Clinton, NJ: New Win Publishing Inc.
    1970   *The Cotton Patch Version of Matthew and John.* Clinton, NJ: New Win Publishing Inc.

Jorgensen, Danny L.
    1989   *Participant Observation: A Methodology for Human Study.* Newbury Park, CA: Sage Publications.

Jorstad, Erling
    1972a   "From Drugs to Jesus." *Catholic Mind* 70(December):14:n.p.
    1972b   *That New Time Religion: The Jesus Revival in America.* Minneapolis, MN: Augsburg.
    1990   *Holding Fast/Pressing On: Religion in America in the 1980s.* New York: Praeger.

Kaiser, Charles
    1988   "In America: Music, Politics, Chaos, Counterculture, and the Shaping of a Generation." New York: Weidenfeld & Nicholson.

Kaiser, Glenn
    1998   Personal interview by John Smith. October 15.
    2001   Personal interview by John Smith. June 19.

Kaldor, Peter
    1987   *Who Goes Where? Who Doesn't Care?* Homebush West, Australia: Lancer Books.

Kaldor, Peter, and Sue Kaldor
    1988   *Where the River Flows: Sharing the Gospel in a Changing Australia.* Homebush West, Australia: Anzea.

Kanter, Rosabeth Moss
    1972   *Commitment and Community: Communes and Utopias in Sociological Perspective.* Cambridge, MA: Harvard University Press.

Keniston, Kenneth
    1967   "The Sources of Student Dissent." *Journal of Social Issues* 23:108-137.

Kennedy, Jon Reid
    1971   "Dropping out Into Jesus." *Vanguard* March:20-21.

Kerlinger, F. N.
    1973   *Foundations of Behavioral Research.* New York: Holt, Rinehart & Winston.

Kerouac, Jack
    1967   *On the Road.* New York: Viking.
    1958   *The Dharma Bums.* New York: Viking.

King, Jonathan
    1992   *Waltzing Materialism.* London, UK: Harper & Row.

Kirk, Michael, and Paul Andrew Ries
    1992   "A Venture in Faith: The History and Philosophy of the Calvary Chapel Movement." A Ministry Focus Submitted to the Faculty of the School of Theology, Fuller Theological Seminary, Pasadena, CA.

Kittler, Glenn D.
    1972   *The Jesus Kids and Their Leaders.* New York: Warner.

Kizilos, Kathy
    1986   "How God's Bikie Spreads the Word." *The Weekend Australian Magazine* June 14-15:n.p.

Klass, Morton
    1995   *Ordered Universes: Approaches to the Anthropology of Religion.* Boulder, CO: Westview Press.

Klein, Rita
    1971   "God, Blessitt, and His Place." *Eternity* January:46-47.

Knight, Walker L.
    1971   *Jesus People Come Alive.* London, UK: Tyndale.

Koch, Klaus
    1982   *The Prophets: The Assyrian Period.* Vol. 1. Margaret Kohl, Trans. London, UK: SCM Press
    1983   *The Prophets: The Babylonian and Persian Periods.* Vol. 2. Margaret Kohl, Trans. London, UK: SCM Press.

Koestler, Arthur
    1967   *The Ghost in the Machine.* London, UK: Hutchinson.

Kraft, Charles H.
    1979   *Christianity in Culture: A Study in Dynamic Biblical Theologizing in Cross-Cultural Perspective.* Maryknoll, NY: Orbis Books.
    1989   *Christianity with Power: Your Worldview and Your Experience of the Supernatural.* Ann Arbor, MI: Vine Books.
    1996a   *Anthropology for Christian Witness.* Maryknoll, NY: Orbis Books.
    1996b   *Communication Theory for Christian Witness.* Maryknoll, NY: Orbis Books.

Laing, R.D.
    1967   *The Politics of Experience.* Harmondsworth, UK: Penguin Books.

Lane, Terry
 1979 *As the Twig is Bent: The Childhood Recollections of Sixteen Prominent Australians.* Melbourne, Australia: Dove Communications.

Larãna, Enrique, Hank Johnston, and Joseph R. Gusfield, eds.
 1994 *New Social Movements: From Ideology to Identity.* Philadelphia, PA: Temple University Press.

Latourette, Kenneth Scott
 1964 *A Short History of the Far East.* New York: The Macmillan Company.
 1975a *A History of Christianity.* Vol. 1. *Beginnings to 1500.* Revised edition. San Francisco, CA: Harper Collins.
 1975b *A History of Christianity.* Vol. 2. *Reformation to the Present.* Revised edition. San Francisco, CA: Harper Collins.

Lawing, n.n.
 1971 "What If?" *Truth* 2(12):13. Melbourne, Australia: Truth & Liberation.

Lawrence, D.H.
 1923 *Kangaroo.* Harmondsworth, Middlesex, UK: Penguin Books.

Lawton, William
 1988 *Being Christian: Being Australian: Contemporary Christianity Down Under.* Homebush West, Australia: Anzea.

Leary, Timothy Francis
 1964 *The Psychedelic Experience: A Manual Based on the Tibetan Book of the Dead.* New York: University Books.
 1968 *The Politics of Ecstasy.* New York: Putnam.

Lee, Jung Young
 1993 *Marginality.* Minneapolis, MN: Fortress Press.

Leffel, Gregory P.
 1995 "Xenos Christian Fellowship: An Experiment in Lay-led Church Growth, 1970-1995." *Journal for the Academy for Evangelism in Theological Education."* 10(1994-1995):59-74.

Leming, Michael R., and Ted C. Smith
 1974 "The Children of God as a Social Movement." *Journal of Voluntary Action Research* 3(July-October):77-83.

Lemons, James Curran
 1984 "The Way International: Historical Development, Theological Critique, and Sociological Assessment." Ph.D. dissertation, Southwestern Baptist Theological Seminary, Fort Worth, TX.

Lennon, John
 1971 "James Taylor: One Man's Family of Rock." *Time* March 1:45.

Lett, James William
 1987 *The Human Enterprise: A Critical Introduction to Anthropological Theory.* Boulder, CO: Westview Press.

Levine, W. Lawrence
    1988   *Highbrow/Lowbrow: The Emergence of Cultural Hierarchy in America*. Cambridge, MA: Harvard University Press.

Lewis, C. S.
    1943   *The Screwtape Letters*. New York: McMillan.

Lienert, Neville
    1972   "Squad in Melbourne." *Encounter for Lutheran Youth* December 2:3.

Lincoln, Y.S., and Guba, E.G.
    1985   *Naturalistic Inquiry*. Beverly Hills, CA:Sage.

Lindsell, Harold
    1969   "Farewell to the Sixties." *Christianity Today* December 19:21-22.

Lindsey, Hal
    1970   *The Late Great Planet Earth*. Grand Rapids, MI: Zondervan.

Linton, Ralph
    1943   "Nativistic Movements." *American Anthropologist* 45:230-240.

Lippy, Charles H.
    1989   *Twentieth-Century Shapers of American Popular Religion.* New York: Greenwood Press.

Lochaas, Phillip
    1976   "The Jesus Movement." Paper presented to the Lutheran Church, Missouri Synod.

Lofland, John, and Rodney Stark
    1959   "Becoming a World-saver: A Theory of Conversion to a Deviant Perspective." *American Sociological Review* 39:862-875.

Lopes, Joao Carlos
    1989   "Revitalization and the Church: A Study of the Renewal Movement in the Sixth Conference of the Brazilian Methodist Church." D.Miss. dissertation. E. Stanley Jones School of World Mission and Evangelism, Asbury Theological Seminary, Wilmore, KY.

Lorenzen, Thorwald
    1995   *Resurrection and Discipleship: Interpretive Models, Biblical Reflections, and Theological Consequences.* Maryknoll, NY: Orbis Books.

Lotz, David W. ed.
    1989   *Altered Landscapes: Christianity in America 1935-1985.* Grand Rapids, MI: William B. Eerdmans.

Lovelace, Richard S.
    1971   "The Shape of the Coming Renewal." *Christian Century* 88:1164-1171.

    1979   *Dynamics of Spiritual Life: An Evangelical Theology of Renewal.* Downers Grove, IL: Inter Varsity Press.

Luce, Henry III, Publisher
    1971   "A Letter from the Publisher." *Time* 97(25[June 21]):9.

Luzbetak, Louis J.
    1988   *The Church and Cultures: New Perspectives in Missiological Anthropology.* Maryknoll, New York: Orbis Books.

Lyra, Synesio, Jr.
    1973   "The Rise and Development of the Jesus Movement." *Calvin Theological Journal* 8:40-61.

Mack, N.
    1971   "The Jesus People: Preaching Christ from the Street Corners." *Milwaukee Journal Insight Magazine* 12(September):8-15, 47-51.

Mackinnon, H., ed.
    1890   *Selected Works of Marcus Clarke*, p.v. Marcus Clarke to Cyril Hopkins, 1866, quoted in C. Hopkins, Biographical notes of the Life and Work of Marcus Clarke (MS. in ML). Melbourne, Australia.

Macpherson, Ian
    1989   "Bring Christ to the Kids." *The Examiner* June 27:11.

Madrid, Patrick
    1994   *Surprised by Truth: Eleven Converts Give the Biblical and Historical Reasons for Becoming Catholic.* San Diego, CA: Basilica Press.

Malone, P., ed.
    1988   Discovering an Australian Theology. Sydney, Australia: St Paul.

Marcuse, Herbert
    1964   *One Dimensional Man.* London, UK: Abacus.

Marquardt, Manfred
    1992   *John Wesley's Social Ethics, Praxis, and Principles.* Nashville, TN: Abingdon.

Martin, Helen
    1986   "Bikies, God and the Man Called Smithy." *Brisbane Courier Mail* October 29:10.
    1989   "Arrested Churchmen to Return to the Philippines." *The Melbourne Herald* July 24:5.

Martin, Joel
    1999 "Revisiting Revitalization." A paper presented at the annual meeting of the American Anthropological Association, November 1999. Joel Martin@acad.fandm.edu.

Martin, William
    1996   *With God on Our Side: The Rise of the Religious Right in America.* New York: Broadway Books.

Marty, Martin E.
- 1970 *Righteous Empire: The Protestant Experience in America.* New York: Dial.
- 1971 "Doing the Jesus Thing." *Context* April 1. Reprinted in *Home Missions* September 42(9):35.
- 1972 "Theological Table Talk: Jesus: the Media and the Message." *Theology Today* January:470-476.
- 1976 *A Nation of Behavers.* Chicago, IL: The University of Chicago Press.

Masel-Walters, Lyne
- 1976b "Modern Fundamentalist Newspapers: The Jesus Press." Paper submitted to the Midwest Pop Culture Association, *Christian Century* 89[November 15]:1171.

Matthews, Leanne
- 1991 "Revving up the Gospel." *The Weekly Times* July 3:33.

Marx, Gary T., and Douglas McAdam
- 1994 *Collective Behavior and Social Movements: Process and Structure.* Englewood Cliffs, NJ: Simon & Schuster.

McAdam, Doug
- 1986 "Recruitment of High Risk Activism: The Case of Freedom Summer." *American Journal of Sociology* 92:64-90.
- 1988 *Freedom Summer: The Idealists Revisited.* New York: Oxford University Press.
- 1989 "The Biographical Consequences of Activism." *American Sociological Review* 54(4):744-60.
- 1999 "The Biographical Impact of Activism." *How Social Movements Matter*, Marco Giugni, Doug McAdam, and Charles Tilly, eds. Pp.117-146. Minneapolis, MN: University of Minnesota Press.

McAdam, Doug, John D. McCarthy, and Mayer N. Zald, eds.
- 1996 *Comparative Perspectives on Social Movements: Political Opportunities, Mobilizing Structures, and Cultural Framings.* Cambridge, UK: Cambridge University Press.

McCallum, Dennis
- 1999a Personal interview by John Smith. August 8.
- 1999b Notes on Personal Conversations with John Smith during travel, August 9.

McClendon, James William Jr.
- 1974 *Biography as Theology: How Life Stories Can Remake Today's Theology.* Nashville, TN: Abingdon.

McDonald, Eileen
- 1998 Personal interview by John Smith. October 11.

McFadden, Michael
- 1972 *The Jesus Revolution.* New York: Harper & Row.

McGraw, James R.
    1973   "Black Lightning and the Jesus Freaks." *Christianity and Crisis* 33/34(May 14):87-89.

McGregor, Mary
    1999   Telephone interview by John Smith. December 17.
    2000   Telephone interview by John Smith. February 22.

McGuire, Barry
    2000   Telephone interview by John Smith. March 28.

McKenna, David
    1971   "Are Jesus Kids Joel's Children? An Evangelical Analysis of the Jesus Movement." *United Evangelical Action* Fall: 9-14.

McKenna, Megan
    1997   *Rites of Justice: The Sacraments and Liturgy as Ethical Imperatives.* Maryknoll, NY: Orbis Books.

McLoughlin, William G.
    1978   *Revivals, Awakenings, and Reform: An Essay on Religion and Social Change in America 1607-1977.* Chicago, IL: University of Chicago Press.

McManners, John, ed.
    1993   *The Oxford Illustrated History of Christianity.* Oxford, UK: Oxford University Press.

Mead, Margaret
    1978[1971]   *Culture and Commitment: A Study of the Generation Gap.* Revised edition. New York: Doubleday.

Mellis, Charles J.
    1976   *Committed Communities: Fresh Streams for World Mission.* South Pasadena, CA: William Carey Library.

Melton, J. Gordon
    1996   "Emerging Religious Movements in North America: Missiological Reflections." *Missiology* 28(1):85-98.
    1998   *Encyclopedia of American Religions.* Detroit, MI: Gale Research.

Melucci, Alberto
    1996a   *Challenging Codes: Collective Action in the Information Age.* Cambridge, UK: Cambridge University Press.
    1996b   *The Playing Self: Person and Meaning in the Planetary Society.* Cambridge, UK: Cambridge University Press.

Merriam, Alan P.
    1964   *The Anthropology of Music.* Evanton, IL: Northwestern University Press.

Merton, Thomas
    1967a   "The Self of Modern Man and the New Christian Consciousness." *The R.M. Bucke Memorial Society Newsletter – Review.* Vol. 2. No.1. Montreal, Quebec.

1967b   *Mystics and Zen Masters.* New York: Farrar, Straus, and Giroux.

Meyer, David
1990   *A Winter of Discontent: the Nuclear Freeze and American Politics.* New York: Praeger.

Meyer, David, and Sidney Tarrow, eds.
1998   *The Social Movement Society: Contentious Politics for a New Century.* Lanham, MD: Rowman & Littlefield Publishers, Inc.

Millay, Grace
1970   "'Jesus People' Established Communes." *Yakima Herald-Republic* June 6:n.p.
1975   "House of Elijah Has Changed Focus." *Yakima Herald-Republic* August 16:7.

Miller, Craig Kennet
1972   *Baby Boomer Spirituality: Ten Values of a Generation.* Nashville, TN: Discipleship Resources.

Miller, David, and Meg Miller
1972   *Grass Roots: Craft and Self-sufficiency for Down to Earth People.* Melbourne, Australia: Waverley Offset Printer.

Miller, Donald E.
1997   *Reinventing American Protestantism: Christianity in the New Millennium.* Berkeley, CA: University of California Press.

Millikan, David
1981   *The Sunburnt Soul: Christianity in Search of an Australian Identity.* Sydney, Australia: Lancer.
1982   "Christianity and Australian Identity." *The Shape of Belief: Christianity in Australia Today.* Dorothy Harris, Douglas Hynd, and David Millikan, eds. Homebush West, Australia: Lancer Books.

Milliken, Bill
1973   *So Long, Sweet Jesus: A Street Worker's Spiritual Odyssey.* New York: Prometheus Press.

Miranda, Jose P.
1977   *Marx and the Bible: A Critique of the Philosophy of Oppression.* London, UK: SCM Press Ltd.

Mohs, Mayo, Richard Ostling, and Margaret Boeth
1971   "The New Rebel Cry: Jesus is Coming!" *Time* 97(25[June 21]):38-49.

Mol, J. J. (Hans)
1971   *The Religion of Australia.* Melbourne, Australia: Nelson.
1985   *The Faith of Australians.* Studies in Society No. 25. North Sydney, Australia: Allan and Irwin Ink.

Moore, T. Inglis
    1971   *Social Patterns in Australian Literature.* Berkeley, CA: University of California Press.

Moreton, Colin
    1973   "Australian Evangelical whose approach is as wide-ranging as it is unusual: Riding with God's Squad to the Outer Fringes of Society." *London Church Times* September 25:8.

Moses, David
    1976   *The Basic Mo Letters: The Basic beliefs of Millions of Children of God around the World on Religion, Politics, Economics, Sex, etc.* Geneva, Switzerland: Children of God.

Moyer, Harold S.
    1972   "The Jesus Revolution." *Brethren Life and Thought* 17(3):167-174.

Moylan Terry, and Jane Phillips,
    1986   "Teenage Suicides up 61% in a Year." *Sun* Melbourne, Australia: October 28:3.

Mulcahy, Joanne
    1991   "Choice Ladies: A Mission from God." *Rider's Choice* December:n.d.

Mumford, Lewis
    1950   *The Myth of the Machine.* Vol. 1. *Technics and Human Development.* New York: Harcourt, Brace & Jovanovich.
    1951   *Myth of the Machine.* Vol. 2. *The Pentagon of Power.* New York: Harcourt, Brace & Jovanovich.

Munger, Robert B.
    1971a   "The New Christians." *Christianity Today* 15(July 16):968-969.
    1971b   "God's Spirit is Breaking Through." *Eternity* August:12-14.
    1971c   "The New Rock: Bittersweet and Low." *Time* [Australian edition] March 1:49. Munroe, Australia.
    1999   Telephone interview by John Smith. December 12.
    2000   Telephone interview by John Smith. February 17.

Murphy, Geanie
    1996   "A Shiloh Sister's Story." *Communities: Journal of Cooperative Living* Fall 92:29-32. Rutledge, MO: Fellowship for Intentional Community.

Murphy, Kevin
    1987   "From Heaven to Hell's Angels." *Australian* December 1:42-43.

Muston, Philip B.
    2001   "John Smith, A Charismatic and Transformational Leader." MA thesis. School of International, Cultural, and Community Studies. Edith Cowan University, Perth, Australia.

Myers, Ched
    1990   *Binding the Strong Man: A Political Reading of Mark's Gospel.* Maryknoll, NY: Orbis Books.
    1994a   "I Will Ask You a Question:' Interrogatory Theology." *Theology without Foundations: Religious Practice & the Future of Theological Truth.* Stanley Hauerwas, Nancey Murphy, and Mark Nation, eds. Pp. 91-116. Nashville TN: Abingdon Press.
    1994b   *Who Will Roll Away the Stone? Discipleship Queries for First World Christians.* Maryknoll, NY: Orbis Books.

Myers, Ched, Marie Dennis, and Joseph Nangle, OFM et al.
    1997   "Say to This Mountain." *Mark's Story of Discipleship.* Karen Lattea, ed. Maryknoll, NY: Orbis Books.

Naisbitt, John
    1982   *Megatrends.* London, United Kingdom: Sidgwick & Jackson.

Nally, Peter
    1988   "We've Got it All: Except Quality of Life." *Gold Coast Bulletin.* September 20:n.p.

Nanus, Burt
    1995   *Visionary Leadership: Creating a Compelling Sense of Direction for Your Organization.* San Francisco, CA: Jossey-Bass.

Nee, Watchman
    1972   *A Table in the Wilderness: Daily Meditations from the Ministry of Watchman Nee.* Fort Washington, PA: Christian Literature Crusade.

Needleman, Jacob
    1970   *The New Religions.* New York: Doubleday.

Neihardt, John G.
    1979[1932]   *Black Elk Speaks.* Lincoln, NE: University of Nebraska Press.

Nethery, Ray
    1999   Personal interview by John Smith. September 3.

Newbigin, Lesslie
    1989   *The Gospel in a Pluralist Society.* Grand Rapids, MI: William B. Eerdmans.
    1994   *A Word in Season: Perspectives on Christian World Missions.* Grand Rapids, MI: William B. Eerdmans.
    1995   *The Open Secret: An Introduction to the Theology of Mission.* Grand Rapids, MI: William B. Eerdmans.

New Life
    1987a   "John Smith's Four Weeks Overseas: Huge Media Coverage in London." 50(September 10):3.
    1987b   "Fourth Melbourne Prayer Breakfast: John Smith focuses on the Nation and Presents the Gospel. 50(December):9
    1988a   "John Smith to Minister on the East Coast of the USA." 50(April 21):8.

1988b "Christianity or Humanism? Lively Debate at Melbourne's La Trobe University." 51(October 13):1-2.
1988c "Ray Martin [TV Midday Show] Interviews John Smith." 51(October 20):2.
1999 "'Jesus people Reunion Celebrates Hippy Revival that Began 30 Years Ago." 61(May 6):2.

Newman, Grover
1999 Phone interview by John Smith. December 21.

Newman, Martyn
1994 *Liberation Theology is Evangelical.* Clifton Hill, Australia: Mallorn Press.

Nida, Eugene A.
1990 *Message and Mission: The Communication of the Christian Faith.* Revised edition. Pasadena, CA: William Cary Library.

Niebuhr, H. Richard
1951 *Christ and Culture.* New York: Harper Row.

Nolan, James
1971 "Now that Jesus is 'In Again'." *Christian Century* 88:767.

Nordhoff, Charles
1960[1875] *The Communistic Societies of the United States: From Personal Visit and Observation.* New York: Hiliary House.

Norman, Larry
1972 "The Outlaw." *Only Visiting This Planet.* Los Angeles, CA: MGM/Verve Records.

Norman, Larry
1972 "The Outlaw." *Only Visiting This Planet.* Los Angeles: CA: MVM/Verve Records.

Obst, Linda Rosen, ed.
1977 "The Sixties: The Decade Remembered now, by the People Who Lived it Then." New York: Random House.

Oakes, Peter
1973 "The Cast with an Amazing Past." *Sunday People.* London, UK: August 15.

On Being
1960 "Mustering Australia's Lost Sheep." 7(2[March]):4-8.
1982a "God Cares." 9(6):4-8.
1982b "The Common People Heard Him Gladly." 9(6[July]):9-11.
1982c "Something's Smoldering in South Oz: Godcares as a Model for Australian Evangelism." 9(6[July]):12-13.
1989a "Why John Smith Went to Prison." 16(9[September]:22-24.
1989b "The Australian Connection. 16(October):20-22.

Ortega, Rueben
1972 *The Jesus People Speak Out!* Elgin, IL: David C. Cook.

Ostling, Joan K.
    1972   "Jesus Movement." *Eternity* 12(January):27-28.

Oved, Yaacov
    1988   *Two Hundred Years of American Communes.* New Brunswick, NJ: Transaction Books, Prometheus Press.

Owen, Bob, and Duane Pederson
    1973   *Jesus Is Alive and Well: The Truths behind the Stickers and Slogans.* Guildford, UK: Lutterworth Press.

Padilla, René
    1985   *Mission Between the Times.* Grand rapids, MI: W. B. Eerdmans.

Padilla, René, ed.
    1976   *The New Face of Evangelism: An International Symposium on the Lausanne Covenant.* Downers Grove, IL: InterVarsity Press.

Painter, John
    1997   *Mark's Gospel: New Testament Readings.* London UK: Routledge.

Palms, Roger C.
    1972   *The Jesus Kids.* London, UK: SCM Press.

Palosaari, Jim
    1973   "The Call of Discipleship." *Street Level: Jesus People Paper of Mid America* January 3:4.
    1999   Telephone interview by John Smith. December 7.

Palosaari, Sue
    1998   Personal correspondence between Sue Palosaari and Mary Steinke.

Parks, Carl
    1971a   "Reproduce!" *Truth* December 2:13. Spokane, WA: Spirit of Elijah
    1971b   "Wilson McKinley." *Truth* December 2:12. Spokane, WA: Spirit of Elijah.

Pascoe, Cindee
    1990a   "Crusader Sees South African Racism Parallel in Australia." *Toowoomba Chronicle* January 3:2.
    1990b   "John Smith has tough advice for Church." *Toowoomba Chronicle* February 26:2.

Patterson, Charles
    1995   *The Civil Rights Movement.* New York: Facts on File.

Peelman, Achiel
    1995   *Christ is a Native American.* Maryknoll, New York: Orbis Books.

Pelto, Pertti J., and Gretel H Pelto
    1978   *Anthropological Research: The Structure of Inquiry.* 2nd edition. Cambridge, UK: Cambridge University Press.

Perkins, John, and Wayne Gordon
    1992   *Christian Community Development Association* 1992-1993 *Membership Directory.* Pasadena, CA: Foundation for Reconciliation & Development.

Perrin, Robin D, and Armand L. Mauss
    1991   "Saints and Seekers: Sources of Recruitment to the Vineyard Christian Fellowship." *Review of Religious Research* 33:97-111.

Perry, Charles
    1984   *The Haight-Ashbury.* New York: Random House.

Peterson, Donald W., and Armand L. Mouss
    1973   "The Cross and the Commune: An Interpretation of the Jesus People." *Religion in Sociological Perspective.* Charles Y. Glock, ed. Pp. 261-279. Belmont, CA: Wadsworth.

Peterson, Joe V.
    1988   "The Unorganizing of the Miracle: The Shiloh Youth Revival Centers Inc. in the Spring of 1978: The Coup." Draft paper of a presentation to the annual meeting of the Scientific Study of Religion. October 28. Chicago, IL.
    1990a   "Jesus People: Christ, Communes and the Counter-Culture of the Late Twentieth Century in the Pacific Northwest: A Brief Overview of the Shiloh Youth Revival Centers, Inc. Highway Missionary Society House of Elijah." MA thesis, Northwest Christian College, Eugene, OR.
    1990b   "Communes and the Youth Movement from the Jesus People to the Bhagwan Shree Rajneesh." Paper presented to the University of Southern Indiana, Center for Communal Studies. February 5. Evansville, IN.
    1996a   "Christian Communities Then and Now. What You Need to Know about Christian Communities." *Communities: Journal of Cooperative Living* 92(Fall):24-27. Rutledge, MO: Fellowship for Intentional Community.
    1996b   "The Rise and Fall of Shiloh." *Communities: Journal of Cooperative Living* 92(Fall):60-65. Rutledge, MO: Fellowship for Intentional Community.
    1996c   "Selections from the Rule of St. Benedict." *Communities: Journal of Cooperative Living* 92(Fall):44. Rutledge, MO: Fellowship for Intentional Community.
    1999a   Personal interview by John Smith. September 28.
    1999b   Telephone interview by John Smith. December 1.
    1999c   Telephone interview by John Smith. December 3.

Pflüg, Melissa A.
    1998   *Ritual and Myth in Odawa Revitalization: Reclaiming a Sovereign Place.* Norman, Oklahoma: University of Oklahoma Press.

Pinnock, Clark
    1971   "The Christian Revolution." *The Post American* Fall:10-11.

Pirrie, Michael
    1994a   "Wheel Turns on Car Crime." *The Herald Sun* June 27:7.
    1994b   "Lucky Escape for Car Chase Youths." *The Herald Sun* June 29:7.

Pirsig, Robert M.
    1974   *Zen and the Art of Motorcycle Maintenance: An Inquiry into Values.* New York: William Morrow/Bantam Books.

Piven, Francis Fox, and Richard A. Cloward
    1979   *Poor People's Movements: Why They Succeed and Why They Fail.* New York: Vintage Books.

Plowman, Edward E.
    1971a   *The Underground Church: Accounts of Christian Revolutionaries in Action.* Elgin, IL: David C. Cook, London, UK: Hodden & Staughton.
    1971b   "Jesus Saves: Our Alienated Youth." *Eternity* 15(August):8-11,31.
    1971c   "Taking Stock of Jesus Rock." *Christianity Today* 15(10[February] 2):512-513.
    1971d   "Demonstrating for Jesus." *Christianity Today* 15(17[May21]):811-812.
    1971e   "Straights Meet Streets." *Christianity Today* 15(0[January 29]):431.
    1971f   "Pacific Northwest: Revival in the Underground." *Christianity Today* 15(January29):431.
    1971g   "Jesus Freaks Move Right On." *Christianity Today* 15(14[March 12]):569.
    1971h   "The Jesus Presses Are Rolling." *Christianity Today* 15(14[April 9]):664.
    1971i   "Shore to Shore: Waves of Witness." *Christianity Today* 15(16[May 7]):762-763.
    1971j   "The Jesus Movement: Now it's in the Hamlets." *Christianity Today* 15(19[June 18]:903-904.
    1972a   "Along the Blessitt Trail: Campaigning for Christ." *Christianity Today* 16(8):379-380.
    1972b   "Godstock in Big D." *Christianity Today* 16(20[July 7]):979-980.
    1972c   "Wave of Witnesses." *Christianity Today* 16(May 7):34.
    1972d   "A Rustling in the Leaves." *Christianity Today* 17(October 13):18-25.
    1973a   "Where Are All the Children Now?" *Christianity Today* 17(15[April 27]):795-796.

1973b "Open Season for Deprogrammers." *Christianity Today* 17(23[August 31]):1208-1209.

1973c "Discovering Jesus." *Christianity Today* 17(23[August 31]):1210-1212.

1975a "The Deepening Rift in the Charismatic Movement." *Christianity Today* 20(October 10):44-46.

1975b "Whatever Happened to the Jesus Movement?" *Today* 20(2[October 24]):102-104.

1976a "Help Us Get Our Children Back." *Christianity Today* 20(March 12):625-626.

1976b "Deprogramming: A Right to Rescue?" *Christianity Today* 20(16[May 7]):846.

Poloma, Margaret
    1982 *The Charismatic Movement: Is There a New Pentecost?* Boston, MA:Twayne Publishers.

Pope, Tom
    1999 Personal interview by John Smith. May 19.

Porter, Muriel
    1991 "John Smith: Australian Evangelist." *Australian Ministry* August:12-15.

Price, Betty, and Everett Hullum, Jr.
    1971 "The Jesus Explosion." *Home Missions* (June-July):13-23.

Pritchett, W. Douglas
    1985 *The Children of God: Family of Love.* New York: Garland Publishing, Inc.

Pulkingham, Betty
    1999 Telephone interview by John Smith. December 21.

Pulkingham, W. Graham
    1972 *Gathered for Power.* New York: Morehouse-Barlow Co.
    1980 *Renewal: An Emerging Pattern.* Dorset, UK: Celebration.

Pulkingham, W. Graham, ed.
    1973 *They Left Their Nets: A Vision for Community Ministry.* London, UK: Hodder & Stoughton.

Punkt
    1986 "Ein Hirte Fur Die Hollenengel." September:20-21.

Quebedeaux, Richard
    1974 *The Young Evangelicals: Revolution in Orthodoxy.* New York: Harper & Row.

Quinn, Kieran
    1971 "What Do You Say to a Jesus Freak?" *The Critique* (September-October):62-64.

Rabey, Steve, ed. contributor, and Dana Key
    1974 *Don't Stop the Music.* Grand Rapids, MI: Zondervan.
    1998 "Age to Age: Ghosts of the Past Whisper Old Stories and Rekindle Ongoing Debates in an In-depth Examination of Chris-

tian Music History." *Contemporary Christian Music: Special. Anniversary Issue. Celebrating Twenty Years of Music, Faith, and Culture* July 18-44.

Radic, Therese
    1984   *A Whip Round for Percy Grainger.* Montmorency, Australia: Yackandandah Playscripts.

Railton, G.S.
    1912   *The Authoritative Life of General William Booth Founder of the Salvation Army.* New York: The Reliance Trading Company.

Rambo, Lewis R.
    1993   *Understanding Religious Conversion.* New Haven, CT: Yale University Press.

Ramsland, John
    1987   *The Struggle against Isolation: A History of the Manning Valley.* The Library of Australian History in Association with Greater Taree City Council. North Sydney, Australia.

Reed, T.V.
    1992   *Fifteen Jugglers, Five Believers: Literary Politics and the Politics of American Social Movements.* Berkeley, CA: University of California Press.

Reich, Charles
    1970   *The Greening of America.* New York: Random House.

Reid, Alvin
    1991   "The Effect of the Jesus Movement on Evangelism Among Southern Baptists." Ph.D. dissertation, Southwestern Baptist Theological Seminary, Fort Worth, TX.

    1995   "The Effect of the Jesus Movement on Evangelism in the Southern Baptist Convention." *Baptist History and Heritage* January 30:41-52.

Reid, W. Stanford
    1971   "Jesus People May Bring About a New Reformation." *Toronto Star* September 18:85.
    1991   "Saints and Seekers: Sources of Recruitment to the Vineyard Christian Fellowship." *Review of Religious Research* 33:97-11.

Reidy, M. T. V., and James T. Richardson
    1975   "Comparative Studies of Neo-Pentecostalism." Paper read at the biannual meeting of the International Conference for the Sociology of Religion, 1975, Spain.

Richardson, Donald
    1973   "Causes and Consequences of the Jesus Movement in the United States." *The Contemporary Metamorphosis of Reli-*

gion. Pp. 393-406. International Conference for the Sociology of Religion, Lille, France: edition du Secrétariat CSIR.

Richardson, Don
    184   *Eternity in Their Hearts.* Ventura, CA: Regal.

    1974   "The Jesus Movement: An Assessment." *Listening: Journal of Religion and Culture* 9:20-42.

Richardson, James T., and M.T.V. Reidy
    1976   "Comparison and Contrast of Two Glossolalic Movements." Paper read at the annual meeting of the Society for the Scientific Study of Religion, October 1976, Philadelphia, PA.
    1980   "Form and Fluidity in Two Contemporary Glossolalic Movements." *Annual Review of the Social Sciences of Religion* 4:183-220.

Richardson, James T., Mary White Stewart, and Robert B. Simmonds
    1979   *Organized Miracles: A Study of a Contemporary, Youth, Communal, Fundamentalist Organization.* New Brunswick, NJ: Transaction Books.

Richardson, James T., Robert B. Simmonds, and Mary White Harder
    1972   "Thought Reform and the Jesus Movement." *Youth and Society* (December):184-202.
    1977   "Conversion Process Models and the Jesus Movement." *American Behavioral Scientist* 20:819-838.
    1979   "The Evolution of a Jesus Movement Organization." *Journal of Voluntary Action Research* (July-October):93-111.

Ricoeur, Paul
    1974   "The Symbol Gives Rise to Thought." *Literature and Religion.* Giles B. Gunn, ed. New York: Harper & Row.
    n.d.   *Interpretation Theory: Discourse and the Surplus of Meaning.* Fort Worth, TX: Texas Christian University Press.

Riesman, David
    1950   *The Lonely Crowd.* New Haven, CT: Yale University Press.

Rifkin, Jeremy
    2000   *The Age of Access: The New Culture of Hypercapitalism: Where All of Life is a Paid-for Experience.* New York: Jeremy P. Tarcher /Penguin Putnam.

Robbins, Thomas
    1984   "Constructing Cultist 'Mind Control.'" *Sociological Analysis* 45(3):241-256.

Roberts, A., and J. Donaldson
    1867   *Ante-Nicene Christian Library I: Apostolic Fathers.* A. Roberts, J. Donaldson, and F. Crombie, trans. Edinburgh: T & T. Clark.

Robertson, Roland
    1979   "Religious Movements and Modern Societies: Toward a Progressive Problem Shift." *Sociological Analysis* 40(4):297-314.

Rogers, Everett M.
    1995   *Diffusion of Innovations.* New York: The Free Press.

Romanowski, William D.
    1990a   "Rock 'n' Religion: A Sociocultural Analysis of the Contemporary Christian Music Industry." Ph.D. dissertation, Bowling Green State University, Bowling Green, KY.
    1990b   "Contemporary Christian Music: The Business of Music Ministry." *American Evangelicals and Mass media.* Quenton J. Schultze ed. Pp. 143-170. Grand Rapids, MI: Zondervan.
    1996   *Pop Culture Wars: Religion and the Role of Entertainment in American Life.* Downers Grove, IL: InterVarsity Press.

Roof, Wade Clark
    1993   *A Generation of Seekers: The Spiritual Journeys of the Baby Boom Generation.* New York: Harper Collins Publishers.
    1999   *Spiritual Marketplace Baby Boomers and the Remaking of American Religion.* Princeton, NJ: Princeton University Press.

Rookmaaker, H.R.
    1968   *Art and Public Today.* Huemoz-sur-Ollon, Switzerland: L'Abri Fellowship Foundation.
    1970   *Modern Art and the Death of a Culture.* Leichester, UK: Inter-Varsity Press.
    1978   *Art Needs No Justification.* Downers Grove, IL: Inter-Varsity Press.
    1987   *The Creative Gift.* Essays on Art and the Christian Life. Westchester, UK: Cornerstone Books.

Roszak, Theodore
    1968   *The Making of a Counterculture: Reflections on the Technocratic Society and Its Youthful Opposition.* London, UK: Faber and Faber.
    1972a   *Sources: An Anthology of Contemporary Materials Useful for Preserving Personal Sanity while Braving the Great Technological Wilderness.* New York: Harper & Row.
    1972b   *Industrial Society.* London, UK: Faber and Faber.
    1972c   *Where the Wasteland Ends: Politics and Transcendence in Post Industrial Society.* New York: Doubleday.
    1995   *The Making of a Counter Culture: Reflections on the Technocratic Society and Its Youthful Opposition.* Revised edition. Berkeley, CA: University of California Press.

Roxborough, Gilbert
    1971   "Fed Up With Formal Service: Worshipers Go Underground." *Toronto Star* April 3:84.

Roxburg, Alan J.
    1996   "Pastoral Role in the Missionary Congregation." *The Church between Gospel and Culture: The Emerging Mission in North America.* George R. Hunsberger, and Craig Van Gelder, eds. Pp. 319-332. Grand Rapids, MI: William B. Eerdmans.

Rudestam, Kjell Erik, and Rae R. Newton
    1992   *Surviving Your Dissertation: A Comprehensive Guide to Content and Process.* Newbury Park, CA: Sage.

Ruhlmann, William
    1992   "Barry McGuire Before and After Eve of Destruction." *Goldmine Magazine* November.

Saliba, John A.
    1995a   *Understanding New Religious Movements.* Grand Rapids, MI: William B. Eerdmans.

Saliba, Philip, Metropolitan
    1997[1987] "Interview: Welcome Home." *Again* 20(1):37-38. Ben Lomond, CA: Conciliar Press.

Sanneh, Lamin
    1983   *West African Christianity: The Religious Impact.* Maryknoll, NY: Orbis Books.
    1989   *Translating the Message: The Missionary Impact on Culture.* Maryknoll, NY: Orbis Books.

Sapwell, Ken
    1989   "Coast Violence Sign of Times, Says John." *Gold Coast Bulletin* January 4:n.p.

Schaeffer, Edith
    1969   *L'Abri.* London, UK: Norfolk Press.

Schaeffer, Frankie
    1997   "Why I became Orthodox." *Again* 20(1):60-61. Ben Lomond, CA: Conciliar Press.

Schaller, Lyle
    1995   Schaller interview. *Worship Leader* January.

Scherer, James A., and Stephen B. Bevans, eds.
    1999   *New Directions in Mission and Evangelization: Faith and Culture.* Maryknoll, NY: Orbis Books.

Schiffmayer, Jeffrey
    1979   "Church of the Redeemer: A New Look." *Acts 29 Newsletter* Pp. 1,3,7.

Schillebeeckx, Edward
    1992   *The Church with a Human Face: A New Expanded Theology of Ministry.* New York: Crossroad.

Schmemann, Alexander
    1995[1963] *For the Life of the World: Sacraments and Orthodoxy.* Crestwood, NY: St Vladimir's Seminary Press.

Schreiter, Robert J.
    1985   *Constructing Local Theologies.* Maryknoll, NY: Orbis Books.
    1994   "Inculturation of Faith or Identification with Culture?" *Concilium* 1994/2: "Christianity and Cultures."
    1997   *The New Catholicity: Theology between the Global and the Local.* Maryknoll, NY: Orbis Books.

Scott, Carolyn
    2000   *The Heavenly Witch: The Story of the Marechale.* London, UK: Hamish Hamilton.

Scott, Dan
    1994   *The Emerging American Church.* Anderson, IN: Bristol Books.

Sczepanski, David
    1961   "Christians In Action: Discipleship Is Doing God's Work." *Logos Journal* (September/October 1975).

Seligman, M.E.P.
    1975   *Helplessness: On Depression, Development and Death.* San Francisco, CA: Freeman.
    1990   "Why Is There so Much Depression Today? The Waxing and Waning of the Commons." *Contemporary Psychological Approaches to Depression.* Rich E. Ingram, ed. New York: Plenum Press/San Francisco, CA: Freeman.

Shaw, Bob
    1985   "God Squad Minister Revs-up for Christ." *The Evening Post* [Wellington, NZ] May 9:n.p.

Sider, Ron
    1977   *Rich Christians in an Age of Hunger.* Downers Grove, IL: InterVarsity Press.

Simcox, Carroll
    1971   "Hooray for Jesus People." *Milwaukee Sentinel* August 7:n.p.
    1977   "Jesus Movement Group." *American Behavioral Scientist* 20(6):909-924.

Simmonds, Robert B., James T. Richardson, and Mary White Harder
    1974   "Organizational Aspects of a Jesus Movement Community." *Social Compass* 21(3):269-281.
    1976   "A Jesus Movement Group: An Adjective CheckList Assessment." *Journal for the Scientific Study of Religion* 15(4[December]):323-337.

Sine, Tom
    1999   Personal interview by John Smith. September 28.

Singer, Peter R.
    1975   *Animal Rights: A New Ethic for Our Treatment of Animals.* New York: Avon Books.

Sitkin, Sim B, and Robert J. Bies

1986 "The Legalization of Organizations: A Multi-Theoretical Perspective." Paper presented at National Academy of Management Meetings titled: "The Law Versus the Manager: The Encroachment of a Litigation Mentality into the Organization."

Slater, Philip
    1971 *The Pursuit of Loneliness: American Culture at the Breaking Point.* Boston, MA: Beacon Press.

Smith, Chuck
    1976a *The Soon to Be Revealed Antichrist.* Costa Mesa, CA: Maranatha Evangelical Association.
    1976b *Snatched Away.* The Word for Today. Costa Mesa, CA: Maranatha Evangelical Association.
    1983 *Charisma vs. Charismania.* Eugene, OR: Harvest House.
    1987 *Harvest.* Old Tappan, NJ: Chosen Books.

Smith, Chuck, and Tal Brooke
    1992 *The History of Calvary Chapel.* Costa Mesa, CA: N.p.

Smith, Chuck, and Hugh Steven
    1972 *The Reproducers: New Life for Thousands.* Glendale, CA: Regal Books.

Smith, John
    1973a "Profile on Dr. Jack Sparks and Michael Eastman." *Truth & Liberation* 2(2):10.
    1973b "Hey Mr. Prime Minister: What is the Answer?" *Truth & Liberation* 2(5):6.
    1974a "Jack Sparks." Interview for *Truth & Liberation* 2(3):4-5.
    1974b *Truth and Liberation Concern Public Relations Leaflet.* Bayswater, Australia: Truth & Liberation Concern.
    1985 "John Smith." *The Home Building Experience: John Archer Talks to Owner Builders.* John Archer ed., Pp. 114-127. Sydney, Australia: Australian Broadcasting Corporation.
    1986 "The Total Package." *Today* September 14.
    1989a *Advance Australia Where?* Revised edition. Homebush West, Australia: Anzea.
    1989b "Johnny B. God." *Sydney Morning Herald: Spectrum* November 18:5.
    1992 *Cutting Edge.* Tunbridge Wells, UK: Monarch Publications.
    2000 "Church of the Redeemer." Unpublished research paper for Jesus Movement Dissertation.

Smith, John, and Alan Harvey
    1996 *Searching for Satisfaction: Rock's Search for Faith and Meaning.* Melbourne, Australia: The Joint Board of Christian Education.

Smith, John, and Malcolm Doney
    1987 *On the Side of the Angels.* Oxford, UK: Lion.

Snyder, Graydon F.
    1995   *Health and Medicine in the Anabaptist Tradition: Care in Community.* Valley Forge, PA: Trinity Press International.

Snyder, Howard A.
    1975   *The Problem of Wineskins: Church Structure in a Technological Age.* Downers Grove, IL: Inter Varsity Press.
    1977   *The Community of the King.* Downers Grove IL: InterVarsity Press.
    1989   *Signs of the Spirit.* Grand Rapids, MI: Zondervan.
    1991   *Models of the Kingdom.* Nashville, TN: Abingdon Press.

Sparks, Jack N.
    1971a   *Letters to Street Christians.* Grand Rapids, MI: Zondervan.
    1971b   *The Street People: Selections from Right On! Berkeley's Underground Student Newspaper.* Valley Forge, PA: Judson Press.
    1973   *Exorcism: How God Counteracts Evil Spirits and Powers.* Berkeley, CA: Christian World Liberation Front.
    1974a   "Jack Sparks." Personal interview by John Smith. *Truth & Liberation.* Vol. 2 (3): 4-5.
    1974b   *God's Forever Family.* Grand Rapids, MI: Zondervan.
    1977   *The Mindbenders: A Look at Current Cults.* Nashville, TN: Thomas Nelson.
    1978   *The Apostolic Fathers.* Nashville, TN: Thomas Nelson.
    1993   *Victory in the Unseen Warfare.* Ben Lomond, CA: Conciliar Press.
    1995   *Virtue in the Unseen Warfare.* Ben Lomond, CA: Conciliar Press.
    1996a   *Tradition and the Early Church.* Elk Grove, CA: St. Athanasius Academy of Orthodox Theology.
    1996b   *Prayer in the Unseen Warfare.* Ben Lomond, CA: Conciliar Press.
    1997   "The Middle Years: A New Foundation." *Again* 20(1):29-31. Ben Lomond, CA: Conciliar Press.
    1999a   Personal interview by John Smith. August 2.
    1999b   Telephone interview by John Smith. November 11.
    1999c   Telephone interview by John Smith. November 12.

Spradley, James P.
    1970   *You Owe Yourself a Drunk: An Ethnography of Urban Nomads.*
        Boston MA: Little, Brown and Company.
    1979   *The Ethnographic Interview.* New York: Holt, Rinehart & Winston. Jovanovich College.
    1980   *Participant Observation.* New York: Holt, Rinehart & Winston.

Spransy, Matthew, and Siv Spransy
    1999   Personal interview by John Smith. June 17.
Stannard, Bruce, and Susan Molloy
    1984   "Inside the Brotherhood of Bikers." *The Bulletin* (Australia) September 18:34-36.
Stark, Rodney
    1984a   "Religion and Conformity: Reaffirming a Sociology of Religion." Presidential Address: The Association for the Sociology of Religion.
    1984b   "A Taxonomy of Religious Experience." Publication A:29:97-116, Survey Research Berkeley, CA: Center University of California.
    1987   "How New Religions Succeed: A Theoretical Model." In David, G. Bromley, and Phillip E. Hammond, eds. *The Future of New Religious Movements*. Macon, GA: Mercer Universal Press.
    1995   "The [court]Testimony of Rodney Stark, Ph.D." *Writings of Watchman Nee and Witness Lee*. Anaheim, CA: Living Stream.
    1996a   *The Rise of Christianity: A Sociologist Reconsiders History*. Princeton, NJ: Princeton University Press.
    1996b   *Sociology*. 6th edition. Belmont, CA: Wadsworth.
Stark, Rodney, and William Sims Bainbridge
    1979   "Of Churches, Sects, and Cults: Preliminary Concepts for a Theory of Religious Movements." *Journal for the Scientific Study of Religion* 18(2):117-131.
    1980a   "Networks of Faith: Interpersonal Bonds and Recruitment to Cults and Sects." *American Journal of Sociology* 85(6):1376-1395.
    1980b   "Towards a Theory of Religion: Religious Commitment." *Journal for the Scientific Study of Religion* 19:114-128.
    1981   "American-Born Sects: Initial Findings." *Journal for the Scientific Study of Religion* 20(2):130-149.
    1983   *The Future of Religion*. Berkeley, CA: University of California Press.
    1985   *The Future of Religion: Secularization, Revival, and Cult Formation*. Berkeley, CA: University of California Press.
    1996a   *A Theory of Religion*. New York: Toronto/Lang.
    1997   *Religion, Deviance, and Social Control*. New York: Rutledge.
Stark, Rodney, William Sims Bainbridge, and Daniel P. Doyle
    1979   "Cults of America: A Reconnaissance in Space and Time." *Sociological Analysis* 40:347-359.

Stark, Rodney, Daniel P. Doyle, and Lori Kent
    1980   "Rediscovering Moral Communities: Church Membership and Crime." *Understanding Crime.* Travis Hirshi, and Michael Gott Fredson eds. Pp. 43-52. Beverly Hills, CA: Sage.

Stark, Rodney, Daniel P. Doyle, and Jesse Lynn Rushing
    1983   "Beyond Durkheim: Religion and Suicide." *Journal for the Scientific Study of Religion* 22(2):120-131.

Stark, Rodney, and Charles Y. Glock
    1968   *American Piety: The Nature of Religious Commitment.* Berkeley, CA: University of California Press.

Stark, Rodney, and Lynne Roberts
    1982   "The Arithmetic of Social Movements: Theoretical Implications." *Sociological Analysis* 43:53-68.

Stegemann, Ekkehard W., and Wolfgang Stegemann
    1999   *The Jesus Movement: A Social History of Its First Century.* Minneapolis, MN: Fortress Press.

Steigerwald, David
    1995   *The Sixties and the End of Modern America.* New York: St. Martin's Press.

Steinke, Brian
    1999   Personal interview by John Smith. June 16.

Steinke, Mary
    1999   Personal interview by John Smith. June 16.

Sterritt, David
    1971   "Rock Finds Religion." *Christian Science Monitor* March 10.

Stewart, Charles J., Craig Allen Smith, and Robert E. Denton Jr.
    1994   *Persuasion and Social Movements.* 3rd edition. Prospect Heights, IL: Waveland Press.

Stones, Christopher R.
    1977   "The Jesus People: Changes in Security and Life-Style as a Function of Nonconformist Religious Influence." *Journal of Psychology* 97:127-133.
    1978   "Jesus People: Fundamentalism and Changes in Factors Associated with Conservatism." *Journal for the Scientific Study of Religion* 1(2):155-158.

Street Level: Jesus People Paper of Mid America
    1971a   "Jesus Christ: Underground?" 1(3):10-11.
    1971b   "Jesus is Making Headlines Everywhere!" 1(8):7-9.
    1971c   "He Is Who He Says He Is." 1(4):10.
    1973   "The Call of Discipleship." 3(1):4.

Streiker, Lowell
    1975   *The Jesus Trip: Advent of the Jesus Freaks.* New York: Abingdon Press.

Strom, Mark
    2000   *Reframing Paul: Conversations in Grace & Community.* Downers Grove, IL: InterVarsity Press.

Stuessy, Joe
    1990   *Rock and Roll: It's Stylistic Development.* Englewood Cliffs, NJ: Prentice Hall.

Segundo, Juan Luis
    1973   *The Community Called Church.* Vol. 1. Theology for Artisans of a New Humanity. Maryknoll, NY: Orbis Books.

Sunday Examiner
    1989   "Born to Stir – John Smith." July 2:n.p.

Tarrow, Sidney
    1998   *Power in Movement: Social Movements and Contentious Politics.* 2nd edition. Cambridge Studies in Comparative Politics. Cambridge, UK: Cambridge University Press.

Taylor, Barry
    1999   Personal interview by John Smith. August 23.

Taylor, Gordon Rattray
    1969   *The Biological Time Bomb.* London, UK: Panther Books.

Taylor, John V.
    1975   *Enough is Enough.* London, UK: SCM Press.

Tesfai, Jacob, ed.
    1994   *The Scandal of a Crucified World: Perspectives on the Cross and Suffering.* Maryknoll, NY: Orbis Books.

Theissen, Gerd
    1978   *Sociology of Early Palestinian Christianity.* Philadelphia, PA: Fortress Press.

Theissen, Gerd, and Annette Merz
    1998   *The Historical Jesus: A Comprehensive Guide.* Minneapolis, MN: Fortress Press.

The Challenge Weekly (New Zealand)
    1991   "Christians 'like Pharisees.'" 49(1[January]):17ff.
    1991   "Chameleon Evangelist Speaks to 'Unreachable' Groups: Changing His Colors to Suit His Environment." 4 (2):24ff.

The Herald
    1972   "Church on Wheels." May 23:1-2.

The Lifewriter
    1992   "The Challenge for Capitalism in the '90's." June:48-49.

The Star Sheffield
    1974   "Flower Children's Song Rocks Sheffield." March 2. N.p.

Theos Sun
    1972   "Is the Future a Bummer? School's Nearly Out. Jesus in the Schools." East Hawthorn, Australia: Y.M. Productions for the Scripture Union of Victoria. October 7:n.p.

Tichy, N.M., and M. Devanna.
    1986   *The Transformational Leader.* New York: John Wiley and Sons.

Tiffin, Gerald C.
    1972   "Cultural Interpretation of the Jesus People." *Fides et Historia* 5(Fall-Spring):79-85.

Tillich, Paul
    1963   *Christianity and the Encounter of the World Religions.* New York: Mentor Books.
    1966   *The Future of Religions.* New York: Harper & Row.

Tilly, Charles
    1978   *From Mobilization to Revolution.* Reading, MA: Addison-Wesley.
    1988   "Social Movements, Old, and New." *Research in Social Movements: Conflicts, and Change.* 10:1-18.
    1993   *European Revolutions,* 1492-1992. Oxford, UK: Basil Blackwell.

Time
    1972   "The Jesus Revolution. The Rebel Cry: Jesus is Coming." *Time* [Australian edition] June 21:1, 38-49.

Tippett, A.R.
    1968   *Solomon Islands Christianity: A Study in Growth and Obstruction.* London, UK: Lutterworth Press.
    n.d.   *The Liminal Years: Selected Essays* 1943-1976. Pasadena, CA: Unpublished.

Tipton, Steven M.
    1982   *Getting Saved from the Sixties.* Berkeley, CA: University of California Press.

Together
    1979   "A Friend of Jesus Today: John Smith, Leader of God's Squad." *Together Religion in Life for Lower Primary Classes.* Unit 1 Lesson 8. Melbourne, Australia: The Joint Board of Christian Education of Australia and New Zealand. The Council for Christian Education in Schools.

Touraine, Alain
    1977   *The Self-Production of Society.* Chicago, IL: University of Chicago Press.
    1988   *Return of the Actor: Social Theory in Post Industrial Society.* Minneapolis, MN: University of Minnesota Press.
    1995   *Critique of Modernity.* Oxford, UK: Blackwell.

Tracey, Phil
    1970   "The Jesus Freaks: Savagery and Salvation on the Sunset Strip." *Commonweal* 93:122-125.

Trafzer, Clifford E.
    1986   *American Indian Prophets.* Sacramento, CA: Sierra Oaks.

Traill, Stewart
    1978   "Diplomat Meeting." Detailed minute instructions to the "lambs" of the Forever Family fold, for November 23:2,4-5, 9-10.

Trueblood, Charles
    1995   "Welcome to the Next Church." *The Atlantic Monthly* 8:37-58.

Trueblood, Elton
    1961   *The Company of the Committed*. New York: Harper & Row.

Truth
    1971a   "What If?" Joint issue with Washington's Spirit of Elijah ministries. 1(12):10. Melbourne, Australia: Truth & Liberation.
    1971b   "Wilson McKinley." Joint issue with Washington's Spirit of Elijah ministries. 1(12):12. Melbourne, Australia: Truth & Liberation.

Truth & Liberation
    1972a   "Truth Sunnies, 'Comparative Religions in a Nutshell'." 1(2):8. Melbourne, Australia: Truth & Liberation.
    1972b   "Dear John: An Open Letter to John Lennon." Joint issue with Washington's Spirit of Elijah ministries. 1(2):1, 5-6. Melbourne, Australia: Truth & Liberation.
    1972c   "The System is Evil." 1(3):14. Melbourne, Australia: Truth & Liberation.
    1972   "Krishna or Christ?" 1(5):13-14. Melbourne, Australia: Truth & Liberation.
    1973a   "Divine or Demonic? The Guru Maharaja Ji." 2(2):6-7. Melbourne, Australia: Truth & Liberation.
    1973b   "Profile on Dr. Jack Sparks and Michael Eastman." 2(2):11; 2(3):1, 9. Melbourne, Australia: Truth & Liberation.
    1973c   "Up From Zen." 2(3):7, 9. Melbourne, Australia: Truth & Liberation.
    1974   "You Are the Orphans of an Age of No Tomorrows." December:1. Melbourne, Australia: Truth & Liberation.

Truzzi, Marcello
    1974   "Reverse Creation." *Truth & Liberation* 4(12):11 Melbourne, Australia.
    1975   "Astrology as Popular Culture." *Journal of Popular Culture* 8:906-911.

Tsitas, Evelyn
    1986   "The Bikie with Words that Bite." *Keilor Messenger* September 23:n.p.

Tuffin, Lindsay
    1986   "He's no Holy Roller." *The Sunday Examiner* March 30:59.

Turner, Harold W.
    1979   *Religious Innovations in Africa: Collected Essays on New Religious Movements.* Boston, MA: G. K. Hall and Co.

Turner, Steve
    1976   *Up To Date.* London, UK: Hodder & Stoughton.
    1994   *A Hard Day's Write: The Stories behind Every Beatles Song.* New York: Harper Perrenial.
    1995   *Hungry for Heaven.* Revised edition. London, UK: Hodder & Stoughton.
    1996   *Jack Kerouac: Angel headed Hipster.* New York: Penguin Books.

Turner, Victor
    1969   *The Ritual Process: Structure and Anti-Structure.* Hawthorn, NY: Aldine de Gruyter.

Turner, Victor, and Edward M. Bruner, eds.
    1986   *The Anthropology of Experience.* Urbana, IL: University of Illinois Press.

Tuttle, L., ed.
    1971   "Report of President and the Jesus Revolution." *World Methodist Conference* 12:17-22, 114-120.

Two Brothers from Berkeley
    1971   *Letters to Street Christians.* Grand Rapids, MI: Zondervan.

Ungar, Andre
    1973   "Jews and Jesus Freaks." *Reconstructionist* 49(December 9):7-11.

Unger, Irwin, and Debi Unger, eds.
    1998   *The Times were a Changin'.* New York: Three Rivers Press.

Uniting
    1984   "Behind the Bikie Image, a Message for Life." August 29:n.p.

U'ren, John
    1999   Personal correspondence with John Smith. Unpublished reflections on the Jesus Movement in Australia as a participator. November 20.

U.S. News & World Report
    1972   "A Day in the Life of the Children of God." March 20:59-65.

Vachon, Brian
    1971   "The Jesus Movement is Upon Us." *Look Magazine* February 9:15-21.

Velikovsky, Immanuel
    1950   *Worlds in Collision.* Garden City, New York: Doubleday.

Van Eldren, Martin
    1971   "The Jesus 'Freaks': Some Thoughts on a Religious Phenomenon." *Reformed Journal* May-June: 16-20.

Van Engen, Charles
    1996   *Mission on the Way: Issues in Mission Theology.* Grand Rapids, MI: Baker Books.

Van Gennep, Arnold
    1960   *The Rites of Passage.* Chicago, IL: University of Chicago Press.

Van Willigen, John
    1993   *Applied Anthropology: An Introduction.* Revised edition. Westport, CT: Bergin and Garbey.

Wagner, C. Peter
    1973   *The New Apostolic Churches.* Ventura, CA: Regal Books.
    1989   *Strategies for Church Growth.* Ventura, CA: Regal Books.

Wagner, Frederick N.
    1971   "A Theological and Historical Assessment of the Jesus Phenomenon." MA thesis, Fuller Theological Seminary, Pasadena, CA.

Wagner, John
    1996   " 'Success' and 'Failure' in Intentional Communities: The Problem of Evaluation." *Communities: Journal of Cooperative Living* 92 (Fall):50.

Vanguard
    1971   "Dropping Out Into Jesus." March:7-9. Pp. 20-22.

Walker, Alan
    1972   "Editorial." *St. Mark's Review* (May):1-4.

Walker, Gordon Thomas
    1997   "Our Entrance into the Orthodox Church." *Again* 20(1):32-35. Ben Lomond, CA: Conciliar Press.
    1999   Personal interview by John Smith. April 8.

Wallace, Anthony F.C.
    1952   "Handsome Lake and the Great Revival in the West." *American Quarterly* 2:149-65.
    1955   "The Disruption of the Individual's Identification with His Culture in Disasters and Other Extreme Situations." Paper read at National Research Council, Committee on Disaster Studies, Conference on Theories of Human Behavior in Extreme Situation, Vassar College.
    1956a   "Mazeway Resynthesis: A Biocultural Theory of Religious Inspiration." *Transactions of the New York Academy of Sciences* 18:626-638.
    1956b   "Revitalization Movements: Some Theoretical Considerations for their Comparative Study." *American Anthropologist* 58:264-281.
    1956c   "Stress and Rapid Personality Change." *International Record of Medicine* 169:761-774.

1957 "The Origins of Iroquois Neutrality: The Grand Settlement of 1701." *Pennsylvania History* 24:223-235.
1958a "Dreams and the Wishes of the Soul." *American Anthropologist* 60:234-248.
1958b "The Dekanawidah Myth Analyzed as the Record of a Revitalization Movement." *Ethnohistory* 5:118-130.
1966 *Religion: An Anthropological View*. New York: Random House.
1969 *The Death and Rebirth of the Seneca*. New York: Random House.
1972 "Mental Illness, Biology, and Culture," In *Psychological Anthropology*. F.L.K. Hsu, ed. 2nd edition. Cambridge, MA: Schenkman.
1980 *Rockdale: The Growth of an American Village in the Early Industrial Revolution*. New York: W.W.Norton.
1990[1949] *King of the Delawares: Teedyuscung* 1700-1763. Revised edition. Syracuse, NY: Syracuse University Press.

Wallerstein, Immanuel
1998 *Utopistics, or Historical Choices of the Twenty-first Century*. New York: The New Press.
1999 *The End of the World as We Know It: Social Science for the Twenty-First Century*. Minneapolis, MN: University of Minnesota Press.
1975 *World Inequity*. Quebec, Montreal: Black Rose Books.

Wallis, Roy
1982 *Millennialism and Charisma*. Belfast, Northern Ireland: The Queen's University.

Ward, Hiley H.
1972 *The Far-Out Saints of the Jesus Communes: A Firsthand Report and Interpretation of the Jesus People Movement*. New York: Association Press.

Ward, Pete
1996 *Growing up Evangelical: Youth Work and the Making of a Subculture*. London, UK: Society for Promoting Christian Knowledge.

Warner, Keith
1996 "Responding to Sexual Misconduct in Christian Community." *Communities: Journal for Cooperative Living* 92(Fall):56-59 Rutledge, MO: Fellowship for Intentional Community.

Watson, David
1983 *You Are My God*. Dunton Green, Kent, UK: Hodder & Stoughton.

Watts, Allan
1950 *The Supreme Identity*. New York: Random House/Panthem.
1959 *Beat Zen, Square Zen, and Zen*. San Francisco: City Lights.

1972 "The Jesus Freaks & Jesus." *New York Times* March 29:43.
Webb, Carolyn
 1992 "God's Biker on the Side of the Angels." *The Herald Sun* February 23:90.
Webber, Robert, and Donald G. Bloesch
 1978 *The Orthodox Evangelicals: Who they are and what They Are Saying*. Nashville, TN: Thomas Nelson.
Weber, Max
 1958[1946] *Max Weber: Essays in Sociology*. H. H. Gerth, and C. Wright Mills, trans. New York: Oxford University Press.
 1964[1947] *The Theory of Social and Economic Organization*. A.M. Henderson and Talcott Parsons, Trans. London, UK: Free Press of Glencoe, Collier-Macmillan.
 1968 *On Charisma and Institution Building: Selected Papers*. S. N. Eisenstadt, ed. Chicago, IL: University of Chicago Press.
 1993 *Basic Concepts in Sociology*. H.P. Secher, trans. New York: Carol Publishing Group/Citadel Press.
Weidman, Hazel H.
 1975 *Concepts as Strategies for Change*. New York: Insight Communications Inc.
Whiteman, Darrell
 1983 *Melanesians and Missionaries*. Pasadena, CA: William Carey Library.
 1984 "The Cultural Dynamics of Religious Movements." *Religious Movements in Melanesia Today* (3). Series 4 Wendy Flannery, ed. Pp.52-76. Goroka, Papua New Guinea.
 1997 "Contextualization: The Theory, the gap, the Challenge." *International Bulletin of Missionary Research* 21(January 1).
Whyte, William H., Jr.
 1956 *The Organization Man*. Garden City, NY: Doubleday.
Wilkerson, Don
 1973 *Coffee House Manual*. Minneapolis, MN: Bethany Fellowship.
Wilkinson, David
 1963 *The Cross and the Switchblade*. Old Tappan, NJ: Fleming H. Revell Co.
 1971 *Get Your Hands off my Throat*. Grand Rapids, MI: Zondervan.
Williams, Donald M.
 1971 "Close Up of the Jesus People." *Christianity Today* 27(8):1033-1035.
Williams, Peter W.
 1989 *Popular Religion in America: Symbolic Change and the Modernization Process in Historical Perspective*. Urbana, IL: University of Illinois Press.

Wilson, B.
    1975   *The Noble Savages: Primitive Origins of Charisma and its Contemporary Survival.* Berkeley, CA: University of California Press.

Wilson, Bruce
    1976   *Can God Survive in Australia?* Sydney, Australia.

Wilson, Bryan R.
    1990   *The Social Dimensions of Sectarianism: Sects and New Religious Movements in Contemporary Society.* Oxford, UK: Oxford University Press.

Wind, James P., and James W. Lewis, eds.
    1994a   *American Congregations.* Vol. 1. *Portraits of Twelve Religious Communities.* Chicago, IL: University of Chicago Press.
    1994b   *American Congregations.* Vol. 2. *New Perspectives in the Study of Congregations.* Chicago, IL: University of Chicago Press.

Windmueller, S.
    1972   "The Jesus Movement: The Jewish Response." *Jewish Frontier* March:23-26.

Winter, Ralph D., and Bruce A. Koch
    1999   "Finishing the Task: The Unreached Peoples Challenge." In *Perspectives on the World Christian Movement: A Reader.* 3rd edition. Ralph D. Winter and Steven C. Hawthorn, eds. Pp. 509-524. Pasadena, CA: William Carey Library.

Witherington, Ben, III
    2000   Personal interview by John Smith. December 7.

Withers, Graeme
    1997   *Life, Learning, and Values. An Evaluation of the Values for Life Seminars Program as a Co-curricular Experience for Australian Young People.* Melbourne: Australian Council for Educational Research.

Woodruff, Jeannie
    1999   Telephone interview by John Smith. December 12.

Woodward, Kenneth L.
    1971   "The Jesus People: Freak Out or Cop-Out?" *Christian Herald* September:12-15.
    1999   "Prophecy. Millennial Visions: What the Bible Says About the End of the World." *Newsweek* November 1:67.

Wormus, J.W.
    1975   "Jesus Movement." *Risk* 11:35-39.

Wright, E.
    1971a   "Report of President and the Jesus Revolution." *World Methodist Conference* 12:17-22, 114-120.
    1971b   "The Jesus People Movement." *Lutheran Witness* October 16.

Wroe, Martin
    1988   "An Unrespectable Prophet." *Strait* Pp. 35-39 London, UK.

Wuthnow, Robert
    1976   *The Consciousness Reformation.* Berkeley and Los Angeles, CA: University of California Press.
    1978   *Experimentation in American Religion: The New Mysticisms and Their Implications for the Churches.* Berkeley, CA: University of California Press.
    1987   *Meaning and Moral Order: Explorations in Cultural Analysis.* Berkeley and Los Angeles, CA: University of California Press.
    1994   *Producing the Sacred: An Essay on Public Religion.* Urbana, IL: University of Illinois Press.
    1997   *The Cricis in the Churches Spiritual Malaise, Fiscal Woe.* New York: Oxford University Press.
    1998   *After Heaven: Spirituality in America Since the 1950s.* Berkeley, CA: University of California Press.

Yin, Robert K.
    1994   *Case Study Research: Design and Methods.* 2nd edition. Applied Social Research Methods Series. Vol. 5. Thousand Oaks, CA: Sage.

Yoder, John Howard
    1972   *The Politics of Jesus.* Grand Rapids, MI: William B. Eerdmans.

Young, Annette
    1986 "Praying for Justice, Crusading for Truth." *The Age* May 12:11.

Young, Louisa
    1986a   "Heaven on a Harley: Dog-collars the Aussie Hell's Angels' Very Own Vicar." *Bike* November.
    1986b   "Out of the Wilderness on a Harley Davidson." *You* November.

Yukl, G.A.
    1998   *Leadership in Organizations.* 4th edition. Inglewood Cliffs, NJ: Prentice-Hall.

Zahniser, Matthias A.H.
    1997   *Symbol and Ceremony: Making Disciples across Cultures.* Monrovia, CA: MARC.

www.ingramcontent.com/pod-product-compliance
Lightning Source LLC
Chambersburg PA
CBHW021112300426

44113CB00006B/130